CORALS OF AUSTRALIA
AND
THE INDO-PACIFIC

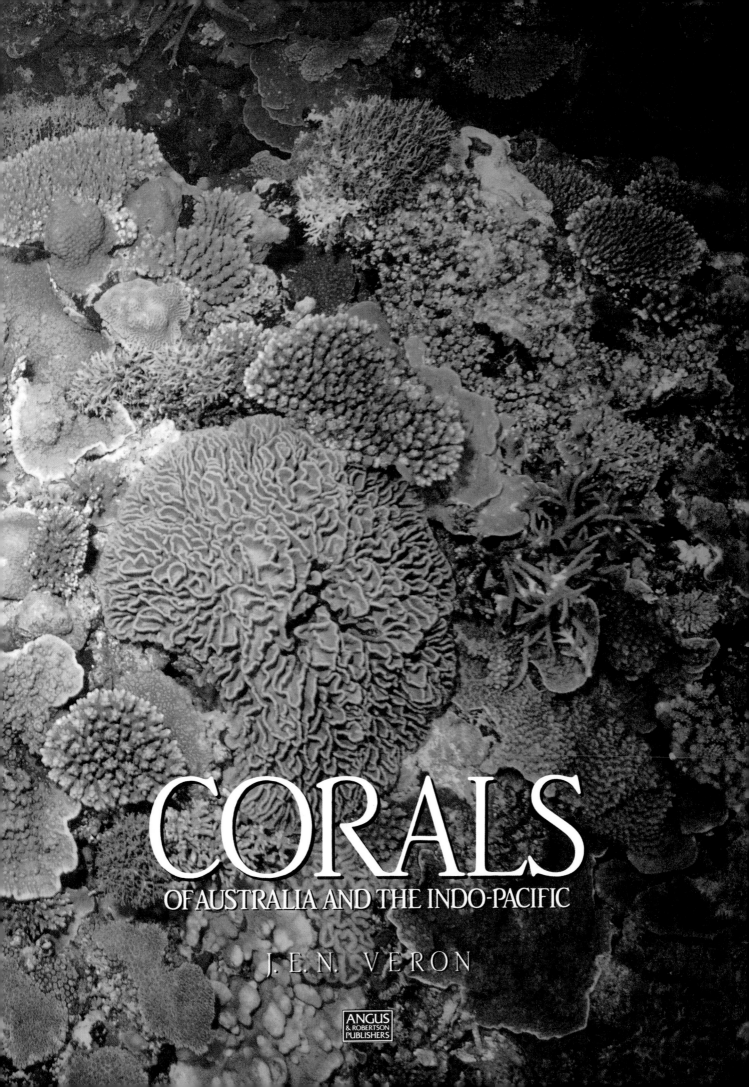

CORALS
OF AUSTRALIA AND THE INDO-PACIFIC

J. E. N. VERON

ANGUS
& ROBERTSON
PUBLISHERS

ANGUS & ROBERTSON PUBLISHERS

Unit 4, Eden Park, 31 Waterloo Road,
North Ryde, NSW, Australia 2113, and
16 Golden Square, London W1R 4BN,
United Kingdom

First published in Australia
by Angus & Robertson Publishers in 1986

National Library of Australia
Cataloguing-in-publication data.

Veron, J.E.N. (John Edward Norwood).
  Corals of Australia and the Indo-Pacific.

    Includes index.
    ISBN 0 207 15116 4.

  1. Anthozoa—Australia—Identification.
  2. Corals—Australia—Identification.
  I. Title.

593.6'0994

Typeset in Bembo by Setrite Typesetters
Printed in Hong Kong

For Noni, who saw the reef for herself,
and wanted me to write this book

The first scuba dive on a reef, at eight years of age.
PHOTOGRAPH: ED LOVELL.

In a small bight on the inner edge of this reef was a sheltered nook where every coral was in full life and luxuriance. Smooth, round masses were contrasted with delicate leaf-like and cup-like expansions with an infinite variety of branching, some with mere finger-shaped projections, others with large, branching stems, and others again exhibiting an elegant assemblage of interlacing twigs of exquisite workmanship. Their colours were unrivalled—vivid greens contrasting with more sober browns and yellows, mingled with rich shades of purple, from pale pink to deep blue.

J. B. Jukes,
Narrative of the Surveying Voyage of H.M.S. Fly,
1847

ACKNOWLEDGEMENTS

This book has been published without any royalty payments to the author or to the photographers.

When it comes to conveying information and to portraying natural beauty, there is no substitute for the right photograph. The author sought such photographs for this book for a long time and in doing so, usually finished up by giving yet another "shopping list" of species to Ed Lovell. To Ed I owe so much, including over half the underwater photographs reproduced here. Thanks Ed.

I particularly want to thank Ron and Valerie Taylor who made their entire photographic library available and sought special photographs for me, and also Len Zell, who filled in many gaps from his own collections. I thank the Great Barrier Reef Marine Park Authority for their aerial photographs and also the Australian Institute of Marine Science. I am grateful to many friends from Townsville for searching through their slides for some photo or other I was looking for, and they include: Terry Done, Vicki Harriott, Dave Fisk, Peter Harrison, Gordon Bull, Alistair Birtles, Carden Wallace, Bette Willis, David Hopley and John Barnett. I thank friends from Western Australia, especially Clay Bryce, also Pat Baker and Barry Wilson and those who contributed photographs of corals from the south coast, including Neville Coleman, Rudi Kuiter, David Staples and Nigel Holmes. I thank Isobel Bennett for over 20 years of encouragement and help. I also thank colleagues from other countries, especially Leon Zann (Fiji) for his aerial photography, and Jim Maragos (Hawaii) and Colin Scrutton (UK) for theirs. Other photographers are acknowledged through the book and I also thank those who sent me photos that I did not use.

To John Wells I owe a great deal and have done so for many years. His all-encompassing knowledge of corals has been a constant support, not only for this book, but for all my endeavours in this field. He has been the source of most of what I have recorded here about Australian ahermatypes and I have used extensively his records of coral distributions.

Special thanks are due to Carden Wallace, Terry Done, Alastair Birtles and Kirsty Veron for their painstaking criticisms of the manuscript, which I found invaluable. I also thank many of my colleagues at the Australian Institute of Marine Science for their criticisms, especially Don Kinsey, Bruce Chalker and David Ayre. Much of the information about coral reproduction recorded here has come from the members of the Coral Reproduction Group at James Cook University, with special thanks to Peter Harrison. Also, at various times I have discussed many of the notions expressed in this book with other colleagues and I especially thank Brian Rosen, Loisette Marsh, Peter Flood, Don Potts and Bob Henderson for their views and information.

Geoff Kelly's artwork speaks for itself. His biologist's eye for detail combined with an artist's hand have done more to elucidate the structure of corals for this book than words could ever do. I thank Les Brady for his painstaking darkroom photography. The manuscript was typed and methodically corrected by Liz Howlett. I thank Elizabeth Perkins and Elizabeth Drew who helped with pronunciations and translations, Marty Thyssen for her graphics and Alan Dartnall for assistance with many aspects of the publication and manuscript preparation.

CONTENTS

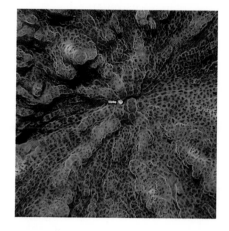

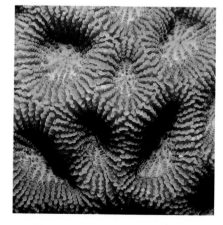

ABOUT THIS BOOK

Coral reefs are magical places, unparalleled in beauty and unmatched in grandeur. Remote from the natural environment of humans, the coral reef confronts the visitor with a surfeit of mystery, wonderment and awe.

These are the feelings of the newcomer to Australia's Great Barrier Reef and, even with experience, they seldom change. The Reef is never familiar. It is too complex to understand in its entirety and its size is not easily imagined. The builders of the Reef, the tiny coral polyps, seem simple enough. But why did they do all this building? Did the same kinds of corals build the reefs of other countries? Have they always done so?

Such questions have been asked by many people in different countries for a century or more. In order to find the answers, marine biologists now spend much time beneath the waves in order to take a close look at corals in their native environment. What they have found are entities which, on the one hand, may be readily identifiable, but on the other, are like Proteus and avoid pursuit by changing their appearance.

The aim of this book is to portray corals in all their natural form and beauty, to show where they live and, finally, to answer some of the multitude of questions asked about them, thus enabling the specialist and non-specialist alike to readily identify a large proportion of the corals found throughout the world today.

For some coral biologists, the Indo-Pacific is like a giant multi-layered jigsaw puzzle containing about 500 pieces—the distribution patterns of the different coral species. Most of these pieces are very large, some extending all the way from the Red Sea to the eastern Pacific. Australia sits right in the middle of this range and is home to about 70 per cent of all Indo-Pacific species. Most other countries have coral faunas differing more in numbers of species than in types, and this book is designed to be useful throughout the whole Indo-Pacific realm.

WHAT ARE CORALS

The term "coral" has several meanings, but is usually the common name for the Order Scleractinia, all members of which have hard limestone skeletons. The Scleractinia are divided into reef-building and non-reef-building groups. The former are mostly *hermatypic* and need sunlight to live, the latter are mostly *ahermatypic* and normally live without sunlight in the ocean depths.

Other organisms build skeletons similar to those of the Scleractinia and these are usually known as *non-scleractinian corals*. Still others resemble corals but have

Opposite: *Australogyra zelli* was first discovered at the Palm Islands, central Great Barrier Reef by the author, where it forms beautifully sculptured colonies.
PHOTOGRAPH: ED LOVELL.

Proteus in Greek mythology, the prophetic old man of the sea, would elude those who tried to consult him by constantly changing his form. But if a captor held him fast, he would return to his proper shape and answer all he was asked.

1

no skeleton, and these are usually known as *soft corals*. The latter are not included in this book.

IDENTIFYING CORALS

The corals constitute a chaotic collection of individuals, and the uncertainty as to what may be considered a species is the first problem that must confront anyone who happens to study corals from his own resources on an isolated coral reef.

Fredric Wood-Jones,
*On the Growth Forms and
Supposed Species in Corals*, 1907.

Some coral species are easily identified simply by finding the right photograph. The photographs in this book have been selected with this in mind, and show characteristics usually seen in well-developed colonies of each species. However, it should also be remembered that corals are mostly colonial organisms that show much variation from one place or habitat type to another. It may be difficult to identify the living colony, in which case it will be necessary to collect a piece of the colony, bleach it, and then use the characteristics of the skeleton to identify it. Such specimens can almost always be readily identified to genus.

Species are recognised easily in some genera, while in others, especially the big genera *Acropora*, *Montipora*, *Porites* and *Fungia*, identification may be difficult. In all cases where there are difficulties, the reader should use the photographs, descriptions and keys in combination with each other. The keys guide the reader to the correct species or group of species and are designed to be used with the species descriptions. Sometimes technical terminology is necessary but this has been kept to a minimum. All terms are explained in the glossary.

DISTRIBUTION OF CORALS

This book contains much information on the distribution of corals, partly because it helps with identification, but also because some of the most interesting problems of coral biology concern distribution.

The distribution maps of reef-building corals included here are compiled from records published in the scientific literature, and from the personal observations of the author with the help of colleagues.

Some of the distributions recorded, especially those of small or uncommon genera, may be extended as more remote reefs are explored, and these maps should be considered as approximations only. However, the overall pattern they show is now well established and does provide an adequate basis for examining many of the "where" and "why" questions of reef coral evolution.

At species level, Indo-Pacific coral distributions are not well known, except for Australia. Those given here are accurate as far as the scientific literature allows but are likely to be greatly extended with further research.

The distribution and depth records given for deep-water Australian corals have been obtained primarily from original museum records and surveys. These will also be greatly extended with further research.

THE COLOURS OF CORALS

All corals have three colours: what you see under water, what you see when you collect them and what comes out in a photograph.

Ed Lovell,
principal photographer for this book.

The best way of appreciating the problems a diver has in recognising colour under water is to collect a piece of blue-coloured coral at about 10 metres' depth, then to swim upwards, watching it all the way. It will gradually change colour and be mauve or pink before reaching the surface. This is because sea water acts as a selective light filter, first removing the longer wave lengths (the reds), then in succession the other colours across the spectrum until, in deep water, everything is a dim bluish-grey. The camera flashlight is designed to correct this effect and the resulting photograph is usually a mixture of natural and artificial (flashlight) colour. Often the photographed colour is unpredictable and the bright-colour patterns of some corals under water stubbornly resist the efforts of the photographer to record them.

The colours of corals indicated in this book are as seen under water by divers and they may therefore differ from the colour in the accompanying photographs. This disparity will vary with depth.

A small proportion of corals have very specific colours or colour patterns and these may help in identification. However, be warned that a species with a characteristic colour in one country may have another colour in another country. The majority of corals have very variable colours, and these are seldom useful in coral taxonomy.

ABUNDANCE

Except for very rare or very common species, abundance is extremely difficult to record. It varies greatly from country to country or from one geographic region to another. It also changes enormously between one habitat and the next, and even then it may be only an apparent abundance because large colonies of conspicuous species will appear to be more abundant than small or inconspicuous yet more numerous colonies of other species. For each species in this book, "abundance" records the author's general impressions, impressions that may mislead the reader in any one particular place.

TYPES AND TAXONOMY

The process of coral taxonomy—the delineation and ordering of corals into a system that expresses their relationships—has had no obvious point of origin and has no sign of an end. The subject is complex and avoided in this book, for this is not a taxonomic work and should not be used as one. The only information of a taxonomic nature that has been included is that which helps in the identification of corals.

To a very significant extent, the complexities of coral taxonomy are man-made and this is largely because many species were first described without any knowledge of the corals' natural variability. Corals make excellent fossils as well as excellent museum specimens for collectors to take back from expeditions. For much of the last century and well into this, corals have attracted the attention of a succession of palaeontologists and museum workers, and while some, like the American James Dana (1813-1895), had good reef experience and did valuable work, most had little or no such experience. (Henry Bernard (1853-1909) is an extreme example of the latter: he wrote more about corals than any other person of his time without ever seeing one alive.) Only in recent times has the subject come into the interest range of the marine biologist.

There is an enormous difference between what marine biologists can see and collect from diving on the reef and what museum workers from the past could learn from the specimens on their shelves. Divers can rapidly observe thousands of corals, all distributed in natural order, and thus can see at first hand how their growth form changes from one habitat to the next. Nevertheless, some of the problems faced by early taxonomists remain, for the rules of nomenclature state that in most cases the oldest name given to a species is the correct name. Thus, taxonomists must know and understand the findings of their predecessors. When deciding on the correct name, they always refer back to the earlier publications as well as to the museum specimens on which original descriptions were based.

These specimens are known as *type specimens* and the place where each was originally collected is called the *type locality* (often not recorded or only recorded vaguely in early descriptions). These localities are recorded in this book because it may be helpful, or interesting, to know where a particular species was originally found.

A final point about coral taxonomy is that, over its history, most species have been described more than once and some have been described many times. This is because the shape and structure of a single species can vary enormously from one place (region, country or ocean) or environmental niche to another. After the oldest name has been selected, the remainder are called *synonyms* and the collective synonyms of all the species of a genus are referred to as the *nominal species* of that genus.

THE FOSSIL RECORD

The jigsaw puzzle of Indo-Pacific species distributions complicated though it is, has another even more complicated dimension—time. As corals make such good fossils, they are used to reconstruct and understand the processes of reef formation and change through the earth's past history. More importantly, the fossil record also gives us an understanding of the phylogeny of genera and families (the family tree) that cannot be gained from the living organisms.

The known geological age of each genus given in this book can be put into context by reference to the family tree of corals (Chapter 5) and the account of reef and coral evolution (Chapter 10). It is emphasised, however, that the fossil record of most coral genera is, at best, very incomplete and for many it is completely absent.

PRONUNCIATION AND COMMON NAMES

The pronunciation of names of corals varies greatly in different countries. Those given in this book, which are correct in terms of modern Latin usage, are commonly used in Britain and Europe and by some Americans, but differ substantially from common Australian usage (where, for example, the syllable stress in *Acropora* is a-*krop*-or-a, not a-kro-*por*-a).

Common names for corals have been mentioned here only in passing. Many common names are widely used, especially in Australia, but there is little uniformity and only a few are applied to specific species or even specific genera.

CORAL REEFS

I am very full of Darwin's new theory of Coral Islands . . .
Let any mountain be submerged gradually, and coral grow in
the sea in which it is sinking, and there will be a ring of coral,
and finally only a lagoon in the centre. Why? For the same
reason that a barrier reef of coral grows along certain coasts:
Australia etc. Coral islands are the last efforts of drowning
continents to lift their heads above water.

Letter from Sir Charles Lyell to Sir John Herschel,
1837.

Intricately organised and immensely diverse, the living
coral reef is the triumphant achievement of coral polyps,
for it is these simple animals that are primarily responsible for the grand limestone ramparts which are spread
around the world's shallow, sunlit tropical oceans. Yet
coral reefs have not always existed as they do today. All
have had a history of change and modification, adjusting
to the great global climatic and geological events which
have shaped the world that we now know. These events
and the changes that they have caused are outlined at the
end of this book; here we look at the similarities and

Opposite: Ambo, South Tarawa, Gilbert Islands, a giant triangular
atoll, 45 km in length with island chains along two sides.
PHOTOGRAPH: LEON ZANN.

Diagram I. Darwin's theory of atoll formation: if a mountain with
a fringing reef subsides slowly enough to allow the reef to keep
growing, it will eventually form a chain of reefs enclosing a lagoon.
DRAWING: MARTY THYSSEN, AIMS.

differences among the main reef types found today.

To a large extent, the general appearance of a reef—
its shape and structure—has little to do with the particular species that built it. All modern reefs have been
built by scleractinian corals, which provide the reef
framework, and coralline algae, which cement the
framework together. It makes little difference which
corals provided the framework and which algae did the
cementing. Only when the algae are sparse or absent, as
is sometimes the case with reefs protected from wave
action or where the water is turbid, is the appearance of
a reef markedly affected.

Where suitable reef-builders are present, the type of
reef developed depends to a large extent on the topography (depth and shape) of the ocean floor, the recent
geological history of the area and on the physical environment, especially temperature and the degree of
exposure to wave action. One of the most basic factors
controlling reef development is the relationship between
the rate of reef growth and the rate of sea-level change.
The sea has not always been at its present level and
changes in the level have had a major effect on all reef
development. But there may also be localised effects due
to the subsidence or uplift of the land under the reef.
This was realised by Charles Darwin, who proposed
that atolls develop where high islands gradually subside
beneath the sea. Coral reefs which begin as fringing
reefs around islands gradually become more and more

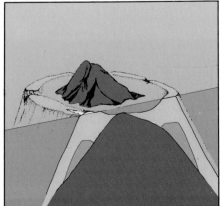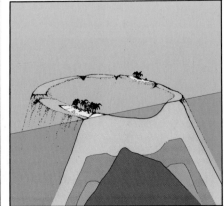

1. Enewetak Atoll, Marshall Islands.
In 1881 Charles Darwin wrote: "I wish that some doubly rich millionaire would take it into his head to have borings made in some of the Pacific and Indian atolls." Darwin's wishes came true, the millionaire was the US Atomic Energy Commission and this is where they finally proved Darwin's theory. Two drill holes hit volcanic basalt at 1267 and 1405 m depth, figures that compare closely with Darwin's predicted thickness of atolls of 5000 feet (1525 m).
PHOTOGRAPH: JIM MARAGOS.

2. Midway Island at the north-western end of the Hawaiian islands is a remnant of former reef-building activity, but now probably has less than 20 surviving genera.
PHOTOGRAPH: DAVID HOPLEY.

3. Funafuti Atoll, Tuvalu. The islet in the foreground is the site of a drill hole made by the Royal Society in 1896 in an unsuccessful attempt to test Darwin's theory of atoll formation.
PHOTOGRAPH: LEON ZANN.

4. Nanumea Atoll, Tuvalu. The ring of islets enclose a small lagoon.
PHOTOGRAPH: LEON ZANN.

Map showing distribution of coral reefs throughout the world.

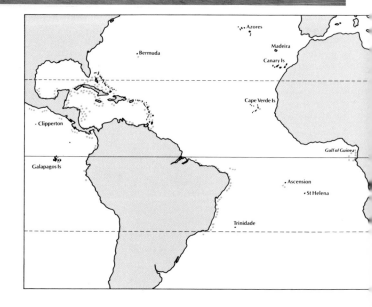

3

4

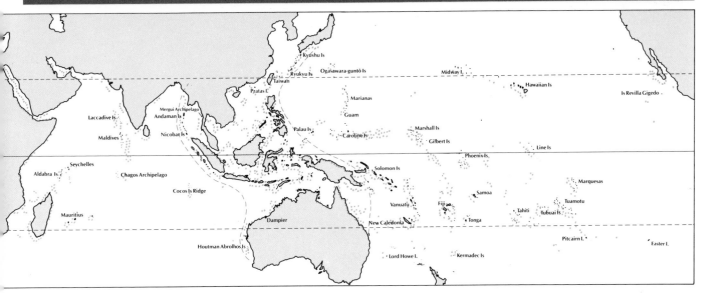

A fossil coral reef raised above the
surrounding sea. Many continental islands
of the western Pacific have the remnants
of former fringing reefs around their
shorelines and even on mountain slopes.
PHOTOGRAPH: AUTHOR.

Fringing reefs are seldom associated with
rainforest because river run-off prevents
coral growth. Here in Palau, reefs and
forests are intermixed in a mosaic made
by reef-building corals and the action of
fresh water at times of low sea-level.
PHOTOGRAPH: LEON ZANN.

Reefs of the Daintree coast. These reefs
are unusual as they fringe the mainland
and also because they occur next to a
rainforest.
PHOTOGRAPH: LEO MEIER,
AUSTRALIAN CONSERVATION FOUNDATION.

distant from the land they fringe until, when the land disappears altogether, what is left is an *atoll*, a circle of reefs enclosing a lagoon. Atolls such as those of the Marshall Islands can be of vast size, and chains of atolls can form from what were originally mountain chains.

Darwin's theory of atolls, which is now generally accepted, does not suppose that all high islands become gradually submerged in order to form reefs. Some submerge too rapidly for any reef construction to take place, others form reefs which become submerged and eventually drown when their upward growth fails to keep pace with the rate of subsidence of their mountain base. The reverse process can also take place. The seabed may rise, and mountains, high islands and atolls emerge out of the sea. This has happened in many places from New Guinea to Taiwan, and what now remains is a succession of exposed fringing reefs which sometimes look like eroded giant stairways, each step being the result of one uplift.

The Great Barrier Reef is, by geological standards, a relatively recent development. Only in the last two million years have reefs existed on the continental margin of north-east Australia. This period was so dominated by sea-level changes (see map, p. 625) that for about three-quarters of its history, the reef areas that we see today have been out of the water. At those times the reefs would have been eroded by rainwater, producing caves, gutters and valleys in the limestone matrix. After they were flooded by the sea, marine life would gradually have re-established and corals would start to grow.

All reefs that we see today, including those of the Great Barrier Reef, are the product of layers of coral and coralline algae growing upon the eroded gutters and valleys of former times. To a large extent, these eroded substrata govern the shapes of modern reefs, but each, in turn, is the result of coral growth and subsequent erosion of an earlier substratum. Consequently, only some reef types reflect clearly the topography of their non-reefal bedrock. Others are the product of layers of coral growth, each layer growing according to the set of environmental conditions that prevailed at the time.

There are no typical atolls in Australian waters. Most Australian reefs either fringe continental islands or the mainland, or are platform or barrier reefs.

Fringing reefs are very common around tropical high islands and sometimes border the main coastline. Because they fringe non-reefal land masses, they usually occur near the mainland and thus have relatively turbid water around them. Being limited by this, these reefs seldom extend into deep water. They have developed only during the last 6000 years when the sea has remained at its present level.

Platform reefs range widely in shape and form. Their size may be immense—over 20 kilometres across—and their geological histories varied.

Barrier reefs are developed typically on the edge of a continental shelf and they may have a Darwinian atoll-like geological history (see Lyell's comments quoted above). One of the world's most spectacular barrier reef systems occurs in the northern Great Barrier Reef where the barrier line extends from Cooktown to eastern Torres Strait, a distance of 670 kilometres.

AUSTRALIAN CORAL REEFS

The world's greatest reef system, possibly the biggest structure ever made by life on earth, extends 2000 kilometres along the north-east coast of Queensland. It includes some 2500 major reefs and almost as many high islands and cays which, collectively, are known worldwide as the Great Barrier Reef (an unfortunate name because the majority of the reefs within the system are not barrier reefs at all).

In size, diversity and complexity, the Great Barrier Reef has no rivals, but it is far from being Australia's only coral reef system. The others, most of which are on the west coast, are much less well known but several are no less scenic and no less interesting.

THE EAST COAST

The Solitary Islands These are a series of five rocky, weather-worn islands, two to 11 kilometres offshore between Coffs Harbour and Grafton. Their barren appearance belies extensive areas of coral, mostly *Acropora* and *Turbinaria*, which cover the rocky sea floor in partly sheltered embayments. These are the most southern coral communities in Australian waters, but they are not reef communities, for there is no sign of there ever

Diagram 2. A diagrammatic cross-section of the Great Barrier Reef showing the principal reef types.
DRAWING: MARTY THYSSEN, AIMS.

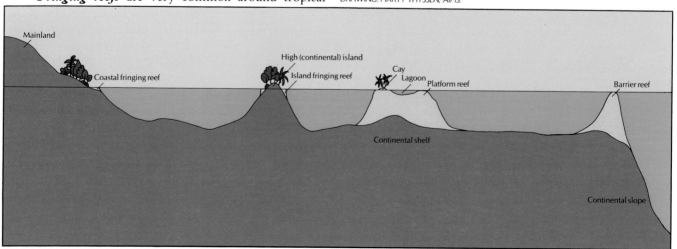

having been any limestone accumulation. Extensive kelp beds also occur around the islands and are usually intermixed with the corals.

Lord Howe Island This high mountainous island has an extensive rugged coastline with several beaches and, on the western side, an extensive lagoon bordered by one of the southernmost coral reefs in the world. In former geological times, this reef was more extensive than it is now, but rich coral communities are still to be found in deeper parts of the lagoon and around the channels which penetrate the reef wall. Although scenically spectacular in places, the reef has a low diversity of corals and many of them are at the southernmost limit of their distribution.

Elizabeth and Middleton Reefs These are the world's southernmost open-ocean platform reefs, about 725 kilometres south of the Great Barrier Reef and just 95 kilometres north of Lord Howe Island. They are littered with wrecks, evidence enough that they occur where reefs are often not expected. The two reefs are similar to each other in all respects except that Elizabeth Reef has a deeper, more extensive lagoon. Broad reef flats are exposed at low tide, when the lagoon waters are ponded well above the level of the surrounding ocean. Although coral species are fewer than on tropical reefs, the corals show few signs of being under any environmental stress.

Flinders Reef (near Moreton Bay) Although this appears to be a coral reef *par excellence*, with a dense cover of corals, the reef itself is thinly disguised sandstone. The diversity of species is extraordinary, considering that the reef area is only about 10 hectares in extent. There are as many coral species here as are found on Elizabeth and Middleton Reefs, each of which is about 2000 hectares in extent.

1. The fringing reef of Lord Howe Island, the southernmost reef of the Pacific, now has some 57 species of coral.
PHOTOGRAPH: JAMES BROWN.

2. The sandstone platform that is Flinders Reef has been carved by the sea so that at first sight it looks like a true limestone reef.
PHOTOGRAPH: ED LOVELL.

3. Flinders Reef near Moreton Bay is a small patch of sandstone surrounded by luxuriant coral growth.
PHOTOGRAPH: ED LOVELL.

The Capricorn and Bunker Groups These are the southernmost reefs of the Great Barrier Reef. Each of the 22 major reefs has a sharply defined margin and a neat rounded shape. Most have shallow lagoons and many have cays, some with dense vegetation. The reefs are separated by deep water allowing for good circulation and, usually, luxuriant coral growth. Although these reefs are at the southern end of the Great Barrier Reef, 72 per cent of all Great Barrier Reef coral species are known to occur there.

The Swain Reefs These are a vast expanse of reef patches of varying shapes and sizes, some with small cays. The eastern and southern reefs are small and, as they are fully exposed to big ocean swells, they have a rugged, wave-washed appearance. Those of the western side are larger, less exposed, and many have lagoons with extensive coral growth. During the Ice Ages these reefs may have been more extensive, but as they are the most remote reefs of the Great Barrier Reef, they have been little studied.

1

2

1. The Hoskyn Islands and reef of the Bunker Group of islands typify the type of reef formation of the southern Great Barrier Reef.
PHOTOGRAPH: LEN ZELL, GREAT BARRIER REEF MARINE PARK AUTHORITY.

2. Lady Musgrave Island of the Bunker Group of islands is one of the southernmost islands of the Great Barrier Reef.
PHOTOGRAPH: LEN ZELL, GREAT BARRIER REEF MARINE PARK AUTHORITY.

3. The Hoskyn Islands.
PHOTOGRAPH: LEN ZELL, GREAT BARRIER REEF MARINE PARK AUTHORITY.

1. Coral growth can fill in lagoons and choke off channels. This has produced most of the mosaic patterns of the Pompey Complex.
PHOTOGRAPH: LEN ZELL, GREAT BARRIER REEF MARINE PARK AUTHORITY.

2. The Pompey Complex of the southern Great Barrier Reef, a navigator's nightmare, is a grand and beautiful sight from the air.
PHOTOGRAPH: AUTHOR.

3. The intricate structure of the Pompey Complex is unlike any other place on the Great Barrier Reef. The reef front, where waves are breaking, is normally protected from the south-east trade winds. The blue hole towards the lower left has been produced by the action of rainwater breaking into the roof of a cave when the sea-level was lower.
PHOTOGRAPH: LEN ZELL, GREAT BARRIER REEF MARINE PARK AUTHORITY.

4. Fringing reefs of the Whitsunday Islands. These have little in common with the limestone ramparts of the outer barrier. They are poorly consolidated but usually have a zone of very active coral growth around their perimeter.
PHOTOGRAPH: LEN ZELL, GREAT BARRIER REEF MARINE PARK AUTHORITY.

The Pompey Complex Seen from the air, the Pompey Complex is a seemingly unending mixture of reefs, channels, sandbars and lagoons, all of awe-inspiring grandeur and beauty. For the mariner, the complex is a warren of reefs of unpredictable shapes, surrounded by deep water and broken up by deep channels which have very strong tidal currents. Indeed, the reefs make such a barrier to tidal-water movement that an observer standing at the right place at a low spring tide can actually see the difference in sea-level between the two sides of the reef. At such times the channels become cascading torrents, but these are short-lived as the flow soon ceases, and then reverses as the tide changes.

The inshore high islands A series of high (continental) island complexes occurs along the coastline from the southern Great Barrier Reef to Princess Charlotte Bay. These usually have complex coastlines, parts of which have strong tidal currents and extensive areas of relatively shallow, turbid water. Such conditions usually produce a wide range of fringing reefs with coral communities adapted to muddy conditions. Species diversity may be very high—higher than that of outer reefs.

The reefs of the central Great Barrier Reef These vary greatly, especially in relation to distance from the coastline. The outermost or shelf-edge reefs have the greatest exposure to wave action and the clearest and deepest water. The innermost reefs are influenced by flood waters of big rivers. The middle or mid-shelf reefs are of varying shapes and sizes and often have very different combinations of coral communities. In this area there are very few cays.

The ribbon reefs A solid wall of barrier reefs extends along the edge of the continental shelf from Cooktown north to Pandora Entrance. The eastern side of these reefs is fully exposed to the open-ocean swell and for 10 months of each year it is pounded by heavy surf. This outer face, plunging down into the abyssal depths of the Queensland Trench, has some of the most spectacular underwater scenery of any reef. The water is very clear and is a photographer's delight. It is on these faces that reef corals probably reach their greatest depth—at 50 metres coral communities are still lush and diverse and many corals have been dredged from over 100 metres.

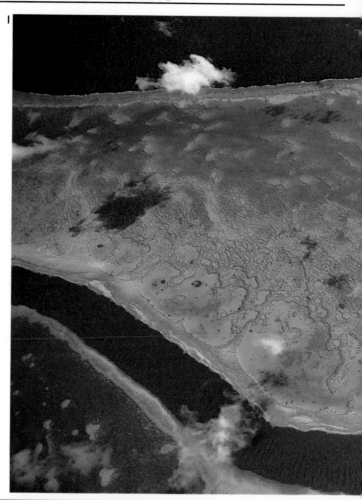

1. Hardy Reef near the Whitsunday Islands. This reef is visited more than any other by tourists wanting access to extensive outer reef flats as well as deep diving sites.
PHOTOGRAPH: LEN ZELL, GREAT BARRIER REEF MARINE PARK AUTHORITY.

2. North Direction Island of the Lizard Island group showing the type of fringing reef usually found around steep rocky islands.
PHOTOGRAPH: LEN ZELL, GREAT BARRIER REEF MARINE PARK AUTHORITY.

3. The fringing reefs of the Palm Islands have an extraordinarily high coral diversity — more species have been recorded here than anywhere else in the world. Eclipse Island in the foreground is a favourite site for coral research.
PHOTOGRAPH: AUTHOR.

4. Ribbon reefs. These form one of the most spectacular reef lines in the world. On the eastern (right) side, the outer slope plunges into very deep water and the upper slope is exposed to pounding surf for most of the year. The reef in the foreground was named after Sir Maurice Yonge, leader of the 1928 expedition to the Great Barrier Reef. The passage between the two reefs in the background was negotiated by Captain James Cook in the *Endeavour* on 14 August, 1770.
PHOTOGRAPH: LEN ZELL, GREAT BARRIER REEF MARINE PARK AUTHORITY.

Over: Lizard Island in the north Great Barrier Reef is unusual in being a high island situated near the outer barrier line. The main island is the site of one of the world's principal reef-research stations.
PHOTOGRAPH: LEN ZELL, GREAT BARRIER REEF MARINE PARK AUTHORITY.

3

4

The deltaic and dissected reefs The barrier line extends north of Pandora Entrance but the shapes of the reefs differ here. Channels between them become narrower and more frequent and they develop a pattern that looks like a series of river deltas. These are the deltaic reefs, which form such a barrier to tidal-water movements that currents through the channels (in the reverse direction for a river delta) may form standing waves up to two metres high. When seen from the air, the deltaic appearance of these reefs is misleading, for they are composed of hard limestone rock, the walls of the smaller channels having been built by corals while those of the main channels have been scoured by tidal currents.

The dissected reefs are at the northern limit of the barrier line where the deltaic pattern breaks up into a complex of reef strips running in an east-west direction. These are the northernmost barrier reefs of the Great Barrier Reef and at their northern extremity they form a series of downward-sloping steps which eventually become submerged in mud from the Gulf of Papua. During periods of monsoonal flooding, large masses of water of low salinity from the rivers of Papua New Guinea move down to these reefs and they can be seen under water as shimmering translucent lenses. They have no apparent effect on the coral communities which remain diverse and luxuriant.

The northern lagoon The vast area between the coastline north from Princess Charlotte Bay, and the outer barrier reefs, referred to as the northern lagoon, contains an immense complex of reefs, cays and high islands. It is shallower than the southern regions of the Great Barrier Reef and the water in places is relatively turbid, but because there are few rivers, extensive reefs grow right up to the coastline.

Torres Strait The western side of Torres Strait is bordered by huge reefs which are little more than mud banks encircled by coral. Westward currents run strongly and the water is turbid. Coral growth is poor and limited in depth. Eastward from this line, the water gets deeper and clearer and reefs and cays are more numerous and rich in coral species. Eastern Torres Strait contains some high islands with extensive reef flats; the eastern edge is composed of the northern extremity of the barrier line—the dissected reefs.

The Coral Sea The Coral Sea can be divided into northern and southern halves. The northern half consists of a broad abyssal plain between the northern Great Barrier

1. The large expanses of reef of western Torres Strait are little more than mud banks fringed with coral.
PHOTOGRAPH: AUTHOR.

2. At its far northern limit, the outer barrier line breaks up into these dissected reefs.
PHOTOGRAPH: AUTHOR.

3. The Murray Islands of eastern Torres Strait are surrounded by wide fringing reefs which, like those of Lizard Island, are continually bathed in clear oceanic water.
PHOTOGRAPH: AUTHOR.

2

3

2 Reef and Vanuatu. The southern half contains a number of sea mounts, some capped by coral reef, cays and atolls, lying between the central and southern Great Barrier Reef and New Caledonia. These reefs are all widely separate from each other and have little in common. Most are very rich in *Acropora* and a few other coral genera, but none has the diversity found on the Great Barrier Reef.

THE WEST COAST

The Houtman Abrolhos Islands These are divided into three groups each consisting of a complex of reefs, cays, lagoons and channels. Seventy per cent of the coral genera of Western Australia extend south to the Houtman Abrolhos Islands and this is the southern limit of two-thirds of these. The reef slopes of the complex are characterised by large quantities of *Sargassum* and other macro-algae (see p. 40) intermixed with the corals, and are thus very distinct from those of tropical reefs. There is little tidal range and little reef flat development.

Shark Bay This is Australia's largest enclosed bay and it has irregular fringing reefs surrounding the arc of continental islands which enclose the western side of the bay. The tidal range is very small, leaving pockets of very saline water in southern parts of the bay which probably restricts coral growth, but which is home for algal stromatolites, similar to some of the world's oldest fossils.

Ningaloo Reef Track An extensive line of fringing reef occurs just north of the Tropic of Capricorn. These are the largest fringing reefs of Australia and can exist close to the mainland because there are no large rivers in the vicinity.

Dampier Archipelago There are many groups of continental islands between North West Cape and Port Hedland. Most of these have extensive fringing reefs similar in general appearance to the Whitsunday Islands of the east coast. Like the fringing reefs of the Whitsunday Islands, those of the Dampier Archipelago are mostly submerged in turbid water, stirred by strong tidal currents.

1. Looking south along Long Island of the Wallaby Group of the Houtman Abrolhos Islands. In places, these islands look atoll-like and are quite unlike any other Australian reef.
PHOTOGRAPH: PAT BAKER, WESTERN AUSTRALIAN MUSEUM.

2. Beacon Island of the Wallaby Group of the Houtman Abrolhos Islands is the site of the marine research station of the Western Australian Museum. It is also the site of Australia's oldest known shipwreck, that of the *Batavia*, which ran aground in 1629.
PHOTOGRAPH: PAT BAKER, WESTERN AUSTRALIAN MUSEUM.

3. The Ningaloo Reef Tract is Australia's largest fringing reef. It owes its existence to the semidesert conditions of the adjacent coastline.
PHOTOGRAPH: RICHARD MAY.

3

Clerke Reef, one of the three reefs of the Rowley Shoals. These are very unusual in being open oceanic reefs with a very great tidal range. At low tide, the water in the lagoon and the surrounding reef flat are left high above the surrounding sea.
PHOTOGRAPH: GRAEME HENDERSON, WESTERN AUSTRALIAN MUSEUM.

Rowley Shoals, Scott and Seringapatam Reefs These reefs are situated beyond the broad Sahul Shelf of north-western Australia. Rowley Shoals are actually three large, ecliptical, open-ocean platform reefs surrounded by deep water. Each reef has an extensive lagoon surrounded by a broad reef flat which is penetrated by small entrance channels. Although the reefs are 290 kilometres from the coastline, the tidal range is high and water is ponded in the lagoons about two metres above low-tide level. Scott Reef is actually two reefs, one forming a crescent-shaped arc south of the other. Both

Rowley Shoals and Scott Reef have a rich coral cover, comparable in scenic beauty to the outer reefs of the Great Barrier Reef. Coral diversity is less than that of the Great Barrier Reef, but is more similar in composition to the latter than it is to the closer reefs of the western coastline. Seringapatam Reef is small, with a deep lagoon devoid of clear entrance channels through the reef flat. Much of the reef front is bordered by an extensive coralline algal terrace, a rarity on Australian reefs.

The Sahul Shelf The Kimberley and far north-western coastlines are characterised by a rugged terrain, a shallow continental shelf and a high tidal range. The area contains extensive complexes of island groups and mud banks. However, strong tidal currents with turbid water prevent extensive reef development.

The Timor and Arafura Seas Extensive reefs occur only towards the Indonesian Archipelago, beyond the shallows of the Sahul Shelf. On the western end of the shelf are Scott, Seringapatam and Ashmore Reefs which differ as greatly from each other as do the reefs of the Coral Sea.

CORAL COMMUNITIES

Nowhere else in the sea is there such a bewildering range of living things, and perhaps nowhere else is the physical and biological pattern so uniform, characteristic and widespread as in the coral reef.

John Wells,
Recent Corals of the Marshall Islands, 1957.

Like a patchwork of miniature forests, the coral reef is a microcosm of different communities, each separate, but linked to the next by a complex web of ecological interactions. These communities are distinctive because, on a single reef, they form a series of narrow bands or zones, each having a particular place in an array of rapidly changing environmental gradients.

The most important factors controlling community composition are light availability, wave action, sediment load, salinity and tidal range. On a broader scale, available food and inorganic nutrients, temperature and bathymetry (topography of the sea floor) are also important. These factors are clearly interrelated, especially where wave action affects the sediment load which, in turn, affects light availability.

THE PHYSICAL ENVIRONMENT

LIGHT

All hermatypic corals require adequate light for photosynthesis of the algae in their tissues. This light changes rapidly, both in intensity and composition, with depth. The changing intensity is not visible to divers because their eyes compensate for it, but the underwater photographer knows that a camera flashlight must be used at depths of over a few metres to restore both light intensity and colour balance, even in clear water.

The visibility of reef waters (a good measure of water clarity) may exceed 50 metres in open-ocean reefs and may be less than one metre after storms around fringing reefs. This range controls the depths at which corals grow, and different species have different tolerances to both maximum and minimum light levels. It is also a major cause of variation in reef community structures.

Opposite: A fish-eye lens can sometimes capture the ever-changing composition of coral communities.
PHOTOGRAPH: GRAPHIC FILMS CORP.

WAVE ACTION

The second controlling factor, wave action, reaches extremes on reef fronts and outer reef flats. On a very calm day a reef front has a benign appearance, the odd wave or two doing little to disrupt its peace and tranquillity. Yet during a storm that same place can be the site of indescribable violence. Huge waves build up on the reef slope, then come crashing down on the outer flat. Only a few species of corals can survive these conditions and those that do are usually gnarled and stunted. Compare such an environment with the lower reef slope, near the lower limit of coral growth. Waves may be pounding the shallow reef front, but on the lower reef slope, only a few hundred metres away, there may be almost no water movement at all.

SEDIMENTATION

Many different types of sediment occur on and around reefs. These include coarse coral rubble, various types of sand and also fine mud. The type of sediment found in any one place depends upon the degree of exposure to currents and wave action and also upon the origin of the sediment. Outer reefs away from the coastline usually have light calcareous sediments produced by algae, notably *Halimeda*, and corals. These sediments are readily transported and have relatively little effect on the water clarity. Near the coastline the sediment comes from the land primarily through river run-off. Such sediment, which often has a high organic component, is readily stirred up by waves and may remain suspended in the water for long periods of time, making the water turbid and reducing light penetration. Also, as it settles from suspension after a major or prolonged disturbance, it can kill organisms such as corals, either by completely burying them or by choking polyps that cannot clear it away quickly enough.

SALINITY

Only in rare instances does the salinity of sea water become high enough to have a widespread effect on coral communities. One such place is Shark Bay (Western Australia) where a large expanse of land-locked water is combined with a low tidal range (and thus little tidal flushing) to produce a salinity which, in the southern part, is high enough to be lethal to corals.

Low salinities have a much more common and important effect, both on reef distribution and coral zonation. Reefs cannot develop in areas that are periodically inundated with river water, a primary factor controlling coral distributions along coastlines. The main effect of salinity on coral zonation is due to rainwater. Reef-flat corals are generally tolerant of short periods of low salinity, but when very heavy or cyclonic rainfall coincides with very low tides, reef-flat communities may be damaged, even completely destroyed.

TIDAL RANGE

Tidal ranges vary greatly from one reef region to another, a variation that has a marked effect on the zonation of reef-front and reef-flat communities. The greater the tide, the greater is the effect of tidal flushing and consequent nutrient transport, and also the greater are the various effects of emersion. In general, the greater the tidal range, the more pronounced are the coral and coralline algae zones on the outer reef slopes. Reef lagoons are often much less affected as the lagoon water may become entrapped at low tide, resulting in a much higher water level in the lagoon than in the surrounding sea.

FOOD AND INORGANIC NUTRIENTS

Corals, like all other forms of life, require both food and inorganic nutrients to live. For reef organisms, both are dissolved in sea water and may be extracted from it by a variety of means. Food may also be suspended in the water as particles which include live plankton. On reefs, as elsewhere, one organism gets its food from others, or the remains of others, and so food webs are formed in which all plant and animal groups are interlinked. When considering food and nutrient requirements of reef organisms, it is important to distinguish between the needs of single species or groups of species and the needs of the reef as a whole, because in order to achieve long-term stability, an overall balance of nutrient cycles must be achieved.

Reefs both import and export nutrients, but trade with the surrounding sea is small compared with their own internal economy of continual recycling. Imported nutrients are usually transported to the reefs from rivers; but if there are no rivers, as with reefs remote from land masses, nutrients can come only by surface ocean circulation. Often this supply is poor, and thus the vast ocean expanses have been referred to as "nutrient deserts". The Indo-Pacific has many huge atolls in these supposed deserts which testify to the resilience of reefs, but the corals themselves may lack the lush appearance of those of more fertile waters. Many reefs have another major supply of inorganic nutrients as, under certain conditions, surface currents moving against a reef face may cause deep ocean water to be drawn to the surface. This "upwelled" water is often rich in phosphorus and other essential chemicals.

Many reefs have seasonal fluctuations in their nutrient budgets, especially the high-latitude reefs where seasonal effects are more pronounced. These changes are primarily due to macro-algae, which appear and disappear with changing temperature, and number of daylight hours. The specific role of corals in the overall productivity and budgeting of reefs is less clearly understood, partly because it is not easily measured and partly because the different groups of corals have very different methods of obtaining nutrients. These subjects are discussed in the next chapter.

TEMPERATURE AND BATHYMETRY

The above factors are all major aspects of the physical environment, which controls community structure. A more remote control is also exercised by temperature, which limits coral growth and reef development as a whole (see Chapter 11). Also, the bathymetry of an area primarily controls the shape of a reef and the steepness and depth of its outer slopes. These factors, in turn, greatly affect or control light availability, turbulence, currents, etcetera.

THE BIOLOGICAL ENVIRONMENT

Important though the physical environment is in determining the composition of coral communities, it is the "biological environment" that creates the wealth of species that is so characteristic of coral reefs. This diversity can exist only after a series of ecological balances is achieved: not only balances between the corals themselves, but between the corals and other organisms, including predators and parasites, and also between other organisms that have little to do with corals directly, such as the balance between herbivorous fish and macro-algae (the latter would rapidly overgrow most coral communities if it were not continually held in check).

As far as the corals themselves are concerned, each species has its own array of growth strategies, food requirements and reproductive capacities. Each has its own response to disruption by storms or predators, diseases and plagues. Each species competes with others for space, light and other resources. The net result of all these interactions and balances (each of which is considered separately in the next chapter) is to make coral communities among the most diverse of any communities on earth.

COMMUNITY TYPES

Two examples of variation in coral communities are taken here: the communities of a generalised outer reef and those of an inner fringing reef.

OUTER REEFS

The lower slope Just what sort of coral communities occur on lower reef slopes at the depth limit for coral growth is, as yet, a matter for speculation. On outer slopes where the water is clear, extensive coral growth may occur at more than 100 metres' depth, but such depths are not found around most reefs. The corals are mostly thin, brittle, encrusting plates, and light availability is the main factor limiting their depth range. At 50 metres' depth, coral cover may be very dense and become moderately diverse. Flat plates of *Turbinaria, Porites* and various faviids are sometimes conspicuously dominant, but more often extensive colonies of one species or genus will be replaced by another in an apparently random fashion. Water clarity, currents and the steepness of the reef slope are probably the main influences on coral community composition. On flat substrates, bottlebrush *Acropora* may be dominant.

Upper reef slopes In this zone, about 0–20 metres in depth, light is not a limiting factor for coral growth. At 20 metres, species diversity is at a maximum. The large monospecific stands found in deeper water are replaced mostly by a very mixed community without a single dominant species. Corals have very varied growth forms which depend in part on the slope of the substrate. At shallower depths, extensive stands of staghorn *Acropora* usually predominate if the substrate does not slope too steeply.

Reef fronts The reef front is the narrow zone that becomes exposed at low tide and is the part of the reef which takes much of the force of the ocean swell. Corals are short and stocky and have the appearance of being mowed down. *Acropora palifera* (east coast only) and pocilloporids are the most common corals in areas exposed to extreme wave action; but in less extreme areas, *Acropora humilus* and *Acropora robusta* and their allies are usually very common. With slightly more protection, *Acropora hyacinthus* may be dominant.

Coral-collecting at 60 m on a reef slope. At this depth everything appears blue-grey and corals adapt their growth form to catch what little light is available.
PHOTOGRAPH: TERRY DONE.

Diagram 3. The zones of a barrier or outer reef.
DRAWING: MARTY THYSSEN, AIMS.

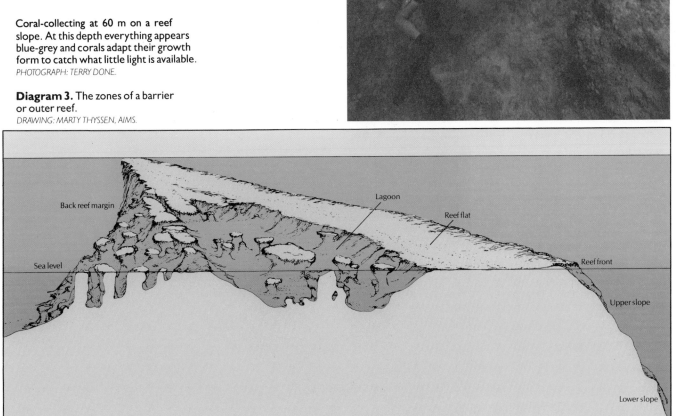

Back reef margin

Lagoon

Reef flat

Sea level

Reef front

Upper slope

Lower slope

1. The upper reef slope of Myrmidon Reef, central Great Barrier Reef, is exposed to open-ocean waves. Many of the more delicate plate corals in this area will not survive the next cyclonic storm.
PHOTOGRAPH: ED LOVELL.

2. Looking down a reef slope at Broadhurst Reef, central Great Barrier Reef. Coral communities change rapidly with increasing depth.
PHOTOGRAPH: ED LOVELL.

3, 4. The shallow upper slopes of outer reefs may have very different coral communities, depending mostly on exposure to wave action.
PHOTOGRAPHS: RON AND VALERIE TAYLOR (Top) AND ED LOVELL (Middle).

5. The common appearance of a reef front pounded by surf. Grooves are cut into the hard limestone surface by the continual movement of rubble.
PHOTOGRAPH: AUTHOR.

1. The reef front of Seringapatam Reef, north-western Australia, consists of a terrace of coralline algae, seen here at low spring tide.
PHOTOGRAPH: AUTHOR.

2. *Acropora* encrusts the limestone of an exposed front of a ribbon reef. Only a few coral species can survive the rigours of this environment.
PHOTOGRAPH: AUTHOR.

3. A partly protected reef front at Myrmidon Reef exposed at a very low tide. Corals growing here are all sturdy and able to withstand the force of big waves.
PHOTOGRAPH: TERRY DONE.

4. The outer reef flat at Heron Island, Great Barrier Reef.
PHOTOGRAPH: RON AND VALERIE TAYLOR.

3

4

Outer reef flats This wave-hammered terrain is usually very sparsely populated. On some equatorial reefs exposed to heavy surf there may be an algal crest or terrace (a zone composed primarily of coralline algae) between the reef front and the outer reef flat, but this is poorly developed on most Australian reefs. Nevertheless, the outer reef flat is usually the highest point of the reef and is also the least populated by corals.

Inner reef flats There is usually a sharp distinction between the outer and inner reef flats because the latter has much loose rubble and only a partly consolidated substrate. Tongues of sand and rubble are intermixed with solid reef rock which generally has a good coverage of corals, mostly *Acropora* and faviids.

Lagoons The rocky substrates of many inner reef flats are often completely eroded, leaving a sandy floor which is usually a few metres deep. These lagoons are surrounded by reef, but usually have a good water circulation from tidal currents. Lagoons may be devoid of coral or have large stands of branching *Acropora* growing on sand, or they may contain large mounds of consolidated or unconsolidated rock overgrown by a wide variety of corals. These are protected from strong wave action and their growth forms may be elaborately developed. Deep lagoons may contain much soft sediment and extensive stands of corals such as *Goniopora*, *Leptoseris*, *Pachyseris* and *Montipora*, which tolerate sediments.

Back reef margins These are often places of very active coral growth and usually consist of sections of reef flat divided by sandy-floored fissures. Such areas, protected from very strong wave action, are usually dominated by *Porites* and faviids, but a very wide range of other corals also may be present. This zone usually changes markedly from place to place along the reef.

1. Reef flat communities are usually mixtures of sand, rubble and scattered coral colonies.
PHOTOGRAPH: ED LOVELL.

2. The lagoon of Elizabeth Reef, eastern Australia, is full of delicate *Acropora* thickets.
PHOTOGRAPH: ED LOVELL.

3. The back-reef margin of Broadhurst Reef, central Great Barrier Reef, is a favourite study site.
PHOTOGRAPH: ED LOVELL.

4. A peaceful and quiet lagoon.
PHOTOGRAPH: RON AND VALERIE TAYLOR.

5. The back-reef margin of Broadhurst Reef, central Great Barrier Reef.
PHOTOGRAPH: ED LOVELL.

4

5

Back reef slopes These are usually less regular than outer reef slopes and may have interesting overhangs, caves and deep canyons. Coral growth may be very lush and varied on slopes which do not plunge steeply, but steep or vertical slopes are usually bare. Many of the rarer genera are found in this region. The lower back reef slopes often have spectacular soft coral communities, often with gorgonians, "black coral" and the like, fauna that are also found at a greater depth on outer slopes.

The inter-reef sea floor Depending on location, the sea floor between reefs is covered with rubble, sand or mud. Corals usually play a minor role in most inter-reef communities but these communities are often rich in a wide variety of other organisms. The types of corals present vary according to the substrate, turbidity and depth and are seldom predictable. One common community type consists entirely of solitary free-living *Diaseris, Cycloseris, Trachyphyllia, Heteropsammia* and *Heterocyathus* in varying combinations.

1. A diver recording the coral species diversity of a lower back-reef slope. *PHOTOGRAPH: TERRY DONE.*

2. Coral growth may be very lush and varied on back-reef slopes which do not plunge steeply. *PHOTOGRAPH: ED LOVELL.*

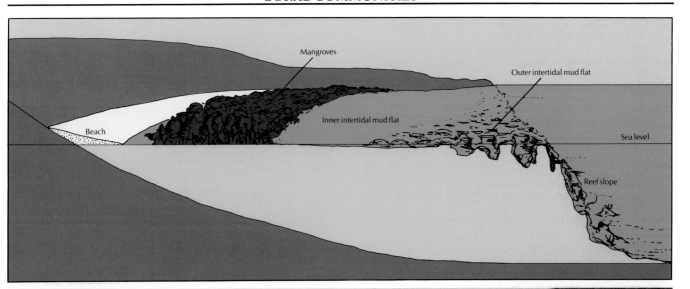

FRINGING REEFS

Fringing reefs are found around "continental" (or "high") islands or along the mainland foreshore. Most fringing reefs are structurally similar, with extensive intertidal mudflats enclosed by a short outer slope.

Inner intertidal mudflats Bays protected from strong wave action may have extensive mangrove swamps. Often there is no clear demarcation between mangrove swamps and the true intertidal reef flat. Some corals, especially pocilloporids, may even occur in the mangroves, growing on the trees' roots.

Outer intertidal mudflats Mudflats always slope towards the sea. As they get progressively deeper, the cover of corals increases. Many of these are shaped as

Diagram 4. The zones of a fringing reef.
DRAWING: MARTY THYSSEN, AIMS.

Above: The outer flat of the fringing reef at Pioneer Bay, Orpheus Island, Palm Islands, the site of the marine research station of James Cook University of north Queensland (and a favourite retreat of the author).
PHOTOGRAPH: AUTHOR.

"micro-atolls", so called because shallow water prevents their upward growth and thus they expand only horizontally leaving dead, eroded centres. Faviids, especially *Goniastrea*, some *Acropora* species (such as *A. aspera* and *A. millepora*) and *Porites* are common in shallow water, but diversity increases rapidly with depth.

1. Fringing reef slopes protected from wave action often have very diverse communities, especially of scleractinian corals and soft corals.
PHOTOGRAPH: ED LOVELL.

2. The upper slope of a fringing reef at the Dampier Archipelago, Western Australia. In reefs such as this, where the water is clear and the circulation good, the community structure may be similiar to that of outer reefs.
PHOTOGRAPH: ED LOVELL.

3. Plate *Acropora* giving way to *Sargassum* on an upper reef slope of the Houtman Abrolhos Islands, Western Australia.
PHOTOGRAPH: ED LOVELL.

4. A reef slope at the Houtman Abrolhos Islands. The slope, dominated by *Sargassum,* is quite unlike that of any other Australian reef except the fringing reef of Lord Howe Island.
PHOTOGRAPH: ED LOVELL.

The outer slope The top of the outer slope is usually exposed only at very low tides and consists of a broad bank of massive coral colonies often dominated by *Porites*. In protected, turbid bays, the slope seldom extends down for more than 10 metres before reaching the flat sea floor. The slope may be more extensive where the water is clearer or where the sea floor is deeper. In either case, and in contrast to the reef slopes of outer reefs, the outer slopes of fringing reefs are usually relatively poor in *Acropora* species, but correspondingly rich in most other genera as well as soft corals. Some species of *Pavona, Goniopora, Porites, Turbinaria* and other genera may form huge monospecific stands, among the largest of all coral colonies. The lower slope may have specialised zones of otherwise rare corals, such as *Anacropora* and *Palauastrea* (both east coast only) and in clearer water there are often extensive areas of fungiids.

OTHER COMMUNITY TYPES

Such is the enormous variation in coral communities that only a small proportion of them can be fitted, by any stretch of the imagination, into the categories described above. Some of the more familiar additions to the above list include the following categories.

Corals of rocky shores Corals may occur well south of any limestone reefs and may also occur on rocky headlands. These corals grow directly on the exposed rock substrate. If this decays easily (for example, basalt), the colonies may never attain a large size, but if the substrate is durable, the resulting community may resemble closely a true reef community (such as Flinders Reef near Moreton Bay in southern Queensland). In either case, the accumulation of coral debris may itself form a suitable substrate for later generations of coral growth.

Corals in algal communities The predominance of beds of kelp and other macro-algae on shallow rocky foreshores south of the tropics is probably one of the main factors limiting the southern extension of coral communities. Some corals, notably *Turbinaria* species and *Pocillopora damicornis*, may compete successfully with the algae but the latter's enormous seasonal growth

1, 2. Extensive communities of one species, usually termed "monospecific stands", occur only in particular environmental conditions. These are two such stands at the Houtman Abrolhos Islands.
PHOTOGRAPHS: ED LOVELL.

3, 4. Many types of coral communities are composed of a number of different species all with similar growth forms, as in these communities of branching *Acropora* (top) and massive faviids (middle).
PHOTOGRAPHS: ED LOVELL (TOP) AND DAVE FISK (MIDDLE).

5. Clusters of brightly coloured *Tubastraea* on the roof of a cave.
PHOTOGRAPH: RON AND VALERIE TAYLOR.

3 smothers most other species. Only at the Houtman Abrolhos Islands in the west and Lord Howe and the Solitary Islands in the east do extensive beds of algae coexist with extensive coral communities.

Communities of one coral species or growth form In some reef situations, a single species or group of species may be overwhelmingly dominant, excluding all others. The result can be a spectacular sight, but usually this happens only in deep or turbid water. Often the dominant species is uncommon in more normal communities (for example, *Euphyllia divisa*, *Leptoseris gardineri*, *Pavona clavus*, *Alveopora catalai* and *Palauastrea ramosa*) and sometimes they almost never occur in other situations (such as *Anacropora* species).

Some communities may be composed of several species, all with the same growth form. The most common are those dominated by bottlebrush or staghorn *Acropora* and those dominated by flat or foliaceous colonies of *Turbinaria*, *Echinopora* and *Montipora*.

Caves During the Ice Ages, when the sea-level periodically fell and left all reefs high out of the water, the reefs were readily eroded by fresh water and this led to the formation of caves of all shapes and sizes. Some of these remain today, submerged below the sea, and populated by gaudy ahermatypic *Tubastraea* and *Dendrophyllia* species, *Distichopora*, *Stylaster* and Bryozoa. Very often these caves are extensive but, unless there is good water circulation, their inner reaches are mostly devoid of life.

Deep-water communites All that is known of the corals **4** of the vast ocean depths comes from the recovery of samples brought to the surface in dredges and other collecting devices. More often than not, dredge samples contain few if any corals but sometimes they are present in thousands. These are ahermatypes, living near or below the maximum depth of light penetration, and they are usually solitary and free-living. *Flabellum* and *Caryophyllia* are the most common genera and may be present in vast numbers over immense areas of fine sandy substrate.

In deeper water, *Stephanocyathus* may also form extensive communities. This is one of the most beautiful of all corals, yet it lives hidden from view in the still, black, near-freezing depths of the continental slopes. Unlike the reef-building hermatypic corals which are largely restricted to tropical and subtropical oceans, the **5** very deep-water ahermatypes are distributed from the Antarctic to the Arctic. They occupy one continuous world ocean with one temperature, which is about 4°C.

CORAL BIOLOGY

HERMATYPIC AND AHERMATYPIC CORALS
Millions of hectares of coral reefs dominate much of the world's tropical coastline. These massive structures result from the accumulation and cementation of skeletons of innumerable corals over thousands of years. Yet, imposing as they are, the existence of modern coral reefs is the result of a most intricate and subtle relationship between the coral polyp and the minute single-celled algae which live symbiotically within the cells of the polyp. These algae, which are commonly called *zooxanthaellae*, belong to a group of unicellular brown plants known as *dinoflagellates*. Most dinoflagellates are a part of the phytoplankton of shallow tropical oceans, where they are a major food source for zooplankton, including small drifting animals and animal larvae. A few members of this group are less benign, occasionally causing lethal "red tides" and shellfish poisoning. Like land plants, the zooxanthellae are able to use the process of photosynthesis to capture the sun's energy and use it to make their own organic food from carbon dioxide, inorganic nutrients and water. Not all corals contain zooxanthellae. Those that do are referred to as *hermatypic* or reef-building corals, and those that do not are called *ahermatypic*.

Symbiotic algae benefit hermatypic corals in two ways. Firstly, 94–98 per cent of all organic carbon produced by zooxanthellae leaks out of the algal cells to be used as a food source by the coral polyp. Secondly, due to photosynthesis by zooxanthellae, hermatypic corals are able to deposit their limestone skeletons two to three times faster in light than in darkness. It is this light-enhanced rate of calcification that enables reefs to grow faster than they are eroded by the action of the sea and eroding organisms.

Even the larvae of hermatypic corals have zooxanthellae, obtained directly from the parent polyp or by "infection" during their free-swimming stage. The algae multiply as the coral grows and are responsible for the brown colours in most hermatypic corals. They may, however, be expelled by the coral as a result of environmental stress (light levels that are too high or too low, low salinity, high temperature) or disease, in which case the coral turns almost white.

Ahermatypic corals, which do not have zooxanthellae, are not restricted to sunlit waters and can grow at any depth. All their nutrition must come from the capture of plankton. Some ahermatypes, notably *Tubastraea, Dendrophyllia* and *Balanophyllia*, are found often on reefs, especially in caves or other places where lack of light prevents the more vigorously growing hermatypes from displacing them. Less than one-third of all ahermatypes are colonial. Those that are usually have poorly interconnected, widely spaced tubular polyps—it is only the hermatypes that have compact, integrated colonies, with well-defined shapes.

These observations raise several interesting questions about coral evolution. Which evolved first, reefs or algal symbiosis? Was the evolution of algal symbiosis a single occurrence or did it evolve at different times in different scleractinian families? Were the corals that helped build Palaeozoic reefs (see Chapter 10) hermatypic? Unfortunately, no accurate way is yet known of distinguishing fossil hermatypes from ahermatypes, except by analogy with modern corals and the sediment types with which they are associated, but it is very likely that the earliest (Triassic) scleractinians lived in a reefal environment. The majority of ahermatypic corals are caryophylliids and these first appeared in the Jurassic period. Since then many other families have evolved deep-water forms independently. Their evolutionary pathway has thus

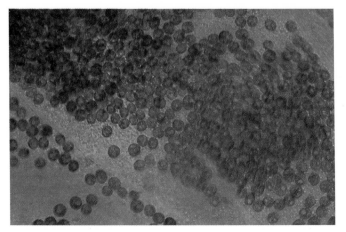

Opposite: Orange egg-and-sperm bundles of *Platygyra sinensis* can be seen through extended tentacles, at night, just before spawning takes place.
PHOTOGRAPH: PETER HARRISON.

Zooxanthellae, the single-celled microscopic algae that are the key to the success of reef-building corals.
PHOTOGRAPH: ED LOVELL.

stretched from shallow reefs and algal symbiosis to an ahermatypic life in the ocean depths. Comparisons with Palaeozoic reefs are difficult, because they were built by organisms, including rugose and tabulate corals, which have no modern equivalents and which built their skeletons from a different form of calcium carbonate (calcite rather than aragonite). It seems likely that algal symbiosis played some role in Palaeozoic reef development, but perhaps a lesser one than it does today.

FOOD

ORGANIC NUTRIENTS

Hermatypic corals have two major food sources: organic compounds produced and excreted by the zooxanthellae in their tissues, and their prey. In return for a place to live and animal waste products, such as phosphates and nitrates which are used as nutrients, the algae supply the coral with as much as 98 per cent of its total food requirements.

Corals growing in shallow clear water where illumination is good, for example, *Acropora*, pocilloporids, etcetera, usually have small polyps. They are able to supplement their diet with minute zooplankton which they are well equipped to catch and which are plentiful on reefs at night. Capture is usually by direct contact: the prey swims onto a tentacle where it is immobilised by some stinging cells and ensnared by others. The struggling victim stimulates the coral to further ensnare its prey and then to swallow it. Corals have the capacity to "taste" their prey and will readily ingest pieces of paper soaked in suitable chemical stimulants. The feeding behaviour of these species appears to vary from region to region. In some areas, such as the Houtman Abrolhos Islands, polyps of many corals, including *Acropora*, remain extended day and night, while in other areas, polyps of the same species will not extend during the day or even on moonlit nights. Perhaps the latter have "learned" that either they, or the plankton they catch, need the protective cover of darkness.

A large number of hermatypic corals grow in relatively dark conditions. These have relatively slower growth rates, and smaller nutritional needs which may be met by algae especially adapted to low-light conditions. They may also consume organic debris and bacteria which are entrapped in the large quantities of mucus which is secreted by specialised epidermal cells and transported to the polyps by movement created by a fine coat of tiny cilia. They may also directly absorb dissolved organic material from sea water.

Another group of corals, including *Euphyllia*, *Cataphyllia* and *Goniopora*, inhabit turbid water and have large fleshy polyps which remain extended during the day. They do not have batteries of stinging cells on their tentacles as do nocturnal plankton feeders. Their food source is unknown, but it may be primarily organic debris.

Many groups of corals appear to have highly specialised feeding habits, which are as yet unknown; for example, the tentacles of *Fungia* and *Heliofungia* could hardly be more different from each other but in all other respects these genera are very similar—presumably they depend on very different food sources.

Ahermatypic corals, which do not have nutrient-supplying symbiotic algae in their tissues, are all carnivorous. Like anemones, they will feed on almost anything they can paralyse with their stinging cells, including worms and fish, and even sea-urchins.

INORGANIC NUTRIENTS

Most coral reefs exist in an environment poor in inorganic nutrients, such as phosphates, nitrates and iron, yet they have a productivity that is similar to that of rainforests. Coral colonies and their zooxanthellae may absorb dissolved nutrients from sea water or obtain them from food captured by the polyps. Since the reefs themselves may receive only low levels of these nutrients from the surrounding ocean, they must have a great capacity to conserve and recycle nutrients. This efficiency can be achieved only when the various groups of animals and plants, and the communities they form, are in balance with each other. This involves many self-regulating processes, which, when combined, make up the nutrient cycle of the reef.

Two special circumstances may supplement the supply of inorganic nutrients on reefs. Firstly, many microscopic filamentous blue-green algae have the ability to absorb nitrogen gas from sea water and convert it to nitrate. When these algae are eaten, this nutrient becomes available to other coral reef organisms. The algae are so efficient and abundant that small amounts of surplus nitrate are often lost to the waters surrounding the reef. Secondly, reefs at the edge of continental shelves may receive periodic inputs of deep, cold, nutrient-rich waters through upwelling. The significance and relative importance of this phenomenon is as yet unknown.

GROWTH

The great evolutionary achievement of the Scleractinia—the development that has allowed them to exploit algal symbiosis to the fullest extent in order to build reefs—is their capacity to form complex colonies by asexual multiplication of polyps. By producing colonies composed of hundreds or thousands of individuals, corals are liberated from all the limitations of the single polyp. They can grow to a very great size, achieve great age, produce enormous quantities of larvae, grow fast enough to outmanoeuvre competitors and can construct plankton-catching sieves on a grand scale.

In *Acropora* growth is achieved by specialised axial polyps which, in some species, bud radial corallites in a precisely determined pattern to produce large complex structures in a very short time; for example, *A. hyacinthus* tables can grow outward at up to 10 centimetres per year. Branching colonies are also capable of rapid growth, with the fast-growing "staghorn" *Acropora* species increasing their branch lengths by up to 15 centimetres per year. In these cases, the competitive strategy of the species is to outgrow and overgrow neighbouring species and this strategy continues until the colony breaks apart under its own weight, or through the

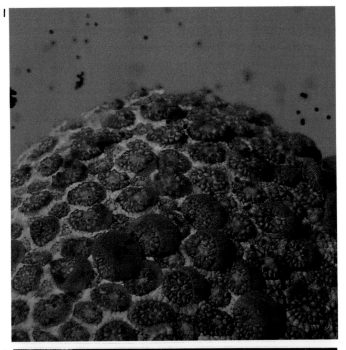

action of boring organisms and waves.

Virtually no other corals can grow as fast as the staghorns. However, other corals have different means of competing for space when growth rate is not all-important. Some produce sturdy colonies able to withstand strong wave action; others produce encrusting colonies, maximising their surface area, and so survive where light is limited. A wide range of species have massive growth forms where rapid growth is sacrificed for long-term endurance and stability. The most extreme examples are the massive *Porites* colonies which grow only about nine millimetres per year. Yet these colonies may reach eight metres in height and may thus be nearly 1000 years old!

Colony growth may also be a way of increasing colony numbers, and many species, including staghorn *Acropora*, are broken up and dispersed during storms. For some corals this type of dispersal is purely accidental; for others it is a major aspect of the growth strategy of the species. This strategy is taken to an extreme in *Diaseris fragilis*, where solitary individuals, not whole colonies, develop weak joints in their skeleton so that they break apart at the slightest touch and form several daughter colonies.

REPRODUCTION

Corals are inventive reproducers and it is very likely that many of the mechanisms employed are still undiscovered. Asexual duplication of polyps occurs not only in colony growth. *Goniopora stokesi* can produce "satellite" colonies (each with their own small skeleton) within the soft tissues of the parent colony. In some corals individual polyps may "bail out" of their skeletons, become detached from the parent colony and develop into new colonies. This bail-out results from stress but it may be a very effective mechanism for short-distance dispersal. Similarly, *Fungia* produces daughter polyps from the tissues of the parent if it is stressed, one example being by burial in mud. All corals, however, devote a substantial part of their available energy to sexual reproduction and the range of methods they employ is extraordinary.

The products of sexual reproduction, the planula larvae, have two functions: they are the means of long-distance dispersal, and they are the means by which corals can cross genetically with each other. These very essential needs create many problems for corals because, being immobile, they cannot move into sexual contact. For coral polyps that have gonads of both sexes, there is the possibility that they may fertilise themselves, but this has yet to be shown to occur. Otherwise, coral have two choices: either males release sperm that swim to

1, 2. *Goniopora* have separate male and female colonies. At the top is a close-up of a female colony (with polyps retracted) releasing dark-coloured egg bundles into the water. At the bottom is a male colony releasing sperm into the water, giving the water a milky appearance.
PHOTOGRAPHS: BETTE WILLIS (TOP) AND GORDON BULL (BOTTOM)

females for internal fertilisation, or both males and females release their gametes (sperm and eggs) into the water for external fertilisation. Both methods have major problems for organisms attached to reefs where currents are strong and gametes disperse quickly. Corals that fertilise internally presumably depend on the existence of other colonies of the same species in close proximity, which release sperm within swimming range. The number of larvae produced is relatively small and the chance that fertilisation will not take place must be very great. Corals that fertilise externally have the advantages of a greater amount of genetic mixing, but they face the enormous problem of having their gametes washed away before fertilisation can occur. To combat this, different colonies of the same species synchronise their spawning, and they do this on the Great Barrier Reef by releasing their gametes shortly after sunset. But which sunset? To synchronise themselves to the correct day, they follow the phases of the moon. When the moon is full, the tides are at their weakest (neap tides). The corals wait for this. But which full moon? To solve this problem they choose the time of the year when water temperature is increasing most rapidly after winter.

The result of all this synchrony is one of the most dramatic events on the reef's yearly calendar. At least half of all the corals of the entire Great Barrier Reef release their gametes just after dark about five days after the full moon in late spring. This incredible mass spawning phenomenon, discovered only in 1982, is the corals' main answer to the great problem of how to get sperm and eggs together from parents that are separated widely and that live in an environment of never-ending water movement.

Most species have polyps that are hermaphrodite (both sexes occur in the one individual) but some colonies have separate sexes. (So far, it has not been shown that individual polyps in the one colony have different sexes.) Hermaphrodite species may release eggs and sperm separately or they may be bundled together. In the latter case, the bundles break apart rapidly after release, well before the eggs are ready for fertilisation. In some species eggs and sperm are ejected vigorously, in others they are extruded slowly. Egg and sperm bundles have a wide variety of colours, but are most commonly pink or yellow.

Species that release gametes for external fertilisation may be hermaphrodite or sexed separately and virtually all of these participate in synchronised mass spawning. Species that brood larvae after internal fertilisation may also be hermaphrodite or sexed separately, but as these keep their eggs safe within the body of the parent, they have less need to coordinate their reproduction. Some, like the pocilloporids, reproduce all year round; others, like *Turbinaria*, reproduce annually but in late autumn.

It appears likely that most ahermatypic corals brood their larvae after internal fertilisation. For those dwelling in deep water, where there is little seasonal variation in temperature and where the cycles of the moon or sun have no effect, it would be very difficult to synchronise gamete-release other than by chemical messages, and it would also be difficult for male and female gametes to make contact in their three-dimensional environment.

1. Orange egg-and-sperm bundles of *Platygyra sinensis* can be seen through extended tentacles, at night, just before spawning takes place.
PHOTOGRAPH: PETER HARRISON.

2. Egg-and-sperm bundles of *Goniastrea retiformis* in the process of being released at Lizard Island, northern Great Barrier Reef.
PHOTOGRAPH: BETTE WILLIS.

3. *Acropora valida* releasing egg-and-sperm bundles during synchronised mass spawning at Magnetic Island, near Townsville.
PHOTOGRAPH: PETER HARRISON.

4. A polyp of *Goniastrea palauensis* shoots out its egg-and-sperm bundle like a ball out of a cannon.
PHOTOGRAPH: PETER HARRISON.

5. A cloud of egg-and-sperm bundles being released from *Platygyra sinensis*. The coral mouths can be seen clearly in the valleys.
PHOTOGRAPH: JAMIE OLIVER.

6. A colony of *Merulina ampliata* joins in the annual mass spawning, filling the water with a cloud of egg-and-sperm bundles.
PHOTOGRAPH: GORDON BULL.

7. The egg-and-sperm bundles of *Acropora tenuis* floating on the water surface. These soon break apart releasing the sperm to fertilise eggs from the same colony or other colonies.
PHOTOGRAPH: PETER HARRISON.

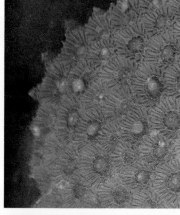

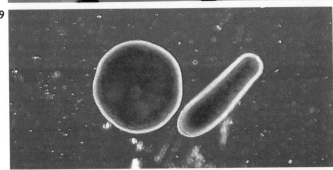

Whatever the coral or its method of sexual reproduction, the products are always planulae larvae. Yet, even here, at least one species (*Pocillopora damicornis*) does the unexpected and produces planulae asexually (without fertilisation) as well as sexually (with internal fertilisation in this case). Asexual production of larvae may be widespread in corals as, like self-fertilisation, it is an effective way of ensuring a maximum rate of larvae production, and adds yet another option to a coral's formidable array of alternative reproductive strategies.

Planula larvae are up to 1.6 millimetres long, have a variety of shapes which change as they develop, and swim actively using minute hair-like cilia. In some corals the planulae settle within a few hours; in others (including most reef-building corals) they may drift on or near the water surface as plankton. They may continue drifting for days, weeks or even months and cover

8. Early development of the planula larvae of *Acropora hyacinthus*. Some are unfertilised eggs, the others are clusters of cells undergoing rapid division.
PHOTOGRAPH: JAMIE OLIVER.

9. During later development, the planula larvae of *Acropora tenuis* change shape. At this stage they are composed of large numbers of cells, many of which have a coating of hair-like cilia allowing the larvae to swim actively.
PHOTOGRAPH: PETER HARRISON.

10. After a planula larva settles on a suitable substrate, it starts to build a skeleton, as shown here.
PHOTOGRAPH: CARDEN WALLACE.

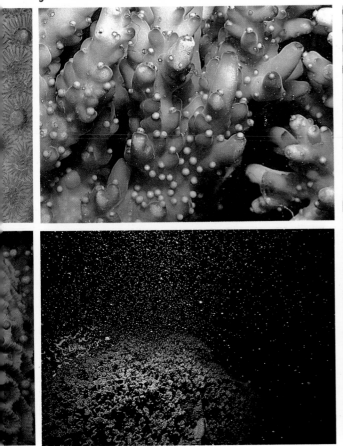

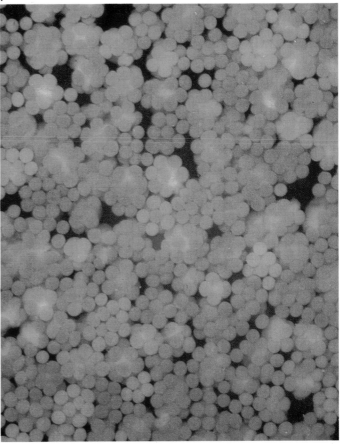

great distances before they detect the proximity of a substrate (presumably by chemical means) and settle. Before settling, they usually search actively for unoccupied space. Once they become attached to a chosen piece of substrate, they start to deposit their skeleton, but even at this stage they may abandon the site and redevelop into a mobile larva. Larvae may settle in very large numbers on suitable substrates, and so only a small proportion of these survive to build new colonies.

TERRITORIALITY AND AGGRESSION

To the daytime observer there are few signs that corals are in any sense "aggressive" towards each other, except when one colony overgrows another. However, at night when tentacles are extended, corals can, and often do, attack one another. Some corals, such as *Galaxea*, *Euphyllia*, *Goniopora*, mussids and the free-living fungiids, are especially aggressive towards other species within their reach, and they may extrude mesenteric filaments which digest the tissues of their neighbours. Other species develop a small number of very long tentacles, called sweeper tentacles, which sting other colonies, sometimes at a distance of several centimetres. As a result of these encounters, many coral colonies cease to grow or develop dead margins when close to other species.

Aggression is more obvious when colonies compete for space by outgrowing or overgrowing each other. Massive colonies (faviids, *Porites* etcetera), which are slow-growing, are the most easily overgrown in this way, but they are the least easily damaged by storms or boring organisms which destroy their faster-growing neighbours. The latter (especially *Acropora*) are usually the early colonisers of areas denuded by cyclones or crown-of-thorns starfish, but they may not be the final dominants in the community structure that develops.

Some community types are predictable and change little from reef to reef. These are sometimes called *climax communities* and appear to be relatively stable. Others are less predictable and probably change continually as one species becomes dominant over another in an endless succession of interactions between different species, and also between those species and their physical and biological environments.

1. The encrusting *Montipora* was kept at a distance by the more dominant *Goniastrea* for about one year before the latter was overgrown and killed.
PHOTOGRAPH: ED LOVELL.

2. A *Euphyllia* (right) using sweeper tentacles to attack a *Goniopora* (left) after these colonies were placed in an aquarium.
PHOTOGRAPH: CHARLES SHEPPARD.

3. A *Favia* (above) growing over an *Astreopora* (below). The whitish band between the colonies is the distance that the stinging tentacles of the *Favia* can reach.
PHOTOGRAPH: ED LOVELL.

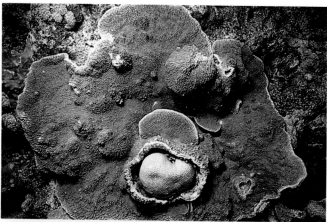

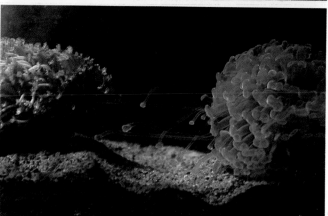

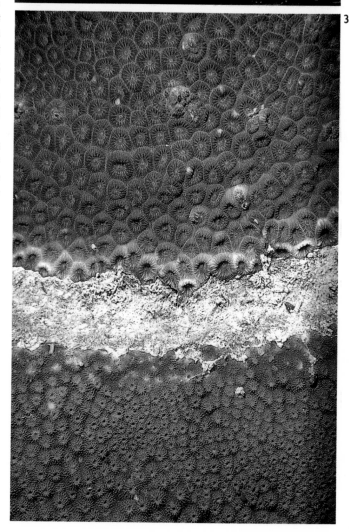

ENEMIES OF CORAL

From the earliest larval stage to the full-grown colony, corals are beset by a host of organisms that feed on them. By far the most prominent of these is the crown-of-thorns starfish (*Acanthaster planci*), notorious for its capacity to multiply to plague numbers which decimate large areas of reef.

The crown-of-thorns starfish was prevalent in the Great Barrier Reef throughout the 1960s and did widespread damage, destroying almost all the corals on some reef slopes. On most reefs, however, the starfish avoids large massive corals, and thus large colonies (especially *Porites* and *Diploastrea*) usually survive attacks. Further substantial outbreaks have occurred on the Great Barrier Reef from the early 1980s and the starfish have been observed by the author as far south as Lord Howe and the Solitary Islands. On the west coast of Australia they have not been seen south of the Ningaloo Reef Tract.

Crown-of-thorns starfish have been recorded throughout the Indo-Pacific from the Red Sea to the far-eastern Pacific, with major outbreaks occurring at approximately the same time throughout most of this range. Just what triggers off these outbreaks and how frequently they might be expected to occur is far from certain. Increases in numbers of starfish larvae have been correlated with rainfall and increases in nutrients from rivers during floods. It appears that the outbreaks are not human-induced, but humans may have increased their severity by collecting shells, several of which are natural predators of the starfish, and also by increasing the survival of starfish larvae by adding nutrients to rivers, and hence reef waters, through clearing forests and fertilising crops. Reefs recover rapidly from starfish attacks, so that five years after denudation coral re-growth is well established, and after 10 years reefs are usually completely recovered. Slow-growing species, especially those forming massive colonies, take longer to re-establish and for that reason the starfish probably has a substantial effect on the structure of coral communities.

Several other organisms may cause destructive outbreaks on reefs. The most notable of these is the small gastropod, *Drupella*, which has caused extensive damage to reefs of the western Pacific, especially southern Japan

4. The crown-of-thorns starfish (*Acanthaster planci*) can cause widespread damage to coral reefs when its numbers reach plague proportions. The starfish itself is a mobile fortress of poisonous spines which few predators can penetrate.
PHOTOGRAPH: ED LOVELL.

5. The crown-of-thorns starfish feeds by everting its stomach through its mouth, wrapping it around its coral prey and digesting the polyps in their own skeletons. Even the most spiny corals are engulfed readily by the delicate folds of stomach seen here after the starfish was removed from its meal.
PHOTOGRAPH: RON AND VALERIE TAYLOR.

6. The aftermath of a crown-of-thorns starfish attack. All the coral is dead and has become encrusted with algae.
PHOTOGRAPH: TERRY DONE.

and Micronesia. Several other coral-eating gastropods have been reported from other countries.

Plague outbreaks on reefs, like fires in forests, cause dramatic, often alarming damage to corals, but boring organisms (for example, the date mussel, *Lithophaga lessepsiana*, various worms including the peacock worm, *Spirobranchus giganteus*, and boring sponges) may also have a great long-term effect on some coral communities. However, by far the greatest predators of coral are fish, many of which have teeth adapted to biting off and then crushing pieces of coral or scraping off polyps. In some regions fish are estimated to consume about one-third of the annual growth of coral. This may have an even greater impact on coral community structure than the crown-of-thorns starfish and may even have an effect on broad-scale coral distributions.

As yet, little is known about the diseases of coral. By far the most common disease is called *coral bleaching*. The coral expels its symbiotic algae or the algae die, the coral turns white and it slowly dies. This bleaching is very widespread and often large areas of reef are affected by it. Another disease may commence when a colony is damaged. An apparent infection of the damaged area spreads until the whole colony gradually dies.

Like most organisms, corals also suffer from what appears to be a form of cancer. Part of a coral colony grows much more rapidly than the rest of the colony and in extreme development may overgrow the original structure. The corallites in these so-called *neoplasms* are usually lightly calcified and have a structure normally associated with deep-water colonies.

Coral Commensals

Many animals live with corals without doing them any apparent harm under normal circumstances. These are commensal organisms and they include a variety of flatworms, polychaete worms, shrimps, crabs, brittle-stars, molluscs and fish. In most instances the relationship between the coral and the commensal is somewhat arbitrary, and the commensal is able to live with a variety of different coral species or live independently. In other instances the relationship is very specific: the commensal has an obligatory association with a particular coral species, or group of species, and modifies its colour, behaviour and even reproductive cycle accordingly.

Perhaps the most common coral commensal is a tiny flatworm, approximately two millimetres long, which lives on the surface of the coral polyp. It has no gut of its own and presumably obtains nutrients from the coral mucus. These worms are found on virtually all corals, usually in low numbers, but they are occasionally found in dense concentrations. They often kill corals that have been placed in aquaria.

The best-known coral commensals are the more conspicuous shrimps and crabs. Several shrimps occur only on the fleshy tentacles of *Euphyllia*, *Goniopora* and *Heliofungia*, while others occur only on branching corals, especially *Acropora* and pocilloporids. At least 40 obligate commensal shrimps have been recorded. Still better known is the gall crab, *Hapalocarcinus marsupialis* (see

p. 80) and the xanthid crab, *Trapezia cymodoce*, which is found on *Acropora divaricata* and most pocilloporids.

A closer association exists between *Fungia* species and the bivalve mollusc *Fungiacava eilatensis*, which lives within the coral's body cavity, and also between *Montastrea* species and the tiny polychaete worm, *Toposyllis*, which is responsible for making grooves between the polyps (see p. 502). There are many such associations between corals and other organisms and often the dividing line between commensalism and parasitism becomes uncertain. There is only one instance (apart from algal symbiosis) where a coral is dependent on another organism: the tiny free-living corals, *Heteropsammia*, *Heterocyathus* and *Psammoseris* are all dependent on sipunculid worms for their continued existence (see pp. 576, 558 and 610).

The Recorders of History

It has long been known that many corals (especially *Porites*) act as biological clocks, depositing layers of skeleton in seasonal cycles. These bands vary in width and density and can be counted like the growth rings of trees, thus indicating something of past environmental conditions. Near-shore corals also show fluorescent bands when they are exposed to ultraviolet light, the amount and intensity of fluorescence varying according to the degree of annual monsoonal flooding. This discovery is important because it is now possible to trace the periods of monsoonal flooding back in time for the entire life of a giant *Porites* colony, perhaps 1000 years, and to do so quite accurately. By studying past atmospheric conditions, it is thus possible to make predictions about the future. It is also possible to learn something about the major changes that periodically take place in ocean circulation patterns. These colonies have therefore probably recorded some of the recent history of the spread of their own species.

1. The surface of a *Porites* colony showing the effects of a large coral-eating wrasse. Large colonies can be damaged extensively within seconds if attacked by schools of coral-grazing fish.
PHOTOGRAPH: RON AND VALERIE TAYLOR.

2. A large *Porites* colony riddled with peacock worms and other borers.
PHOTOGRAPH: ED LOVELL.

3. Tiny arms of brittle-stars project from grooves in the surface of a *Cyphastrea* colony. These brittle-stars have the ability to modify the growth forms of the coral.
PHOTOGRAPH: AUTHOR.

4. Small shrimps are often found on *Euphyllia*; their bodies are transparent except for the tiny skeletal plates.
PHOTOGRAPH: AUTHOR.

5. The common coral-bleaching disease. The white colonies have no algae in their tissues and will soon die. The brown colonies in the centre are already dead and covered with algae.
PHOTOGRAPH: ED LOVELL.

STRUCTURE AND CLASSIFICATION

Coral reefs are grand in size and complex in character, but the organisms that build them are the exact opposite, for corals belong to the coelenterates, a group of simply structured organisms which also includes an enormous range of jellyfish, soft corals, anemones, hydroids and many others. All coelenterates have a body built of two layers. The only multicellular animals that have a more simple organisation are the sponges; all others have their tissues and organs derived from three primordial cell layers and thus are essentially distinct from coelenterates.

The coral polyp is basically an anemone-like animal that secretes a skeleton. Some corals are solitary and look just like anemones when their tentacles are extended. Others are colonial and these are the familiar corals of coral reefs.

THE CORAL POLYP

THE POLYP SKELETON

Although corals are primitive organisms, their skeletons, like those of many other primitive organisms, are often very complex. Fortunately, it is not necessary to understand most of this complexity in order to identify corals. A general account of the structure of the polyp

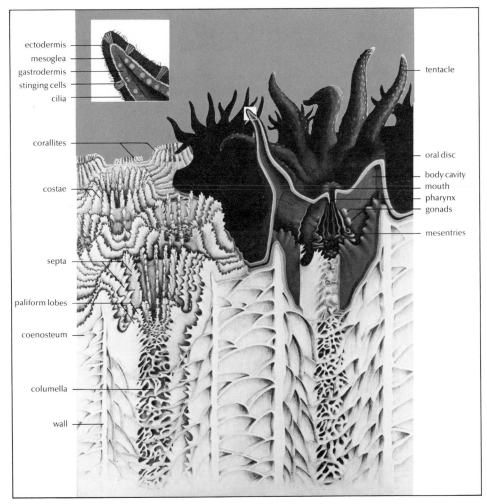

ectodermis
mesoglea
gastrodermis
stinging cells
cilia

corallites

costae

septa

paliform lobes

coenosteum

columella

wall

tentacle

oral disc
body cavity
mouth
pharynx
gonads

mesentries

Diagram 5. The structure of a coral.
DRAWING: GEOFF KELLY.

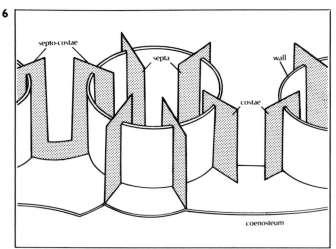

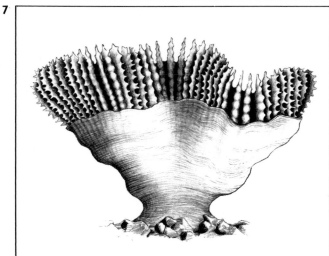

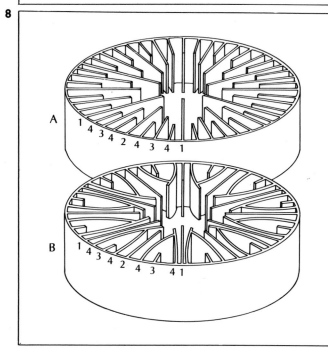

Diagram 6. Diagrammatic representation of the skeletal elements of a polyp.

Diagram 7. The epitheca of *Trachyphyllia geoffroyi*.
DRAWING: GEOFF KELLY.

Diagram 8.
Septal cycles in corals:
a. normal cyclical order,
b. Pourtalès Plan. (Numbers indicate cycles.)

skeleton is given here and this is supplemented, where necessary, with more detail in the introduction to individual families.

The skeleton of the polyp, called the *corallite*, is a tube that contains vertical plates radiating from the tube's centre. The tube itself is the corallite wall and the plates are the *septo-costae*. The tubes are joined together by horizontal plates and other structures, collectively called the *coenosteum*. Some polyps have an additional thin film of skeleton around the wall called the *epitheca*.

The *wall* is usually formed by three skeletal elements which vary in proportion in the different coral families. Some have walls composed primarily of septo-costae which become thickened within the wall. Some have walls composed primarily of coenosteum, while others have walls composed primarily of horizontal rods connected to the septo-costae. In some ahermatypes, the wall may be composed primarily of epitheca. The wall is very prominent in some corals and is hardly formed at all in others.

The septo-costae are the radial elements of the corallite and are divided by the wall into two components: the *septa* which are inside the wall, and the *costae* which are outside. The septa seldom join at the centre of the corallite. Instead, their inner margins usually have fine inward-projecting teeth which, in most corals, become intertwined, forming a complex tangle called the *columella*. Many corals also have a pillar-like projection on the inner margin of some or all of their septa. These are the *paliform lobes* and they often form a neat circle around the columella. The costae seldom extend far beyond the wall, except in corallites that do not project much above the surrounding skeleton. In the latter case the costae often join one corallite to the next.

The coenosteum is usually a matrix of tiny blister-shaped plates which join one corallite to the next. In some corals the plates are fused into a solid layer, while in others they develop very elaborate structures which can become larger and more prominent than the corallites themselves.

The epitheca is the first skeletal element to be produced by the coral planula larva. It is cemented to the substrate and then grows up the side of the polyp. In many corals it becomes obliterated, but in others it forms a dead film resembling tissue paper where the coral is in contact with the substrate. This film is often encrusted with fouling organisms. It often grows independently of the rest of the colony, and may even overgrow and kill corallites.

SYMMETRY

Patterns of radial symmetry, especially of the septa, are used extensively in coral taxonomy.

As a polyp grows, it first forms a cycle of six septa, called the first septal cycle. Then a second cycle of six is formed which alternates with the first. This may be followed by a third cycle of 12, a fourth cycle of 24, and so on. These cycles often remain distinct in fully developed corallites, the first cycle being the largest and the higher cycles becoming progressively smaller.

There are several exceptions to this, the most important of which is called Pourtalès Plan. Corals with septa following this plan have longer fourth-cycle septa than third-cycle septa and they fuse so that the third cycle is enclosed. The pattern formed, which may be repeated in higher cycles, is readily recognisable and often used in identification.

The Polyp Tissues

A coral polyp is essentially a sac with a single *mouth* at the top which is surrounded by tentacles. The mouth leads into a short tube, the *pharynx*, which opens into the body cavity. This is partitioned by vertical *mesenteries* which connect the pharynx to the wall in a radial fashion, and the wall is usually thrown into similar folds by the presence of the septa. A series of coiled filaments, the *mesenteric filaments*, are packed along the inner edge of the mesenteries.

The body wall of the polyp, as with all coelenterates, is composed of two cell layers: the *ectodermis* on the outside and the *gastrodermis* on the inside. These layers are separated by the *mesoglea*, which is initially non-cellular but which may contain a wide range of cell types after initial growth.

The extended polyp, with its anemone-like appearance, has tubular tentacles composed of the same two cell layers. The whole of this structure sits above the skeleton in a manner that allows the lower polyp wall to cover the skeleton. As the latter has a complex shape, the lower polyp wall is also complex for it is the ectodermis of this part of the polyp that secretes the skel-

eton. The ectodermis of the upper part of the polyp has a wide range of specialised cells. Some are stinging cells which are usually grouped into wart-like *batteries*, clearly visible to the naked eye. Other cells secrete large amounts of slimy mucus, which always covers the polyp. The mucus is moved around by minute hair-like *cilia*. This helps in food capture and in the removal of sediment.

The coelenterates are the simplest organisms to have discrete nervous, muscular and reproduction systems, and in corals all are well developed. A simple nerve net, composed of both ectodermal and gastro-dermal cells, permeates the body wall with connections to a variety of specialised cells responsible for sensing mechanical and chemical stimuli as well as light.

A muscular system, consisting primarily of fibres either side of the mesoglea, allows polyps to extend and retract in response to signals from the nerve net. These signals are also transmitted readily from polyp to polyp.

1. The nervous system of a *Goniopora* colony in action. The polyps in the foreground have retracted and the stimulus to retract is spreading to the other polyps in the colony. The whole process takes only a few seconds.
PHOTOGRAPH: CLAY BRYCE.

2. Female gonads (ovaries) of an *Acropora* polyp seen after the skeleton was dissolved in acid. Each gonad is associated with one mesentery.
PHOTOGRAPH: CARDEN WALLACE.

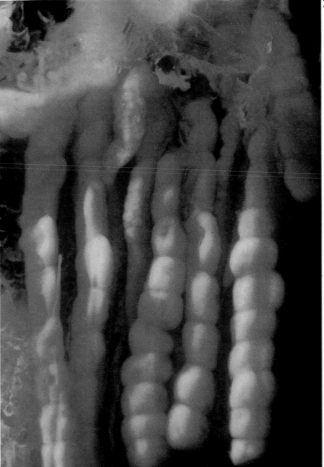

The reproductive organs develop within the mesoglea of the mesenteries. This happens on an annual cycle in most species, after which the organs disappear, only to re-form the next year. Some species of corals may have separate male and female colonies or both sexes may be present in the same polyps (hermaphrodites). In either case the gonads are arranged around the base of the pharynx in a regular fashion. In some hermaphrodite corals, male and female gonads are on different mesenteries, in others the testes are above the ovaries on the same mesenteries and in still others testes and ovaries grow together.

The gastrodermis, the inner-cell layer, has an array of specialised cells for digestion, part of which occurs in the body cavity and part inside the gastrodermal cells themselves. Because the body cavities of neighbouring polyps are interconnected, the polyps of a colony share nutrients rather than compete with each other.

The gastrodermis is also the layer that contains the zooxanthellae, the unicellular symbiotic algae which exist within gastrodermal cells themselves and are essential to the growth and survival of hermatypic corals. These algae are minute, approximately 0.008–0.012 millimetres in diameter, and they occur in enormous numbers in the polyp tissue.

THE CORAL COLONY

Important though the structure of the individual polyp may be in the identification of most corals, both the pattern of colony formation and the growth form of mature colonies may be equally important.

COLONY FORMATION

All corals that form colonies do so by a process of budding, where the parent polyp divides into two or more polyps (*intratentacular budding*), or daughter polyps form on the side of the parent (*extratentacular budding*), or polyps lose their identity as individuals and form continuous valleys. The growth form of the colony that results depends on the type of budding in some corals, but is completely independent of it in others.

If the corallites of a colony have their own walls, they are called *plocoid* or *phaceloid*, depending on how elongate they are. If they share common walls they are called *meandroid* or *cerioid*, depending on whether they form valleys or not. In addition, corals are termed *flabello-meandroid* if they form valleys which do not have common walls.

A variety of other types of colony formation are found in corals, but these are uncommon. Far from being mutually exclusive, some species (even some

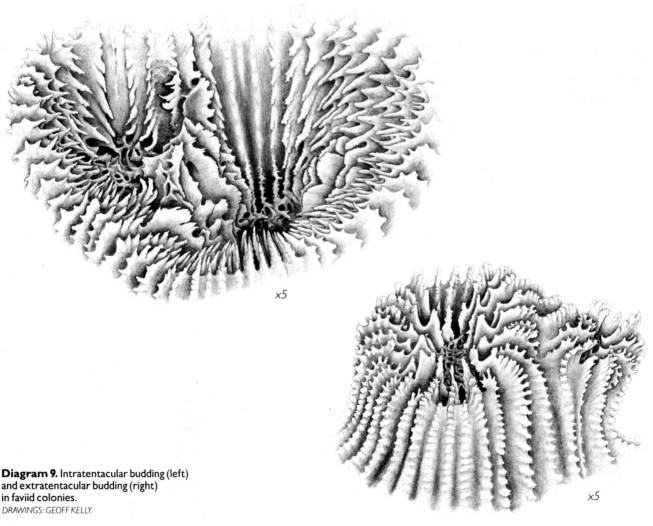

x5

x5

Diagram 9. Intratentacular budding (left)
and extratentacular budding (right)
in faviid colonies.
DRAWINGS: GEOFF KELLY.

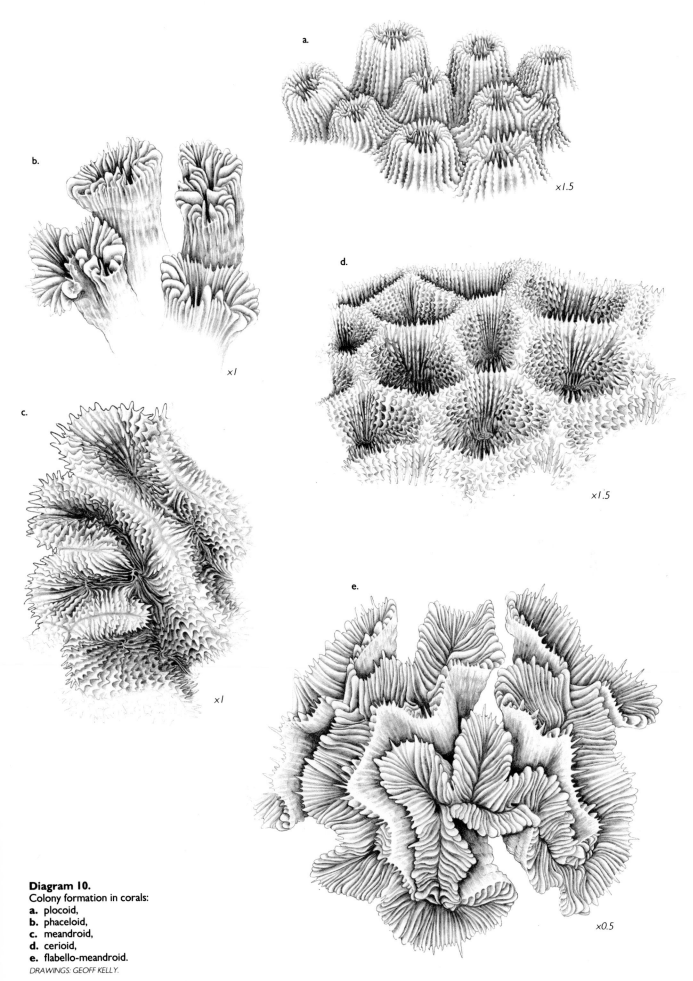

a.

×1.5

b.

×1

c.

×1

d.

×1.5

e.

×0.5

Diagram 10.
Colony formation in corals:
a. plocoid,
b. phaceloid,
c. meandroid,
d. cerioid,
e. flabello-meandroid.
DRAWINGS: GEOFF KELLY.

59

individual colonies) may exhibit more than one type of colony formation and others are intermediate between one type and the next.

GROWTH FORM

Colonies that have phaceloid and flabello-meandroid types of colony formation have distinctive growth forms, usually described by those same names. Other modes of colony formation may result in widely differing growth forms which are usually described by their shape rather than their structure.

The most common terms used are: *massive* (similar in all dimensions), *columnar* (forming columns), *encrusting* (adhering to the substrate), *branching* (arborescent or tree-like to digitate or finger-like), *foliaceous* (leaf-like) and *laminar* (plate-like). Other terms are used for particular families; all are explained in the glossary.

GROWTH-FORM VARIATION

Colony development has allowed corals to be free of many of the limitations of the solitary individual. It allows them to build complex structures which are variable in shape, size and design to meet the demands of different parts of the reef's wide array of environmental conditions. With corals these developments have not taken place through the evolution of a large number of different species, but have occurred within species, giving many species a wide range of growth-form options, each suited to a different set of environmental conditions.

Growth-form variations in corals are very readily seen on a reef slope. Corals on the upper slope, exposed to continual pounding from the ocean waves, are small, stunted and solidly constructed. Further down the slope, where wave action is less, coral colonies become larger and more delicate, and a much wider range of forms appears. Still deeper, where there is no wave action but where light availability becomes reduced, the shapes of colonies are different again and broad delicate tables and plates and lightly structured branching forms become the most common.

These sorts of changes occur in response to change in any major environmental gradient, especially wave action, light availability, and turbidity. Sometimes, like forests on a mountain slope, they are due to one species or group of species replacing others. But often the one species persists from one environment to the next by modifying its skeleton structure.

One or other aspect of the physical environment is usually the most likely cause of growth-form variation in corals. However, the biological environment may be equally important because corals have the capacity to modify their growth form in response to the activities of neighbouring corals, and sometimes even in response to neighbouring polyps of the same colony. Thus a number of growth strategies may be used to overgrow a neighbouring colony and the budding pattern of an individual polyp may reflect the size of the colony or the degree of crowding.

The genetic control of growth-form variation is another matter again. Like all other aspects of a coral's growth and development, its capacity for growth-form variation is genetically programmed. This can be done by allowing a single species to have a wide range of genetically determined forms, so that each form is suited to a particular environmental niche. Alternatively, it can be done by allowing growth form to be as free as possible from genetic constraints.

Whatever its cause and control, growth-form variation affects greatly the concepts coral taxonomists have about species, and it must be taken into account by anyone attempting to identify a coral. Most coral species

Diagram 11.
The growth forms of corals:
a. massive,
b. columnar,
c. encrusting,
d. branching,
e. foliaceous, forming a whorl,
f. laminar, forming a tier,
g. free-living.
DRAWINGS: GEOFF KELLY.

do not have a particular growth form or precise corallite characterisation. Individual corallites vary on different parts of the same colony and colonies vary in different parts of a reef, in different regions and in different countries. The species is the sum of all this variation and this has given corals a bad reputation amongst biologists as a particularly difficult group of animals to classify.

CLASSIFICATION

But as a Darwinian I have the clearest idea of what a species is . . . it is one which works very well, because the numbers of well-marked, and at first sight good species, which yet show a complete transition to other species, are very few indeed compared with the very large number which show no such transition.

Alfred R. Wallace,
in a letter to Henry Bernard, 1900.

The appearance of the living coral under water—its growth form and the shape and colour of its polyps—is usually an important aid in species identification and is used by all who work with corals. In order to classify corals, however, the taxonomist needs much more information, the nature of which depends on whether he or she is dealing with a species, a genus or a family.

At species level, the coral taxonomist is concerned mostly with details of corallite structure and with growth form and how these vary along environmental gradients in one particular region, and finally, how they vary from one region to the next. In most instances he or she must work with groups of species in order to distinguish between true species and what are simply growth-form or geographic variants of true species. The work of delineating true species, therefore, involves combinations of underwater and laboratory studies.

At generic level, the emphasis changes. Species are true biological units, but the genus is a human-made concept. The taxonomist assigns a species to one genus or another depending on how closely it is considered to be related to the other species in the genus. This is a simple task for most corals because the generic groupings of corals are usually distinct. Where doubt exists, the taxonomist relies entirely on details of skeletal structure.

At family level, the emphasis changes again because any one family of corals may include an enormous range of growth forms, solitary and colonial species, hermatypes and ahermatypes, corals from any ocean and fossil corals from any time in the entire evolution of the Scleractinia. The characters of families may therefore be particularly difficult to determine with precision, and taxonomists often resort to ultra-fine details of skeletal

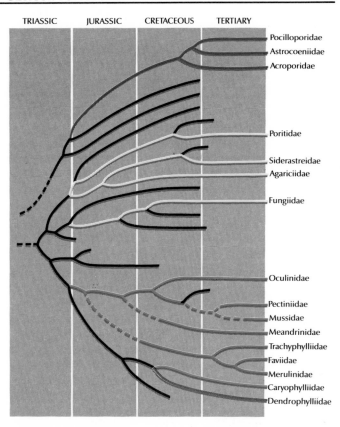

Diagram 12. The family tree of Scleractinia showing the relationships between hermatypic families.
DRAWING: MARTY THYSSEN, AIMS.

structure, especially details of the structure of the individual septo–costae.

The task of establishing species, genera and families, complicated though it often is, does not end with the corals that exist now. The same system of classification must also incorporate fossils. With corals, which often form good fossils, this is an important aspect of taxonomy. The variability of skeletal structures seen in living coral species confronts the coral palaeontologist with insuperable problems because, even with large numbers of good fossils, a means of distinguishing true species characters from growth-form variations is seldom available. For genera and families, however, taxonomic characters of fossils may be as good as those of existing corals. What is generally lacking is completeness (it is seldom possible to get anywhere near a complete inventory of genera from fossils), and then there is the enormous difficulty of having to grapple with the dimensions of time as well as space.

The fossil record will never be good enough to show how most corals change their distribution and their structure with time, but it does tell us much about the evolutionary history of major coral groups and it is a major component of family-level classification.

REEF-BUILDING SCLERACTINIA
Australian Species

Opposite: *Australogyra zelli* is basically a meandroid species with prominent valleys, but forms branching colonies.
PHOTOGRAPH: ED LOVELL.

FAMILY
ASTROCOENIIDAE

(pronounced ass-tro-see-nee-id-ee)

KOBY, 1890

THE GENERA

Only one living genus, *Stylocoeniella*, is included in this otherwise fossil
family of colonial, hermatypic corals.
Stylocoeniella has close affinities with the Pocilloporidae.

EARLIEST FOSSILS

Some of the oldest scleractinian fossils, from the Triassic, are included in this family.

Opposite: *Stylocoeniella* is usually found intermixed with other encrusting corals
in out-of-the-way places such as this rock ledge at Scott Reef, Western Australia.
PHOTOGRAPH: AUTHOR.

GENUS
STYLOCOENIELLA

(pronounced <u>sty</u>-lo-<u>see</u>-nee-<u>el</u>-la)

Yabe & Sugiyama, 1935

The most remarkable aspect of the biology of this little-known genus is that it only forms big colonies on temperate reefs, near the limit of coral reef distribution. Thus on the southernmost reefs of the east and west coasts of Australia, colonies over two metres in diameter grow in shallow water and look like *Porites*. In the tropics, *Stylocoeniella* is uncommon and is usually restricted to turbid environments where it forms only small encrusting colonies.

TYPE SPECIES
Porites armata Ehrenberg, 1834.

FOSSIL RECORD
Eocene to Recent from the USA, West Indies and Indo-Pacific.

NUMBER OF SPECIES
Three nominal species, two true species, both Australian.

CHARACTERS
Colonies are massive, columnar or encrusting. Corallites are immersed, circular, with two unequal cycles of septa and a style-like columella. The coenosteum is covered with fine spinules and also by larger pointed styles which are almost as numerous as the corallites.
Polyps have not been observed extended.

SIMILAR GENERA
Stylocoeniella resembles *Porites* and *Palauastrea* under water. Both the latter are distinguished by their lack of coenosteum styles. Corallites of *Stylocoeniella*, *Palauastrea*, and *Stylaraea* are curiously similar, considering that they belong to three different families.

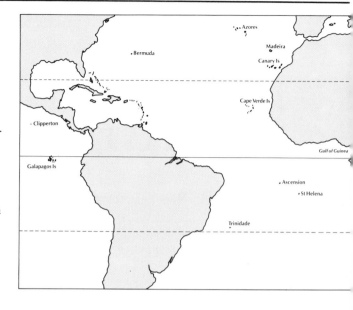

Stylocoeniella guentheri
BASSETT-SMITH, 1890

TYPE LOCALITY
South China Sea.

IDENTIFYING CHARACTERS
Calices are about 0.8 mm in diameter and are flush with the coenosteum. Septa are in two very unequal cycles.

COLOUR
Dark or pale greenish-brown, with white polyps.

SIMILAR SPECIES
S. armata.

DISTRIBUTION
From Madagascar east to the Marshall Islands.
Around Australia: the Great Barrier Reef, Coral Sea and south to Sydney in the east, and south to the Houtman Abrolhos Islands on the west coast.

ABUNDANCE
Usually uncommon but more abundant than *S. armata*. Large colonies (greater than 0.5 m in diameter) are found in higher latitudes only.

1. *Stylocoeniella guentheri* from Lord Howe Island, eastern Australia. At Elizabeth Reef, eastern Australia, and the Houtman Abrolhos Islands, Western Australia, colonies grow larger and tend to be more spherical.
PHOTOGRAPH: JOHN BARNETT.
2. The common appearance of *Stylocoeniella guentheri*.
PHOTOGRAPH: AUTHOR.
3. The polyps of *Stylocoeniella armata*.
PHOTOGRAPH: AUTHOR.

x5

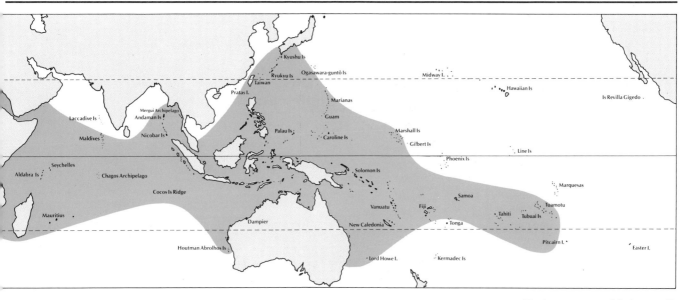

The known range of *Stylocoeniella*.

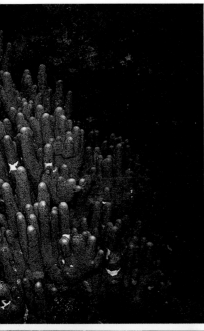

Stylocoeniella armata
(EHRENBERG, 1834)

TYPE LOCALITY
  Red Sea.

IDENTIFYING CHARACTERS
  Calices are about 1.3 mm in diameter and form excavations in the coenosteum. Septa are in two equal or sub-equal cycles.

COLOUR
  Dark or pale brown or green.

SIMILAR SPECIES
  S. guentheri

DISTRIBUTION
  From the Red Sea east to the Tuamotu Archipelago. Around Australia: the Great Barrier Reef, Coral Sea and south to Elizabeth Reef in the east, and the Rowley Shoals and Scott Reef on the west coast.

ABUNDANCE
  Rare, cryptic.

x5

3

FAMILY
POCILLOPORIDAE

(pronounced po-sil-oh-por-id-ee)

GRAY, 1842

The Pocilloporidae contains three common genera, *Pocillopora, Seriatopora* and *Stylophora*, which have very similar biological characteristics, and two uncommon genera, *Palauastrea* and *Madracis*, which are different in most respects, especially the latter which is composed of mostly ahermatypic species, although the Australian species is hermatypic.

The common genera all abound on upper reef slopes exposed to strong wave action and are also found in deep water and in lagoons. They are all highly polymorphic and all show similar growth forms in response to wave action and light availability.

Unlike the majority of corals, most species brood planula larvae after internal fertilisation rather than release gametes into the water. They brood at regular or irregular intervals throughout the year. Mature colonies are hermaphrodite.

CHARACTERS
Colonial and mostly hermatypic. Colonies are submassive, ramose or arborescent. Corallites are immersed to conical, small, have well–developed columellae and neatly arranged septa of two cycles or less, some usually fused with the columella. The coenosteum is covered with spinules.

RELATED FAMILIES
Astrocoeniidae and Acroporidae.

EARLIEST FOSSILS
Cretaceous.

THE GENERA
The five genera *Pocillopora, Seriatopora, Stylophora, Palauastrea* and *Madracis,* all occur in Australia.

KEY TO GENERA OF POCILLOPORIDAE

Colonies covered with verrucae . . . *Pocillopora* (p. 70)

Colonies branching, without verrucae

  Branches fine, anastomosing, corallites in rows . . . *Seriatopora* (p. 80)

  Branches usually over 15 mm thick, corallites with hoods . . . *Stylophora* (p. 84)

  Branches pencil to finger thickness, corallites immersed, without hoods . . . *Palauastrea* (p. 86)

Colonies encrusting or with club-shaped columns, corallites subcerioid . . . *Madracis* (p. 88)

Opposite: New life on the reef. Pocilloporids and *Acropora* are early colonisers of denuded reefs.
PHOTOGRAPH: RON AND VALERIE TAYLOR.

Genus
POCILLOPORA

(pronounced <u>po</u>-sil-oh-<u>por</u>-a)

Lamarck, 1816

In the collections there are over 50 specimens and in addition I have examined a very large number in the British Museum ... and I am doubtful whether all these so-called species should not rather be described as varieties of one species, the characters of which would be the characters of the whole genus.

J. Stanley Gardiner,
*On Some Collections of Corals of
the Family Pocilloporidae from
the S.W. Pacific Ocean, 1897.*

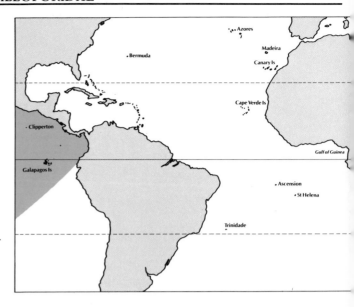

The genus *Pocillopora* is easily identified by the presence of wart-like growths, called verrucae, which cover the colonies. The three common species, *P. damicornis, P. verrucosa* and *P. eydouxi*, would also be easily recognised were it not for the presence of the two uncommon species, *P. meandrina* and *P. woodjonesi. P. meandrina* is easily confused with *P. verrucosa; P. woodjonesi* is easily confused with *P. eydouxi*.

Pocillopora is characteristically a polymorphic genus. Each species, particularly *P. damicornis* and *P. verrucosa*, shows marked changes in growth form according to environmental conditions and geographic location. On shallow reef fronts exposed to heavy wave action, all species of *Pocillopora* are relatively stunted, while in deep water, branches are thin and open. The effects of environment are so marked that colonies of different species on reef fronts may resemble each other more than colonies of the same species from deeper water. The effect of geographic location may be almost as pronounced. For example, colonies of *P. damicornis* from different isolated localities at the southern limit of its distribution (such as Lord Howe and the Solitary Islands) all look very different and thus the species can readily be divided into a series of geographic subspecies.

Hardy, widespread and common, *Pocillopora* is often the experimental "guineapig" of the coral world. Indeed, most of the early discoveries about the growth and reproduction of corals were made with *P. damicornis* at Low Isles during the 1928 expedition to the Great Barrier Reef. This species is still studied widely and it has recently been shown that the coral can produce asexual as well as sexual larvae, a discovery of considerable importance in coral genetics. The larvae can remain free-swimming for several weeks and can even become partly polyp-like, enabling feeding to occur before settling and commencing skeleton formation. Unlike the majority of corals, *Pocillopora* (like other pocilloporids) release planula larvae after internal fertilisation. The polyps are hermaphrodites, each with four sets of male and four sets of female gonads on alternate mesenteries.

x5

KEY TO SPECIES OF *POCILLOPORA*

Verrucae intergrade with branches ... *P. damicornis* (p. 72)

Verrucae distinct, smaller than branches

    Colony consists of uniform dividing branches, not laterally flattened columns

        Branches have an upright form ... *P. verrucosa* (p. 74)

        Branches have a sprawling form ... *P. meandrina* (p. 76)

    Colony consists of stout, laterally flattened columns

        Branches irregular, oar-shaped, coenosteum heavily granulated ... *P. woodjonesi* (p. 77)

        Branches very stout, upright, coenosteum not heavily granulated ... *P. eydouxi* (p. 78)

Note: This key is a guide only and should be used in conjunction with descriptions of the species.

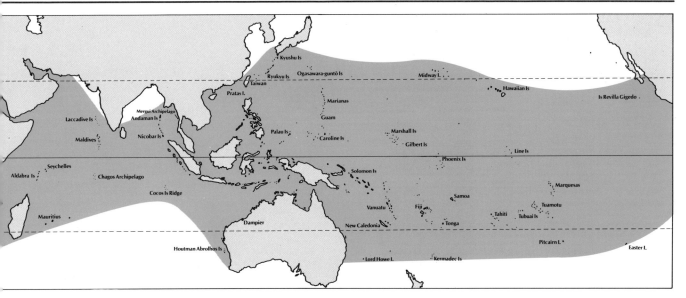

The known range of *Pocillopora*.

TYPE SPECIES
Pocillopora acuta Lamarck, 1816 from the "Indian Ocean".

FOSSIL RECORD
Eocene to Recent from the West Indies and Indo–Pacific.

NUMBER OF SPECIES
Approximately 35 nominal species, seven to 10 true species, five of which are Australian.

CHARACTERS
Colonies are submassive to ramose with branches tending to be blade-like or else fine and irregular. Colonies are covered with verrucae.
Corallites are immersed. They may be devoid of internal structures or have a low solid columella and two unequal cycles of septa. The coenosteum is usually covered by granules.
Polyps are usually extended only at night.

SIMILAR GENERA
Pocillopora is a well-defined genus readily distinguishable from others by the presence of verrucae.

The wart-like verrucae of *Pocillopora*.
PHOTOGRAPH: ED LOVELL.

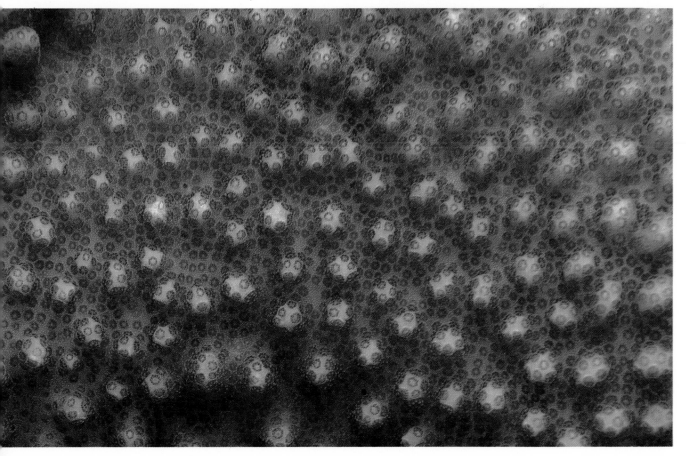

Pocillopora damicornis

(LINNAEUS, 1758)

TYPE LOCALITY
"Oceanus Asiatico"

IDENTIFYING CHARACTERS
Verrucae and branches intergrade. Branches may be fine and widely separated (in calm environments) to very compact (on upper reef slopes).

COLOUR
Pale brown, greenish or pink.

SIMILAR SPECIES
P. verrucosa.

DISTRIBUTION
Occurs throughout the full range of *Pocillopora.*
Around Australia: the Great Barrier Reef, Coral Sea and south to Sydney in the east, and south to Rottnest Island on the west coast.

ABUNDANCE
Very common. Occurs in all shallow-water habitats from wharf piles and mangrove swamps to exposed reef fronts.

1. *Pocillopora damicornis* from the Solitary Islands, eastern Australia, showing thick, widely spaced branches. Particular growth forms such as this are often restricted to remote localities and form recognisable subspecies.
PHOTOGRAPH: ED LOVELL.

2. A finely structed *Pocillopora damicornis* from Broadhurst Reef, Great Barrier Reef. This growth form is characteristic of reef slopes protected from strong wave action.
PHOTOGRAPH: ED LOVELL.

3. *Pocillopora damicornis* with polyps extended.
PHOTOGRAPH: AUTHOR.

4. *Pocillopora damicornis* is recognised readily because verrucae intergrade with branches.
PHOTOGRAPH: ED LOVELL.

5. *Pocillopora damicornis* often occurs on reef flats exposed to strong wave action. In such environments, branches become thick and compact.
PHOTOGRAPH: AUTHOR.

4

5

Pocillopora verrucosa

(ELLIS & SOLANDER, 1786)

TYPE LOCALITY
Not recorded.

IDENTIFYING CHARACTERS
Colonies are composed of uniform upright branches clearly distinct from the verrucae, but the latter are irregular in size. They have permanently coloured red-brown stalks.

COLOUR
Usually cream, pink or blue.

SIMILAR SPECIES
P. damicornis and P. meandrina.

DISTRIBUTION
From the Red Sea and eastern Africa east to Hawaii. Around Australia: the Great Barrier Reef and Coral Sea in the east, and south to Shark Bay on the west coast.

ABUNDANCE
Common. Occurs in most shallow-water environments from fringing reefs to exposed reef fronts.

1. *Pocillopora verrucosa* from an upper reef slope of Myrmidon Reef, Great Barrier Reef, exposed to strong wave action. Branches are sturdy and tend to be plate-like.
PHOTOGRAPH: ED LOVELL.

2. *Pocillopora verrucosa* on an exposed reef flat showing extreme thickening of branches.
PHOTOGRAPH: AUTHOR.

3. A characteristic view of *Pocillopora verrucosa*. Note the compact branches which do not intergrade with the verrucae.
PHOTOGRAPH: ED LOVELL.

4. *Pocillopora verrucosa* from a reef slope.
PHOTOGRAPH: ED LOVELL.

3

4

Pocillopora meandrina

DANA, 1846

TYPE LOCALITY
Hawaii.

IDENTIFYING CHARACTERS
Colonies are composed of uniform sprawling branches with small uniform verrucae.

COLOUR
Usually cream, or pink.

SIMILAR SPECIES
P. verrucosa and *P. meandrina* may be difficult to distinguish unless both species are collected together.

DISTRIBUTION
From Australia east to Samoa, the Marshall Islands and Hawaii. Around Australia: the northern and central Great Barrier Reef and Coral Sea in the east, and south to Houtman Abrolhos Islands on the west coast.

ABUNDANCE
Uncommon except on exposed reef fronts and Coral Sea reefs. Colonies may be over 1 m in diameter.

1. The usual appearance of *Pocillopora meandrina.*
PHOTOGRAPH: ED LOVELL.

2. *Pocillopora meandrina* (right) next to *P. eydouxi* (left) from an upper reef slope.
PHOTOGRAPH: VICKI HARRIOTT.

3. *Pocillopora meandrina* from an upper reef slope exposed to strong wave action. Such colonies resemble closely *P. verrucosa.*
PHOTOGRAPH: ED LOVELL.

Pocillopora woodjonesi
VAUGHAN, 1918

TYPE LOCALITY
Cocos-Keeling Islands.

IDENTIFYING CHARACTERS
Colonies are composed of upright flattened branches. The coenosteum is covered with fine granules.

COLOUR
Pink or brown.

SIMILAR SPECIES
P. eydouxi has a similar shape but branches are bigger.

DISTRIBUTION
Australia and the Cocos-Keeling Islands.
Around Australia: the Great Barrier Reef in the east, and south to Dampier Archipelago on the west coast.

ABUNDANCE
Uncommon except on upper reef slopes exposed to strong wave action.

1. A large colony of *Pocillopora woodjonesi* from an upper reef slope of Myrmidon Reef, Great Barrier Reef. A small colony of *P. verrucosa* is seen at the lower left.
PHOTOGRAPH: ED LOVELL.

2. *Pocillopora woodjonesi* at the Dampier Archipelago, Western Australia.
PHOTOGRAPH: BARRY WILSON.

Pocillopora eydouxi

EDWARDS & HAIME, 1860

TYPE LOCALITY
"Pacific Ocean".

IDENTIFYING CHARACTERS
Colonies are composed of stout, upright, flattened branches. They may be widely separated, or compact, especially where currents are strong.

SIMILAR SPECIES
P. woodjonesi.

COLOUR
Pale to dark green or brown.

DISTRIBUTION
From the Red Sea south to Mozambique and east to Hawaii. Around Australia: the northern and central Great Barrier Reef and Coral Sea in the east, and south to Houtman Abrolhos Islands on the west coast.

ABUNDANCE
Common, especially on exposed reef fronts and where currents are strong. May form mono-specific stands of several metres in diameter.

1. *Pocillopora eydouxi* at Broadhurst Reef, Great Barrier Reef. The white tips to the branches are caused by grazing fish. This species is often very conspicuous and is a favourite for collectors.
PHOTOGRAPH: ED LOVELL.

2. The branches of large *Pocillopora eydouxi* may become flattened or paddle-shaped.
PHOTOGRAPH: ED LOVELL.

3. A coral zone dominated by *Pocillopora eydouxi* at the Dampier Archipelago, Western Australia.
PHOTOGRAPH: ED LOVELL.

4, 5. Two common growth forms of *Pocillopora eydouxi.*
PHOTOGRAPHS: ED LOVELL.

78

Genus
SERIATOPORA

(pronounced see-ree-at-oh-por-a)

Lamarck, 1816

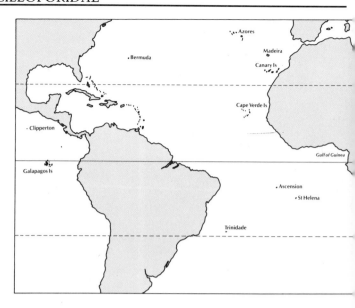

One of the most curious methods of asexual reproduction in corals was discovered in *Seriatopora* in an aquarium where polyps were seen to detach themselves from a dying colony. The skeletonless polyps were then able to form new colonies by normal budding. This extraordinary process, called polyp bail-out, has since been discovered in several other corals, and has also been found to occur under natural conditions.

Seriatopora shows similar variations in growth form in response to depth and wave action as *Pocillopora* and *Stylophora*; colonies from shallow water exposed to strong wave action tend to have short, thick branches while those from deep or turbid water have long, fine ones. Parts of colonies of these genera also show remarkable modifications caused by other organisms, the most notable of which is the gall-forming crab *Hapalocarcinus marsupialis*. Female crabs influence the growing tips of the coral to form a "gall", which is effectively a cage that permanently encloses the crab. Male crabs, which are much smaller than the females, are able to enter the cage to mate. The female spends her whole life in self-imposed captivity producing broods of larvae inside the protective walls of her coral cage.

TYPE SPECIES
Seriatopora subulata Lamarck, 1816 from the West Indies.

FOSSIL RECORD
Miocene to Recent from the Indo-Pacific.

NUMBER OF SPECIES
Twenty-six nominal species, approximately five true species, two of which are Australian.

CHARACTERS
Colonies form compact bushes with thin anastomosing branches.
Corallites are arranged in neat rows along the branches. They are mostly immersed and have poorly developed internal structures except for solid style-like columellae. Usually one, sometimes two cycles of septa are developed and are fused to the columella. The coenosteum is covered by fine spinules.
Polyps are extended only at night.

SIMILAR GENERA
Seriatopora is a well-defined genus closest to, but clearly distinct from, *Stylophora*.

×5

1

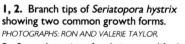

1, 2. Branch tips of *Seriatopora hystrix* showing two common growth forms.
PHOTOGRAPHS: RON AND VALERIE TAYLOR.

3. Several species of crabs can modify the growth of *Seriatopora* and other corals to meet their own needs. Here females of the gall-crab, *Hapalocarcinus marsupialis*, have induced the coral to form a cage like a pair of cupped hands. The females become entrapped in their own prison but can be visited by the much smaller males who crawl between the finger-like bars.
PHOTOGRAPH: AUTHOR.

2

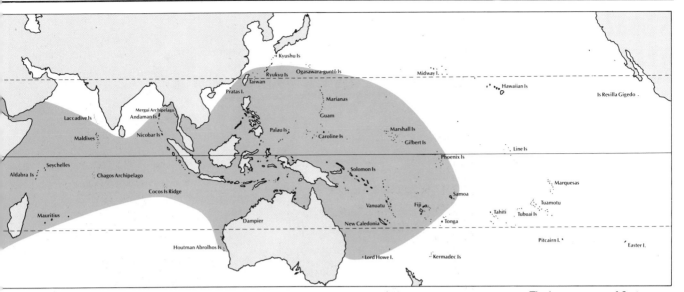

The known range of *Seriatopora*.

3

Seriatopora hystrix

DANA, 1846

TYPE LOCALITY
   Fiji.

IDENTIFYING CHARACTERS
   Branches are tapered to a point;
   they may be either widely spaced
   or compact.

COLOUR
   Cream, blue or pink.

SIMILAR SPECIES
   S. caliendrum, distinguished by
   having thicker branches which do
   not taper.

DISTRIBUTION
   Occurs throughout the full range
   of *Seriatopora*.
   Around Australia: the Great
   Barrier Reef, Coral Sea and south
   to Flinders Reef (Moreton Bay)
   and Lord Howe Island in the east,
   and south to North West Cape
   on the west coast.

ABUNDANCE
   Common in all shallow reefal
   environments.

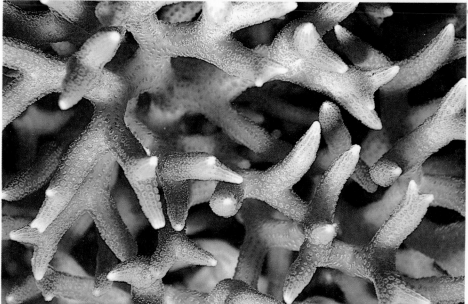

1. A finely branched colony of
Seriatopora hystrix, commonly called
"needle coral", from Broadhurst Reef,
Great Barrier Reef. Colonies such as this
are common on most reef slopes.
PHOTOGRAPH: ED LOVELL.

2, 3. *Seriatopora hystrix* has a wide
range of colours and growth forms. The
sharply pointed branches provide a haven
for small reef fish.
PHOTOGRAPHS: ED LOVELL.

Seriatopora caliendrum

EHRENBERG, 1834

TYPE LOCALITY
Red Sea.

IDENTIFYING CHARACTERS
Branches do not taper, they may be widely spaced or compact. Corallites tend to have a *Stylophora*-like hood.

COLOUR
Cream or brown.

SIMILAR SPECIES
S. *hystrix.*

DISTRIBUTION
From the Red Sea and eastern Africa east to New Caledonia. Around Australia: the Great Barrier Reef, Coral Sea and south to Elizabeth Reef in the east; and south to Houtman Abrolhos Islands on the west coast.

ABUNDANCE
Uncommon except on some upper reef slopes.

1. *Seriatopora caliendrum* from Willis Island, Great Barrier Reef.
PHOTOGRAPH: ED LOVELL.

2. Adjacent colonies of *Seriatopora hystrix* (left) and *Seriatopora caliendrum* (right) illustrating their contrasting appearance under water.
PHOTOGRAPH: ED LOVELL.

GENUS
STYLOPHORA
(pronounced sty-loh-for-a)

Schweigger, 1819

Stylophora pistillata is one of the tramp species of the coral world. Larvae readily attach themselves to floating pumice, or sometimes pieces of wood, where they can grow into colonies several centimetres across. These colonies may be transported hundreds, even thousands of kilometres and can produce more larvae *en route*. It is therefore no wonder the species is so widely distributed.

    Stylophora species, along with most other Pocilloporidae, are hermaphrodites, although young colonies have been reported to be male only. Eggs are brooded inside the parent polyp until they are fertilised by sperm from another colony and are then released as planula larvae. Larval release occurs after sunset. The green fluorescent larvae swim actively and may even be capable of swallowing food.

TYPE SPECIES
Stylophora pistillata Esper, 1797 from the east Indian Ocean.

FOSSIL RECORD
Eocene to Recent from Europe, North America, South America and the Indo–Pacific.

NUMBER OF SPECIES
Twenty-four nominal species, at least four true species, one from Australia.

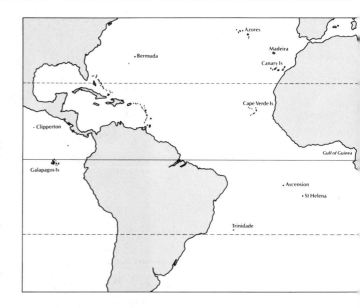

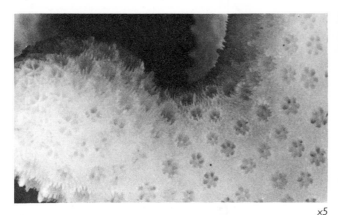

x5

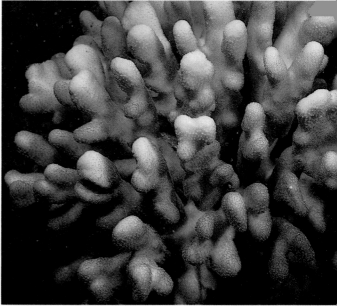

I. The two most common colours of *Stylophora pistillata*.
PHOTOGRAPH: ED LOVELL.

2. An uncommon green *Stylophora pistillata* at Heron Island, Great Barrier Reef, with polyps becoming extended.
PHOTOGRAPH: RON AND VALERIE TAYLOR.

3. *Stylophora pistillata* develops very sturdy branches on upper reef slopes exposed to strong wave action.
PHOTOGRAPH: AUTHOR.

4. The most common appearance of *Stylophora pistillata* on a back reef slope.
PHOTOGRAPH: ED LOVELL.

5. A very finely branched *Stylophora pistillata* in the lagoon of Scott Reef, north-western Australia.
PHOTOGRAPH: AUTHOR.

4

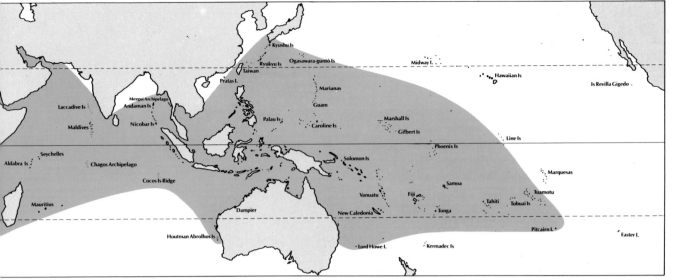

The known range of *Stylophora*.

2

3

Stylophora pistillata

ESPER, 1797

TYPE LOCALITY
"East Indian Ocean".

IDENTIFYING CHARACTERS
Colonies are branching with blunt-ended branches becoming thick and submassive.
Corallites are immersed, conical or hooded. They have a solid style-like columella, six primary septa which may be short or fused with the columella, and sometimes six short secondary septa. The coenosteum is covered by fine spinules.
Polyps are extended only at night.

COLOUR
Uniform cream, pink, blue or green.

SIMILAR SPECIES
Stylophora is a well-defined genus closest to, but clearly distinct from, *Seriatopora*. Under water it can be confused with *Palauastrea ramosa*.

DISTRIBUTION
Throughout the full range of *Stylophora*.
Around Australia: the Great Barrier Reef and south to Lord Howe Island and the Solitary Islands in the east, and south to Houtman Abrolhos Islands on the west coast.

ABUNDANCE
Common in most shallow-water reefal areas exposed to strong wave action and may be a dominant on exposed reef fronts.

5

GENUS
PALAUASTREA

(pronounced pal-oh-ass-tree-a)

Yabe & Sugiyama, 1941

The existence of *Palauastrea ramosa* on the Great Barrier Reef was not suspected until the author took a close look at what appeared to be a colony of *Porites cylindrica* growing on a sandy substrate. The resemblance between the two species is remarkable, but it ends on close inspection of the corallites.

TYPE SPECIES
Palauastrea ramosa Yabe & Sugiyama, 1941.

FOSSIL RECORD
None.

NUMBER OF SPECIES
One.

1. A branch of *Palauastrea ramosa* with some polyps partly extended. On closer inspection, the tiny polyps appear star-like.
PHOTOGRAPH: ED LOVELL.

2. *Palauastrea ramosa* from a turbid lagoon in the Swain Reefs, Great Barrier Reef, showing its characteristic appearance.
PHOTOGRAPH: ED LOVELL.

3. *Palauastrea ramosa* with polyps extended during the day.
PHOTOGRAPH: AUTHOR.

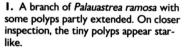

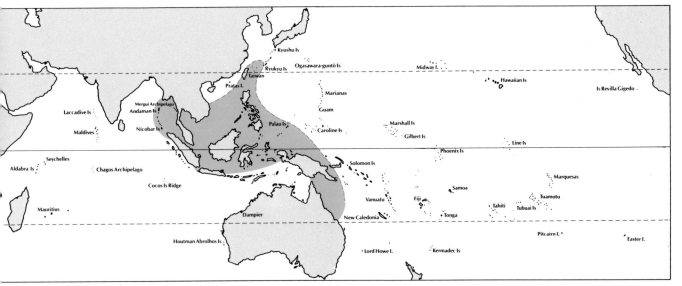

The known range of *Palauastrea ramosa*.

x5

Palauastrea ramosa

YABE & SUGIYAMA, 1941

TYPE LOCALITY
Palau.

IDENTIFYING CHARACTERS
Colonies are ramose with anastomosing blunt-ended, terete branches.
Corallites are immersed, circular, with a blunt style-like columella and two unequal cycles of septa that do not fuse with the columella. The coenosteum is covered by fine spinules.
Polyps are usually extended only at night.

COLOUR
Cream or pinkish-brown.

SIMILAR SPECIES
Palauastrea is most readily confused under water with the much more abundant *Porites cylindrica* which may have exactly the same colony shape. Corallites of *Palauastrea* appear star-like on closer inspection. They resemble those of *Stylocoeniella* without the coenosteum styles, but these genera are readily distinguished by their differing growth forms.

DISTRIBUTION
Around Australia: the Great Barrier Reef in the east, and the Houtman Abrolhos Islands on the west coast.

ABUNDANCE
Usually found in turbid water with a sandy substrate, but is seldom abundant.

GENUS
MADRACIS

(pronounced mad-ray-sis)

Edwards & Haime, 1849

Madracis is much more widespread than any other genus of purely reef-building corals. It occurs in tropical and temperate oceans around the world including the Mediterranean. Although the Australian species is hermatypic, most species are ahermatypic and are usually found only in deep water.

TYPE SPECIES
Madracis asperula Edwards & Haime, 1850 from Madeira.

FOSSIL RECORD
Cretaceous to Recent from Europe, the Indo-Pacific, North America and the West Indies.

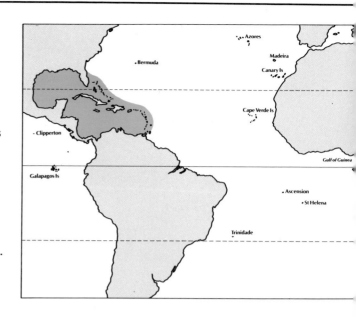

Madracis kirbyi

VERON & PICHON, 1976

TYPE LOCALITY
Palm Islands (Great Barrier Reef).

IDENTIFYING CHARACTERS
Colonies are laminar, encrusting or columnar, columns being club-shaped.
Corallites are subcereoid, closely compacted, angular in outline, with a solid conical columella. Usually 10 septa are present and these are fused with the columella. The coenosteum is covered by fine spinules. Polyps are extended only at night.

COLOUR
The oral disc is green, the coenosteum brown.

SIMILAR SPECIES
Madracis is a well-defined genus. It can be confused under water with *Stylocoeniella* because both genera are basically encrusting and cryptic but the larger, angular corallites of *Madracis* and lack of coenosteum styles make these genera easy to distinguish on close inspection.

DISTRIBUTION
Australia, Thailand, Indonesia and the Philippines; may also occur in the western Indian Ocean.
Around Australia: the Great Barrier Reef in the east; not found on the west coast.

ABUNDANCE
Rare.

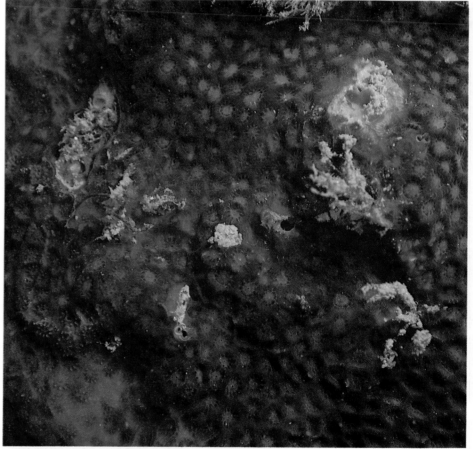

1. *Madracis kirbyi* is one of the most cryptic of corals. On the rare occasions when it is seen, it is usually encrusting.
PHOTOGRAPH: ED LOVELL.

2. Club-shaped branches of *Madracis kirbyi*.
PHOTOGRAPH: AUTHOR.

x5

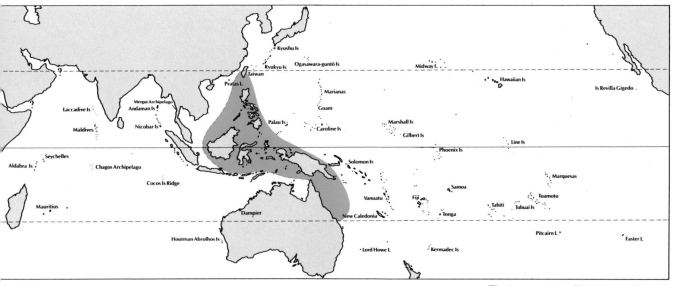

The known range of hermatypic *Madracis*.

2

FAMILY
ACROPORIDAE

(pronounced akro-por-id-ee)

VERRILL, 1902

CHARACTERS

Colonial, hermatypic, mostly extant. Colonies have all growth forms known
for hermatypic corals.
Corallites (except *Astreopora*) are small with septa in two cycles or less,
columellae are poorly developed.

RELATED FAMILIES

Pocilloporidae and Astrocoeniidae.

EARLIEST FOSSILS

Cretaceous.

THE GENERA

The Acroporidae is composed of four extant hermatypic genera, *Montipora*,
Anacropora, *Acropora* and *Astreopora*, all of which occur around Australia.

Opposite: *Acropora* species are the main builders of most coral reefs.
They are also the preferred food of the crown-of-thorns starfish.
PHOTOGRAPH: TERRY DONE.

GENUS
MONTIPORA

(pronounced mon-tee-por-a)

de Blainville, 1830

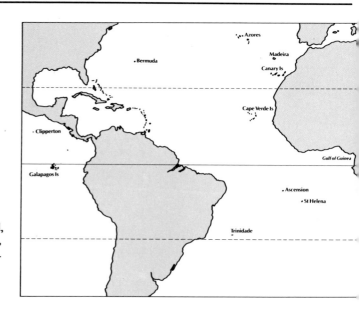

The influence on the mind of the puzzled worker of such a group [Montipora] of many individuals showing great variations yet undoubtedly, specifically identical, leads him as a rule temporarily to a wholesale lumping of other specimens, until his courage fails him, when the more striking individual variations are once more separately described as new types.

Henry Bernard,
Catalogue of Madreporaria, Volume III,
British Museum (Natural History), 1897.

Although *Montipora* is the second-largest coral genus in terms of species, it has been studied less than any other of the major genera. One reason for this is that almost half the species are inconspicuous, either encrusting or forming small plates. Another reason is that the corallites are the smallest of all corals and appear almost structureless to the unaided eye.

The general resemblance between *Montipora* and *Porites* is entirely superficial and divers soon learn to distinguish between them. The corallites of *Porites* are filled with septa and associated structures, while those of *Montipora* are mostly empty, the septa consisting of vertical rows of inwardly projecting spines.

With few exceptions, *Montipora* are difficult to identify from underwater photographs. Not only do species vary in general appearance but often one species looks much like another.

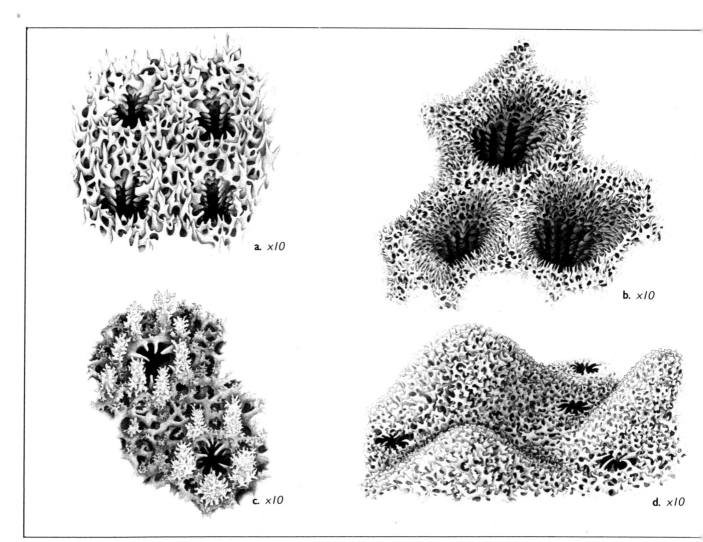

a. ×*10*

b. ×*10*

c. ×*10*

d. ×*10*

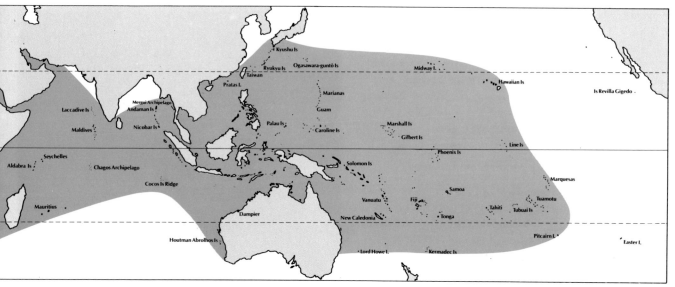

The known range of *Montipora*.

TYPE SPECIES
Porites verrucosa Lamarck, 1816.

FOSSIL RECORD
Eocene to Recent from the Indo-Pacific.

NUMBER OF SPECIES
Two hundred and eleven nominal species. The number of true species is unknown, but at least 38 have been recognised from Australia.

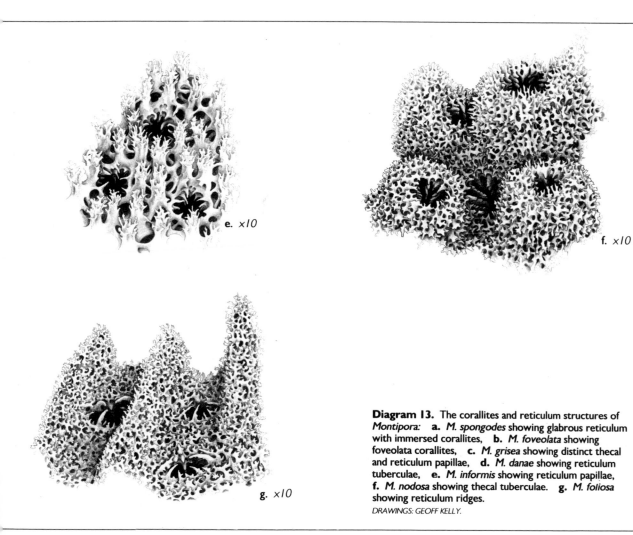

Diagram 13. The corallites and reticulum structures of *Montipora*: **a.** *M. spongodes* showing glabrous reticulum with immersed corallites, **b.** *M. foveolata* showing foveolata corallites, **c.** *M. grisea* showing distinct thecal and reticulum papillae, **d.** *M. danae* showing reticulum tuberculae, **e.** *M. informis* showing reticulum papillae, **f.** *M. nodosa* showing thecal tuberculae. **g.** *M. foliosa* showing reticulum ridges.
DRAWINGS: GEOFF KELLY.

CHARACTERS
Colonies are submassive, laminar, foliaceous, encrusting or branching.
Corallites are very small. Septa are in two cycles with inward-projecting teeth. Columellae are absent.
Corallite walls and the coenosteum are porous and may be highly elaborated.
Polyps are usually extended only at night.

SIMILAR GENERA
Montipora is most readily confused with *Porites*.

STRUCTURE AND IDENTIFICATION
In one important aspect *Montipora* are unlike all other corals: there are major differences in the structure of the coenosteum among the different species and these differences are very useful for identification. In some species the coenosteum is plain, without any elaborations, and the corallites are found either immersed in the coenosteum or situated at the base of funnel-shaped depressions. Other species develop various elaborations, or ornamentations, on their coenosteum. These are all of essentially similar structure but for convenience are called "papillae" if they are smaller than the corallite and "tuberculae" if they are larger. If they are grouped around the corallite, they are termed "thecal papillae" or "thecal tuberculae", and if scattered between the corallites, they are termed "reticulum papillae" or "reticulum tuberculae". Sometimes these structures are fused into "ridges".

Different species of *Montipora* have different combinations of these coenosteum structures and these are used in combination with growth form characters for identification. In some species, especially those that are massive or form thick plates without additional upward growth (such as nodules or branches), there is little variation in growth form. Others show enormous variation and these are the ones that are initially difficult to identify. In the following key, the first set of choices, which are based on growth form, may be misleading.

KEY TO SPECIES OF *MONTIPORA*

Colonies massive or thick plates, without additional upward growths
    Corallites both immersed and exsert
        Tuberculae absent, papillae present *M. grisea* (p. 116), *M. crassituberculata* (p. 121)
        Tuberculae present, papillae absent *M. monasteriata* (p. 96), *M. tuberculosa* (p. 97)
        Tuberculae and papillae absent *M. venosa* (p. 110)
    Corallites all or almost all immersed or funnel-shaped
        Tuberculae and/or papillae present
            Tuberculae large, smooth, regular, dome-shaped, papillae absent *M. verrucosa* (p. 107), *M. danae* (p. 106)
            Tuberculae not as above, papillae present or absent
                Corallites in, as well as between, tuberculae *M. hoffmeisteri* (p. 98), *M. floweri* (p. 100)
                Corallites mostly between tuberculae
                    Corallites minute *M. millepora* (p. 99)
                    Corallites over 1 mm in diameter *M. caliculata* (p. 111), *M. crassituberculata* (p. 121)
            Tuberculae absent, papillae present
                Thecal and reticulum papillae differentiated *M. peltiformis* (p. 101), *M. efflorescens* (p. 115), *M. nodosa* (p. 114)
                Thecal and reticulum papillae undifferentiated *M. calcarea* (p. 101), *M. informis* (p. 118)
        Without tuberculae or papillae
            Corallites with funnel-shaped openings *M. foveolata* (p. 109), *M. caliculata* (p. 111)
            Corallites without funnel-shaped openings *M. capricornis* (p. 102), *M. turgescens* (p. 101)
Colonies thick plates with additional upward growths (columns, nodules etcetera), or irregular
    Corallites both immersed and exsert
        Tuberculae absent, papillae present *M. hispida* (p. 113)
        Tuberculae present *M. incrassata* (p. 108), *M. australiensis* (p. 114)
    Corallites all or almost all immersed
        Tuberculae and/or papillae present
            Tuberculae large, smooth, regular, dome-shaped, papillae absent *M. danae* (p. 106), *M. verrucosa* (p. 107)
            Tuberculae not as above, papillae present *M. mollis* (p. 100), *M. undata* (p. 105)
            Tuberculae absent, papillae present *M. turtlensis* (p. 100), *M. peltiformis* (p. 101), *M. corbettensis* (p. 114)
        Without tuberculae or papillae *M. spongodes* (p. 103), *M. spumosa* (p. 104), *M. capricornis* (p. 102)
Colonies thin plates
    With upright branches *M. stellata* (p. 117), *M. hispida* (p. 113)
    Without upright branches
        Tuberculae large, smooth, regular, dome-shaped *M. danae* (p. 106)
        Tuberculae/papillae in ridges perpendicular to colony margin *M. foliosa* (p. 119)
        Tuberculae/papillae irregular *M. aequituberculata* (p. 120)
Colonies primarily branching or digitate
    With encrusting bases
        Corallites immersed *M. angulata* (p. 111)
        Corallites immersed and exsert *M. undata* (p. 105), *M. hispida* (p. 113)
    Without encrusting bases *M. digitata* (p. 112)

Note: This key is a guide only and should be used in conjunction with descriptions of the species.
The key assumes that the usual growth form of the species is well developed. The same species may key out in more than one place.

1. Most *Montipora* species have a wide range of growth forms. Some of this range can sometimes be seen in a single large colony.
PHOTOGRAPH: ED LOVELL.

2. The extended polyps of *Montipora* species are similar in appearance and are among the smallest of all corals.
PHOTOGRAPH: DAVE FISK.

3. *Montipora* (left) and *Porites* (right) may have similar growth forms and both have small polyps. However, on closer inspection, these two genera are easily separated: *Porites* calices are filled with septa, while *Montipora* calices are almost empty and are usually surrounded by elaborate skeletal structures.
PHOTOGRAPH: ED LOVELL.

Montipora monasteriata
(FORSKÅL, 1775)

TYPE LOCALITY
 Red Sea.

IDENTIFYING CHARACTERS
 Colonies are massive or are
 unifacial or bifacial thick plates.
 Corallites are mostly immersed.
 The reticulum is covered with
 papillae and/or tuberculae.

COLOUR
 Pale brown or pink with pink or
 white margins.

SIMILAR SPECIES
 M. incrassata and *M. tuberculosa.*
 The latter has smaller corallites
 and papillae only.

DISTRIBUTION
 From the Red Sea east to Hawaii.
 Around Australia: the Great
 Barrier Reef, Coral Sea and also
 the Elizabeth and Middleton
 Reefs in the east, and south to
 Shark Bay on the west coast.

ABUNDANCE
 Common on reef slopes.

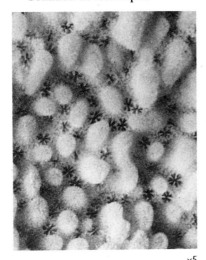

x5

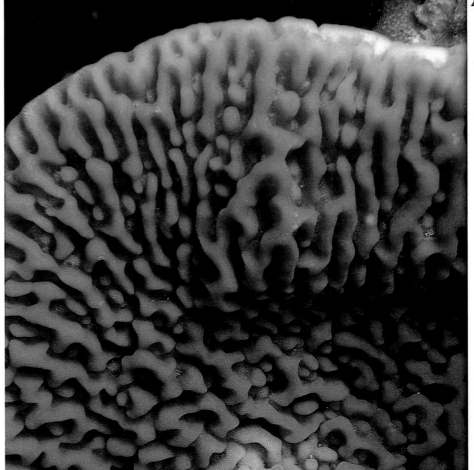

I. A common form of *Montipora
monasteriata.*
PHOTOGRAPH: ED LOVELL.

2. The surface detail of a *Montipora
monasteriata* colony.
PHOTOGRAPH: ED LOVELL.

Montipora tuberculosa

(LAMARCK, 1816)

TYPE LOCALITY
Unrecorded.

IDENTIFYING CHARACTERS
Colonies are submassive or plate-like. Corallites are small, some exsert, some immersed. Corallites are separated by papillae/tuberculae of about one corallite in diameter.

COLOUR
Usually dull brown or green, may be bright blue.

SIMILAR SPECIES
M. monasteriata.

DISTRIBUTION
Widespread, but the full range is not known.
Around Australia: the Great Barrier Reef and south to Flinders Reef (Moreton Bay) in the east, and south to Ningaloo Reefs on the west coast.

ABUNDANCE
Common over a wide range of habitats.

x5

1. A plate-like colony of *Montipora tuberculosa*.
PHOTOGRAPH: ED LOVELL.

2. Two overlapping colonies of *Montipora tuberculosa* at the Palm Islands, Great Barrier Reef.
PHOTOGRAPH: ED LOVELL.

Montipora hoffmeisteri

WELLS, 1956

TYPE LOCALITY
  Marshall Islands.

IDENTIFYING CHARACTERS
  Colonies are thick plates.
  Corallites are immersed. The
  reticulum is covered with
  tuberculae which may contain
  corallites.

COLOUR
  Cream or brown, occasionally
  brightly coloured.

SIMILAR SPECIES
  M. floweri has smaller corallites.

DISTRIBUTION
  Recorded from the Marshall
  Islands and Australia.
  Around Australia: the Great
  Barrier Reef and Coral Sea in the
  east, and south to Houtman
  Abrolhos Islands on the west
  coast.

ABUNDANCE
  Very common over a wide range
  of habitats, but inconspicuous.

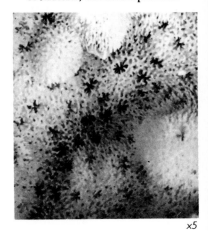

x5

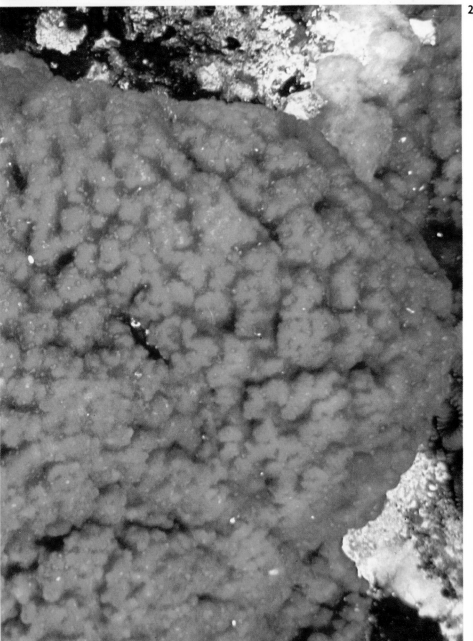

1, 2. *Montipora hoffmeisteri.* Colonies
are usually a drab cream or brown.
PHOTOGRAPHS: ED LOVELL.

98

Montipora millepora

CROSSLAND, 1952

TYPE LOCALITY
Great Barrier Reef.

IDENTIFYING CHARACTERS
Colonies are massive or encrusting. Corallites are very small, immersed. The reticulum has tuberculae which seldom contain corallites.

COLOUR
Dark green or brown.

SIMILAR SPECIES
M. floweri has evenly distributed corallites. Also resembles *Stylocoeniella guentheri* under water.

DISTRIBUTION
Known only from Australia: the Great Barrier Reef and Coral Sea in the east, and south to Ningaloo Reefs on the west coast.

ABUNDANCE
Occurs in crevices and under overhangs; very inconspicuous.

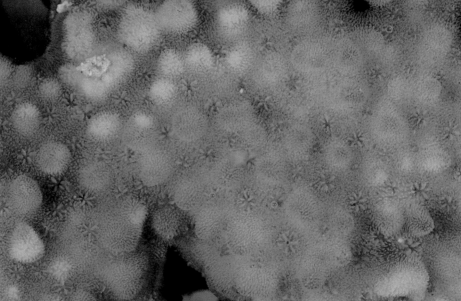

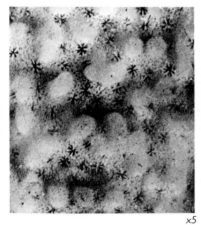

x5

1. *Montipora millepora* (above) and *M. turgescens* (below) encrust a polychaete worm tube.
PHOTOGRAPH: ED LOVELL.

2. The surface detail of *Montipora millepora.*
PHOTOGRAPH: AUTHOR.

Montipora floweri
WELLS, 1956

TYPE LOCALITY
Marshall Islands.

IDENTIFYING CHARACTERS
Colonies are submassive. Corallites are very small, immersed and evenly distributed. The reticulum is covered with fused tuberculae.

COLOUR
Usually dark brown or green.

SIMILAR SPECIES
M. hoffmeisteri and M. millepora.

DISTRIBUTION
Recorded from the Marshall Islands and Australia. Around Australia: the Great Barrier Reef and Coral Sea in the east, and the Rowley Shoals and Scott Reef on the west coast.

ABUNDANCE
Common on some upper reef slopes of the Coral Sea, rare and inconspicuous elsewhere.

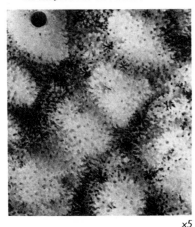

x5

The surface detail of Montipora floweri.
PHOTOGRAPH: AUTHOR.

Montipora mollis
BERNARD, 1897

TYPE LOCALITY
Palm Islands and Torres Strait, Great Barrier Reef.

IDENTIFYING CHARACTERS
Colonies are irregular clumps, columns and plates. Corallites are mostly immersed. The reticulum is coarse. Low tuberculae are sometimes present.

COLOUR
Uniform brown.

SIMILAR SPECIES
M. turtlensis and M. turgescens.

DISTRIBUTION
From the Persian Gulf to Australia. Around Australia: the Great Barrier Reef, Coral Sea, Flinders Reef (Moreton Bay) and Lord Howe Island in the east, and south to Geographe Bay on the west coast.

ABUNDANCE
Common on subtidal mudflats and in turbid reef habitats.

x5

Montipora turtlensis
VERON & WALLACE, 1984

TYPE LOCALITY
Turtle Islands, Great Barrier Reef.

IDENTIFYING CHARACTERS
Colonies are flat plates with nodular upward growths at their centre. Corallites are closely compacted, immersed. Thecal and reticulum papillae are present.

COLOUR
Brown, green or purple with cream tips to nodules.

SIMILAR SPECIES
M. mollis and M. peltiformis.

DISTRIBUTION
Known only from Australia: the Great Barrier Reef, Coral Sea and south to Lord Howe Island in the east, and south to Houtman Abrolhos Islands on the west coast.

ABUNDANCE
Common in turbid water habitats.

x5

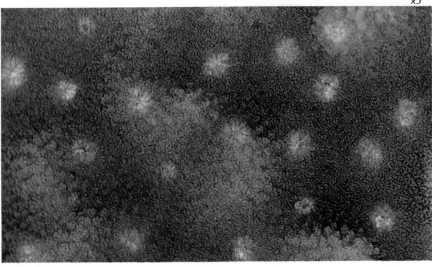

Montipora peltiformis

BERNARD, 1897

TYPE LOCALITY
Indonesia.

IDENTIFYING CHARACTERS
Colonies are submassive or are flat plates, with or without nodular upward growths. Corallites are mostly immersed. Thecal and reticulum papillae are present.

COLOUR
Pale brown.

SIMILAR SPECIES
M. turtlensis and M. calcarea.

DISTRIBUTION
From Madagascar east to Australia and the Philippines. Around Australia: the Great Barrier Reef, Coral Sea and south to Flinders Reef (Moreton Bay) in the east, and south to Houtman Abrolhos Islands on the west coast.

ABUNDANCE
Uncommon. Found on shallow reef slopes.

x5

Montipora calcarea

BERNARD, 1897

TYPE LOCALITY
Tonga.

IDENTIFYING CHARACTERS
Colonies are irregular thick plates. Corallites are immersed. The reticulum is covered with fine papillae. The corallum usually has a light texture.

COLOUR
Pale brown.

SIMILAR SPECIES
M. peltiformis.

DISTRIBUTION
Australia and Tonga. Around Australia: south to Houtman Abrolhos Islands on the west coast; not found in the east.

ABUNDANCE
Uncommon.

x5

Montipora turgescens

BERNARD, 1897

TYPE LOCALITY
Southern Great Barrier Reef.

IDENTIFYING CHARACTERS
Colonies are massive, flat, hemispherical or columnar with the surface raised into mounds. Corallites are immersed. The reticulum is smooth.

COLOUR
Brown, cream or purple.

SIMILAR SPECIES
M. mollis and M. capricornis.

DISTRIBUTION
From the western Indian Ocean east to the Ellice Islands and Samoa. Around Australia: the Great Barrier Reef, Coral Sea and south to Lord Howe Island in the east, and south to Houtman Abrolhos Islands on the west coast.

ABUNDANCE
Common over a wide range of habitats.

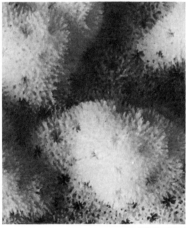

x5

Montipora capricornis

VERON, 1985

TYPE LOCALITY
Llewellyn Reef, Great Barrier Reef.

IDENTIFYING CHARACTERS
Colonies are flat plates in tiers or whorls, sometimes with columns. Corallites are immersed. There are no tuberculae or papillae. The reticulum is coarse.

COLOUR
Uniform purple, blue or brown.

SIMILAR SPECIES
M. turgescens has smaller calices and a finer reticulum.

DISTRIBUTION
Known only from Australia: the southern Great Barrier Reef in the east, and south to Houtman Abrolhos Islands on the west coast.

ABUNDANCE
Sometimes common in lagoons, rare elsewhere.

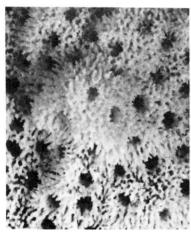

x5

1. A large colony of *Montipora capricornis*. This species may also develop an upright growth form.
PHOTOGRAPH: ED LOVELL.

2. The beautiful *Montipora capricornis* in the lagoon of Llewellyn Reef, Great Barrier Reef.
PHOTOGRAPH: ED LOVELL.

Montipora spongodes

BERNARD, 1897

TYPE LOCALITY
Not designated.

IDENTIFYING CHARACTERS
Colonies have encrusting or plate-like bases which may have rootlets. Plates have upward projecting ridges developing into anastomosing columns. Corallites are widely spaced and immersed, the reticulum is smooth.

COLOUR
Uniform pale cream or pink or deep grey.

SIMILAR SPECIES
None.

DISTRIBUTION
From the western Indian Ocean east to Japan and the Great Barrier Reef.
Around Australia: the Great Barrier Reef and south to Lord Howe Island in the east. and south to Port Denison on the west coast.

ABUNDANCE
Usually uncommon.

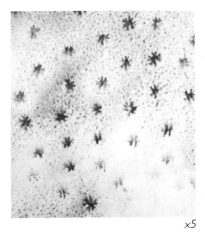

x5

1. *Montipora spongodes* at the Houtman Abrolhos Islands, Western Australia.
PHOTOGRAPH: ED LOVELL.

2. *Montipora spongodes*. Polyps are widely spaced and the colony surface is smooth.
PHOTOGRAPH: JOHN BARNETT.

3. A tightly compacted colony of *Montipora spongodes*.
PHOTOGRAPH: AUTHOR.

Montipora spumosa
(LAMARCK, 1816)

TYPE LOCALITY
Unrecorded.

IDENTIFYING CHARACTERS
Colonies are encrusting, plate-like or columnar, the columns frequently being tubular. Encrusting colonies may have rootlets. Corallites are immersed, without papillae. The reticulum is very coarse (this can be seen under water).

COLOUR
Usually mottled or uniform brown, cream or blue, sometimes with pink margins.

SIMILAR SPECIES
M. spumosa is very distinctive.

DISTRIBUTION
Central Indo–Pacific east to Fiji. Around Australia: the Great Barrier Reef, Coral Sea and Flinders Reef (Moreton Bay) in the east, and south to Houtman Abrolhos Islands on the west coast.

ABUNDANCE
Common over a wide range of habitats.

×5

1. The most common growth form of *Montipora spumosa* in turbid water environments.
PHOTOGRAPH: ED LOVELL.

2. *Montipora spumosa* at Elizabeth Reef, eastern Australia.
PHOTOGRAPH: ED LOVELL.

3. The characteristic appearance of *Montipora spumosa* in the Great Barrier Reef.
PHOTOGRAPH: RON AND VALERIE TAYLOR.

Montipora undata

BERNARD, 1897

TYPE LOCALITY
Moluccas.

IDENTIFYING CHARACTERS
Colonies are horizontal to vertical plates or tubes, also thick columns and branches. Corallites are immersed, and indistinct. The reticulum has tuberculae fused into ridges forming the same pattern as *Porites rus*.

COLOUR
Purple, pink or brown, with pale-growing margins.

SIMILAR SPECIES
M. danae.

DISTRIBUTION
Australia, the Philippines and Indonesia.
Around Australia: the Great Barrier Reef and Coral Sea in the east, and south to the Dampier Archipelago on the west coast.

ABUNDANCE
Common, especially on upper reef slopes.

×5

1. The usual appearance of *Montipora undata*.
PHOTOGRAPH: ED LOVELL.

2. The surface detail of *Montipora undata*.
PHOTOGRAPH: AUTHOR.

Montipora danae

(EDWARDS & HAIME, 1851)

TYPE LOCALITY
Fiji.

IDENTIFYING CHARACTERS
Colonies are columns or plates with surfaces covered with tuberculae which are dome-shaped or fused into radiating ridges. Corallites are small, immersed, crowded between the tuberculae.

COLOUR
Usually pale brown with paler margins. Polyps are often brightly coloured.

SIMILAR SPECIES
M. verrucosa has much larger, more open corallites. Also *M. undata*.

DISTRIBUTION
From the Red Sea east to the Marshall Islands.
Around Australia: all localities except the Solitary Islands in the east, and south to Houtman Abrolhos Islands on the west coast.

ABUNDANCE
Common on upper reef slopes and lagoons.

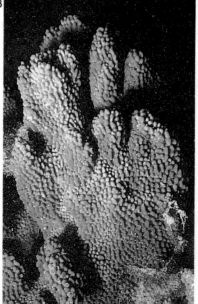

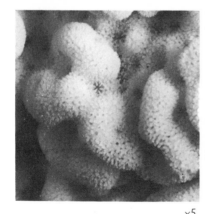

×5

1. An encrusting *Montipora danae* from an upper reef slope exposed to strong wave action.
PHOTOGRAPH: ED LOVELL.

2. The small polyps of *Montipora danae* are dotted in between much larger, somewhat irregular tuberculae.
PHOTOGRAPH: AUTHOR.

3. A columnar colony of *Montipora danae.*
PHOTOGRAPH: ED LOVELL.

4. The characteristic appearance of a flat plate of *Montipora danae.*
PHOTOGRAPH: ED LOVELL.

Montipora verrucosa

(LAMARCK, 1816)

TYPE LOCALITY
Unrecorded.

IDENTIFYING CHARACTERS
Colonies are submassive or plate-like with the surface uniformly covered with tuberculae, like those of *M. danae*. Corallites are immersed between tuberculae.

COLOUR
Blue or brown, uniform or mottled. Bright-blue or green polyps are extended during the day.

SIMILAR SPECIES
M. danae.

DISTRIBUTION
From the Red Sea east to the Marshall Islands.
Around Australia: the Great Barrier Reef and Coral Sea in the east, and south to Houtman Abrolhos Islands the west coast.

ABUNDANCE
Common on upper reef slopes and lagoons.

x5

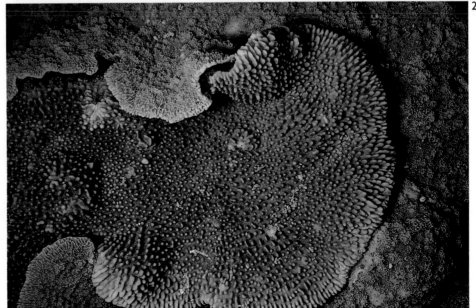

1. A columnar colony of *Montipora verrucosa.*
PHOTOGRAPH: ED LOVELL.

2. An encrusting colony of *Montipora verrucosa* (centre) competes with *M. crassituberculata* for space.
PHOTOGRAPH: ED LOVELL.

107

Montipora incrassata

(DANA, 1846)

TYPE LOCALITY
Fiji.

IDENTIFYING CHARACTERS
Colonies are thick plates with or without contorted nodular columns or branches. Corallites are both immersed and exsert. The reticulum is covered with tuberculae which may be fused into ridges.

COLOUR
Mottled or uniform purple or brown, usually with white polyps.

SIMILAR SPECIES
Plate-like colonies may resemble *M. monasteriata*.

DISTRIBUTION
Australia and Fiji.
Around Australia: the Great Barrier Reef, Coral Sea and Elizabeth and Middleton Reefs in the east, and south to Houtman Abrolhos Islands on the west coast.

ABUNDANCE
Occurs primarily on upper reef slopes; uncommon.

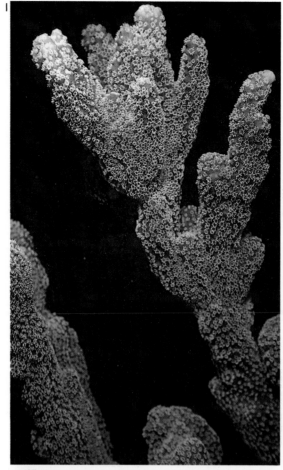

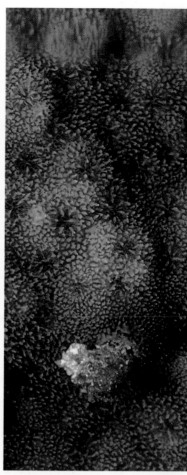

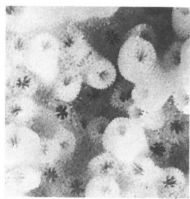

 x5

1, 2. *Montipora incrassata*, a common, but often cryptic species.
PHOTOGRAPHS: ED LOVELL.
3. The surface detail of *Montipora incrassata*.
PHOTOGRAPH: AUTHOR.

Montipora foveolata

(DANA, 1846)

TYPE LOCALITY
Fiji.

IDENTIFYING CHARACTERS
Colonies are massive or form thick plates. Corallites are funnel-shaped, immersed in the reticulum, with the opening of the corallite being at the base of the funnel. Tuberculae and papillae are absent.

COLOUR
Usually pale brown, pink or cream but may be brightly coloured, sometimes with bright-blue or green polyps partly extended during the day.

SIMILAR SPECIES
M. venosa.

DISTRIBUTION
Australia and the central western Pacific.
Around Australia: the Great Barrier Reef, Coral Sea and Flinders Reef (Moreton Bay) in the east, and south to Shark Bay on the west coast.

ABUNDANCE
Seldom common but relatively distinctive.

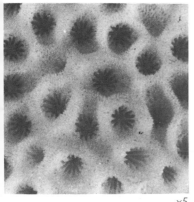

×5

1, 2. *Montipora foveolata,* one of the best-known and most easily recognised *Montipora.*

PHOTOGRAPHS: ED LOVELL.

Montipora venosa

(EHRENBERG, 1834)

TYPE LOCALITY
Unrecorded.

IDENTIFYING CHARACTERS
Coralla are massive. Corallites are a mixture: some slightly exsert, others funnel-shaped. Tuberculae and papillae are absent.

COLOUR
Pale brown.

SIMILAR SPECIES
M. venosa is like a diminutive *M. foveolata*. Also resembles *M. caliculata*.

DISTRIBUTION
From the Red Sea east to the Marshall Islands.
Around Australia: the Great Barrier Reef and Flinders Reef (Moreton Bay) in the east, and south to Houtman Abrolhos Islands on the west coast.

ABUNDANCE
Rare.

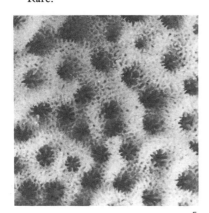

x5

1. *Montipora venosa* with polyps partly extended.
PHOTOGRAPH: RON AND VALERIE TAYLOR.
2. *Montipora venosa*.
PHOTOGRAPH: ED LOVELL.

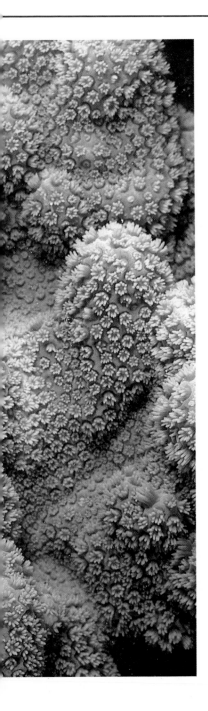

Montipora caliculata
(DANA, 1846)

TYPE LOCALITY
Fiji.

IDENTIFYING CHARACTERS
Colonies are massive. Corallites are a mixture of immersed and funnel-shaped, the latter usually being irregular. Tuberculae may be present.

COLOUR
Brown or blue.

SIMILAR SPECIES
M. venosa.

DISTRIBUTION
Australia and the western Pacific. Around Australia: the Great Barrier Reef, Coral Sea and Flinders Reef (Moreton Bay) in the east, and south to Houtman Abrolhos Islands on the west coast.

ABUNDANCE
Uncommon.

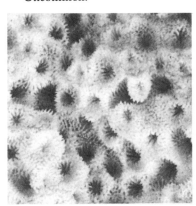

x5

Montipora angulata
(LAMARCK, 1816)

TYPE LOCALITY
"Eastern Ocean".

IDENTIFYING CHARACTERS
Colonies have extensive encrusting bases with irregularly contorted branches. Corallites are immersed and evenly distributed. The reticulum is smooth.

COLOUR
Pale brown.

SIMILAR SPECIES
None.

DISTRIBUTION
From the Gulf of Mannar east to the western Pacific. Around Australia: the northern and central Great Barrier Reef in the east, and south to Houtman Abrolhos Islands on the west coast.

ABUNDANCE
Uncommon except on some fringing reef flats.

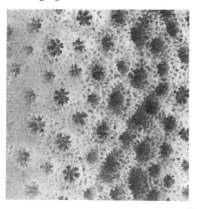

x5

111

Montipora digitata

(DANA, 1846)

TYPE LOCALITY
Fiji.

IDENTIFYING CHARACTERS
Colonies are digitate or arborescent with anastomosing upright branches. Corallites are immersed and are small (especially colonies from very shallow water).

COLOUR
Pale cream or brown.

SIMILAR SPECIES
None.

DISTRIBUTION
From the western Indian Ocean east to Fiji.
Around Australia: the northern and central Great Barrier Reef in the east, and south to Port Denison on the west coast.

ABUNDANCE
Common. May be a dominant species on shallow mudflats.

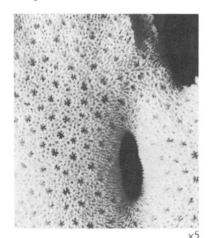

x5

1, 2. *Montipora digitata*, one of the most distinctive of all Australian *Montipora*.
PHOTOGRAPHS: ED LOVELL.

Montipora hispida
(DANA, 1846)

TYPE LOCALITY
Singapore.

IDENTIFYING CHARACTERS
Colonies may be submassive, plate-like, columnar or digitate or various combinations of these forms. Plate-like and digitate forms are usually found in turbid water; massive and columnar forms occur on reef slopes. Corallites are both immersed and exsert, the latter with thecal papillae; shorter papillae also occur on the reticulum, which is coarse.

COLOUR
Pale brown, sometimes with white branch tips.

SIMILAR SPECIES
M. nodosa and M. grisea.

DISTRIBUTION
From Sri Lanka east to Hawaii. Around Australia: the Great Barrier Reef and Coral Sea in the east, and south to Houtman Abrolhos Islands on the west coast.

ABUNDANCE
Common, especially in turbid water.

x5

1

2

1, 2. *Montipora hispida*, a common species in turbid environments.
PHOTOGRAPHS: ED LOVELL.

Montipora australiensis

BERNARD, 1897

TYPE LOCALITY
Houtman Abrolhos Islands.

IDENTIFYING CHARACTERS
Colonies are thick bifacial plates which may develop columns at their centre. Corallites are both immersed and exsert, the latter with thecal papillae. Ridges of reticulum join corallites forming a network.

COLOUR
Pale brown.

SIMILAR SPECIES
M. nodosa.

DISTRIBUTION
Australia east to Tahiti.
Around Australia: the Coral Sea in the east; not found on the west coast.

ABUNDANCE
Very rare.

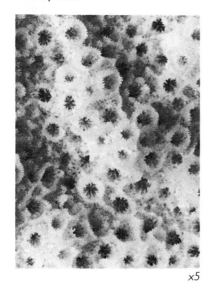

x5

Montipora nodosa

(DANA, 1846)

TYPE LOCALITY
Fiji.

IDENTIFYING CHARACTERS
Colonies are massive or are unifacial plates. Corallites are immersed or exsert and are surrounded by fused thecal papillae. Reticulum papillae are usually present.

COLOUR
Pale brown.

SIMILAR SPECIES
M. hispida, also M. grisea and M. australiensis.

DISTRIBUTION
Western Pacific.
Around Australia: the Great Barrier Reef, Coral Sea and Elizabeth and Middleton Reefs in the east, and Houtman Abrolhos Islands on the west coast.

ABUNDANCE
Common in the Coral Sea; usually uncommon elsewhere and rare on the west coast of Australia.

x5

Montipora corbettensis

VERON & WALLACE, 1984

TYPE LOCALITY
Corbett Reef, Great Barrier Reef.

IDENTIFYING CHARACTERS
Colonies are massive or are thick unifacial or bifacial plates, usually with irregularly shaped upward growths near their centre. Corallites are immersed. Reticulum papillae are large.

COLOUR
Yellowish or pale brown.

SIMILAR SPECIES
M. informis.

DISTRIBUTION
Known only from Australia: the northern and central Great Barrier Reef in the east; not found on the west coast.

ABUNDANCE
Rare.

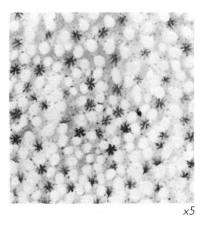

x5

Montipora efflorescens

BERNARD, 1897

TYPE LOCALITY
Unrecorded.

IDENTIFYING CHARACTERS
Colonies are massive, the surface being an irregular series of mounds. Corallites are immersed. The reticulum is covered with papillae; there are also thecal papillae which are slightly longer.

COLOUR
Usually bright or dark green, sometimes cream, blue or pink.

SIMILAR SPECIES
M. informis.

DISTRIBUTION
From Chagos Islands east to Tahiti.
Around Australia: the Great Barrier Reef, Coral Sea and Elizabeth and Middleton Reefs in the east, and south to Houtman Abrolhos Islands on the west coast.

ABUNDANCE
Common on upper reef slopes.

 x5

1. A brightly coloured *Montipora efflorescens* on an upper reef slope.
PHOTOGRAPH: RON AND VALERIE TAYLOR.

2. *Montipora efflorescens* (centre), a common colourful species on most reefs.
PHOTOGRAPH: ED LOVELL.

115

Montipora grisea

BERNARD, 1897

TYPE LOCALITY
Tonga.

IDENTIFYING CHARACTERS
Colonies are massive or are thick unifacial plates. Corallites are mostly exsert, surrounded by partly fused thecal papillae. Reticulum papillae are also present.

COLOUR
Usually dark brown or green but may be pale colours or bright blue or pink.

SIMILAR SPECIES
M. nodosa, also *M. hispida*.

DISTRIBUTION
Australia to New Ireland and Tonga.
Around Australia: the Great Barrier Reef and Coral Sea in the east, and south to North West Cape on the west coast.

ABUNDANCE
Usually common on upper reef slopes.

x5

The surface detail of *Montipora grisea*.
PHOTOGRAPH: AUTHOR.

Montipora stellata

BERNARD, 1897

TYPE LOCALITY
Great Barrier Reef.

IDENTIFYING CHARACTERS
Colonies are small, composed of contorted laminae, sometimes in whorls or tiers, and upright contorted branches which are irregularly anastomosed. Corallites are immersed with irregular thecal papillae. Reticulum papillae are numerous and are not fused into ridges.

COLOUR
Cream, pink or brown, often with white ridges.

SIMILAR SPECIES
None.

DISTRIBUTION
Australia, Solomon Islands and the Philippines.
Around Australia: the northern and central Great Barrier Reef in the east, and south to Houtman Abrolhos Islands on the west coast.

ABUNDANCE
Common, sometimes a dominant in shallow turbid water.

x5

1, 2. *Montipora stellata* at the Houtman Abrolhos Islands, Western Australia (top) and the Palm Islands, Great Barrier Reef (bottom).
PHOTOGRAPHS: PAT BAKER (TOP) AND ED LOVELL (BOTTOM).

117

Montipora informis

BERNARD, 1897

TYPE LOCALITY
Great Barrier Reef.

IDENTIFYING CHARACTERS
Colonies are massive to encrusting. Corallites are evenly distributed, immersed. The reticulum is densely covered with elongate papillae of uniform length.

COLOUR
Brown or mottled brown and white. Papillae may have white or purple tips. White polyps may be extended during the day.

SIMILAR SPECIES
M. efflorescens and *M. corbettensis*.

DISTRIBUTION
From Madagascar to New Caledonia.
Around Australia: the Great Barrier Reef and Coral Sea in the east, and south to Houtman Abrolhos Islands on the west coast.

ABUNDANCE
Common on upper reef slopes.

x5

1. A massive colony of *Montipora informis*. The hillocky surface is due to an infestation of date mussels and barnacles.
PHOTOGRAPH: ED LOVELL.

2. The most common appearance of *Montipora informis*, with white-tipped papillae.
PHOTOGRAPH: ED LOVELL.

3. A large colony of *Montipora informis* at Scott Reef, north-western Australia.
PHOTOGRAPH: AUTHOR.

Montipora foliosa
(PALLAS, 1766)

TYPE LOCALITY
Unrecorded.

IDENTIFYING CHARACTERS
Colonies are encrusting with broad laminar margins sometimes forming tiers or whorls. Corallites are arranged in rows between reticulum ridges which are conspicuous and usually perpendicular to the corallum margin.

COLOUR
Usually cream, pink or brown.

SIMILAR SPECIES
M. aequituberculata is primarily distinguished from *M. foliosa* by its lack of reticulum ridges.

DISTRIBUTION
From the Red Sea east to the New Hebrides and Fiji. Around Australia: the Great Barrier Reef and Coral Sea in the east, and south to Houtman Abrolhos Islands on the west coast.

ABUNDANCE
Very common, especially on protected upper reef slopes.

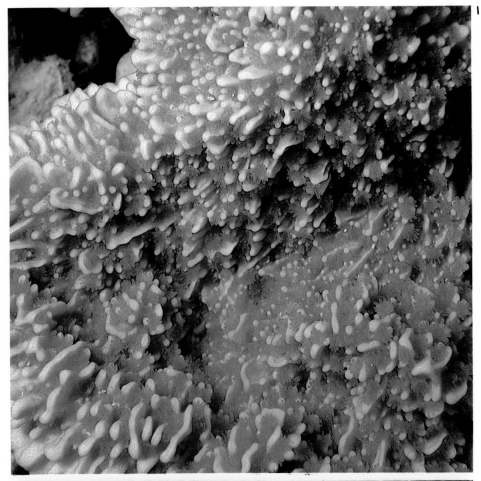

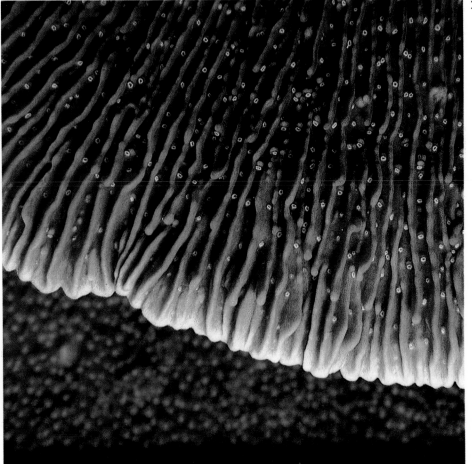

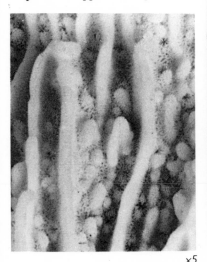

x5

1. *Montipora foliosa* with pink polyps extended.
PHOTOGRAPH: ED LOVELL.

2. A flat *Montipora foliosa* plate showing the distinctive appearance of fully developed colonies. Tuberculae are fused into long ridges running perpendicular to the plate margins.
PHOTOGRAPH: ED LOVELL.

119

Montipora aequituberculata

BERNARD, 1897

TYPE LOCALITY
Torres Strait, Great Barrier Reef.

IDENTIFYING CHARACTERS
Colonies are composed of thin laminae often arranged in oblique overlapping whorls. Corallites are immersed or exsert and are surrounded by thecal papillae. These are frequently fused into short ridges and may form hoods over the corallites. Reticulum papillae are thick and highly fused.

COLOUR
Usually a uniform brown, cream or purple, sometimes with pale margins.

SIMILAR SPECIES
M. foliosa and *M. crassituberculata*.

DISTRIBUTION
Possibly occurs throughout the full west—east range of *Montipora*.
Around Australia: the Great Barrier Reef, Coral Sea, Elizabeth and Middleton Reefs and Lord Howe Island in the east, and south to Houtman Abrolhos Islands on the west coast.

ABUNDANCE
Very common and may be a dominant species on sheltered upper reef slopes.

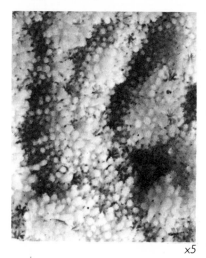

x5

1, 2. Two large colonies of *Montipora aequituberculata* at the Houtman Abrolhos Islands, Western Australia, appear very different, making this species, the most common of all *Montipora*, difficult to recognise under water.
PHOTOGRAPHS: ED LOVELL.

3. The usual appearance of thick plates of *Montipora aequituberculata*.
PHOTOGRAPH: ED LOVELL.

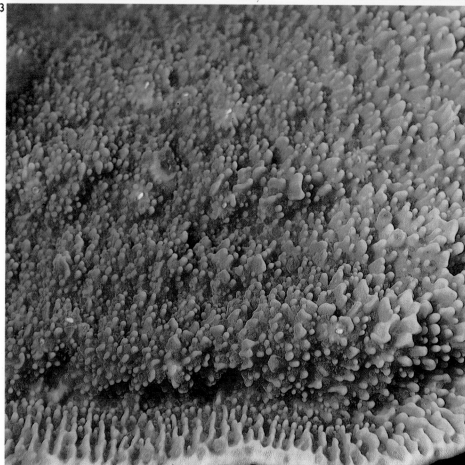

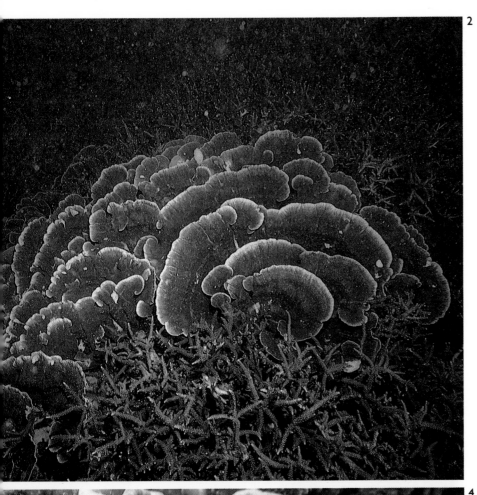

2 # *Montipora crassituberculata*
BERNARD, 1897

TYPE LOCALITY
Houtman Abrolhos Islands.

IDENTIFYING CHARACTERS
Colonies are submassive or are subencrusting plates. Corallites are immersed or exsert (intermixed), the latter being conical with thick thecae. Thecal and reticulum papillae are both thick.

COLOUR
Usually brown or blue.

SIMILAR SPECIES
M. aequituberculata may be similar but has smaller corallites and fewer papillae.

DISTRIBUTION
Known only from Australia: the Great Barrier Reef and Coral Sea in the east, and south to Houtman Abrolhos Islands on the west coast.

ABUNDANCE
Common on upper and lower reef slopes.

4

x5

4. Convoluted *Montipora aequituberculata* at Heron Island, Great Barrier Reef. Such colonies are found only in shallow water.
PHOTOGRAPH: RON AND VALERIE TAYLOR.

GENUS
ANACROPORA

(pronounced an-akro-por-a)

Ridley, 1884

There are no long and puzzling series. Each type of growth can be described by itself without fear of reproach for needless multiplication of new species.

Henry Bernard,
Catalogue of Madreporaria, Volume III,
British Museum (Natural History), 1897.

Anacropora are essentially branching *Montipora*. They have no axial corallites like the *Acropora*; rather, new corallites are budded from the smooth tissue of the branch tip. The result, in comparison with *Acropora*, is a slow-growing, irregular colony. *Anacropora* appear to be poor competitors and survive only in muddy niches usually unoccupied by other corals. Not surprisingly, they are seldom seen by divers.

TYPE SPECIES
Anacropora forbesi Ridley, 1884.

FOSSIL RECORD
None.

NUMBER OF SPECIES
Ten nominal species, six true species, four of which are Australian.

CHARACTERS
Colonies are arborescent with thin tapered branches, without axial corallites.
All corallites are radial, and are small and immersed. Septa are in two cycles with inward-projecting teeth. Columellae are absent. Corallite walls and the coenosteum are porous, without elaborations. Polyps are extended day and night and are widely spaced; they are small, with fine tentacles.

SIMILAR GENERA
Anacropora has *Montipora*-like corallites combined with an *Acropora*-like arborescent growth form. Unlike *Acropora*, there are no terminal corallites.

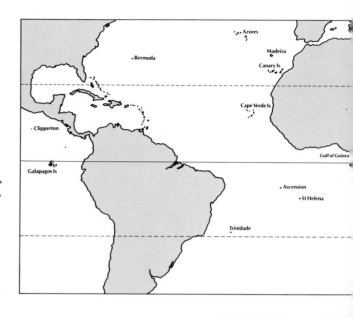

Anacropora forbesi
RIDLEY, 1884

TYPE LOCALITY
Cocos-Keeling Islands.

IDENTIFYING CHARACTERS
Branches are widely spaced, less than 10 mm in diameter, tapering, with blunt tips. Spinules are distributed evenly on the coenosteum.

COLOUR
Pale brown with white branch tips.

SIMILAR SPECIES
A. reticulata and *A. puertogalerae.*

DISTRIBUTION
From the Seychelles and Providence Islands east to the Marshall Islands and Fiji. Around Australia: the central Great Barrier Reef in the east, and known only from Cocos-Keeling Island near the west coast.

ABUNDANCE
Rare, but more abundant than other *Anacropora.*

I. *Anacropora forbesi* with polyps partly extended.
PHOTOGRAPH: AUTHOR.

2. *Anacropora forbesi* at Torres Strait. This is the most common of the *Anacropora* species and is found only in turbid water.
PHOTOGRAPH: LEN ZELL.

3. A large colony of *Anacropora forbesi* on a muddy substrate at 20 m depth.
PHOTOGRAPH: AUTHOR.

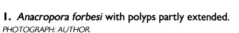

x5

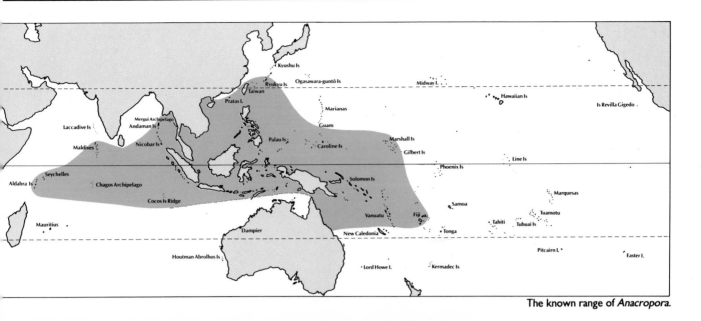

The known range of *Anacropora*.

Anacropora puertogalerae

NEMENZO, 1964

TYPE LOCALITY
  The Philippines.

IDENTIFYING CHARACTERS
  Branches are compact, less than 13 mm in diameter, tapering to a point. Spines may project below corallites.

COLOUR
  Pale brown, sometimes with white branch tips.

SIMILAR SPECIES
  A. forbesi.

DISTRIBUTION
  Australia and the Philippines. Around Australia: the central Great Barrier Reef in the east, and Scott Reef on the west coast.

ABUNDANCE
  Rare.

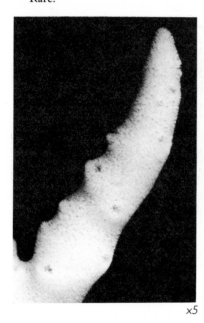

x5

1. *Anacropora puertogalerae* at the Palm Islands, Great Barrier Reef. The gnarled, pointed branches make this species an easily recognised one.
PHOTOGRAPH: ED LOVELL.

2. *Anacropora puertogalerae* is very abundant at Scott Reef, but no *Anacropora* has been found at any other Western Australian reef.
PHOTOGRAPH: AUTHOR.

Anacropora reticulata

VERON & WALLACE, 1984

TYPE LOCALITY
Palm Islands, Great Barrier Reef.

IDENTIFYING CHARACTERS
Branches are widely spaced, up to 14 mm in diameter, tapering, with blunt tips. The coenosteum is composed of fine rows of fused spinules (visible under water).

COLOUR
Pale brown.

SIMILAR SPECIES
A. forbesi, which has finer branches and a non-reticulate coenosteum.

DISTRIBUTION
Known only from Australia: the central Great Barrier Reef in the east; not found on the west coast.

ABUNDANCE
Very rare.

Anacropora matthai

PILLAI, 1973

TYPE LOCALITY
Indonesia.

IDENTIFYING CHARACTERS
Branches are less than 5 mm in diameter and do not taper. Corallites are tubular, up to 1.5 mm exsert.

COLOUR
Brown with pale-brown or cream branch tips. Polyps may be extended day and night.

SIMILAR SPECIES
A. matthai is distinct from other Australian species.

DISTRIBUTION
Australia and East Indies. Around Australia: the central Great Barrier Reef in the east; not found on the west coast.

ABUNDANCE
Rare but may cover extensive areas on horizontal muddy substrates with clear water.

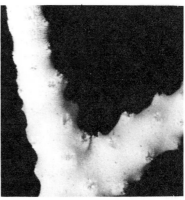

x5

x5

The rare *Anacropora reticulata* in turbid water.
PHOTOGRAPH: ED LOVELL.

Anacropora matthai. Colonies are so delicate that they fall apart when disturbed.
PHOTOGRAPH: LEN ZELL.

GENUS
ACROPORA
(pronounced <u>akro-por</u>-a)

Oken, 1815

The protean scleractinian genus, with bewildering speciation, and reef-former par excellence.

John Wells,
*A Survey of the Distribution of Reef Coral Genera
in the Great Barrier Reef Region,*
Cornell University, 1955.

This is an apt description of *Acropora*. Like the Greek god Proteus and the flowers named after him, *Acropora* can have many guises—"staghorns", bushes, thickets, plates, columns and tables, all different species, all growing in lush profusion on all Indo–Pacific reefs.

Why is *Acropora* so successful? One reason is that most species have light skeletons which allow them to grow quickly and overcome their neighbours. Another, probably more important reason is that the task of budding new corallites has been taken over by specialised "axial" corallites. As a result, all the corallites of a colony are closely interconnected and can grow in a coordinated fashion, almost as if they were parts of the same individual. This allows some species to form the tall staghorn colonies that are probably the best known of all corals. It also allows other species to form the large, delicately engineered plates and tables that are found on most reef slopes. The latter are probably the coral world's greatest and most recent architectural achievement.

Most *Acropora* sexually reproduce simultaneously on the Great Barrier Reef. This occurs after dark soon after the full moon from October to December. Pinkish egg bundles can be seen protruding from the radial corallites and these are released in a stream to be fertilised by sperm released from other polyps at the same time. When thousands of colonies spawn synchronously, the water surface becomes milky with eggs, sperm and larvae. Some larvae settle quickly on the same reef, others drift around, perhaps for months, and may settle on reefs hundreds of kilometres away.

The identification of *Acropora* species is often a major task for reef biologists. Even a small patch of reef may have hundreds of *Acropora* colonies growing on it, expressing an almost endless array of shapes, sizes and colours. The initial impression is, however, the most bewildering. On closer inspection, the differences between species are usually masked only by colour; colonies can usually be grouped into species or probable species. When a good idea has been formed of what that species looks like generally, it should be possible to identify it from the photographs and descriptions given here.

TYPE SPECIES
Millepora muricata Linnaeus, 1758 from the West Indies.

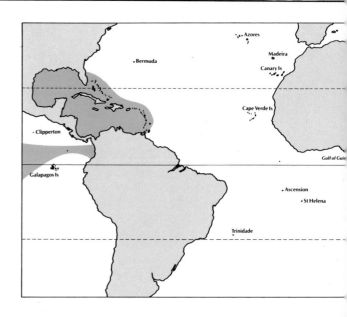

FOSSIL RECORD
Eocene to Recent from Europe, West Indies, North America and the Indo–Pacific.

NUMBER OF SPECIES
Three hundred and sixty-eight nominal species. The number of true species is unknown, but 73 species have been recognised from eastern Australia, 54 from Western Australia. All but three west-coast species are found in the east.

CHARACTERS
Colonies are usually ramose to arborescent, bushy or plate-like, rarely encrusting or submassive.
Corallites are of two types, axial and radial. Septa are usually in two cycles. Columellae are absent. Corallite walls and the coenosteum are porous.
Polyps are usually extended only at night.

SIMILAR GENERA
Only two *Cyphastrea* species and the ahermatypic *Arcohelia* have distinct axial and radial corallites.

GROWTH FORMS AND CORALLITE SHAPES
The most common growth forms of *Acropora* are:
table- or *plate-like*: colonies are flat, either with one central leg or attached to the substrate at one side.
pillow-like: colonies are composed of fine branches and grow as thick pillow-like clumps.
arborescent: colonies are composed of tree-like branches.
corymbose: colonies are composed of horizontal anastomosing branches and short vertical branchlets.
caespitose: colonies are bushy, being composed of anastomosing branches inclined at varying angles.
digitate: colonies are composed of short non-dividing, non-anastomosing branches like the fingers of a hand.

Almost every coral colony in this shallow water community is one of the many species of *Acropora*. This genus displays an enormous range of size and shape and dominates most upper reef slopes where the water is clear.
PHOTOGRAPH: ED LOVELL.

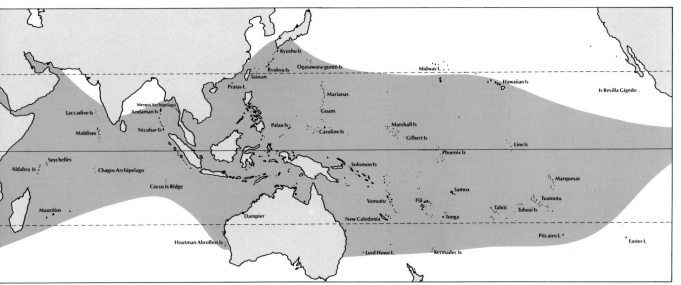

The known range of *Acropora*.

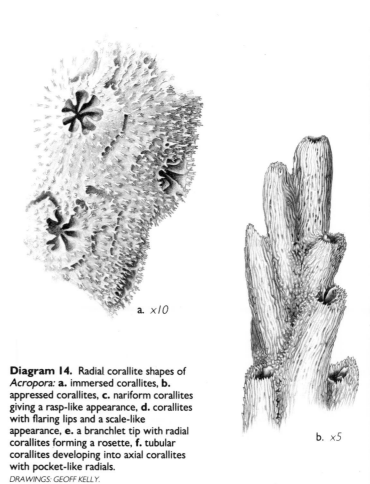

a. ×10

Diagram 14. Radial corallite shapes of *Acropora*: **a.** immersed corallites, **b.** appressed corallites, **c.** nariform corallites giving a rasp-like appearance, **d.** corallites with flaring lips and a scale-like appearance, **e.** a branchlet tip with radial corallites forming a rosette, **f.** tubular corallites developing into axial corallites with pocket-like radials.
DRAWINGS: GEOFF KELLY.

b. ×5

Acropora have axial and radial polyps; the latter are budded off in a regular fashion during growth. Much of the colour of the branch comes from algae in the coral polyp tissues. Rapidly growing branch tips are usually pale-coloured because the algae have not had time to saturate the newly forming tissue of the polyp.
PHOTOGRAPH: ED LOVELL.

Diagram 15. The growth forms of *Acropora*: **a.** tables and plates, **b.** massive, **c.** arborescent, **d.** caespitose, **e.** digitate, **f.** corymbose, **g.** bottlebrush.
DRAWINGS: GEOFF KELLY.

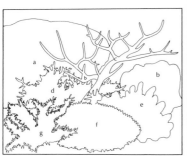

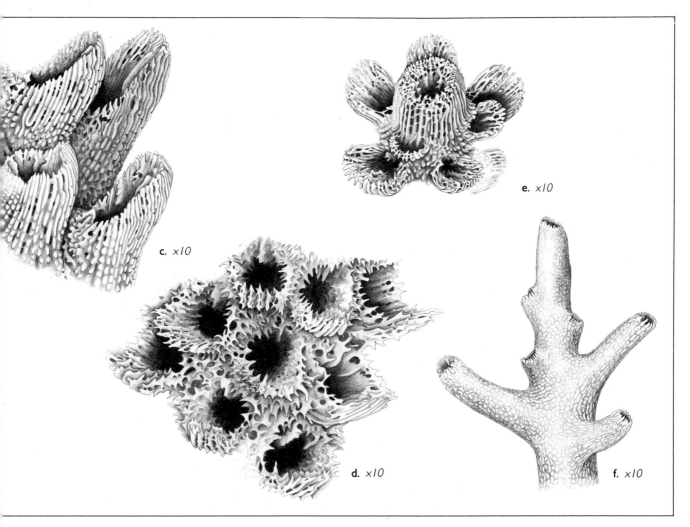

c. ×10

e. ×10

d. ×10

f. ×10

encrusting: colonies adhere to the substrate—most species have encrusting bases.
bottlebrush: colonies have short side branchlets projecting out from the main branch.
prostrate: colonies sprawl over the substrate.
massive: colonies are similar in all dimensions.

Other *Acropora* colonies form *ridges* and *columns*. Various terms are also applied to the shape of the radial corallites. These may be immersed (imbedded in the branch), tubular, nariform (shaped like an upside-down Roman nose), appressed (adhering closely to the branch) and may have lips (the outer rim of the corallite) of various shapes (for example, flaring, spiny, scale–like and rasp–like).

SPECIES

The identification of small specimens of *Acropora* is usually a specialist's job.★ The common species, however, are usually not difficult to recognise if the shape of the whole colony is known, and especially if the colony has been observed under water.

Although *Acropora* displays the greatest variety of growth forms of any coral genus, only two subgenera can be distinguished: subgenus *Isopora*, containing three species, and subgenus *Acropora*, containing all the remaining species. Some of these species may be

★*For a key to* Acropora *see* Scleractinia of Eastern Australia. Part V: Acroporidae, *Veron and Wallace, Australian Institute of Marine Science Monograph Series, Vol. 6, ANU Press, 485 pp.*

superficially similar (for example, they form "staghorns" or "plates") but have different structural detail; others are similar in structural detail but have quite different growth forms. In general, *Acropora* are divisible into non-taxonomic groups, some of which are distinct, others more arbitrary. Species usually resemble other species in the same group but this is not always the case. To identify an *Acropora* species, the reader should become familiar with these groups as described and illustrated here.

There are 15 groups:

Subgenus *Isopora* (p. 132)
A. palifera, A. cuneata, A. brueggemanni
This group is distinguished by having more than one "axial" corallite per branch. Branches are correspondingly thick and have cross-sections of varying shape, depending on the grouping of the "axial" corallites. The group is distinguished further by the fine structure of the coenosteum, which bears uniformly distributed spinules with very elaborated tips.

The *Acropora humilis* group (p. 136)
A. humilis, A. gemmifera, A. monticulosa, A. samoensis, A. digitifera, A. multiacuta
The first three species are closely related and closely resemble each other on upper reef slopes where they are very common. The latter three are less common (the last is rare) and more distinctive.

The *Acropora lovelli* group (p. 142)
A. bushyensis, A. verweyi, A. lovelli, A. glauca
This is an arbitrary group composed of species which
resemble the *A. humilis* group. They are uncommon,
except in very specific habitats of particular reefs.

The *Acropora robusta* group (p. 146)
A. robusta, A. danai, A. palmerae, A. nobilis, A. polystoma,
A. listeri
These species all have very similar radial corallites,
which are of two sizes, and a coarse coenosteum. They
are all restricted to shallow reef habitats, especially those
exposed to strong wave action.

The *Acropora formosa* group (p. 153)
A. grandis, A. formosa, A. abrolhosensis, A. acuminata,
A. valenciennesi
These species all have an arborescent or modified
arborescent growth form. The first two resemble
arborescent species in other groups, especially *A. nobilis*.

The *Acropora horrida* group (p. 158)
A. microphthalma, A. kirstyae, A. horrida, A. tortuosa,
A. vaughani, A. austera
All these species show at least some resemblance to
A. horrida, and all species except *A. austera* may have a
similar growth form.

The *Acropora aspera* group (p. 164)
A. aspera, A. pulchra, A. millepora
These species are very polymorphic, both in growth
form and in corallite structure. They are characterised by
having radial corallites with no upper wall and a lower
wall with rounded or flaring lips.

The *Acropora selago* group (p. 167)
A. tenuis, A. selago, A. donei, A. dendrum, A. yongei
This is an arbitrary group of species: *A. tenuis* and
A. selago are clearly similar and so are *A. donei* and
A. yongei. Both pairs of species have similar radial
corallites with flaring or pointed lower lips.

The *Acropora hyacinthus* group (p. 172)
A. cytherea, A. microclados, A. paniculata, A. hyacinthus,
A. spicifera, A. anthocercis
All these species except *A. anthocercis* form plate- or
table-like colonies composed of fine anastomosed
horizontal branches and fine upward projecting
branchlets with small corallites.

The *Acropora latistella* group (p. 178)
A. latistella, A. subulata, A. nana, A. aculeus, A. azurea
These species all have small appressed corallites and
slender branchlets. *A. latistella* and *A. subulata* may form
very large table-like colonies. *A. nana* and *A. azurea* are
both rare.

The *Acropora nasuta* group (p. 182)
A. cerealis, A. nasuta, A. valida, A. secale, A. lutkeni
These species have similar corallites and a similar
coenosteum. With the exception of *A. lukteni*, they all
have corymbose or caespito-corymbose growth forms,
all have similar habitat preferences and all show similar
growth-form modifications in response to
environmental conditions.

It is common for these species to be found together
on upper reef slopes where *Acropora* diversity is high.
This tends to assist identification because the different
species can be compared directly under water.

The *Acropora divaricata* group (p. 188)
A. clathrata, A. divaricata, A. solitaryensis, A. stoddarti
These species are grouped together because they have
similar nariform to tubo-nariform corallites and a
similar coenosteum between the corallites.

The *Acropora echinata* group (p. 192)
A. echinata, A. subglabra, A. carduus, A. elseyi,
A. longicyathus
These are the "bottlebrush" corals. They are most
commonly found on lower reef slopes or on sandy
lagoon floors. All species have pocket-like radial
corallites and numerous tubular axial corallites. All have
a similar coenosteum and are clearly related.

The *Acropora loripes* group (p. 197)
A. loripes, A. chesterfieldensis, A. granulosa, A. caroliniana,
A. willisae
These species have a wide range of growth forms but
nevertheless appear to be related because they have
similar structural detail, including a fine, smooth
Turbinaria-like coenosteum.

All species are found most commonly in habitats
with clear water protected from strong wave action
where *Acropora* diversity is high.

The *Acropora florida* group (p. 202)
A. florida, A. sarmentosa
These two species have general similarities and are
distinct from the other *Acropora*.

2

1. An outer reef flat at low tide. Most of the corals here are *Acropora*, but other corals with small polyps may also be common.
PHOTOGRAPH: ED LOVELL.

2. The undersurface of a large *Acropora* table. Built by many thousands of polyps growing in a highly coordinated manner, these colonies are the masterpieces of coral architecture.
PHOTOGRAPH: RON AND VALERIE TAYLOR.

3. One of the most dramatic sights on a coral reef: the synchronised night-time release of countless millions of egg-and-sperm bundles by an entire community of *Acropora* and other corals.
PHOTOGRAPH: GORDON BULL.

SUBGENUS *ISOPORA*

Acropora (Isopora) palifera
(LAMARCK, 1816)

TYPE LOCALITY
"Southern Ocean".

IDENTIFYING CHARACTERS
Colonies are encrusting plates, ridges or columns, without axial corallites.

COLOUR
Pale cream or brown.

SIMILAR SPECIES
A. cuneata may be difficult to distinguish from *A. palifera*. The former has smaller, usually flatter branches, and corallites are finer, with round rather than elongate calices.

DISTRIBUTION
From Madagascar and Diego Garcia east to the Marshall Islands and Samoa.
Around Australia: the Great Barrier Reef, Coral Sea and south to Lord Howe Island in the east, and the Rowley Shoals and Scott Reef on the west coast.

ABUNDANCE
The most abundant coral species along the coast of eastern Australia and the primary builder of outer barrier reefs. Occurs in all reef environments.
Uncommon in Western Australia.

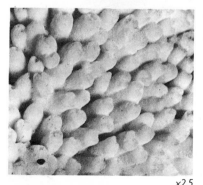

×2.5

1. An upper reef slope community exposed to very strong wave action. Such communities of east Australian reefs are usually dominated by *Acropora palifera*, seen here as short rounded ridges. *Pocillopora verrucosa* (foreground) is a common subdominant species.
PHOTOGRAPH: ED LOVELL.

2. The most common appearance of *Acropora palifera* on upper reef slopes exposed to moderate wave action. *Acropora cerealis* is seen in the foreground.
PHOTOGRAPH: ED LOVELL.

3. Sprawling colonies of *Acropora palifera* at Scott Reef, north-western Australia.
PHOTOGRAPH: AUTHOR.

4. A tall columnar form of *Acropora palifera* from the lower slope of an outer reef where the water is clear.
PHOTOGRAPH: ED LOVELL.

5. *Acropora palifera* also has a branching growth form in partly turbid water, such as in lagoons.
PHOTOGRAPH: ED LOVELL.

3

2

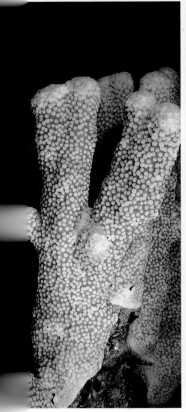

4

Acropora (Isopora) *cuneata*

(DANA, 1846)

TYPE LOCALITY
  Fiji.

IDENTIFYING CHARACTERS
  Colonies are solid plates or short flattened branches, without axial corallites.

COLOUR
  Pale cream or brown.

SIMILAR SPECIES
  A. palifera.

DISTRIBUTION
  From Madagascar east to the Marshall Islands.
  Around Australia: the Great Barrier Reef and Coral Sea in the east; not found on the west coast.

ABUNDANCE
  Common, but much less common than *A. palifera*. Occurs in all reef environments especially upper reef slopes and reef flats.

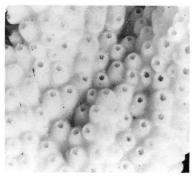

x2.5

Acropora cuneata looks like A. palifera and is sometimes difficult to distinguish from it unless both species occur together.
PHOTOGRAPH: ED LOVELL.

Acropora *(Isopora)* *brueggemanni*
(BROOK, 1893)

TYPE LOCALITY
Singapore.

IDENTIFYING CHARACTERS
Colonies are arborescent or prostrate with tapering branches with blunt ends and one or more immersed axial corallites.

COLOUR
Pale or dark brown.

SIMILAR SPECIES
None.

DISTRIBUTION
Indo-Malayan region, the Philippines and Australia. Around Australia: the Great Barrier Reef and Coral Sea in the east, and the Rowley Shoals and Scott Reef on the west coast.

ABUNDANCE
Common in shallow water, including exposed upper reef slopes and reef flats.

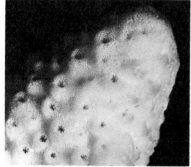

x2.5

1. *Acropora brueggemanni* on a lower reef slope with *A. echinata* (foreground) and *A. carduus* (behind, between the *Porites*).
PHOTOGRAPH: ED LOVELL.

2. *Acropora brueggemanni* may closely resemble branching *A. palifera* but is readily distinguished from it by its axial polyps.
PHOTOGRAPH: ED LOVELL.

SUBGENUS *ACROPORA*

Acropora humilis
(DANA, 1846)

TYPE LOCALITY
Fiji.

IDENTIFYING CHARACTERS
Colonies are corymbose. Branches are thick, tapering to a large axial corallite. Radial corallites are of two sizes, usually in rows.

COLOUR
Many colours, but most commonly cream, brown or blue with blue or cream tips.

SIMILAR SPECIES
A. gemmifera and *A. monticulosa*.

DISTRIBUTION
From the Red Sea east to the Marshall Islands, Tuamotu Archipelago and Hawaii. Around Australia: the Great Barrier Reef and Coral Sea in the east, and south to Dampier Archipelago on the west coast.

ABUNDANCE
Very common on the east coast of Australia and sometimes dominant on exposed upper reef slopes and on reef flats. Usually uncommon on the west coast.

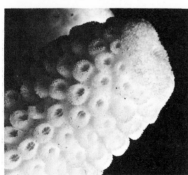

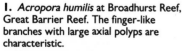

x2.5

1. *Acropora humilis* at Broadhurst Reef, Great Barrier Reef. The finger-like branches with large axial polyps are characteristic.
PHOTOGRAPH: ED LOVELL.

2. *Acropora humilis* sometimes has a partly prostrate growth form.
PHOTOGRAPH: ED LOVELL.

3. *Acropora humilis* exposed at low tide. Colonies exposed to strong wave action have sturdier branches than this.
PHOTOGRAPH: ED LOVELL.

Acropora gemmifera

(BROOK, 1892)

TYPE LOCALITY
Great Barrier Reef.

IDENTIFYING CHARACTERS
Colonies are digitate to corymbose, branches are thick, tapering to a small axial corallite. Radial corallites are of two sizes, usually in rows. Large-sized corallites increase in length towards branch bases.

COLOUR
Usually blue, cream or brown, with blue or white branch tips.

SIMILAR SPECIES
A. humilis and A. monticulosa.

DISTRIBUTION
Possibly extends west to the Red Sea and east to New Caledonia and Fiji.
Around Australia: the Great Barrier Reef, Coral Sea and south to Elizabeth Reef in the east, and south to Dampier Archipelago on the west coast.

ABUNDANCE
Common on exposed upper reef slopes and on reef flats.

x2.5

1. The difference between *Acropora gemmifera* (left) and *A. humilis* (right) is usually clear on the reef, but these species have been confused by taxonomists.
PHOTOGRAPH: ED LOVELL.

2. A large compound colony of *Acropora gemmifera*. This species, as well as *A. humilis*, *A. monticulosa* and *A. lutkeni*, forms these sorts of colonies on outer reefs where the water is very clear and turbulent.
PHOTOGRAPH: ED LOVELL.

3. *Acropora gemmifera* has radial polyps which increase in size down the branch sides.
PHOTOGRAPH: RON AND VALERIE TAYLOR.

Acropora monticulosa
(BRÜGGEMANN, 1879)

TYPE LOCALITY
Rodriguez.

IDENTIFYING CHARACTERS
Colonies are corymbose to digitate, branches are thick, tapering to a small axial corallite. Radial corallites are uniform in size, usually arranged in rows.

COLOUR
Blue or cream, usually with pale branch tips of various colours.

SIMILAR SPECIES
A. humilis and *A. gemmifera*.

DISTRIBUTION
Australia and Rodriguez. Around Australia: the Great Barrier Reef, except the Capricorn and Bunker groups, and Coral Sea in the east, and Rowley Shoals and Scott Reef on the west coast.

ABUNDANCE
Seldom abundant. May form large colonies on upper reef slopes.

x2.5

1. A compound colony of *Acropora monticulosa* at Myrmidon Reef, Great Barrier Reef.
PHOTOGRAPH: ED LOVELL.

2. The usual appearance of *Acropora monticulosa*. Axial polyps are small and radial polyps are of uniform size.
PHOTOGRAPH: ED LOVELL.

138

Acropora samoensis

(BROOK, 1891)

TYPE LOCALITY
Samoa.

IDENTIFYING CHARACTERS
Colonies are corymbose or prostrate, branches are terete. Radial corallites are of two sizes, thick-walled. Axial corallites are larger, with very thick walls.

COLOUR
Usually purple or cream.

SIMILAR SPECIES
A. sarmentosa and *A. humilis*.

DISTRIBUTION
Probably restricted to the central southern Indo-Pacific. Around Australia: the Great Barrier Reef, except the Capricorn and Bunker groups, in the east, and south to Dampier Archipelago on the west coast.

ABUNDANCE
Uncommon, usually found only on upper reef slopes.

x2.5

1. *Acropora samoensis* at Middleton Reef, eastern Australia. Outer branches of colonies tend to sprawl irregularly.
PHOTOGRAPH: ED LOVELL.

2. A branch end of *Acropora samoensis* showing radial polyps of two different sizes.
PHOTOGRAPH: RON AND VALERIE TAYLOR.

Acropora digitifera
(DANA, 1846)

TYPE LOCALITY
Unrecorded.

IDENTIFYING CHARACTERS
Colonies are corymbose to digitate with small terete branches. Resembles a diminutive *A. humilis*.

COLOUR
Purple, pale brown, cream or yellow, often with pale-blue, cream or yellow branch tips.

SIMILAR SPECIES
A. humilis.

DISTRIBUTION
From Madagascar east to Samoa. Around Australia: the Great Barrier Reef, Coral Sea and south to Flinders Reef (Moreton Bay) in the east, and south to Houtman Abrolhos Islands on the west coast.

ABUNDANCE
Usually rare except for wave-washed back margins of some reefs, where it may be dominant.

x2.5

2

1. *Acropora digitifera* (right) is much smaller than *A. humilis* or *A. gemmifera* (top centre), otherwise these species are similar.
PHOTOGRAPH: ED LOVELL.

2. *Acropora digitifera* may be the dominant species of wave-washed reef backs.
PHOTOGRAPH: ED LOVELL.

Acropora multiacuta

NEMENZO, 1967

TYPE LOCALITY
The Philippines.

IDENTIFYING CHARACTERS
Colonies are small and branches have extremely long naked axial corallites.

COLOUR
Pastel colours, usually cream.

SIMILAR SPECIES
None.

DISTRIBUTION
Nicobar Islands, the Philippines and Australia.
Around Australia: the northern and central Great Barrier Reef in the east; not found on the west coast.

ABUNDANCE
Rare, occurs only on wave-washed lagoon margins of a few reefs.

x2.5

1. *Acropora multiacuta*, a rare but beautiful species.
PHOTOGRAPH: ED LOVELL.

2. Branch tips of *Acropora multiacuta*.
PHOTOGRAPH: ED LOVELL.

Acropora bushyensis

VERON & WALLACE, 1984

TYPE LOCALITY
Bushy Island, Great Barrier Reef.

IDENTIFYING CHARACTERS
Colonies are digitate, with mostly terete branches and outward-facing corallites with wide empty calices.

COLOUR
Pale brown or cream, occasionally with blue branch tips.

SIMILAR SPECIES
May resemble *A. digitifera*.

DISTRIBUTION
Known only from Australia: the southern Great Barrier Reef in the east; not found on the west coast.

ABUNDANCE
Common in Bushy Island lagoon; very rare elsewhere.

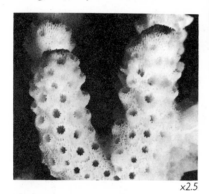

×2.5

Acropora bushyensis always has this appearance and colour.
PHOTOGRAPH: ED LOVELL.

142

Acropora verweyi

VERON & WALLACE, 1984

TYPE LOCALITY
  Magdelaine Cay, Coral Sea.

IDENTIFYING CHARACTERS
  Colonies have irregular terete branches with radial corallites arranged in rows. Axial corallites are prominent.

COLOUR
  A uniform creamy-brown with yellow axial corallites on the northern and central Great Barrier Reef; a variety of other colours elsewhere.

SIMILAR SPECIES
  A. austera.

DISTRIBUTION
  Known only from Australia: the Great Barrier Reef, Coral Sea and south to Flinders Reef (Moreton Bay) in the east, and south to Houtman Abrolhos Islands on the west coast.

ABUNDANCE
  Usually uncommon. Occurs on upper reef slopes, especially those exposed to heavy wave action or currents.

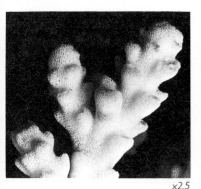

x2.5

1. *Acropora verweyi* at Myrmidon Reef, Great Barrier Reef. The delicate colonies usually fall apart if an attempt is made to collect them.
PHOTOGRAPH: ED LOVELL.

2, 3. *Acropora verweyi* is always delicately coloured. In the central Great Barrier Reef (2), it always has yellow axial polyps; at Heron Island, southern Great Barrier Reef (3), it is pinkish-brown.
PHOTOGRAPHS: ED LOVELL (2) AND RON AND VALERIE TAYLOR (3).

Acropora lovelli

VERON & WALLACE, 1984

TYPE LOCALITY
Middleton Reef.

IDENTIFYING CHARACTERS
Colonies are caespitose or bottlebrush with tall upright branches.

COLOUR
Pale brown or blue.

SIMILAR SPECIES
A. florida, sometimes *A. samoensis*.

DISTRIBUTION
Known only from Australia: the Great Barrier Reef and south to Lord Howe Island in the east, and south to Houtman Abrolhos Islands on the west coast.

ABUNDANCE
Common on Elizabeth and Middleton Reefs and Lord Howe Island, extremely rare on the Great Barrier Reef.

x2.5

1, 2. *Acropora lovelli* is named after Ed Lovell, the principal photographer for this book. This species is common in the lagoon of Middleton Reef, eastern Australia.
PHOTOGRAPHS: ED LOVELL.

3. The branches of *Acropora lovelli*, exposed to some wave action, develop short *A. florida*-like side branches.
PHOTOGRAPH: ED LOVELL.

Acropora glauca
(BROOK, 1893)

TYPE LOCALITY
"West Australia".

IDENTIFYING CHARACTERS
Colonies are corymbose plates with or without upward branches. Radial corallites have wide openings and thick lips.

COLOUR
Brown, cream or green.

SIMILAR SPECIES
A. clathrata and *A. solitaryensis*.

DISTRIBUTION
Known only from Australia: the Great Barrier Reef and southern localities except the Solitary Islands in the east, and south to Port Denison on the west coast.

ABUNDANCE
Extremely rare on the Great Barrier Reef but abundant on all reefs to the south. The dominant coral of Boat Harbour, Lord Howe Island. Relatively common on the west coast of Australia.

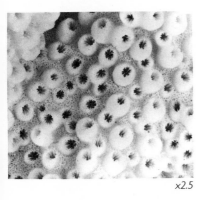

x2.5

Acropora glauca is similar in general appearance to *A. solitaryensis*, and both species, as well as *A. lovelli*, are found in abundance only at far-southern localities.
PHOTOGRAPH: ED LOVELL.

Acropora robusta

(DANA, 1846)

TYPE LOCALITY
Fiji.

IDENTIFYING CHARACTERS
Colonies are irregular in shape with thick conical branches at the centre and with thinner prostrate branches with upturned ends at the periphery. Radial corallites are of mixed sizes and shapes but are generally rasp-like.

COLOUR
Bright green with deep-pink branch tips or pinky brown, yellow-brown or cream.

SIMILAR SPECIES
A. danai.

DISTRIBUTION
From Chagos east to Tahiti. Around Australia: the Great Barrier Reef and Coral Sea in the east, and south to Houtman Abrolhos Islands on the west coast.

ABUNDANCE
Restricted to shallow reef environments, common on reef margins exposed to strong wave action.

x2.5

1. *Acropora robusta* is an anarchist among corals. Different parts of the same colony can have very different growth forms, as seen here.
PHOTOGRAPH: RON AND VALERIE TAYLOR.

2. *Acropora robusta* is a common inhabitant of the reef flat.
PHOTOGRAPH: ED LOVELL.

3. A large, sprawling *Acropora robusta* at Seringapatam Reef, north-western Australia.
PHOTOGRAPH: AUTHOR.

4. A fully developed *Acropora robusta* at Torres Strait. This species is restricted to shallow water where there is seldom space for the unrestricted growth shown by this colony.
PHOTOGRAPH: ED LOVELL.

1

3

2

4

Acropora danai

(EDWARDS & HAIME, 1860)

TYPE LOCALITY
Unrecorded.

IDENTIFYING CHARACTERS
Colonies consist of sprawling prostrate branches with upwardly projecting pointed ends at the periphery. Radial corallites are like those of *A. robusta*.

COLOUR
Deep pinkish-brown or greenish-grey.

SIMILAR SPECIES
A. robusta is distinguished from *A. danai* by its thick central branches.

DISTRIBUTION
From Madagascar east to Tahiti. Around Australia: the Great Barrier Reef, Coral Sea and all southern localities in the east, and south to Houtman Abrolhos Islands on the west coast.

ABUNDANCE
Usually restricted to shallow reef environments. Common on reef margins exposed to strong wave action.

x2.5

1. *Acropora danai*, like *A. robusta*, forms irregular colonies often consisting of both sprawling and upright branches.
PHOTOGRAPH: ED LOVELL.

2. When fully developed, *Acropora danai* has spire-like upright branches.
PHOTOGRAPH: ED LOVELL.

3. Upright branches of *Acropora danai* are usually pointed, as shown here. Such colonies may be very extensive on upper reef slopes.
PHOTOGRAPH: ED LOVELL.

148

Acropora palmerae

WELLS, 1954

TYPE LOCALITY
Marshall Islands.

IDENTIFYING CHARACTERS
Colonies are encrusting with or without short irregularly shaped branches. Radial corallites are mostly rasp-like except that they face in different directions.

COLOUR
Greenish- or pinkish-brown.

SIMILAR SPECIES
None.

DISTRIBUTION
Marshall Islands and Australia. Around Australia: the Great Barrier Reef and all southern localities except Lord Howe Island in the east; not found on the west coast.

ABUNDANCE
Very rare, except on some outer reefs and Flinders Reef (Moreton Bay). Restricted to intertidal reef flats exposed to extreme wave action where colonies may exceed 2 m in diameter.

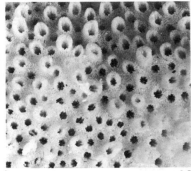

×2.5

In contrast to its relatives, *Acropora palmerae* is the least impressive of all *Acropora*. It is usually entirely encrusting and seldom develops the branches shown here.
PHOTOGRAPH: DAVE FISK.

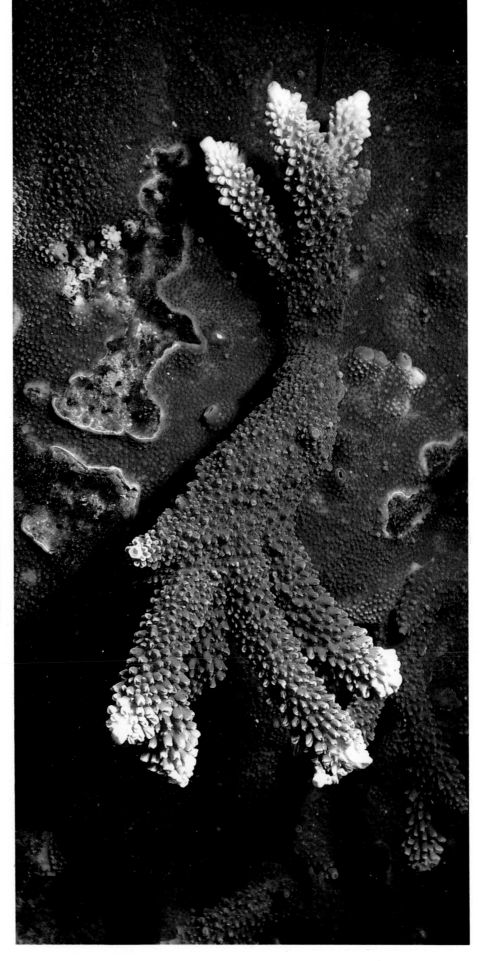

Acropora nobilis

(DANA, 1846)

TYPE LOCALITY
Singapore.

WELL-KNOWN SYNONYM
A. intermedia (Brook, 1891).

IDENTIFYING CHARACTERS
Colonies are arboresent, usually staghorn–like. Radial corallites are of mixed sizes and shapes and are similar to those of *A. robusta* and *A. danai*.

COLOUR
Cream, brown, blue, yellow and green. Individual colonies are uniform in colour except for the branch ends which are pale.

SIMILAR SPECIES
A. formosa and *A. grandis* may have similar growth forms but radial corallites are markedly different.

DISTRIBUTION
Australia and western Pacific. Around Australia: the Great Barrier Reef, Coral Sea and Flinders Reef (Moreton Bay) in the east, and south to Houtman Abrolhos Islands on the west coast.

ABUNDANCE
Very common in deep sandy lagoons where extensive monospecific stands frequently occur. Also common on upper reef slopes.

x2.5

1. *Acropora nobilis*, the most "staghorn"-like *Acropora*, exposed at low tide.
PHOTOGRAPH: ED LOVELL.

2. A branch end of *Acropora nobilis* showing radial polyps of mixed sizes.
PHOTOGRAPH: RON AND VALERIE TAYLOR.

3. The usual appearance of an *Acropora nobilis* thicket.
PHOTOGRAPH: ED LOVELL.

4. *Acropora nobilis* (cream) intermixed with *A. formosa* (purple). These similar species often grow together, especially in lagoons.
PHOTOGRAPH: ED LOVELL.

Acropora polystoma

(BROOK, 1891)

TYPE LOCALITY
  Mauritius.

IDENTIFYING CHARACTERS
  Colonies are corymbose, with thick irregular branches. Radial corallites are very irregular giving a spiny appearance.

COLOUR
  Cream or yellow.

SIMILAR SPECIES
  A. listeri also has a spiny appearance; *A. lutkeni* may have the same colony shape.

DISTRIBUTION
  Mauritius and the Red Sea east to Samoa.
  Around Australia: the northern and central Great Barrier Reef and Coral Sea in the east; not found on the west coast.

ABUNDANCE
  Uncommon, restricted to upper reef slopes exposed to strong wave action.

x2.5

The usual appearance of *Acropora polystoma*.
PHOTOGRAPH: ED LOVELL.

Acropora listeri

(BROOK, 1893)

TYPE LOCALITY
Tonga.

IDENTIFYING CHARACTERS
Colonies are composed of thick horizontal branches becoming corymbose plates with or without thick vertical branches. Radial corallites are very irregular, giving a spiny appearance.

COLOUR
Cream or brown.

SIMILAR SPECIES
A. *polystoma*.

DISTRIBUTION
Indonesia and eastern Australia east to Samoa.
Around Australia: the Great Barrier Reef, Coral Sea and south to Elizabeth Reef in the east; not found on the west coast.

ABUNDANCE
Rare, restricted to upper reef slopes exposed to strong wave action.

x2.5

Acropora listeri at Tijou Reef, Great Barrier Reef. This species is found only on upper reef slopes where wave action is strong. Its pointed polyps give it a spiny appearance.
PHOTOGRAPH: ED LOVELL.

Acropora grandis

(BROOK, 1892)

TYPE LOCALITY
Palm Island, Great Barrier Reef.

IDENTIFYING CHARACTERS
Colonies are arborescent, usually staghorn-like. Radial corallites are of mixed sizes and shapes. Those near branch tips are long and tubular and outwardly projecting.

COLOUR
Usually dark reddish-brown with very pale branch ends. Other colours include blue, purple and green, usually with paler branch ends.

SIMILAR SPECIES
A. nobilis is usually distinguished from *A. grandis* by its radial corallites and also by its colour under water.

DISTRIBUTION
Australia, the Philippines and Samoa.
Around Australia: the Great Barrier Reef, Coral Sea and Flinders Reef (Moreton Bay) in the east, and south to Houtman Abrolhos Islands on the west coast.

ABUNDANCE
Seldom common but found in a wide variety of environments. Most common on upper reef slopes where individual colonies may be up to 7 m across.

x2.5

1. In murky water, *Acropora grandis* has relatively thin, frail branches.
PHOTOGRAPH: ED LOVELL.

2. The most common growth form of *Acropora grandis* with branches tending to sprawl horizontally. The tips of branches crumble easily when pinched, aiding underwater recognition.
PHOTOGRAPH: ED LOVELL.

Acropora formosa

(DANA, 1846)

TYPE LOCALITY
Fiji and Sulu Sea.

IDENTIFYING CHARACTERS
Colonies are arborescent, usually forming thickets. Radial corallites may be similar or varied in size, and uniformly or erratically distributed.

COLOUR
Usually cream, brown or blue, usually with pale branch ends.

SIMILAR SPECIES
A. nobilis and *A. microphthalma* are larger and smaller respectively than *A. formosa*.

DISTRIBUTION
From Madagascar east to the Marshall and Phoenix Islands. Around Australia: the Great Barrier Reef and Coral Sea in the east, and south to Houtman Abrolhos Islands on the west coast.

ABUNDANCE
Very common and frequently the dominant species of lagoons and some fringing reef.

x2.5

1. A large stand of *Acropora formosa* at Broadhurst Reef, Great Barrier Reef. The different colonies which make up the stand often have different colours.
PHOTOGRAPH: ED LOVELL.

2. The tangled colony in the foreground and the upright colony in the background are both *Acropora formosa* (at Houtman Abrolhos Islands, Western Australia). This type of growth-form variation is usually the result of differences in colony age and space availability.
PHOTOGRAPH: ED LOVELL.

3. The usual appearance of a single *Acropora formosa* colony in a lagoon.
PHOTOGRAPH: RON AND VALERIE TAYLOR.

4. The branch tips of *Acropora formosa*.
PHOTOGRAPH: RON AND VALERIE TAYLOR.

Acropora abrolhosensis

VERON, 1985

TYPE LOCALITY
Houtman Abrolhos Islands.

IDENTIFYING CHARACTERS
Colonies are arborescent with straight branches. Axial corallites are large and prominent. Radial corallites are large with outward-facing, circular openings.

COLOUR
Brown, blue or pink with pale branch tips.

SIMILAR SPECIES
A. nobilis and *A. grandis* are both arborescent with large corallites.

DISTRIBUTION
Known only from Australia: south to Houtman Abrolhos Islands on the west coast; not found in the east.

ABUNDANCE
Common in lagoons or reef slopes protected from strong wave action.

1

2

x2.5

1. A large stand of *Acropora abrolhosensis* at the Houtman Abrolhos Islands, Western Australia. Such stands may be over 20 m across in shallow lagoons protected from strong wave action.
PHOTOGRAPH: ED LOVELL.

2. *Acropora abrolhosensis* has distinctively large axial polyps. Polyps are often extended during the day, giving colonies a hairy appearance.
PHOTOGRAPH: ED LOVELL.

Acropora acuminata

(VERRILL, 1864)

TYPE LOCALITY
Gilbert Islands.

IDENTIFYING CHARACTERS
Colonies are caespito-corymbose, forming corymbose tables. Horizontal branches are anastomosed. Branches curve up towards the ends which taper to a point. Skeletons have a permanent dark colour.

COLOUR
Usually bright or pale blue or brown.

SIMILAR SPECIES
A. valenciennesi forms colonies of similar shape but these are much larger.

DISTRIBUTION
South China Sea, Gilbert and Marshall Islands and Australia. Around Australia: the Great Barrier Reef and Coral Sea in the east, and Houtman Abrolhos Islands on the west coast.

ABUNDANCE
Uncommon. Found in turbid or clear water on upper or lower reef slopes.

x2.5

I. The spiky appearance of *Acropora acuminata* from an exposed upper reef slope.
PHOTOGRAPH: ED LOVELL.

2. A thicket of *Acropora acuminata.* The general growth form is similar to that of *A. valenciennesi* but branches are much smaller.
PHOTOGRAPH: ED LOVELL.

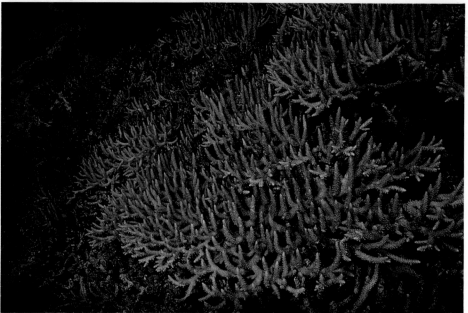

156

Acropora valenciennesi

(EDWARDS & HAIME, 1860)

TYPE LOCALITY
Torres Strait, Great Barrier Reef.

WELL-KNOWN SYNONYM
A. splendida (Nemenzo, 1967).

IDENTIFYING CHARACTERS
Colonies develop into open corymbose tables composed of horizontal widely spaced branches and upturned branch ends.

COLOUR
Mixtures of brown, blue and green with pale branch ends.

SIMILAR SPECIES
A. acuminata is like *A. valenciennesi* but all structures are much smaller.

DISTRIBUTION
From Sri Lanka east to the Philippines, Palau and Fiji. Around Australia: the Great Barrier Reef and Coral Sea in the east, and south to Houtman Abrolhos Islands on the west coast.

ABUNDANCE
Common on upper and lower reef slopes and inter-reef channels.

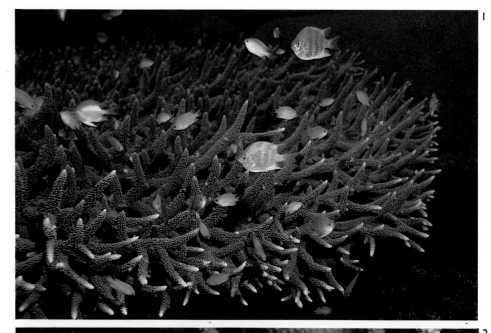

x2.5

I. *Acropora valenciennesi* colonies are always composed of interlocking branches with pointed upturned ends. They are amongst the most beautiful and distinctive of all *Acropora* species.
PHOTOGRAPH: ED LOVELL.

2. The branch ends of *Acropora valenciennesi.*
PHOTOGRAPH: ED LOVELL.

3. A large colony of *Acropora valenciennesi* at Scott Reef, north-western Australia.
PHOTOGRAPH: AUTHOR.

Acropora microphthalma

(VERRILL, 1859)

TYPE LOCALITY
Ryukyu Islands.

IDENTIFYING CHARACTERS
Colonies are arborescent, small, usually forming thickets. Branches are slender and straight. Radial corallites are small, numerous and of the same size.

COLOUR
Usually pale grey, sometimes pale brown or cream.

SIMILAR SPECIES
A. microphthalma is the smallest and finest of the arborescent *Acropora*. Closest to *A. formosa*, *A. horrida* and *A. vaughani*.

DISTRIBUTION
From Madagascar east to the Marshall Islands and north to the Ryukyu Islands.
Around Australia: the Great Barrier Reef and Coral Sea in the east, and south to Houtman Abrolhos Islands on the west coast.

ABUNDANCE
Occupies most reef environments but is uncommon except in turbid water or in sandy lagoons where colonies frequently exceed 2 m in diameter.

x2.5

I. *Acropora microphthalma* commonly forms these small thickets. It is like *A. formosa* but smaller.
PHOTOGRAPH: ED LOVELL.

2. A thicket of *Acropora microphthalma*.
PHOTOGRAPH: ED LOVELL.

Acropora kirstyae

VERON & WALLACE, 1984

TYPE LOCALITY
Palm Islands, Great Barrier Reef.

IDENTIFYING CHARACTERS
Colonies are caespitose, composed of fine branches with very small corallites.

COLOUR
Uniform pale orange-brown.

SIMILAR SPECIES
None.

DISTRIBUTION
Known only from Australia: the central and southern Great Barrier Reef in the east; not found on the west coast.

ABUNDANCE
Rare, restricted to shallow water protected from wave action.

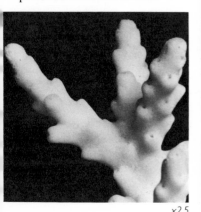

×2.5

1. Named after the author's wife; *Acropora kirstyae* is composed of delicate interlocking branches.
PHOTOGRAPH: ED LOVELL.

2. The fine fluted polyps of *Acropora kirstyae.*
PHOTOGRAPH: ED LOVELL.

Acropora horrida

(DANA, 1846)

TYPE LOCALITY
Fiji.

IDENTIFYING CHARACTERS
Colonies are arborescent to caespitose. Corallites are irregular and the surface of branches is very rough. Polyps are usually extended during the day.

COLOUR
Usually pale blue, sometimes dark blue or pale yellow or brown. Polyps are pale blue or white.

SIMILAR SPECIES
A. tortuosa is very similar; *A. microphthalma* and *A. vaughani* are also small arborescent species.

DISTRIBUTION
From the Red Sea east to the Marshall Islands.
Around Australia: the Great Barrier Reef, Coral Sea and Elizabeth and Middleton Reefs in the east, and south to Houtman Abrolhos Islands on the west coast.

ABUNDANCE
Uncommon except in turbid water around fringing reefs. Arborescent colonies are usually associated with turbid water, bushy colonies occur on upper reef slopes and in lagoons.

x2.5

1. In shallow lagoons, *Acropora horrida* branches may be tall and closely clustered, even bushy. They always have a gnarled appearance and usually appear powder-blue. The colour seen here, the true colour, is produced with a flashlight.
PHOTOGRAPH: RON AND VALERIE TAYLOR.

2. *Acropora horrida* usually has white or pale-blue polyps extended during the day.
PHOTOGRAPH: ED LOVELL.

3, 4. In turbid water, *Acropora horrida* often occurs as a tangle of twisted branches (3) and in clear water it is usually bottlebrush-shaped (4).
PHOTOGRAPHS: ED LOVELL.

Acropora tortuosa

(DANA, 1846)

TYPE LOCALITY
Fiji.

IDENTIFYING CHARACTERS
Colonies are caespitose to bottlebrush. Corallites are irregular and the surface of branches is usually rough. Polyps are not extended during the day.

COLOUR
Deep blue or brown; usually mauve in photographs.

SIMILAR SPECIES
A. horrida is very similar; polyps are not extended during the day, corallites are smaller and septal teeth are more prominent.

DISTRIBUTION
Fiji, Caroline Islands and Australia.
Around Australia: the Great Barrier Reef and Elizabeth and Middleton Reefs in the east, and Houtman Abrolhos Islands on the west coast.

ABUNDANCE
Very rare on the Great Barrier Reef but abundant in the lagoon of Elizabeth and Middleton Reefs; uncommon at the Houtman Abrolhos Islands.

x2.5

Acropora tortuosa at Elizabeth and Middleton Reefs, eastern Australia. This species is very similar to *A. horrida* but is seldom found.
PHOTOGRAPH: ED LOVELL.

Acropora vaughani

WELLS, 1954

TYPE LOCALITY
  Marshall Islands.

IDENTIFYING CHARACTERS
  Colonies are arborescent to caespitose. Corallites are widely spaced. The coenosteum is fine, thus giving branches a smooth appearance.

COLOUR
  Uniform blue, cream or pale brown.

SIMILAR SPECIES
  A. horrida may have a similar growth form but has markedly different corallites and coenosteum.

DISTRIBUTION
  West Australian coast east to the Marshall Islands and Micronesia. Around Australia: the northern and central Great Barrier Reef and Coral Sea in the east, and south to Houtman Abrolhos Islands on the west coast.

ABUNDANCE
  Uncommon except in turbid water around fringing reefs. Growth forms and habitat preferences are similar to those of *A. horrida*.

x2.5

Acropora vaughani is often found with *A. horrida*. Branches have a porcelain-like smooth surface, the opposite of *A. horrida*.
PHOTOGRAPH: ED LOVELL.

Acropora austera

(DANA, 1846)

TYPE LOCALITY
Unrecorded.

IDENTIFYING CHARACTERS
Colonies are arborescent to caespitose. Corallites project outwards and have wide calices.

COLOUR
Many colours, most commonly blue or cream. Axial corallites are frequently yellow.

SIMILAR SPECIES
A. austera does not resemble closely any other species but its wide range of growth forms sometimes makes it difficult to identify.

DISTRIBUTION
From Madagascar east to the Marshall Islands.
Around Australia: the Great Barrier Reef, Coral Sea and south to Elizabeth Reef in the east, and south to Houtman Abrolhos Islands on the west coast.

ABUNDANCE
Occupies a wide range of environments but is usually uncommon except on upper reef slopes of outer reefs.

x2.5

1. The distinctive appearance of *Acropora austera* with pointed main branches and irregular sub-branches.
PHOTOGRAPH: ED LOVELL.

2. Branch ends of *Acropora austera* have polyps of irregular shapes and sizes.
PHOTOGRAPH: ED LOVELL.

3. The common growth form of *Acropora austera.*
PHOTOGRAPH: ED LOVELL.

Acropora aspera
(DANA, 1846)

TYPE LOCALITY
Fiji.

IDENTIFYING CHARACTERS
Colonies are subcorymbose with short thick branches. Radial corallites are of two sizes, are crowded and have prominent lower lips giving a scale-like appearance.

COLOUR
Commonly pale blue-grey, green or cream; less commonly bright blue.

SIMILAR SPECIES
A. millepora is readily distinguished by having all radial corallites the same size; *A. pulchra* is similar but corallites are much smaller.

DISTRIBUTION
From the Cocos-Keeling Islands east to Fiji.
Around Australia: the Great Barrier Reef, Coral Sea and Elizabeth and Middleton Reefs in the east, and south to Houtman Abrolhos Islands on the west coast.

ABUNDANCE
Abundant on reef flats and shallow lagoons. Uncommon on exposed upper reef slopes and deep water.

×2.5

1. *Acropora aspera* is a common species in lagoons and on reef flats. Like *A. millepora,* polyps are scale-like but they are in two sizes.
PHOTOGRAPH: ED LOVELL.

2. Branch tips of an *Acropora aspera* thicket.
PHOTOGRAPH: ED LOVELL.

Acropora pulchra
(BROOK, 1891)

TYPE LOCALITY
Cocos-Keeling Islands.

IDENTIFYING CHARACTERS
Colonies are arborescent to caespito–corymbose. Radial corallites are of mixed sizes, are widely spaced and small, with projecting lower lips.

COLOUR
Pale to dark brown or blue, often with pale-blue tips.

SIMILAR SPECIES
A. aspera is the nearest species but corallites are much larger and scale–like.

DISTRIBUTION
From the Cocos-Keeling Islands east to Fiji.
Around Australia: the Great Barrier Reef and Elizabeth and Middleton Reefs in the east, and south to Houtman Abrolhos Islands on the west coast.

ABUNDANCE
Uncommon, restricted to shallow back-reef margins where it occurs with *A. aspera*.

x2.5

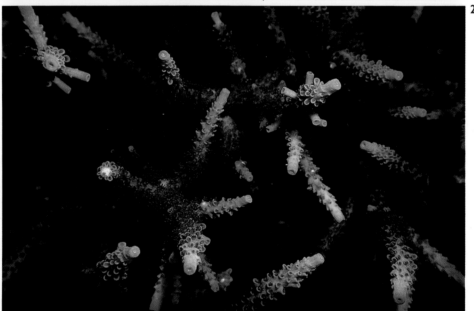

1. *Acropora pulchra* in a protected lagoon at the Houtman Abrolhos Islands, Western Australia.
PHOTOGRAPH: ED LOVELL.

2. Branch tips of an *Acropora pulchra* ticket with radial polyps partly extended
PHOTOGRAPH: ED LOVELL.

3. A finely branched *Acropora pulchra* on a lower reef slope.
PHOTOGRAPH: ED LOVELL.

Acropora millepora

(EHRENBERG, 1834)

TYPE LOCALITY
"Indian Ocean".

IDENTIFYING CHARACTERS
Colonies are corymbose to tubular, with short branches. Radial corallites are all the same size and have prominent lower lips giving a scale-like appearance.

COLOUR
Commonly green with orange tips; also bright salmon-pink, bright orange, or pale green, blue or pink.

SIMILAR SPECIES
A. aspera has similar radial corallites but they are of two intermixed sizes.

DISTRIBUTION
From Sri Lanka and Thailand east to the Marshall Islands and Tonga.
Around Australia: all localities except Lord Howe Island in the east, and south to Houtman Abrolhos Islands on the west coast.

ABUNDANCE
Common. Restricted to shallow water, usually reef flats, but also lagoons and upper reef slopes.

x2.5

I. *Acropora millepora* at Tijou Reef, Great Barrier Reef.
PHOTOGRAPH: ED LOVELL.

2. The polyps of *Acropora millepora* have a very distinctive, neat scale-like appearance which makes this species easily recognisable.
PHOTOGRAPH: RON AND VALERIE TAYLOR.

Acropora tenuis

(DANA, 1846)

TYPE LOCALITY
Unrecorded.

IDENTIFYING CHARACTERS
Colonies are corymbose plates with neat, evenly spaced branches. Radial corallites have wide lower lips giving them a neat rosette-like appearance when viewed from above.

COLOUR
Cream or blue. Colours may be bright with distinctively coloured radial corallite lips.

SIMILAR SPECIES
A. selago is similar but *A. tenuis* is recognised readily by the above characters.

DISTRIBUTION
From Mauritius east to the Marshall Islands.
Around Australia: the Great Barrier Reef, Coral Sea and Elizabeth and Middleton Reefs in the east, and south to Houtman Abrolhos Islands on the west coast.

ABUNDANCE
Common where *Acropora* diversity is moderate or high, especially upper reef slopes.

x2.5

1. *Acropora tenuis* from an upper reef slope.
PHOTOGRAPH: RON AND VALERIE TAYLOR.

2. *Acropora tenuis* at Keeper Reef, Great Barrier Reef. The neatly arranged wide-lipped radial polyps allow this species to be easily recognised.
PHOTOGRAPH: ED LOVELL.

3. The polyps of *Acropora tenuis*.
PHOTOGRAPH: ED LOVELL

Acropora selago
(STUDER, 1878)

TYPE LOCALITY
New Ireland.

WELL-KNOWN SYNONYM
A. delicatula (Brook, 1893).

IDENTIFYING CHARACTERS
Colonies are caespito–corymbose with thin branches. Radial corallites are scale–like, lightly structured and do not have a rosette–like appearance. Polyps are frequently extended during the day.

COLOUR
Pale cream or brown.

SIMILAR SPECIES
A. tenuis.

DISTRIBUTION
From the central–western Pacific east to the Marshall and Solomon Islands.
Around Australia: the Great Barrier Reef and Coral Sea in the east, and south to Port Gregory on the west coast.

ABUNDANCE
Seldom common but occurs in a wide variety of environments from exposed upper reef slopes to turbid lagoons.

x2.5

Acropora selago may have much finer branches than shown here. It has a delicate appearance and was once appropriately named *A. delicatula.*
PHOTOGRAPH: ED LOVELL.

Acropora donei

VERON & WALLACE, 1984

TYPE LOCALITY
Turtle Islands, Great Barrier Reef.

IDENTIFYING CHARACTERS
Colonies are caespito–corymbose or corymbose plates and tables. Branches are highly anastomosed. Radial corallites are usually in two sizes, the larger of which have flaring lips. The coenosteum is coarse, giving a rough appearance to branches.

COLOUR
Green, white or cream; rarely pale brown.

SIMILAR SPECIES
A. yongei has similar corallites but is much less corymbose.

DISTRIBUTION
Known only from Australia: the Great Barrier Reef, Coral Sea and Flinders Reef (Moreton Bay) in the east, and south to Houtman Abrolhos Islands on the west coast.

ABUNDANCE
Uncommon but distinctive. Restricted to shallow fringing reefs and upper reef slopes where *Acropora* diversity is high.

x2.5

1. A large colony of *Acropora donei*, named after the author's colleague, Terry Done.
PHOTOGRAPH: ED LOVELL.

2. *Acropora donei* has rasp-like radial polyps, similar to *A. yongei*.
PHOTOGRAPH: ED LOVELL.

Acropora dendrum

(BASSETT-SMITH, 1890)

TYPE LOCALITY
  South China Sea.

IDENTIFYING CHARACTERS
  Colonies are corymbose plates
  with tapering branches and
  corallites are non-exsert.

COLOUR
  Pale brown or cream.

SIMILAR SPECIES
  Corymbose *A. valida*.

DISTRIBUTION
  South China Sea, Arafura Sea and
  Australia.
  Around Australia: the Great
  Barrier Reef and Coral Sea in the
  east, and south to Houtman
  Abrolhos Islands on the west
  coast.

ABUNDANCE
  Rare, occurs only on upper reef
  slopes where *Acropora* diversity is
  high. Colonies are usually 0.5–1
  m in diameter.

x2.5

1, 2. *Acropora dendrum* has little
variation. The small upward-projecting
branchlets taper and radial polyps are
almost immersed within them.
PHOTOGRAPHS: ED LOVELL.

Acropora yongei

VERON & WALLACE, 1984

TYPE LOCALITY
Britomart Reef, Great Barrier Reef.

IDENTIFYING CHARACTERS
Colonies are arborescent or prostrate or form caespito-corymbose bushes. Branches are up to 20 mm thick. Radial corallites have projecting lower lips.

COLOUR
Uniform cream, yellow or pale brown.

SIMILAR SPECIES
A. subulata and *A. tenuis* may be similar but branches are much thinner. See also *A. donei*.

DISTRIBUTION
Australia and the Philippines. Around Australia: the Great Barrier Reef and all southern localities except the Solitary Islands in the east, and south to Houtman Abrolhos Islands on the west coast.

ABUNDANCE
Common, occurs in a wide variety of environments. Colonies are frequently over 2 m in diameter and may form monospecific stands (for example, at Lord Howe Island).

x2.5

I. *Acropora yongei* at the Houtman Abrolhos Islands, Western Australia. This species was named after Sir Maurice Yonge, leader of the 1928 expedition to the Great Barrier Reef.
PHOTOGRAPH: ED LOVELL.

2. A large stand of *Acropora yongei* at Broadhurst Reef, Great Barrier Reef. The thicker branches of *A. danai* protrude above the stand while pinkish *A. horrida* can be seen in the foreground.
PHOTOGRAPH: ED LOVELL.

3. The characteristic appearance of *Acropora yongei* branches. Radial polyps have rasp-like lower lips.
PHOTOGRAPH: ED LOVELL.

Acropora cytherea
(DANA, 1846)

TYPE LOCALITY
Tahiti.

IDENTIFYING CHARACTERS
Colonies are wide flat tables which are thin and finely structured. Fine upward projecting branchlets have exsert axial corallites. Polyps are frequently extended during the day.

COLOUR
Uniform pale cream, brown or blue.

SIMILAR SPECIES
A. hyacinthus is similar except that branchlets do not have exsert axial corallites and have radial corallites arranged in a rosette.

DISTRIBUTION
From the Mascarene Archipelago east to Tahiti and Hawaii. Around Australia: all localities except Lord Howe and Solitary Islands in the east, and south to Houtman Abrolhos Islands on the west coast.

ABUNDANCE
One of the most abundant corals of upper reef slopes and it may occur in lagoons and lower reef slopes.

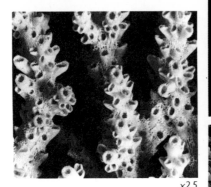

×2.5

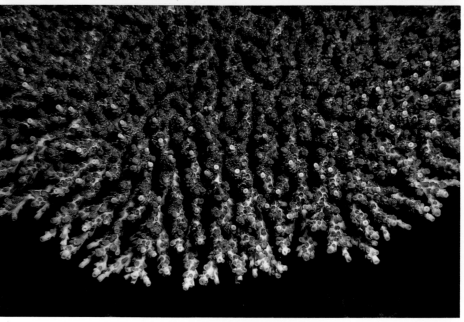

1. Plates of *Acropora cytherea* (upper and lower left) and *A. hyacinthus* (right).
PHOTOGRAPH: ED LOVELL.

2. A plate of *Acropora cytherea* in shallow water. These are so delicate that they can be cut with a knife, yet are damaged only by severe storms.
PHOTOGRAPH: ED LOVELL.

3. The characteristic appearance of an *Acropora cytherea* plate. The axial polyps are elongate and do not have radial polyps arranged around them in a neat rosette like *A. hyacinthus*.
PHOTOGRAPH: ED LOVELL.

Acropora microclados

(EHRENBERG, 1834)

TYPE LOCALITY
Unrecorded.

IDENTIFYING CHARACTERS
Colonies are corymbose plates with branches up to 10 mm thick which are tapering, evenly spaced and curving upward to a uniform height.

COLOUR
Always a distinctive pale pinky brown. Pale-grey tentacles are often extended during the day.

SIMILAR SPECIES
Closest to *A. cytherea* which has finer branches and corymbose *A. cerealis* which has subdividing branches of irregular lengths.

DISTRIBUTION
Australia and Indonesia. Around Australia: the Great Barrier Reef, except the Capricorn and Bunker groups, and Coral Sea in the east, and Rowley Shoals and Scott Reef on the west coast.

ABUNDANCE
Uncommon except on some upper reef slopes. Colonies are up to approximately 1m in diameter.

x2.5

Acropora microclados at Broadhurst Reef, Great Barrier Reef.
PHOTOGRAPH: ED LOVELL.

Acropora paniculata

VERRILL, 1902

TYPE LOCALITY
Probably Fiji.

IDENTIFYING CHARACTERS
Colonies are large plates or tables which are up to 25 mm thick and finely structured. Corallites are long, thin and tubular.

COLOUR
Cream or blue.

SIMILAR SPECIES
A. hyacinthus and *A. cytherea* both form plates which are thinner and have different corallites.

DISTRIBUTION
Australia, Fiji and Hawaii. Around Australia: the Great Barrier Reef, except the Capricorn and Bunker groups, and Coral Sea in the east, and recorded from Christmas Island, but not from the west coast.

ABUNDANCE
Uncommon. Colonies are conspicuous, frequently over 1 m in diameter. Occurs only on upper reef slopes.

×2.5

Acropora paniculata, which looks like a much-thickened *A. cytherea*. Branch ends have many elongate polyps seen here with tentacles partly extended. As with many corals, the polyps may extend only one tentacle during the day, which hangs downward, apparently lifeless.

PHOTOGRAPH: ED LOVELL.

Acropora hyacinthus
(DANA, 1846)

TYPE LOCALITY
Fiji.

IDENTIFYING CHARACTERS
Colonies are wide, flat tables which are thin and finely structured. Fine upward projecting branchlets have a rosette-like arrangement of radial corallites. Axial corallites are not exsert.

COLOUR
Uniform cream, brown or green with or without blue- or pink-growing margins.

SIMILAR SPECIES
A. cytherea.

DISTRIBUTION
From the Mascarene Archipelago east to Tahiti.
Around Australia: all localities including Lord Howe and the Solitary Islands in the east, and south to Jurien Bay on the west coast.

ABUNDANCE
One of the most abundant corals of upper reef slopes and outer reef flats.

x2.5

1. A favourite study site at Broadhurst Reef, Great Barrier Reef, dominated by *Acropora hyacinthus*. In this picture the reef flat is exposed during a low spring tide.
PHOTOGRAPH: ED LOVELL.

2. An *Acropora hyacinthus* forms a large two-tiered spiral.
PHOTOGRAPH: ED LOVELL.

3. The branchlets of *Acropora hyacinthus* are easily recognised.
PHOTOGRAPH: AUTHOR.

Acropora spicifera

(DANA, 1846)

TYPE LOCALITY
Singapore and Fiji.

IDENTIFYING CHARACTERS
Colonies are wide, flat plates and tables. Curved, tapered, upward-projecting branchlets have a rosette-like arrangement of radial corallites.

COLOUR
Grey, with a broad white border to the plates.

SIMILAR SPECIES
A. hyacinthus has much smaller and finer branchlets. *A. dendrum* has less prominent corallites and colonies are less plate-like.

DISTRIBUTION
Australia, east to Fiji. Around Australia: south to Houtman Abrolhos Islands on the west coast; not found in the east.

ABUNDANCE
One of the dominant corals of upper reef slopes of the Houtman Abrolhos Islands.

x2.5

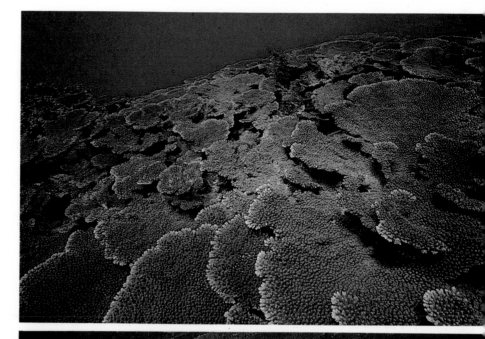

1. A large stand of *Acropora spicifera* at the Houtman Abrolhos Islands, Western Australia.
PHOTOGRAPH: ED LOVELL.

2. *Acropora spicifera* colonies often consist of irregularly divided plates. These usually have pale borders.
PHOTOGRAPH: ED LOVELL.

3. An *Acropora spicifera* plate with polyps extended.
PHOTOGRAPH: ED LOVELL.

Acropora anthocercis

(BROOK, 1893)

TYPE LOCALITY
Palm Islands, Great Barrier Reef.

IDENTIFYING CHARACTERS
Colonies are thick corymbose plates. Branches are upward-projecting, thick, with several axial corallites which are thick, exsert and tapered. Radial corallites have thick walls.

COLOUR
Colonies are a mixture of colours: blue, mauve, purple and grey being the most common.

SIMILAR SPECIES
A. hyacinthus is similar, but is much less solid.

DISTRIBUTION
From Madagascar and possibly the Red Sea east to the Great Barrier Reef.
Around Australia: the Great Barrier Reef, Coral Sea and Elizabeth and Middleton Reefs in the east, and south to Houtman Abrolhos Islands on the west coast.

ABUNDANCE
Usually uncommon except on upper reef slopes exposed to strong wave action.

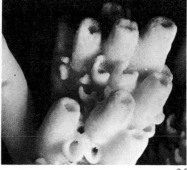

x2.5

1. *Acropora anthocercis* on a protected slope of Fitzroy Reef, Great Barrier Reef.
PHOTOGRAPH: ED LOVELL.

2. *Acropora anthocercis* at Tijou Reef, Great Barrier Reef, where it is exposed to strong wave action. The general appearance is like a solid *A. hyacinthus* except that branchlets have several axial polyps.
PHOTOGRAPH: ED LOVELL.

177

Acropora latistella

(BROOK, 1891)

TYPE LOCALITY
Great Barrier Reef.

IDENTIFYING CHARACTERS
Colonies are corymbose, corymbose plates or caespitose. Branches are 5-9 mm thick, straight or uniformly curved. Radial corallites are usually in rows and are appressed with rounded calices.

COLOUR
Uniform pale cream, grey or brown, sometimes green or purple. Branch ends are sometimes yellow.

SIMILAR SPECIES
A. subulata, A. valida and *A. cerealis.*

DISTRIBUTION
Australia, the Philippines and Samoa.
Around Australia: all localities except the Solitary Islands in the east, and south to Exmouth Gulf on the west coast.

ABUNDANCE
Common, occurs in a wide range of environments, but can be difficult to recognise except when it forms corymbose plates.

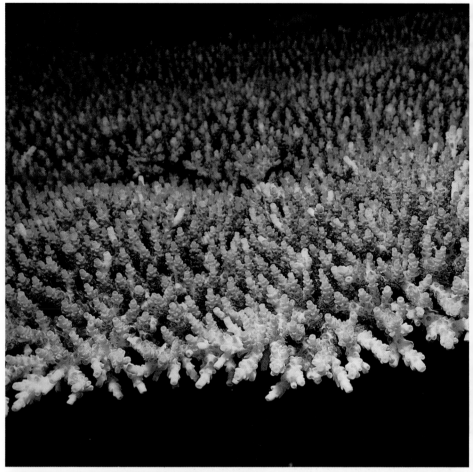

x2.5

I. The fine branchlets at the side of an *Acropora latistella* colony. The branchlets are very evenly spaced and give large colonies a neat appearance.
PHOTOGRAPH: ED LOVELL.

2. *Acropora latistella* with polyps partly extended during the day.
PHOTOGRAPH: ED LOVELL.

Acropora subulata

(DANA, 1846)

TYPE LOCALITY
Fiji.

IDENTIFYING CHARACTERS
Colonies form large circular tables often over 2 m in diameter, with a fine structure consisting of a network of horizontal branches and fine, evenly spaced branchlets. The whole structure is soft and crumbles readily when touched. Small colonies are usually pillow-shaped.

COLOUR
Usually pale grey or brown, sometimes blue or green. Branchlet lips may be pale. Most colonies have a 10 cm wide pale border.

SIMILAR SPECIES
A. latistella has coarser and larger skeletal structures.

DISTRIBUTION
❨ Australia, the Philippines and Fiji.
Around Australia: the Great Barrier Reef and Coral Sea in the east, and south to Houtman Abrolhos Islands on the west coast.

ABUNDANCE
Restricted to shallow reef slopes with a high *Acropora* diversity but protected from strong wave action. Very conspicuous.

x2.5

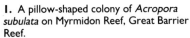

1. A pillow-shaped colony of *Acropora subulata* on Myrmidon Reef, Great Barrier Reef.
PHOTOGRAPH: ED LOVELL.

2. Two colonies of *Acropora subulata* that have joined together to grow as one.
PHOTOGRAPH: ED LOVELL.

Acropora nana

(STUDER, 1878)

TYPE LOCALITY
Fiji.

IDENTIFYING CHARACTERS
Colonies consist of compact thickets of long, terete, straight branches radiating from a solid base. Radial corallites are appressed.

COLOUR
Cream, blue or pink, usually with pale branch tips.

SIMILAR SPECIES
A. aculeus and *A. azurea*.

DISTRIBUTION
Australia, Cocos-Keeling Islands and Fiji.
Around Australia: the Great Barrier Reef, Coral Sea and Flinders Reef (Moreton Bay) in the east, and south to Houtman Abrolhos Islands on the west coast.

ABUNDANCE
Uncommon, found only where currents or wave actions are strong.

x2.5

I. *Acropora nana*, primarily characterised by straight branches radiating from a small base. Colonies fall apart readily if disturbed yet they can withstand heavy wave action.
PHOTOGRAPH: ED LOVELL.

2. Despite its delicate appearance, *Acropora nana* is a common species of outer reef flats.
PHOTOGRAPH: AUTHOR.

Acropora aculeus

(DANA, 1846)

TYPE LOCALITY
Fiji.

IDENTIFYING CHARACTERS
Colonies are corymbose or pillow-like. Horizontal branches are thin and spreading. Upward-projecting branchlets are fine and radial corallites have flaring lips.

COLOUR
Usually grey or bright blue-green or yellow. Tips of branches may be yellow, lime green, pale blue or brown.

SIMILAR SPECIES
A. nana and A. latistella.

DISTRIBUTION
From Sri Lanka east to the Marshall Islands and Samoa. Around Australia: the Great Barrier Reef and Coral Sea in the east, and south to Houtman Abrolhos Islands on the west coast.

ABUNDANCE
Very common, especially on upper reef slopes and in lagoons, where its pillow shape is best developed.

×2.5

1, 2. Colonies of *Acropora aculeus* are usually pillow-like with a few horizontal main branches.
PHOTOGRAPHS: ED LOVELL.

3. Polyps of *Acropora aculeus*, one of the most brightly coloured *Acropora*.
PHOTOGRAPH: ED LOVELL.

181

Acropora azurea

VERON & WALLACE, 1984

TYPE LOCALITY
Myrmidon Reef, Great Barrier Reef.

IDENTIFYING CHARACTERS
Colonies are composed of fine, irregular, anastomosing branches arising from a solid base. Radial corallites are very small, appressed to the branch.

COLOUR
Uniform sky-blue.

SIMILAR SPECIES
A. nana.

DISTRIBUTION
Known only from Australia: Myrmidon Reef (Great Barrier Reef) in the east; not found on the west coast.

ABUNDANCE
Extremely rare. Despite its delicate appearance, it forms a narrow zone on an upper reef slope exposed to very strong wave action.

x2.5

Acropora cerealis

(DANA, 1846)

TYPE LOCALITY
Sulu Sea.

IDENTIFYING CHARACTERS
Colonies are caespitose or corymbose, composed of highly anastomosed branches which are thin, with most of their width occupied by corallites.

COLOUR
Mostly pale brown, cream or white, with purple, pink, blue or cream branch tips.

SIMILAR SPECIES
A. latistella, A. nasuta and A. valida.

DISTRIBUTION
From the Philippines and Indonesia east to the Marshall Islands and Tonga.
Around Australia: the Great Barrier Reef and Coral Sea in the east, and south to Dampier Archipelago on the west coast.

ABUNDANCE
Abundant on upper reef slopes.

x2.5

I. The branches of a colourful *Acropora cerealis.*
PHOTOGRAPH: ED LOVELL.

2. A side view of a small *Acropora cerealis* colony.
PHOTOGRAPH: RON AND VALERIE TAYLOR.

3. *Acropora cerealis* showing its usual neat, compact appearance.
PHOTOGRAPH: ED LOVELL.

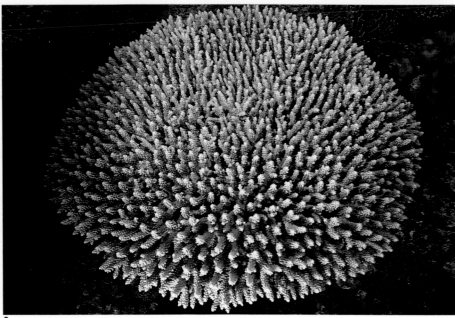

3

Acropora nasuta

(DANA, 1846)

TYPE LOCALITY
Tahiti.

IDENTIFYING CHARACTERS
Colonies are irregularly corymbose with tapering branches up to 12 mm wide. Radial corallites are usually in neat rows and are nariform in shape.

COLOUR
Cream or pale brown with blue branch tips, cream with brown corallites or greenish-brown with purple or blue corallites.

SIMILAR SPECIES
A. cerealis and *A. valida*.

DISTRIBUTION
From the Red Sea east to Tahiti. Around Australia: all localities south to Elizabeth Reef in the east, and south to Houtman Abrolhos Islands on the west coast.

ABUNDANCE
Occurs in almost all *Acropora* assemblages but is especially common on upper reef slopes.

x2.5

1. *Acropora nasuta* is so named because its radial polyps are nose-shaped, the "noses" being upside down and in neat rows.
PHOTOGRAPH: ED LOVELL.

2. Branch tips of *Acropora nasuta*.
PHOTOGRAPH: ED LOVELL.

3. A side view of a finely branched *Acropora nasuta* colony with polyps partly extended.
PHOTOGRAPH: RON AND VALERIE TAYLOR.

Acropora valida

(DANA, 1846)

TYPE LOCALITY
Fiji.

IDENTIFYING CHARACTERS
Colonies are mostly caespitose-corymbose but have a wide range of forms from compact bushes to tables. Radial corallites are usually a mixture of sizes and are strongly appressed with small openings.

COLOUR
Cream brown or yellow, sometimes brown with purple branch tips and cream corallites, a colour shared by *A. secale* and other species.

SIMILAR SPECIES
A. cerealis and *A. nasuta* are similar but the strongly appressed radial corallites of *A. valida* are distinctive.

DISTRIBUTION
From the Red Sea east to central America. Found on most temperate reefs and is the most widely distributed *Acropora* species. Around Australia: the Great Barrier Reef, Coral Sea and south to Elizabeth Reef in the east, and south to Houtman Abrolhos Islands on the west coast.

ABUNDANCE
Very abundant and occurs in a wide range of environments. Is a dominant species of the upper reef slopes of Elizabeth and Middleton Reefs. Colonies seldom exceed 0.5 m in diameter.

x2.5

1. *Acropora valida* is one of the most widespread and abundant of all corals. Colonies usually occur in neat clumps, as seen here.
PHOTOGRAPH: ED LOVELL.

2, 3. The two most common colours of *Acropora valida*. Radial polyps are appressed against the branches and have small openings and are usually easily recognised.
PHOTOGRAPHS: RON AND VALERIE TAYLOR (2) AND ED LOVELL (3).

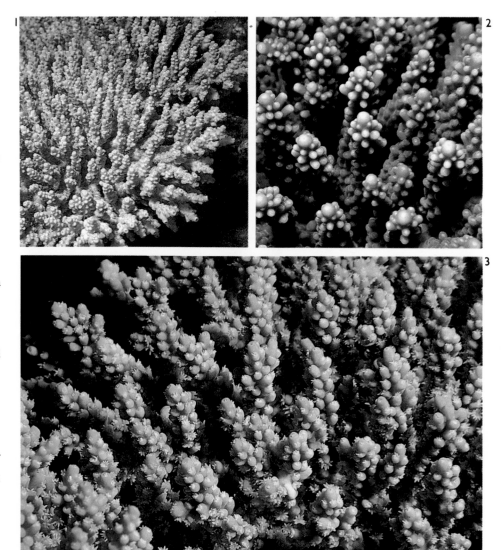

4. Adjacent corals of *Acropora valida* and *Goniastrea retiformis* in an outer reef flat, where both these species are common.
PHOTOGRAPH: AUTHOR.

Acropora secale

(STUDER, 1878)

TYPE LOCALITY
 Sri Lanka.

WELL-KNOWN SYNONYM
 A. diversa (Brook, 1891).

IDENTIFYING CHARACTERS
 Colonies are mostly corymbose. Branches are tapered, up to 25 mm in diameter. Corallites are of mixed sizes, sometimes alternating in vertical rows, and are large and conspicuous.

COLOUR
 Colonies are colourful, usually mixtures of cream, blue, purple, brown and yellow.

SIMILAR SPECIES
 None, but *A. secale* can be confused with *A. gemmifera*.

DISTRIBUTION
 From Mauritius east to the Marshall Islands and the Tuamotu Archipelago. Around Australia: the Great Barrier Reef, Coral Sea and south to Flinders Reef (Moreton Bay) in the east, and south to North West Cape on the west coast.

ABUNDANCE
 Common in shallow reef environments especially upper reef slopes and outer reef flats.

x2.5

1. *Acropora secale* at Keeper Reef, Great Barrier Reef. Colonies are often more compact than this one.
PHOTOGRAPH: ED LOVELL.

2. *Acropora secale* on an upper reef slope exposed to moderate wave action.
PHOTOGRAPH: ED LOVELL.

3. The branch ends of *Acropora secale* are gaudy. Polyps are solidly constructed and their shape, as seen here, is distinctive.
PHOTOGRAPH: ED LOVELL.

Acropora lutkeni

CROSSLAND, 1952

TYPE LOCALITY
Great Barrier Reef.

IDENTIFYING CHARACTERS
Colonies have a wide variety of growth forms ranging from bottlebrush to corymbose. They are always very sturdy, with thick tapering branches. Radial corallites are irregular and have a wide range of shapes and sizes but are characteristically thick-walled with rounded margins.

COLOUR
Uniform grey, creamy brown or purple.

SIMILAR SPECIES
A. humilis and *A. gemmifera* may appear similar under water but have much more regular growth forms and regularly arranged corallites.

DISTRIBUTION
Known only from Australia: the Great Barrier Reef, Coral Sea and south to Flinders Reef (Moreton Bay) in the east; not found on the west coast.

ABUNDANCE
Restricted to shallow upper reef slopes exposed to strong wave action or currents. May be very abundant, even dominant, on outer barrier reefs and Coral Sea reefs.

x2.5

1. *Acropora lutkeni* looks like *A. humilis* and its relatives at a distance, but its polyps are a mixture of shapes and sizes. This species is common on exposed slopes of outer reefs where colonies have a wide range of forms.
PHOTOGRAPH: ED LOVELL.

2. The usual growth form of *Acropora lutkeni* exposed to moderate or heavy wave action.
PHOTOGRAPH: ED LOVELL.

Acropora clathrata

(BROOK, 1891)

TYPE LOCALITY
Mauritius.

IDENTIFYING CHARACTERS
Colonies are tables with generally horizontal radiating, anastomosing branches which may form an almost solid plate. There is usually no development of vertical branches.

COLOUR
Brown or green, often with pale margins.

SIMILAR SPECIES
Only *A. glacua* from far southern localities can be confused with *A. clathrata*.

DISTRIBUTION
From Madagascar east to the Tuamotu Archipelago. Around Australia: the Great Barrier Reef, Coral Sea and south to Flinders Reef (Moreton Bay) in the east, and south to Dampier Archipelago on the west coast.

ABUNDANCE
Common on upper reef slopes, back reef margins and fringing reefs.

x2.5

1. The distinctive appearance of *Acropora clathrata*. Colonies have the same shape as those of *A. cytherea* and *A. hyacinthus*, but the horizontal interlocking branches do not have upright branchlets.
PHOTOGRAPH: ED LOVELL.

2. A large *Acropora clathrata* table.
PHOTOGRAPH: ED LOVELL.

Acropora divaricata

(DANA, 1846)

TYPE LOCALITY
Fiji.

IDENTIFYING CHARACTERS
Colonies are caespitose, bowl-shaped, or are thick tables, with branches 6-12 mm thick. Axial corallites are often devoid of radial corallites on their upper surface. Radial corallites are all of the one type, and change shape and size along the branch.

COLOUR
Usually dark brown or greenish-brown, sometimes with light-brown or blue branch tips or dark blue with whitish tips.

SIMILAR SPECIES
A. secale may be similar but has radial corallites of two sizes.

DISTRIBUTION
From the Seychelles east to Fiji. Around Australia: the Great Barrier Reef, Coral Sea and south to Flinders Reef (Moreton Bay) in the east, and south to Houtman Abrolhos Islands on the west coast.

ABUNDANCE
Abundant on upper reef slopes, also commonly found in lagoons and on fringing reefs. May be a dominant species.

×2.5

1

2

3

I. *Acropora divaricata* has one of the widest range of growth forms of any *Acropora*, yet is usually readily recognisable because its upright branches are interconnected in a manner similar to the horizontal branches of corymbose colonies. This specimen has unusually thick branches and a solid appearance.
PHOTOGRAPH: ED LOVELL.

2. A finely branched *Acropora divaricata*.
PHOTOGRAPH: ED LOVELL.

3. The polyps of a finely branched *Acropora divaricata*.
PHOTOGRAPH: ED LOVELL.

Acropora solitaryensis

VERON & WALLACE, 1984

TYPE LOCALITY
Solitary Islands.

IDENTIFYING CHARACTERS
Branch pattern is like *A. divaricata* but with basal branches fused into a perforated or solid horizontal plate.

COLOUR
Dark brown or green.

SIMILAR SPECIES
A. glauca, A. divaricata and *A. stoddarti.*

DISTRIBUTION
Known only from Australia: the Great Barrier Reef and all southern localities in the east, and south to Houtman Abrolhos Islands on the west coast.

ABUNDANCE
Extremely rare on the Great Barrier Reef, but abundant on all reefs to the south and one of the dominant corals of the Solitary Islands where it commonly forms plates over 2 m in diameter. Common at most west coast localities.

×2.5

1, 2. *Acropora solitaryensis* at the Solitary Islands, eastern Australia (1), and at Dampier Archipelago, Western Australia (2). This species forms a solid basal plate from which *A. divaricata*-like branches sometimes grow.
PHOTOGRAPHS: ED LOVELL.

3. The basal plate of *Acropora solitaryensis* can become completely fused. This specimen, from Dampier Archipelago, Western Australia, is an extreme case and looks more like a *Montipora* than an *Acropora* species.
PHOTOGRAPH: ED LOVELL.

Acropora stoddarti

PILLAI & SCHEER, 1976

TYPE LOCALITY
  Maldive Islands.

IDENTIFYING CHARACTERS
  Colonies consist of fused branches which are prostrate, becoming plate-like. Branches are also flattened, especially the lower ones. Corallites are widely spaced and immersed.

COLOUR
  Brown or green with pale margins.

SIMILAR SPECIES
  A. divaricata.

DISTRIBUTION
  Maldive Islands and Australia. Around Australia: the Houtman Abrolhos Islands on the west coast; not found in the east.

ABUNDANCE
  Uncommon except at the Houtman Abrolhos Islands.

x2.5

1. *Acropora stoddarti*.
PHOTOGRAPH: ED LOVELL.

2. *Acropora stoddarti*, named after the reef geographer and explorer David Stoddart, has a flattened, sprawling appearance.
PHOTOGRAPH: ED LOVELL.

Acropora echinata

(DANA, 1846)

TYPE LOCALITY
Fiji and Sulu Sea.

IDENTIFYING CHARACTERS
Colonies are bottlebrush, composed of sprawling, sometimes intertwined branches. Secondary branchlets are fine and uniform.

COLOUR
Usually cream with blue or purple branchlet tips. Occasionally entirely blue.

SIMILAR SPECIES
A. *subglabra*.

DISTRIBUTION
From the Maldive Islands east to the Marshall Islands and Samoa. Around Australia: the northern and central Great Barrier Reef and Coral Sea in the east; not found on the west coast.

ABUNDANCE
Usually restricted to protected reef backs and relatively clear deep water. Usually uncommon but very conspicuous.

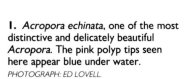
x2.5

1. *Acropora echinata*, one of the most distinctive and delicately beautiful *Acropora*. The pink polyp tips seen here appear blue under water.
PHOTOGRAPH: ED LOVELL.

2. *Acropora echinata* at Tijou Reef, Great Barrier Reef, displaying its bottlebrush growth form.
PHOTOGRAPH: ED LOVELL.

Acropora subglabra
(BROOK, 1891)

TYPE LOCALITY
Singapore.

IDENTIFYING CHARACTERS
Colonies are bottlebrush, forming thickets of intertwining branches, usually with the distal 10-20 cm only alive. Branches divide irregularly, usually at intervals of less than 5 cm.

COLOUR
Pale brown, usually with yellow branchlet tips.

SIMILAR SPECIES
A. echinata and *A. carduus*.

DISTRIBUTION
Central Indo-Pacific, north to the Ryukyu Islands and south to the Great Barrier Reef and Fiji. Around Australia: the northern and central Great Barrier Reef and Coral Sea in the east, and Rowley Shoals and Scott Reef on the west coast.

ABUNDANCE
Uncommon, usually restricted to protected reef backs with clear water and soft substrates. Usually found with *A. echinata*.

1. *Acropora subglabra* is similar to *A. echinata* but has shorter branchlets and main branches divide more frequently.
PHOTOGRAPH: ED LOVELL.

2. *Acropora subglabra* in a lagoon at Scott Reef, north-western Australia.
PHOTOGRAPH: AUTHOR.

Acropora carduus

(DANA, 1846)

TYPE LOCALITY
Fiji.

IDENTIFYING CHARACTERS
Colonies are bottlebrush, forming thickets with upright or prostrate main branches. Branches are evenly spaced, corallites are small and exsert.

COLOUR
Uniform pale brown or cream, rarely blue or mauve.

SIMILAR SPECIES
A. subglabra and *A. longicyathus* have smaller and larger corallites and branches respectively. Also *A. elseyi*.

DISTRIBUTION
Western Pacific, north to Japan and south to the Great Barrier Reef and Fiji.
Around Australia: the northern and central Great Barrier Reef and Coral Sea in the east; not found on the west coast.

ABUNDANCE
Abundant in deep water or protected reef backs and in lagoons.

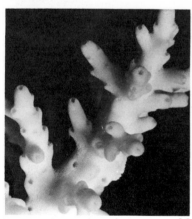

×2.5

Acropora carduus specimens may be difficult to distinguish from those of *A. subglabra*, but under water these species are distinct.
PHOTOGRAPH: ED LOVELL.

Acropora elseyi

(BROOK, 1892)

TYPE LOCALITY
Great Barrier Reef.

IDENTIFYING CHARACTERS
Colonies are shaped like pine trees, with bottlebrush radiating branches of variable length.

COLOUR
Yellow or cream with pale branch tips.

SIMILAR SPECIES
A. carduus and *A. longicyathus* are occasionally similar, the former having similar corallite dimensions.

DISTRIBUTION
Maldive Islands and Australia. Around Australia: the Great Barrier Reef, except the Capricorn and Bunker groups, and Coral Sea; not found on west coast.

ABUNDANCE
Very common and often dominant on fringing reefs of continental islands where it may form extensive monospecific stands. Also common in lagoons and on some lower reef slopes.

x2.5

1. The branches of a bushy colony of *Acropora elseyi*. This species is very common on protected fringing reefs and may form extensive stands.
PHOTOGRAPH: ED LOVELL.

2. A tall bottlebrush form of *Acropora elseyi* at Broadhurst Reef, Great Barrier Reef.
PHOTOGRAPH: ED LOVELL.

Acropora longicyathus

(EDWARDS & HAIME, 1860)

TYPE LOCALITY
Unrecorded.

IDENTIFYING CHARACTERS
Colonies are sub-arborescent, bottlebrush, with upright main branches. Corallites are elongate tubes with round calices.

COLOUR
Usually uniform pale to dark brown, occasionally blue.

SIMILAR SPECIES
A. elseyi and bottlebrush forms of *A. loripes.*

DISTRIBUTION
Western Pacific from the Philippines to the Great Barrier Reef.
Around Australia: the Great Barrier Reef and Coral Sea in the east, and Scott Reef on the west coast.

ABUNDANCE
Abundant over a wide range of environments and may be a dominant species on unconsolidated substrates.

×2.5

1. The most common growth form of *Acropora longicyathus.*
PHOTOGRAPH: ED LOVELL.·

2. *Acropora longicyathus* with short irregular branches.
PHOTOGRAPH: ED LOVELL.

3. The polyps of a bushy colony of *Acropora longicyathus.* Although this species has many growth forms, the appearance of the elongate blunt-ended axial polyps allows it to be easily recognised.
PHOTOGRAPH: ED LOVELL.

Acropora loripes

(BROOK, 1892)

TYPE LOCALITY
Great Barrier Reef.

IDENTIFYING CHARACTERS
Colonies have many shapes and may be bottlebrush, caespitose or plate-like. Corallites may be tubular or have thickened walls becoming tubular. Tubular axial corallites may have no radial corallites on one side (like *A. divaricata*).

COLOUR
Usually pale blue or brown. Axial corallites are usually whitish.

SIMILAR SPECIES
This species is so variable it is readily confused with several others, especially *A. granulosa* and *A. longicyathus*. The former is distinguished by its smaller, tapering corallites, which are not clearly divisible into axial and radial. The latter species has thinner branches and shorter branchlets, giving a more arborescent appearance. See also *A. chesterfieldensis*.

DISTRIBUTION
The Philippines and Australia. Around Australia: the Great Barrier Reef and Coral Sea in the east; not found on the west coast.

ABUNDANCE
Very abundant on upper reef slopes but occurs in a wide range of environments.

x2.5

1, 2. Whatever its growth form, *Acropora loripes* can be recognised by its long axial polyps which are usually tubular and are often without radial polyps on one side.
PHOTOGRAPHS: ED LOVELL.

3, 4. *Acropora loripes* may have a flat plate-like (left) or an upright bushy growth form (right).
PHOTOGRAPHS: ED LOVELL.

Acropora chesterfieldensis

VERON & WALLACE, 1984

TYPE LOCALITY
Chesterfield Reefs, eastern Coral Sea.

IDENTIFYING CHARACTERS
Colonies are corymbose to caespitose. Branches are terete and divide irregularly.

COLOUR
Cream or yellow.

SIMILAR SPECIES
A. loripes is very similar but differs in having often tubular axial corallites with no radial corallites on one side and in having bottlebrush and plate-like, not corymbose, growth forms.

DISTRIBUTION
Known only from Australia: the Coral Sea (not recorded from Great Barrier Reef) in the east; not found on the west coast.

ABUNDANCE
Common on the Chesterfield Reefs, rare elsewhere.

×2.5

Acropora chesterfieldensis at the Chesterfield Reefs, Great Barrier Reef.
PHOTOGRAPH: ED LOVELL.

Acropora granulosa
(EDWARDS & HAIME, 1860)

TYPE LOCALITY
Bourbon Island.

IDENTIFYING CHARACTERS
Colonies are semicircular horizontal plates less than 1 m across, composed of regularly spaced horizontal branches with short upright branchlets with tapering tubular corallites.

COLOUR
Usually uniform cream, grey or pale blue, but may be other colours.

SIMILAR SPECIES
A. loripes and *A. caroliniana*.

DISTRIBUTION
From Madagascar east to Tahiti. Around Australia: the Great Barrier Reef and Coral Sea in the east, and south to Houtman Abrolhos Islands on the west coast.

ABUNDANCE
Seldom found in shallow water but common on lower reef slopes.

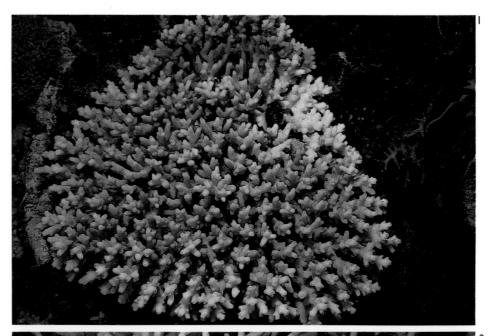

x2.5

1. A common shape and appearance of *Acropora granulosa* colonies.
PHOTOGRAPH: ED LOVELL.

2. *Acropora granulosa* has elongate tubular axial polyps.
PHOTOGRAPH: ED LOVELL.

3. Branch tips of *Acropora granulosa*.
PHOTOGRAPH: VICKI HARRIOTT.

Acropora caroliniana

NEMÉNZO, 1976

TYPE LOCALITY
  The Philippines.

IDENTIFYING CHARACTERS
  Colonies are thick horizontal plates composed of horizontal branches and short upright branchlets. The latter have large tapering corallites curving upwards or pointing in different directions.

COLOUR
  Whitish-brown or pale blue.

SIMILAR SPECIES
  A. granulosa.

DISTRIBUTION
  Australia and the Philippines. Around Australia: the Great Barrier Reef and Coral Sea in the east, and Rowley Shoals and Scott Reef on the west coast.

ABUNDANCE
  Uncommon.

x2.5

I. *Acropora caroliniana* is similar to *A. granulosa* except that polyps are larger and usually curve to point in different directions.
PHOTOGRAPH: ED LOVELL.

2. *Acropora caroliniana* from shallow water exposed to strong wave action.
PHOTOGRAPH: ED LOVELL.

Acropora willisae

VERON & WALLACE, 1984

TYPE LOCALITY
Britomart Reef, Great Barrier Reef.

IDENTIFYING CHARACTERS
Colonies are corymbose plates with short branchlets bearing numerous elongate thin-walled corallites.

COLOUR
Pale cream or brown.

SIMILAR SPECIES
A. granulosa has similar corallites but is not corymbose.

DISTRIBUTION
Known only from Australia: the Great Barrier Reef in the east, and south to Houtman Abrolhos Islands on the west coast.

ABUNDANCE
Uncommon but occupies a wide range of habitats from flats to lagoons.

x2.5

Acropora willisae at the Houtman Abrolhos Islands, Western Australia.
PHOTOGRAPH: ED LOVELL.

Acropora florida

(DANA, 1846)

TYPE LOCALITY
  Fiji.

IDENTIFYING CHARACTERS
  Colonies consist of thick upright
  or prostrate branches covered
  with short stubby branchlets.
  Corallites are of even size and
  distribution.

COLOUR
  Usually pinkish-brown,
  sometimes yellow-brown,
  occasionally green (east
  Australia), bright green (west
  Australia).

SIMILAR SPECIES
  A. sarmentosa; see also *A. grandis*.

DISTRIBUTION
  From the Maldive Islands east to
  the Marshall Islands.
  Around Australia: the Great
  Barrier Reef and Flinders Reef
  (Moreton Bay) in the east, and
  south to Houtman Abrolhos
  Islands on the west coast.

ABUNDANCE
  Common, may occur in any
  Acropora assemblage. Colonies in
  turbid water may attain great
  sizes (over 15 m across).

x2.5

I. The characteristic appearance of an
Acropora florida branch.
PHOTOGRAPH: ED LOVELL.

202

2

3

2, 3. *Acropora florida* may have many growth forms but is always easily recognised by its knobbly branchlets.
PHOTOGRAPHS: ED LOVELL.

4. *Over:* Flattened, spreading bright-green *Acropora florida* colonies are usually abundant on reefs of Western Australia.
PHOTOGRAPH: ED LOVELL.

5. *Over:* A large colony of *Acropora florida* in a shallow lagoon pinnacle of Scott Reef, north-western Australia.
PHOTOGRAPH: AUTHOR.

Acropora sarmentosa
(BROOK, 1892)

TYPE LOCALITY
Great Barrier Reef.

IDENTIFYING CHARACTERS
Colonies consist of prostrate main branches with bottlebrush or corymbose secondary branching. Axial corallites are large and rounded.

COLOUR
Dull greenish-grey or brown with pale-brown or pink branch tips.

SIMILAR SPECIES
A. florida and *A. samoensis*.

DISTRIBUTION
The Philippines, Australia and Fiji.
Around Australia: the Great Barrier Reef, Coral Sea and south to Elizabeth Reef in the east, and North West Cape on the west coast.

ABUNDANCE
Common on upper reef slopes, but may occur in most *Acropora* assemblages.

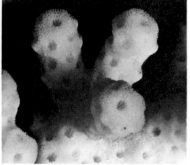

x2.5

1. *Acropora sarmentosa* colonies are usually prostrate and sprawling.
PHOTOGRAPH: ED LOVELL.

2. All *Acropora sarmentosa* branch ends have this general appearance, which make the species easily recognised under water.
PHOTOGRAPH: ED LOVELL.

Genus
ASTREOPORA

(pronounced ass-tree-oh-por-a)

de Blainville, 1830

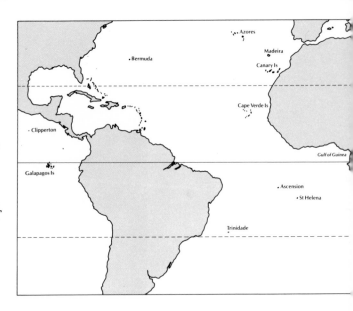

As an example of the difference between pure museum work and observations on the reef, compare Bernard's division of this genus into explanate, pulvinate and glomerate forms with Waugh's demonstration that all these forms frequently occur in the one colony.

Cyril Crossland,
*Scientific Reports of the Great Barrier
Reef Expedition 1928-29*, Volume 6, 1952.

Some species of *Astreopora* are very distinct and easily identified. Others, especially those with a massive growth form, may be difficult to distinguish with certainty. This is partly because they have few distinctive characters and partly because there is only one common species, *A. myriophthalma*.

Although *Astreopora* clearly belongs in the Acroporidae, it is very distinct from the other three genera of the family. Superficially it more closely resembles *Turbinaria* and has been grouped with *Turbinaria* by most early taxonomists.

Like most other Acroporidae, *Astreopora* reproduces sexually by releasing egg bundles and sperm for external fertilisation. They are hermaphrodite.

TYPE SPECIES
Astraea myriophthalma Lamarck, 1816.

FOSSIL RECORD
Cretaceous to Recent from Europe, the West Indies and the Indo-Pacific.

NUMBER OF SPECIES
Twenty-eight nominal species, approximately 15 true species, nine of which are Australian.

CHARACTERS
Colonies are massive, laminar, encrusting or foliaceous. Corallites are immersed or conical with short,

numerous, neatly spaced short septa. Columellae are deep-seated and compact. Corallite walls are slightly porous and the coenosteum and walls have few elaborations.
Polyps are extended only at night.

SIMILAR GENERA
Astreopora is a well-defined genus which can be confused only with *Turbinaria*.

The upper face of *Astreopora explanata* plates at the Houtman Abrolhos Islands, Western Australia.
PHOTOGRAPH: ED LOVELL.

KEY TO SPECIES OF *ASTREOPORA*

Colony hemispherical or dome-shaped
    Corallites mostly conical *A. myriophthalma* (p. 208), *A. ocellata* (p. 212)
    Corallites mostly immersed *A. listeri* (p. 209), *A. gracilis* (p. 210)
Colony thick flat plates
    Colony with very large corallites *A. ocellata* (p. 212), *A. macrostoma* (p. 212)
    Colony without very large corallites
        Colony with rootlets *A. moretonensis* (p. 211), *A. cucullata* (p. 212)
        Colony without rootlets
            Corallites face different directions *A. cucullata* (p. 212)
            Corallites mostly immersed *A. listeri* (p. 209), *A. ocellata* (p. 212)
Colony encrusting *A. moretonensis* (p. 211)
Colony foliaceous *A. explanata* (p. 213)

---

*Note: This key is a guide only and should be used in conjunction with descriptions of the species.
Some species may key out in more than one place.*

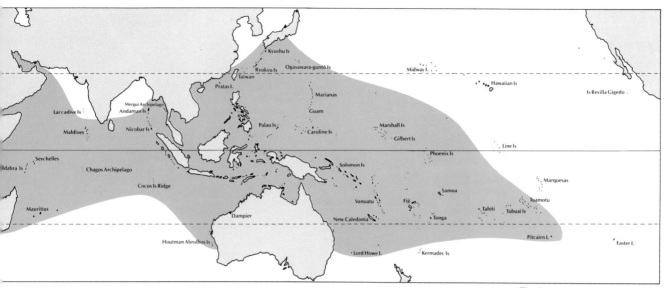

The known range of *Astreopora*.

Astreopora myriophthalma
(LAMARCK; 1816)

TYPE LOCALITY
Unrecorded.

IDENTIFYING CHARACTERS
Colonies are hemispherical, with an even surface. Corallites are evenly spaced and conical with rounded calices.

COLOUR
Cream, brownish-blue or yellow, sometimes mottled.

SIMILAR SPECIES
A. listeri.

DISTRIBUTION
From the Red Sea east to the Tuamotu Archipelago. Around Australia: the Great Barrier Reef, Coral Sea and Flinders Reef (Moreton Bay) in the east, and south to Houtman Abrolhos Islands on the west coast.

ABUNDANCE
By far the most common species of *Astreopora*, found in most reef habitats except in very turbid water.

x2.5

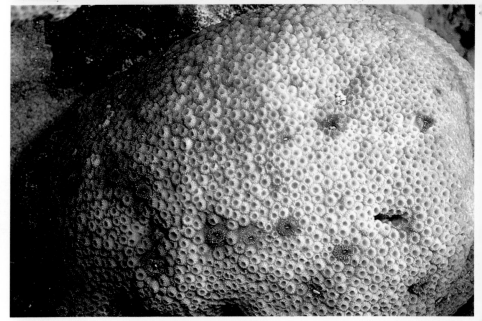

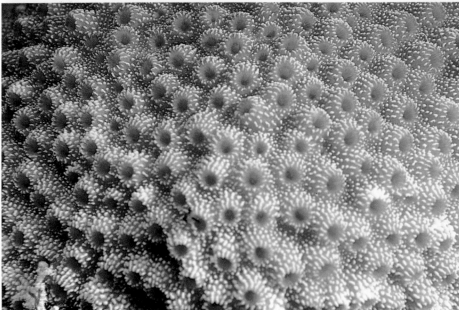

1, 2. Two common colours of *Astreopora myriophthalma.*
PHOTOGRAPHS: ED LOVELL.

3. The polyps of *Astreopora myriophthalma.* These superficially resemble *Turbinaria* rather than other Acroporidae.
PHOTOGRAPH: ED LOVELL.

Astreopora listeri

BERNARD, 1896

TYPE LOCALITY
Tonga.

IDENTIFYING CHARACTERS
Colonies are hemispherical or flattened. Corallites are immersed, crowded, with rounded calices surrounded by feathery spinules giving the colony a spiny appearance.

COLOUR
Cream, grey or brown.

SIMILAR SPECIES
A. myriophthalma.

DISTRIBUTION
From the Nicobar Islands east to the Marshall Islands.
Around Australia: the Great Barrier Reef, Coral Sea and south to Elizabeth Reef in the east; not found on the west coast.

ABUNDANCE
Found in a wide range of environments but common only in intertidal pools.

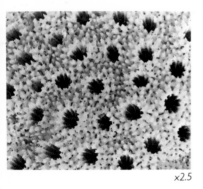

x2.5

A comparison between *Astreopora myriophthalma* (left) and *A. listeri* (right). The difference between these species is often indistinct.
PHOTOGRAPH: ED LOVELL.

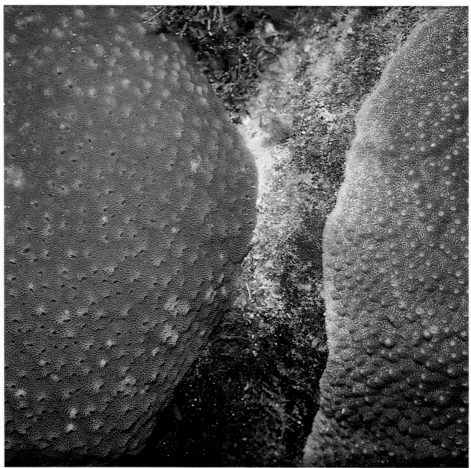

Astreopora gracilis

BERNARD, 1896

TYPE LOCALITY
Solomon Islands.

IDENTIFYING CHARACTERS
Colonies are hemispherical with irregular corallites and a smooth coenosteum. Corallites are immersed to conical and usually face different directions.

COLOUR
Pale cream or brown.

SIMILAR SPECIES
Difficult to distinguish from *A. myriophthalma* unless the above characters are clearly developed.

DISTRIBUTION
From Australia east to the Marshall Islands.
Around Australia: the Great Barrier Reef and Coral Sea in the east; south to the Houtman Abrolhos Islands on the west coast.

ABUNDANCE
Rare except in the Coral Sea where it is usually uncommon.

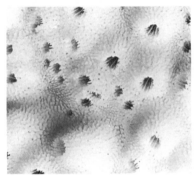

x2.5

1. *Astreopora gracilis* with characteristically irregular polyps.
PHOTOGRAPH: AUTHOR.

2. *Astreopora gracilis.*
PHOTOGRAPH: ED LOVELL.

Astreopora moretonensis

VERON & WALLACE, 1984

TYPE LOCALITY
Middleton Reef.

IDENTIFYING CHARACTERS
Colonies are plate-like or encrusting, sometimes with irregular tubes or columns on the upper surface and rootlets on the lower surface. Corallites are mostly immersed but may be conical.

COLOUR
Cream or brown.

SIMILAR SPECIES
May resemble *A. ocellata*.

DISTRIBUTION
Known only from Australia: the Great Barrier Reef, Coral Sea and all localities south to Lord Howe Island in the east; not found on the west coast.

ABUNDANCE
Rare in the tropics but common in temperate localities.

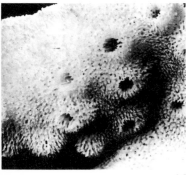

×2.5

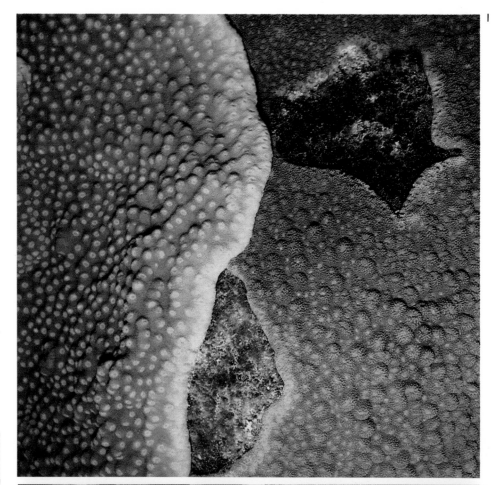

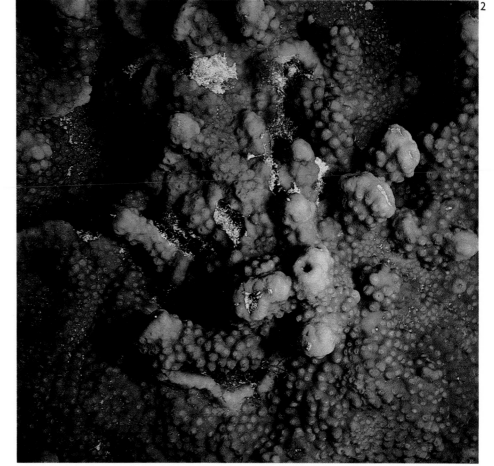

1. Two encrusting colonies of *Astreopora* species at Middleton Reef, eastern Australia: *A. listeri* (left) and *A. moretonensis* (right). These species are not separable without close inspection.
PHOTOGRAPH: ED LOVELL.

2. *Astreopora moretonensis* at Middleton Reef, eastern Australia.
PHOTOGRAPH: ED LOVELL.

Astreopora cucullata

LAMBERTS, 1980

TYPE LOCALITY
Samoa and the Marshall Islands.

IDENTIFYING CHARACTERS
Colonies are thick or encrusting plates, sometimes with short rootlets. Corallites are irregular, immersed on concave surfaces, exsert on convex ones, the latter usually facing the colony margins. Spinules around the corallites have a feathery appearance.

COLOUR
Cream or pale brown.

SIMILAR SPECIES
May be difficult to distinguish from *A. myriophthalma* unless the above characters are clearly developed.

DISTRIBUTION
Australia, Samoa and Marshall Islands.
Around Australia: the Coral Sea, southern Great Barrier Reef and Flinders Reef (Moreton Bay) in the east; not found on the west coast.

ABUNDANCE
Rare.

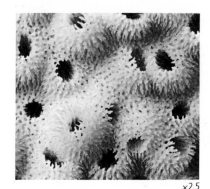

×2.5

Astreopora ocellata

BERNARD, 1896

TYPE LOCALITY
Great Barrier Reef.

IDENTIFYING CHARACTERS
Colonies are dome-shaped or flat. Corallites are compact, large, with wide calices. Small corallites usually occur between the large ones. The coenosteum is coarse.

COLOUR
Cream or yellow.

SIMILAR SPECIES
Corallites are substantially larger than those of other *Astreopora*, except *A. macrostoma*.

DISTRIBUTION
Australia, Micronesia, Palau and Marshall Islands.
Around Australia: the Great Barrier Reef, Coral Sea and Elizabeth and Middleton Reefs in the east, and North West Cape on the west coast.

ABUNDANCE
Usually rare.

×2.5

Astreopora macrostoma

VERON & WALLACE, 1984

TYPE LOCALITY
Chesterfield Reefs, eastern Coral Sea.

IDENTIFYING CHARACTERS
Colonies are submassive plates, sometimes with short rootlets. Corallites are very large and widely spaced, either immersed or curved, and facing different directions.

COLOUR
Yellow-brown.

SIMILAR SPECIES
None, corallites are much bigger than other *Astreopora*.

DISTRIBUTION
Known only from Australia: the Chesterfield Reefs in the east; not found on the west coast.

ABUNDANCE
Very rare.

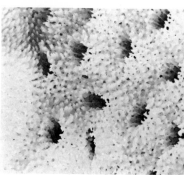

×2.5

Astreopora explanata
VERON, 1985

TYPE LOCALITY
Houtman Abrolhos Islands.

IDENTIFYING CHARACTERS
Colonies consist of flat bifacial plates arranged in tiers or whorls. Corallites are small.

COLOUR
Brown to dark green, usually with pale margins.

SIMILAR SPECIES
M. myriophthalma on lower reef slopes may become plate-like.

DISTRIBUTION
Known only from Australia: south to Houtman Abrolhos Islands on the west coast; not found in the east.

ABUNDANCE
Usually uncommon.

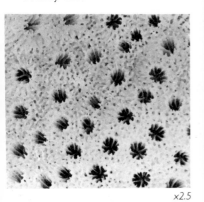

x2.5

1. The thin tiered plates of *Astreopora explanata* seen from the side.
PHOTOGRAPH: ED LOVELL.

2. The polyps of *Astreopora explanata* are relatively inconspicuous.
PHOTOGRAPH: ED LOVELL.

FAMILY
PORITIDAE

(pronounced por-eye-tid-ee)

GRAY, 1842

CHARACTERS
Colonial, hermatypic, mostly extant. Colonies usually massive, laminar or ramose. Corallites have a wide size range but are usually compacted with little or no coenosteum. Walls and septa are porous.

RELATED FAMILIES
None.

EARLIEST FOSSILS
Cretaceous.

THE GENERA
The Poritidae is an isolated family which includes four extant hermatypic genera, *Porites, Stylaraea, Goniopora* and *Alveopora*, all of which are Australian. *Stylaraea* is very rare, monospecific, and clearly related to *Porites* (and has previously been considered a subgenus of *Porites*). *Porites* and *Goniopora* are very different, but can be shown to be related by their patterns of septal fusion. *Alveopora* has very tenuous affinities with *Goniopora*. Family Poritidae, therefore, is essentially a heterogeneous assembly of distantly related genera.

Opposite: Large colonies of *Porites* are usually found in turbid water, but they may occur in any reef situation, such as this outer reef slope.
PHOTOGRAPH: TERRY DONE.

215

Genus
PORITES

(pronounced por-eye-tees)

Link, 1807

. . . The difficulties presented by the skeleton in Porites, *with its minute calices, were most discouraging. So great, indeed, is its apparent complexity, showing so many subtle differences which baffle all attempts to define or even to describe, that the student stands long before the task in despair.*

Henry Bernard,
Catalogue of Madreporaria, Volume V,
British Museum (Natural History), 1905.

Henry Bernard may well have despaired at the task of separating *Porites* species from collections of specimens in museums. To attempt to do so is to attempt the impossible, for taxonomists can only find reliable characters for doing this by studying the differences between species collected from the same habitat. Once these characters have been established, *Porites* species are not difficult to identify with the aid of a hand lens.

Like *Montipora*, *Porites* have very small corallites. Nevertheless they form some of the largest of all coral colonies, some near-spherical giants reaching 8 m in height. With average growth rates of about 9 mm per year, such colonies may be nearly 1000 years old, among the oldest of all forms of animal life.

Porites, like *Goniopora*, have different male and female colonies. With few exceptions, the polyps of female colonies do not release egg bundles into the water like the majority of corals, but brood planulae in

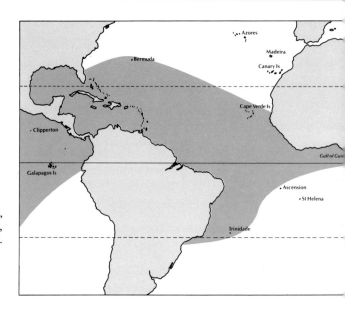

their body cavity. Fertilisation is therefore internal and must depend on free-swimming sperm from male colonies reaching the female.

TYPE SPECIES
Porites polymorphus Link, 1807 = *Porites porites* Pallas, 1766.

FOSSIL RECORD
Eocene to Recent, cosmopolitan.

NUMBER OF SPECIES
Approximately 122 nominal species, the majority of which are invalid. The number of true species is unknown, at least 16 are Australian.

KEY TO SPECIES OF *PORITES*

Corallites minute (less than 0.7 mm in diameter), shallow, concentrated on concave surfaces *P. rus* (p.232)
Corallites not as above
    Colonies foliaceous or columnar or irregular *P. lichen* (p. 228), *P. annae* (p. 230), *P. vaughani* (p. 231), *P. heronensis* (p. 229)
    Colonies arborescent *P. cylindrica* (p. 226), *P. nigrescens* (p. 227)
    Colonies basically massive
        Pali absent *P. solida* (p. 219)
        Pali present
            Columella absent
                Denticles absent *P. densa* (p. 225), *P. mayeri* (p. 225)
                Denticles present *P. murrayensis* (p. 223), *P. stephensoni* (p. 225)
            Columella present
                Triplet fused *P. lutea* (p. 224), *P. australiensis* (p. 222)
                Triplet not fused
                    8 pali present
                        2 denticles per septum *P. lobata* (p. 220), *P. australiensis* (p. 222), *P. myrmidonensis* (p. 220)
                        1 denticle per septum *P. stephensoni* (p. 225)
                    4 or 5 pali present
                        Denticles mostly absent *P. mayeri* (p. 225)
                        1 denticle per septum *P. murrayensis* (p. 223)
                        2 denticles per septum *P. lobata* (p. 220)

Note: This key is a guide only and should be used in conjunction with descriptions of species and diagrams. The same species may key out in more than one place.

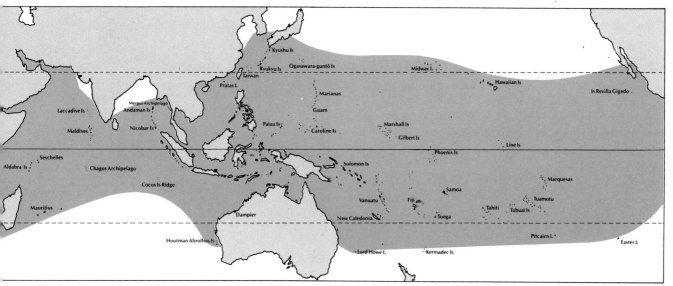

The known range of *Porites*.

CHARACTERS

Colonies are flat (foliaceous or encrusting), massive or branching. Massive colonies are spherical or hemispherical when small and helmet- or dome-shaped when large, and are commonly over 5 m in diameter. Corallites are small, immersed, with calices less than 2 mm in diameter and filled with septa.
Polyps are usually extended only at night.

SIMILAR GENERA

Porites resemble *Montipora* and also *Stylaraea*.
Porites differ from *Montipora* by many differences in growth form. Corallites are usually larger and more compacted and lack the elaborate thecal and reticulum papillae and tuberculae which characterise *Montipora*. *Porites* also have corallites filled with septa, whereas those of *Montipora* contain only inward-projecting septal teeth.

SPECIES

An initial grouping of species can be made as follows:
(*a*) Species forming very large, massive, generally hemispherical or helmet–shaped colonies with ledges around their bases: *P. lobata, P. australiensis* and *P. lutea* are very abundant, *P. solida* is common and *P. mayeri* and *P. myrmidonensis* are relatively rare.
(*b*) Species forming massive hemispherical or spherical colonies which do not attain large sizes: *P. murrayensis* and *P. densa* are sometimes common, *P. stephensoni* is rare.
(*c*) Species forming branching colonies: *P. cylindrica* and *P. nigrescens* are both very common and are readily separated by minor differences in growth form and major differences in corallite characters.
(*d*) Species forming flat plates or columns or irregular branches: *P. lichen* is very abundant, *P. annae* and *P. vaughani* are both common, *P. heronensis* is usually uncommon. These species are the most difficult to recognise as they all lack conservative skeletal characters.
(*e*) *P. rus* is unlike other *Porites* species and is separated into subgenus *Synaraea*. It has very small corallites and can be readily confused with *Montipora*.

IDENTIFICATION

Diagrams summarising the most useful diagnostic characters of *Porites* species are given below with each species. To understand the diagrams it is first necessary to understand some of the skeletal characters they illustrate.
septa: These are named according to a convention. As illustrated, each corallite has one *dorsal directive* and one *ventral directive* septum, four *lateral pairs* of septa arranged symmetrically and two more septa either side of the ventral directive which, together with the ventral directive, form the *triplet*. The inner margins of the triplet may be free or fused. In the latter case they may be fused along their inner margins or each outer septum may be fused to the sides of the ventral directive by a cross bar.

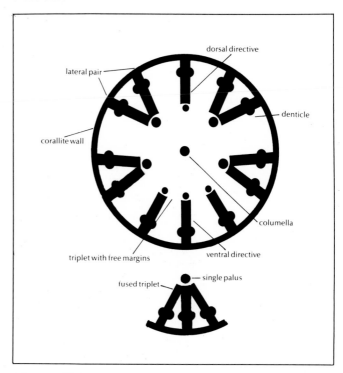

Diagram 16. Diagrammatic representation of a *Porites* corallite showing septal structures used in species identification.

pali: The pali are vertical pillars positioned as illustrated. The four pali associated with the lateral pairs of septa are the largest. A fifth palus is usually associated with the dorsal directive septum. One, two or three pali may be associated with the triplet: one palus if the triplet is fused as illustrated; two pali if they are fused by a cross bar; and three pali if the triplet is not fused.

denticles: These are vertical pillars resembling pali and are arranged along the top of the septa at fixed intervals. The pali and denticles may form concentric circles.

radii: These usually occur deep within the corallite and connect the pali to the columella. The columella, pali and denticles are all covered with granules and may be similar in appearance.

I. *Porites* is very common on most reef flats.
PHOTOGRAPH: AUTHOR.

2. When polyps are extended, all *Porites* colonies have a furry appearance that makes species impossible to recognise under water.
PHOTOGRAPH: ED LOVELL.

SUBGENUS
PORITES

Porites solida
(FORSKÅL, 1775)

TYPE LOCALITY
Red Sea.

IDENTIFYING CHARACTERS
See diagram below.
Colonies are massive and may be several metres in diameter.

COLOUR
Brown or greenish-yellow.

SIMILAR SPECIES
P. lobata, which has weakly developed pali. *P. solida* is easily recognised under water.

DISTRIBUTION
From the Red Sea east to Hawaii. Around Australia: the Great Barrier Reef, Coral Sea and Elizabeth and Middleton Reefs in the east, and south to Houtman Abrolhos Islands on the west coast.

ABUNDANCE
Common.

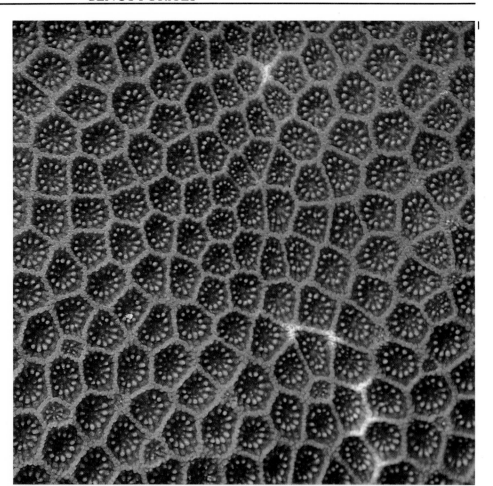

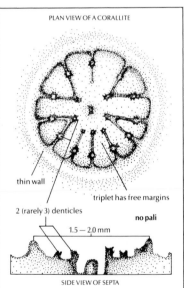

PLAN VIEW OF A CORALLITE

thin wall

triplet has free margins

2 (rarely 3) denticles

no pali

1.5 — 2.0 mm

SIDE VIEW OF SEPTA

1, 2. *Porites solida* can be readily recognised under water, especially with a magnifying lens.

PHOTOGRAPHS: ED LOVELL (TOP) AND AUTHOR (BOTTOM).

Porites myrmidonensis

VERON, 1985

TYPE LOCALITY
Myrmidon Reef, Great Barrier Reef.

IDENTIFYING CHARACTERS
See diagram below.
Colonies are massive with a hillocky surface. Corallites are in deeply excavated pits.

COLOUR
Uniform or mottled green or brown.

SIMILAR SPECIES
P. solida.

DISTRIBUTION
Known only from Australia: the Great Barrier Reef and Coral Sea in the east; not found on the west coast.

ABUNDANCE
Uncommon.

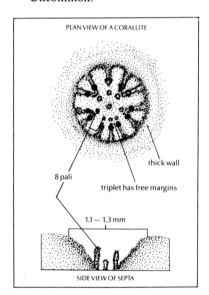

PLAN VIEW OF A CORALLITE

thick wall
8 pali
triplet has free margins
1.1 — 1.3 mm
SIDE VIEW OF SEPTA

Porites lobata

DANA, 1846

TYPE LOCALITY
Fiji.

IDENTIFYING CHARACTERS
See diagram below.
Colonies are hemispherical or helmet-shaped and may be very large.

COLOUR
Usually cream or pale brown but may be bright blue, purple or green in shallow water.

SIMILAR SPECIES
P. solida and P. australiensis, especially the latter, which is distinguished by having taller pali, especially on the lateral pairs of septa.

DISTRIBUTION
From the Nicobar Islands east to Hawaii, Bonin Island and the Galapagos.
Around Australia: the Great Barrier Reef, Coral Sea and Flinders Reef (Moreton Bay) in the east, and south to Houtman Abrolhos Islands on the west coast.

ABUNDANCE
Very common and frequently a dominant, with P. lutea and P. australiensis, of back reef margins, lagoons and some fringing reefs.

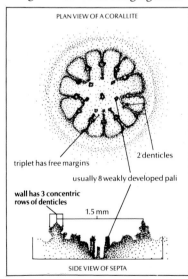

PLAN VIEW OF A CORALLITE

2 denticles
triplet has free margins
usually 8 weakly developed pali
wall has 3 concentric rows of denticles
1.5 mm
SIDE VIEW OF SEPTA

1. A 'micro-atoll' of Porites lobata. Only the outer perimeter is alive as upward growth is stopped by exposure at low tide.
PHOTOGRAPH: ED LOVELL.

2. Porites lobata at Mellish Reef, Great Barrier Reef. Large colonies such as this are common in lagoons and partly protected reef slopes.
PHOTOGRAPH: ED LOVELL.

3. Polyps of Porites lobata.
PHOTOGRAPH: ED LOVELL.

1

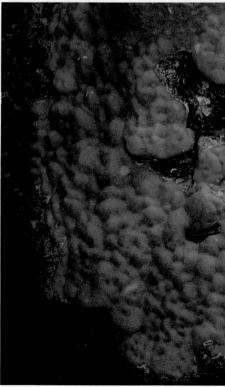

2

3

Porites australiensis

VAUGHAN, 1918

TYPE LOCALITY
Great Barrier Reef.

IDENTIFYING CHARACTERS
See diagram below.
Colonies are hemispherical to helmet-shaped and may be very large, with a surface of irregular humps and nodules.

COLOUR
Usually cream or yellow but may be bright colours in shallow water.

SIMILAR SPECIES
P. lobata.

DISTRIBUTION
From Chagos east to the Marshall Islands.
Around Australia: the Great Barrier Reef, Coral Sea and Flinders Reef (Moreton Bay) in the east; not found on the west coast.

ABUNDANCE
Very common and occurs with *P. lutea* and *P. lobata* on back reef margins, lagoons and fringing reefs.

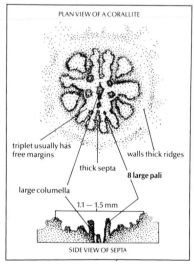

Porites australiensis from Willis Islet, Coral Sea.

PHOTOGRAPH: ED LOVELL.

Porites murrayensis

VAUGHAN, 1918

TYPE LOCALITY
Murray Islands, Torres Strait.

IDENTIFYING CHARACTERS
See diagram below.
Colonies are hemispherical or spherical, up to 200 mm in diameter.

COLOUR
Usually cream or brown, but may be bright colours in shallow water.

SIMILAR SPECIES
P. lobata is distinguished by its longer septa and less-well-developed pali.

DISTRIBUTION
From the Maldive and Nicobar Islands east to Samoa and the Marshall Islands.
Around Australia: the Great Barrier Reef, Coral Sea and Flinders Reef (Moreton Bay) in the east, and Rowley Shoals and Scott Reef on the west coast.

ABUNDANCE
Sometimes common, found in shallow clear water, especially reef flats.

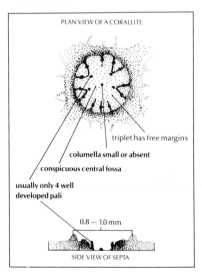

PLAN VIEW OF A CORALLITE

triplet has free margins
columella small or absent
conspicuous central fossa
usually only 4 well developed pali

0.8 – 1.0 mm

SIDE VIEW OF SEPTA

Porites murrayensis showing characterically thick and rounded polyp walls.
PHOTOGRAPH: ED LOVELL.

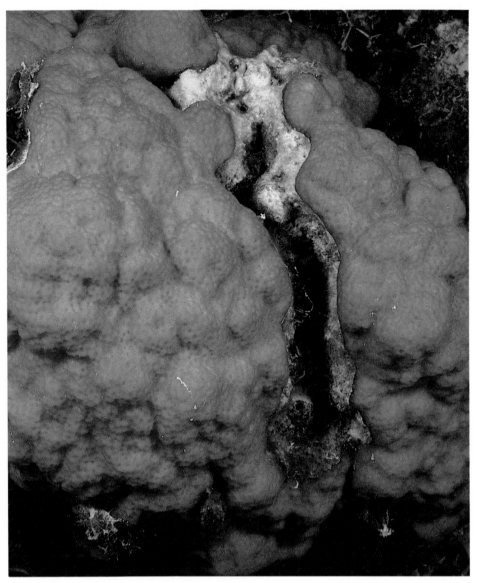

Porites lutea

EDWARDS & HAIME, 1860

TYPE LOCALITY
Fiji.

IDENTIFYING CHARACTERS
See diagram below.
Colonies are hemispherical or helmet-shaped and may be very large. The surface is usually smooth.

COLOUR
Usually cream or yellow but may be bright colours in shallow water.

SIMILAR SPECIES
P. australiensis is similar but the five tall pali with radii are readily recognisable even under water.

DISTRIBUTION
Red Sea east to the Tuamotu Archipelago.
Around Australia: the Great Barrier Reef, Coral Sea and Flinders Reef (Moreton Bay) in the east, and south to Houtman Abrolhos Islands on the west coast.

ABUNDANCE
Very common and occurs with *P. lobata* and *P. australiensis* on back reef margins, lagoons and fringing reefs.

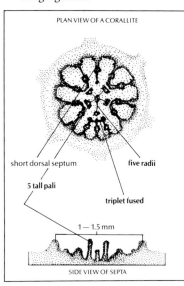

PLAN VIEW OF A CORALLITE

short dorsal septum   five radii

5 tall pali

triplet fused

1 — 1.5 mm

SIDE VIEW OF SEPTA

1. Two colonies of *Porites lutea* at Torres Strait. Colonies of this size are hundreds of years old.
PHOTOGRAPH: ED LOVELL.

2. The polyps of *Porites lutea.*
PHOTOGRAPH: ED LOVELL.

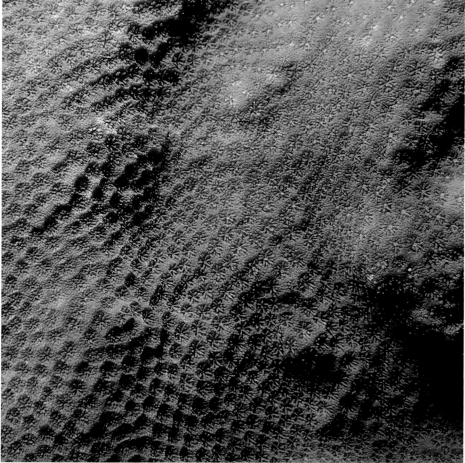

Porites stephensoni

CROSSLAND, 1952

TYPE LOCALITY
Low Isles, Great Barrier Reef.

IDENTIFYING CHARACTERS
See diagram below.
Colonies are spherical, hemispherical or columnar and are usually less than 100 mm in diameter.

COLOUR
Not known.

SIMILAR SPECIES
P. murrayensis.

DISTRIBUTION
Australia and the Philippines. Around Australia: the Great Barrier Reef in the east; not found on the west coast.

ABUNDANCE
Rare, occurs only on reef flats.

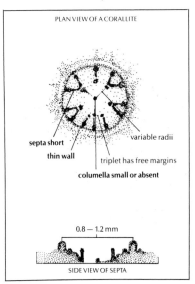

Porites mayeri

VAUGHAN, 1918

TYPE LOCALITY
Murray Islands, Torres Strait.

IDENTIFYING CHARACTERS
See diagram below.
Colonies are hemispherical with a smooth, even or lobed surface. They may be very large.

COLOUR
Cream or brown.

SIMILAR SPECIES
P. stephensoni and *P. densa.*

DISTRIBUTION
Known only from Australia: the Great Barrier Reef in the east; not found on the west coast.

ABUNDANCE
Seldom common, found on back reef margins, lagoons and fringing reefs.

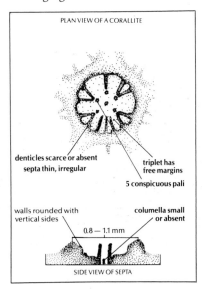

Porites densa

VAUGHAN, 1918

TYPE LOCALITY
Great Barrier Reef.

IDENTIFYING CHARACTERS
See diagram below.
Colonies are spherical or hemispherical, less than 150 mm in diameter.

COLOUR
Cream or brown.

SIMILAR SPECIES
P. mayeri. The deeply excavated calices of *P. densa* are readily recognisable even under water.

DISTRIBUTION
Known only from Australia: the Great Barrier Reef in the east; not found on the west coast.

ABUNDANCE
Sometimes common, found primarily on back reef margins.

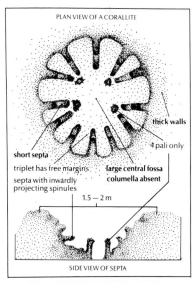

Porites cylindrica

DANA, 1846

TYPE LOCALITY
Fiji.

IDENTIFYING CHARACTERS
See diagram below.
Colonies are branching,
sometimes with an encrusting
base. Corallites are very shallow.

COLOUR
Usually cream, yellow, blue or
green.

SIMILAR SPECIES
P. nigrescens is distinguished
readily under water by its deeper
calices. *P. cylindrica* is confused
more readily with *Palauastrea*
under water.

DISTRIBUTION
From Madagascar and the
Mascarene Archipelago east to
the Marshall Islands and Tonga.
Around Australia: the Great
Barrier Reef and Coral Sea in the
east, and south to North West
Cape on the west coast.

ABUNDANCE
Very common and may be a
dominant in lagoons or on back
reef margins.

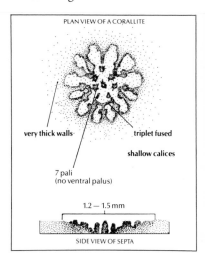

PLAN VIEW OF A CORALLITE

very thick walls

triplet fused

shallow calices

7 pali
(no ventral palus)

1.2 — 1.5 mm

SIDE VIEW OF SEPTA

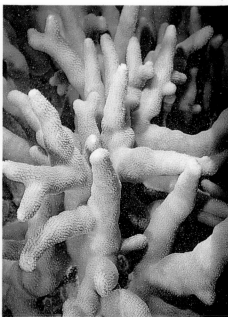

1. *Porites cylindrica* at Fitzroy Island,
Great Barrier Reef, showing compact,
finger-like branches.
PHOTOGRAPH: ED LOVELL.

2. Branches of *Porites cylindrica* at the
Swain Reefs, southern Great Barrier Reef,
showing smooth branch surfaces.
PHOTOGRAPH: ED LOVELL.

3. A "micro-atoll" of *Porites cylindrica*
at Heron Island, Great Barrier Reef.
PHOTOGRAPH: ISOBEL BENNETT.

4. Large stands of *Porites cylindrica* are
common in lagoons.
PHOTOGRAPH: AUTHOR.

Porites nigrescens

DANA, 1848

TYPE LOCALITY
Fiji.

IDENTIFYING CHARACTERS
See diagram below.
Colonies are branching, sometimes with an encrusting base. Concave calices give the surface a pitted appearance. Polyps are frequently extended during the day.

COLOUR
Brown or cream.

SIMILAR SPECIES
P. cylindrica.

DISTRIBUTION
From Madagascar east to Fiji and Tonga.
Around Australia: the Great Barrier Reef and Coral Sea in the east, and south to Ningaloo Reefs on the west coast.

ABUNDANCE
Common; occurs frequently with *P. cylindrica* but also common on lower reef slopes.

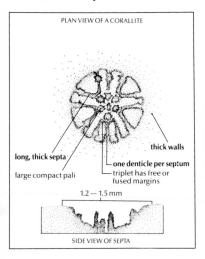

PLAN VIEW OF A CORALLITE

long, thick septa

large compact pali

thick walls

one denticle per septum

triplet has free or fused margins

1.2 — 1.5 mm

SIDE VIEW OF SEPTA

1. *Porites cylindrica* (above) and *Porites nigrescens* (below) at Lizard Island, Great Barrier Reef.
PHOTOGRAPH: ED LOVELL.

2. *Porites nigrescens* on a shallow upper reef slope.
PHOTOGRAPH: ED LOVELL.

3. *Porites nigrescens* at the Swain Reefs, Great Barrier Reef. Shallow pits, which are the polyps, cover the branch surface.
PHOTOGRAPH: ED LOVELL.

4. Branch ends of *Porites cylindrica* (left) and *Porites nigrescens* (right) at Scott Reef, Western Australia.
PHOTOGRAPH: AUTHOR.

Porites lichen
DANA, 1846

TYPE LOCALITY
Fiji.

IDENTIFYING CHARACTERS
See diagram below.
Colonies form flat laminae or plates, or fused nodules and columns. Corallites are usually aligned in irregular rows separated by low ridges. Septal structures are variable and irregular.

COLOUR
Usually bright yellowish-green, sometimes brown.

SIMILAR SPECIES
P. annae.

DISTRIBUTION
From the Red Sea east to the Marshall Islands and Samoa. Around Australia: the Great Barrier Reef, Coral Sea, Elizabeth and Middleton Reefs and Lord Howe Island in the east, and south to Houtman Abrolhos Islands on the west coast.

ABUNDANCE
Very common and frequently a dominant of lagoons and reef slopes. Usually conspicuous, both by colouration and abundance.

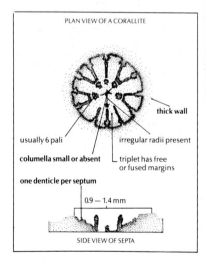

PLAN VIEW OF A CORALLITE

thick wall

usually 6 pali

irregular radii present

columella small or absent

triplet has free or fused margins

one denticle per septum

0.9 — 1.4 mm

SIDE VIEW OF SEPTA

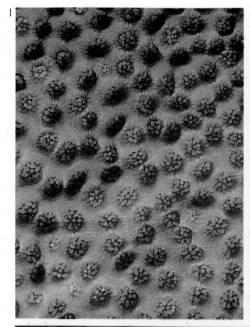

1. Polyps of *Porites lichen*.
PHOTOGRAPH: ED LOVELL.

2. *Porites lichen* may form large, beautifully sculptured colonies in clear water protected from strong wave action.
PHOTOGRAPH: RON AND VALERIE TAYLOR.

3. *Porites lichen* showing a combination of laminar and nodular growth forms.
PHOTOGRAPH: RON AND VALERIE TAYLOR.

4. An oyster in a *Porites lichen* colony. This is a common colour of the species.
PHOTOGRAPH: ED LOVELL.

Porites heronensis

VERON, 1985

TYPE LOCALITY
Heron Island, Great Barrier Reef.

IDENTIFYING CHARACTERS
See diagram below.
Colonies are massive, encrusting or columnar.

COLOUR
Cream, green, brown or mottled.

SIMILAR SPECIES
P. lichen has a similar growth form.

DISTRIBUTION
Known only from Australia: the Great Barrier Reef south to Solitary Islands in the east, and between Dampier Archipelago and Houtman Abrolhos Islands on the west coast.

ABUNDANCE
Common in temperate localities, rare in the tropics.

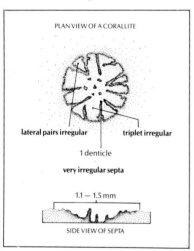

PLAN VIEW OF A CORALLITE

lateral pairs irregular   triplet irregular

1 denticle

very irregular septa

1.1 — 1.5 mm

SIDE VIEW OF SEPTA

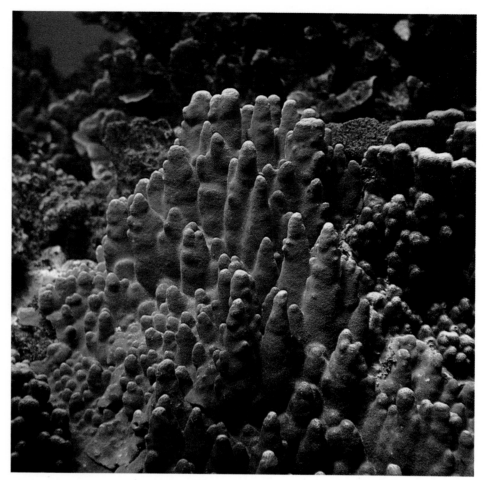

Porites heronensis at Lord Howe Island, eastern Australia, showing its common columnar growth form.
PHOTOGRAPH: JAMES BROWN.

Porites annae

CROSSLAND, 1952

TYPE LOCALITY
Low Isles, Great Barrier Reef.

IDENTIFYING CHARACTERS
See diagram below.
Colonies have knobby anastomosing branches or columns with encrusting or laminar bases.

COLOUR
Pale or dark green, yellow, purple or brown.

SIMILAR SPECIES
P. lichen is best distinguished by its different growth forms. It usually has larger corallites although the size range is similar.

DISTRIBUTION
Known only from Australia: the Great Barrier Reef in the east; not found on the west coast.

ABUNDANCE
Common, may form monospecific stands on sloping reef faces in clear or turbid water. In turbid water, colonies are predominantly laminar.

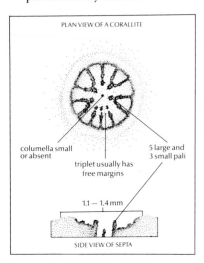

PLAN VIEW OF A CORALLITE

columella small or absent

triplet usually has free margins

5 large and 3 small pali

1.1 — 1.4 mm

SIDE VIEW OF SEPTA

1, 3. The characteristically irregular appearance of *Porites annae*.
PHOTOGRAPHS: ED LOVELL.

2. *Porites annae*.
PHOTOGRAPH: RON AND VALERIE TAYLOR.

Porites vaughani
CROSSLAND, 1952

TYPE LOCALITY
Low Isles, Great Barrier Reef.

IDENTIFYING CHARACTERS
See diagram below.
Colonies are plate-like or form columns. Corallites are widely spaced, separated by ridges. Corallites are uniform in size within the same colony. Those from exposed upper reef slopes are relatively small.

COLOUR
Usually pale cream, pink or brown but may be bright green or purple.

SIMILAR SPECIES
P. annae and *P. lichen*.

DISTRIBUTION
South China Sea and Australia. Around Australia: the Great Barrier Reef in the east, and Rowley Shoals and Scott Reef on the west coast.

ABUNDANCE
Sometimes common and found over a wide range of environments.

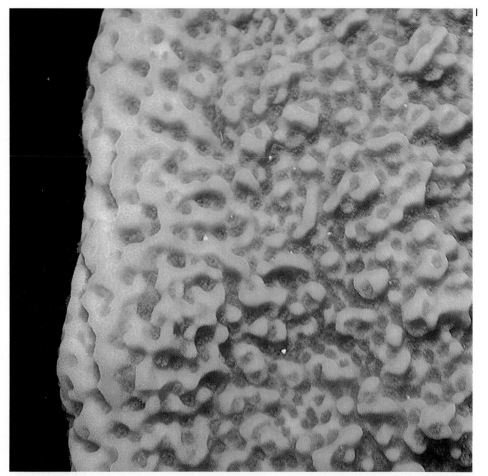

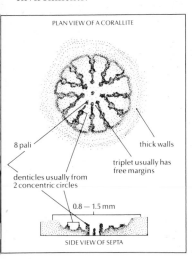

PLAN VIEW OF A CORALLITE

8 pali

thick walls

triplet usually has
free margins

denticles usually from
2 concentric circles

0.8 — 1.5 mm

SIDE VIEW OF SEPTA

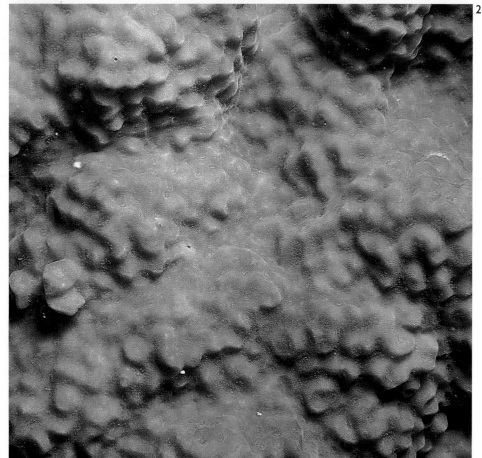

1, 2. *Porites vaughani*, showing the small, widely spaced polyps.
PHOTOGRAPHS: ED LOVELL.

SUBGENUS
SYNARAEA

Porites (*Synaraea*)
rus
(FORSKÅL, 1775)

TYPE LOCALITY
  Red Sea.

IDENTIFYING CHARACTERS
  See diagram below.
  Colonies are laminar or contorted
  anastomosing branches and
  columns. Corallites are very
  small. They are separated into
  groups by ridges which
  characteristically converge
  towards each other forming
  flame-shaped patterns.

COLOUR
  Pale cream or yellow, or dark
  bluish-brown, often with pale
  branch tips.

SIMILAR SPECIES
  P. rus can be confused with
  Montipora under water.

DISTRIBUTION
  From the Red Sea to Hawaii and
  the Society Islands.
  Around Australia: the Great
  Barrier Reef in the east, and
  Dampier Archipelago on the west
  coast.

ABUNDANCE
  Usually uncommon but occurs in
  a wide range of habitats.

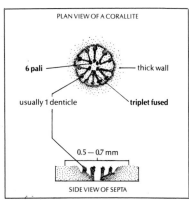

PLAN VIEW OF A CORALLITE

6 pali — thick wall

usually 1 denticle — **triplet fused**

0.5 — 0.7 mm

SIDE VIEW OF SEPTA

1. *Porites rus*, showing the characteristic
appearance of colonies with contorted
anastomosing branches.
PHOTOGRAPH: RON AND VALERIE TAYLOR.

2. The laminar growth form of *Porites
rus.*
PHOTOGRAPH: RON AND VALERIE TAYLOR.

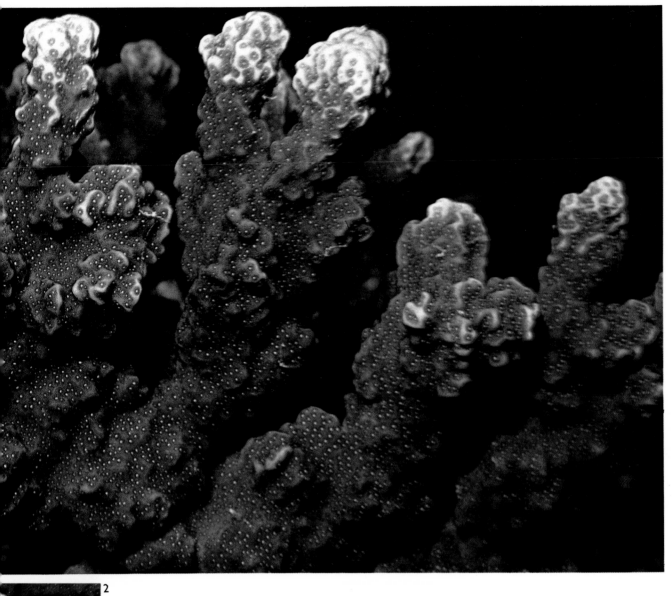

2

GENUS
STYLARAEA

(pronounced sty-la-ree-a)

Edwards & Haime, 1851

TYPE SPECIES
Porites punctata Linnaeus, 1758.

FOSSIL RECORD
None.

NUMBER OF SPECIES
One.

SIMILAR GENERA
Stylaraea resembles *Porites* except that septa are short, are in two cycles and do not fuse.

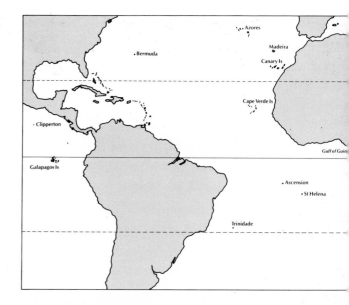

Stylaraea punctata
(LINNAEUS, 1758)

TYPE LOCALITY
Fossil from Europe?

IDENTIFYING CHARACTERS
Colonies are circular, encrusting. They are less than 15 mm in diameter and are thus smaller than any other coral.
Colonies have up to 12 corallites which resemble those of *Porites*.

DISTRIBUTION
Around Australia: the Great Barrier Reef in the east; not recorded on the west coast.

ABUNDANCE
Very rare. The species is always found in shallow-water environments uninhibited by other corals.

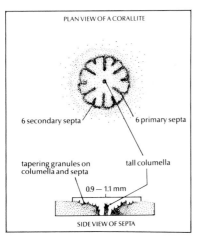

PLAN VIEW OF A CORALLITE

6 secondary septa   6 primary septa

tapering granules on columella and septa   tall columella

0.9 — 1.1 mm

SIDE VIEW OF SEPTA

×14

1. One of eleven specimens of *Stylaraea punctata* collected from Low Isles reef in 1928 and illustrated by Cyril Crossland in 1952.
2. Corallum of *Stylaraea punctata* magnified with an electron microscope.
ELECTRONMICROGRAPH: AUTHOR.

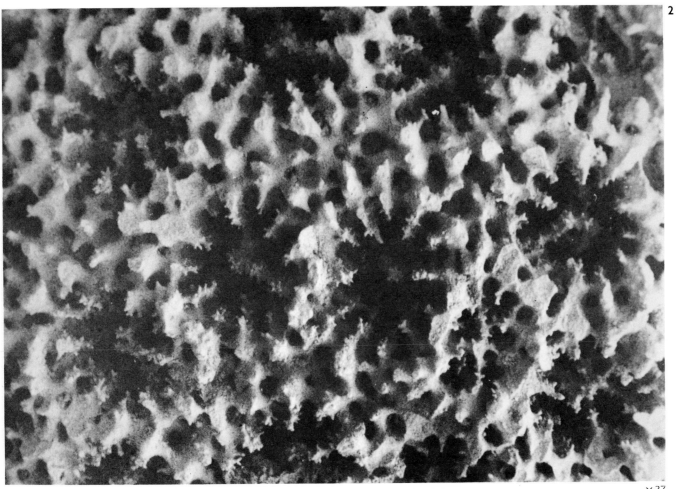

The known range of *Stylaraea punctata*.

×37

2

Genus
GONIOPORA

(pronounced go-nee-oh-por-a)

de Blainville, 1830

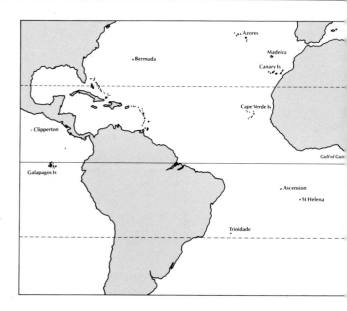

I have no hesitation in asserting that in the present state of our knowledge coral species are indeterminable. The long list of names which were steadily growing as I proceeded to designate every apparent different form of Porites and Goniopora in the old way, got completely out of hand.

Henry Bernard,
Catalogue of Madreporaria, Volume IV,
British Museum (Natural History), 1903.

The synonymy of this genus [Goniopora] *is in a hopeless condition. Bernard's obsession with growth forms naturally led him to abandon attempts at synonymy, and spoils his descriptions.*

Cyril Crossland,
*Scientific Reports of the Great Barrier
Reef Expedition 1928-29*, Volume 6, 1952.

Regrets are often expressed that we possess as a rule merely the dried skeleton remains of the Stony Corals. These regrets I do not share . . .

Henry Bernard.

These extracts illustrate the hopelessness of early attempts to define the species of genera like *Goniopora* without first studying them under water.

Most species of *Goniopora* can be identified from collected specimens, most can be identified on sight under water, but the task is much easier if the characters of both the skeleton and the living polyp are known.

Goniopora are most commonly found in turbid water protected from strong wave action. Colonies may be many metres across and sometimes whole sections of a reef face are covered by one branching *Goniopora* species or another to the exclusion of all other corals. *Goniopora* are generally aggressive corals. They do not have sweeper tentacles but polyps sometimes become enormously extended (over 40 cm) and attack any other coral within reach. Thus it is unusual to see other corals growing up close to a *Goniopora* species in a natural situation.

KEY TO SPECIES OF *GONIOPORA*

Colonies free-living *G. stokesi* (p. 240)

Colonies attached

Colonies forming columns or branches or submassive

Calices large (over 3 mm in diameter)

Columellae dome-shaped, divided into 6 septal deltas *G. djiboutiensis* (p. 238)

Columellae flat, diffuse (upper corallites especially) *G. stokesi* (p. 240), *G. columna* (p. 243)

Columellae small, septa long *G. lobata* (p. 241)

Calices small (less than 3 mm in diameter)

Colonies with no submassive base *G. pandoraensis* (p. 248), *G. eclipsensis* (p. 250)

Colonies with submassive base *G. palmensis* (p. 249), *G. fruticosa* (p. 252)

Colonies massive, without columns or branches

Calices large (over 3 mm in diameter)

Columellae broad *G. djiboutiensis* (p. 238), *G. stokesi* (p. 240), *G. pendulus* (p. 242)

Columellae small *G. lobata* (p. 241)

Calices small (less than 3 mm in diameter)

Paliform lobes present *G. tenuidens* (p. 245), *G. minor* (p. 246)

Paliform lobes absent *G. norfolkensis* (p. 247)

Colonies flat, plate-like or encrusting

Calices large (over 3 mm in diameter), shallow *G. somaliensis* (p. 244)

Calices small (less than 3 mm in diameter), shallow *G. stutchburyi* (p. 253)

Note: This key is a guide only and should be used in conjunction with descriptions of the species. Some species may key out in more than one place.

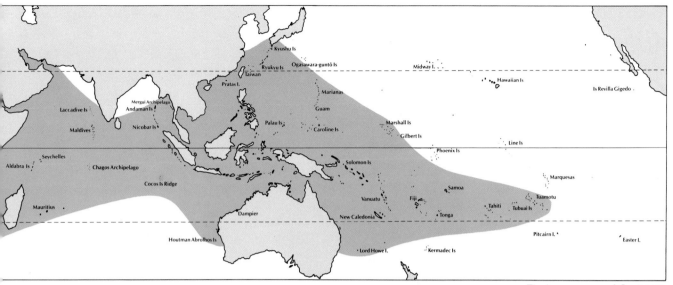

The known range of *Goniopara*.

Like *Porites, Goniopora* colonies have separate sexes, but unlike *Porites*, gametes are released into the water for external fertilisation rather than planula larvae being brooded by the mother polyp after internal fertilisation.

TYPE SPECIES
Goniopora pedunculata Quoy & Gaimard, 1833 from Papua New Guinea.

FOSSIL RECORD
Cretaceous to Recent in Europe and the Indo-Pacific.

NUMBER OF SPECIES
Thirty-nine nominal species, an unknown number of true species, 14 from Australia.

CHARACTERS
Colonies are usually columnar or massive but may be encrusting.
Corallites have thick but porous walls and calices are filled with compacted septa and columellae.
Polyps are long and fleshy and are normally extended day and night. They have 24 tentacles. Different species have polyps of different shapes and colours, which allow them to be identified under water.

SIMILAR GENERA
Goniopora is like *Alveopora* but, as illustrated, all skeletal structures are better developed. Polyps of these genera are similar except that *Goniopora* has 24 tentacles while *Alveopora* has 12.

1. The polyps of *Goniopora* colonies sometimes become greatly extended and will attack any other coral they can reach. Other corals usually keep their distance.
PHOTOGRAPH: LEN ZELL.

2. *Goniopora* species often form large monospecific stands. These are usually composed of branches which are club-shaped due to the mass of extended polyps at the ends.
PHOTOGRAPH: ED LOVELL.

Goniopora djiboutiensis

VAUGHAN, 1907

TYPE LOCALITY
Somalia.

IDENTIFYING CHARACTERS
Colonies are submassive or are short thick columns. Calices are up to 4.5 mm in diameter. Columellae are prominent, dome-shaped, divided into six parts, each being a delta of four septa. Polyps have large oral cones.

COLOUR
Pale or dark brown or green. Oral cones are usually white.

SIMILAR SPECIES
G. djiboutiensis is recognised readily under water by its large oral cones. Cleaned skeletons may resemble *G. lobata, G. stokesi* and *G. somaliensis.*

DISTRIBUTION
From the western Indian Ocean east to Fiji and probably the Marshall Islands.
Around Australia: the Great Barrier Reef, Coral Sea and Flinders Reef (Moreton Bay) in the east, and south to Houtman Abrolhos Islands on the west coast.

ABUNDANCE
Common, especially in turbid water. May form large monospecific stands.

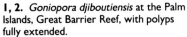

×2.5

1, 2. *Goniopora djiboutiensis* at the Palm Islands, Great Barrier Reef, with polyps fully extended.
PHOTOGRAPHS: ED LOVELL.

3, 4. The polyps of *Goniopora djiboutiensis* have very wide, conspicuous oral cones.
PHOTOGRAPHS: ED LOVELL.

Goniopora stokesi

EDWARDS & HAIME, 1851

TYPE LOCALITY
Unrecorded.

IDENTIFYING CHARACTERS
Colonies are free-living or attached, hemispherical or short thick columns. Calices are 3-6 mm in diameter with high walls which have a ragged appearance. Columellae are broad and irregular. Small daughter colonies often occur imbedded in the living tissue of parent colonies. Polyps are of mixed sizes, the larger being very elongate.

COLOUR
Uniform brown or green.

SIMILAR SPECIES
G. lobata, G. djiboutiensis, G. columna.

DISTRIBUTION
From eastern Africa east to the Philippines, Indonesia and Australia.
Around Australia: the Great Barrier Reef and Coral Sea in the east, and south to Houtman Abrolhos Islands on the west coast.

ABUNDANCE
Uncommon. Usually found free-living, on sandy substrates.

×2.5

1. A free-living *Goniopora stokesi* with satellite daughter colonies growing in the soft tissue of the parent colony. The largest daughter colony is under the holder's thumb.
PHOTOGRAPH: ED LOVELL.

2. Satellite daughter colonies form lumps on the side of a *Goniopora stokesi* colony. The polyps are partly or fully retracted.
PHOTOGRAPH: ED LOVELL.

Goniopora lobata

EDWARDS & HAIME, 1860

TYPE LOCALITY
Red Sea.

IDENTIFYING CHARACTERS
Colonies are hemispherical or short thick columns. Calices are 3-5 mm in diameter. Columellae are small. Living colonies have very large polyps.

COLOUR
Usually brown, yellow or green.

SIMILAR SPECIES
G. columna, also *G. stokesi* which is distinguished by its high ragged walls and broad columellae.

DISTRIBUTION
From eastern Africa and the Red Sea east to Fiji and Samoa. Around Australia: the Great Barrier Reef, Coral Sea and south to Elizabeth Reef in the east; south to Shark Bay on the west coast.

ABUNDANCE
Common, forms large monospecific stands, especially in turbid water.

x2.5

1, 2. The polyps of *Goniopora lobata*. These are similar to those of *G. djiboutiensis* except that the oral cones are smaller.

PHOTOGRAPHS: ED LOVELL.

Goniopora pendulus

VERON, 1985

TYPE LOCALITY
Houtman Abrolhos Islands.

IDENTIFYING CHARACTERS
Colonies are hemispherical. Calices are 3-4 mm in diameter. Columellae are large. Living colonies have large polyps with drooping tentacles.

COLOUR
Greenish-brown.

SIMILAR SPECIES
G. *djiboutiensis,* G. *stokesi* and G. *lobata.*

DISTRIBUTION
Known only from Australia: south to Houtman Abrolhos Islands on the west coast; not found in the east.

ABUNDANCE
Common at the Houtman Abrolhos Islands, especially on protected reef slopes.

×2.5

1. *Goniopora pendulus* has long, thin, mop-like tentacles.
PHOTOGRAPH: ED LOVELL.

2. Only when there is no water movement are the tentacles of *Goniopora pendulus* widely spaced.
PHOTOGRAPH: AUTHOR.

Goniopora columna

DANA, 1846

TYPE LOCALITY
  Fiji.

IDENTIFYING CHARACTERS
  Colonies are short columns, oval in transverse section. Calices are 3.5-4.5 mm in diameter. Those near the tops of columns have fine irregular septa and diffuse columellae. Those on the sides of columns have broad compact columellae and short septa. Living colonies have large polyps.

COLOUR
  Brown, green or yellow. Contracted polyps usually have distinctly different colours.

SIMILAR SPECIES
  G. *stokesi*, also G. *lobata*, the latter being distinguished by having corallites with small columellae.

DISTRIBUTION
  From the Red Sea east to Fiji. Around Australia: the Great Barrier Reef and Coral Sea in the east; south to Houtman Abrolhos Islands on the west coast.

ABUNDANCE
  Common, forms large monospecific stands especially in turbid water.

x2.5

1. A large colony of *Goniopora columna* that has been damaged, revealing the branching columns of which the colony is composed.
PHOTOGRAPH: LEN ZELL.

2. The characteristic appearance of *Goniopora columna* viewed from above.
PHOTOGRAPH: ED LOVELL.

3. The compact polyps of *Goniopora columna*.
PHOTOGRAPH: ED LOVELL.

Goniopora somaliensis

VAUGHAN, 1907

TYPE LOCALITY
Somalia.

IDENTIFYING CHARACTERS
Colonies are thick or thin encrusting plates with shallow calices forming a smooth surface. Calices are 2.8–4 mm in diameter. Polyps are short and cylindrical with pointed tentacles. They are usually retracted during the day.

COLOUR
Usually grey.

SIMILAR SPECIES
None.

DISTRIBUTION
East Africa and Australia. Around Australia: the Great Barrier Reef, Coral Sea and Flinders Reef (Moreton Bay) in the east; not found on the west coast.

ABUNDANCE
Uncommon, large colonies (which may be over 2 m in diameter) are conspicuous. They are usually found under overhangs.

x2.5

I. A large colony of *Goniopora somaliensis* at Magdelaine Cay. Colonies are flat and look like shaggy carpet.
PHOTOGRAPH: ED LOVELL.

2. The usual appearance of *Goniopora somaliensis* polyps.
PHOTOGRAPH: ED LOVELL.

3. The polyps of *Goniopora somaliensis* are usually short and have short tentacles. They project upwards vertically.
PHOTOGRAPH: ED LOVELL.

Goniopora tenuidens

(QUELCH, 1886)

TYPE LOCALITY
  The Philippines.

IDENTIFYING CHARACTERS
  Colonies are massive, hemispherical or irregular. Calices are 2.5-3.1 mm in diameter. They have six very prominent pali. Polyps are elongate with tentacles of even length.

COLOUR
  Uniform blue, green or brown, sometimes with white tips to the tentacles.

SIMILAR SPECIES
  G. minor has thick pali forming a crown. *G. norfolkensis* is also similar, but lacks pali.

DISTRIBUTION
  From the Nicobar Islands east to the South China Sea, the Philippines and New Caledonia. Around Australia: the Great Barrier Reef, Coral Sea, Elizabeth and Middleton Reefs and Lord Howe Island in the east, and south to Onslow on the west coast.

ABUNDANCE
  Very common in east Australia over a wide range of habitats and may be a dominant in lagoons; uncommon in west Australia.

×2.5

1. *Goniopora tenuidens* in Redbill Reef lagoon, Great Barrier Reef.
PHOTOGRAPH: ED LOVELL.

2, 3. The polyps of *Goniopora tenuidens* are easily recognised because their tentacles look as if they have been neatly cropped.
PHOTOGRAPHS: ED LOVELL.

Goniopora minor

CROSSLAND, 1952

TYPE LOCALITY
Low Isles, Great Barrier Reef.

IDENTIFYING CHARACTERS
Colonies are hemispherical or encrusting. Calices are 2.5-4 mm in diameter, circular in outline, with thick walls. There are usually six thick pali which are in contact forming a crown. All septal structures are heavily granulated.

COLOUR
Brown or green, usually with distinctively coloured oral discs and pale tips to the tentacles.

SIMILAR SPECIES
G. tenuidens.

DISTRIBUTION
South China Sea, the Philippines and Australia.
Around Australia: the Great Barrier Reef, Coral Sea and Elizabeth and Middleton Reefs in the east, and south to Dampier Archipelago on the west coast.

ABUNDANCE
Common in east Australia, especially in shallow water; uncommon in west Australia.

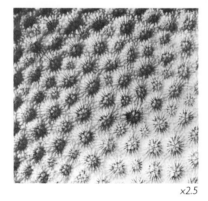

×2.5

The polyps of *Goniopora minor* have short, pointed tentacles.
PHOTOGRAPH: ED LOVELL.

Goniopora norfolkensis

VERON & PICHON, 1982

TYPE LOCALITY
Palm Islands, Great Barrier Reef.

IDENTIFYING CHARACTERS
Colonies are hemispherical to encrusting. Calices are 2.5-4 mm in diameter with small columellae and long, regular, steeply plunging septa. Pali are absent.

COLOUR
Brown or green, usually with distinctively coloured oral discs and pale tips to the tentacles.

SIMILAR SPECIES
G. tenuidens and *G. minor* are both distinguished by the presence of pali and/or broad columellae.

DISTRIBUTION
Hong Kong, Australia and Norfolk Island.
Around Australia: the Great Barrier Reef and Coral Sea in the east; not found on the west coast.

ABUNDANCE
Uncommon but occurs over a wide range of habitats.

x2.5

The polyps of *Goniopora norfolkensis* have distinctive white tips.
PHOTOGRAPH: ED LOVELL.

Goniopora pandoraensis
VERON AND PICHON, 1982

TYPE LOCALITY
Pandora Reef, Great Barrier Reef.

IDENTIFYING CHARACTERS
Colonies are small branched columns, usually oval in transverse section. Corallites have thick walls and septa. Calices are 2.7–3.1 mm in diameter. Six thick pali form a crown.

COLOUR
Always dark grey-brown with white mouths and tentacle tips.

SIMILAR SPECIES
G. columna has larger and *G. eclipsensis* has smaller columns and corallites. *G. pandoraensis* and *G. eclipsensis* can be reliably distinguished only if both species occur together (as is usually the case) or by the colour of the polyps.

DISTRIBUTION
Known only from Australia: the Great Barrier Reef in the east; not found on the west coast

ABUNDANCE
Common in shallow turbid waters of inshore fringing reefs.

x2.5

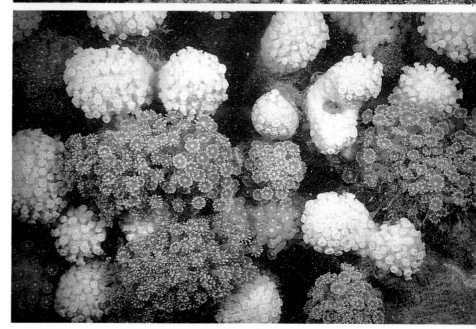

1. A stand of mixed *Goniopora* species. Here the species are *G. pandoraensis* (upper right), *G. eclipsensis* (centre) and *G. djiboutiensis* (left).
PHOTOGRAPH: ED LOVELL.

2. *Goniopora pandoraensis* (left and right) with *G. djiboutiensis* (centre).
PHOTOGRAPH: ED LOVELL.

3. For unknown reasons, many corals periodically turn white by expelling their zooxanthellae. Here a colony of *Goniopora pandoraensis* has some normal-coloured branches intermixed with white branches.
PHOTOGRAPH: ED LOVELL.

Goniopora palmensis

VERON & PICHON, 1982

TYPE LOCALITY
Palm Islands, Great Barrier Reef.

IDENTIFYING CHARACTERS
Colonies are submassive or branching. Branches seldom anastomose. Corallites are very uniform, circular in outline. Calices are 2.2-3 mm in diameter. Polyps have large oral cones and short pointed tentacles.

COLOUR
Brown, green or cream, often with white tentacle tips.

SIMILAR SPECIES
G. *fruticosa*.

DISTRIBUTION
Australia and possibly Mauritius. Around Australia: the Great Barrier Reef in the east, and south to Onslow on the west coast.

ABUNDANCE
Common in shallow turbid waters of inshore fringing reefs.

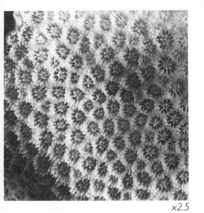

x2.5

1, 2. The polyps of *Goniopora palmensis* are characteristically short and pointed and sometimes have white tips.

PHOTOGRAPHS: ED LOVELL.

249

Goniopora eclipsensis

VERON & PICHON, 1982

TYPE LOCALITY
Palm Islands, Great Barrier Reef.

IDENTIFYING CHARACTERS
Colonies are small, branched, cylindrical columns. Corallites are circular in outline, with thick walls and septa. Calices are 2-2.5 mm in diameter. Six paliform lobes form a crown.

COLOUR
Uniform brown with or without paler tentacle tips.

SIMILAR SPECIES
G. eclipsensis resembles a diminutive *G. pandoraensis*.

DISTRIBUTION
Known only from Australia: the Great Barrier Reef in the east; not found on the west coast.

ABUNDANCE
Uncommon, usually found with *G. pandoraensis*.

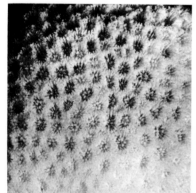

x2.5

1, 2. *Goniopora djiboutiensis* (right), *G. eclipsensis* (centre) and *G. pandoraensis* (left) at the Palm Islands, Great Barrier Reef, where stands of mixed species are very common and form spectacular "flower gardens".
PHOTOGRAPHS: ED LOVELL.

3. The polyps of *Goniopora eclipsensis* (right) and *G. columna* (left).
PHOTOGRAPH: ED LOVELL.

Goniopora fruticosa

SAVILLE-KENT, 1893

TYPE LOCALITY
Great Barrier Reef.

IDENTIFYING CHARACTERS
Colonies are encrusting or branching with highly anastomosed branches. Calices are 2–2.5 mm in diameter. Polyps have fine tapering tentacles.

COLOUR
Always dark brown with white oral discs.

SIMILAR SPECIES
G. fruticosa has a distinctive growth form. It is closest to *G. palmensis*.

DISTRIBUTION
South China Sea, Malaysia and Australia.
Around Australia: the Great Barrier Reef and Elizabeth and Middleton Reefs in the east; not found on the west coast.

ABUNDANCE
Uncommon, occurs on upper reef slopes protected from strong wave action.

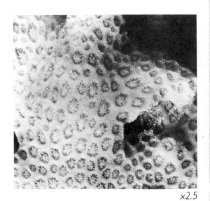

x2.5

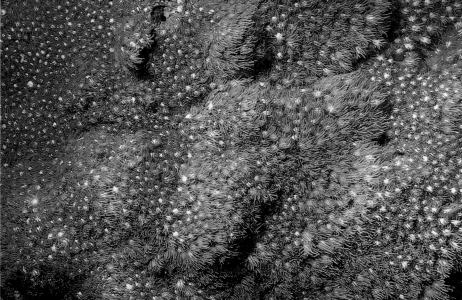

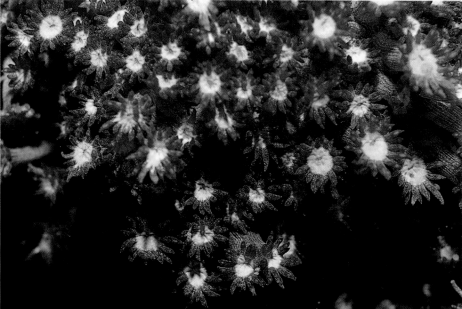

1. *Goniopora fruticosa* in an aquarium with polyps slightly extended.
PHOTOGRAPH: ED LOVELL.

2. *Goniopora fruticosa* at the Dampier Archipelago, Western Australia. East and west Australian colonies have exactly the same colouration.
PHOTOGRAPH: ED LOVELL.

3. The distinctive polyps of *Goniopora fruticosa*. Tentacles may be pale or dark brown but the oral disc is always white.
PHOTOGRAPH: ED LOVELL.

Goniopora stutchburyi

WELLS, 1955

TYPE LOCALITY
Moreton Bay.

IDENTIFYING CHARACTERS
Colonies are submassive to encrusting. Calices are small, (1.6-2.9 mm in diameter) and very shallow, giving colonies a smooth surface. Polyps have short tapering tentacles which may not be extended during the day.

COLOUR
Usually pale brown or cream, sometimes with pale blue mouths.

SIMILAR SPECIES
None, but could be confused with *Porites*.

DISTRIBUTION
India, South China Sea, Malaysia and Australia.
Around Australia: the Great Barrier Reef, Coral Sea and south to Elizabeth Reef in the east, and south to Houtman Abrolhos Islands on the west coast.

ABUNDANCE
Uncommon but occurs in most shallow-water habitats.

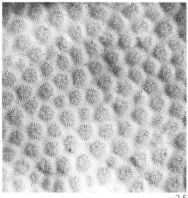

×2.5

1, 2. *Goniopora stutchburyi* with its polyps retracted (top) and extended (right). The polyps are the smallest of the *Goniopora* and are not much larger than some *Porites* species.
PHOTOGRAPHS: ED LOVELL.

GENUS
ALVEOPORA

(pronounced al-vee-oh-por-a)

de Blainville, 1830

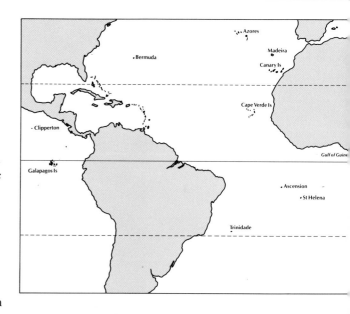

Alveopora were once considered to be in a family or subfamily of their own, with little or no affinity with *Goniopora* or *Porites*. On the other hand, more recently a taxonomist has claimed that *Alveopora* and *Goniopora* are "hardly separable". Perhaps the truth lies somewhere in between. The skeletons of the two genera are distinct, but have a lot in common. Likewise, the polyps can be distinguished readily by the number of tentacles present (12 in *Alveopora*, 24 in *Goniopora*), but are otherwise similar in appearance and behaviour.

No species of *Alveopora* is common, and perhaps more than any other genus of corals, their occurrence on reefs is unpredictable. The different species tend to occupy very different habitats, for example, *A. catalai* and *A. gigas* are found in turbid water protected from wave action, while *A. verrilliana* is found in clear water on reef slopes. Seldom are more than two or three species encountered in the same area of reef.

The polyps, like those of *Goniopora* species, retract promptly if disturbed. The nervous stimulation that causes retraction is transmitted to neighbouring polyps and this wave of contraction usually spreads out over the whole colony.

As yet nothing is known about the reproductive cycle of *Alveopora*. When this has been determined, the affinities between *Alveopora* and *Goniopora* may be clearer than they are now.

TYPE SPECIES
Madrepora daedalea Forskål, 1775 from the Red Sea.

FOSSIL RECORD
Eocene to Recent from Europe and the Indo-Pacific.

NUMBER OF SPECIES
Twenty-seven nominal species have been described, at least 16 of these are true species, eight are from Australia.

CHARACTERS
Colonies are massive or branching, often with irregular shapes.
The skeletal structure is very light, consisting of interconnecting rods and spines. Corallites have walls that are very perforated and septa that are mostly composed of fine spines which may meet in the centre forming a columella tangle.
Polyps are large and fleshy and are normally extended day and night. They have 12 tentacles, often with swollen knob-like tips.

SIMILAR GENERA
Alveopora are like *Goniopora*.

Alveopora catalai.
PHOTOGRAPH: AUTHOR.

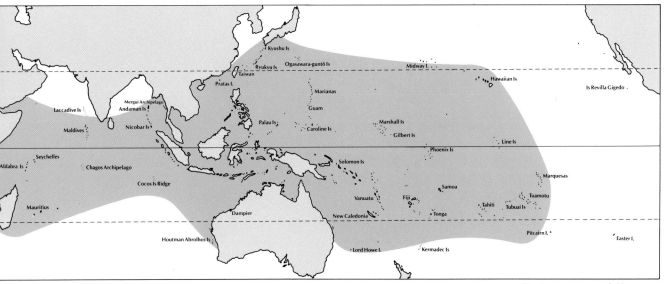

The known range of *Alveopora*.

Alveopora catalai

WELLS, 1968

TYPE LOCALITY
New Caledonia.

IDENTIFYING CHARACTERS
Colonies are composed of gnarled branches that divide irregularly. Corallites are large, composed of an interlocking network of rods and spines. Polyps are large with knob-like tentacle tips.

COLOUR
Pale brownish-pink when polyps are retracted. Extended polyps are amber or yellowish with white oral discs and sometimes white tips to the tentacles.

SIMILAR SPECIES
None.

DISTRIBUTION
New Caledonia and Australia. Around Australia: the Great Barrier Reef in the east, and Scott Reef on the west coast.

ABUNDANCE
Occurs only on soft substrates in deep water or in shallow turbid water protected from wave action and currents. It may form stands over 10 m in diameter.

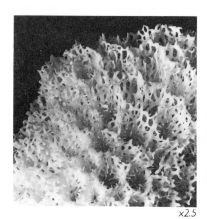

x2.5

I. *Alveopora catalai* at Scott Reef, Western Australia, growing between *Porites nigrescens* (left) and *Acropora tenuis* (right).
PHOTOGRAPH: AUTHOR.

2. The polyps of *Alveopora catalai*, the largest of the genus. Note that, as with other *Alveopora*, there are only 12 tentacles compared with the 24 tentacles of *Goniopora* polyps.
PHOTOGRAPH: ED LOVELL.

256

Alveopora allingi

HOFFMEISTER, 1925

TYPE LOCALITY
Samoa.

IDENTIFYING CHARACTERS
Colonies are encrusting or have short irregular lobes with rounded surfaces. Corallites are 3.5-4.5 mm in diameter with walls of interconnected rods and spines and long spine-like septa. A columella is usually present, and is sometimes well developed. Polyps are tightly compacted and long, with knobs on tentacle tips.

COLOUR
Usually yellow, green or brown with white bases to the tentacles.

SIMILAR SPECIES
Corallites are almost as large as *A. catali* but the growth form is similar to that of *A. marionensis*.

DISTRIBUTION
From the Maldive Islands east to the Philippines and Samoa. Around Australia: the Great Barrier Reef, Coral Sea and south to Lord Howe Island in the east, and south to Houtman Abrolhos Islands on the west coast.

ABUNDANCE
Usually uncommon.

x2.5

The polyps of *Alveopora allingi* at Pandora Reef, Great Barrier Reef. Colour variation in the polyps makes this species difficult to recognise although colonies are larger than those of other *Alveopora*, except *A. catalai*.
PHOTOGRAPH: ED LOVELL.

Alveopora gigas

VERON, 1985

TYPE LOCALITY
Houtman Abrolhos Islands.

IDENTIFYING CHARACTERS
Colonies are composed of blunt-ended irregular columns. Corallites are 4.3-7.6 mm in diameter, with thin, highly perforated walls of interconnected rods and spines. Polyps are up to 100 mm long and 20 mm across when fully extended.

COLOUR
Tentacles have white tips and white bases, the rest of the polyps are brown or greenish-brown.

SIMILAR SPECIES
This is the largest Australian *Alveopora*. *A. allingi* has similar skeletal structures; *A. catalai* has similar polyps.

DISTRIBUTION
Known only from Australia: south to Houtman Abrolhos Islands on the west coast; not found in the east.

ABUNDANCE
Common and very conspicuous at the Houtman Abrolhos Islands, uncommon elsewhere.

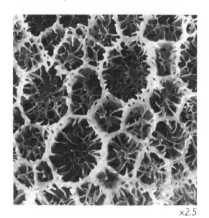

x2.5

1, 4. *Alveopora gigas* at the Houtman Abrolhos Islands, Western Australia. Large colonies like this are an impressive sight.
PHOTOGRAPHS: ED LOVELL.

2, 3. The polyps of *Alveopora gigas*. This species has the largest polyps and builds the largest colonies of any Australian *Alveopora*.
PHOTOGRAPHS: ED LOVELL (LEFT) AND PAT BAKER (RIGHT).

1

2

258

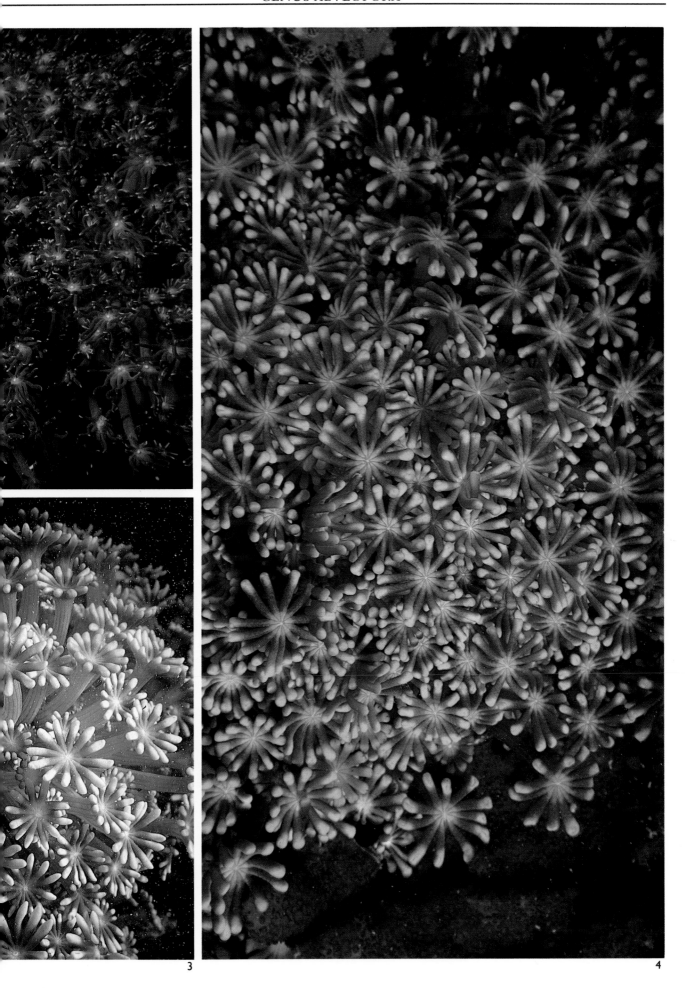

3

4

Alveopora marionensis

VERON & PICHON, 1982

TYPE LOCALITY
Marion Reef, Coral Sea.

IDENTIFYING CHARACTERS
Colonies are composed of short irregular lobes. Corallites are 2.8–3.2 mm in diameter with walls composed of compacted rods and spines. Septa are composed of tapering spines which are only connected lower down the corallite. Polyps have short straight tentacles.

COLOUR
Uniform grey or brown or pinkish, sometimes with white tentacle tips.

SIMILAR SPECIES
A. *fenestrata*.

DISTRIBUTION
Known only from Australia: the Coral Sea in the east; not found on the west coast.

ABUNDANCE
Abundant on Marion Reef, rare elsewhere.

×2.5

1. *Alveopora marionensis* from Marion Reef, Coral Sea.
PHOTOGRAPH: ED LOVELL.

2. The polyps of *Alveopora marionensis*, which are indistinguishable from *A. fenestrata* under water.
PHOTOGRAPH: ED LOVELL.

260

Alveopora fenestrata

(LAMARCK, 1816)

TYPE LOCALITY
"Southern Ocean".

IDENTIFYING CHARACTERS
Colonies are generally hemispherical with the surface divided into lobes. Corallites are 2.1–3 mm in diameter and are similar in structure to those of *A. marionensis*. Polyps are long with long thin tentacles, giving a ragged appearance.

COLOUR
Uniform grey or greenish-brown.

SIMILAR SPECIES
A. fenestrata has a growth form intermediate between *A. marionesis* and *A. verrilliana*. Only larger colonies can be distinguished by their growth form.

DISTRIBUTION
Known only from Australia: the Great Barrier Reef and Coral Sea in the east, and south to Houtman Abrolhos Islands on the west coast.

ABUNDANCE
Always uncommon.

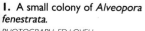

x2.5

1. A small colony of *Alveopora fenestrata*.
PHOTOGRAPH: ED LOVELL.

2. *Alveopora verrilliana* with polyps extended (left) growing around an *A. fenestrata* colony with polyps retracted (right), at Marion Reef, Coral Sea.
PHOTOGRAPH: ED LOVELL.

261

Alveopora verrilliana

DANA, 1872

TYPE LOCALITY
Hawaii.

IDENTIFYING CHARACTERS
Colonies are composed of short irregularly dividing knob-like branches. Corallites are 1.7-2 mm in diameter with short blunt septal spines and a few similar vertical spines surrounding the corallites. Polyps are long when extended.

COLOUR
Dark greenish-brown or grey (east Australia) or chocolate with white centres (west Australia).

SIMILAR SPECIES
A. fenestrata. A. verrilliana is distinguished by its growth form and the spines around its corallites.

DISTRIBUTION
From Australia to Hawaii. Around Australia: the Great Barrier Reef, Coral Sea and Elizabeth and Middleton Reefs in the east, and south to Houtman Abrolhos Islands on the west coast.

ABUNDANCE
Usually uncommon.

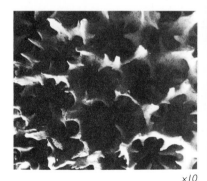

×10

1. *Alveopora verrilliana* with polyps retracted, showing the colony shape.
PHOTOGRAPH: ED LOVELL.

2. *Alveopora verrilliana* from the Houtman Abrolhos Islands, Western Australia, where this species is more abundant than it is on the east coast.
PHOTOGRAPH: ED LOVELL.

3. *Alveopora verrilliana* with polyps at varying stages of retraction.
PHOTOGRAPH: ED LOVELL.

Alveopora spongiosa

DANA, 1846

TYPE LOCALITY
Fiji.

IDENTIFYING CHARACTERS
Colonies are thick plates or pillows with a flat or undulating upper surface. Corallites are 1.9–2.6 mm in diameter, with long or short fine septal spines which seldom meet. Tips of polyp tentacles may be pointed or knob-like. Sometimes six large tentacles alternate with six small ones.

COLOUR
Usually uniform pale or dark brown, rarely green. Polyps sometimes have white tentacle tips.

SIMILAR SPECIES
A. tizardi.

DISTRIBUTION
Western Pacific from the Banda Sea to Tahiti.
Around Australia: the Great Barrier Reef, Coral Sea and south to all localities except the Solitary Islands in the east, and south to Houtman Abrolhos Islands on the west coast.

ABUNDANCE
Usually uncommon but colonies may be over 1 m across in protected parts of upper reef slopes, and are conspicuous.

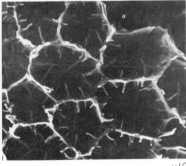

x10

1. A lobed colony of *Alveopora spongiosa* at the Houtman Abrolhos Islands, Western Australia.
PHOTOGRAPH: ED LOVELL.

2, 4 *(over)*. Two unusual colour combinations in *Alveopora spongiosa*. The species is usually brown and looks like chocolate cake under water.
PHOTOGRAPHS: ED LOVELL.

3. *Over:* The usual colour and appearance of *Alveopora spongiosa*. The delicate skeleton can be sliced readily with a knife.
PHOTOGRAPHS: ED LOVELL

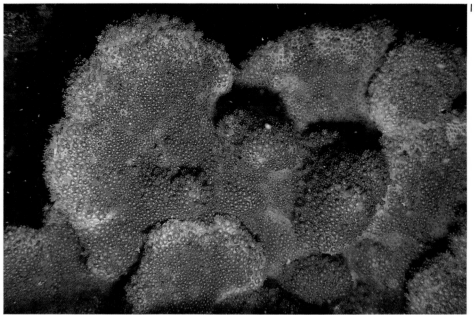

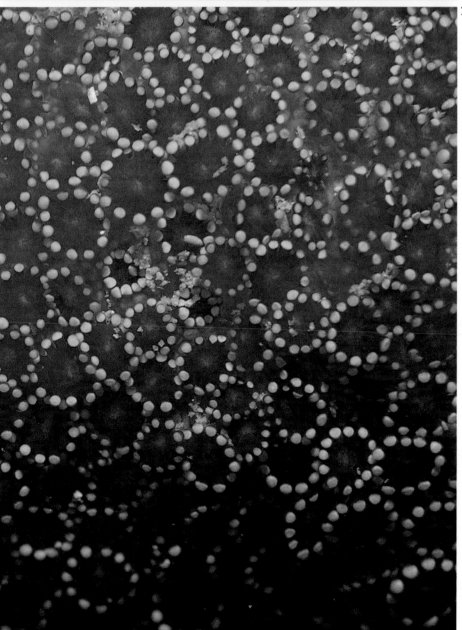

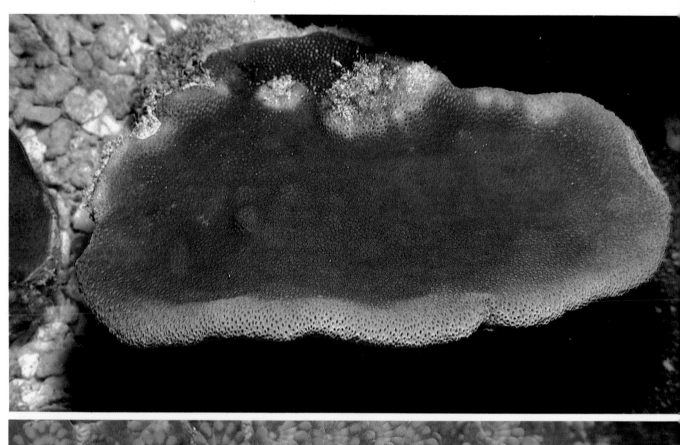

Alveopora tizardi

BASSETT-SMITH, 1890

TYPE LOCALITY
South China Sea.

IDENTIFYING CHARACTERS
Colonies are flat or undulating plates. Corallites are 1.2-1.7 mm in diameter, usually with regularly tapered septal spines. Polyps are short with knob-like tentacle tips.

COLOUR
Pale pinkish-brown to bright pink, sometimes with grey oral discs and tentacle tips.

SIMILAR SPECIES
A. spongiosa has larger corallites and polyps and is usually reliably distinguished by its brown colour.

DISTRIBUTION
South China Sea and Australia. Around Australia: the Great Barrier Reef in the east, and south to Houtman Abrolhos Islands on the west coast.

ABUNDANCE
Rare, found only on protected fringing reefs.

×10

Alveopora tizardi at the Palm Islands, Great Barrier Reef. The polyps are almost identical to those of *A. spongiosa*.
PHOTOGRAPH: ED LOVELL.

FAMILY
SIDERASTREIDAE

(pronounced sigh-der-ass-tree-id-ee)

VAUGHAN & WELLS, 1943

This family is composed largely of an assemblage of genera which have doubtful relationships. All but two genera (*Psammocora* and *Coscinaraea*) are small and have relatively restricted distributions. *Siderastrea radians*, however, is probably unique among hermatypic coral species in being found in both the Atlantic and the Indo-Pacific.

As far as is known, all siderastreids have colonies of separate sex.

CHARACTERS

Colonial (except for some fossil genera), hermatypic, mostly extant. Corallites are immersed with poorly defined walls formed by thickening of the septo-costae. Septa are usually fused along their inner margins to form fan-like groups, they have granulated upper margins and are closely compacted and equally spaced.

RELATED FAMILY

Agariciidae.

EARLIEST FOSSILS

Cretaceous.

THE GENERA

The Siderastreidae includes six extant hermatypic genera, three of which, *Pseudosiderastrea, Psammocora* and *Coscinaraea*, are Australian. *Siderastrea* is from the Atlantic and Indian Ocean and the Red Sea, and *Anomastrea* and *Horastrea* are from the western Indian Ocean. The distinction between *Psammocora* and *Coscinaraea* may be uncertain with some species. *Pseudosiderastrea* is monospecific.

Opposite: *Coscinaraea exesa*, one of the hermatypic Australian genera in Family Siderastreidae.
PHOTOGRAPH: RON AND VALERIE TAYLOR.

GENUS
PSEUDO-SIDERASTREA

(pronounced su-doh-sigh-der-ass-tree-a)

Yabe & Sugiyama, 1935

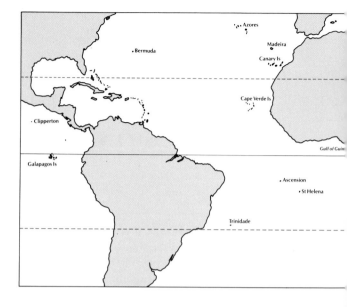

TYPE SPECIES
Pseudosiderastrea tayami Yabe & Sugiyama, 1935.

FOSSIL RECORD
None.

NUMBER OF SPECIES
Three nominal species, one true species.

Pseudosiderastrea tayami

YABE & SUGIYAMA, 1935

TYPE LOCALITY
Arafura Sea.

IDENTIFYING CHARACTERS
Colonies are encrusting to massive, dome-shaped, up to 160 mm in diameter.
Corallites are cerioid, polygonal, 3-6 mm in diameter. Septa are evenly spaced and fuse with each other in fan-like groups. They have fine, saw-like teeth.
Columellae consist of one to four pinnules.

COLOUR
Pale grey with distinctive white corallite walls.

SIMILAR GENERA
Pseudosiderastrea is a well-defined genus which may resemble *Coscinaraea* and superficially resembles *Coeloseris* and *Leptastrea*.
Coscinaraea has true affinities with *Pseudosiderastrea* but corallites are not cereoid and septa are coarser and have their own distinctive patterns.
Coeloseris has no columella and has smooth-sided septa which seldom fuse.
Leptastrea is subcerioid (that is, corallites are separated by a groove), septa seldom fuse and only rarely do they have saw-like teeth.

DISTRIBUTION
Around Australia: the northern and central Great Barrier Reef in the east, and south to Dampier Archipelago on the west coast.

ABUNDANCE
Uncommon throughout its range.

x5

Pseudosiderastrea tayami always has white polyp walls and always looks similar to this colony.
PHOTOGRAPH: LEN ZELL.

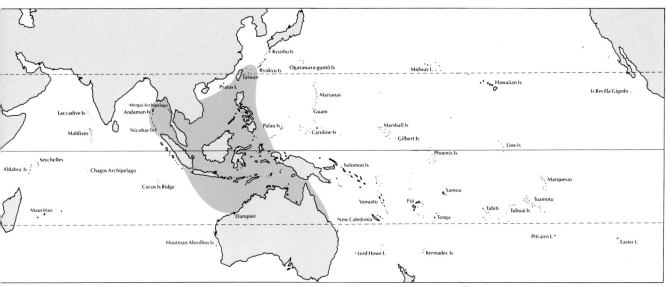

The known range of *Pseudosiderastrea tayami*.

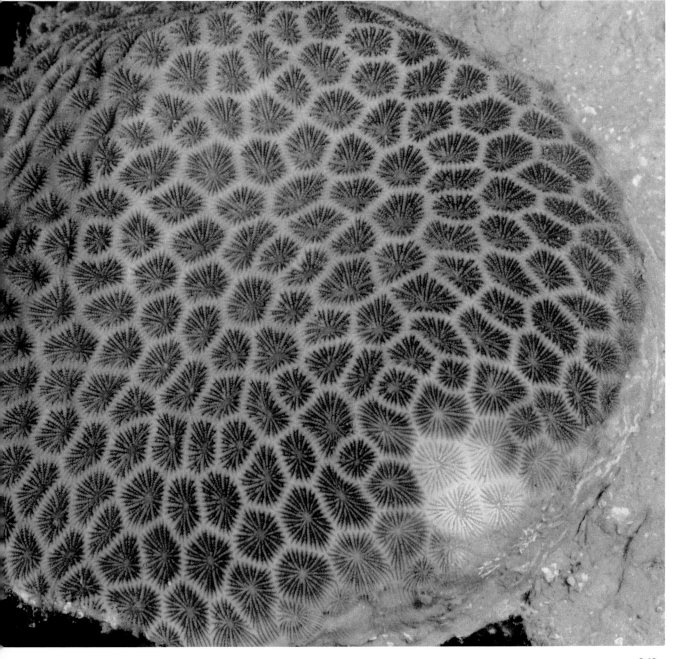

GENUS
PSAMMOCORA

(pronounced sam-oh-kor-a)

Dana, 1846

This genus has previously been included, by the present author and others, in the Family Thamnasteriidae Vaughan and Wells, 1943 but is now believed to have closer affinities with the Siderastreidae, especially *Coscinaraea*.

TYPE SPECIES
Pavonia obtusangulata Lamarck, 1816 from the "Indian Ocean".

FOSSIL RECORD
Miocene to Recent from the West Indies and Indo-Pacific.

NUMBER OF SPECIES
Approximately 27 nominal species, an unknown number of true species, seven from Australia.

CHARACTERS
Colonies are massive, columnar, laminar, foliaceous or encrusting.
Corallites are very small and shallow, sometimes in shallow valleys. Walls are indistinct. A small number of primary septo-costae are imbedded in secondary septo-costae, forming distinctive species-specific patterns. Septo-costae have finely granulated margins. Columellae consist of groups of pinnules.
Polyps are usually extended only at night.

SIMILAR GENERA
Psammocora is readily confused with *Coscinaraea*. The latter is initially distinguished by having larger corallites with much larger calices. *Psammocora explanulata*, in particular, is like *Coscinaraea wellsi*.

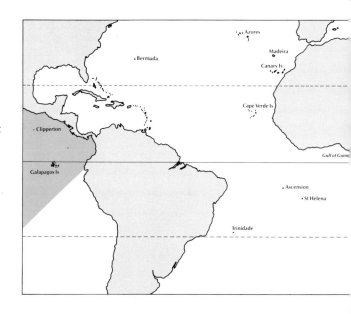

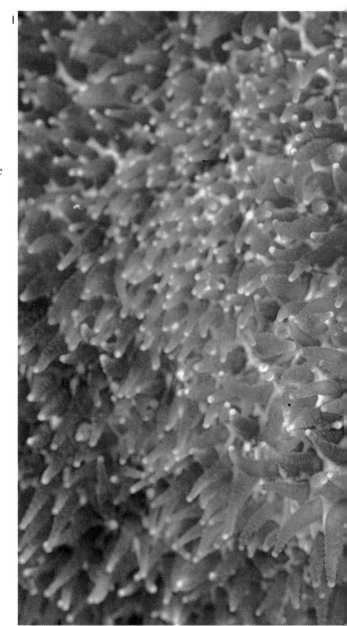

I. *Psammocora digitata* with tentacles extended at night.
PHOTOGRAPH: ED LOVELL.

2. Branch tops of *Psammocora digitata* at Ningaloo Reef Tract, Western Australia.
PHOTOGRAPH: BARRY WILSON.

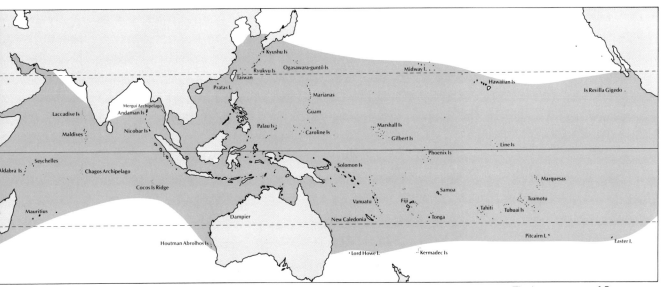

The known range of *Psammocora*.

2

Psammocora digitata

EDWARDS & HAIME, 1851

TYPE LOCALITY
China Sea.

IDENTIFYING CHARACTERS
Colonies are composed of plates and/or columns. Corallites are small and shallow, each with a few slightly exsert petaloid primary septa.

COLOUR
Purple, grey or brown.

SIMILAR SPECIES
The growth form is unlike any other *Psammocora* species, but colonies of *Coscinaraea exesa* may be similar in shape. Corallites are similar to those of *P. contigua*, but are larger.

DISTRIBUTION
From the Seychelles Islands east to Fiji.
Around Australia: the Great Barrier Reef and Flinders Reef (Moreton Bay) in the east, and south to Houtman Abrolhos Islands on the west coast.

ABUNDANCE
Occurs in a wide range of habitats and is distinctive, although usually uncommon.

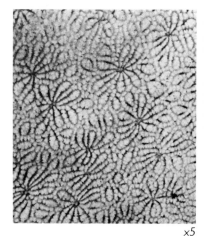

x5

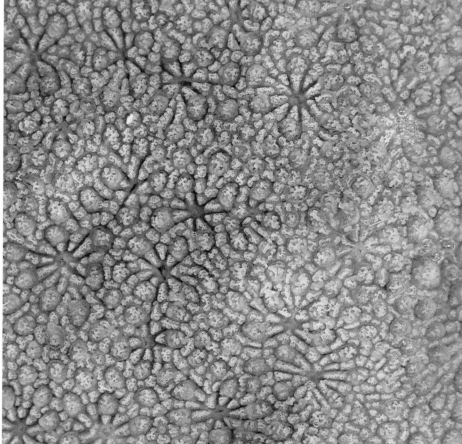

1. A fully developed *Psammocora digitata* colony showing the characteristic growth form of the species.
PHOTOGRAPH: ED LOVELL.

2. The surface detail of a branch of *Psammocora digitata*.
PHOTOGRAPH: AUTHOR.

Psammocora contigua
(ESPER, 1797)

TYPE LOCALITY
  Unrecorded.

IDENTIFYING CHARACTERS
  Colonies are a mixture of flattened branches or columns or irregular nodules. They are sometimes found free-living. Corallites are very fine and shallow, giving colonies a smooth surface.

COLOUR
  Pale to dark grey-brown.

SIMILAR SPECIES
  P. digitata.

DISTRIBUTION
  From eastern Africa and the Red Sea east to Samoa.
  Around Australia: the Great Barrier Reef, Coral Sea and all southern localities except the Solitary Islands in the east, and south to Shark Bay on the west coast.

ABUNDANCE
  Common over a wide range of environments.

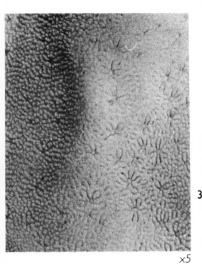

×5

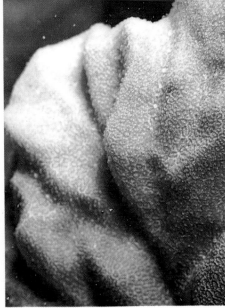

I. A fully developed *Psammocora contigua* colony. Colonies of this species have very variable shapes but it is the only branching Australian *Psammocora*.
PHOTOGRAPH: LEN ZELL.

2. Some of the branch tips of a *Psammocora contigua* colony 3 m in diameter.
PHOTOGRAPH: AUTHOR.

3. The usual appearance of a compact *Psammocora contigua* colony on an upper reef slope.
PHOTOGRAPH: ED LOVELL.

4. The surface detail of a *Psammocora contigua* branch.
PHOTOGRAPH: ED LOVELL.

Psammocora superficialis

GARDINER, 1898

TYPE LOCALITY
Marshall Islands.

IDENTIFYING CHARACTERS
Colonies are thick plates with low irregular ridges and small shallow corallites which are irregularly distributed.

COLOUR
Pale to dark grey or brown.

SIMILAR SPECIES
P. niestraszi has similar corallites but with well-defined ridges.

DISTRIBUTION
From east Africa and the Gulf of Aden east to the Marshall Islands and Samoa.
Around Australia: the Great Barrier Reef, Elizabeth and Middleton Reefs and the Solitary Islands in the east, and south to Houtman Abrolhos Islands on the west coast.

ABUNDANCE
Relatively common over a wide range of habitats but usually very inconspicuous.

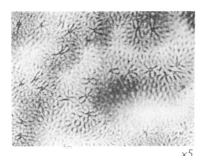

x5

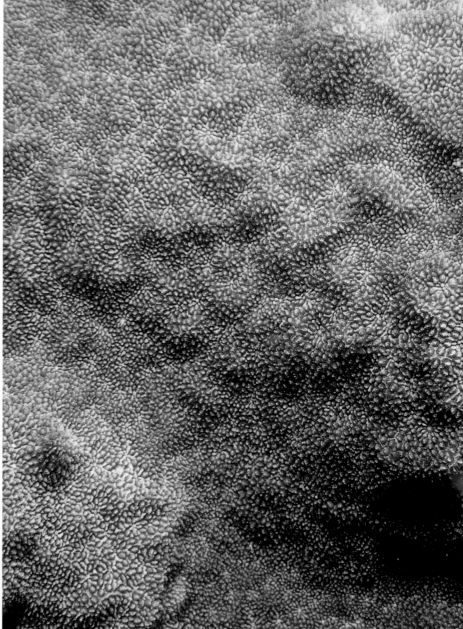

1, 2. The surface detail of *Psammocora superficialis*.
PHOTOGRAPHS: AUTHOR (1) AND ED LOVELL (2).

Psammocora profundacella

GARDINER, 1898

TYPE LOCALITY
Marshall Islands.

IDENTIFYING CHARACTERS
Colonies are submassive or plate-like. Corallites are in short valleys. Primary septo-costae are not petaloid or only slightly so.

COLOUR
Grey, brown or cream.

SIMILAR SPECIES
P. superficialis and *P. haimeana.*

DISTRIBUTION
From South Africa and the western Indian Ocean east to the Line Islands.
Around Australia: the Great Barrier Reef in the east, and south to Houtman Abrolhos Islands on the west coast.

ABUNDANCE
Uncommon.

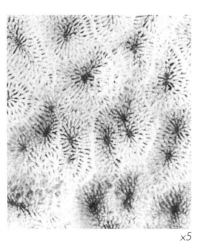

×5

Psammocora profundacella.
PHOTOGRAPH: AUTHOR.

Psammocora haimeana

EDWARDS & HAIME, 1851

TYPE LOCALITY
  Seychelles Islands.

IDENTIFYING CHARACTERS
  Colonies are submassive.
  Corallites are situated at the
  bottom of shallow depressions or
  short non-meandering valleys.
  Primary septo-costae are petaloid
  but not exsert.

COLOUR
  Grey or brown.

SIMILAR SPECIES
  P. profundacella is similar except
  that primary septo-costae are not
  petaloid.

DISTRIBUTION
  From South Africa and the Red
  Sea east to the Marshall Islands.
  Around Australia: the Great
  Barrier Reef, Flinders Reef
  (Moreton Bay) and Elizabeth and
  Middleton Reefs in the east, and
  south to Houtman Abrolhos
  Islands on the west coast.

ABUNDANCE
  Rare.

×5

1, 2. The surface detail of *Psammocora haimeana*.
PHOTOGRAPHS: AUTHOR.

Psammocora nierstraszi

VAN DER HORST, 1921

TYPE LOCALITY
Indonesia.

IDENTIFYING CHARACTERS
Colonies are massive and are primarily characterised by highly meandering valleys with steep walls. Corallites are distributed largely independently of the valleys.

COLOUR
Grey or cream.

SIMILAR SPECIES
P. profundacella also has valleys but corallites are aligned along the valley floors. See also *P. superficialis*.

DISTRIBUTION
From Aldabra and the Maldive Islands east to Samoa and the Marshall Islands.
Around Australia: the Great Barrier Reef and Elizabeth and Middleton Reefs in the east, and Dampier Archipelago on the west coast.

ABUNDANCE
Rare, may be restricted to outer reefs.

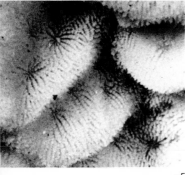

×5

Psammocora explanulata

VAN DER HORST, 1922

TYPE LOCALITY
Amirante and Providence Islands.

IDENTIFYING CHARACTERS
Colonies are thin plates or encrusting with a flat surface. Corallites are large for *Psammocora*, regularly distributed, and have very distinctive exsert petaloid primary septo-costae.

COLOUR
Pale or dark brown or green, frequently mottled.

SIMILAR SPECIES
Resembles *Coscinaraea wellsi* more than other *Psammocora*.

DISTRIBUTION
From Mozambique east to the Marshall Islands.
Around Australia: the northern and central Great Barrier Reef in the east; not found on the west coast.

ABUNDANCE
Rare.

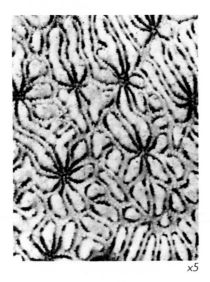

×5

277

GENUS
COSCINARAEA

(pronounced ko-sin-a-ree-a)

Edwards & Haime, 1848

There are six species of Australian *Coscinaraea*, two of which, *C. mcneilli* and *C. marshae*, are restricted to southern temperate waters and are never found on tropical coral reefs. Only one other Australian hermatypic coral, *Scolymia australis*, has a comparable distribution. Just why these species are able to tolerate temperatures that are lethal to most reef corals is unknown.

TYPE SPECIES
Madrepora monile Forskål, 1775 from the Red Sea.

FOSSIL RECORD
Extends only back to the Pleistocene.

NUMBER OF SPECIES
Approximately 14 nominal species, eight true species, six of which are Australian.

CHARACTERS
Colonies are massive, columnar, encrusting or laminar. Corallites are in short valleys or are irregularly scattered and shallow. Corallite walls are indistinct. Columellae consist of groups of pinnules. Septo-costae are fused in distinctive patterns and have finely serrated to heavily granulated margins.
Polyps are usually extended at night and sometimes during the day. Retracted polyps have a rough appearance.

SIMILAR GENERA
Coscinaraea resembles *Pseudosiderastrea* but is readily confused with *Psammocora*, being primarily distinguished by the larger size of the corallites.

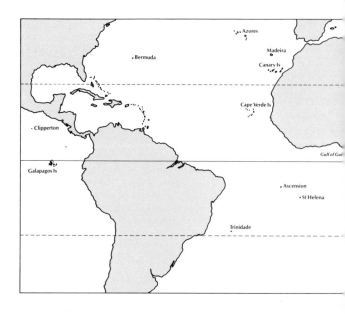

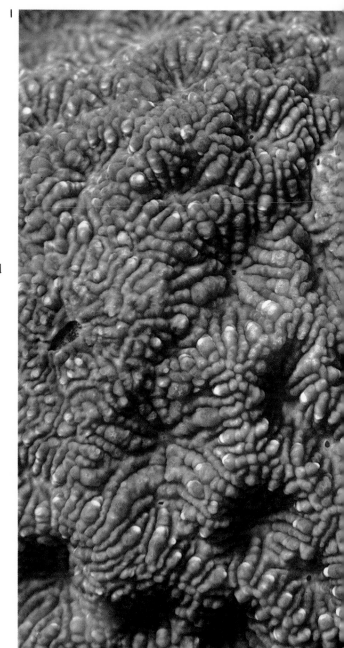

1. *Coscinaraea columna* with polyps retracted during the day.
PHOTOGRAPH: ED LOVELL.

2. *Coscinaraea exesa* at the Swain Reefs, Great Barrier Reef, showing columns which develop especially well in lagoons.
PHOTOGRAPH: ED LOVELL.

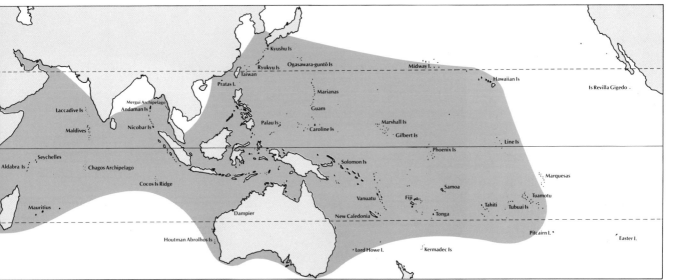

The known range of *Coscinaraea*.

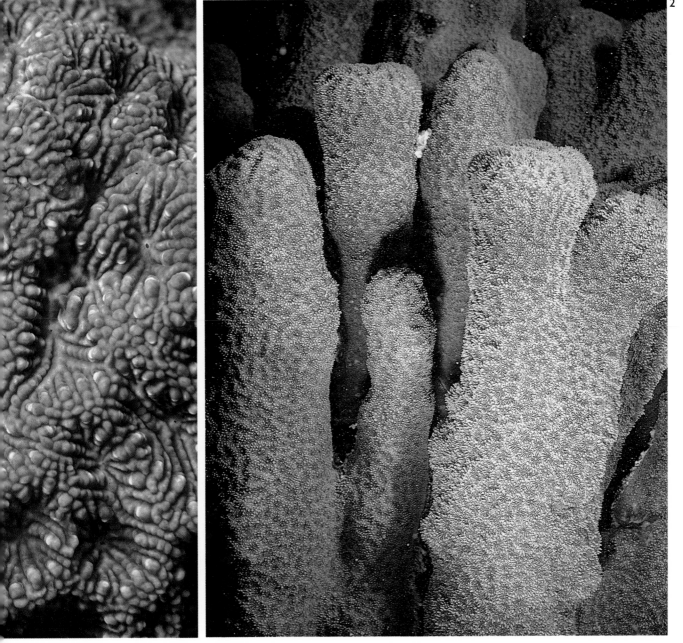

2

Coscinaraea exesa

(DANA, 1846)

TYPE LOCALITY
Fiji.

IDENTIFYING CHARACTERS
Colonies are columnar. Corallites are in shallow depressions or valleys. Septo–costae are usually granulated.

COLOUR
Dark grey or brown.

SIMILAR SPECIES
C. columna, also *Psammocora digitata* which may have a similar growth form but has much finer corallites.

DISTRIBUTION
The Philippines, Australia and Fiji.
Around Australia: the Great Barrier Reef, Coral Sea and Elizabeth and Middleton Reefs in the east, and south to Houtman Abrolhos Islands on the west coast.

ABUNDANCE
Common in shallow water, especially lagoons where colonies may be several metres in diameter.

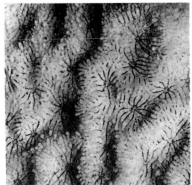

x2.5

I. *Coscinaraea exesa* with polyps extended.
PHOTOGRAPH: RON AND VALERIE TAYLOR.

2. The characteristic appearance of *Coscinaraea exesa*.
PHOTOGRAPH: RON AND VALERIE TAYLOR.

Coscinaraea columna

(DANA, 1846)

TYPE LOCALITY
Fiji.

IDENTIFYING CHARACTERS
Colonies are encrusting or massive, sometimes hillocky. Columellae are compacted pinnules set well below the septo-costae.

COLOUR
Grey or bright yellow.

SIMILAR SPECIES
C. exesa is distinguished by its columnar growth form. Corallites are usually shallower and larger and have granulated septo-costae.

DISTRIBUTION
From Madagascar east to Samoa and the Tuamotu Archipelago. Around Australia: the Great Barrier Reef, Coral Sea and all localities south to Lord Howe Island except the Solitary Islands in the east, and south to Houtman Abrolhos Islands on the west coast.

ABUNDANCE
Seldom common but occurs in a wide range of shallow-water habitats.

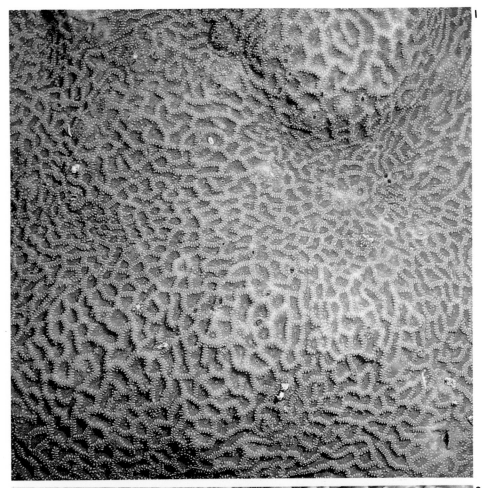

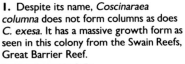

x2.5

1. Despite its name, *Coscinaraea columna* does not form columns as does *C. exesa*. It has a massive growth form as seen in this colony from the Swain Reefs, Great Barrier Reef.
PHOTOGRAPH: ED LOVELL.

2. *Coscinaraea columna* with polyps extended at night (right).
PHOTOGRAPH: ED LOVELL.

Coscinaraea mcneilli

WELLS, 1962

TYPE LOCALITY
  Sydney.

IDENTIFYING CHARACTERS
  Colonies are flat plates with corallites aligned in shallow depressions parallel to the corallum margin. Septo–costae are neatly arranged, perpendicular to the corallum margin.

COLOUR
  Dark grey, brown or green.

SIMILAR SPECIES
  C. marshae and *C. crassa*.

DISTRIBUTION
  Known only from Australia: south-eastern Australia north to Byron Bay, southern Australia and south-western Australia north to Jurien Bay.

ABUNDANCE
  Usually uncommon throughout its range.

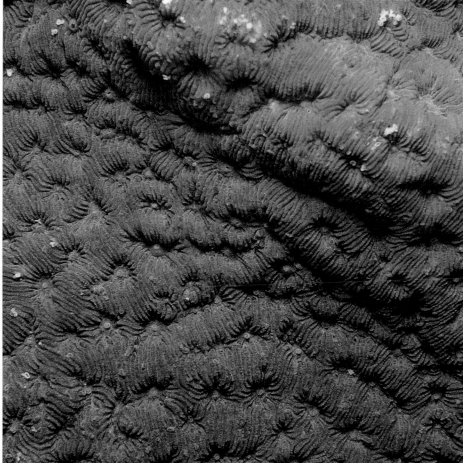

x2.5

1. *Coscinaraea mcneilli* at the Solitary Islands, eastern Australia, where colonies take the form of large flat plates.
PHOTOGRAPH: ED LOVELL.

2. *Coscinaraea mcneilli* from South Australia.
PHOTOGRAPH: NIGEL HOLMES.

Coscinaraea marshae

WELLS, 1962

TYPE LOCALITY
Rottnest Island, west Australia.

IDENTIFYING CHARACTERS
Colonies are flat plates with corallites aligned between *Leptoseris*-like folds parallel to the corallum margin.

COLOUR
Brown or yellow-brown, sometimes mottled.

SIMILAR SPECIES
C. mcneilli.

DISTRIBUTION
Known only from Australia: south-western Australia between Recherche Archipelago and Houtman Abrolhos Islands; not found in the east.

ABUNDANCE
Usually uncommon.

x2.5

1. *Coscinaraea marshae* from near Perth. Polyps are distinctly arranged in concentric rows.
PHOTOGRAPH: PAT BAKER.

2. Tiered colonies of *Coscinaraea marshae* near Dunsborough, Western Australia.
PHOTOGRAPH: BARRY WILSON.

3. The usual appearance of *Coscinaraea marshae* in shallow water.
PHOTOGRAPH: ED LOVELL.

Coscinaraea wellsi

VERON & PICHON, 1980

TYPE LOCALITY
Marshall Islands.

IDENTIFYING CHARACTERS
Colonies are thin, often overlapping laminae, with lobed margins. Corallites are irregularly distributed, with deep-seated columellae and thick granulated septo–costae.

COLOUR
Brown or red-brown, with white perimeters.

SIMILAR SPECIES
May be confused with *Psammocora explanulata* which has smaller corallites and petaloid septo–costae. Also resembles *Leptoseris scabra*.

DISTRIBUTION
From Madagascar east to the Marshall Islands.
Around Australia: the Great Barrier Reef, Coral Sea, Elizabeth and Middleton Reefs and Lord Howe Island in the east; not found on the west coast.

ABUNDANCE
Uncommon except when encrusting vertical or overhang faces.

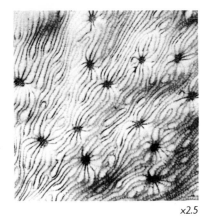

x2.5

The delicate laminae of *Coscinaraea wellsi* at Lord Howe Island, eastern Australia.
PHOTOGRAPH: LEN ZELL.

Coscinaraea crassa

VERON & PICHON, 1980

TYPE LOCALITY
Ashmore Reef, Torres Strait.

IDENTIFYING CHARACTERS
Colonies are large plates with large compact corallites. Different-sized septo-costae alternate slightly. Columellae are single fused bosses.

COLOUR
Not known.

SIMILAR SPECIES
Superficially resembles *Podabacia crustacea*. Structurally resembles an enlarged *C. mcneilli*.

DISTRIBUTION
Known only from Australia: Ashmore Reef, northern Great Barrier Reef in the east; not found on the west coast.

ABUNDANCE
Very rare.

x2.5

FAMILY
AGARICIIDAE

(pronounced ag-a-ree-see-id-ee)

GRAY, 1847

With a couple of exceptions, the agariciid corals are recognised easily. They are mostly uncommon on reef flats or slopes exposed to wave action, but are often found on protected reef slopes and are common in lagoons. Agariciids have very fine tentacles which are seldom extended during the day (except for *Pavona explanulata*). Little is known about their sexual reproduction, except that different species may be separately sexed or hermaphrodite and may brood planula larvae or release gametes.

CHARACTERS
Colonial (except for some fossil genera), hermatypic. Colonies are massive, laminar or foliaceous. Corallites are immersed with poorly defined walls formed by thickening of the septo–costae. Septa seldom fuse and are continuous between adjacent corallite centres. They have smooth or finely serrated margins and are closely packed.

SIMILAR FAMILY
Siderastreidae.

EARLIEST FOSSILS
Cretaceous.

THE GENERA
The Agariciidae includes six extant hermatypic genera: *Pavona, Leptoseris, Gardineroseris, Coeloseris,* and *Pachyseris*, which are Australian, as well as *Agaracia* from the West Indies. The distinction between *Pavona* and *Leptoseris* may be uncertain with some species, the remainder are well defined.

Opposite: a giant colony of *Pavona minuta* a member of Family Agariciidae. The name must refer to the size of the polyps, as the species forms some of the largest colonies of all corals, rivalled only by *Porites*. The colonies always have a beautifully rounded, sculptured appearance.

PHOTOGRAPH: RON AND VALERIE TAYLOR.

GENUS
PAVONA
(pronounced pa-voh-na)

Lamarck, 1801

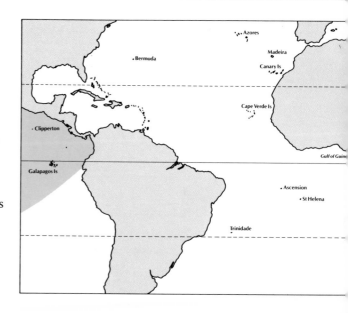

Pavona species can be divided into two groups: leafy species and non-leafy species. The former group has the greatest number of nominal species, (and perhaps true species) but these are poorly represented in Australian waters. These leafy *Pavona* are usually distinguished from *Leptoseris* by the presence of corallites on both sides of the fronds or "leaves".

Most *Pavona* species, including all Australian species, are widespread in the Indian as well as the Pacific Oceans.

TYPE SPECIES
Madrepora cristata Ellis & Solander, 1786 from an unknown locality.

FOSSIL RECORD
Miocene to Recent from Europe, the West Indies and the Indo-Pacific.

NUMBER OF SPECIES
Approximately 50 nominal species, at least 12 true species, eight of which are Australian.

CHARACTERS
Colonies are massive, laminar or foliaceous, the latter usually being bifacial.
Corallites have poorly defined walls. They are small shallow depressions, usually with a central columella, sometimes separated by ridges. Corallites are interconnected by prominent septo-costae.
Except for *P. explanulata*, polyps are extended only at night.

SIMILAR GENERA
Pavona is close to *Leptoseris* which has similar corallites but finer septo-costae. Foliaceous colonies are unifacial in *Leptoseris* but the distinction between these genera may sometimes be unclear.

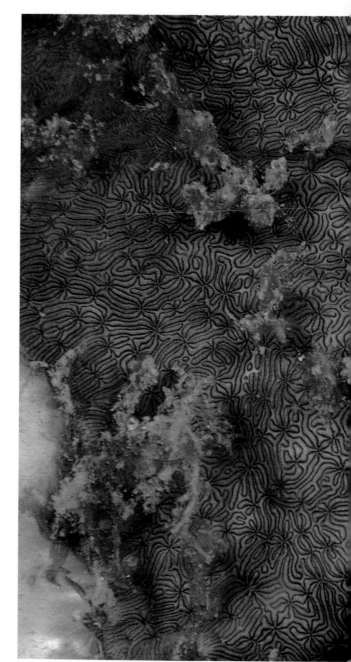

A small encrusting colony of *Pavona minuta* being overgrown by *P. explanulata.*
PHOTOGRAPH: LEN ZELL.

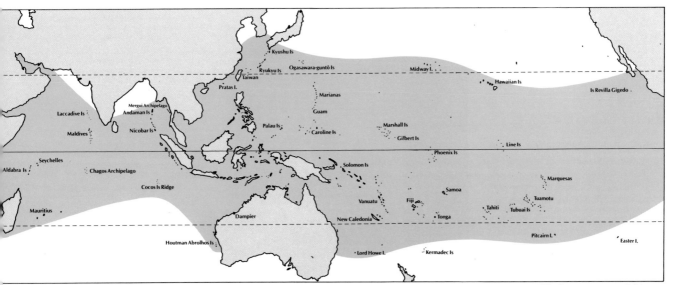

The known range of *Pavona*.

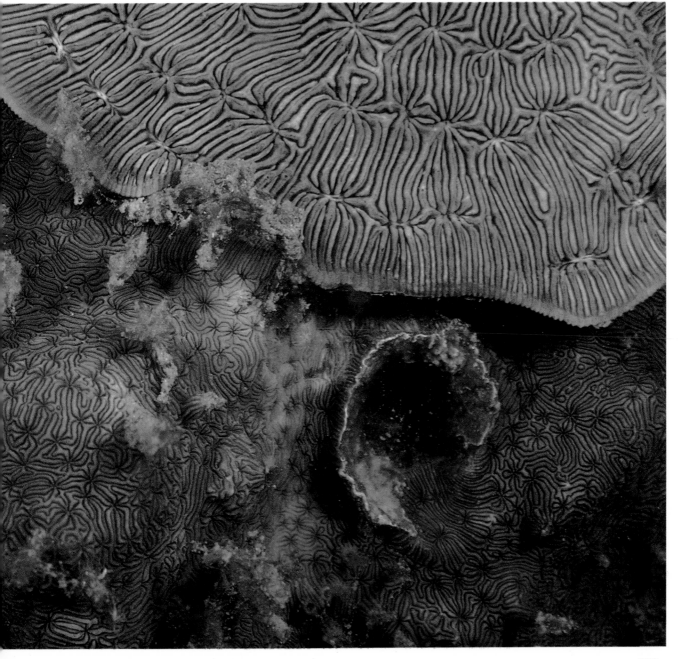

Pavona cactus

(FORSKÅL, 1775)

TYPE LOCALITY
Red Sea.

IDENTIFYING CHARACTERS
Colonies are thin, contorted, bifacial, upright fronds with or without thickened branching bases. Corallites are fine and shallow, and aligned in irregular rows parallel to the margins.

COLOUR
Pale brown or greenish-brown.

SIMILAR SPECIES
None.

DISTRIBUTION
From the Red Sea to the Marshall Islands.
Around Australia: the Great Barrier Reef in the east, and Rowley Shoals and Scott Reef on the west coast.

ABUNDANCE
Abundant in some lagoons and on upper reef slopes, especially those of fringing reefs, and in turbid water protected from wave action, where colonies frequently exceed 10 m in diameter.

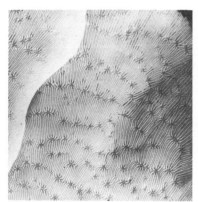

x2.5

1, 2. *Pavona cactus* forming thin convoluted fronds (1) and twisted branches (2).
PHOTOGRAPHS: LEN ZELL.

Pavona decussata

(DANA, 1846)

TYPE LOCALITY
Fiji.

IDENTIFYING CHARACTERS
Colonies are thick, interconnecting, bifacial upright laminae. or are submassive, with or without lobed horizontal margins and upright laminae. Corallites are irregular, deep-seated, sometimes aligned parallel to margins or to radiating ridges.

COLOUR
Brown, creamy yellow or greenish.

SIMILAR SPECIES
None.

DISTRIBUTION
From the Red Sea east to Samoa. Around Australia: the Great Barrier Reef, Coral Sea and Elizabeth and Middleton Reefs in the east, and south to Houtman Abrolhos Islands on the west coast.

ABUNDANCE
Common over a wide range of shallow-water environments.

x2.5

1. *Pavona decussata* forming anastomosing upright fronds.
PHOTOGRAPH: RON AND VALERIE TAYLOR.

2. The polyps of *Pavona decussata* as illustrated by James Dana in 1849.

3. The usual appearance of *Pavona decussata*. The species may become almost submassive but remains readily recognisable.
PHOTOGRAPH: RON AND VALERIE TAYLOR.

4. The polyps of *Pavona decussata*.
PHOTOGRAPH: ED LOVELL.

Pavona explanulata

(LAMARCK, 1816)

TYPE LOCALITY
Unrecorded.

IDENTIFYING CHARACTERS
Colonies are encrusting or thin unifacial laminae, sometimes submassive or columnar. Corallites are usually widely spaced, circular, with pillar-like columellae and smooth alternating septo–costae.

COLOUR
Grey, brown, pink, purple, green or yellow, sometimes mottled.

SIMILAR SPECIES
Distinct from other *Pavona* but may resemble *Leptoseris explanata*.

DISTRIBUTION
From Madagascar east to the Philippines and eastern Australia. Around Australia: the Great Barrier Reef, Coral Sea and south to Lord Howe Island excluding the Solitary Islands in the east, and south to Houtman Abrolhos Islands on the west coast.

ABUNDANCE
Occurs in a wide range of shallow habitats but is seldom common.

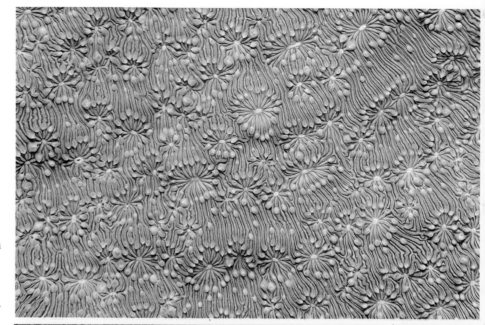

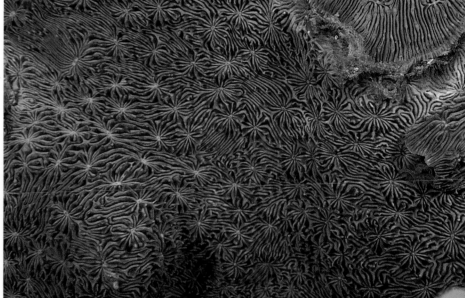

×2.5

1, 2. Two common colour variants of *Pavona explanulata*.
PHOTOGRAPHS: ED LOVELL (1) AND LEN ZELL (2).

3. *Pavona explanulata* with polyps extended during the day. The species is easily recognised under water.
PHOTOGRAPH: ED LOVELL.

Pavona clavus
(DANA, 1846)

TYPE LOCALITY
Fiji.

IDENTIFYING CHARACTERS
Colonies are columnar or laminar, or both. Columns divide but do not anastomose. Corallites are thick-walled. Columellae are short or absent.

COLOUR
Uniform pale grey, cream or brown.

SIMILAR SPECIES
None, although the corallites are like *P. minuta*.

DISTRIBUTION
From the Mascarene Archipelago and Red Sea east across the Pacific to the Galapagos Islands. Around Australia: the Great Barrier Reef and Coral Sea in the east, and Rowley Shoals and Scott Reef on the west coast.

ABUNDANCE
Common on some shallow upper reef slopes exposed to currents, and may be a dominant coral forming extensive monospecific stands.

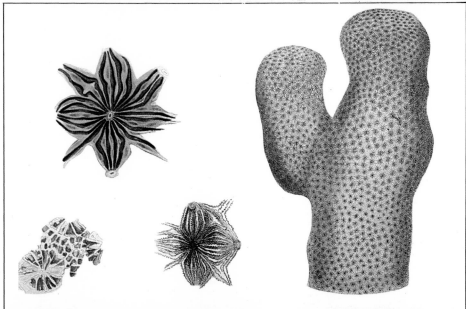

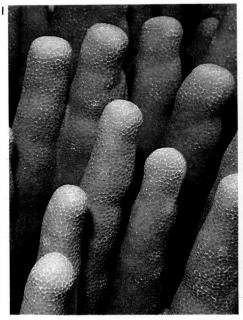

1. On some outer reef slopes, *Pavona clavus* may occur as extensive monospecific stands of these tall, straight columns. These form excellent refuges for schools of larger reef fish.
PHOTOGRAPH: RON AND VALERIE TAYLOR.

2. *Pavona clavus* often forms flat plates. Sometimes, in deep water, whole colonies are composed of these plates, and sometimes they surround the base of columns.
PHOTOGRAPH: LEN ZELL.

3. *Pavona clavus* as illustrated by James Dana in 1849, showing the corallum (right) and a corallite (left). The drawings are very accurate and readily recognisable.

4. *Pavona clavus* forming short columns.
PHOTOGRAPH: LEN ZELL.

Pavona minuta

WELLS, 1956

TYPE LOCALITY
   Marshall Islands.

IDENTIFYING CHARACTERS
   Colonies are massive, divided into parallel or irregular ridges or hillocks. Corallites are small, giving colonies a smooth appearance; they have strongly alternating septo-costae.

COLOUR
   Uniform grey.

SIMILAR SPECIES
   None. Corallites are like *P. clavus* but smaller, with more exsert primary septo–costae.

DISTRIBUTION
   From the Nicobar Islands east to the Marshall Islands.
   Around Australia: the Great Barrier Reef, Coral Sea and south to Lord Howe Island excluding the Solitary Islands in the east, and south to Houtman Abrolhos Islands on the west coast.

ABUNDANCE
   Uncommon but colonies may be very large, over 10 m in diameter.

x2.5

1. *Pavona minuta*, showing its most common growth form on the Great Barrier Reef.
PHOTOGRAPH: RON AND VALERIE TAYLOR.

2. *Pavona minuta* at the Ryukyu Islands, Japan.
PHOTOGRAPH: AUTHOR.

Pavona varians

VERRILL, 1864

TYPE LOCALITY
Hawaii.

IDENTIFYING CHARACTERS
Colonies are submassive, laminar or encrusting or various combinations of these. Corallites are in short irregular valleys, or are aligned between ridges perpendicular to margins, or are irregularly distributed on flat surfaces. Septa are in a two alternating orders.

COLOUR
Yellow, green and brown.

SIMILAR SPECIES
P. venosa has similar corallites, but walls between valleys are acute and septa are generally in three orders; columellae are less developed and septa are more widely spaced.

DISTRIBUTION
From the Red Sea east to Hawaii and Tahiti.
Around Australia: the Great Barrier Reef and south to Lord Howe Island excluding the Solitary Islands in the east, and south to Houtman Abrolhos Islands on the west coast.

ABUNDANCE
Occurs in a very wide range of habitats and may be common in some lagoons and sheltered upper reef slopes.

×2.5

1. A large colony of *Pavona varians* with irregular horizontal laminae, the most common growth form of the species.
PHOTOGRAPH: ED LOVELL.

2. *Pavona varians* at the Whitsunday Islands, Great Barrier Reef. Such colonies closely resemble *P. venosa* and *Leptoseris mycetoseroides.*
PHOTOGRAPH: LEN ZELL.

3. Surface detail of *Pavona varians.*
PHOTOGRAPH: ED LOVELL.

Pavona venosa

(EHRENBERG, 1834)

TYPE LOCALITY
Red Sea.

IDENTIFYING CHARACTERS
Colonies are massive or columnar. Corallites are nearly subcerioid or are in short valleys with acute walls. Septo-costae are generally in three orders, and are widely spaced. Columellae are poorly developed or absent.

COLOUR
Yellow-brown or pinkish-brown, sometimes mottled.

SIMILAR SPECIES
P. varians.

DISTRIBUTION
From the Red Sea east to the Marshall Islands.
Around Australia: the Great Barrier Reef and Coral Sea in the east, and south to North West Cape on the west coast.

ABUNDANCE
Occurs in a wide range of habitats but is uncommon.

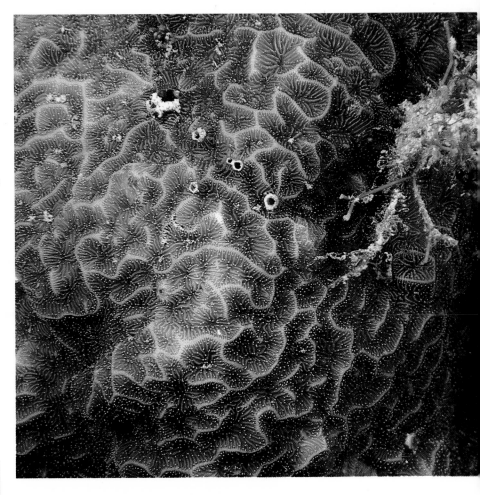

x2.5

Pavona venosa at Torres Strait, Great Barrier Reef, showing the short valleys and acute walls which characterise the species.
PHOTOGRAPH: LEN ZELL.

Pavona maldivensis

(GARDINER, 1905)

TYPE LOCALITY
Maldive Islands.

IDENTIFYING CHARACTERS
Colonies are columnar, or thin horizontal plates, or mixtures of these. Corallites are circular, plocoid, usually of irregular sizes. Those near plate margins may be aligned in parallel rows.

COLOUR
Pale or dark grey-brown or green, sometimes bright orange.

SIMILAR SPECIES
None.

DISTRIBUTION
From Madagascar east to the Marshall Islands.
Around Australia: the Great Barrier Reef, Coral Sea and south to Lord Howe Island excluding the Solitary Islands in the east, and Rowley Shoals and Scott Reef on the west coast.

ABUNDANCE
May be common on upper reef slopes and outer reef flats. The columnar form is usually found where wave action is strong.

x2.5

1. *Pavona maldivensis* at the Swain Reefs, Great Barrier Reef, showing the most common growth form in shallow water. In deeper water, the columns have flat plates around their bases or, rarely, consist only of flat plates.
PHOTOGRAPH: ED LOVELL.

2. The tops of *Pavona maldivensis* columns.
PHOTOGRAPH: ED LOVELL.

3. The characteristic appearance of the polyps of *Pavona maldivensis*. In shallow water, such colonies may be a striking iridescent orange colour which the camera with flashlight fails to capture.
PHOTOGRAPH: RON AND VALERIE TAYLOR.

GENUS
LEPTOSERIS

(pronounced lep-toe-seer-is)

Edwards & Haime, 1849

Leptoseris colonies are generally found on lower reef slopes, especially under overhangs and in the openings of caverns, on lagoon floors and also on the ocean floor between reefs. Most species have a delicate leafy appearance. They are usually uncommon and found only by scuba divers.

TYPE SPECIES
Leptoseris fragilis Edwards & Haime, 1849 from the Bourbon Islands. .

FOSSIL RECORD
Oligocene to Recent from the West Indies and Indo-Pacific.

NUMBER OF SPECIES
Twenty-five nominal species, approximately 14 true species, eight of which are Australian.

CHARACTERS
Colonies are foliaceous, sometimes laminar or encrusting, the former being usually unifacial. They frequently have a distinctive central corallite. Corallites have poorly defined walls. They are small shallow depressions with a central columella, usually separated by ridges and interconnected by fine septo-costae.

SIMILAR GENERA
Leptoseris is close to *Pavona*.

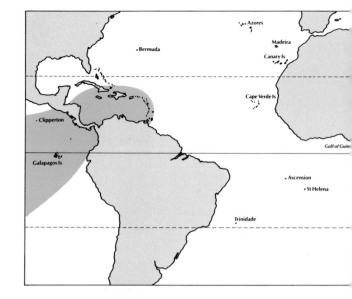

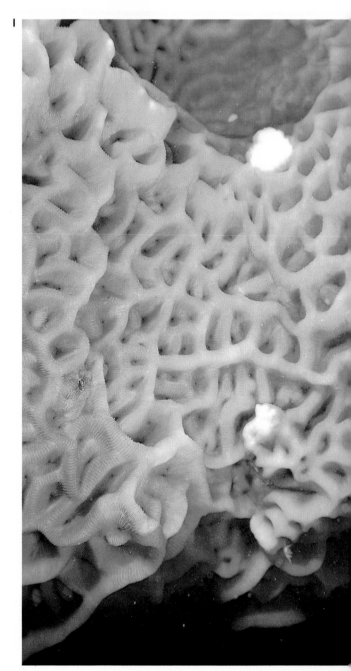

1. *Leptoseris mycetoseroides* is often composed of a series of small folds arranged perpendicularly to each other.
PHOTOGRAPH: ED LOVELL.

2. The common appearance of *Leptoseris yabei*, composed of laminae with radiating ridges.
PHOTOGRAPH: ED LOVELL.

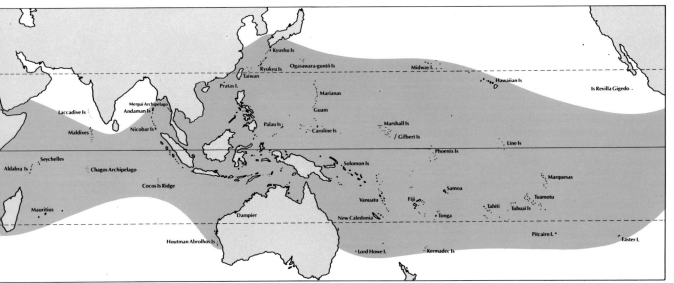

The known range of *Leptoseris*.

2

Leptoseris papyracea

(DANA, 1846)

TYPE LOCALITY
Sulu Sea.

IDENTIFYING CHARACTERS
Colonies are delicate, unifacial, contorted and with irregularly divided fronds, each frond with a few corallites.

COLOUR
Pale-brown upper surface, white undersurface.

SIMILAR SPECIES
L. gardineri is larger and coarser.

DISTRIBUTION
Madagascar and the Amirante Islands east to Hawaii and possibly the far eastern Pacific. Around Australia: the northern and central Great Barrier Reef in the east, and Scott Reef on the west coast.

ABUNDANCE
Restricted to inter-reef areas on soft horizontal substrates where there is little sediment movement. Usually uncommon.

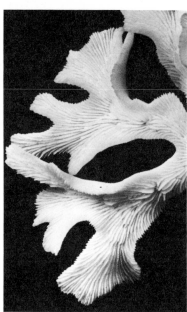

x2.5

Part of a large colony of *Leptoseris papyracea* at the Mergui Archipelago, Thailand.
PHOTOGRAPH: AUTHOR.

Leptoseris gardineri

VAN DER HORST, 1921

TYPE LOCALITY
Indonesia.

IDENTIFYING CHARACTERS
Colonies are horizontal, unifacial, subdividing fronds. Corallites are aligned on the centre of narrow parts of fronds or several may be aligned transversely on broad parts.

COLOUR
Pale or orangy-brown.

SIMILAR SPECIES
L. papyracea is like a diminutive *L. gardineri*.

DISTRIBUTION
From the Maldive Islands east to the Marshall Islands and Samoa. Around Australia: the Great Barrier Reef in the east; not found on the west coast.

ABUNDANCE
Uncommon except on some lower reef slopes with soft substrates where monospecific stands may be over 10 m in diameter.

x2.5

1. *Leptoseris gardineri* at the Swain Reefs, Great Barrier Reef. Such colonies, which may be very extensive, are found only in turbid water.
PHOTOGRAPH: ED LOVELL.

2. The distinctive, beautifully sculptured polyps of *Leptoseris gardineri*.
PHOTOGRAPH: ED LOVELL.

Leptoseris explanata

YABE & SUGIYAMA, 1941

TYPE LOCALITY
Palau.

IDENTIFYING CHARACTERS
Colonies are composed of unifacial laminae which may be horizontal with entire or lobed margins, or contorted and partly upright. Corallites are widely spaced and outwardly inclined. Septo–costae alternate strongly, forming fine but conspicuous radiating ridges.

COLOUR
Pale brown or yellow-brown, often with white margins.

SIMILAR SPECIES
Closest to *L. gardineri* and *L. scabra*.

DISTRIBUTION
From the Red Sea to Palau and Australia.
Around Australia: the Great Barrier Reef, Coral Sea and Elizabeth and Middleton Reefs in the east, and south to Houtman Abrolhos Islands on the west coast.

ABUNDANCE
Seldom common except on vertical or overhang faces, especially of lower reef slopes.

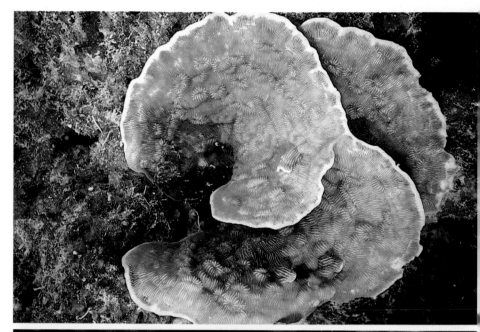

x2.5

1. The usual appearance of *Leptoseris explanata* on the Great Barrier Reef.
PHOTOGRAPH: ED LOVELL.

2. The polyps of *Leptoseris explanata*.
PHOTOGRAPH: ED LOVELL.

302

Leptoseris scabra

VAUGHAN, 1907

TYPE LOCALITY
Hawaii.

IDENTIFYING CHARACTERS
Colonies are composed of encrusting unifacial laminae which may become highly contorted, forming hollow columns or tubes and fronds. Corallites become more widely spaced towards the colony perimeter. They are not outwardly inclined. Septo–costae alternate strongly.

COLOUR
Dull grey, brown or green, usually with white margins.

SIMILAR SPECIES
Resembles many species, especially *L. hawaiiensis* which is distinguished by its deep, rounded corallites and a very smooth coenosteum.

DISTRIBUTION
From Mauritius east to Hawaii and Tahiti.
Around Australia: the Great Barrier Reef, Coral Sea, Elizabeth and Middleton Reefs and Lord Howe Island in the east, and south to Houtman Abrolhos Islands on the west coast.

ABUNDANCE
Found usually on vertical or overhang walls.

1

2

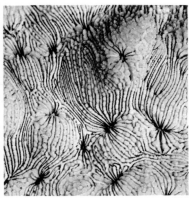

x2.5

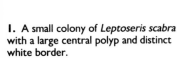

1. A small colony of *Leptoseris scabra* with a large central polyp and distinct white border.
PHOTOGRAPH: LEN ZELL.

2. The common appearance of *Leptoseris scabra*.
PHOTOGRAPH: ED LOVELL.

Leptoseris hawaiiensis

VAUGHAN, 1907

TYPE LOCALITY
 Hawaii.

IDENTIFYING CHARACTERS
 Colonies are encrusting laminae.
 Corallites are deep and rounded,
 irregularly distributed and
 slightly inclined towards the
 perimeter. Septo-costae are very
 even, giving the coenosteum a
 smooth appearance.

COLOUR
 Brown or green, usually mottled.

SIMILAR SPECIES
 L. scabra.

DISTRIBUTION
 From the Mascarene Archipelago
 and Red Sea east to Hawaii and
 Tahiti.
 Around Australia: the Great
 Barrier Reef, Coral Sea and Lord
 Howe Island in the east, and
 south to Houtman Abrolhos
 Islands on the west coast.

ABUNDANCE
 Uncommon, found on vertical or
 overhanging walls.

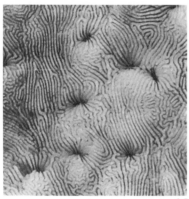

x2.5

Leptoseris hawaiiensis at Torres Strait,
showing the characteristic appearance of
the polyps.
PHOTOGRAPH: LEN ZELL.

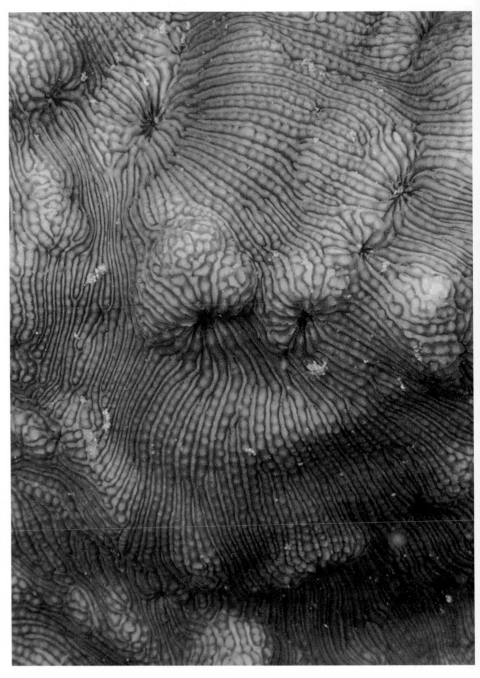

Leptoseris mycetoseroides

WELLS, 1954

TYPE LOCALITY
Marshall Islands.

IDENTIFYING CHARACTERS
Colonies are encrusting or laminar with a surface of small irregular folds. Corallites are crowded between the folds except towards the periphery where they are aligned in rows parallel to the margins. They are outwardly inclined. Septo-costae are fine and even.

COLOUR
Mottled brown and green, usually dark colours if in shade.

SIMILAR SPECIES
L. foliosa and *L. yabei*, also *Pavona varians*.

DISTRIBUTION
From Madagascar east to the Marshall Islands.
Around Australia: the Great Barrier Reef and Coral Sea in the east, and south to Houtman Abrolhos Islands on the west coast.

ABUNDANCE
Sometimes common on reef slopes protected from wave action especially on steeply sloping or vertical walls, where they frequently exceed 1 m in diameter.

×2.5

1. The most common appearance of *Leptoseris mycetoseroides*, Torres Strait, Great Barrier Reef.
PHOTOGRAPH: LEN ZELL.

2. *Leptoseris mycetoseroides* at the Swain Reefs, Great Barrier Reef, showing the relatively smooth surface of colonies from lower reef slopes.
PHOTOGRAPH: ED LOVELL.

Leptoseris yabei
(PILLAI & SCHEER, 1976)

TYPE LOCALITY
Maldive Islands.

IDENTIFYING CHARACTERS
Colonies are laminar plates, in whorls or tiers or vase-shaped. Corallites are situated between radiating ridges or folds and are separated by secondary folds parallel to the margins. Septo-costae alternate and are exsert.

COLOUR
Usually pale brown or yellowish, sometimes with white margins.

SIMILAR SPECIES
L. mycetoseroides.

DISTRIBUTION
Maldive Islands and Australia. Around Australia: the Great Barrier Reef and Coral Sea in the east, and south to Houtman Abrolhos Islands on the west coast.

ABUNDANCE
Common on flat substrates. Colonies may exceed 1 m in diameter and are usually conspicuous.

×2.5

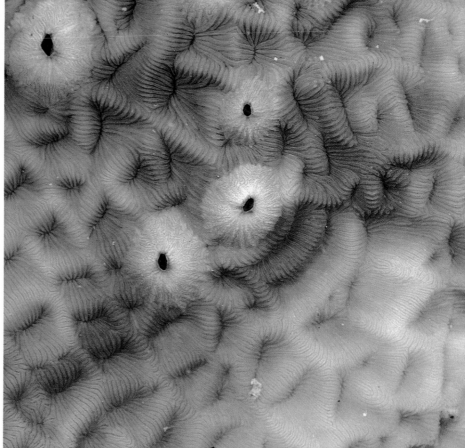

1. A large colony of *Leptoseris yabei*, composed of encrusting and tiered laminae.
PHOTOGRAPH: LEN ZELL.

2. The surface detail of *Leptoseris yabei*. Polyps are grouped into pockets, each pocket being separated by radiating, as well as concentric, ridges.
PHOTOGRAPH: LEN ZELL.

Leptoseris foliosa

DINESEN, 1980

SYNONYM

Previously called *L. tenuis* by the author.

TYPE LOCALITY

Lizard Island, Great Barrier Reef.

IDENTIFYING CHARACTERS

Colonies are laminar plates either encrusting or in whorls or tiers, with or without radiating folds. Corallites are in irregular rows parallel to the margins, and are small and shallow. Columellae are conspicuous. Septo-costae are fine.

COLOUR

Cream or brown.

SIMILAR SPECIES

L. mycetoseroides.

DISTRIBUTION

From the Amirante and Providence Islands east to the Solomon and Paternoster Islands. Around Australia: the Great Barrier Reef and Coral Sea in the east, and south to Houtman Abrolhos Islands on the west coast.

ABUNDANCE

Uncommon, found on vertical or overhang walls.

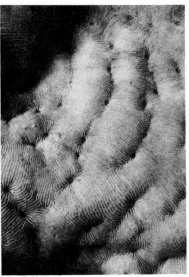

×2.5

Leptoseris foliosa at Torres Strait. Colonies are seldom better developed than this one and lack distinctive characters.

PHOTOGRAPH: LEN ZELL.

Genus GARDINEROSERIS

(pronounced gar-din-ner-oh-seer-is)

Scheer & Pillai, 1974

COMMON SYNONYM
Agariciella Ma, 1937.

TYPE SPECIES
Agaracia ponderosa Gardiner, 1905 from the Maldive Islands.

FOSSIL RECORD
None.

NUMBER OF SPECIES
Two species, only one of which has been named.

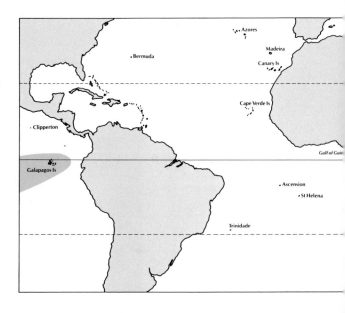

Gardineroseris planulata

(DANA, 1846)

TYPE LOCALITY
Unrecorded.

IDENTIFYING CHARACTERS
Colonies are massive to encrusting, sometimes with laminar margins. Corallites have poorly defined walls but are separated by acute ridges so that each corallite or group of corallites is at the bottom of a neat excavation. Columellae are present and septo-costae are very fine and even. Polyps are rarely extended and only at night.

COLOUR
Usually purple-grey, sometimes brown or yellow.

SIMILAR SPECIES
A second species of *Gardineroseris* with finer corallites has been recorded from Thailand. Otherwise the species is distinct.

DISTRIBUTION
The full range of the genus. Around Australia: the Great Barrier Reef and the Solitary Islands in the east, and south to Houtman Abrolhos Islands on the west coast.

ABUNDANCE
Uncommon throughout its range except on some walls or under overhangs. Usually requires clear water.

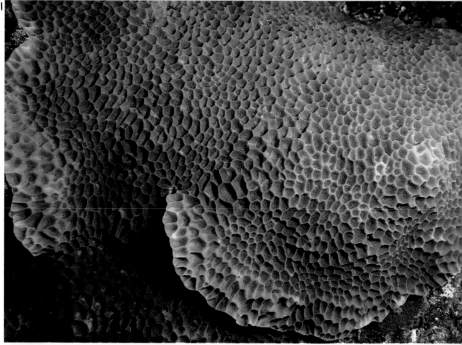

x2.5

1. A large colony of *Gardineroseris planulata* on an upper reef slope.
PHOTOGRAPH: ED LOVELL.

2. The surface detail of *Gardineroseris planulata*.
PHOTOGRAPH: AUTHOR.

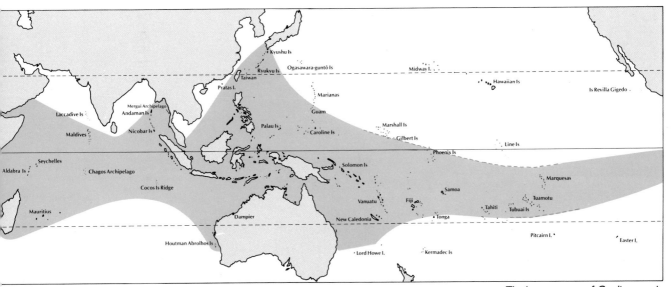

The known range of *Gardineroseris*.

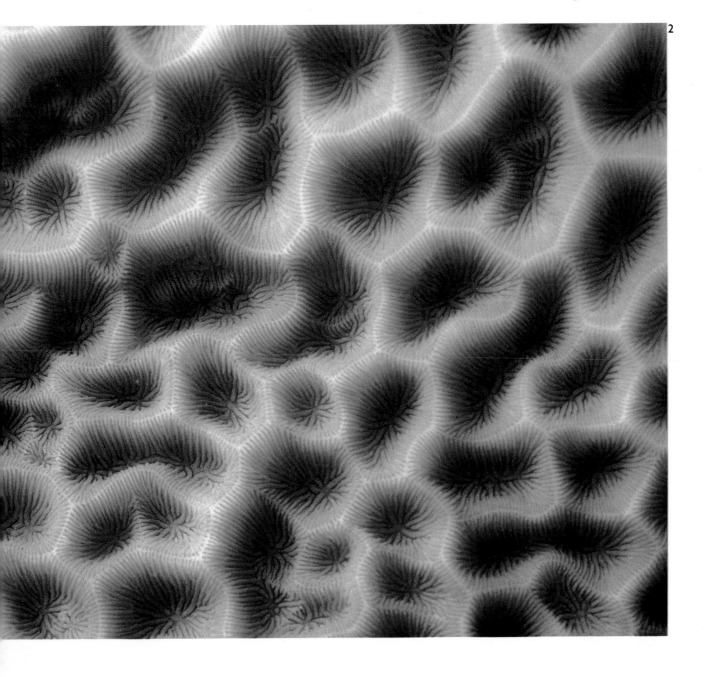

2

GENUS
COELOSERIS

(pronounced *see-loh-seer-is*)

Vaughan, 1918

TYPE SPECIES
Coeloseris mayeri Vaughan, 1918.

FOSSIL RECORD
Pliocene to Recent.

NUMBER OF SPECIES
Three nominal species, one true species.

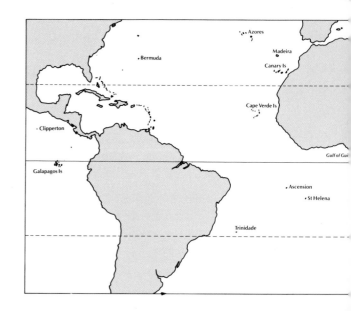

Coeloseris mayeri
VAUGHAN, 1918

TYPE LOCALITY
Torres Strait, Great Barrier Reef.

IDENTIFYING CHARACTERS
Colonies are massive either rounded or hillocky. Corallites are cerioid, without columellae and with *Pavona*-like septo-costae. Polyps are extended only at night.

COLOUR
Pale green, yellow or brown with darker calices.

SIMILAR SPECIES
Coeloseris is a well-defined genus closest to *Pavona*. Superficially it looks like a faviid, especially *Goniastrea* and *Leptastrea*.

DISTRIBUTION
Around Australia: the Great Barrier Reef and Elizabeth and Middleton Reefs in the east, and Rowley Shoals and Scott Reef on the west coast.

ABUNDANCE
May be common on some upper reef slopes and lagoons of the northern and central Great Barrier Reef. Rare elsewhere.

x2.5

1. A large colony of *Coeloseris mayeri*.
PHOTOGRAPH: ED LOVELL.
2. Polyps of *Coeloseris mayeri*.
PHOTOGRAPH: ED LOVELL.

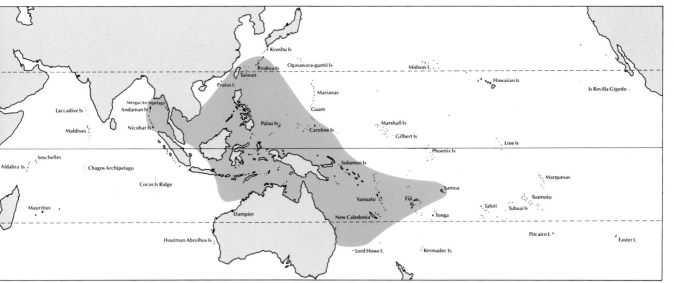

The known range of *Coeloseris mayeri*.

GENUS
PACHYSERIS
(pronounced pak-ee-seer-is)

Edwards & Haime, 1849

TYPE SPECIES
Agaricia rugosa Lamarck, 1801.

FOSSIL RECORD
Miocene to Recent from the Indo-Pacific.

NUMBER OF SPECIES
Twelve nominal species, most of which are synonyms
of the two true Australian species.

CHARACTERS
Colonies are laminar and unifacial, to branching and
bifacial. Branches are usually highly contorted. The
surface is a series of concentric ridges parallel with the
margins.
Corallite centres are not discernable. Valleys are
concentric and parallel to the corallum edge. Columellae
are wall-like with lobed upper margins or absent. Septo-
costae are very fine, even and tightly compacted.
Extended polyps have never been observed day or night.

SIMILAR GENERA
Pachyseris is a well-defined genus resembling only
Agaricia from the West Indies.

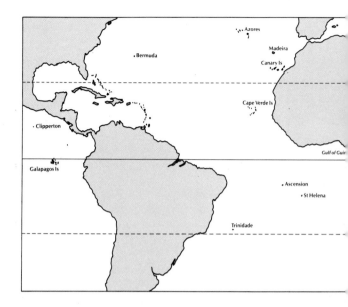

I. *Pachyseris rugosa* in a lagoon at Scott
Reef, Western Australia.
PHOTOGRAPH: AUTHOR.
2. The tall fronds of a large colony of
Pachyseris rugosa.
PHOTOGRAPH: ED LOVELL.

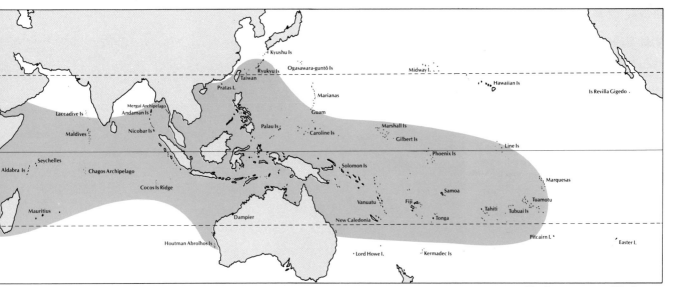

The known range of *Pachyseris*

2

Pachyseris rugosa
(LAMARCK, 1801)

TYPE LOCALITY
"Southern Ocean".

IDENTIFYING CHARACTERS
Colonies consist of upright irregular, usually contorted, anastomosing bifacial plates. Columellae are wall-like lobes.

COLOUR
Deep bluish-grey or brown.

SIMILAR SPECIES
P. speciosa.

DISTRIBUTION
From the Red Sea east to the Marshall Islands, Micronesia and Samoa.
Around Australia: the Great Barrier Reef in the east, and south to Houtman Abrolhos Islands on the west coast.

ABUNDANCE
Common, may develop into mound-shaped colonies over 8 m in diameter in shallow turbid water, but smaller colonies occur in a wide range of habitats.

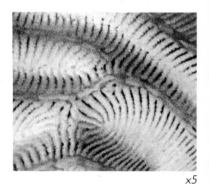

×5

1. A very large colony of *Pachyseris rugosa* in a lagoon in the Swain Reef, Great Barrier Reef.
PHOTOGRAPH: ED LOVELL.
2. Surface detail of *Pachyseris rugosa.*
PHOTOGRAPH: ED LOVELL.

Pachyseris speciosa

(DANA, 1846)

TYPE LOCALITY
"East Indies".

IDENTIFYING CHARACTERS
Colonies are unifacial laminae, usually horizontal, but may develop upright ridges or columns. More than one row of corallites may occur between ridges. Columellae are absent.

COLOUR
Pale brown to deep grey.

SIMILAR SPECIES
P. rugosa, readily distinguished by its growth form and the presence of columellae.

DISTRIBUTION
From the Red Sea east to the Line Islands, Samoa and Tahiti. Around Australia: the Great Barrier Reef and Coral Sea in the east, and south to Houtman Abrolhos Islands on the west coast.

ABUNDANCE
Common over a wide range of habitats, colonies are seldom over 2 m in diameter.

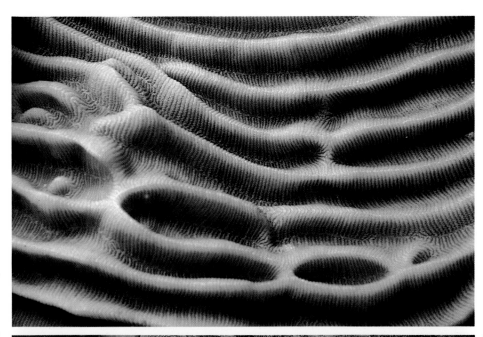
1

2

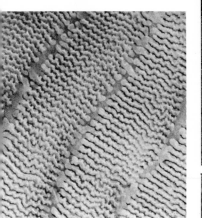

x5

3

1, 3. Surface detail of *Pachyseris speciosa*.
PHOTOGRAPHS: AUTHOR.

2. The usual appearance of a small *Pachyseris speciosa* colony.
PHOTOGRAPH: LEN ZELL.

315

FAMILY
FUNGIIDAE

(pronounced fun-dgee-id-ee)

DANA, 1846

Most free-living (unattached) corals found on reefs are fungiids and these are a common sight on almost all Indo-Pacific reefs. They include the common "mushroom corals" (*Fungia*), the "slipper corals" (*Herpetoglossa* and *Polyphyllia*) and "Neptune's Cap" (*Halomitra*) which possesses one of the oldest common names given to any coral.

As most reef fungiids are free-living it might be expected that they would also be abundant in deep oceanic water (as ahermatypic species) where free-living forms predominate, but this is not so—only one living ahermatypic genus, *Fungiacyathus*, is known.

The majority of fungiids are solitary. The polyps are among the largest of all corals—in the case of *Heliofungia*, polyps frequently reach a diameter of over 50 cm, including their long anemone-like tentacles. These solitary forms have a long fossil history extending back to the early origins of the Scleractinia. It is therefore likely that the colonial genera have evolved from the solitary ones, rather than the reverse. This theory is supported by the fact that the structure of the septa of each colonial genus has an equivalent in one of the subgenera of *Fungia*.

Comparisons between free-living fungiids raise the question: when does an individual polyp cease to be an individual and become a colony? Most individuals of *Diaseris* and *Fungia* have one mouth and are clearly solitary, but abnormal specimens of many species may have two or more mouths. *Fungia simplex* always has a series of mouths (and is thus usually placed in a genus of its own) but in all other respects is clearly related closely to *F. echinata*, which has one mouth. Is one specimen of *Polyphyllia* a colony where the individual has almost no separate identity except for a mouth and one tentacle, or is it an individual, with a clearly defined structure which includes mouths all over the upper surface of its body? As a general rule, corals with one mouth are called solitary and those with many mouths are called colonial, but clearly this distinction is not always well defined, nor is it basic to the structural organisation of several species.

Like most corals, fungiids display several methods of asexual as well as sexual reproduction, but some of these are rarely found in other groups. Most solitary fungiids are able to regenerate after damage, but *Diaseris* regularly undergoes natural autotomy: individuals break apart and regenerate as two or more individuals. Many species of *Fungia* are able to generate daughter polyps (acanthocauli) on their upper or lower surface if they become partly buried or damaged. This appears to be a form of asexual budding in some instances, but could also be the result of sexually or asexually produced planulae in others. In the normal cycle of sexual reproduction, acanthocauli develop from planula larvae which attach themselves to any solid substrate. A vase-shaped polyp is formed which develops a spreading upper surface that may reach several centimetres in diameter before it becomes detached from the substrate through degeneration of the stalk, a process helped by boring sponges. *Heliofungia* species have been reported to be hermaphrodite while *Fungia* have separate sexes. It is likely, however, that the whole family has separate sexes, the females either brooding planulae or releasing gametes.

Opposite: *Fungia (Pleuractis) scutaria.* PHOTOGRAPH: ED LOVELL

Little is known about many important aspects of the biology of free-living fungiids, especially their population dynamics, food sources and growth rates. One distinctive aspect of the daily existence of all but the heaviest fungiids is that they are at least partially mobile. Most can extract themselves from sand when buried, and *Cycloseris*, *Diaseris* and most *Fungia* are capable of lateral movement. *Cycloseris* and *Diaseris* are readily able to right themselves if overturned and both are able to climb over obstacles by using their tentacles and inflating their body cavities.

CHARACTERS

Solitary or colonial, free-living or attached, mostly hermatypic and extant. Colonial genera are derived from solitary genera and each has septo-costal structures corresponding to those of a solitary genus. These septo-costae radiate from the mouth on the upper surface (as septa) and from the centre of the undersurface (as costae).

SIMILAR FAMILIES
None.

EARLIEST FOSSILS
Cretaceous.

THE GENERA

The Fungiidae includes 11 extant genera—*Cycloseris*, *Diaseris*, *Heliofungia*, *Fungia*, *Herpolitha*, *Polyphyllia*, *Halomitra*, *Sandalolitha*, *Lithophyllon*, *Podabacia* and *Zoopilus*. They are an Indo-Pacific family with all extant genera occurring in Australia except *Zoopilus*. *Zoopilus* is a very distinctive genus forming large dome-shaped, free-living colonies which are very delicate and have septo-costae like *Fungia* (*Ctenactis*).
Fungiacyathus is the only extant ahermatype.

KEY TO GENERA OF AUSTRALIAN FUNGIIDAE

Corallum solitary

Corallum consists of 1 to several fan-shaped segments . . . *Diaseris* (p. 326)

Corallum not as above

Septal teeth and costal spines fine, corallum small . . . *Cycloseris* (p. 320)

Septal teeth and/or costal spines coarse

Septal teeth large broad lobes, polyps with very large tentacles . . . *Heliofungia* (p. 328)

Septal teeth not broad lobes, polyps with small tentacles . . . *Fungia* (p. 330)

Corallum colonial

Colony free-living

Colony elongate with an axial furrow

Secondary centres outside axial furrow absent . . . *Fungia simplex* (p. 347)

Secondary centres present

Primary septa long, with large lobes . . . *Herpolitha* (p. 348)

Primary septa short, petaloid . . . *Polyphyllia* (p. 352)

Colony rounded, dome-shaped, without an axial furrow

Colony heavily constructed with lobed septa . . . *Sandalolitha* (p. 356)

Colony lightly constructed with toothed septa . . . *Halomitra* (p. 354)

Colony attached

Septo-costae low, compact, granular . . . *Lithophyllon* (p. 358)

Septo-costae large, lobed . . . *Podabacia* (p. 360)

Note: This key is a guide only and should be used in conjunction with descriptions of the genera.

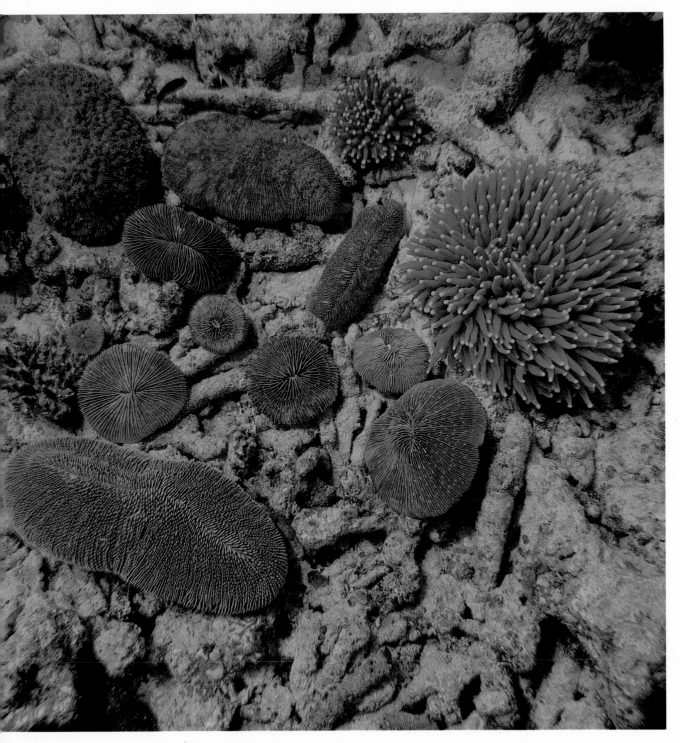

Free-living fungiids.
PHOTOGRAPH: ED LOVELL.

GENUS *CYCLOSERIS*

(pronounced sigh-klo-seer-is)

Edwards & Haime, 1849

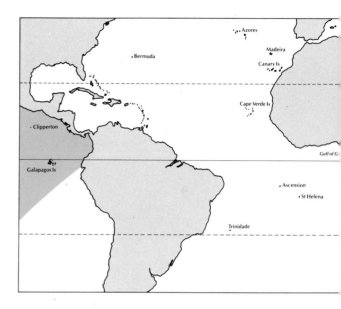

Cycloseris species are seldom found in any habitat other than on flat sandy substrates between reefs. Even here, however, there is only one common species, *C. cyclolites*, with *C. patelliformis* being the only other species that is not rare. *C. cyclolites* may occur in large numbers in association with other free-living corals, notably *Heteropsammia*, *Heterocyathus*, *Trachyphyllia* and *Diaseris*. All of these are well adapted to living on soft substrates and can readily uncover themselves if buried. They can also right themselves if turned upside down and all except *Trachyphyllia* are highly mobile. As far as *Cycloseris* is concerned, much of this mobility appears to be achieved by the action of ciliary hairs on the body surface, by the inflation of the body cavity with water and, reportedly, by the use of tentacles.

C. *cyclolites* is recognised easily by its neat, fine, symmetrical structure and concave lower surface. *C. patelliformis* is likewise neat and finely structured. The other species of *Cycloseris* are more easily confused with immature *Fungia* (*Verrillofungia*) species.

TYPE SPECIES
Fungia cyclolites Lamarck, 1816.

FOSSIL RECORD
Cretaceous to Recent from Eurasia and the Indo-Pacific.

NUMBER OF SPECIES
Fifteen nominal species, seven true species from Australia.

CHARACTERS
Corals are solitary, free-living, flat or dome-shaped, circular or slightly oval in outline, with a central mouth. Septa have fine teeth, costae are fine, without undersurface pits.
Polyps are usually extended only at night. Fine tentacles cover the upper surface of the disc.

SIMILAR GENERA
Cycloseris is close to *Fungia* and resembles *Diaseris*. *Fungia* grows to much larger sizes than *Cycloseris*, may be elongate, has septa with larger teeth, and costae composed of rows of spines.
Diaseris is composed of wedge-shaped segments giving an irregular shape, septa are thick with blunt teeth.

×25

Diagram 17. The fine structure of the septal teeth (above) and costal spines (below) of *Cycloseris*.
DRAWINGS: GEOFF KELLY.

Right: Two solitary free-living corals at the Palm Islands, Great Barrier Reef: *Cycloseris cyclolites* and the smaller *Diaseris distorta*. These species are often found together on soft sandy substrates where both are highly mobile.
PHOTOGRAPH: ED LOVELL.

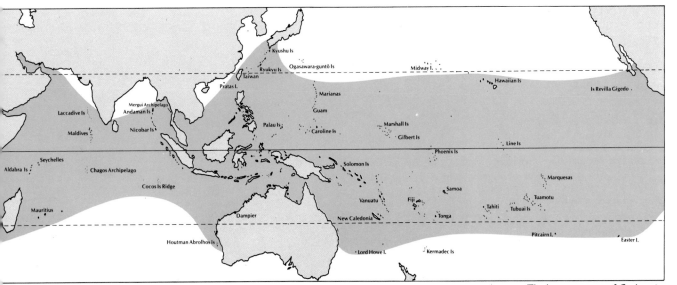

The known range of *Cycloseris*.

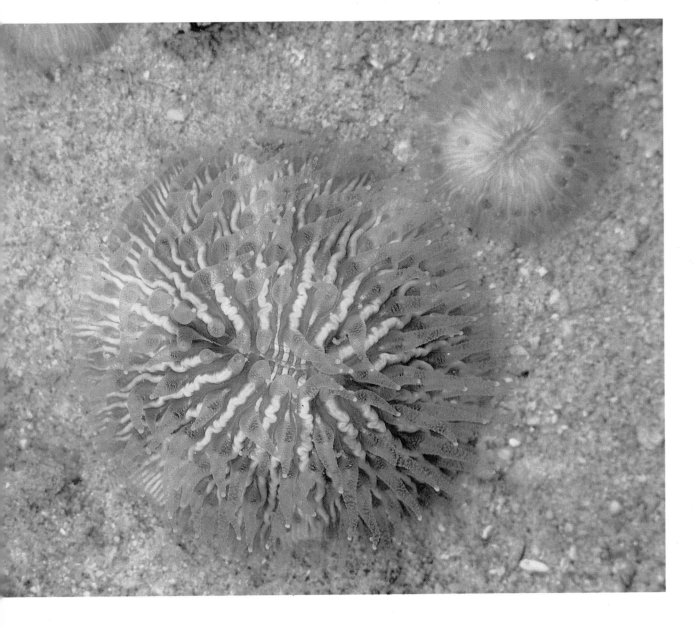

Cycloseris cyclolites

(LAMARCK, 1801)

TYPE LOCALITY
"Southern Ocean".

IDENTIFYING CHARACTERS
Corals are circular domes up to 40 mm in diameter with a concave undersurface. Septa are straight and symmetrical. Primary septa are thick and exsert around the mouth.

COLOUR
Pale cream or greenish.

SIMILAR SPECIES
C. costulata, but *C. cyclolites* is very distinctive.

DISTRIBUTION
From the Red Sea east to Japan, Palau and Australia.
Around Australia: the Great Barrier Reef in the east, and south to Dirk Hartog Island on the west coast.

ABUNDANCE
Common on flat inter-reef soft substrates.

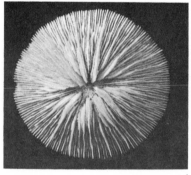

x1

Cycloseris cyclolites with polyps extended. This is by far the most common species of *Cycloseris* and the only one occurring in any quantities. It is usually found on soft sandy substrates between reefs.
PHOTOGRAPH: RON AND VALERIE TAYLOR.

Cycloseris costulata

(ORTMANN, 1889)

TYPE LOCALITY
Sri Lanka.

IDENTIFYING CHARACTERS
Corals are circular, helmet-shaped, up to 76 mm in diameter with a concave undersurface. Primary septa are thick and exsert around the mouth.

COLOUR
Pale cream or brown.

SIMILAR SPECIES
C. cyclolites.

DISTRIBUTION
From the Maldive Islands east to the Bismark Archipelago. Around Australia: the Great Barrier Reef, and south to Elizabeth and Middleton Reefs and the Solitary Islands in the east; not found on the west coast.

ABUNDANCE
Rare, found unpredictably on lower reef slopes and inter-reef habitats.

x1

Cycloseries somervillei

(GARDINER, 1909)

TYPE LOCALITY
Seychelles Islands.

IDENTIFYING CHARACTERS
Corals are oval, flat, with a central dome and a flat undersurface. Primary septa are exsert on the central dome.

COLOUR
Not known.

SIMILAR SPECIES
C. patelliformis.

DISTRIBUTION
From the Seychelles Islands east to Fiji.
Around Australia: the Murray Islands only in the east; not found on the west coast.

ABUNDANCE
Very rare.

x1

Cycloseris erosa

(DÖDERLEIN, 1901)

TYPE LOCALITY
Unrecorded.

IDENTIFYING CHARACTERS
Corals are circular or subcircular, nearly flat to strongly convex with a flat or concave undersurface. Septa have ragged margins.

COLOUR
Not known.

SIMILAR SPECIES
None.

DISTRIBUTION
Japan, Indonesia and Australia. Around Australia: the Great Barrier Reef in the east; not found on the west coast.

ABUNDANCE
Very rare.

x1

Cycloseris patelliformis
(BOSCHMA, 1923)

TYPE LOCALITY
Indonesia.

IDENTIFYING CHARACTERS
Corals are circular to slightly oval, with a central dome and a nearly flat undersurface.

COLOUR
Pale brown or cream, sometimes with a dark perimeter.

SIMILAR SPECIES
C. somervillei, which is clearly oval.

DISTRIBUTION
From the Seychelles Islands east to Samoa.
Around Australia: Lizard Island only in the east, and south to Houtman Abrolhos Islands on the west coast.

ABUNDANCE
Usually uncommon.

 x1

1. *Cycloseris patelliformis* at the Dampier Archipelago, Western Australia.
PHOTOGRAPH: ED LOVELL.

2. *Cycloseris patelliformis* is much less common than *C. cyclolites* but all other *Cycloseris* species are rare. The neat symmetrical appearance seen here is typical of the species.
PHOTOGRAPH: ED LOVELL.

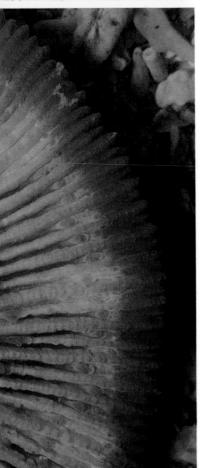

Cycloseris vaughani
(BOSCHMA, 1923)

TYPE LOCALITY
Hawaii.

IDENTIFYING CHARACTERS
Corals are circular, generally dome-shaped, with a flat undersurface. Costae near the perimeter are in distinctly different orders.

COLOUR
Not known.

SIMILAR SPECIES
This species is distinguished only by its costae.

DISTRIBUTION
From the Nicobar Islands east to Hawaii and the Easter Islands. Around Australia: Lizard Island only in the east, and south to Houtman Abrolhos Islands on the west coast.

ABUNDANCE
Very rare.

x1

Cycloseris marginata
(BOSCHMA, 1923)

TYPE LOCALITY
Indonesia.

IDENTIFYING CHARACTERS
Corals are circular and flat. Septa are in markedly different orders but each septum is uniform throughout its length, like *Diaseris*.

COLOUR
Not known.

SIMILAR SPECIES
None.

DISTRIBUTION
From the Red Sea east to Hawaii. Around Australia: Lizard Island only in the east; not found on the west coast.

ABUNDANCE
Very rare.

x1

GENUS
DIASERIS
(pronounced dye-a-seer-is)

Edwards & Haime, 1849

Diaseris is a small distinct genus related to *Cycloseris*. It is usually found in the same habitats as *Cycloseris cyclolites* and other free-living corals. It is seldom encountered by divers but where it does occur it is usually found in large numbers, either spread over the ocean floor or aggregated in patches.

The single distinctive feature of *Diaseris* is that it reproduces asexually by natural autotomy, so that a single individual will break up into several wedge-shaped daughter segments. Each of these can regenerate a mouth near the point of the wedge, and new growth occurs outward from this point. As a result, most individuals in any given population are at various stages of regeneration and differ greatly in size and shape.

TYPE SPECIES
Fungia distorta Michelin, 1843.

FOSSIL RECORD
None.

NUMBER OF SPECIES
Four nominal species, two true species are Australian.

CHARACTERS
Corals are solitary, free-living discs, flat, composed of several fan-shaped segments, with a mouth situated at the point of divergence of the segments. Septa are thick with blunt teeth resembling rows of granules.

SIMILAR GENERA
Diaseris resembles only *Cycloseris*.

1. At 20 m depth this area of flat sand and mud at the Palm Islands, Great Barrier Reef, is covered with *Diaseris distorta*. Concentrations of individuals to this degree are uncommon and seldom seen because they occur away from reefs.
PHOTOGRAPH: ED LOVELL.

2. The corallum of *Diaseris distorta* is covered by fine, delicate polyp tissue with short tentacles. These individuals may move several cm per day and can readily climb obstacles.
PHOTOGRAPH: ED LOVELL.

3. Showing the method of polyp fragmentation which *Diaseris* use in asexual reproduction.
PHOTOGRAPH: ED LOVELL.

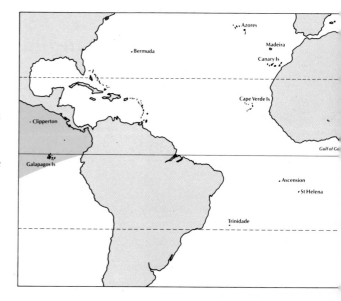

Diaseris distorta
(MICHELIN, 1843)

TYPE LOCALITY
Unrecorded.

IDENTIFYING CHARACTERS
Corals consist of fan-shaped segments up to 40 mm in diameter. Thick beaded septa are of unequal height.

COLOUR
Cream or brown, sometimes mottled.

SIMILAR SPECIES
D. fragilis is larger, with thinner margins and has septa of uniform height.

DISTRIBUTION
From the Red Sea east to Central America.
Around Australia: the Great Barrier Reef in the east, and Houtman Abrolhos Islands on the west coast.

ABUNDANCE
Restricted to soft substrates exposed to currents. Rarely found but plentiful where it occurs.

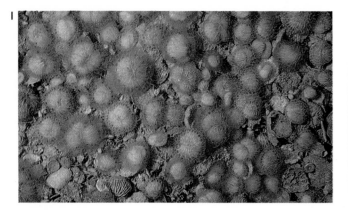

x2.5

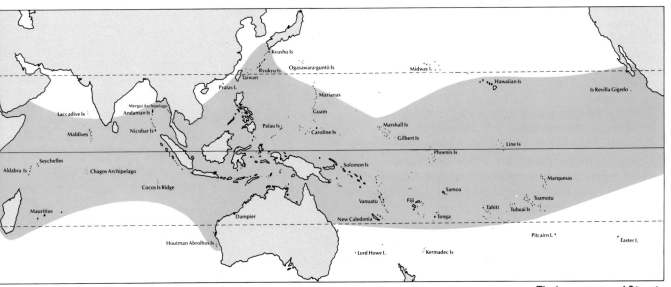

The known range of *Diaseris*.

Diaseris fragilis
ALCOCK, 1893

TYPE LOCALITY
Andaman Sea.

IDENTIFYING CHARACTERS
Corals are irregular in outline, up to 70 mm in diameter, generally composed of several wedge-shaped sectors which break apart readily. Thick beaded septa are approximately equal in height.

COLOUR
Greyish-yellow or beige, often with green margins or centres.

SIMILAR SPECIES
D. distorta.

DISTRIBUTION
From the Seychelles Islands east to the Marshall Islands and Hawaii.
Around Australia: the Great Barrier Reef in the east, and Houtman Abrolhos Islands on the west coast.

ABUNDANCE
Found on a wide range of lower reef slopes or flat substrates. Rarely found but plentiful where it occurs.

×2.5

4

5

4. *Diaseris fragilis* with its short tentacles fully extended. This specimen has been kept in an aquarium where it has become overlarge and developed several mouths (green).
PHOTOGRAPH: ED LOVELL.

5. *Diaseris fragilis* may occur in dense aggregations like *D. distorta* but large numbers of these species seldom occur together.
PHOTOGRAPH: AUTHOR.

GENUS
HELIOFUNGIA

(pronounced heel-ee-oh-fun-dgee-a)

Wells, 1966

Before coral biologists became aware of the difference between the size and shape of living polyps of *Heliofungia* and *Fungia*, the former was considered to be a subgenus of the latter. This difference in the polyps is all the more remarkable for the fact that the skeletons of the two genera differ in detail only, and that both genera occupy similar habitats.

TYPE SPECIES
Fungia actiniformis Quoy & Gaimard, 1833.

FOSSIL RECORD
None.

NUMBER OF SPECIES
One.

Heliofungia actiniformis
(QUOY & GAIMARD, 1833)

TYPE LOCALITY
Cocos-Keeling Islands.

IDENTIFYING CHARACTERS
Corals are solitary, free-living (except for juveniles), flat, with a central mouth. Septa have large lobed teeth.
Polyps are extended day and night and are the largest of all corals. They have long dark-purple or green tentacles with pale tips, very similar to those of giant anemones. The oral disc is striped and there is one mouth up to 30 mm wide.

SIMILAR SPECIES
Heliofungia skeletons are essentially similar to those of *Fungia*. *Fungia* polyps have short tapering tentacles extended only at night.

DISTRIBUTION
Around Australia: the Great Barrier Reef in the east, and south to Admiralty Gulf on the west coast.

ABUNDANCE
Commonly found on flat soft or rubble substrates, usually in reef lagoons. Very conspicuous.

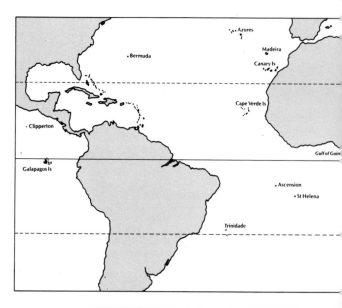

1. *Heliofungia actiniformis*. This solitary free-living species has the largest polyps of all corals. Specimens such as this exceed 50 cm in diameter. They closely resemble giant anemones, but never harbour fish. Polyps contract only vigorously disturbed. The white substance on the tentacle tips is sticky and comes off if touched.
PHOTOGRAPH: RON AND VALERIE TAYLOR.

x0.5

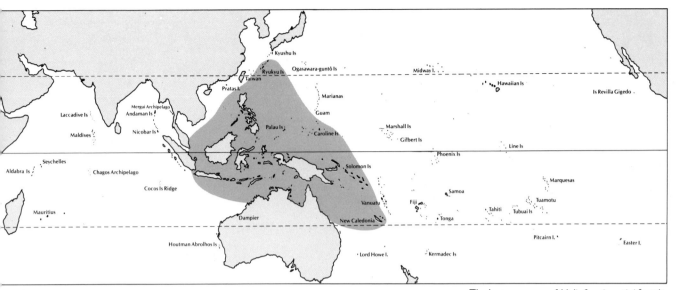

The known range of *Heliofungia actini formis*.

2. The long tentacles of *Heliofungia actiniformis* are able to retract slowly between the large teeth of the septa.
PHOTOGRAPH: RON AND VALERIE TAYLOR.

3. An immature *Heliofungia actiniformis* still attached to the substrate. The striped oral disc is typical of the species.
PHOTOGRAPH: JOHN BARNETT.

Genus
FUNGIA

(pronounced fun-dgee-a)

Lamarck, 1801

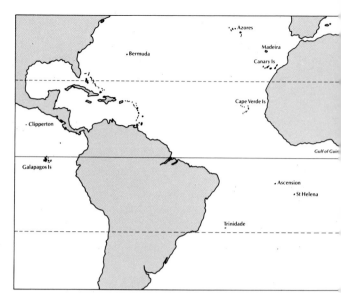

Fungia, universally known as mushroom corals, are the most abundant and widespread of the fungiids. Because they are all free-living, and are thus readily moved by waves, *Fungia* are usually found below the depth of strong wave action. They are especially common on the slopes of fringing reefs where many species are usually found together.

Most *Fungia* species are restricted to tropical or subtropical latitudes, either because they are intolerant of lower temperatures or because their larvae have limited powers of dispersal. *Fungia scutaria* is an exception to this rule: it is found in high-latitude reefs and is also exceptional in inhabiting exposed upper reef slopes where thick heavy specimens are commonly found wedged into crevices.

All *Fungia* species have similar short tapering tentacles with batteries of stinging nematocysts like those of *Cycloseris* and *Diaseris*, but are very distinct from those of *Heliofungia*. They are usually extended only at night and are readily retracted if disturbed. All species have wide slit-like mouths. Occasionally parasites reside inside the mouth and one species, the bivalve gastropod *Fungiacava eilatensis*, is found nowhere else.

Very young *Fungia*, called acanthocauli, bear little resemblance to the adult form. They are produced both asexually and sexually. Asexually produced acanthocauli apparently can develop from partly buried, damaged or dying parent tissue. They also develop from planula larvae. In either case, the result is a vase-shaped polyp that gradually grows into a flattened disc on a stalk. The septa, which were originally inside the corallite, develop on the upper surface while the costae, originally on the outside of the corallite, develop on the lower surface. The stalk becomes weakened by boring organisms and breaks near the disc leaving a central scar which is gradually overgrown. *Fungia* reproduce sexually by the release of gametes into the water. Sexes are separate.

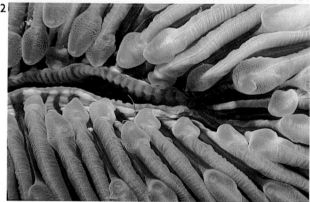

1. All *Fungia* species extend short, tapered tentacles at night.
PHOTOGRAPH: ED LOVELL.

2. The large mouth of *Fungia*. Sometimes a small bivalve, *Fungiacava eilatensis*, lives in the mouth. Why *Fungia* should have such large mouths is not clear, but they are sometimes seen feeding on jellyfish and this may be their main food source.
PHOTOGRAPH: RON AND VALERIE TAYLOR.

3. A partly dead *Fungia* in an aquarium. Small regenerating polyps (acanthocauli) can be seen budding from the remains of the parent.
PHOTOGRAPH: LEN ZELL.

4. The tentacles of *Fungia*. These are fully extended but show no similarity with those of *Heliofungia*.
PHOTOGRAPH: AUTHOR.

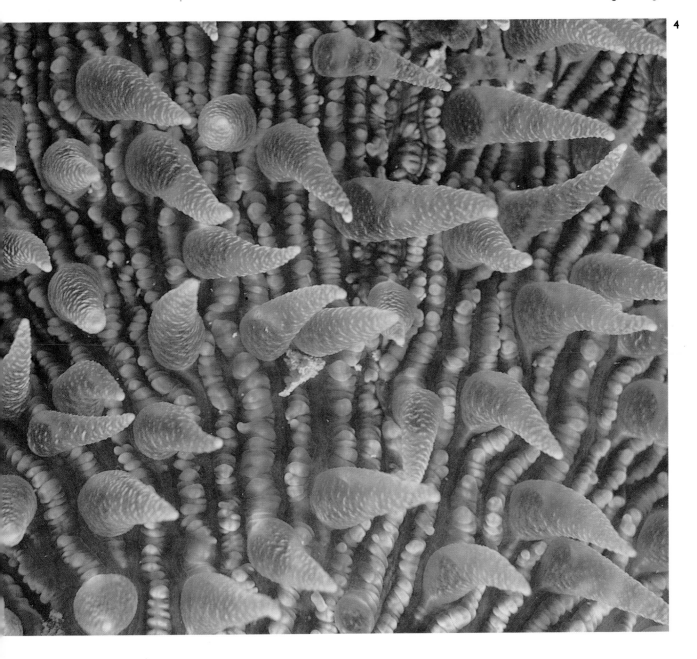

The known range of *Fungia*.

4

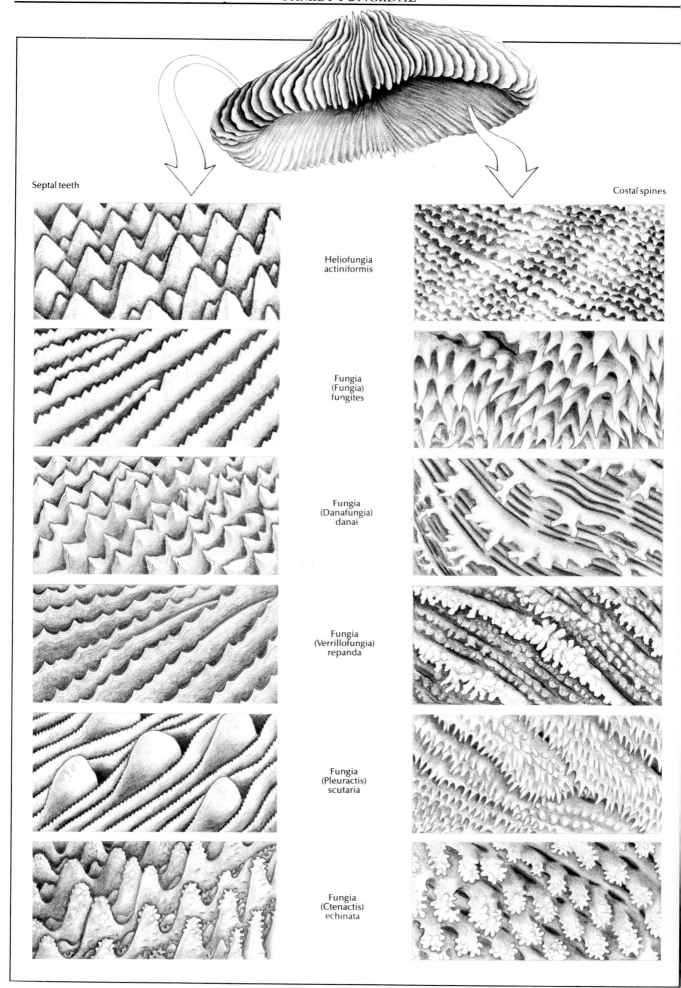

Septal teeth

Costal spines

Heliofungia
actiniformis

Fungia
(Fungia)
fungites

Fungia
(Danafungia)
danai

Fungia
(Verrillofungia)
repanda

Fungia
(Pleuractis)
scutaria

Fungia
(Ctenactis)
echinata

Some species of *Fungia*, especially the elongate ones of the subgenera *Pleuractis* and *Ctenactis*, are easy to recognise, but this is not so for the disc-shaped species. Immature specimens may be difficult to identify and may even be confused with *Cycloseris*. Mature specimens are best identified to subgenus first, then to species, and this is done by using the skeletal characters given here. The septa on the upper (oral) surface and costae on the lower surface are both arranged like the spokes of a wheel, the primary septa or costae being relatively large and separated by smaller septa or costae of increasingly higher orders. The septa have teeth and sometimes also have a lobe (very obvious in *F. scutaria*) where they are "inserted"—this is called the tentacular lobe because the living polyp has a single tentacle above it. The costae have spines and sometimes pits are seen between the costae. The species of *Fungia* are identified according to differences in the details of these structures.

COMMON SYNONYM
Herpetoglossa Wells, 1966.

TYPE SPECIES
Madrepora fungites Linnaeus, 1758.

FOSSIL RECORD
Miocene to Recent from the Indo-Pacific.

NUMBER OF SPECIES
Approximately 65 nominal species, 25 true species, 15 of which are Australian.

CHARACTERS
Corals are solitary (except for *F. simplex* and occasionally other species), free-living (except for juveniles), flat or dome-shaped, circular or elongate in

Diagram 18. The fine structure of the septal teeth and costal spines of *Heliofungia* and the five subgenera of *Fungia*.
DRAWINGS: GEOFF KELLY.

1. A *Fungia* showing acanthocauli in early stages of development.
PHOTOGRAPH: ED LOVELL.

2. A small button-like *Fungia* on a stalk. At about this stage, the polyp becomes detached and starts its free-living existence.
PHOTOGRAPH: RON AND VALERIE TAYLOR.

3. Acanthocauli growing on the skeleton of the now-dead parent *Fungia*.
PHOTOGRAPH: AUTHOR.

4. An uncommon view of a male *Fungia* releasing sperm into the water. Female polyps release egg bundles at the same time, once each year. Fertilisation takes place on the water surface to produce planula larvae which settle on a solid substrate to develop into acanthocauli.
PHOTOGRAPH: PETER HARRISON.

outline, with a central mouth. Septa have large or small, rounded to pointed teeth, costae consist mostly of rows of spines. The disc often has pits between the costae on the lower surface.

Polyps are usually extended only at night and have short widely spaced tentacles.

SIMILAR GENERA

Fungia is distinguished from *Heliofungia* by the latter's large lobed septal teeth and large anemone-like polyps. *Fungia* is distinguished from *Cycloseris* by growing much larger, frequently being elongate, often having septa with large teeth and costae with large spines and sometimes having pits on the lower surface.

THE SUBGENERA OF FUNGIA

As an aid to species identification, *Fungia* can be divided into five subgenera as follows:

Subgenus *Fungia*—one species
    Corals are circular.
    Septal teeth are triangular, pointed.
    Costal spines are conical, smooth.

Subgenus *Danafungia*—six species
    Corals are circular.
    Septal teeth are large, each tooth having a thickened rib.
    Costal spines are elongate, those on larger (low order) costae being much larger than those on smaller (high order) costae.

Subgenus *Verrillofungia*—four species
    Corals are circular.
    Septal teeth are fine, usually with a series of ridges parallel to the margin.
    Costal spines are blunt or granular, with those of different orders not markedly different in size.

Subgenus *Pleuractis*—three species
    Corals are elongate.
    Septal teeth and costal spines are fine.

Subgenus *Ctenactis*—two species
    Corals are elongate.
    Septal teeth and costal spines are coarse.

KEY TO SPECIES OF *FUNGIA*

Corals are elongate or oval
    Septal teeth large (Subgenus *Ctenactis*)
        A single mouth present . . . *F.(C.) echinata* (p. 346)
        A series of mouths present . . . *F.(C.) simplex* (p. 347)
    Septal teeth fine (Subgenus *Pleuractis*)
        Primary septa inserted at regular intervals from mouth to perimeter . . . *F.(P.) scutaria* (p. 343)
        Most primary septa extend to the mouth
            Undersurface with little or no attachment scar . . . *F.(P.) paumotensis* (p. 344)
            Undersurface with conspicuous attachment scar . . . *F.(P.) moluccensis* (p. 345)

Corals are circular or nearly so
    Septal teeth large, each with a thickened rib, costal spines elongate with major differences in size between high and low orders (Subgenus *Danafungia*)
        Undersurface with pits between costae
            Costae widely spaced, spines rarely branching . . . *F.(D.) corona* (p. 336)
            Costae compact
                Spines usually branching . . . *F.(D.) danai* (p. 336)
                Spines simple and compact . . . *F.(D.) scruposa* (p. 337)
        Undersurface without pits between costae
            Septa and septal teeth neat, costal spines small . . . *F.(D.) klunzingeri* (p. 339)
            Septal teeth irregular, costal spines long
                Teeth very large, triangular . . . *F.(D.) valida* (p. 338)
                Teeth not so large, rounded . . . *F.(D.) horrida* (p. 337)
    Septal teeth triangular, costal spines tall, smooth, conical (Subgenus *Fungia*) . . . *F.(F.) fungites* (p. 335)
    Septal teeth fine, with parallel ridges, costal spines usually granular, orders not markedly different (Subgenus *Verrillofungia*)
        Septal teeth triangular
            Septal teeth and costal spines clearly visible, undersurface with pits . . . *F.(V.) repanda* (p. 340)
            Septal teeth minute, undersurface mostly unpitted, costal spines small . . . *F.(V.) concinna* (p. 341)
        Septal teeth conical, granular, minute
            Septa thin, undersurface without pits . . . *F.(V.) scabra* (p. 342)
            Septa thick, wavy, with granular sides, undersurface pitted . . . *F.(V.) granulosa* (p. 342)

Note: This key is a guide only and should be used in conjunction with descriptions of the species.

SUBGENUS *FUNGIA*

Lamarck, 1801

Fungia (Fungia) fungites

(LINNAEUS, 1758)

TYPE LOCALITY
Red Sea.

IDENTIFYING CHARACTERS
Corals are circular or subcircular, up to 280 mm in diameter. Septal teeth are triangular, pointed, costal spines are tall, smooth and conical.

COLOUR
Brown, sometimes mottled.

SIMILAR SPECIES
F. danai is sometimes confused with *F. fungites*.

DISTRIBUTION
From Mozambique and the Red Sea east to the Marquesas and the Tuamotu Archipelago.
Around Australia: the Great Barrier Reef and Coral Sea in the east, and south to Ningaloo Reef Tract on the west coast.

ABUNDANCE
Very common.

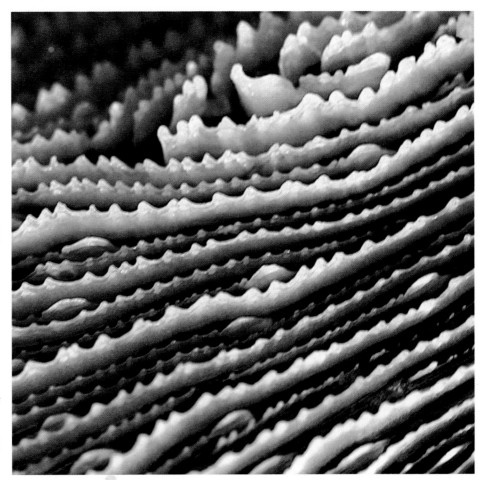

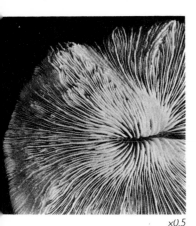

x0.5

The septa of *Fungia (Fungia) fungites*, showing their pointed triangular teeth.
PHOTOGRAPH: ED LOVELL.

SUBGENUS
DANAFUNGIA

Wells, 1966

Fungia (Danafungia) *danai*

EDWARDS & HAIME, 1851

TYPE LOCALITY
The Philippines.

IDENTIFYING CHARACTERS
Corals are circular, up to 300 mm in diameter, not heavily calcified. Septal teeth are very prominent. Costae are compact, with branching spines of different sizes on different orders. The undersurface has pits between the costae.

COLOUR
Usually brown, sometimes mottled.

SIMILAR SPECIES
F. corona and F. scruposa, also F. fungites.

DISTRIBUTION
From Madagascar east to Tahiti and the Tuamotu Archipelago. Around Australia: the Great Barrier Reef in the east; not found on the west coast.

ABUNDANCE
Common.

Fungia (Danafungia) *corona*

DÖDERLEIN, 1901

TYPE LOCALITY
Singapore.

IDENTIFYING CHARACTERS
Corals have an irregular outline and are generally flat, thin and light. Septa are of markedly different sizes and have large teeth. Costae are widely spaced. The undersurface has pits between the costae.

COLOUR
Pale brown.

SIMILAR SPECIES
F. danai and F. scruposa, sometimes F. horrida.

DISTRIBUTION
From Chagos east to Singapore and Australia.
Around Australia: the Great Barrier Reef and Coral Sea in the east; not found on the west coast.

ABUNDANCE
Uncommon.

x0.5

x0.5

Fungia (Danafungia) danai, a common reef species.
PHOTOGRAPH: ED LOVELL.

Fungia *(Danafungia)* scruposa

KLUNZINGER, 1879

TYPE LOCALITY
  Red Sea.

IDENTIFYING CHARACTERS
  Corals are circular or oval, up to 240 mm in diameter, not strongly arched, and thick and heavy. Costae are compact, with simple spines. The undersurface has pits between costae.

COLOUR
  Usually brown.

SIMILAR SPECIES
  F. danai, also *F. corona*.

DISTRIBUTION
  From the Red Sea east to Australia.
  Around Australia: the Great Barrier Reef in the east, and Dampier Archipelago on the west coast.

ABUNDANCE
  Uncommon.

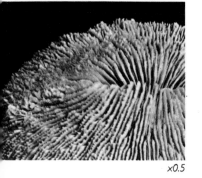

x0.5

Fungia *(Danafungia)* horrida

DANA, 1846

TYPE LOCALITY
  Fiji.

IDENTIFYING CHARACTERS
  Corals are circular, up to 200 mm in diameter, with a strong central arch. Septa have large irregular teeth. Costae are very unequal, with long spines. There are no pits between the costae.

COLOUR
  Usually brown.

SIMILAR SPECIES
  F. valida, sometimes *F. corona*.

DISTRIBUTION
  From the Red Sea east to Tahiti. Around Australia: the Great Barrier Reef in the east, and Rowley Shoals and Scott Reef on the west coast.

ABUNDANCE
  Common.

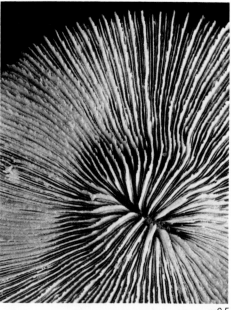

x0.5

Fungia (Danafungia) horrida.
PHOTOGRAPH: ED LOVELL.

Fungia (Danafungia) valida

VERRILL, 1864

TYPE LOCALITY
Zanzibar.

IDENTIFYING CHARACTERS
Corals are circular, generally thick and flat. Septal teeth are very large, triangular and irregular. Costal spines are long. There are no pits between the costae.

COLOUR
Usually brown or mottled.

SIMILAR SPECIES
F. horrida.

DISTRIBUTION
From Zanzibar east to the Phoenix Islands.
Around Australia: the Great Barrier Reef in the east; not found on the west coast.

ABUNDANCE
Uncommon.

x0.5

The surface of *Fungia (Danafungia) valida,* showing large, conspicuous septal teeth.
PHOTOGRAPH: ED LOVELL.

Fungia (Danafungia) *klunzingeri*

DÖDERLEIN, 1901

TYPE LOCALITY
 Red Sea.

IDENTIFYING CHARACTERS
 Corals are circular, not strongly arched. Septa are very neat and regular. Costal spines are fine. There are no pits between the costae.

COLOUR
 Usually brown, sometimes patterned with pale septa.

SIMILAR SPECIES
 None.

DISTRIBUTION
 From the Red Sea to Australia. Around Australia: the northern Great Barrier Reef in the east, and Rowley Shoals and Scott Reef on the west coast.

ABUNDANCE
 Usually uncommon.

x0.5

Fungia (Danafungia) klunzingeri has symmetrical septa with relatively neat, regular teeth.
PHOTOGRAPH: ED LOVELL.

SUBGENUS *VERRILLIO-FUNGIA*
Wells, 1966

Fungia (Verrillofungia) repanda
DANA, 1846

TYPE LOCALITY
"East Indies" and Fiji.

IDENTIFYING CHARACTERS
Corals are circular, up to 30 cm in diameter, thick, flat or strongly arched. Septal teeth are fine but clearly visible, coral spines are granular. The undersurface has pits between the costae.

COLOUR
Usually brown.

SIMILAR SPECIES
F. concinna.

DISTRIBUTION
From the Red Sea east to the Tuamotu Archipelago. Around Australia: the Great Barrier Reef and Coral Sea in the east, and south to the Ningaloo Reef Tract on the west coast.

ABUNDANCE
Very common.

x0.5

The very common *Fungia (Verrillofungia) repanda* with small septal teeth and no tentacular lobes.
PHOTOGRAPH: LEN ZELL.

Fungia
(Verrillofungia)
concinna

VERRILL, 1864

TYPE LOCALITY
Zanzibar.

IDENTIFYING CHARACTERS
Corals are circular, up to 160 mm in diameter, generally flat. Septal teeth and costal spines are very small. The undersurface is usually without pits.

COLOUR
Usually brown.

SIMILAR SPECIES
F. repanda.

DISTRIBUTION
From the Red Sea east to the Tuamotu Archipelago. Around Australia: the Great Barrier Reef and Coral Sea in the east, and the Ningaloo Reef Tract on the west coast.

ABUNDANCE
Very common.

×0.5

Fungia (Verrillofungia) concinna with almost smooth septal margins.
PHOTOGRAPH: ED LOVELL.

Fungia
(Verrillofungia)
scabra
DÖDERLEIN, 1901

TYPE LOCALITY
"East Indies".

IDENTIFYING CHARACTERS
Corals are usually circular and flat. Septa are thin with fine conical or granular teeth. Costae are fine. There are no pits between the costae.

COLOUR
Usually brown.

SIMILAR SPECIES
F. granulosa.

DISTRIBUTION
The Philippines, Singapore, Indonesia and Australia. Around Australia: the Great Barrier Reef in the east; not found on the west coast.

ABUNDANCE
Rare.

x0.5

Fungia
(Verrillofungia)
granulosa
KLUNZINGER, 1879

TYPE LOCALITY
Red Sea.

IDENTIFYING CHARACTERS
Corals are circular, up to 135 mm in diameter, flat or with a central arch. Septa are thick, wavy, with finely granulated margins. Costae are fine. The undersurface has pits between the costae.

COLOUR
Usually brown.

SIMILAR SPECIES
F. scabra.

DISTRIBUTION
From the Red Sea east to the Philippines and Australia. Around Australia: the Great Barrier Reef and Coral Sea in the east, and Rowley Shoals and Scott Reef on the west coast.

ABUNDANCE
Usually uncommon.

x0.5

SUBGENUS *PLEURACTIS*

Verrill, 1864

Fungia (Pleuractis) scutaria

LAMARCK, 1801

TYPE LOCALITY
"Indian Ocean".

IDENTIFYING CHARACTERS
Corals oval, thick and heavy, up to 170 mm long. Primary septa are inserted with a tall tentacular lobe and these are distributed at regular intervals from the mouth to the perimeter.

COLOUR
Usually brown or yellow, often with bright-green tentacular lobes.

SIMILAR SPECIES
None.

DISTRIBUTION
From South Africa and the Red Sea east to Hawaii and the Tuamotu Archipelago.
Around Australia: the Great Barrier Reef, Coral Sea and Elizabeth and Middleton Reefs in the east, and south to Coral Bay on the west coast.

ABUNDANCE
Very common and distinctive. Found with other *Fungia* species and also on upper reef slopes exposed to strong wave action.

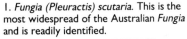
x0.5

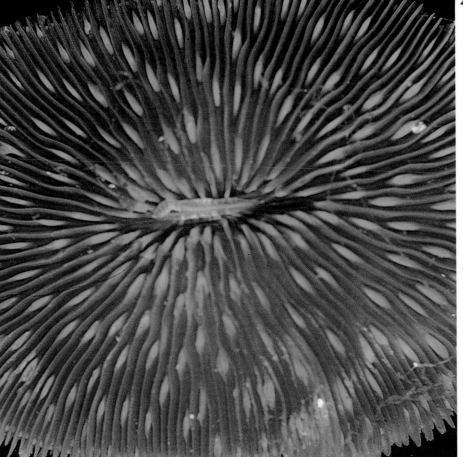

1. *Fungia (Pleuractis) scutaria.* This is the most widespread of the Australian *Fungia* and is readily identified.
PHOTOGRAPH: RON AND VALERIE TAYLOR.

2. *Fungia (Pleuractis) scutaria.* The septa have large, thick tentacular lobes at their inner end. Each lobe has a corresponding tentacle. See also p. 316.
PHOTOGRAPH: ED LOVELL.

Fungia
(Pleuractis)
paumotensis
STUTCHBURY, 1833

TYPE LOCALITY
  Paumotu Islands.

IDENTIFYING CHARACTERS
  Corals are elongate, up to
  250 mm long with almost parallel
  sides, and thick and heavy,
  usually with a strong central
  arch. Most primary septa extend
  from the mouth to the perimeter.
  There are no attachment scars
  except on immature specimens.

COLOUR
  Usually brown.

SIMILAR SPECIES
  F. moluccensis.

DISTRIBUTION
  From Madagascar and the Red
  Sea east to Japan, Hawaii and the
  Tuamotu Archipelago.
  Around Australia: the Great
  Barrier Reef and Coral Sea in the
  east, and south to Passage Island
  on the west coast.

ABUNDANCE
  Common.

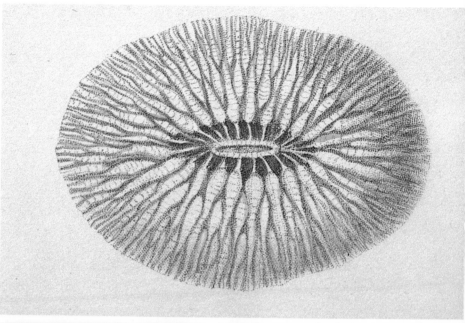

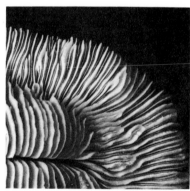

x0.5

1. *Fungia (Pleuractis) paumotensis* as
illustrated by James Dana in 1849.
2. *Fungia (Pleuractis) paumotensis.*
PHOTOGRAPH: AUTHOR.

344

Fungia
(Pleuractis)
moluccensis
VAN DER HORST. 1919

TYPE LOCALITY
Indonesia.

IDENTIFYING CHARACTERS
Corals are usually attached to, or encrust, the substrate. They may be shaped like *F. paumotensis* or be very contorted. They usually have a strong central arch. In uncontorted specimens, primary septa extend from the mouth to the perimeter. An attachment scar is usually prominent.

COLOUR
Brown, cream or mottled.

SIMILAR SPECIES
F. *paumotensis*.

DISTRIBUTION
From the Red Sea east to the Philippines and Australia. Around Australia: the Great Barrier Reef in the east; not found on the west coast.

ABUNDANCE
Usually uncommon.

×0.5

Unlike other *Fungia* species, *F. (Pleuractis) moluccensis* frequently remains attached to the substrate. As seen here, they may become very distorted and may have more than one mouth. The coral with the tentacles is *Heliofungia actiniformis*.
PHOTOGRAPH: ED LOVELL.

SUBGENUS *CTENACTIS*

Verrill, 1864

Fungia (Ctenactis) echinata

(PALLAS, 1766)

TYPE LOCALITY
  "Indian Ocean".

IDENTIFYING CHARACTERS
  Corals are elongate. Septal teeth
  and costal spines are both
  strongly developed. A single
  mouth only is present.

COLOUR
  Usually brown.

SIMILAR SPECIES
  F. simplex has a series of mouths;
  septal teeth are similar.

DISTRIBUTION
  From the Red Sea east to Japan
  and the Society Islands.
  Around Australia: the Great
  Barrier Reef in the east, and
  south to North West Cape on the
  west coast.

ABUNDANCE
  Very common.

×0.5

1. *Fungia (Ctenactis) echinata*, a very
common and distinctive species.
PHOTOGRAPH: ED LOVELL.

2. A side view of *Fungia (Ctenactis)
echinata*, showing the characteristic
appearance of large-toothed septa.
PHOTOGRAPH: ED LOVELL.

Fungia
(Ctenactis)
simplex
GARDINER, 1905

Note: This species was previously placed in a separate genus of its own, *Herpetoglossa* Wells, 1966. It appears, however, to be more closely related to *Fungia echinata* than the latter is to other *Fungia* species. *Herpetoglossa* was distinguished from *Fungia* by the presence of several mouths along the axial furrow giving it a quasicolonial status. Multiple mouths are, however, sometimes found in other *Fungia* species, notably *F. moluccensis* and occasionally several species of *Danafungia*.

TYPE LOCALITY
Maldive Islands.

IDENTIFYING CHARACTERS
Corals are elongate, with an axial furrow extending almost to the corallum ends. Several centres, corresponding with mouths, are arranged along the axial furrow but do not occur outside the furrow.

COLOUR
Pale brown.

SIMILAR SPECIES
F. echinata has a single mouth; septa teeth are similar.

DISTRIBUTION
Australia: the northern and central Great Barrier Reef in the east, and south to North West Cape on the west coast.

ABUNDANCE
Seldom abundant but found frequently on reef slopes protected from strong wave action and on sandy-floored reef lagoons.

x0.5

1. *Fungia (Ctenactis) simplex* is like *F. echinata* but has a series of slit-like mouths down the axial furrow which extends to the ends of the corallum.
PHOTOGRAPH: ED LOVELL.

2. The septal teeth of *Fungia (Ctenactis) simplex*.
PHOTOGRAPH: ED LOVELL.

GENUS
HERPOLITHA
(pronounced herp-oh-lee-tha)

Eschscholtz, 1825

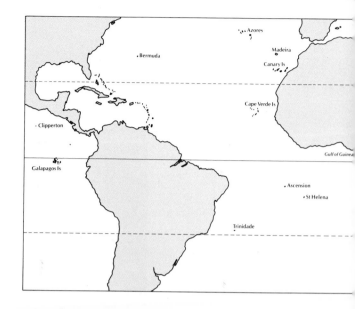

This genus is easily recognised. Of the two known species, *H. limax* is the more common by far. Colonies may be larger than 1 m and become very heavily calcified, the heaviest of all the free-living corals.

TYPE SPECIES
Madrepora limax Houttuyn, 1772.

FOSSIL RECORD
Pliocene.

NUMBER OF SPECIES
Nine nominal species, two true species, both of which are Australian.

CHARACTERS
Colonies are free-living, elongate, with an axial furrow that may extend to the corallum ends. Several centres, corresponding with mouths, are arranged along the furrow and secondary centres are distributed over the rest of the upper surface. Septa are similar in structure to those of *Fungia (Pleuractis)*. Polyps are extended only at night. Tentacles are short and widely spaced, like *Fungia*. Secondary centres have single tentacles.

SIMILAR GENERA
Herpolitha is similar in shape to *Fungia (Ctenactis)*. It also has similarities with *Polyphyllia*, although the latter has very distinct septa and more numerous centres.

Herpolitha limax has mouths down the axial furrow like *Fungia simplex*, but it also has lateral mouths.
PHOTOGRAPH: ED LOVELL.

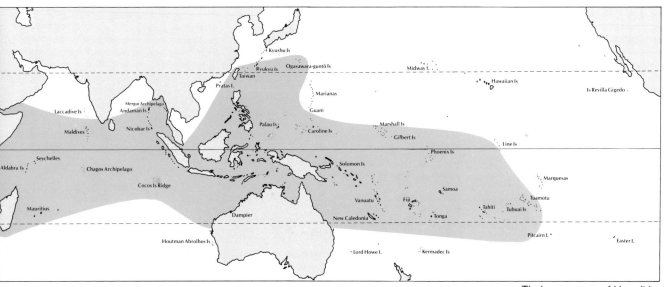

The known range of *Herpolitha*.

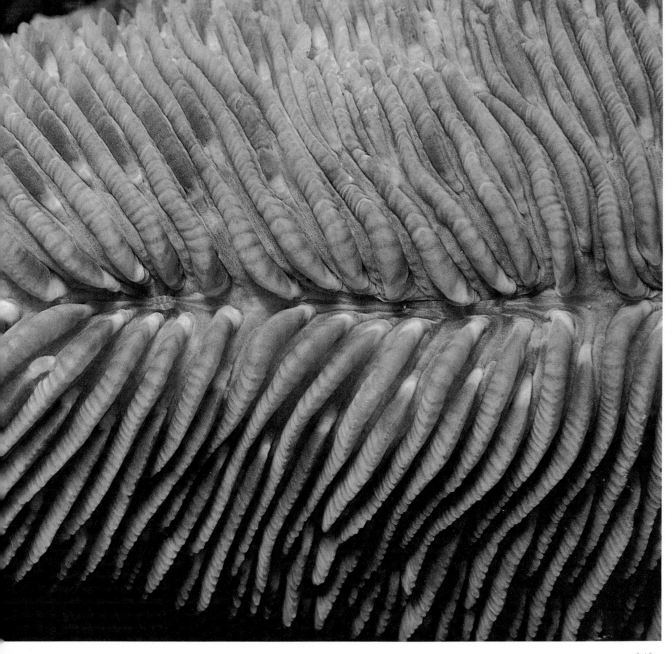

Herpolitha limax

HOUTTUYN, 1772

TYPE LOCALITY
Unrecorded.

IDENTIFYING CHARACTERS
Colonies are elongate with rounded ends. Secondary centres are numerous. Few primary septa extend from the axial furrow to the perimeter. Some colonies develop forked axial furrows and become Y-, T-, or X-shaped.

COLOUR
Pale or dark brown or greenish-brown.

SIMILAR SPECIES
H. weberi.

DISTRIBUTION
From the Red Sea east to the Tuamotu Archipelago. Around Australia: the Great Barrier Reef and Coral Sea in the east, and south to North West Cape on the west coast.

ABUNDANCE
Common on partly protected reef slopes where *Fungia* occur.

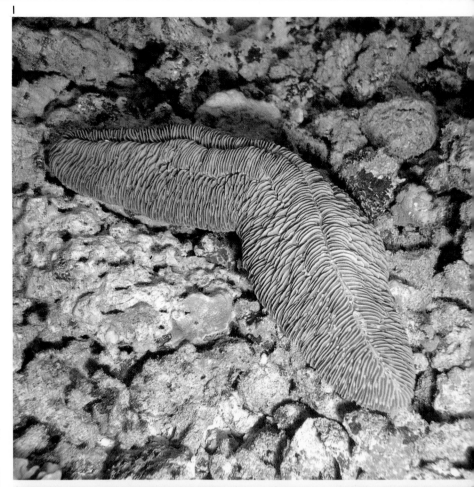

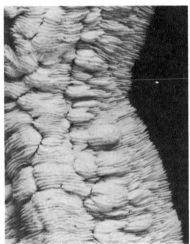

x0.5

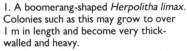

1. A boomerang-shaped *Herpolitha limax*. Colonies such as this may grow to over 1 m in length and become very thick-walled and heavy.
PHOTOGRAPH: ED LOVELL.

2. Some *Herpolitha limax* colonies become flat and wide.
PHOTOGRAPH: ED LOVELL.

3. Y- or even X-shaped colonies of *Herpolitha limax* are not uncommon.
PHOTOGRAPH: ED LOVELL.

2

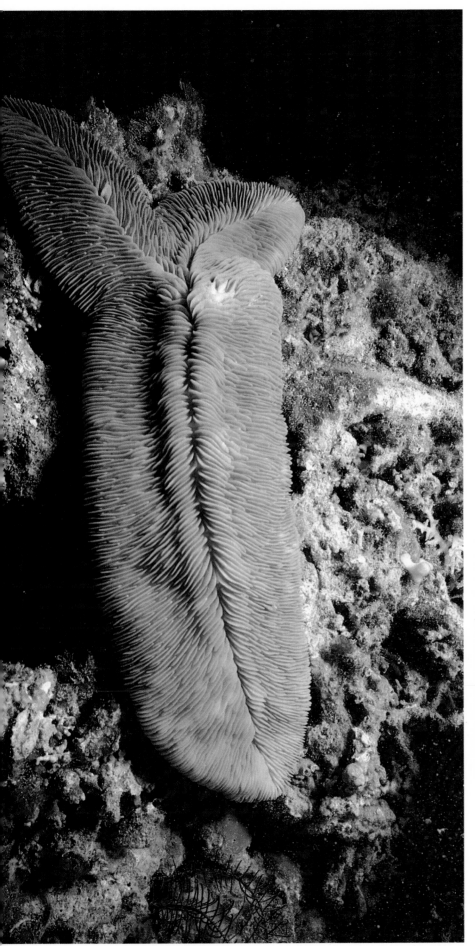

3

Herpolitha weberi

VAN DER HORST, 1921

TYPE LOCALITY
Indonesia.

IDENTIFYING CHARACTERS
Colonies are elongate with pointed ends. There are few secondary centres. Most primary septa extend from the axial furrow to the perimeter.

COLOUR
Usually pale brown.

SIMILAR SPECIES
Immature colonies may be difficult to distinguish from *H. limax*.

DISTRIBUTION
Maldive Islands east to Palau and the Great Barrier Reef. Around Australia: the Great Barrier Reef and Coral Sea in the east, and Rowley Shoals on the west coast.

ABUNDANCE
Much less common than *H. limax*.

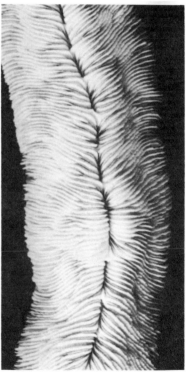

x0.5

GENUS
POLYPHYLLIA

(pronounced polly-fill-ee-a)

Quoy & Gaimard, 1833

Polyphyllia is generally regarded as a colonial genus because "colonies" have many mouths. These are distributed over the whole upper surface, with larger mouths aligned along the axial furrow, which extends down the midline of the colony. However, some colonies may be almost circular, without any axial furrow, in which case all the mouths are small and the whole colony has the appearance of being a single individual. Despite the small mouths, the tentacles are long, shaggy and mop-like. They are always extended but can retract slowly if vigorously disturbed.

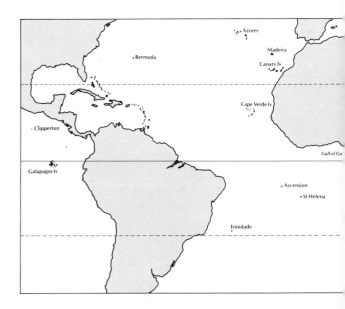

TYPE SPECIES
Fungia talpina Lamarck, 1801.

FOSSIL RECORD
None.

NUMBER OF SPECIES
Eleven nominal species, three true species, one of which is Australian.

Polyphyllia talpina

LAMARCK, 1801

TYPE LOCALITY
"East Indies".

IDENTIFYING CHARACTERS
Colonies are free-living, elongate, with an axial furrow that may become indistinct. Centres are evenly distributed over the upper surface. Primary septa are short, elliptical or petaloid, secondary septa usually fuse around the primaries to form a fused background matrix. Polyps are usually extended during the day. Tentacles are long and numerous.

COLOUR
Grey, greenish or cream, with white tentacle tips.

SIMILAR SPECIES
None.

DISTRIBUTION
From Madagascar east to Fiji and Tonga. Around Australia: the Great Barrier Reef in the east, and south to North West Cape on the west coast.

ABUNDANCE
Common on reef slopes, especially where *Fungia* is common.

1. The usual appearance of free-living *Polyphyllia talpina* on a reef slope.
PHOTOGRAPH: LEN ZELL, GREAT BARRIER REEF MARINE PARK AUTHORITY.

2. *Polyphyllia talpina* always has its tentacles extended, and resembles a small, elongate mop.
PHOTOGRAPH: ED LOVELL.

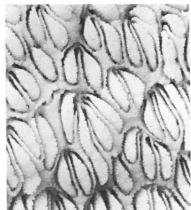

×2.5

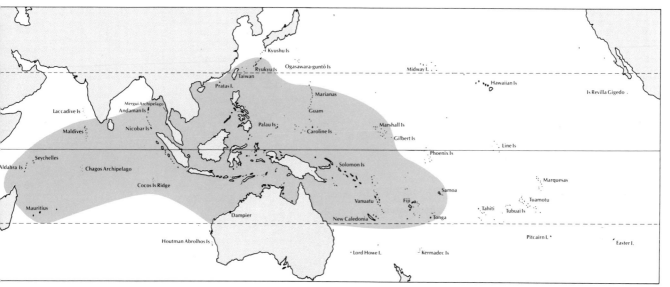

The known range of *Polyphyllia*.

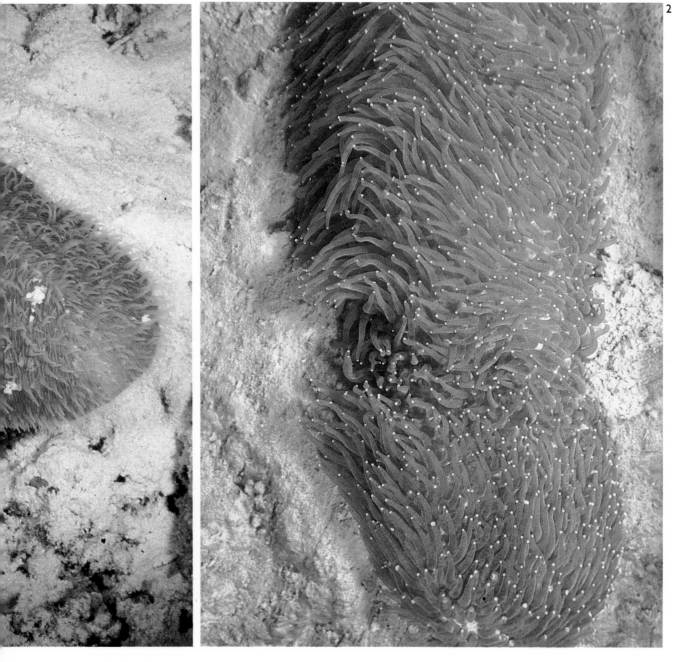

2

GENUS
HALOMITRA
(pronounced hal-oh-my-tra)

Dana, 1846

TYPE SPECIES
Madrepora pileus Linnaeus, 1758.

FOSSIL RECORD
Miocene.

NUMBER OF SPECIES
Six nominal species, probably only one true species.

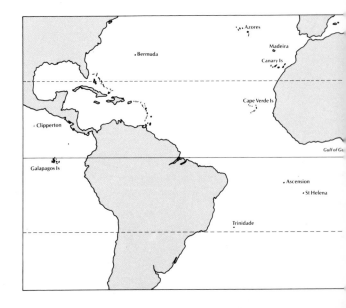

Halomitra
pileus
(LINNAEUS, 1758)

TYPE LOCALITY
   "East Indies".

IDENTIFYING CHARACTERS
   Colonies are large and free-
   living, circular, dome- or bell-
   shaped, thin and delicate and
   without an axial furrow.
   Corallites are widely spaced.
   Septo-costae are similar to those
   of *Fungia fungites*.
   Polyps are extended only at
   night. Tentacles are small and
   widely spaced.

COLOUR
   Pale brown, frequently with
   bright-pink or purple margins.

SIMILAR SPECIES
   Halomitra is similar to
   Sandalolitha. The latter is of much
   heavier construction, corallites
   are closer together and septo-
   costae are more prominent and
   have the characters of *Fungia*
   (Verrillofungia) and *Podabacia*.

DISTRIBUTION
   Around Australia: the northern
   and central Great Barrier Reef in
   the east; not found on the west
   coast.

ABUNDANCE
   Occurs on middle to lower reef
   slopes and in lagoons on soft
   substrates. Usually uncommon.

x0.5

Halomitra pileus, commonly called
Neptune's Cap, at Rib Reef, Great Barrier
Reef.
PHOTOGRAPH: ED LOVELL.

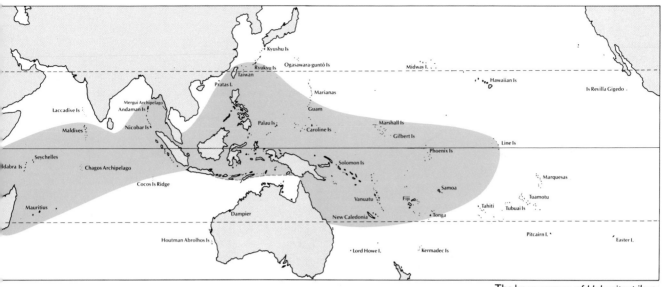

The known range of *Halomitra pileus*.

GENUS
SANDALOLITHA

(pronounced <u>san</u>-da-<u>loh</u>-<u>lee</u>-tha)

Quelch, 1884

TYPE SPECIES
Sandalolitha dentata Quelch, 1884 from Tahiti.

WELL-KNOWN SYNONYM
Parahalomitra Wells, 1937.

FOSSIL RECORD
Miocene.

NUMBER OF SPECIES
Four nominal species, two true species, one of which is Australian.

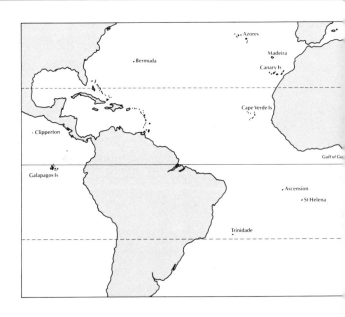

Sandalolitha robusta

QUELCH, 1886

x0.5

TYPE LOCALITY
Indonesia.

IDENTIFYING CHARACTERS
Colonies are large, free-living, circular to oval, dome-shaped, heavily constructed and without an axial furrow. Corallites are compacted. Septo-costae are similar to those of *Fungia (Verrillofungia)* and *Podabacia*. Polyps are extended only at night.

COLOUR
Usually pale or dark brown, sometimes with purple margins and white centres.

SIMILAR SPECIES
Sandalolitha is similar to *Halomitra*. The latter is of much lighter construction, corallites are further apart and septo-costae have the characters of *Fungia fungites*.

DISTRIBUTION
Occurs throughout the full range of the genus.
Around Australia: the Great Barrier Reef and Coral Sea in the east, and south to North West Cape on the west coast.

ABUNDANCE
Common.

1. *Sandalolitha robusta*.
PHOTOGRAPH: ED LOVELL.

2. A small, flattened *Sandalolitha robusta*, a common shape in turbid water.
PHOTOGRAPH: ED LOVELL.

3. The characteristically coarse, gnarled surface of *Sandalolitha robusta*, at the Swain Reefs, Great Barrier Reef.
PHOTOGRAPH: ED LOVELL.

4. *Sandalolitha robusta* with its short tentacles extended at night.
PHOTOGRAPH: ED LOVELL.

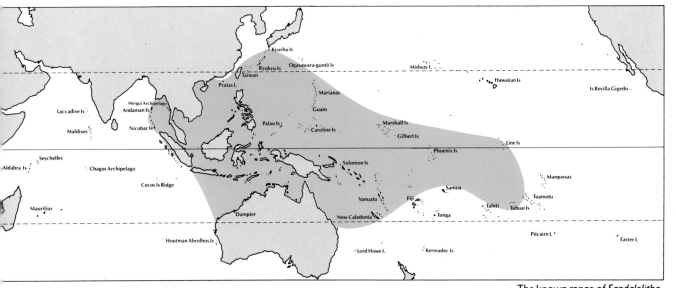

The known range of *Sandalolitha*.

3

4

Genus
LITHOPHYLLON

(pronounced lith-oh-fill-on)

Rehberg, 1892

TYPE SPECIES
Lithophyllon undulatum Rehberg, 1892 from an unrecorded locality.

FOSSIL RECORD
Oligocene to Recent from Europe and the Indo-Pacific.

NUMBER OF SPECIES
Seven nominal species, two true species, one of which is Australian.

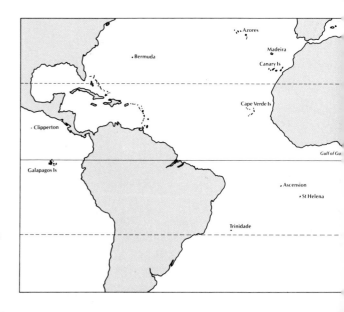

Lithophyllon edwardsi
ROUSSEAU, 1854

TYPE LOCALITY
Unrecorded.

IDENTIFYING CHARACTERS
Colonies are attached, encrusting or laminar, unifacial. Colonies are up to 80 mm in diameter on the Great Barrier Reef but may be several metres in diameter in other parts of the species' range, including Western Australia.
A central corallite is usually distinguishable in small colonies.
Septo-costae are similar to *Diaseris*.
Polyps are usually extended only at night.

COLOUR
Dull green, grey or brown, sometimes with white margins or white centres.

SIMILAR SPECIES
Lithophyllon is most similar to *Podabacia*.

DISTRIBUTION
Probably occurs throughout the full range of the genus.
Around Australia: the northern and central Great Barrier Reef in the east, and south to North West Cape on the west coast.

ABUNDANCE
Found on lower reef slopes.
Always uncommon.

1. *Lithophyllon edwardsi* at the Dampier Archipelago, Western Australia. Colonies never reach this size on the Great Barrier Reef, but they are common in more northerly localities.
PHOTOGRAPH: ED LOVELL.

2. *Lithophyllon edwardsi* with tentacles extended during the day.
PHOTOGRAPH: ED LOVELL.

×1

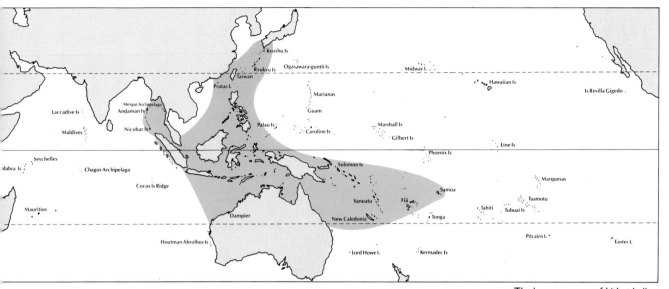

The known range of *Lithophyllon*.

2

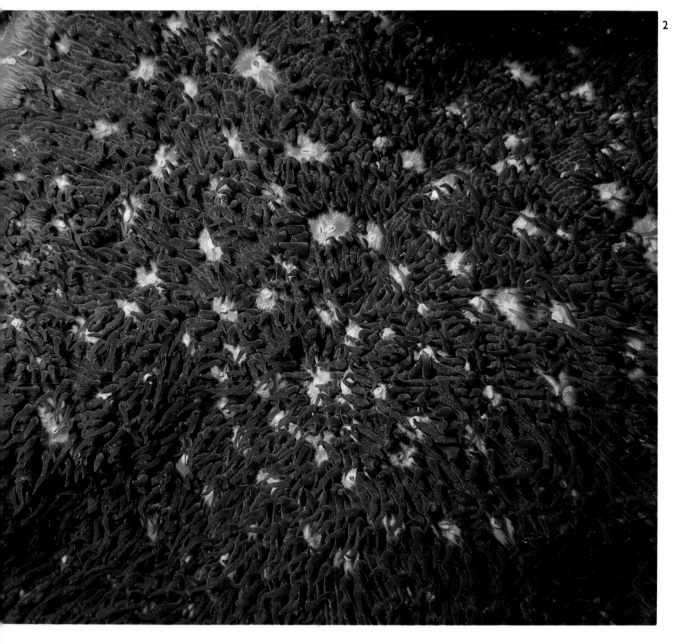

Genus
PODABACIA
(pronounced poh-da-bay-see-a)

Edwards & Haime, 1849

TYPE SPECIES
Madrepora crustacea Pallas, 1766.

FOSSIL RECORD
None.

NUMBER OF SPECIES
Four nominal species, one true species.

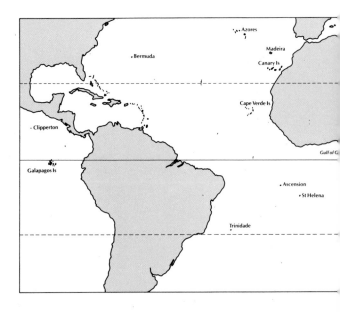

Podabacia crustacea
(PALLAS, 1766)

TYPE LOCALITY
  Unrecorded.

IDENTIFYING CHARACTERS
  Colonies are attached, encrusting or laminar, unifacial, up to 1.5 m across.
  A central corallite is sometimes distinguishable. Septo-costae are similar to those of *Fungia (Verrillofungia)* and, especially, *Sandalolitha.*
  Polyps may be extended day or night.

COLOUR
  Dark-coloured, except for the septo-costae which are cream.

SIMILAR SPECIES
  Podabacia is most similar to *Lithophyllon*. A small piece of corallum may be confused easily with *Sandalolitha robusta*.

DISTRIBUTION
  Probably occurs throughout the full range of the genus.
  Around Australia: the Great Barrier Reef and the Coral Sea in the east, and south to North West Cape on the west coast.

ABUNDANCE
  Found in most reef habitats but is seldom abundant.

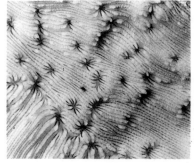

×1

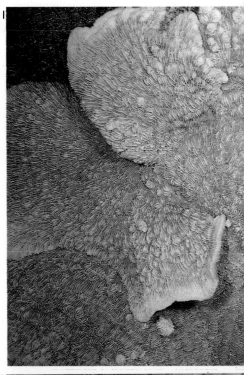

1. *Podabacia crustacea* at the Palm Islands, Great Barrier Reef.
PHOTOGRAPH: LEN ZELL.

2. A flat, heavily calcified plate of *Podabacia crustacea* at Broadhurst Reef, Great Barrier Reef.
PHOTOGRAPH: ED LOVELL.

3. The polyps of *Podabacia crustacea.* These may be very similar in structure to those of *Sandalolitha robusta* but different colonies vary greatly in their degree of calcification.
PHOTOGRAPH: ED LOVELL.

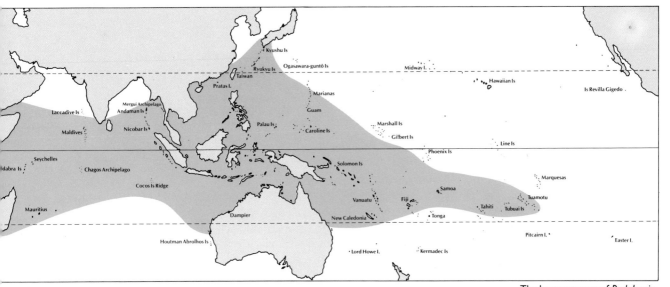

The known range of *Podabacia*.

3

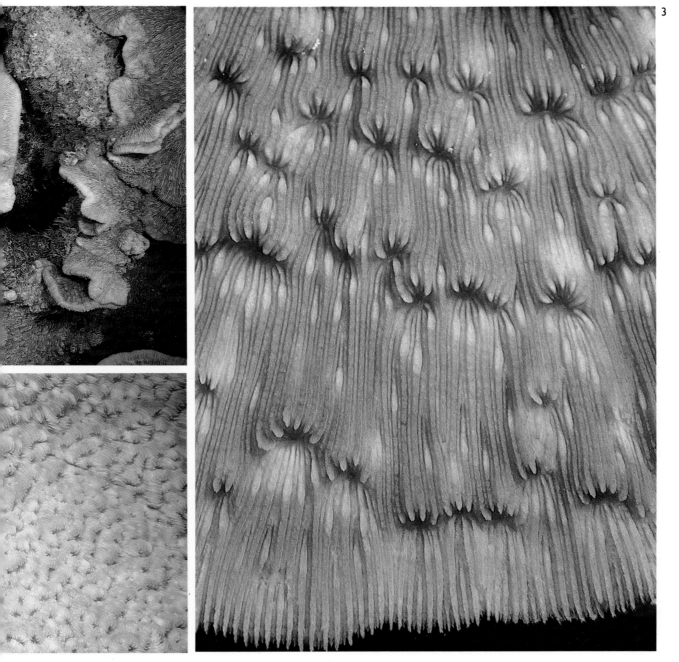

FAMILY
OCULINIDAE

(pronounced ok-you-line-id-ee)

GRAY, 1847

The two genera of oculinids found on coral reefs have polyps which are amongst the most beautiful of all corals. Each polyp has a circle of delicate sabre-like septa surrounded by an outer circle of softly coloured translucent tentacles, which usually have white tips.

Acrhelia is truly a coral of the outer reef, growing only in clear water where light availability is good. *Galaxea* is found usually at the opposite end of the environmental range and thrives in turbid water, especially around inshore fringing reefs. The majority of the oculinid genera, however, are not found around tropical reefs. They are ahermatypic and do not require light for survival. Some, such as *Archohelia* and *Cyathelia*, are found in shallow water, but the majority grow in the permanent darkness of the ocean depths. Unlike most other ahermatypes, the oculinids are always colonial, sometimes forming extensive monospecific stands.

All oculinids on the Great Barrier Reef are hermaphrodite and release gametes during the period of mass spawning. However, both *Galaxea* and *Acrhelia* are known to brood planula larvae at Palau.

CHARACTERS
Colonial, hermatypic and ahermatypic, extant and fossil.
Corallites are thickened and linked by a smooth coenosteum. Septa are very exsert.

RELATED FAMILIES
Rhizangiidae.

EARLIEST FOSSILS
Cretaceous.

THE GENERA
The Oculinidae are ahermatypic except for the two Australian genera *Galaxea* and *Acrhelia*, which are readily distinguished by their different growth forms—the former being massive, encrusting, columnar or irregular; the latter being arborescent or bushy.

Opposite: A member of the Family Oculinidae, *Galaxea fascicularis*, is one of the most beautiful of reef corals. See also p. 367.
PHOTOGRAPH: ED LOVELL.

Genus
GALAXEA

(pronounced gal-aks-ee-a)

Oken, 1815

Galaxea colonies are essentially groups of long, branching, tubular corallites linked together by layers of tiny blister-like plates, the outermost layer of which is covered by the living tissue. When these colonies die and break up, only the tubular corallites remain. These are often a major component of coral rubble on beaches but are seldom recognised as being *Galaxea*.

　　Galaxea often dominates inshore fringing reefs, sometimes to the exclusion of all other corals. Colonies may be of enormous size and usually vary in shape according to local conditions, but the growth form is also affected by boring organisms, especially the date mussel *Lithophaga*. Major infestations of the latter can cause big colonies to break apart; they may also cause colonies to develop a sub-branching growth form.

TYPE SPECIES
Madrepora fascicularis Linnaeus, 1767.

FOSSIL RECORD
Miocene from Indonesia and North America, and Pliocene, from the Western Pacific.

NUMBER OF SPECIES
Approximately 24 nominal species, less than five true species, two of which are Australian.

CHARACTERS
Colonies are massive, columnar, encrusting or irregular. Corallites are cylindrical, thin-walled and separated by a blistery coenosteum. Columellae are weak or absent. Septa are very exsert.
Polyps are sometimes extended during the day.

SIMILAR GENERA
Galaxea is close to *Acrhelia* which differs in being arborescent or bushy.

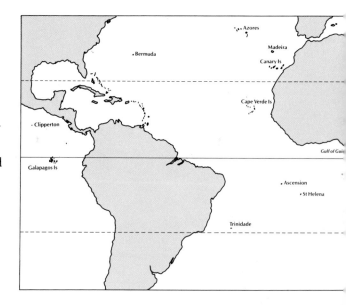

1. The tubular polyps of *Galaxea astreata*.
PHOTOGRAPH: AUTHOR.

2. A castle-like colony of *Galaxea astreata*.
PHOTOGRAPH: AUTHOR.

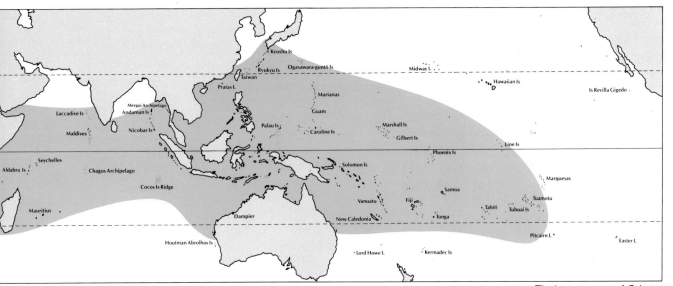

The known range of *Galaxea*.

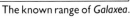

2

Galaxea astreata

(LAMARCK, 1816)

TYPE LOCALITY
"Indian Ocean".

COMMON SYNONYM
Galaxea clavus Dana, 1846.

IDENTIFYING CHARACTERS
Colonies are submassive, columnar or encrusting, with uniform corallites 3-4.5 mm in diameter. Usually eight to 12 septa reach the corallite centre. Polyps are seldom extended during the day.

COLOUR
Usually pink, grey, green or brown.

SIMILAR SPECIES
G. fascicularis.

DISTRIBUTION
From the Red Sea east to Indonesia and Fiji.
Around Australia: the Great Barrier Reef and Coral Sea in the east, and south to the Ningaloo Reef Tract on the west coast.

ABUNDANCE
Common in any habitat protected from very strong wave action. Encrusting colonies may exceed 2 m in diameter in turbid water.

x2.5

1. *Galaxea astreata* at Ningaloo Reef Tract, Western Australia. Columnar colonies such as this are common in Western Australia but tend to be encrusting or massive on the Great Barrier Reef.
PHOTOGRAPH: BARRY WILSON.

2. *Galaxea astreata* at Torres Strait. Encrusting or pillow-like colonies of this species are common because columns are usually developed only when colonies reach a large size.
PHOTOGRAPH: LEN ZELL.

3. *Galaxea astreata* with polyps extended.
PHOTOGRAPH: ED LOVELL.

Galaxea fascicularis

(LINNAEUS, 1767)

TYPE LOCALITY
Torres Strait, Great Barrier Reef.

IDENTIFYING CHARACTERS
Small colonies are cushion-shaped or low domes or irregular. Large colonies are columnar or develop irregular short sub-branches. Corallites are of mixed sizes, commonly up to 6 mm in diameter with numerous septa reaching the corallite centre.

COLOUR
Usually green, red and brown in various mixtures. Polyps are frequently extended during the day, and tentacles often have conspicuous white tips.

SIMILAR SPECIES
G. astreata, also stunted *Acrhelia*. The latter always has much thinner branches.

DISTRIBUTION
From the Red Sea east to Fiji and Samoa.
Around Australia: the Great Barrier Reef and Coral Sea in the east, and south to Houtman Abrolhos Islands on the west coast.

ABUNDANCE
Very common in a wide range of habitats and may be dominant on inshore fringing reefs, where columnar colonies frequently exceed 5 m in diameter.

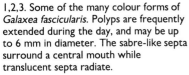

×2.5

1,2,3. Some of the many colour forms of *Galaxea fascicularis*. Polyps are frequently extended during the day, and may be up to 6 mm in diameter. The sabre-like septa surround a central mouth while translucent septa radiate.
PHOTOGRAPHS: RON AND VALERIE TAYLOR.

4. A sub-branching colony of *Galaxea fascicularis*. These colonies look very different from the large, even-surfaced, massive colonies this species may also form. Sometimes the full range of growth forms occurs in the same place.
PHOTOGRAPH: LEN ZELL.

GENUS
ACRHELIA
(pronounced ak-rell-ee-a)

Edwards & Haime, 1849

TYPE SPECIES
Acrhelia sebae Edwards & Haime, 1849 from an unrecorded locality.

FOSSIL RECORD
Miocene from Indonesia and Pliocene and Pleistocene from the Marshall Islands.

NUMBER OF SPECIES
One.

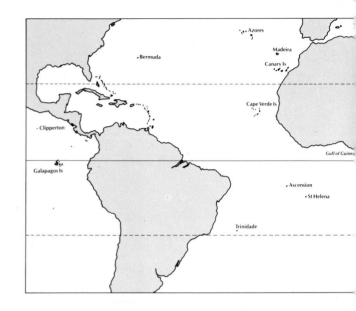

Acrhelia horrescens
(DANA, 1846)

TYPE LOCALITY
Torres Strait, Great Barrier Reef.

IDENTIFYING CHARACTERS
Colonies are arborescent, either bushy or open-branched. Corallites are tubular, thin-walled with flaring rims. Columellae are absent. Septa are very exsert. Polyps are extended usually only at night. They have tapering translucent tentacles with white tips.

COLOUR
Pale brown, yellow or green, sometimes with white branch ends.

SIMILAR SPECIES
Acrhelia is close to *Galaxea* which differs primarily in not being arborescent.

DISTRIBUTION
Around Australia: the Great Barrier Reef in the east, and Rowley Shoals and Scott Reef on the west coast.

ABUNDANCE
Uncommon and is restricted to reefal areas with good water circulation and light availability.

×2.5

1. *Acrhelia horrescens* at Torres Strait. The species develops only short, compact branches like this in clear, shallow water.
PHOTOGRAPH: ED LOVELL.

2. The most common appearance of *Acrhelia horrescens* on upper reef slopes.
PHOTOGRAPH: ED LOVELL.

3. The polyps of *Acrhelia horrescens* are similar to those of *Galaxea*.
PHOTOGRAPH: VICKI HARRIOTT.

4. The polyps of *Acrhelia horrescens*.
PHOTOGRAPH: RON AND VALERIE TAYLOR.

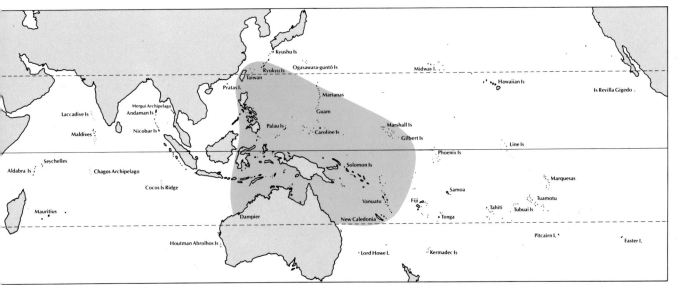

The known range of *Acrhelia horrescens*.

3

4

369

FAMILY
PECTINIIDAE

(pronounced pek-tin-ee-id-ee)

VAUGHAN & WELLS, 1943

The pectiniids, except *Pectinia*, have mussid-like polyps, typically thick and fleshy and usually very colourful. Polyps are extended only at night; they usually have long, thin, translucent tentacles.
As far as is known, pectiniids are hermaphrodites and release gametes during periods of mass spawning for external fertilisation.

CHARACTERS
There is one solitary fossil genus, the remainder are colonial and hermatypic. Colonies are basically laminar, composed of thin plates. Corallite walls are absent or formed by the non-porous costate coenosteum of the laminae.

RELATED FAMILY
Mussidae.

EARLIEST FOSSILS
Oligocene.

THE GENERA
The Pectiniidae is a small distinct family with only five extant genera, all hermatypic, comprised of *Physophyllia* and the four Australian genera, *Echinophyllia, Oxypora, Mycedium* and *Pectinia*.

KEY TO GENERA OF AUSTRALIAN PECTINIIDAE

Colonies with wide valleys and high acute walls or spines . . . *Pectinia* (p. 384)
Colonies laminar with or without secondary thickening, without valleys
    Coenosteum pitted at insertion of septo-costae
        Septa widely and irregularly spaced . . . *Oxypora* (p. 378)
        Septa compact, regular . . . *Echinophyllia* (p. 372)
    Coenosteum not pitted, corallites face outward . . . *Mycedium* (p. 382)

Opposite: *Mycedium elephantotus*, a member of the Pectiniidae family, at Broadhurst Reef, Great Barrier Reef. See also p. 382
PHOTOGRAPH: ED LOVELL.

Genus
ECHINOPHYLLIA

(pronounced ee-kine-oh-fill-ee-a)

Klunzinger, 1879

TYPE SPECIES
Madrepora aspera Ellis & Solander, 1786.

FOSSIL RECORD
Miocene from Indonesia, and Pliocene from the Ryukyu Islands.

NUMBER OF SPECIES
Five nominal species, four true species from Australia.

CHARACTERS
Colonies are encrusting, laminar or foliaceous. Calices are round or oval in shape, immersed to tubular, not strongly inclined on the corallum surface. Septa are numerous, columellae are well developed. The coenosteum is pitted at the insertion of new septo-costae.
Polyps are extended only at night.

SIMILAR GENERA
Echinophyllia is readily confused with *Oxypora* and also with *Echinopora* and *Mycedium*.

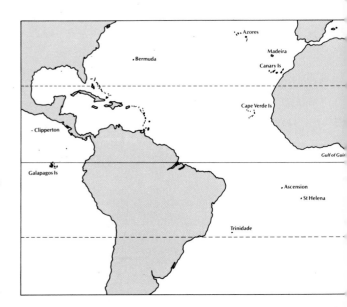

Diagram 19. A corallite of *Echinophyllia orphiensis* showing pits at the insertion of new costae. Similar pits are found in *Oxypora,* and several subgenera of *Fungia.*
DRAWING: GEOFF KELLY.

Right: The wide range of colours and polyp shapes of *Echinophyllia aspera* often make this species hard to recognise.
PHOTOGRAPH: ED LOVELL.

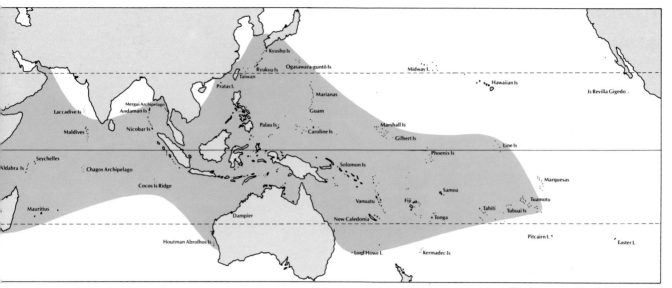

The known range of *Echinophyllia*.

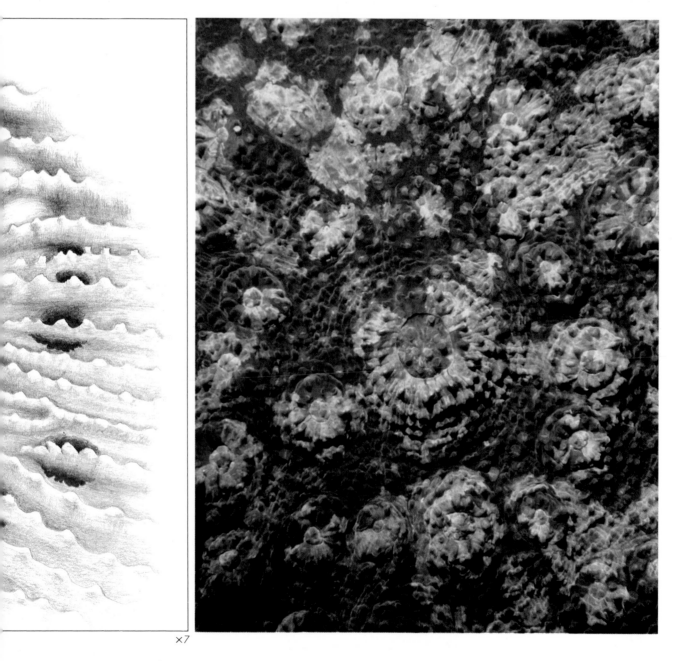

×7

Echinophyllia aspera

(ELLIS & SOLANDER, 1788)

TYPE LOCALITY
"Eastern Indian Ocean".

IDENTIFYING CHARACTERS
Colonies are partly encrusting laminae. Central parts may be hillocky and submassive, peripheral parts may be contorted or form whorls and tiers. Corallites have toothed rather than beaded costae and no paliform lobes.

COLOUR
Brown, green and red are most common, usually with red or green oral discs, often mottled.

SIMILAR SPECIES
E. orpheensis and *E. echinata*. The former is distinguished by its generally exsert corallites with thick beaded costae and paliform lobes. Closely resembles *Oxypora lacera* under water.

DISTRIBUTION
From Madagascar and the Red Sea east to Tahiti.
Around Australia: the Great Barrier Reef, Coral Sea and south to Lord Howe Island except the Solitary Islands in the east, and south to Houtman Abrolhos Islands on the west coast.

ABUNDANCE
Common over a wide range of habitats, especially lower reef slopes, lagoons and fringing reefs.

x2.5

1. The most common appearance of *Echinophyllia aspera* polyps.
PHOTOGRAPH: ED LOVELL.

2. *Echinophyllia aspera* at Broadhurst Reef, Great Barrier Reef, with thick polyp walls.
PHOTOGRAPH: ED LOVELL.

Echinophyllia orpheensis

VERON & PICHON, 1980

TYPE LOCALITY
Palm Islands, Great Barrier Reef.

IDENTIFYING CHARACTERS
Colonies are submassive with exsert corallites becoming laminar around the periphery. Costae are thick and beaded. Paliform lobes are usually well developed.

COLOUR
Usually cream or pale brown, sometimes with green centres.

SIMILAR SPECIES
E. aspera. Can be mistaken for *Barabattoia amicorum.*

DISTRIBUTION
Japan south to Australia. Around Australia: the Great Barrier Reef, Coral Sea and Elizabeth and Middleton Reefs in the east, and south to South Passage on the west coast.

ABUNDANCE
Usually uncommon but occurs in a wide range of habitats. Colonies are less than 0.4 m in diameter.

x2.5

1. Plate-like *Echinophyllia orpheensis* usually have polyps facing different directions.
PHOTOGRAPH: LEN ZELL.

2. Polyps of *Echinophyllia orpheensis*.
PHOTOGRAPH: ED LOVELL.

3. *Echinophyllia orpheensis* with characteristically thick, exsert polyps.
PHOTOGRAPH: LEN ZELL.

Echinophyllia echinata

(SAVILLE-KENT, 1871)

TYPE LOCALITY
Solomon Islands.

IDENTIFYING CHARACTERS
Colonies are thin, flat to vase-shaped laminae, with a conspicuous central corallite and widely spaced radial corallites. Costae are prominent, smooth or toothed.

COLOUR
Mottled brown, green and red.

SIMILAR SPECIES
Closely resembles immature *Pectinia* and *Mycedium*.

DISTRIBUTION
Possibly extends from the Maldive Islands east to the Solomon Islands and New Caledonia.
Around Australia: the Great Barrier Reef and Coral Sea in the east; not found on the west coast.

ABUNDANCE
Usually rare, found only on vertical or overhang substrates, or on lower reef slopes of fringing reefs.

x2.5

The central polyp of *Echinophyllia echinata*.
PHOTOGRAPH: RON AND VALERIE TAYLOR.

376

Echinophyllia echinoporoides

VERON & PICHON, 1980

TYPE LOCALITY
Whitsunday Islands, Great Barrier Reef.

IDENTIFYING CHARACTERS
Colonies are flat laminae with small corallites.

COLOUR
Usually a uniform cream to dark brownish-green.

SIMILAR SPECIES
Unlike other *Echinophyllia*, but superficially resembles *Echinopora lamellosa*. It is readily distinguished by its prominent costae.

DISTRIBUTION
Australia and the Celebes. Around Australia: the northern and central Great Barrier Reef in the east; not found on the west coast.

ABUNDANCE
Uncommon, found only in turbid water on protected steeply sloping substrates.

x2.5

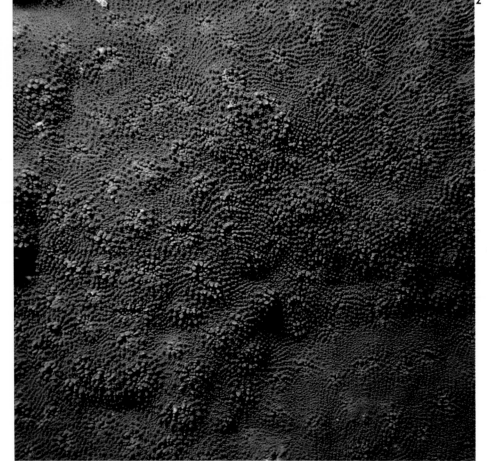

1. *Echinophyllia echinoporoides* at Torres Strait.
PHOTOGRAPH: LEN ZELL.

2. *Echinophyllia echinoporoides* at the Ryukyu Islands.
PHOTOGRAPH: AUTHOR.

GENUS
OXYPORA

(pronounced oks-ee-por-a)

Saville–Kent, 1871

TYPE SPECIES
Trachypora lacera Verrill, 1864.

FOSSIL RECORD
None.

NUMBER OF SPECIES
Five nominal species, two true species, both of which are Australian.

CHARACTERS
Colonies are primarily foliaceous, usually with very thin folia.
Calices are round or oval in shape, irregular, shallow, not strongly inclined on the corallum surface. Septa are few, columellae are poorly developed. The coenosteum is pitted at the insertion of new septo-costae.
Polyps are extended only at night.

SIMILAR·GENERA
Oxypora is readily confused with *Echinophyllia*, especially when colonies become thickened. See also *Echinopora* and *Mycedium*.

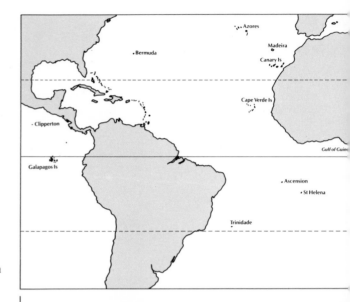

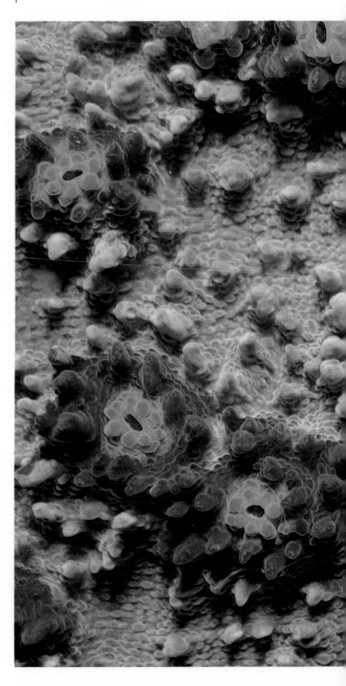

The most common colouration of *Oxypora lacera*.
PHOTOGRAPH: ED LOVELL.

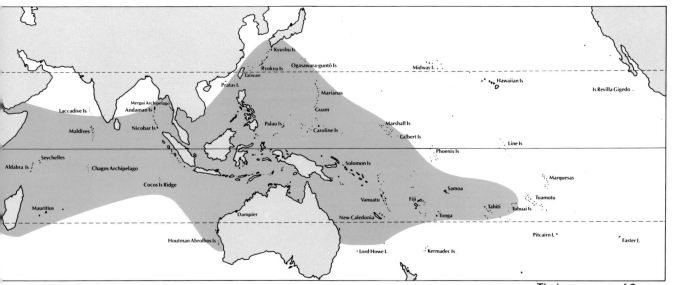

The known range of *Oxypora*.

Oxypora lacera

(VERRILL, 1864)

TYPE LOCALITY
Singapore.

IDENTIFYING CHARACTERS
Colonies may be submassive, encrusting or laminar. Corallites may be fine and delicate on thin laminae to grossly thickened on submassive parts of the same colony. Costae are always toothed.

COLOUR
Usually pale brown or greenish, either uniform or with green or red oral discs.

SIMILAR SPECIES
O. glabra is distinguished by its lack of teeth on the costae. May resemble *Echinophyllia aspera* under water.

DISTRIBUTION
From the Red Sea east to the Marshall and Loyalty Islands. Around Australia: the Great Barrier Reef, Coral Sea and Elizabeth and Middleton Reefs in the east, and south to Houtman Abrolhos Islands on the west coast.

ABUNDANCE
Common, especially in shallow protected reef slopes.

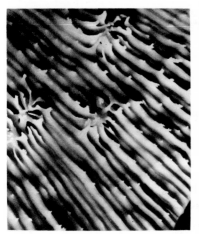

x2.5

1. *Oxypora lacera* at Torres Strait.
PHOTOGRAPH: LEN ZELL.

2. The polyps of *Oxypora lacera*. These resemble closely those of *Echinophyllia aspera* under water, but coralla of these species are easily distinguished.
PHOTOGRAPH: RON AND VALERIE TAYLOR.

Oxypora glabra

NEMENZO, 1959

TYPE LOCALITY
The Philippines.

IDENTIFYING CHARACTERS
Colonies are thin encrusting laminae. Costae do not have teeth. Septa and columellae are twisted, forming a short, usually clockwise spiral.

COLOUR
Dark brown.

SIMILAR SPECIES
O. lacera.

DISTRIBUTION
The Philippines, New Caledonia and Australia.
Around Australia: the Great Barrier Reef in the east, and south to Houtman Abrolhos Islands on the west coast.

ABUNDANCE
Rare on the east coast; common on the west coast.

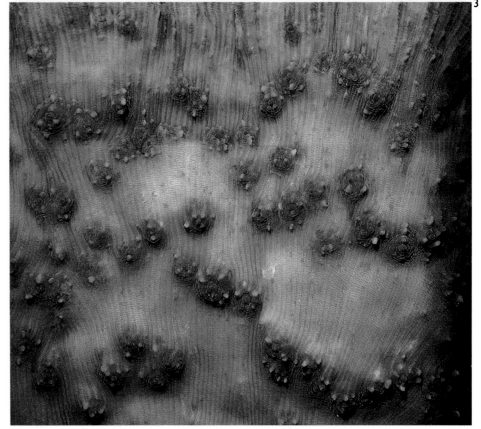

×2.5

1. *Oxypora glabra* at the Rowley Shoals.
PHOTOGRAPH: AUTHOR.

2. *Oxypora glabra* is common at the Houtman Abrolhos Islands, Western Australia, where it usually forms colonies of this shape.
PHOTOGRAPH: ED LOVELL.

3. The polyps of *Oxypora glabra*.
PHOTOGRAPH: ED LOVELL.

Genus
MYCEDIUM
(pronounced my-see-dee-um)

Oken, 1815

Mycedium elephantotus from Moreton Bay displays . . . such wide variation from thin, widely spaced, to close, thick, irregularly and spinosely dentate septa, and from superficial through pocket-shaped to irregularly elevated, cylindrical calices, as to make it probable that the various 'species' of this genus . . . are actually a single variable species.

John Wells
Recent and Subfossil Corals from Moreton Bay,
Queensland, 1955.

TYPE SPECIES
Mycedium elephantotus Pallas, 1766.

FOSSIL RECORD
Known only from the Pliocene.

NUMBER OF SPECIES
Three nominal species, two true species, one from Australia.

SIMILAR GENERA
Mycedium is closest to *Echinophyllia* but is distinguished by its outwardly inclined nose–shaped corallites and the absence of pits in the coenosteum.

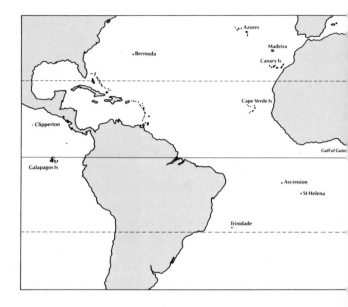

1. *Mycedium elephantotus* at Davies Reef, Great Barrier Reef, showing concentric rows of polyps facing towards the edge of the colony.
PHOTOGRAPH: ED LOVELL.

2. A common rough appearance of *Mycedium elephantotus*, due to prominent irregular costae.
PHOTOGRAPH: ED LOVELL.

3. *Mycedium elephantotus* at Heron Island, Great Barrier Reef, with smooth-walled polyps.
PHOTOGRAPH: RON AND VALERIE TAYLOR.

4. *Mycedium elephantotus* at Lord Howe Island, eastern Australia.
PHOTOGRAPH: JOHN BARNETT.

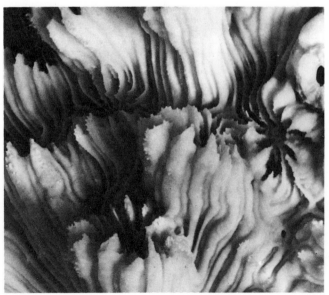

×2.5

Mycedium elephantotus
(PALLAS, 1766)

TYPE LOCALITY
"Indian Ocean".

IDENTIFYING CHARACTERS
Colonies are laminar or foliaceous.
Corallites are nose–shaped, facing outward towards the corallum perimeter. Septa and columellae are well developed and costae form outwardly radiating ribs on the corallum surface which may become highly elaborated on corallite walls. The coenosteum is never pitted at the insertion of new septo–costae.
Polyps are extended only at night.

COLOUR
Usually a uniform brown, grey, green or pink but may have green or red oral discs and may have a coloured margin around the colony.

SIMILAR SPECIES
None.

DISTRIBUTION
From the Red Sea east to Tahiti. Around Australia: the Great Barrier Reef, Coral Sea and Lord Howe Island in the east, and south to Houtman Abrolhos Islands on the west coast.

ABUNDANCE
Common over a wide range of habitats.

2

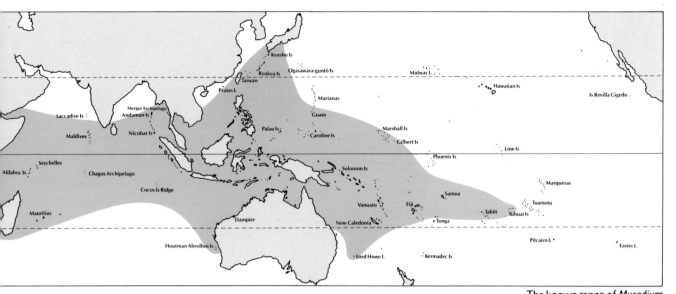

The known range of *Mycedium*.

3

4

GENUS
PECTINIA
(pronounced pek-tin-ee-a)

Oken, 1815

The synonymy . . . is in a hopeless state. A critical reading of the available literature on the genus Pectinia *with careful comparison of the various figures of species will show how difficult it is to pin down the different species. The so-called characters of specimens identified by various authors . . . overlap.*

Georg Scheer and Gapinadha Pillai,
Report on the Scleractinia from the Nicobar Islands, 1974.

Pectinia is a distinctive genus which includes some of the most beautifully coloured colonies to be found in the coral world. These are mostly autumn colours: reds, browns and greens. The genus has several common names like hibiscus coral, and carnation coral.

Tentacles are long and tubular and are widely spaced around the mouth.

TYPE SPECIES
Madrepora lactuca Pallas, 1766.

WELL-KNOWN SYNONYM
Tridacophyllia de Blainville, 1830.

FOSSIL RECORD
None.

NUMBER OF SPECIES
Fourteen nominal species, seven true species, four of which are Australian.

CHARACTERS
Colonies are laminar to sub-arborescent, covered with high, thin, acute irregular walls usually arranged as short wide valleys. Valleys may be as short as they are wide and the walls may form tall spires, becoming sub-arborescent.
Corallite centres occur in any position. Septo-costae are well developed and may form the start of walls or spires. Polyps are extended only at night and then only rarely.

SIMILAR GENERA
Pectinia resembles only *Physophyllia*, which is not found in Australia.

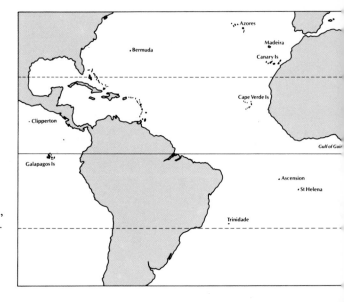

Pectinia lactuca
(PALLAS, 1766)

TYPE LOCALITY
Unrecorded.

IDENTIFYING CHARACTERS
Colonies have elongate valleys and walls, the latter of relatively uniform height. Most valleys can be traced from the colony margins to the centre.

COLOUR
Uniform grey, brown or green.

SIMILAR SPECIES
This is the most distinctive of the Australian *Pectinia*.

DISTRIBUTION
From Madagascar east to Vanuatu and Fiji.
Around Australia: the Great Barrier Reef in the east, and south to Ningaloo Reef Tract on the west coast.

ABUNDANCE
Common on lower reef slopes and in turbid water habitats where colonies frequently exceed 1 m in diameter.

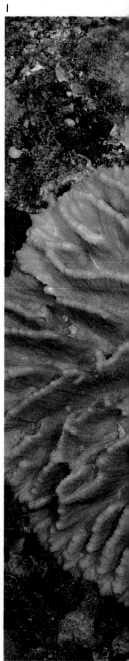

I. A small colony of *Pectinia lactuca.*
PHOTOGRAPH: LEN ZELL.

2. *Pectinia lactuca* showing the long radiating valleys which best characterise the species.
PHOTOGRAPH: AUTHOR.

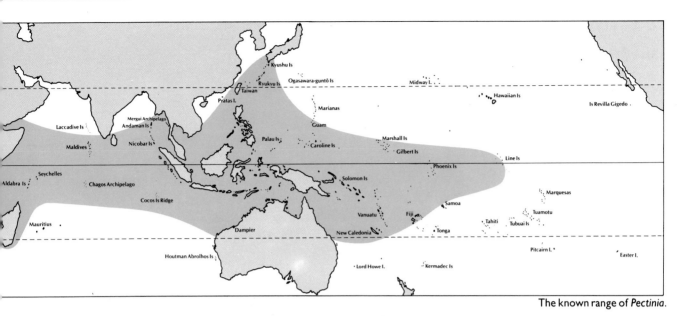

The known range of *Pectinia*.

2

Pectinia paeonia
(DANA, 1846)

TYPE LOCALITY
Fiji.

IDENTIFYING CHARACTERS
Colonies never have extended valleys, but consist of irregular clusters of fluted thin laminae with very prominent costae forming upwardly projecting spires. Columellae are weakly developed. Septa are smooth or have small teeth.

COLOUR
Uniform brown or grey.

SIMILAR SPECIES
P. alcicornis is distinguished by its more solid structures and tall spires, its well-developed columellae and also by the strong teeth on the costae.

DISTRIBUTION
Widely distributed, at least from Sri Lanka east to New Caledonia and Fiji.
Around Australia: the Great Barrier Reef in the east, and south to North West Cape on the west coast.

ABUNDANCE
Common in turbid water habitats, especially on fringing reefs.

1. *Pectinia paeonia* at Broadhurst Reef, Great Barrier Reef, showing the most common of the species's many growth forms.
PHOTOGRAPH: ED LOVELL.

2. *Pectinia paeonia* colonies may have almost frond-like laminae.
PHOTOGRAPH: AUTHOR.

3. A large colony of *Pectinia paeonia* showing clusters of thin, fluted laminae.
PHOTOGRAPH: RON AND VALERIE TAYLOR.

4. *Pectinia paeonia* is often one of the most delicately coloured of all corals. These colours can be photographed but not preserved or copied.
PHOTOGRAPH: RON AND VALERIE TAYLOR.

3

4

Pectinia alcicornis

(SAVILLE-KENT, 1871)

TYPE LOCALITY
Solomon Islands.

IDENTIFYING CHARACTERS
Colonies are as described for *P. paeonia* except that most structures are more solid. Upward-projecting spires may be very tall and the dominant part of the colony. Columellae are well developed. Costae are characteristically toothed.

COLOUR
Mixtures of greens, yellows and browns. Central parts of colonies are usually darker than outer parts.

SIMILAR SPECIES
P. paeonia.

DISTRIBUTION
Indonesia, south to Australia and east to the Solomon Islands. Around Australia: the Great Barrier Reef in the east, and Seringapatam Reef on the west coast.

ABUNDANCE
Common in turbid water, especially on horizontal substrates.

Pectinia alcicornis at Torres Strait showing a characteristic spire-like growth form.
PHOTOGRAPH: LEN ZELL.

Pectinia teres

NEMENZO, 1981

TYPE LOCALITY
The Philippines.

IDENTIFYING CHARACTERS
Colonies consist of clumps of pointed branches each composed of prominent costae. Corallites are conspicuous.

COLOUR
Grey.

SIMILAR SPECIES
P. paeonia and P. lactuca.

DISTRIBUTION
Australia and the Philippines. Around Australia: the Rowley Shoals and Scott and Seringapatam Reefs on the west coast; not found in the east.

ABUNDANCE
Rare.

Pectinia teres from the Rowley Shoals, Western Australia, showing the development of branches rather than laminae.
PHOTOGRAPH: AUTHOR.

Symphyllia wilsoni has a very wide colour range and is one of
the most beautiful corals of south-western Australia.
A member of Family Mussidae, this species is found
nowhere else. See also p. 421.

PHOTOGRAPH: ED LOVELL.

Family
Mussidae

(pronounced muss-id-ee)

ORTMANN, 1890

Mussids are usually recognised easily; they have heavily constructed skeletons with large teeth on the septa. Polyps are usually thick, fleshy and colourful. The genera of the Mussidae are well defined and easily identified. Most are widespread, and *Lobophyllia* and *Symphyllia* are readily found on most Indo-Pacific reefs.

Polyps are extended only at night. Polyps of the different genera are generally similar with large numbers of sturdy tentacles that appear well suited for capturing actively swimming zooplankton.

Acanthastrea, Lobophyllia and *Symphyllia* are hermaphrodites and release eggs and sperm into the water for external fertilisation.

CHARACTERS
All genera are hermatypic, solitary or colonial, extant or fossil. Skeletal structures are solid. Corallites and valleys are large. Septa have large teeth or lobes. Columellae and walls are thick and well developed.

RELATED FAMILY
Pectiniidae.

EARLIEST FOSSILS
? Eocene.

THE GENERA
All Indo-Pacific genera (*Blastomussa, Cynarina, Scolymia, Australomussa, Acanthastrea, Lobophyllia* and *Symphyllia*) occur in Australia. All are restricted to the Indo-Pacific except *Scolymia* which also occurs in the West Indies and Brazil. There are five more mussid genera restricted to the Atlantic: *Mussa, Isophyllia, Isophyllastrea* and *Mycetophyllia* from the West Indies and *Mussismillia* from Brazil.

KEY TO GENERA OF AUSTRALIAN MUSSIDAE

Corals solitary

    Septa plunge steeply, with 1 to 3 large lobed teeth . . . *Cynarina* (p. 396)

    Septa slope evenly, with numerous similar teeth . . . *Scolymia* (p. 400)

Corals colonial

    Colonies with 1 central centre and with lateral centres

        Lateral centres in shallow valleys . . . *Australomussa* (p. 404)

        Lateral centres not in valleys . . . *Scolymia* (p. 400)

    Colonies meandroid

        Valleys shallow, with indistinct walls, septa with low blunt teeth . . . *Australomussa* (p. 404)

        Valleys with distinct walls, septa with sharp spiny teeth . . . *Symphyllia* (p. 420)

    Colonies meandro-phaceloid . . . *Lobophyllia* (p. 412)

    Colonies phaceloid

        Corallites less than 15 mm in diameter, with gently sloping septa and small teeth . . . *Blastomussa* (p. 392)

        Corallites over 15 mm in diameter, with sharp spiny teeth . . . *Lobophyllia* (p. 412)

    Colonies cerioid or subplocoid . . . *Acanthastrea* (p. 406)

Note: This key is a guide only and should be used in conjunction with the descriptions of the genera. It assumes colonies are well developed.

GENUS
BLASTOMUSSA
(pronounced blasto-muss-a)

Wells, 1961

Although most corals display a range of colours, some of which are characteristic of the species, only *Blastomussa* has two distinct colour morphs: one red, the other brown or greenish-brown.

As *Blastomussa* colonies grow, the individual corallites often lose all organic connection. The colony, by usual definition, then ceases to be a colony and becomes a clone of solitary individuals, presumably competing with each other for food and space.

TYPE SPECIES
Blastomussa merleti Wells, 1961.

FOSSIL RECORD
Pleistocene.

NUMBER OF SPECIES
Three true species, two from Australia.

CHARACTERS
Colonies are phaceloid with irregularly spaced sprawling corallites.
Corallites have one centre with a weakly developed columella. Septa slope gently to the corallite centre and have lobed teeth. Corallite walls are enveloped with, and often joined by, epitheca.
Polyps have fleshy mantles extended during the day to form a continuous cover obliterating the phaceloid colony structure underneath. Polyps are extended only at night. Both species have two colour morphs, one being red.

SIMILAR GENERA
Caulastrea also has phaceloid colonies which are usually green but corallites do not have mantles and septa are fine, without lobed teeth.

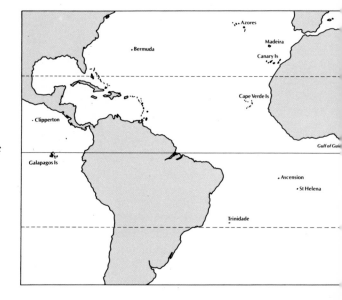

Blastomussa merleti
(WELLS, 1961)

TYPE LOCALITY
New Caledonia.

IDENTIFYING CHARACTERS
Corallites are less than 7 mm in diameter. Septa are in three cycles, of which only the first two reach the columella.

COLOUR
Dark red or greenish-brown (two colour morphs).

SIMILAR SPECIES
B. wellsi has much larger corallites with more numerous septa.

DISTRIBUTION
From Madagascar east to New Caledonia.
Around Australia: the Great Barrier Reef in the east, and south to Houtman Abrolhos Islands on the west coast.

ABUNDANCE
Uncommon.

1. A large colony of *Blastomussa merleti* at the Houtman Abrolhos Islands, Western Australia.
PHOTOGRAPH: ED LOVELL.

2. The polyps of *Blastomussa merleti* at Lizard Island, Great Barrier Reef. These often lose organic contact and become a group of solitary individuals.
PHOTOGRAPH: LEN ZELL.

3. *Blastomussa merleti* at Endeavour Reef, Great Barrier Reef.
PHOTOGRAPH: AUTHOR.

x2.5

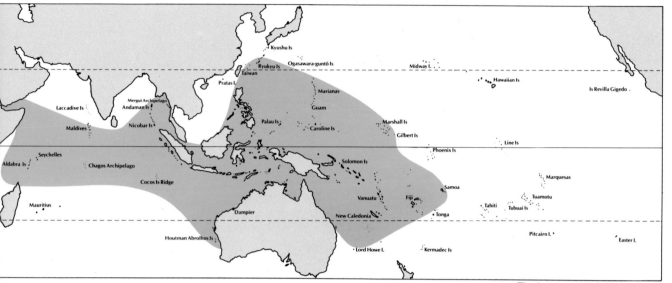

The known range of *Blastomussa*.

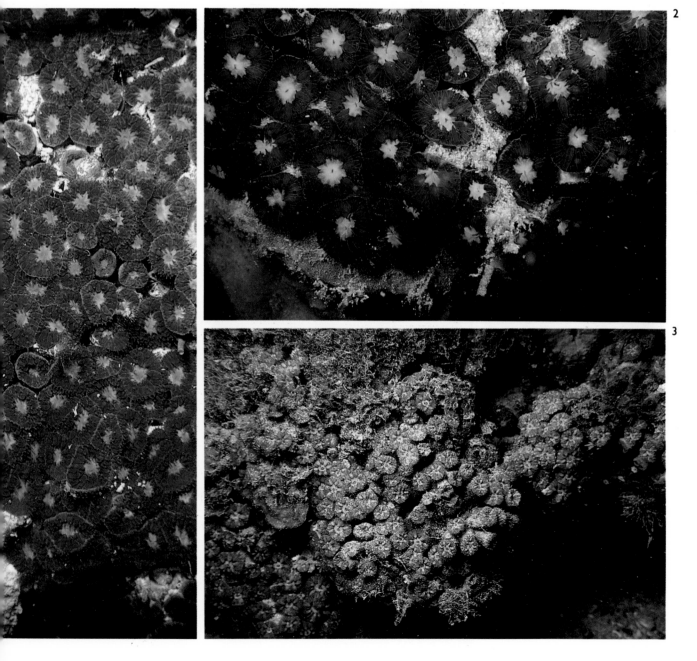

2

3

Blastomussa wellsi

WIJSMAN-BEST 1973

TYPE LOCALITY
New Caledonia.

IDENTIFYING CHARACTERS
Corallites are 9-14 mm in diameter. Septa are not arranged in cycles and are numerous.

COLOUR
Dark red or green (two colour morphs).

SIMILAR SPECIES
B. merleti.

DISTRIBUTION
New Caledonia and Australia. Around Australia: the Great Barrier Reef, Coral Sea and Elizabeth and Middleton Reefs in the east, and Houtman Abrolhos Islands on the west coast.

ABUNDANCE
Uncommon except on some lower reef slope habitats.

x2.5

1,3. The red colour morph of *Blastomussa wellsi*. Polyps have their fleshy mantle extended (right), and retracted after being disturbed (left).
PHOTOGRAPHS: ED LOVELL.

2. The green colour morph of *Blastomussa wellsi*.
PHOTOGRAPH: LEN ZELL.

4. Polyps of *Blastomussa wellsi*.
PHOTOGRAPH: ED LOVELL.

GENUS
CYNARINA
(pronounced sigh-na-ree-na)

Brüggemann, 1877

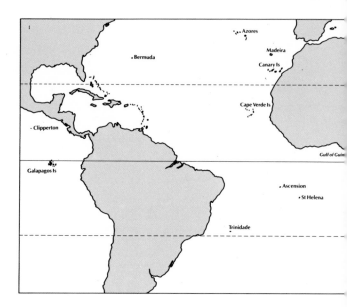

This is of the most delicately beautiful of all corals. During the day the body cavity is inflated with water, forming a series of radiating lobes, each lobe corresponding to a major septum. The body wall is translucent, allowing the septa to be seen through patterns of delicate pastel colours which are different in each individual. At night the lobes contract and delicate translucent tentacles are extended. These are folded inward in an anemone-like fashion if the coral is disturbed, or if prey is caught.

Cynarina species are usually found on lower reef slopes attached to rock walls or under overhangs. Sometimes they are found free-living on soft substrates.

Despite their delicate appearance, *Cynarina*, alone among the mussids, are tolerant of a wide range of environmental conditions and make good aquarium specimens.

TYPE SPECIES
Cynarina savignyi Brüggemann, 1877 from the Red Sea.

FOSSIL RECORD
Miocene from the East Indies.

NUMBER OF SPECIES
Nine nominal species, one or two true species, one from Australia.

x1

Diagram 20. The large-lobed septal teeth of *Cynarina*. Such teeth are characteristic of mussids.
DRAWING: GEOFF KELLY.

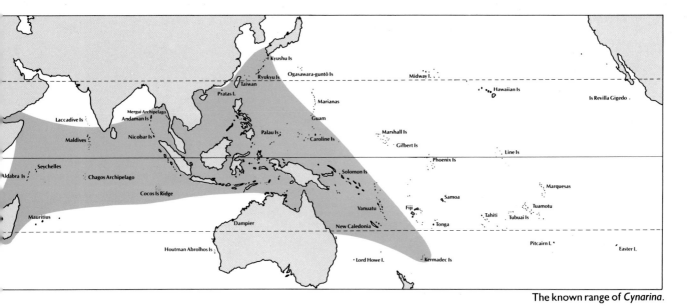

The known range of *Cynarina*.

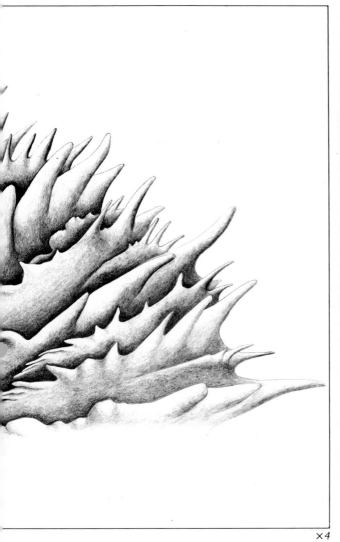

×4

Above and 1 over: Two common colour combinations of *Cynarina lacrymalis.*
PHOTOGRAPHS: ED LOVELL (ABOVE) AND RON AND VALERIE TAYLOR (OVER).

397

Cynarina lacrymalis

(EDWARDS & HAIME, 1848)

TYPE LOCALITY
The Philippines.

IDENTIFYING CHARACTERS
Corals are monocentric (oval or circular), cylindrical, with a base for attachment or with a pointed base, and free-living.
Primary septa are thick and have very large teeth. Paliform lobes are usually well developed. Columellae are broad and compact.
Polyps are extended only at night. They are translucent so that the toothed primary septa are seen clearly within lobes of the polyp wall.

COLOUR
Various mixtures of almost all colours.

SIMILAR SPECIES
Cynarina does not closely resemble any other genus.

DISTRIBUTION
The full range of the genus. Around Australia: the Great Barrier Reef and Coral Sea in the east; not found on the west coast.

ABUNDANCE
Seldom common but always conspicuous.

1. See previous page.
2. The mouth of *Cynarina lacrymalis*. The large primary septa are seen clearly through the transparent polyp wall.
PHOTOGRAPH: ED LOVELL.

3. At night the lobed polyp wall of *Cynarina lacrymalis* is retracted and tentacles are extended.
PHOTOGRAPH: ED LOVELL.

4. If *Cynarina lacrymalis* is disturbed while tentacles are extended, the polyp retracts in an anemone-like manner.
PHOTOGRAPH: ED LOVELL.

5. *Cynarina lacrymalis* from the Swain Reefs, Great Barrier Reef, a spectacular solitary coral and a favourite of photographers.
PHOTOGRAPH: LEN ZELL.

3

5

GENUS
SCOLYMIA
(pronounced skolly-my-a)

Haime, 1852

This was formerly believed to be an Atlantic Ocean genus with *Parascolymia* being its Indo–Pacific tropical homologue. A third genus, *Homophyllia*, was used for a separate species (*S. australis*) from the southern coastline of Australia. These forms have essentially similar skeletal characters and the polyps, in contrast to those of *Cynarina*, are also similar.

TYPE SPECIES
Madrepora lacera Pallas, 1766 from the Caribbean.

SYNONYMS
Homophyllia Brüggemann, 1877; *Parascolymia* Wells, 1964.

FOSSIL RECORD
Miocene from Indonesia.

NUMBER OF SPECIES
Six nominal species, two true species from the Indo–Pacific (found in Australia), and two nominal species from the Atlantic.

CHARACTERS
Corals are usually monocentric, rarely polycentric. Secondary centres may occur inside or outside the original calice and calices may divide. Walls are indistinct beneath the septo–costae. Septa slope evenly, with little fusion. Primary septa have large, regular, blunt teeth. Columellae are broad and compact. Polyps are extended only at night.

SIMILAR GENERA
The skeletal structure of *Scolymia* resembles that of *Australomussa*.
Scolymia species do not have large polyps like *Cynarina*.

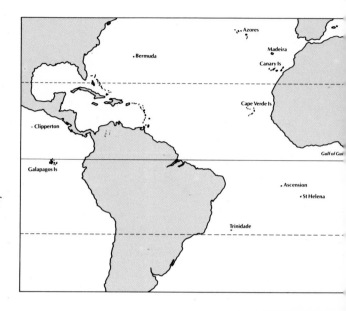

Scolymia vitiensis
BRÜGGEMANN, 1877

TYPE LOCALITY
Fiji.

IDENTIFYING CHARACTERS
There is wide latitudinal variation in this species. In temperate localities it is usually solitary, saucer-shaped and less than 60 mm in diameter. In the tropics it becomes colonial and septo-costae slope up from the centre to an indistinct wall, then down to the periphery. Secondary centres may occur near the colony centre and also around the periphery. Septo–costae are sturdy with large blunt teeth.

COLOUR
Usually dark green.

SIMILAR SPECIES
S. australis may be indistinguishable from juvenile *S. vitiensis*.

DISTRIBUTION
Australia and east to Fiji and the Marshall Islands.
Around Australia: the Great Barrier Reef, Coral Sea and south to Elizabeth and Middleton Reefs in the east; not found on the west coast.

ABUNDANCE
Seldom common but occurs in a wide range of environments.

x1

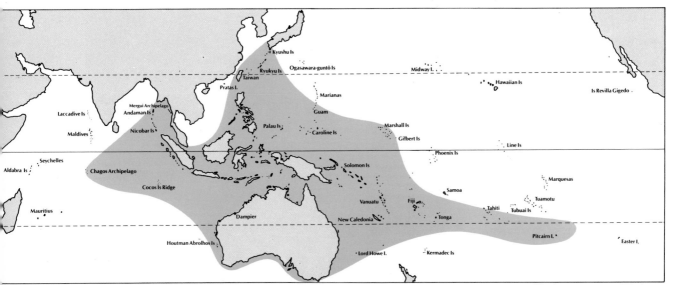

The known range of *Scolymia*.

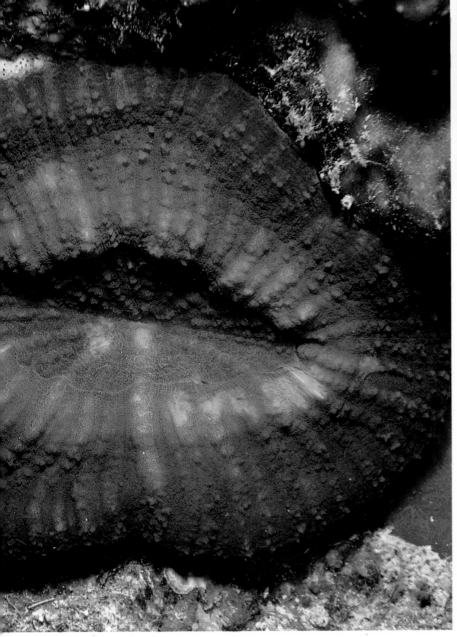

1. The distinctive appearance of a mature *Scolymia vitiensis*.
PHOTOGRAPH: RON AND VALERIE TAYLOR.

2. A small *Scolymia vitiensis*. These closely resemble *S. australis* from southern localities.
PHOTOGRAPH: LEN ZELL.

Scolymia australis

(EDWARDS & HAIME, 1849)

TYPE LOCALITY
Port Lincoln, South Australia.

IDENTIFYING CHARACTERS
Usually solitary, sometimes with two to four centres in the one or more separate corallites. Corallites are less than 60 mm in diameter and saucer-shaped. Septo-costae are sturdy with blunt saw-like teeth.

COLOUR
Colourful, commonly mixtures of cream, red, blue and green.

SIMILAR SPECIES
S. *vitiensis*.

DISTRIBUTION
Known only from Australia: the eastern and southern coast, and the west coast north to Rottnest Island.

ABUNDANCE
Relatively common at Elizabeth and Middleton Reefs, Lord Howe Island and the south-west coast; uncommon elsewhere but always conspicuous.

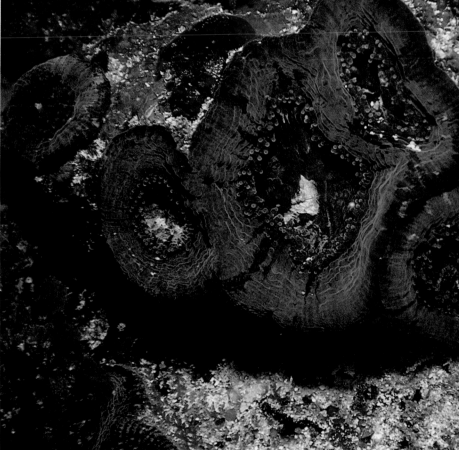

1,2,3. Colour combinations of *Scolymia australis* from southern Australia.
PHOTOGRAPHS: RON AND VALERIE TAYLOR (1), NIGEL HOLMES (2) AND NEVILLE COLEMAN A.M.P.I. (3).

4. *Scolymia australis* sometimes forms a colony of several polyps, but this is rare
PHOTOGRAPH: NIGEL HOLMES.

5. *Scolymia australis* with tentacles extended.
PHOTOGRAPH: RON AND VALERIE TAYLOR.

3

GENUS
AUSTRALOMUSSA
(pronounced ostral-oh-muss-a)

Veron, 1985

This genus has only one species, *A. rowleyensis*, first seen by the author at the Rowley Shoals off north-western Australia. It was then seen at several places down the Western Australian coast and was thought to be endemic to the coast (hence its name). It is, however, one of the most common mussids of the Mergui Archipelago and western Thailand and is now known to have a wider Indo–Pacific distribution.

TYPE SPECIES
Australomussa rowleyensis Veron, 1985.

FOSSIL RECORD
None.

NUMBER OF SPECIES
One.

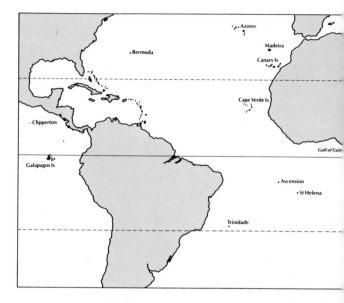

Australomussa rowleyensis
VERON, 1985

TYPE LOCALITY
Dampier Archipelago, Western Australia.

IDENTIFYING CHARACTERS
Colonies are flattened, helmet- or dome-shaped and are covered with short, shallow valleys 8–20 mm wide and separated by thick walls.

COLOUR
A uniform blue-grey, or valleys may have concentric cream and green colours. In Thailand colonies have a much wider range of colours including bright red, yellow and green.

SIMILAR SPECIES
None.

DISTRIBUTION
Around Australia: South to Dampier Archipelago; not found in the east.

ABUNDANCE
Rare.

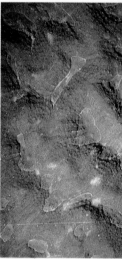

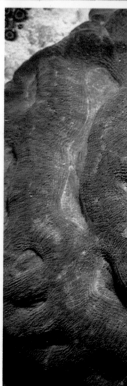

1. Polyps of *Australomussa rowleyensis*.
PHOTOGRAPH: ED LOVELL.

2. *Australomussa rowleyensis* at the Mergui Archipelago, Thailand, where it is common and often brightly coloured.
PHOTOGRAPH: AUTHOR.

3. The first *Australomussa rowleyensis* sighted by the author, at the Rowley Shoals, Western Australia.
PHOTOGRAPH: AUTHOR.

4. The polyps of *Australomussa rowleyensis* at Dampier Archipelago, Western Australia.
PHOTOGRAPH: ED LOVELL.

5. A large *Australomussa rowleyensis* colony at Dampier Archipelago, Western Australia.
PHOTOGRAPH: ED LOVELL.

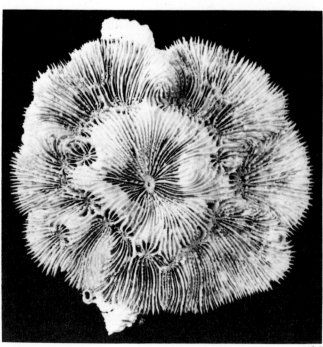

x0.5

4

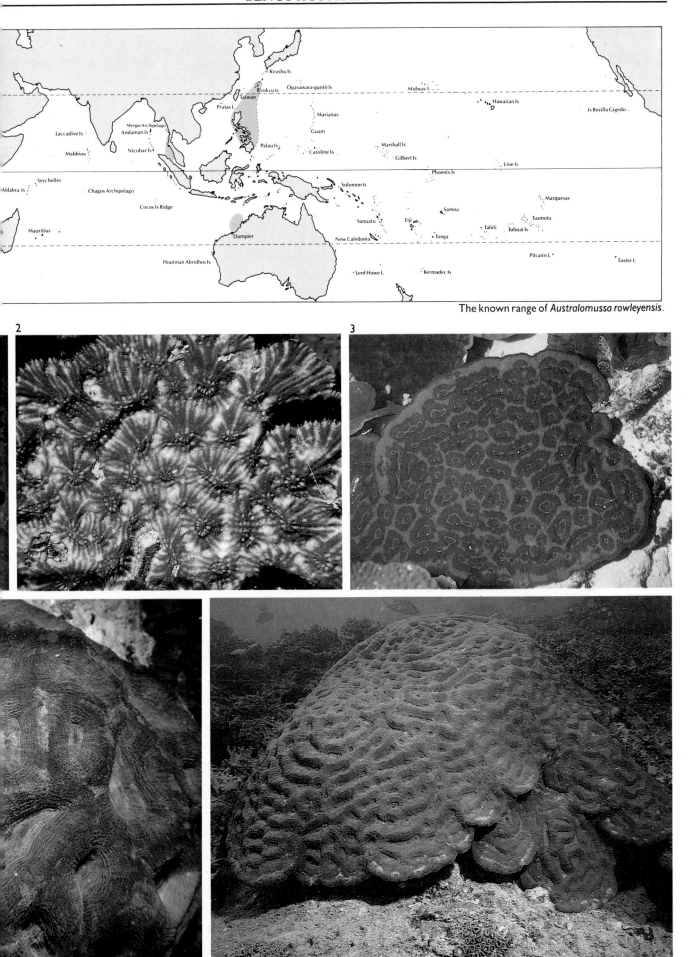

The known range of *Australomussa rowleyensis*.

2

3

5

Genus
ACANTHASTREA
(pronounced ak-an-thas-tree-a)

Edwards & Haime, 1848

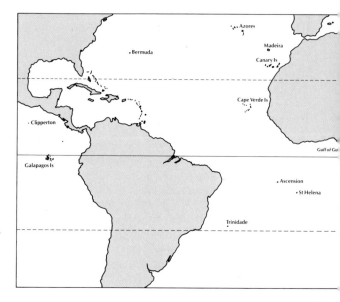

Specimens of *Acanthastrea*, alone among the mussids, may present identification problems because of similarities with faviids, especially *Favia, Favites* and *Moseleya*. They are identified much more readily under water, where thick fleshy polyps obscure underlying skeletal structures, just as they do with most other mussids.

There is only one common *Acanthastrea, A. echinata*, on most tropical reefs. The other species are generally more abundant in temperate latitudes.

TYPE SPECIES
Acanthastrea spinosa Edwards & Haime, 1848 = *Astrea echinata* Dana, 1846 from Tonga.

FOSSIL RECORD
Miocene to Recent from the Indo-Pacific.

NUMBER OF SPECIES
Approximately 13 nominal species, approximately six true species, four of which are Australian.

CHARACTERS
Colonies are massive, usually flat.
Corallites are cerioid or subplocoid, monocentric, either circular or angular in shape. Septo-costae are thick near the corallite wall, becoming thin near the columella, and have tall mussid teeth.
Polyps are thick-walled and are extended only at night.

SIMILAR GENERA
Acanthastrea does not resemble any other mussid genus, with the exception of *A. hillae* which is sometimes *Symphyllia*-like. However, *Acanthastrea* species are readily confused with Faviidae, especially *Favites* (in the case of *A. echinata*) and *Moseleya* (in the case of *A. hillae* and *A. bowerbanki*).

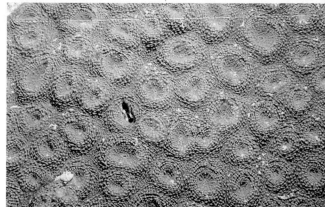

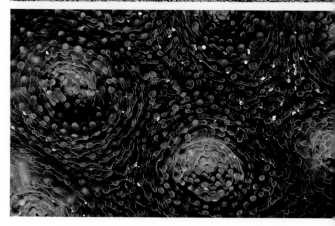

1. *Acanthastrea* at night. All species extend a thick tangle of tentacles.
PHOTOGRAPH: LEN ZELL.

2. *Acanthastrea echinata* at Heron Island, Great Barrier Reef. This is the most common colour of the species.
PHOTOGRAPH: JOHN BARNETT.

3,4. The polyps of *Acanthastrea echinata*. Note the thick, fleshy appearance which conceals the underlying skeleton. This makes this common species easy to distinguish under water from any faviid.
PHOTOGRAPHS: RON AND VALERIE TAYLOR.

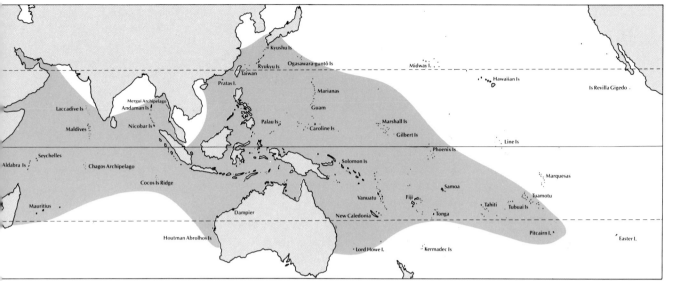

The known range of *Acanthastrea*.

Acanthastrea echinata

(DANA, 1846)

TYPE LOCALITY
Fiji.

IDENTIFYING CHARACTERS
Corallites are cerioid or subplocoid, circular, with thick walls. When retracted, polyps have thick concentric folds.

COLOUR
Uniform dull brown, grey or green.

SIMILAR SPECIES
A. hillae is cerioid with angular walls and usually has larger corallites. May be confused with *Favites*, but not under water where the fleshy polyps are prominent.

DISTRIBUTION
From the Red Sea east to the Marshall Islands and the Tuamotu Archipelago. Around Australia: the Great Barrier Reef, Coral Sea and south to Elizabeth Reef in the east, and south to Houtman Abrolhos Islands on the west coast.

ABUNDANCE
Common over a wide range of habitats. Rarely occurs over 1 m in diameter.

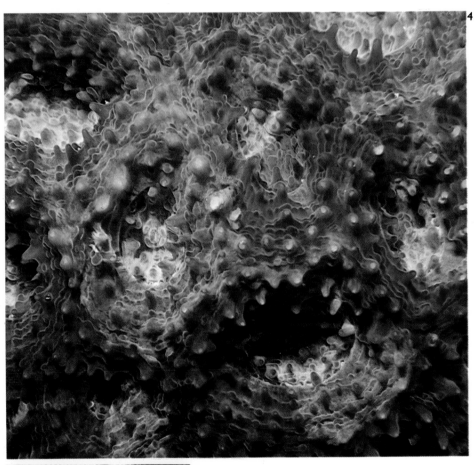

x1

Acanthastrea hillae

WELLS, 1955

TYPE LOCALITY
Moreton Bay.

IDENTIFYING CHARACTERS
Colonies are cerioid. Corallites have irregular shapes and sometimes become valleys with several centres. Polyps are fleshy when retracted.

COLOUR
Red, cream and brown, sometimes in mottled patterns.

SIMILAR SPECIES
Closest to *A. bowerbanki* which has non-fleshy polyps, thinner and more numerous septa and smaller, more diffuse columellae.

DISTRIBUTION
New Caledonia and Australia. Around Australia: the Great Barrier Reef and south to Solitary Islands in the east, and south to Houtman Abrolhos Islands on the west coast.

ABUNDANCE
Common south of the Great Barrier Reef except the Solitary Islands. Colonies may exceed 1.5 m in diameter and are conspicuous.

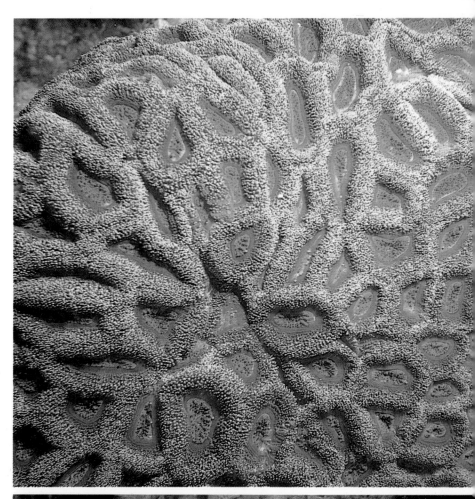

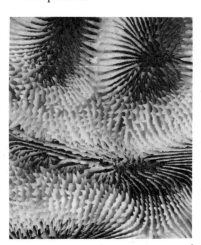

x1

1. *Acanthastrea hillae* at the Solitary Islands, eastern Australia. This conspicuous species is common at southern localities, especially Lord Howe Island, but is seldom encountered in the tropics.
PHOTOGRAPH: ED LOVELL.

2. The polyps of *Acanthastrea hillae*. As with *A. echinata*, the thick, fleshy polyps make the species immediately recognisable under water. In some colonies, some of the polyps are very elongate, almost *Symphyllia*-like.
PHOTOGRAPH: CLAY BRYCE.

Acanthastrea bowerbanki

EDWARDS & HAIME, 1851

TYPE LOCALITY
"Australia".

IDENTIFYING CHARACTERS
Colonies are cerioid. Corallites have irregular angular shapes and a central corallite may be conspicuous. Septa are relatively thin and compact and the columellae small. Polyps are not fleshy.

COLOUR
Commonly pale grey, brown or rust-coloured, often mottled.

SIMILAR SPECIES
A. hillae, also Moseleya. If a central corallite is inconspicuous it resembles Favites, especially under water.

DISTRIBUTION
Recorded from Australia and Rodriguez Island.
Around Australia: the southern Great Barrier Reef, Coral Sea and south to Lord Howe Island in the east; not found on the west coast.

ABUNDANCE
Rare except at Lord Howe Island where colonies may exceed 2 m in diameter.

×1

1. *Acanthastrea bowerbanki* from Lord Howe Island, eastern Australia.
PHOTOGRAPH: LEN ZELL.

2. The polyps of *Acanthastrea bowerbanki*. Unlike other *Acanthastrea*, the polyps are not thick and fleshy and thus may resemble those of *Favites* under water.
PHOTOGRAPH: LEN ZELL.

3. A small colony of *Acanthastrea bowerbankii* showing the large central polyp from which daughter polyps bud in concentric rows.
PHOTOGRAPH: JOHN BARNETT.

Acanthastrea lordhowensis

VERON & PICHON, 1982

TYPE LOCALITY
Lord Howe Island.

IDENTIFYING CHARACTERS
Colonies are cerioid with laterally compressed corallites of uneven heights. Walls are very acute, septa are thick with very large teeth. Columellae are barely developed. Living colonies have fleshy polyps.

COLOUR
Very colourful: red, purple and green are the most common colours.

SIMILAR SPECIES
None.

DISTRIBUTION
Hong Kong, the Philippines and Australia.
Around Australia: the Flinders Reef (Moreton Bay), Elizabeth and Middleton Reefs, Lord Howe and Solitary Islands in the east, and Dampier Archipelago and Burrup Peninsula on the west coast.

ABUNDANCE
Sometimes common. Usually conspicuous.

x1

1-6. *Acanthastrea lordhowensis* is a common species in temperate localities. These are just some of the colour combinations.
PHOTOGRAPHS: JOHN BARNETT (1), LEN ZELL (2, 4 AND 5), ED LOVELL (3) AND NEVILLE COLEMAN A.M.P.I. (6).

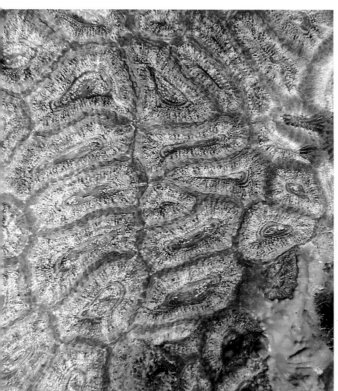
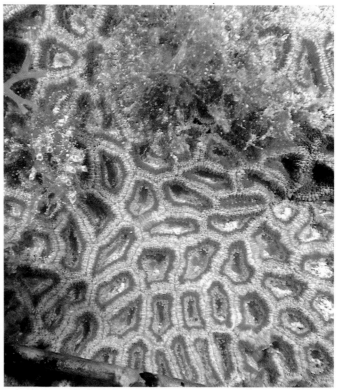

5

6

GENUS
LOBOPHYLLIA

(pronounced lobo-fill-ee-a)

de Blainville, 1830

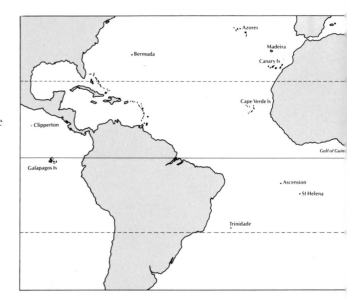

Lobophyllia are by far the most common mussids and are usually found on all but the most exposed reef slopes. This widespread abundance is due to a single species, *L. hemprichii*, which is easily recognised once its extraordinary range of growth forms and colours are appreciated. The other *Lobophyllia* species are seldom common in any habitat and show little variation in growth form or colour.

TYPE SPECIES
Madrepora corymbosa Forskål, 1775.

FOSSIL RECORD
Miocene from Indonesia.

NUMBER OF SPECIES
Twenty-two nominal species, five true species from Australia.

CHARACTERS
Colonies are phaceloid to flabello-meandroid, either flat-topped or dome-shaped.
Corallites and/or valleys are large. Septa are large with very long teeth. Columella centres are broad and compact.
Polyps are extended only at night. Tentacles usually have white tips.

SIMILAR GENERA
Only *Symphyllia* has coarse skeletal structures comparable to *Lobophyllia*, but only *L. hattai*, which is partly meandroid, can be confused with *Symphyllia*.

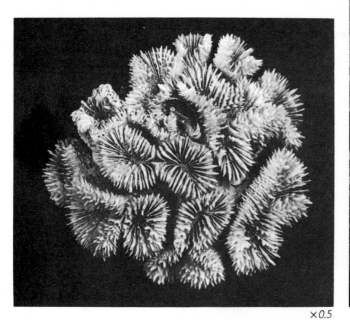

×0.5

1. *Lobophyllia* hardly ever extend their polyps during the day. At night the different species look similar.
PHOTOGRAPH: LEN ZELL.

412

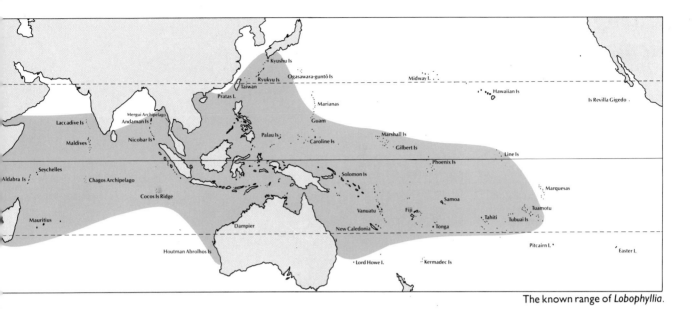

The known range of *Lobophyllia*.

2. Two colonies of *Lobophyllia hemprichii*.

PHOTOGRAPH: RON AND VALERIE TAYLOR.

Lobophyllia hemprichii

(EHRENBERG, 1834)

TYPE LOCALITY
Red Sea.

IDENTIFYING CHARACTERS
Colonies are flat to hemispherical, phaceloid to flabello-meandroid, the latter with valleys dividing irregularly as growing space permits. Septa taper in thickness from the wall to the columella and have tall sharp teeth. Retracted polyps are thick and fleshy, with either smooth or rough surfaces.

COLOUR
Colonies may be uniform in colour or have two or more colours concentrically around the mouths or valleys. All corallites of the same colony have the same colours.

SIMILAR SPECIES
Whereas *L. hemprichii* is very polymorphic, other *Lobophyllia* species show little variation. Phaceloid *L. hemprichii* are similar to *L. corymbosa* and *L. pachysepta*. Under water it is easily confused with *Symphyllia* as the thick fleshy polyps mask the underlying growth form.

DISTRIBUTION
From eastern Africa and the Red Sea east to Tahiti and the Tuamotu Archipelago.
Around Australia: the Great Barrier Reef, Coral Sea and Flinders Reef (Moreton Bay) in the east, and south to Houtman Abrolhos Islands on the west coast.

ABUNDANCE
Very common and frequently a dominant on upper reef slopes where different colonies may form monospecific stands.

1,2. A compound colony of *Lobophyllia hemprichii* at Wistari Reef, Great Barrier Reef. This species may be very abundant on some reef slopes protected from strong wave action, and separate colonies may grow together and take the shape of a single colony. The skeletons of the different original colonies shown here were very similar, but the polyps reflect the wide range of colours and textures this species always displays.
PHOTOGRAPHS: JOHN BARNETT.

3. A *Lobophyllia hemprichii* at an early stage of colony formation.
PHOTOGRAPH: ED LOVELL.

4. Polyps of *Lobophyllia hemprichii* often have a coarse texture but others may be almost smooth.
PHOTOGRAPH: RON AND VALERIE TAYLOR.

5. *Lobophyllia hemprichii* at Middleton Reef, eastern Australia, showing a mixture of polyp shapes.
PHOTOGRAPH: ED LOVELL.

4

5

Lobophyllia diminuta

VERON, 1985

TYPE LOCALITY
Swain Reefs, Great Barrier Reef.

IDENTIFYING CHARACTERS
Colonies are phaceloid, each corallite has one to three centres. Corallites average 16 mm in diameter and have very elongate septal spines.

COLOUR
Mottled orange and white.

SIMILAR SPECIES
L. diminuta is like a diminutive *L. hemprichii*.

DISTRIBUTION
Known only from Australia: the Swain Reefs (Great Barrier Reef) in the east; not found on the west coast.

ABUNDANCE
Very rare.

Lobophyllia diminuta at the Swain Reefs, Great Barrier Reef. This rare species is readily distinguished by its small polyps and large septal teeth.
PHOTOGRAPH: AUTHOR.

Lobophyllia corymbosa
(FORSKÅL, 1775)

TYPE LOCALITY
Red Sea.

IDENTIFYING CHARACTERS
Colonies are usually hemispherical, with one to three centres per branch. Calices are deep with well defined walls. Septa are thick near the walls and thin within the calice. Septal teeth are tall and blunt, decreasing in size towards the columella.

COLOUR
Colonies are a dull greenish-brown with pale centres.

SIMILAR SPECIES
L. corymbosa differs from phaceloid *L. hemprichii* by the shape of the calices and septa. *L. pachysepta* has thickened primary septa with large–lobed dentations. These species are distinct under water.

DISTRIBUTION
From eastern Africa and the Red Sea east to Tahiti and the Tuamotu Archipelago. Around Australia: the Great Barrier Reef, Coral Sea and Flinders Reef (Moreton Bay) in the east, and south to Houtman Abrolhos Islands on the west coast.

ABUNDANCE
Sometimes common on upper reef slopes but much less so than *L. hemprichii*. Colonies seldom exceed 0.5 m in diameter.

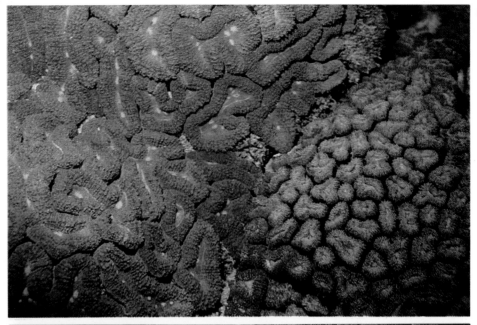

1. A comparison between *Lobophyllia hemprichii* (left) and *L. corymbosa* (right).
PHOTOGRAPH: LEN ZELL.

2. *Lobophyllia corymbosa* has little variation and this colony is typical.
PHOTOGRAPH: ED LOVELL.

3. The polyps of *Lobophyllia corymbosa*.
PHOTOGRAPH: ED LOVELL.

Lobophyllia pachysepta

CHEVALIER, 1975

TYPE LOCALITY
Chesterfield Reefs, eastern Coral Sea.

IDENTIFYING CHARACTERS
Colonies are flat or hemispherical, phaceloid or partly flabello-meandroid. Primary septa are very thick with three to five long lobed teeth.

COLOUR
Uniformly dark green with yellowish primary septa.

SIMILAR SPECIES
L. pachysepta is readily distinguished by its large-lobed primary septa, and under water by its colour.

DISTRIBUTION
Maldive Islands east to Australia. Around Australia: the Great Barrier Reef, Coral Sea and Elizabeth and Middleton Reefs in the east; not found on the west coast.

ABUNDANCE
Usually uncommon. Occurs on protected upper reef slopes and in lagoons.

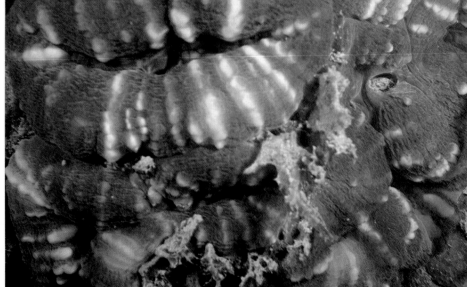

1. A single polyp of *Lobophyllia pachysepta*. Note the yellowish septal teeth visible beneath the polyp—this is characteristic of the species, although not always as clearly seen as here.
PHOTOGRAPH: ED LOVELL.

2. *Lobophyllia pachysepta* at the Whitsunday Islands, Great Barrier Reef. Colonies are always small and are usually composed of a few irregular polyps, as shown here.
PHOTOGRAPH: LEN ZELL.

Lobophyllia hataii

YABE, SUGIYAMA & EGUCHI, 1936

TYPE LOCALITY
Palau.

IDENTIFYING CHARACTERS
Colonies are meandro-phaceloid at the periphery, sometimes becoming submeandroid at the centre. Valleys are shallow with flat floors. Columellae are usually in two rows except at valley ends.

COLOUR
Usually brown or green. Valley floors and walls are usually of different colours.

SIMILAR SPECIES
Resembles *Symphyllia valenciennesii* more than other *Lobophyllia* species.

DISTRIBUTION
Maldive Islands east to the South China Sea, the Philippines and New Caledonia.
Around Australia: the Great Barrier Reef and Coral Sea in the east, and south to Houtman Abrolhos Islands on the west coast.

ABUNDANCE
Rare, found on upper reef slopes protected from wave action.

Lobophyllia hattai at Gould Reef, Great Barrier Reef. This species is difficult to distinguish under water.
PHOTOGRAPH: JOHN BARNETT.

GENUS
SYMPHYLLIA
(pronounced sim-fill-ee-a)

Edwards & Haime, 1848

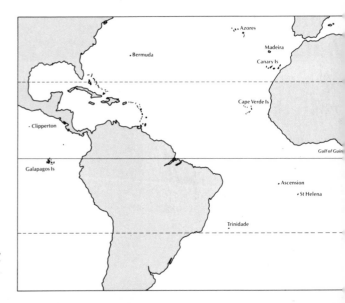

It is very unfortunate that Dana's greatly damaged and now quite worthless specimens were preserved and used as a basis for the resuscitation of his names nobilis and recta. The result is that a well-known name is altered, with no advantage to anyone ... also that, instead of the identification of later specimens depending upon Dana's types it is those types which are only recognisable from later specimens and work done upon them. Dana's samples should have been ignored.

Cyril Crossland,
Scientific Reports of the Great Barrier Reef Expedition, 1928-29, Volume 6, 1952.

There are three common and widely spread species, *S. recta, S. radians* and *S. agaricia*. These are generally recognised under water as having relatively small, middle-sized and large valleys respectively. Where different species cannot be directly compared, other characters can be used for identification.

Collecting specimens of *Symphyllia* for identification is usually no easy matter because they have the largest valleys of all corals and specimens large enough to show the shape of the valleys sometimes need to be 0.5 m wide.

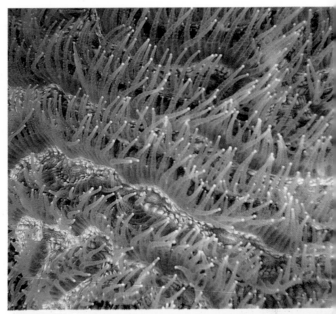

TYPE SPECIES
Meandrina sinuosa Quoy & Gaimard, 1833 from New Ireland.

FOSSIL RECORD
Pliocene.

NUMBER OF SPECIES
Thirteen nominal species, five true species from Australia.

CHARACTERS
Colonies are meandroid, either flat-topped or dome-shaped.
Valleys are wide. A groove usually runs along the top of the walls. Septa are large with very long teeth.
Columella centres are broad and compact.
Polyps are extended only at night.

SIMILAR GENERA
Only *Lobophyllia* has coarse skeletal structures comparable to *Symphyllia*.

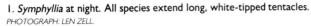

1. *Symphyllia* at night. All species extend long, white-tipped tentacles.
PHOTOGRAPH: LEN ZELL.

2. A large colony of *Symphyllia wilsoni* encrusting a rock in shallow water.
PHOTOGRAPH: CLAY BRYCE.

3, 4. Surface detail of two colour variants of *Symphyllia wilsoni*. There is almost always a groove along the tops of the valley walls.
PHOTOGRAPHS: AUTHOR (3) AND CLAY BRYCE (4).

×0.5

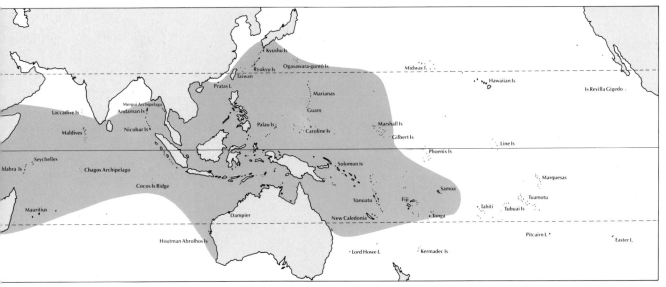

The known range of *Symphyllia*.

Symphyllia wilsoni

VERON, 1985

TYPE LOCALITY
Houtman Abrolhos Islands.

IDENTIFYING CHARACTERS
Colonies are massive or submassive and flattened. Valleys are irregular in length and shape. All skeletal structures are very small for a *Symphyllia*, with septa being generally like those of *Acanthastrea*. Polyps are fleshy, with a groove along the tops of valley walls.

COLOUR
A wide range of mottled, green, grey, purple and brown.

SIMILAR SPECIES
None. *S. wilsoni* is superficially more *Platygyra*-like than *Symphyllia*-like.

DISTRIBUTION
Known only from Australia: Rottnest and Houtman Abrolhos Islands and coastal localities between Shark and Geographe Bays on the west coast; not found in the east.

ABUNDANCE
Usually uncommon but very conspicuous.

2

3

4

Symphyllia recta

(DANA, 1846)

TYPE LOCALITY
Wake Island.

IDENTIFYING CHARACTERS
Colonies are dome-shaped or hemispherical. Valleys are 12–15 mm in diameter and sinuous. Septa are relatively fine.

COLOUR
Usually dull brown, grey or green, sometimes red. Valley floors and the tops of walls are often distinctly coloured.

SIMILAR SPECIES
S. radians.

DISTRIBUTION
Maldive Islands east to the Marshall Islands and Samoa. Around Australia: the Great Barrier Reef and Coral Sea in the east, and south to Dampier Archipelago on the west coast.

ABUNDANCE
Common on upper reef slopes and fringing reefs.

1. A large colony of *Symphyllia recta* at Torres Strait, Great Barrier Reef.
PHOTOGRAPH: LEN ZELL.

2. *Symphyllia recta* at Broadhurst Reef, Great Barrier Reef, showing the most common shape and colour of the species.
PHOTOGRAPH: ED LOVELL.

3. The branching, sinuous valleys of *Symphyllia recta.*
PHOTOGRAPH: RON AND VALERIE TAYLOR.

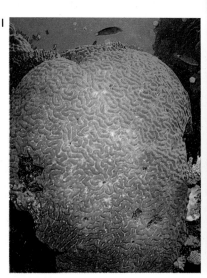

Symphyllia radians

EDWARDS & HAIME, 1849

TYPE LOCALITY
  "East Indies".

IDENTIFYING CHARACTERS
  Colonies are hemispherical to flat. Valleys are 20-25 mm in diameter, irregularly meandroid, becoming straight in flat colonies.

COLOUR
  A wide range of colours; valleys and walls are usually coloured differently.

SIMILAR SPECIES
  S. radians has valleys and septa intermediate in size between the small *S. recta* and the large *S. agaricia*. *S. recta* has more sinuous valleys, *S. agaricia* has a double row of columellae.

DISTRIBUTION
  Laccadive and Maldive Islands east to New Caledonia and Fiji. Around Australia: the Great Barrier Reef and Coral Sea in the east, and south to the Ningaloo Reef Tract on the west coast.

ABUNDANCE
  Very common and may be a dominant on upper reef slopes and fringing reefs.

1. *Symphyllia radians* at Broadhurst Reef, Great Barrier Reef.
PHOTOGRAPH: ED LOVELL.

2. *Symphyllia radians*, showing the straight valleys usually occurring with flat colonies.
PHOTOGRAPH: ED LOVELL.

Symphyllia agaricia

EDWARDS & HAIME, 1849

TYPE LOCALITY
Unrecorded.

IDENTIFYING CHARACTERS
Colonies are hemispherical to flat. Valleys are sinuous or straight, averaging 35 mm in diameter, and are usually separated by a narrow groove. Septa are thick with very large teeth. Columellae are in two rows.

COLOUR
Brown, green or red, valleys and walls are usually contrastingly coloured.

SIMILAR SPECIES
S. radians and *S. valenciennesii*.

DISTRIBUTION
From eastern Africa and the Red Sea east to Samoa.
Around Australia: the Great Barrier Reef and Coral Sea in the east, and south to Ningaloo Reef Tract on the west coast.

ABUNDANCE
Uncommon, found only on exposed upper reef slopes.

1. *Symphyllia agaricia* at Dampier Archipelago, Western Australia. This species is best recognised under water by its large valleys. Coralla have two rows of columellae and thus colonies have two rows of mouths in each valley, but these are often indistinct.
PHOTOGRAPH: ED LOVELL.

2. A small colony of *Symphyllia agaricia* at the Swain Reefs, Great Barrier Reef. Valleys of this species may be straight or sinuous.
PHOTOGRAPH: ED LOVELL.

Symphyllia valenciennesii

EDWARDS & HAIME, 1849

TYPE LOCALITY
Singapore.

IDENTIFYING CHARACTERS
Colonies are usually flat. Valleys radiate from a central area and have steep sides and flat floors. Valleys are separated by a well-defined groove. Septa are thick, with large teeth.

COLOUR
Usually grey or mottled with valley floors and walls of different colours.

SIMILAR SPECIES
S. agaricia, also *Lobophyllia hataii*.

DISTRIBUTION
From Aldabra east to New Caledonia and Tonga. Around Australia: the Great Barrier Reef and Coral Sea in the east, and south to Dampier Archipelago on the west coast.

ABUNDANCE
Rare.

Symphyllia valenciennesii at the Swain Reefs, Great Barrier Reef. This species is rare but even small colonies are conspicuous.
PHOTOGRAPH: ED LOVELL.

FAMILY
MERULINIDAE

(pronounced merry-you-line-id-ee)

VERRILL, 1866

Although the four Australian genera of the Merulinidae are quite distinct and easily recognised, they have had a long history of confusion for coral taxonomists. *Hydnophora* has been continually confused with *Merulina*, the former usually being considered to belong to the Faviidae. *Paraclavarina* has also been confused with the now invalid genus *Clavarina* because little was known about the type species on which the name *Clavarina* was based. Merulinids are hermaphrodites and, as far as is known, they all release gametes for external fertilisation.

CHARACTERS
All genera are extant, hermatypic and colonial.
Skeletal structures are faviid–like but are highly fused, without paliform lobes. Valleys are superficial or may become obscured because of fanwise spreading or contortions.

RELATED FAMILIES
Faviidae and Trachyphylliidae.

EARLIEST FOSSILS
Cretaceous

THE GENERA
The Merulinidae is composed of five genera, *Hydnophora, Merulina, Paraclavarina* and *Scapophyllia*, which are Australian, and *Boninastrea* from the north-west Pacific.

Opposite: A member of the Merulinidae family, *Merulina ampliata* at Torres Strait, growing as a mixture of horizontal and vertical plates. See also p. 436.
PHOTOGRAPH: LEN ZELL.

GENUS
HYDNOPHORA

(pronounced hide-no-for-a)

Fischer de Waldheim, 1807

This genus has traditionally been included in the family Faviidae. However, the structural similarities between the branch tips of *Hydnophora* and *Merulina* and the similarities between the extended polyps of *H. pilosa* and *Scapophyllia cylindrica* leave very little doubt as to the former's real affinities.

   Hydnophora is a common genus easily distinguished from all others by the beautifully sculptured conical hydnophores which cover the colony surface.

TYPE SPECIES
Hydnophora demidovii Fischer de Waldheim, 1807 from the "Indian Ocean".

FOSSIL RECORD
Cretaceous to Recent from Eurasia, West Indies, South America and the Indo-Pacific.

NUMBER OF SPECIES
Approximately 22 nominal species, probably five true species, four from Australia.

CHARACTERS
Colonies are massive, encrusting or arborescent. The genus is characterised by the presence of hydnophores formed where sections of common wall between corallites intersect and develop into conical mounds. Hydnophores cover the colony surface and make this genus immediately recognisable.
Polyps are usually extended only at night (except *H. exesa* and *H. pilosa*). Short tentacles surround the base of each hydnophore, one tentacle between each pair of septa.

SIMILAR GENERA
Hydnophora may superficially resemble *Australogyra* but the latter does not have hydnophores. Fine branch tips of *Hydnophora* have sometimes been confused with *Merulina* and also resemble *Paraclavarina*.

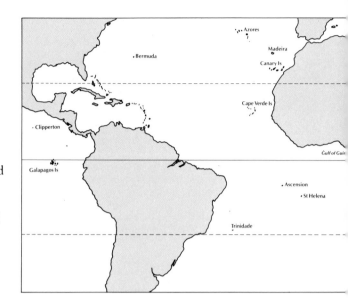

Diagram 21. The hydnophores of *Hydnophora*.
DRAWING: GEOFF KELLY.

The irregular, tangled branches of *Hydnophora rigida*.
PHOTOGRAPH: ED LOVELL.

×1

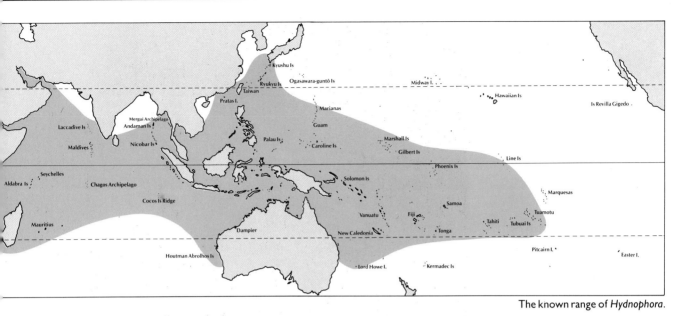

The known range of *Hydnophora*.

×8

Hydnophora rigida

(DANA, 1846)

TYPE LOCALITY
 Fiji.

IDENTIFYING CHARACTERS
 Colonies are arborescent, without encrusting bases.

COLOUR
 Cream or green.

SIMILAR SPECIES
 H. pilosa has an encrusting base but similar branches.

DISTRIBUTION
 From the Nicobar Islands east to Fiji.
 Around Australia: the Great Barrier Reef and Coral Sea in the east, and south to North West Cape on the west coast.

ABUNDANCE
 Sometimes common, especially in lagoons and on protected reef slopes.

1. *Hydnophora rigida* colonies consist only of branches—they have no encrusting base.
PHOTOGRAPH: ED LOVELL.

2. A branch of *Hydnophora rigida*. The hydnophores are the lumps on the branches.
PHOTOGRAPH: LEN ZELL.

3. *Hydnophora rigida* with polyps extended at night.
PHOTOGRAPH: ED LOVELL.

Hydnophora pilosa

VERON, 1985

TYPE LOCALITY
Elizabeth Reef, eastern Australia.

IDENTIFYING CHARACTERS
Colonies have encrusting, laminar and submassive bases with short columns or branches. Branches are flattened towards their tips and are finely structured. Polyps are extended day and night and have long shaggy tentacles of uniform length.

COLOUR
Polyps are dark brown or blue-grey, tentacles have white tips.

SIMILAR SPECIES
H. rigida has similar branches but colonies do not have encrusting bases. Under water the extended polyps are *Scapophyllia*-like.

DISTRIBUTION
Known only from Australia: Elizabeth and Middleton Reefs in the east, and south to Houtman Abrolhos Islands on the west coast.

ABUNDANCE
Usually uncommon except in some shallow-water habitats protected from strong wave action.

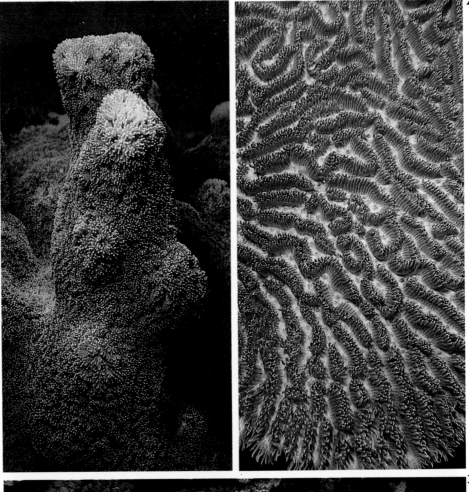

1. *Hydnophora pilosa* at Middleton Reef, eastern Australia, with polyps extended during the day. These colonies look like *Scapophyllia* but hydnophores are clearly visible when the polyps retract.
PHOTOGRAPH: ED LOVELL.

2. A flat plate of *Hydnophora pilosa* at the Houtman Abrolhos Islands, Western Australia.
PHOTOGRAPH: ED LOVELL.

3. *Hydnophora pilosa* at Dampier Archipelago, Western Australia. The polyps have retracted after being disturbed, revealing a typical *Hydnophora* skeleton.
PHOTOGRAPH: ED LOVELL.

Hydnophora exesa

(PALLAS, 1766)

TYPE LOCALITY
"Indian Ocean".

IDENTIFYING CHARACTERS
Colonies are submassive, encrusting or sub-arborescent with much of this variation occurring in the one colony. Hydnophores are 5-8 mm in diameter.

COLOUR
Cream or dull green.

SIMILAR SPECIES
H. microconos, which is massive and rounded with smaller hydnophores.

DISTRIBUTION
From the Red Sea east to Tuvalu. Around Australia: the Great Barrier Reef, Coral Sea and south to Lord Howe Island in the east, and south to Houtman Abrolhos Islands on the west coast.

ABUNDANCE
Common, especially in lagoons and on protected reef slopes.

1. *Hydnophora exesa* often forms irregular laminae.
PHOTOGRAPH: ED LOVELL.

2. The hydnophores of *Hydnophora exesa*. Polyps have tentacles partly extended.
PHOTOGRAPH: AUTHOR.

3. The characteristic appearance of *Hydnophora exesa*.
PHOTOGRAPH: ED LOVELL.

Hydnophora microconos
(LAMARCK, 1816)

TYPE LOCALITY
Unrecorded.

IDENTIFYING CHARACTERS
Colonies are massive, rounded, with hydnophores 2-3 mm in diameter.

COLOUR
Dull cream, brown or green.

SIMILAR SPECIES
H. exesa.

DISTRIBUTION
From the Red Sea east to the Cook Islands.
Around Australia: the Great Barrier Reef, Coral Sea and Flinders Reef (Moreton Bay) in the east, and south to the Ningaloo Reef Tract on the west coast.

ABUNDANCE
Seldom common, occurs primarily in lagoons and on protected reef slopes.

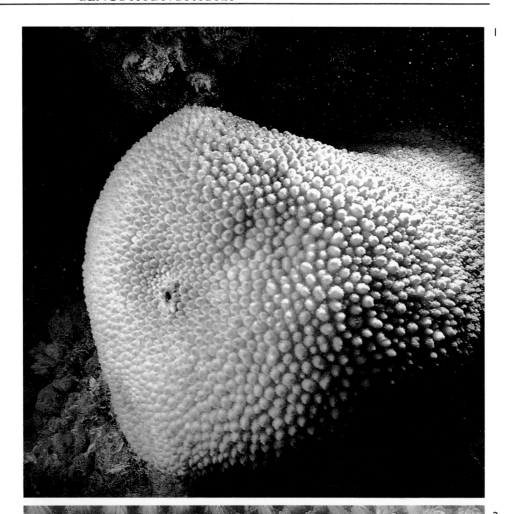

1. *Hydnophora microconos* at Rib Reef, Great Barrier Reef, showing its usual rounded appearance.
PHOTOGRAPH: ED LOVELL.

2. *Hydnophora microconos*: the hydnophores are small and uniform.
PHOTOGRAPH: ED LOVELL.

GENUS
MERULINA
(pronounced merry-you-line-a)

Ehrenberg, 1834

TYPE SPECIES
Madrepora ampliata Ellis & Solander, 1786.

FOSSIL RECORD
Miocene from Indonesia.

NUMBER OF SPECIES
Six nominal species, at least two true species, both of which are Australian.

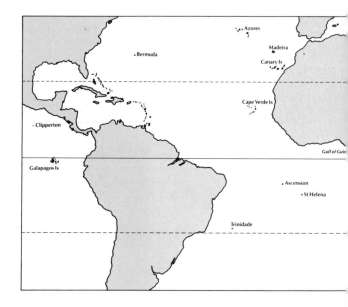

×0.5

The most common growth form and colours of *Merulina ampliata*.
PHOTOGRAPH: ED LOVELL.

434

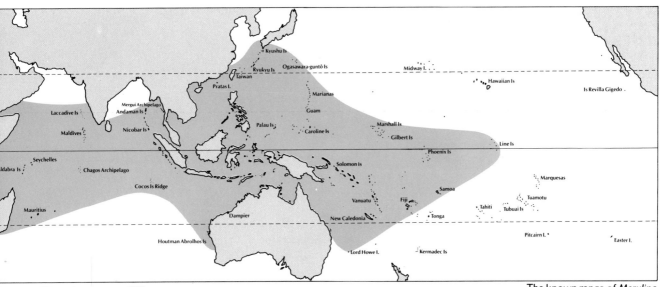

The known range of *Merulina*.

Merulina ampliata

(ELLIS & SOLANDER, 1786)

TYPE LOCALITY
Unrecorded.

IDENTIFYING CHARACTERS
Colonies are laminar and foliaceous or sub-arborescent with different growth forms characteristically occurring in the one colony.
Valleys are short, straight and spread fanwise, then divide. They radiate from the colony centre on flat surfaces but are highly contorted on branches. Flat surfaces often have concentric growth lines.
Polyps are usually extended only at night.

COLOUR
A variety of pale colours, usually pink or pale brown.

SIMILAR SPECIES
M. scabricula. Branch tips may resemble *Paraclavarina* and *Hydnophora*. Laminar pieces have the same skeletal structure as *Scapophyllia* except that the latter do not have valleys spreading fanwise.

DISTRIBUTION
The full range of the genus. Around Australia: the Great Barrier Reef, Coral Sea and Lord Howe Island in the east, and south to Houtman Abrolhos Islands on the west coast.

ABUNDANCE
Common. Occurs in a wide variety of reefal habitats but is most abundant in lagoons.

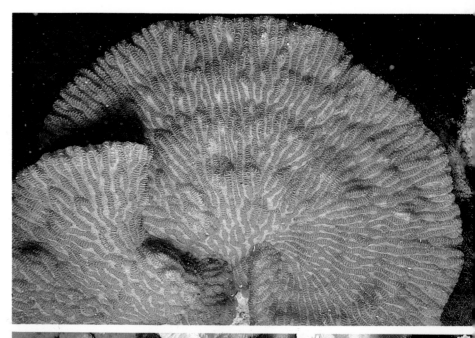

1. A *Merulina ampliata* colony at the Swain Reefs, Great Barrier Reef, showing no development of upright plates or branches. This growth form is common on southern reefs of the east and west coasts.
PHOTOGRAPH: ED LOVELL.

2. A *Merulina ampliata* colony consisting primarily of contorted upright branches.
PHOTOGRAPH: ED LOVELL.

3. *Merulina ampliata* colonies commonly consist of tiers of plates at the Houtman Abrolhos Islands, Western Australia. These colonies are found on sloping reef faces in protected lagoons.
PHOTOGRAPH: ED LOVELL.

Merulina scabricula

DANA, 1846

TYPE LOCALITY
  Fiji.

IDENTIFYING CHARACTERS
  Colonies are laminar, and foliaceous or sub-arborescent, with different growth forms characteristically occurring in the one colony.
  Valleys are as described for *M. ampliata*, only shorter.

COLOUR
  A variety of pale colours, usually pink or pale brown.

SIMILAR SPECIES
  M. ampliata has markedly finer plates and branches, and sub-arborescent branches are usually less developed.

DISTRIBUTION
  Mergui Archipelago east to Fiji. Around Australia: the Great Barrier Reef in the east and south to the Ningaloo Reef Tract on the west coast.

ABUNDANCE
  Rare on the Great Barrier Reef, common at Rowley Shoals and Scott Reef, where it occurs in lagoons with *M. ampliata*.

1. *Merulina scabricula* at Scott Reef, Western Australia.
PHOTOGRAPH: AUTHOR.

2. The characteristically delicate appearance of *Merulina scabricula*.
PHOTOGRAPH: AUTHOR.

GENUS
PARACLAVARINA
(pronounced para-klav-a-rine-a)

Veron, 1985

TYPE SPECIES
Clavarina triangularis Veron, Pichon & Wijsman–Best, 1979.

FOSSIL RECORD
None.

NUMBER OF SPECIES
One.

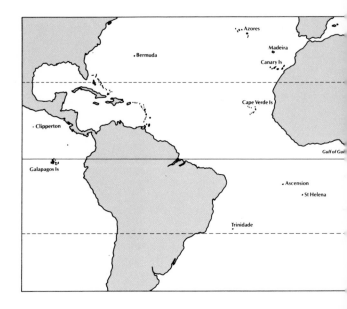

Paraclavarina triangularis
(VERON, PICHON & WIJSMAN-BEST, 1979)

TYPE LOCALITY
Bushy Island, Great Barrier Reef.

IDENTIFYING CHARACTERS
Colonies consist of a network of anastomosing branches, either compacted or open, and are frequently over 2 m in diameter. They are triangular in section. Valleys are short and shallow with thick columellae and septa which, except near branch tips, are fused into one solid structure. Polyps are extended only at night and have long fine tentacles which occupy most of the space between branches.

COLOUR
Pale yellow or cream.

SIMILAR SPECIES
Branch tips of *Paraclavarina* may resemble those of *Hydnophora* and *Merulina* but are readily distinguished from both by their triangular section, shallow valleys and highly fused skeletal elements.

DISTRIBUTION
Known only from Australia: the Great Barrier Reef in the east; not found on the west coast.

ABUNDANCE
Occurs in reefal areas protected from strong wave action. Usually uncommon but may form large colonies in lagoons with soft substrates.

Note: This species was previously placed in the genus Clavarina.

×5

1. *Paraclavarina triangularis* at Torres Strait. Large colonies usually house schools of small reef fish.
PHOTOGRAPH: LEN ZELL.
2. The branches of *Paraclavarina triangularis*.
PHOTOGRAPH: ED LOVELL.
3. The surface detail of *Paraclavarina triangularis* branches. As the name implies, branches are generally triangular in section.
PHOTOGRAPH: LEN ZELL.

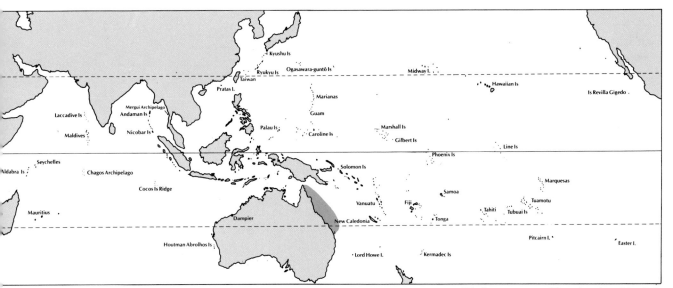

The known range of *Paraclavarina triangularis*.

3

Genus
SCAPOPHYLLIA

(pronounced skap-oh-fill-ee-a)

Edwards & Haime, 1848

TYPE SPECIES
Scapophyllia cylindrica Edwards & Haime, 1848.

FOSSIL RECORD
None.

NUMBER OF SPECIES
One.

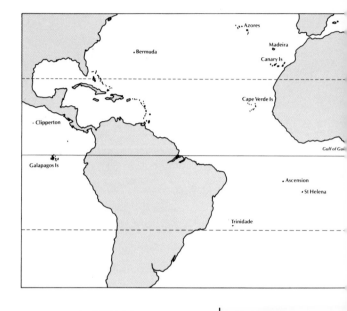

Scapophyllia cylindrica
EDWARDS & HAIME, 1848

TYPE LOCALITY
"South China Sea".

IDENTIFYING CHARACTERS
Colonies are composed of blunt-ended columns which may divide, and thick laminar bases. Valleys are meandroid and sinuous. Septa are thick in the valleys and fuse irregularly with each other and with the few thick septal teeth that comprise each columella.
Polyps are usually extended only at night and have long tapering tentacles of uniform length.

COLOUR
Usually cream or yellow-brown.

SIMILAR SPECIES
Laminar pieces of *Scapophyllia* skeleton resemble *Merulina* but the latter have short valleys spreading fanwise, not sinuous valleys.

DISTRIBUTION
Around Australia: the Great Barrier Reef and Coral Sea in the east, and south to Houtman Abrolhos Islands on the west coast.

ABUNDANCE
Usually found in partly turbid water, such as around fringing reefs and in lagoons, but is seldom common.

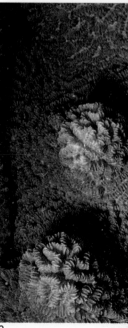

×5

1. The usual appearance of *Scapophyllia cylindrica*.
PHOTOGRAPH: ED LOVELL.

2. *Scapophyllia cylindrica* may form plate-like colonies with long valleys that become sinuous on columns.
PHOTOGRAPH: ED LOVELL.

3. *Scapophyllia cylindrica* columns are beautifully sculptured, and this is best seen when the walls and valleys are contrasting colours.
PHOTOGRAPH: ED LOVELL.

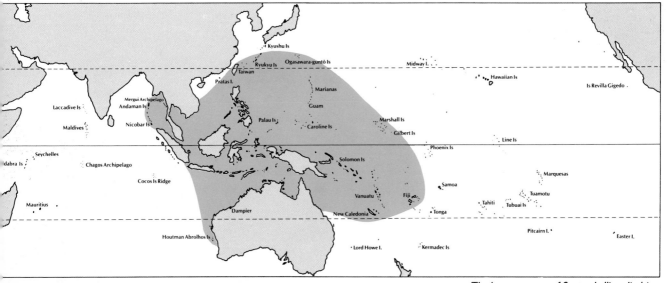

The known range of *Scapophyllia cylindrica*.

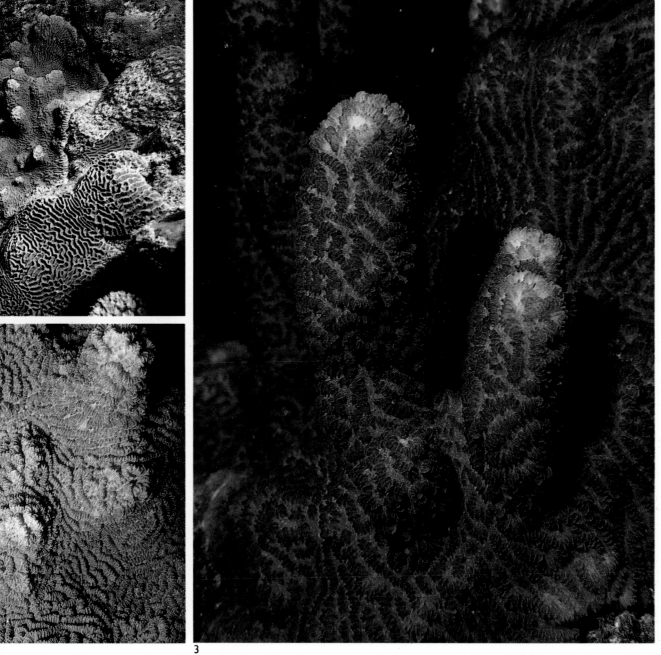

3

FAMILY
FAVIIDAE

(pronounced fav-vee-id-ee)

GREGORY, 1900

The Faviidae is one of the most important families of corals. It is the biggest in terms of number of genera, and ranks next to the Acroporidae in number of species and overall abundance in most reef habitats throughout the Indo-Pacific.

Despite the number of genera, the faviids have a generally similar reproductive cycle. Recent studies have shown that they are major contributors to the mass spawning which takes place on the Great Barrier Reef every year. It is probable that all species are hermaphrodites. During the winter months, egg masses and testes develop on the polyp mesenteries. The gametes are released at night after the full moon in November and December when *Acropora* (and many other genera) also spawn. All species studied up until now conform to this pattern, but there are many differences of reproductive detail between the different species, including the number and colour of egg masses, the behaviour of the polyp and the rate of maturation of the gonads.

CHARACTERS

All extant species are hermatypic and colonial. Septa, paliform lobes, columellae and wall structures, when present, all appear to be structurally similar. Septal structures are simple, columellae are a simple tangle of elongate septal teeth, walls are composed of thickened septa and cross-linkages.

RELATED FAMILIES
Merulinidae and Trachyphylliidae.

EARLIEST FOSSILS
Jurassic.

THE GENERA

Two Indo-Pacific faviids, *Favia* and *Montastrea*, also occur in the Atlantic and there are five Atlantic (West Indian) faviid genera, *Diploria*, *Colpophyllia*, *Manicinia*, *Solenastrea* and *Cladocora*, not found in the Indo-Pacific. Two Indo-Pacific faviids, *Astreosmilia* and *Erythrastrea*, are restricted to the western Indian Ocean and Red Sea respectively. All other genera are Australian and include the following: *Caulastrea*, *Favia*, *Barabattoia*, *Favites*, *Goniastrea*, *Platygyra*, *Australogyra*, *Leptoria*, *Oulophyllia*, *Oulastrea*, *Montastrea*, *Plesiastrea*, *Diploastrea*, *Leptastrea*, *Cyphastrea*, *Echinopora* and *Moseleya*. The majority of faviid genera are easily recognised because they are composed of a small number of species all of which have a number of distinctive characters in common. These are indicated in the key below. However, four genera, *Favia*, *Barabattoia*, *Favites* and *Montastrea* may be confused.

Opposite: A large colony of *Favia stelligera* showing one of the most common growth forms of the species. See also p. 452.

PHOTOGRAPH: ED LOVELL.

Barabattoia is really a group of three species with doubtful affinities but which are grouped together because they have elongate corallites. Only one uncommon species occurs on Australian reefs.

Favia and *Favites* are usually easily separated because they are plocoid and cerioid respectively, but some species, especially *Favia rotumana*, *Favia rotundata* and *Favia veroni*, can be almost completely cerioid (*Favites*-like) in shallow wave-washed habitats.

Similarly *Montastrea*, which is distinguished from *Favia* by having extratentacular rather than intratentacular budding, may be difficult to recognise in colonies that are not actively budding. Even when they are actively budding, some species, especially *M. valenciennesi*, often display both types of budding in different proportions according to environmental conditions. In the case of *Montastrea* the species may be more readily recognised than the genus.

TYPES OF COLONY FORMATION

More than in any other family, the faviids display a lot of variation in the means by which colonies are formed through asexual budding of polyps. They also have corallites of several different structural types which are used to separate many of the genera. These types are:

— *phaceloid*: corallites are tubular and have a uniform height. *Caulastrea* is the only faviid with such corallites.

— *plocoid*: corallites are conical and have their own walls. Two types of budding are possible: *intratentacular budding*, where the parent polyp divides into two daughter polyps; and *extratentacular budding*, where daughter polyps form on the side of the parent polyp.

— *cerioid*: adjacent corallites share common walls and thus can reproduce only by intratentacular budding.

— *meandroid*: valleys, rather than separate corallites, are formed. This is caused by a form of intratentacular budding where polyp formation occurs only at the valley ends and daughter polyps are not divided off by a wall.

These types of colony formation are found in many corals (illustrated on p. 59) but the terms described here are used for faviids more than for other families, partly because there are so many genera involved.

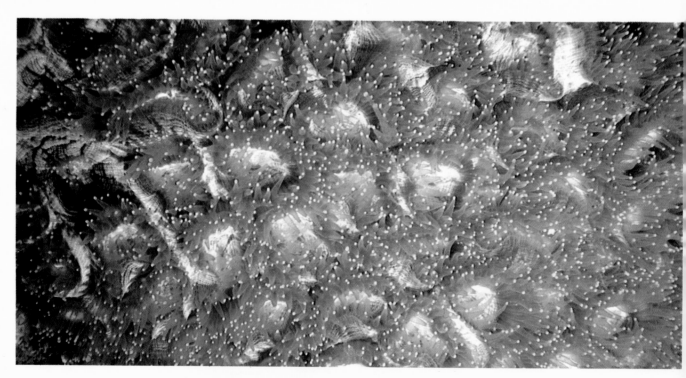

Most faviids look similar at night when tentacles are extended.
PHOTOGRAPH: ED LOVELL.

KEY TO GENERA OF AUSTRALIAN FAVIIDAE

Corallum phaceloid . . . *Caulastrea* (p. 446)

Corallum foliaceous . . . *Echinopora* (p. 526)

Corallum arborescent

    Valleys meandroid or corallites cerioid . . . *Australogyra* (p. 494)

    Corallites plocoid . . . *Echinopora* (p. 526)

Corallum massive

    Valleys meandroid

        Paliform lobes and columella centres absent

            Columellae solid, wall-like . . . *Leptoria* (p. 496)

            Columellae a continuous tangle of spines . . . *Platygyra* (p. 488)

        Paliform lobes and/or columella centres present

            Valleys short, wide . . . *Oulophyllia* (p. 498)

            Valleys elongate . . . *Goniastrea* (p. 478)

    Corallites cerioid

        Paliform lobes absent . . . *Platygyra* (p. 488)

        Paliform lobes present

            Prominent central corallites present . . . *Moseleya* (p. 534)

            Without central corallite . . . *Favites* (p. 468), *Goniastrea* (p. 478)

    Corallites plocoid

        Budding intratentacular . . . *Favia* (p. 450), *Barabattoia* (p. 466)

        Budding extratentacular

            Corallites angular (subplocoid) . . . *Leptastrea* (p. 514)

            Corallites rounded, small (calices less than 3 mm in diameter)

                Coenosteum costate . . *Plesiastrea* (p. 510)

                Coenosteum granulated . . . *Cyphastrea* (p. 520), *Echinopora* (p. 526)

            Corallites rounded, large

                Septa greatly thickened near wall . . . *Diploastrea* (p. 512)

                Septa not thickened . . . *Montastrea* (p. 502)

Note: This key is a guide only and should be used in conjunction with the descriptions of the genera.
It also assumes that the user is aware of the exceptions noted above.
In these cases the species may be more readily recognised than the genus.
The same genus may key out in more than one place.

GENUS
CAULASTREA
(pronounced korl-ass-tree-a)

Dana, 1846

TYPE SPECIES
Caulastrea furcata Dana, 1846.

FOSSIL RECORD
Eocene to Recent from Eurasia and the Indo–Pacific.

NUMBER OF SPECIES
Eight nominal species, probably four true species, all of which are Australian.

CHARACTERS
Colonies are phaceloid.
Corallites have numerous fine septa and well-developed columellae.
Polyps are sometimes extended during the day.

SIMILAR GENERA
Caulastrea is similar to *Astreosmilia* from the western Indian Ocean. Of Australian genera, it has a superficial resemblance to *Blastomussa*.

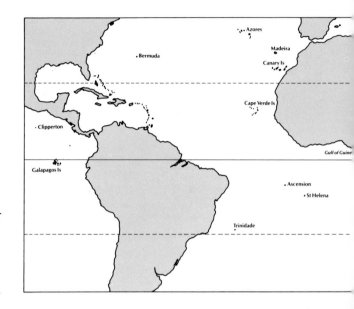

Caulastrea tumida
MATTHAI, 1928

TYPE LOCALITY
King's Sound, Western Australia.

IDENTIFYING CHARACTERS
Colonies have short sturdy corallites, 10-15 mm in diameter. These frequently have more than one mouth. Costae are poorly developed.

COLOUR
Dull cream and grey.

SIMIILAR SPECIES
Closest to *C. echinulata*.

DISTRIBUTION
From Madagascar east to New Caledonia.
Around Australia: the Great Barrier Reef in the east, and south to Houtman Abrolhos Islands on the west coast.

ABUNDANCE
Very rare on the Great Barrier Reef, but common on the west coast where it appears to be the only *Caulastrea* in coastal localities.

×1

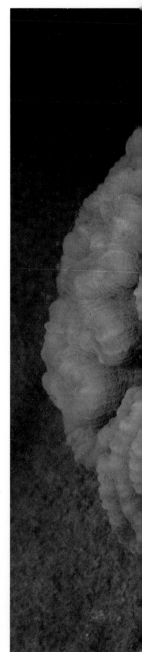

Caulastrea tumida at the Dampier Archipelago. This is the only species of *Caulastrea* recorded from near shore Western Australia and is very distinctive.
PHOTOGRAPH: ED LOVELL.

The known range of *Caulastrea*.

Caulastrea echinulata
(EDWARDS & HAIME, 1849)

TYPE LOCALITY
Singapore.

IDENTIFYING CHARACTERS
Corallites are closely compacted, 10-12 mm in diameter.

COLOUR
Pale brown.

SIMILAR SPECIES
C. *furcata* has less compact corallites but other characters are similar.

DISTRIBUTION
Far western Pacific north to Japan and south to the Great Barrier Reef.
Around Australia: the northern Great Barrier Reef in the east; not recorded on the west coast.

ABUNDANCE
Usually uncommon.

Caulastrea furcata

DANA, 1846

TYPE LOCALITY
Fiji.

IDENTIFYING CHARACTERS
Colonies have diverging corallites averaging 9.5 mm in diameter.

COLOUR
Brown or green with green oral discs. Underlying septa may give pale radiating stripes to the upper corallite wall.

SIMILAR SPECIES
C. echinulata and *C. curvata*.

DISTRIBUTION
Seychelles and Maldive Islands east to Fiji and Tonga.
Around Australia: the Great Barrier Reef and Coral Sea in the east, and Scott Reef on the west coast.

ABUNDANCE
Common on protected reef slopes where the substrate is partly sandy. Forms extensive monospecific stands, sometimes over 5 m in diameter.

1. *Caulastrea furcata* at Rib Reef, Great Barrier Reef.
PHOTOGRAPH: ED LOVELL.

2. Small polyps of a zooanthid (a soft coral) are crowded between the *Caulastrea furcata* polyps.
PHOTOGRAPH: RON AND VALERIE TAYLOR.

3. A common appearance of *Caulastrea furcata* where some polyps have pale stripes radiating from the oral disc and others do not. These stripes probably form only when the polyp is fully retracted.
PHOTOGRAPH: ED LOVELL.

4. The polyps of *Caulastrea furcata*.
PHOTOGRAPH: VICKI HARRIOTT.

Caulastrea curvata

WIJSMAN–BEST, 1972

TYPE LOCALITY
New Caledonia.

IDENTIFYING CHARACTERS
Colonies have sprawling irregular corallites averaging 8 mm in diameter; those at the colony periphery are characteristically curved.

COLOUR
Pale brown.

SIMILAR SPECIES
C. furcata, which can be separated under water by its colour; also corallites are more regular and larger, with more numerous septa and better-developed costae.

DISTRIBUTION
New Caledonia and Australia. Around Australia: the Great Barrier Reef and Coral Sea in the east; not recorded on the west coast.

ABUNDANCE
Uncommon but often found with *C. furcata*. Colonies are seldom over 1 m in diameter.

1. The usual appearance of *Caulastrea curvata*.
PHOTOGRAPH: ED LOVELL.

2. The polyps of *Caulastrea curvata*.
PHOTOGRAPH: DAVE FISK.

GENUS
FAVIA
(pronounced fay-vee-a)

Oken, 1815

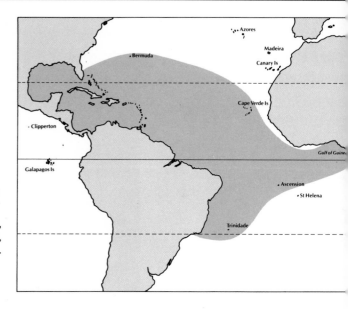

... the classification of other groups, especially the so-called Astraeidae, is in a highly unsatisfactory condition ... Mr Matthai's is the last attempt at classifying them ... I am splitting his genus Favia *into three families, distributing the species among four genera, and am suggesting that a fifth genus may be represented.*

T. W. Vaughan,
*Some Shoal-water Corals from Murray Island (Australia),
Cocos-Keeling Islands, and Fanning Island, 1981.*

The species of *Favia* are the most common corals found in shallow-water communities that are not dominated by *Acropora*. Such communities are found on different types of reef flats and also around fringing reefs and similar places where the water is often turbid.

Almost all *Favia* are strictly night-time feeders. Their tubular polyps are fringed by a mass of translucent tentacles which retract rapidly if disturbed and may even react to torchlight.

TYPE SPECIES
Madrepora fragum Esper, 1795 from the Caribbean.

FOSSIL RECORD
Extensive, extending back to the Cretaceous.

NUMBER OF SPECIES
Approximately 70 nominal species, 11 true species from Australia.

CHARACTERS
Colonies are usually massive, either flat or dome-shaped. Corallites are monocentric and plocoid: each corallite projects slightly above the colony surface and has its own wall. Daughter corallites are formed by intratentacular division.

KEY TO SPECIES OF *FAVIA*

Corallites small (calices less than 6 mm in diameter)
>> Septa and costae thick ... *F. stelligera* (p. 452)
>> Septa and costae thin ... *F. laxa* (p. 454)

Corallites middle-sized (calices 6-12 mm in diameter)
>> Septa conspicuously exsert or with ragged margins
>>> Paliform lobes conspicuous ... *F. matthaii* (p. 460)
>>> Paliform lobes inconspicuous or absent ... *F. rotumana* (p. 461)
>> Septa not conspicuously exsert
>>> Septa irregular
>>>> Corallites conical ... *F. favus* (p. 458)
>>>> Corallites not conical ... *F. pallida* (p. 456)
>>> Septa regular and uniformly spaced
>>>> Corallites and septa both closely compact ... *F. speciosa* (p. 457)
>>>> Corallites widely spaced
>>>>> Septa widely spaced ... *F. lizardensis* (p. 459)
>>>>> Septa closely compact ... *F. helianthoides* (p. 455)

Corallites large (calices over 12 mm in diameter)
>> Septa irregular ... *F. favus* (p. 458)
>> Septa regular and uniformly spaced
>>> Paliform lobes conspicuous ... *F. maxima* (p. 463)
>>> Paliform lobes inconspicuous or absent ... *F. maritima* (p. 464), *F. veroni* (p. 465)

Note: This key is a guide only and should be used in conjunction with the descriptions of the species. It assumes that the reader is aware of problems of species variation noted above.

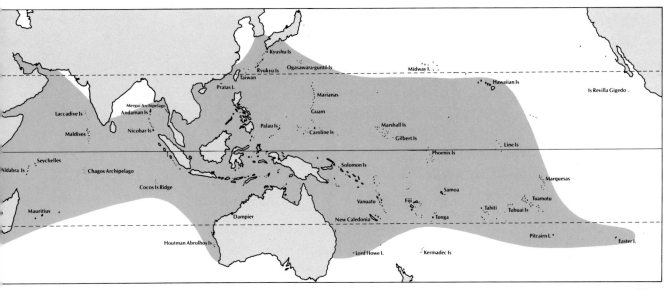

The known range of *Favia*.

Polyps are extended only at night and have a simple circle of tapering tentacles, often with a pigmented tip.

SIMILAR GENERA

Favia is similar to *Favites* but the latter has cerioid corallites. This distinction is sometimes arbitrary, in which case *Favia* corallites are further characterised by subdividing equally, whereas *Favites* corallites usually subdivide unequally, producing daughter corallites of different sizes.

Favia is distinguished from *Barabattoia* by its less protuberant corallites.

SPECIES

Those involved in identifying of *Favia* species should bear in mind that there are often exceptions to most identifying characters. This is because most species have wide depth ranges on reefs, have wide geographic ranges and also are tolerant of a wide range of environmental conditions. As a result, a colony on an intertidal reef flat may be very different from another colony of the same species on the same reef at a depth of 50 m. Both may be very different from other colonies of the same species in similar conditions but from a different country.

In many cases, *Favia* are difficult to recognise under water without much practice. This is due to their colour variation, and also to the living polyp obscuring the underlying skeleton. To identify a *Favia* species satisfactorily, a piece should be collected and its colour and habitat also noted.

Favia species all look similar at night when their tentacles are extended.
PHOTOGRAPH: JOHN BARNETT.

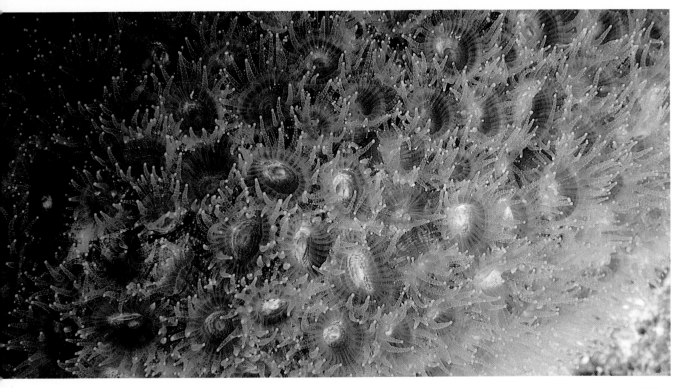

Favia stelligera
(DANA, 1846)

TYPE LOCALITY
Fiji.

IDENTIFYING CHARACTERS
Colonies are spherical, columnar, hillocky or flat. Corallites are evenly distributed, with small calices.

COLOUR
Uniform brown or green.

SIMILAR SPECIES
Resembles *F. laxa* but also species of other genera with small corallites, especially *Montastrea curta* and *Plesiastrea versipora*.

DISTRIBUTION
Red Sea east to Hawaii. Around Australia: the Great Barrier Reef and Coral Sea in the east, and south to North West Cape on the west coast.

ABUNDANCE
Seldom common but occurs in a wide range of habitats.

x2.5

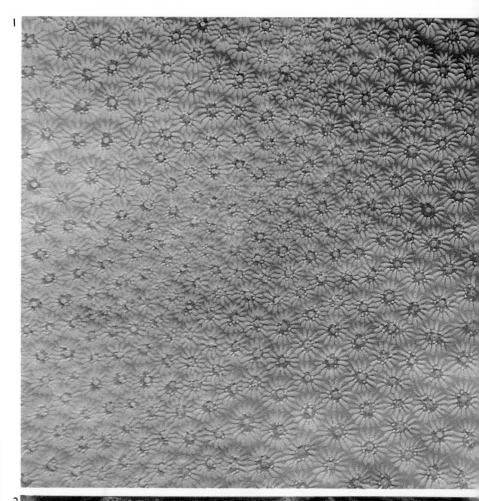

1. *Favia stelligera* is easily recognised by the neat, uniform appearance of the polyps.
PHOTOGRAPH: ED LOVELL.

2. The polyps of *Favia stelligera*. These are the smallest of *Favia* species.
PHOTOGRAPH: RON AND VALERIE TAYLOR.

3. A large colony of *Favia stelligera*, showing a common growth form. See also p. 442.
PHOTOGRAPH: RON AND VALERIE TAYLOR.

Favia laxa

(KLUNZINGER, 1879)

TYPE LOCALITY
Red Sea.

IDENTIFYING CHARACTERS
Colonies are hemispherical. Corallites are conical with calices 3-6 mm in diameter. Paliform lobes form a neat crown. Septa are fine and neatly arranged.

COLOUR
Usually pale brown or pinkish-brown.

SIMILAR SPECIES
F. stelligera has smaller corallites with thicker septa.

DISTRIBUTION
From the Red Sea east to New Caledonia.
Around Australia: the Great Barrier Reef in the east, and Scott Reef on the west coast.

ABUNDANCE
Uncommon.

x1

1. *Favia laxa* at Lizard Island, Great Barrier Reef.
PHOTOGRAPH: LEN ZELL.

2,3. The polyps of *Favia laxa*.
PHOTOGRAPHS: ED LOVELL.

Favia helianthoides

WELLS, 1954

TYPE LOCALITY
Marshall Islands.

IDENTIFYING CHARACTERS
Colonies are small and hemispherical. Corallites are conical, widely spaced with small calices (up to 4 mm in diameter). Septa are fine and closely compacted with a neat crown of paliform lobes.

COLOUR
Usually cream or yellow.

SIMILAR SPECIES
Most closely resembles *Plesiastrea versipora*.

DISTRIBUTION
Australia east to the Marshall Islands.
Around Australia: the Coral Sea in the east, and Scott Reef on the west coast.

ABUNDANCE
Rare.

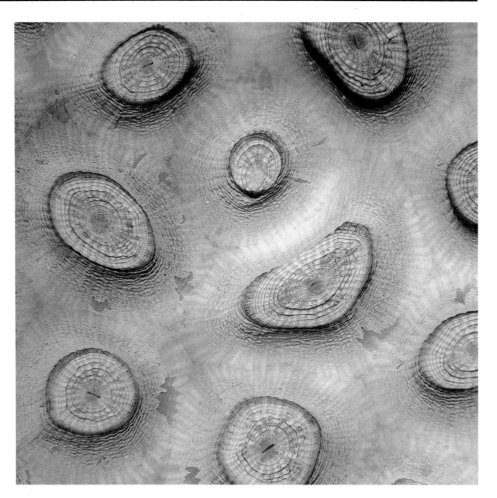

×2.5

The polyps of *Favia helianthoides*. This rare species has a delicate beauty under water.
PHOTOGRAPH: RON AND VALERIE TAYLOR.

Favia pallida

(DANA, 1846)

TYPE LOCALITY
Fiji.

IDENTIFYING CHARACTERS
Colonies are massive. Corallites are circular, with calices 6-10 mm in diameter. Septa are widely spaced and irregular. Paliform lobes are usually poorly developed.

COLOUR
Pale yellow, cream or green, always with dark-brown or green calices.

SIMILAR SPECIES
F. speciosa.

DISTRIBUTION
East Africa and the Red Sea east to Samoa and Tuamotu Archipelago.
Around Australia: all localities except the Solitary Islands in the east, and south to Houtman Abrolhos Islands on the west coast.

ABUNDANCE
The most common faviid and often a dominant of back reef margins.

x1

Favia pallida, the most common Australian faviid. Collected specimens of this species may be difficult to recognise, but under water its usual dark polyp centres distinguish it from other common *Favia*.
PHOTOGRAPH: RON AND VALERIE TAYLOR.

Favia speciosa

(DANA, 1846)

TYPE LOCALITY
"East Indies".

IDENTIFYING CHARACTERS
Colonies are massive. Corallites are crowded together, subcircular, with calices up to 12 mm in diameter. Septa are fine, numerous and regular. Paliform lobes are poorly developed.

COLOUR
Pale grey, green or brown, usually with calices of contrasting colour.

SIMILAR SPECIES
F. pallida.

DISTRIBUTION
Red Sea and east Africa east to Society Islands and Tuamotu Archipelago.
Around Australia: the Great Barrier Reef, Coral Sea and all localities south to Lord Howe Island in the east, and south to Houtman Abrolhos Islands on the west coast.

ABUNDANCE
Uncommon except in southern localities.

×1

1. *Favia speciosa* is difficult to distinguish from *F. pallida* under water; it is seldom found on tropical reefs.
PHOTOGRAPH: RON AND VALERIE TAYLOR.

2. The polyps of *Favia speciosa*.
PHOTOGRAPH: ED LOVELL.

3. *Favia speciosa* at Scott Reef, Western Australia.
PHOTOGRAPH: AUTHOR.

Favia favus

(FORSKAL, 1775)

TYPE LOCALITY
Red Sea.

IDENTIFYING CHARACTERS
Colonies are massive, rounded or flat. Corallites are conical, with calices 12–20 mm in diameter. Septa have an irregular appearance. Paliform lobes are poorly developed.

COLOUR
Usually dark green, brown or grey. It is often mottled and may have pale calices.

SIMILAR SPECIES
F. pallida and *F. lizardensis*.

DISTRIBUTION
Red Sea east to the Marshall Islands and Samoa.
Around Australia: the Great Barrier Reef, Coral Sea and south to Elizabeth Reef in the east, and south to Rottnest Island on the west coast.

ABUNDANCE
Very common (second only to *F. pallida*) and may be a dominant on back reef margins.

×1

1. *Favia favus* is second only to *F. pallida* in abundance. It has a very wide range of colours but is most commonly dark brown, as seen here.
PHOTOGRAPH: ED LOVELL.

2,3. Polyps of *Favia favus*.
PHOTOGRAPHS: RON AND VALERIE TAYLOR.

458

Favia lizardensis
VERON, PICHON & WIJSMAN-BEST, 1977

TYPE LOCALITY
Lizard Island, Great Barrier Reef.

IDENTIFYING CHARACTERS
Colonies are massive. Corallites are circular, with regularly spaced calices 10-13 mm in diameter. Walls have fine rims. Septa are uniformly thin and widely spaced, without paliform lobes. Costae are well developed.

COLOUR
Pinkish-brown with cream or greenish oral discs.

SIMILAR SPECIES
A distinct species when seen under water. Closest to *F. speciosa*.

DISTRIBUTION
Known only from Australia: the Great Barrier Reef in the east, and south to Houtman Abrolhos Islands on the west coast, but may be distributed across the Indian Ocean.

ABUNDANCE
Seldom common.

×1

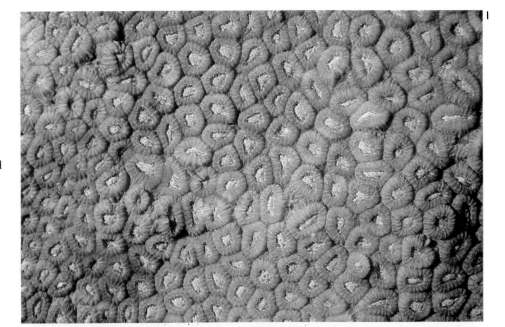

1. *Favia lizardensis* at Lord Howe Island, eastern Australia. This species can be recognised under water by its colour, which seldom varies, and the distinct circular polyp walls.
PHOTOGRAPH: LEN ZELL.

2. The polyps of *Favia lizardensis*.
PHOTOGRAPH: LEN ZELL.

Favia matthaii

VAUGHAN, 1918

TYPE LOCALITY
"Western Indian Ocean".

IDENTIFYING CHARACTERS
Colonies are massive. Corallites are crowded, and circular, with calices 9-12 mm in diameter. Septa are thickened, exsert or ragged, with large teeth near the wall and well-developed paliform lobes forming a crown around the columella.

COLOUR
Usually brown or grey, with dark calices.

SIMILAR SPECIES
F. matthaii is readily distinguished from other *Favia* species with corallites of similar size (*F. pallida*, *F. speciosa*) by its exsert or ragged septa and paliform crown.

DISTRIBUTION
Madagascar east to Indonesia and New Caledonia.
Around Australia: the Great Barrier Reef, Coral Sea and Elizabeth and Middleton Reefs in the east, and south to Dampier Archipelago on the west coast.

ABUNDANCE
Common on upper reef slopes.

1. *Favia matthaii*.
PHOTOGRAPH: RON AND VALERIE TAYLOR.

2. The polyps of *Favia matthaii*. This species may have the same colour as *F. pallida*, but is usually distinguished by its irregularly exsert or ragged septa.
PHOTOGRAPH: ED LOVELL.

Favia rotumana

(GARDINER, 1899)

TYPE LOCALITY
Fiji.

IDENTIFYING CHARACTERS
Colonies are usually flat and subplocoid. Corallites are crowded, irregular in shape and may have up to three centres. Septa are exsert, thin and very irregular; they plunge steeply inside the wall. Paliform lobes are poorly developed or absent.

COLOUR
A wide range, usually with different-coloured corallite walls and oral discs.

SIMILAR SPECIES
F. matthaii. May also be confused with *Platygyra pini*.

DISTRIBUTION
South China Sea south to Australia and east to Samoa. Around Australia: the Great Barrier Reef, Coral Sea, Elizabeth and Middleton Reefs and Lord Howe Island in the east, and south to Barrow Island on the west coast.

ABUNDANCE
Common on upper reef slopes.

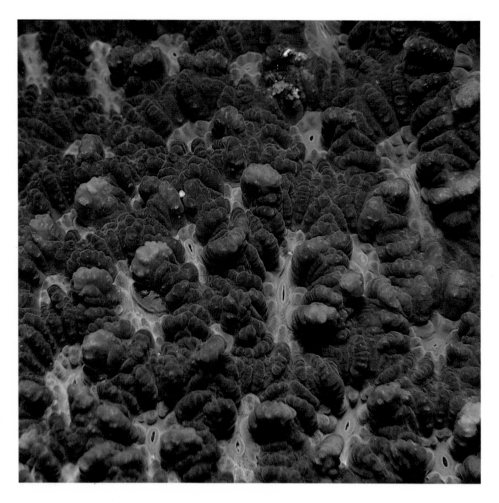

×1

Favia rotumana is one of the most distinctive *Favia* species.
PHOTOGRAPH: ED LOVELL.

Favia rotundata

(VERON, PICHON & WIJSMAN-BEST, 1977)

TYPE LOCALITY
Swain Reefs, Great Barrier Reef.

IDENTIFYING CHARACTERS
Colonies are dome-shaped or flat. Corallites are thick-walled, circular, tending to be subplocoid, with calices 17-20 mm in diameter. Polyps are fleshy and circular in outline.

COLOUR
Pale grey, yellowish or brown.

SIMILAR SPECIES
None, only *F. maxima* and *Favites flexuosa* have similar-sized corallites. This species was formerly considered to belong to genus *Favites* as it was originally described from subplocoid specimens.

DISTRIBUTION
Known only from Australia: the Great Barrier Reef and Coral Sea in the east, and south to Houtman Abrolhos Islands on the west coast.

ABUNDANCE
Uncommon but conspicuous.

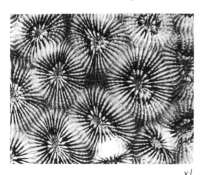

x1

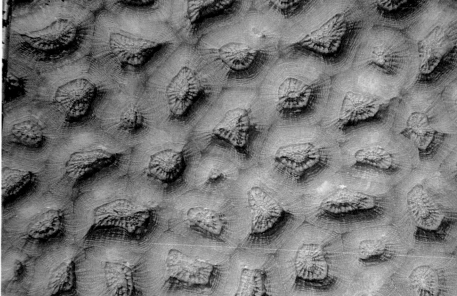

1. *Favia rotundata* at the Swain Reefs, Great Barrier Reef.
PHOTOGRAPH: ED LOVELL.

2. *Favia rotundata* at the Ningaloo Reef Tract, Western Australia.
PHOTOGRAPH: CLAY BRYCE.

3. *Favia rotundata*, so named because its polyps do, indeed, become very rotund.
PHOTOGRAPH: RON AND VALERIE TAYLOR.

Favia maxima

VERON, PICHON & WIJSMAN-BEST, 1977

TYPE LOCALITY
Whitsunday Islands, Great Barrier Reef.

IDENTIFYING CHARACTERS
Colonies are massive. Corallites are circular, large, with calices 20-30 mm in diameter. Septa are very regular, thickened at the wall and with well-developed paliform lobes forming a crown around the columella.

COLOUR
Brown or yellow-brown with dull-green oral discs.

SIMILAR SPECIES
F. veroni.

DISTRIBUTION
Australia and New Caledonia. Around Australia: the Great Barrier Reef and Elizabeth and Middleton Reefs in the east, and south to Houtman Abrolhos Islands on the west coast.

ABUNDANCE
Uncommon. Found on upper reef slopes and is conspicuous.

×1

1. *Favia maxima* at the Swain Reefs, Great Barrier Reef, where small colonies of this conspicuous species are common.
PHOTOGRAPH: ED LOVELL.

2,3. Polyps of *Favia maxima*. These are the largest of *Favia* species.
PHOTOGRAPHS: ED LOVELL (2) AND AUTHOR (3).

Favia maritima

(NEMENZO, 1971)

TYPE LOCALITY
The Philippines.

IDENTIFYING CHARACTERS
Colonies are massive. Corallites are conical, large, with calices up to 18 mm in diameter. Septa are uniform, fine and numerous. Paliform lobes are poorly developed or absent.

COLOUR
Dark brown or greenish.

SIMILAR SPECIES
F. favus has smaller corallites with less numerous, less regular septa.

DISTRIBUTION
The Philippines and Australia. Around Australia: the Great Barrier Reef and Flinders Reef (Moreton Bay) in the east; not found on the west coast.

ABUNDANCE
Rare.

x1

1. *Favia maritima* is rarely found.
PHOTOGRAPH: ED LOVELL.

2. The polyps of *Favia maritima*. Two are undergoing intratentacular budding.
PHOTOGRAPH: ED LOVELL.

464

Favia veroni

MOLL & BOREL-BEST, 1984

TYPE LOCALITY
Indonesia.

IDENTIFYING CHARACTERS
Colonies are massive, with very large calices up to 25 mm in diameter and 10 mm deep. Corallites are compacted together and irregular in outline. Paliform lobes are absent.

COLOUR
Very variable, corallites are usually rich brown, red and/or cream in concentric circles.

SIMILAR SPECIES
F. maxima has similar-sized corallites with conspicuous paliform lobes. *F. maritima* has smaller but prominent widely spaced corallites.

DISTRIBUTION
Australia and Indonesia. Around Australia: the Great Barrier Reef in the east, and south to Passage Island on the west coast.

ABUNDANCE
Uncommon but usually conspicuous.

x1

A colony of *Favia veroni* at a fringing reef near Cape Tribulation, Great Barrier Reef.
PHOTOGRAPH: AUTHOR.

465

GENUS
BARABATTOIA
(pronounced barra-bat-toe-ee-a)

Yabe & Sugiyama, 1941

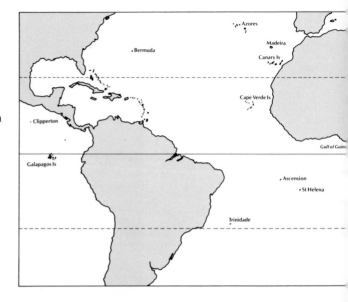

Barabattoia is an ill-defined genus made up of uncommon species which usually have elongate corallites. Sometimes these corallites are so elongate that they anastomose, giving the colonies a "dendroid" structure.

SYNONYM
Bikiniastrea Wells, 1954.

TYPE SPECIES
Barabattoia mirabilis Yabe & Sugiyama, 1941 from the Yap Islands.

FOSSIL RECORD
None.

NUMBER OF SPECIES
Probably four nominal species, three true species as far as is known, one of which is Australian.

Barabattoia amicorum
(EDWARDS & HAIME, 1850)

TYPE LOCALITY
Tonga.

IDENTIFYING CHARACTERS
Colonies are massive.
Corallites are plocoid to subdendroid, that is, they are protuberant tubes rather than conical ones.
Polyps are extended only at night.

COLOUR
Usually mottled brown and green or brown and cream.

SIMILAR SPECIES
B. amicorum was originally included in *Favia* but is distinguished by having subdendroid corallites which resemble those of *Bikiniastrea laddi* Wells, 1954. The latter may also be included in *Barabattoia*.

DISTRIBUTION
Western Pacific.
Around Australia: the Great Barrier Reef in the east, and south to Fremantle on the west coast.

ABUNDANCE
Uncommon except on some back reef margins in shallow water.

1. *Barabattoia amicorum* has very protuberant polyps compared with those of species of *Favia*.
PHOTOGRAPH: ED LOVELL.

2. Polyps of *Barabattoia amicorum* showing a mottled colour pattern.
PHOTOGRAPH: ED LOVELL.

x1

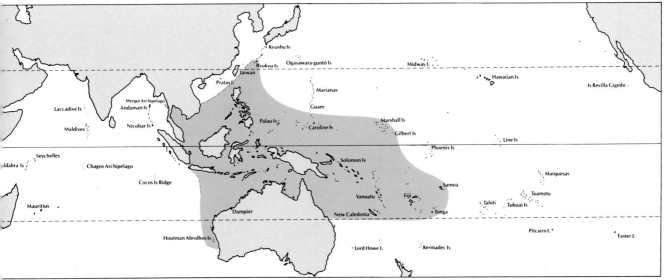

The known range of *Barabattoia*.

2

Genus
FAVITES

(pronounced fav-eye-tees)

Link, 1807

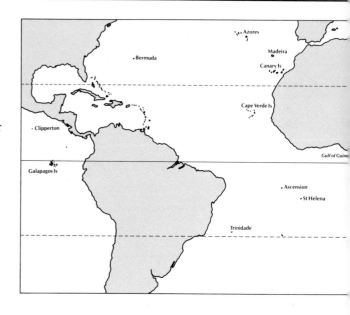

Like *Favia*, *Favites* species are common in shallow-water habitats, especially some reef flats and fringing reefs where the water is often turbid. Like *Favia* also, *Favites* feed at night and have similar tubular polyps when extended.

TYPE SPECIES
Favites astrinus Link, 1807 from an unknown locality.

FOSSIL RECORD
Eocene to Recent from Europe, the West Indies and the Indo-Pacific.

NUMBER OF SPECIES
Approximately 23 nominal species, seven true species from Australia.

CHARACTERS
Colonies are usually massive, either flat or dome-shaped.
Corallites are monocentric and cerioid, occasionally subplocoid. Adjacent corallites mostly share common walls. Paliform lobes are often poorly developed.
Polyps are extended only at night and have a single circle of tapering tentacles like *Favia*.

SIMILAR GENERA
Favites is similar to *Favia* and also to *Goniastrea*. *Goniastrea* may be cerioid like *Favites*, in which case it is distinguished by the presence of prominent paliform lobes, and by having a very regular pattern of septa with relatively fine teeth.

SPECIES
These provide the same sorts of taxonomic problems as *Favia* species because they have similar habitat preferences and geographic ranges. *Favites* are particularly common on temperate reefs and non-reefal habitats where they have relatively well-calcified skeletons and where colonies are generally colourful. Two species formerly considered to belong to *Favites* have been placed in other genera: these are *Favia rotundata* and *Oulophyllia bennettae*.

Right and 2 over: Two colour combinations of *Favites abdita*.
PHOTOGRAPHS: RON AND VALERIE TAYLOR.

KEY TO SPECIES OF *FAVITES*

Corallites very small (calices less than 7 mm in diameter) . . . *F. pentagona* (p. 475)
Corallites middle-sized (calices 7-13 mm in diameter)
    Paliform lobes absent . . . *F. abdita* (p. 470), *F. chinensis* (p. 473)
    Paliform lobes present
        Corallites cerioid, corallites angular . . . *F. complanata* (p. 474), *F. russelli* (p. 476)
        Corallites subplocoid
            Calices rounded . . . *F. halicora* (p. 471)
            Calices angular . . . *F. russelli* (p. 476)
Corallites large (calices over 13 mm in diameter)
    Corallites cerioid, calices angular . . . *F. flexuosa* (p. 472), see *Oulophyllia bennettae* (p. 500)
    Corallites subplocoid, calices rounded . . . see *Favia rotundata* (p. 462)

Note: This key is a guide only and should be used in conjunction with the descriptions of the species.
Two species that have been placed in other genera are also included because they frequently have all the characters of Favites.

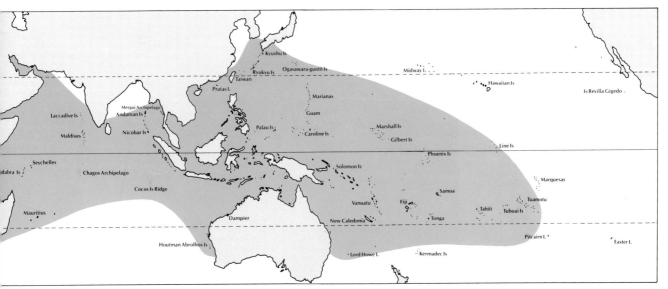

The known range of *Favites*.

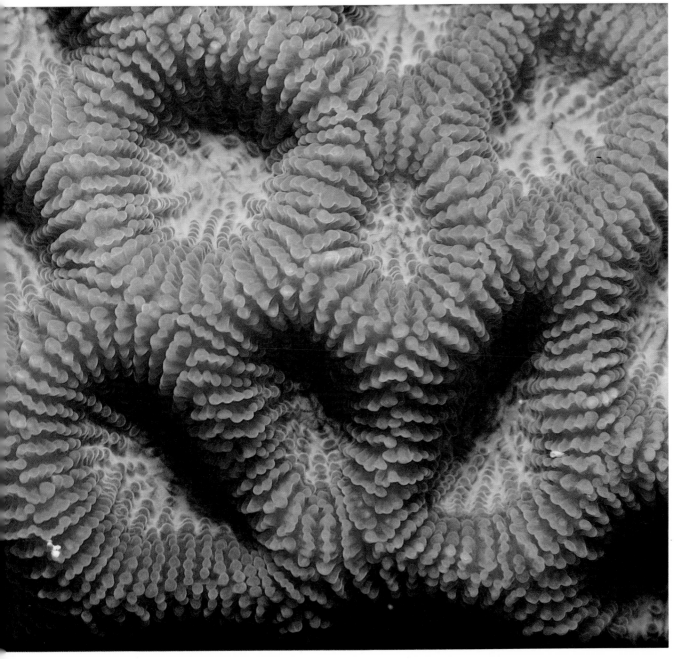

Favites abdita

(ELLIS & SOLANDER, 1786)

TYPE LOCALITY
Unrecorded.

IDENTIFYING CHARACTERS
Colonies are massive, either rounded or hillocky. Walls are thick, calices are 7–12 mm in diameter, septa are straight, with prominent teeth.

COLOUR
Dark in turbid environments, otherwise pale brown with green oral discs.

SIMILAR SPECIES
F. halicora, *F. flexuosa*, also *Acanthastrea echinata*. The latter has larger septal teeth and thick fleshy polyps.

DISTRIBUTION
From the Red Sea east to Samoa. Around Australia: the Great Barrier Reef, Coral Sea and south to Lord Howe and Solitary Islands and Nambucca Heads in the east, and south to Cape Naturaliste on the west coast.

ABUNDANCE
Common and occupies a wide range of habitats with colonies frequently exceeding 1 m in diameter.

x1

1. The most common appearance of *Favites abdita*.
PHOTOGRAPH: LEN ZELL.

2. See previous page.

470

Favites halicora

(EHRENBERG, 1834)

TYPE LOCALITY
Red Sea.

IDENTIFYING CHARACTERS
Colonies are massive, either rounded or hillocky. Corallites have very thick walls and tend to become subplocoid. Calices average 10 mm in diameter. Budding is both intra- and extratentacular. Paliform lobes may be developed.

COLOUR
Usually uniform pale yellowish- or greenish-brown.

SIMILAR SPECIES
F. abdita has more angular corallites with thinner walls and no paliform lobes.

DISTRIBUTION
From the Red Sea east to the Loyalty Islands and Samoa. Around Australia: the Great Barrier Reef, Coral Sea and Elizabeth and Middleton Reefs in the east, and south to Houtman Abrolhos Islands on the west coast.

ABUNDANCE
Usually uncommon.

×1

1. *Favites halicora* at Lizard Island, Great Barrier Reef.
PHOTOGRAPH: LEN ZELL.

2. *Favites halicora* at the Houtman Abrolhos Islands, West Australia. The solid appearance is characteristic of the species.
PHOTOGRAPH: CLAY BRYCE.

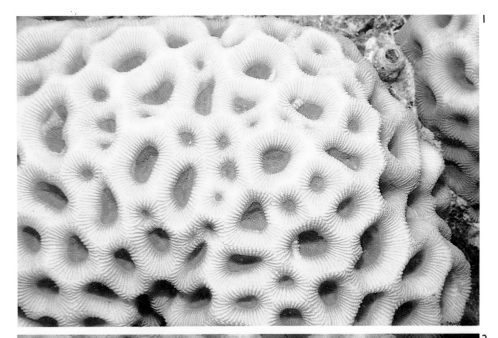

Favites flexuosa

(DANA, 1846)

TYPE LOCALITY
Fiji.

IDENTIFYING CHARACTERS
Colonies are hemispherical or flat. Corallites are angular with calices 15-20 mm in diameter. Septa have large teeth with a tendency to develop paliform lobes.

COLOUR
Green or brown.

SIMILAR SPECIES
F. abdita has smaller, less angular corallites.

DISTRIBUTION
From the Red Sea east at least to Fiji.
Around Australia: the Great Barrier Reef, Coral Sea and south to Lord Howe and Solitary Islands in the east, and south to Houtman Abrolhos Islands on the west coast.

ABUNDANCE
Common over a wide range of habitats.

×1

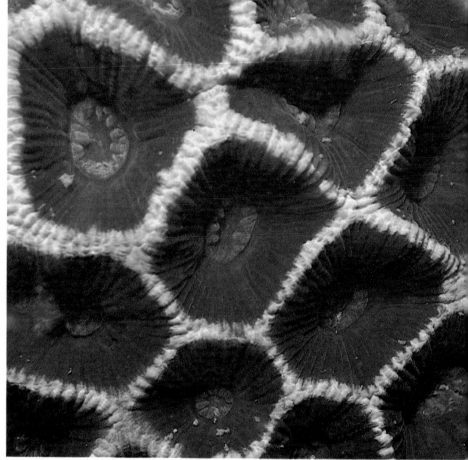

1. *Favites flexuosa* looks much like *F. abdita* under water, but calices are larger.
PHOTOGRAPH: ED LOVELL.

2. A large, colourful *Favites flexuosa*.
PHOTOGRAPH: ED LOVELL.

Favites chinensis

(VERRILL, 1866)

TYPE LOCALITY
Hong Kong.

IDENTIFYING CHARACTERS
Colonies are massive and rounded. Corallites are angular, with thin walls. Calices are 10–13 mm in diameter. Septa are straight and widely spaced, without paliform lobes and are aligned with those of adjacent corallites.

COLOUR
Yellow or greenish-brown.

SIMILAR SPECIES
Can be confused with *Goniastrea aspera* which is primarily distinguished by its paliform lobes.

DISTRIBUTION
From Sri Lanka east to Japan and New Caledonia.
Around Australia: the Great Barrier Reef, Flinders Reef (Moreton Bay) and Elizabeth and Middleton Reefs in the east, and south to Houtman Abrolhos Islands on the west coast.

ABUNDANCE
Uncommon but occurs in a wide range of habitats.

×1

Favites chinensis.
PHOTOGRAPH: LEN ZELL.

473

Favites complanata
(EHRENBERG, 1834)

TYPE LOCALITY
Red Sea.

IDENTIFYING CHARACTERS
Colonies are massive with slightly angular corallites. Calices are 8-12 mm in diameter with strongly alternating septa and weakly developed paliform lobes. Columellae are large.

COLOUR
A wide range but usually brown, sometimes with green oral discs.

SIMILAR SPECIES
F. chinensis is similar but smaller, with thinner walls.

DISTRIBUTION
From the Red Sea east to Tahiti and Tuamotu Archipelago. Around Australia: the Great Barrier Reef, Coral Sea and Lord Howe Island in the east, and south to Geographe Bay on the west coast.

ABUNDANCE
Common on some reefs.

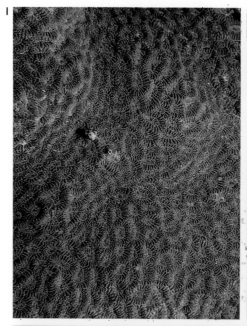

×1

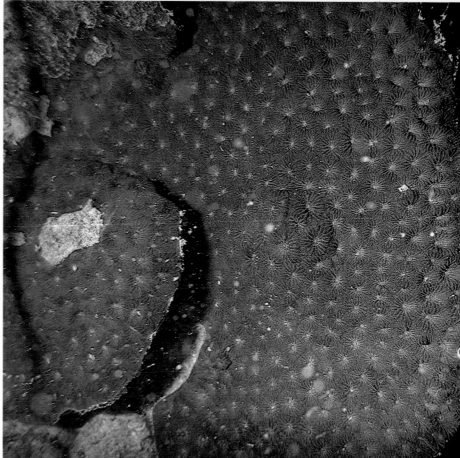

1. The most common appearance of *Favites complanata*.
PHOTOGRAPH: ED LOVELL.

2. *Favites complanata* at the Houtman Abrolhos Islands, Western Australia.
PHOTOGRAPH: ED LOVELL.

3. Polyps of *Favites complanata*.
PHOTOGRAPH: RON AND VALERIE TAYLOR.

Favites pentagona

(ESPER, 1794)

TYPE LOCALITY
"East Indies"

IDENTIFYING CHARACTERS
Colonies are submassive to encrusting, sometimes forming irregular columns. Corallites are thin-walled and angular, with calices usually less than 6 mm in diameter. Septa are few in number, paliform lobes are well developed.

COLOUR
Often brightly coloured, brown or red with green oral discs being common.

SIMILAR SPECIES
F. russelli.

DISTRIBUTION
From the Red Sea east to New Caledonia.
Around Australia: the Great Barrier Reef, Coral Sea and south to Elizabeth Reef in the east, and south to Rottnest Island on the west coast.

ABUNDANCE
Sometimes common (west coast especially), with colonies exceeding 1 m in diameter.

×1

1. *Favites pentagona* from Lizard Island, Great Barrier Reef. The small, usually brightly coloured polyps make this species very distinctive under water.
PHOTOGRAPH: LEN ZELL.

2. *Favites pentagona* at a fringing reef near Cape Tribulation, Great Barrier Reef.
PHOTOGRAPH: AUTHOR.

Favites russelli

(WELLS, 1954)

TYPE LOCALITY
Marshall Islands.

IDENTIFYING CHARACTERS
Colonies are submassive to encrusting. Corallites are cerioid to subplocoid, rounded and thick-walled. Calices average 10 mm in diameter. Paliform lobes are well developed.

COLOUR
Usually green, brown or mottled or concentric green and cream.

SIMILAR SPECIES
F. pentagona has thinner walls and smaller corallites.

DISTRIBUTION
From Australia east to the Marshall Islands.
Around Australia: the Great Barrier Reef, Flinders Reef (Moreton Bay) and Lord Howe Island in the east, and south to Cockburn Sound on the west coast.

ABUNDANCE
Common and occurs in a very wide range of habitats.

x1

1. The usual appearance of *Favites russelli*. The polyps are larger than those of *F. pentagona*.
PHOTOGRAPH: ED LOVELL.

2,4. The polyps of two *Favites russelli* colonies at the Palm Islands, Great Barrier Reef.
PHOTOGRAPHS: AUTHOR (2) AND ED LOVELL (4).

3. A brightly coloured *Favites russelli* at Lord Howe Island, eastern Australia.
PHOTOGRAPH: LEN ZELL.

3

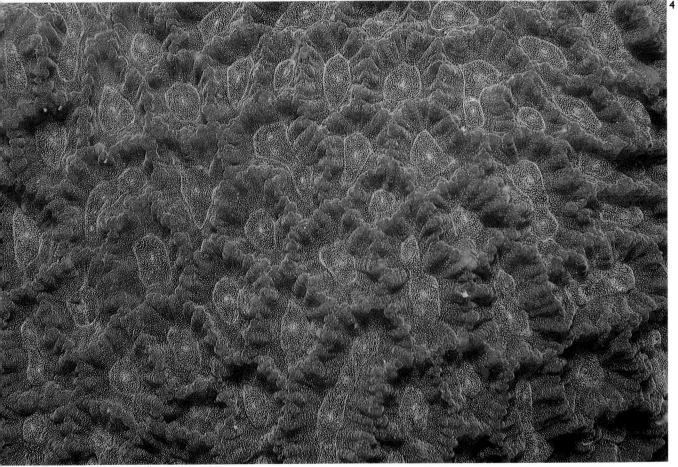

4

GENUS
GONIASTREA

(pronounced go-nee-ass-tree-a)

Edwards & Haime, 1848

Goniastrea species are very commonly found on intertidal flats of fringing reefs and on rocky shorelines, harbour breakwaters etcetera. They are the toughest of all corals and can tolerate several hours of exposure to the tropical sun at low tide and also muddy conditions and low salinity. Not surprisingly, they are encountered frequently in places where no coral might be expected to live.

All species of *Goniastrea* have corallites with a regular neat appearance. Some look like honeycomb and are thus sometimes called "honeycomb corals". Others have meandering valleys (and, with *Platygyra*, are called "brain corals"), but in both cases, all skeletal structures are more precisely arranged than other faviids, except *Leptoria*.

Like other faviids, *Goniastrea* species are hermaphrodite. The egg bundles are large and conspicuous, filling the whole calice of the smaller species.

TYPE SPECIES
Astraea retiformis Lamarck, 1816.

FOSSIL RECORD
Eocene to Recent, from North America, West Indies and Indo-Pacific.

NUMBER OF SPECIES
Approximately 34 nominal species, seven true species from Australia.

CHARACTERS
Colonies are massive, usually spherical or elongate. Corallites are monocentric and cerioid to polycentric and meandroid. Paliform lobes are well developed. Meandroid colonies have well-defined columella centres. Polyps are extended only at night.

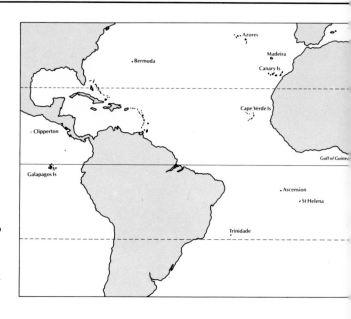

SIMILAR GENERA
Goniastrea has similarities with *Favites*, *Leptoria* and also *Platygyra*. *Platygyra*, like *Goniastrea*, can be cerioid or meandroid but has no paliform lobes and columella centres are seldom distinguishable.

Polyp detail of *Goniastrea retiformis*.
PHOTOGRAPH: ED LOVELL.

KEY TO SPECIES OF *GONIASTREA*

Corallites with calices or valleys less than 7 mm wide
     Cerioid ... *G. retiformis* (p. 480), *G. edwardsi* (p. 481)
     Submeandroid ... *G. favulus* (p. 482)
Corallites with calices or valleys over 7 mm wide
     Cerioid
         Walls thin, calices angular ... *G. aspera* (p. 483), *G. pectinata* (p. 484)
         Walls thick, calices rounded ... *G. palauensis* (p. 487)
     Submeandroid ... *G. favulus* (p. 482), *G. pectinata* (p. 484)
     Meandroid ... *G. australiensis* (p. 485)

Note: This key is a guide only and should be used in conjunction with the descriptions of the species.

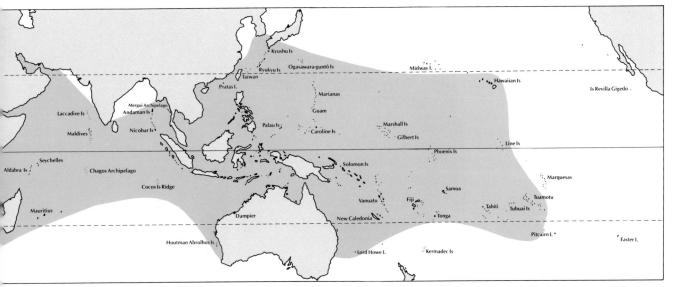

The known range of *Goniastrea*.

Goniastrea retiformis

(LAMARCK, 1816)

TYPE LOCALITY
Unrecorded.

IDENTIFYING CHARACTERS
Colonies are massive or columnar. Calices are 3.5 mm in diameter and four- to six-sided. Septa clearly alternate and are thin and straight with well-developed thin paliform lobes.

COLOUR
Cream or pale brown, occasionally brown, pink or green.

SIMILAR SPECIES
G. edwardsi has thicker walls and septa and more irregular corallites.

DISTRIBUTION
From the Red Sea east to Samoa. Around Australia: the Great Barrier Reef and Coral Sea in the east, and south to Port Gregory on the west coast.

ABUNDANCE
Common and usually a dominant of intertidal habitats. Subtidal colonies frequently exceed 1 m in diameter.

x2.5

1. *Goniastrea retiformis* on an intertidal rock face. This species can tolerate more emersion than any other coral.
PHOTOGRAPH: VICKI HARRIOTT.

2. *Goniastrea retiformis* with egg masses just prior to spawning, five days after the full moon in October.
PHOTOGRAPH: ED LOVELL.

3. The polyps of *Goniastrea retiformis* have thin, angular walls with neatly arranged septa.
PHOTOGRAPH: ED LOVELL.

4. *Goniastrea retiformis* on an outer reef flat.
PHOTOGRAPH: AUTHOR.

Goniastrea edwardsi

CHEVALIER, 1971

TYPE LOCALITY
Seychelles Islands.

IDENTIFYING CHARACTERS
Colonies are massive or columnar. Calices are 3–7 mm in diameter and angular. Septa are irregular in length and taper from the wall to the columella, which is small. Paliform lobes are thick.

COLOUR
Cream or brown.

SIMILAR SPECIES
G. *retiformis*.

DISTRIBUTION
From the Seychelles Islands east to the Loyalty Islands.
Around Australia: the Great Barrier Reef and Coral Sea in the east, and south to Houtman Abrolhos Islands on the west coast.

ABUNDANCE
Common in subtidal communities where colonies frequently exceed 1 m in diameter.

x2.5

Goniastrea edwardsi is similar to *G. retiformis*, but has thicker walls and more rounded polyps.
PHOTOGRAPH: ED LOVELL.

481

Goniastrea favulus

(DANA, 1846)

TYPE LOCALITY
  Fiji.

IDENTIFYING CHARACTERS
  Colonies are mostly massive.
  Corallites are cerioid to
  submeandroid. Walls are thin,
  columellae small and paliform
  lobes well developed.

COLOUR
  Dull green or brown.

SIMILAR SPECIES
  G. favulus is like a submeandroid
  G. retiformis.

DISTRIBUTION
  From the Laccadive Islands east
  to New Caledonia and Fiji.
  Around Australia: the Great
  Barrier Reef, Coral Sea and south
  to Lord Howe Island in the east,
  and south to Houtman Abrolhos
  Islands on the west coast.

ABUNDANCE
  Usually uncommon except in
  intertidal or subtidal habitats but
  occurs in a wide range of other
  habitats.

×2.5

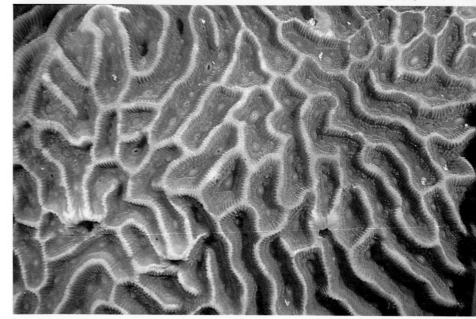

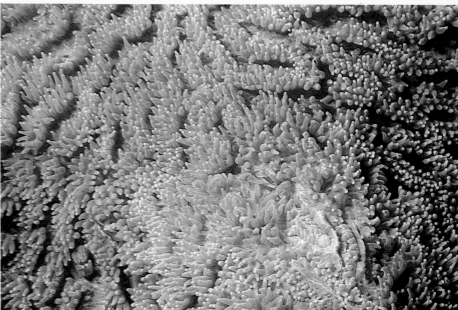

1. A common colony shape of *Goniastrea
favulus*.
PHOTOGRAPH: LEN ZELL.

2. *Goniastrea favulus* is readily recognised
under water by its short valleys with thin
walls. It is much smaller than *Platygyra*
species.
PHOTOGRAPH: LEN ZELL.

3. *Goniastrea favulus* with a carpet of fine
tentacles extended at night.
PHOTOGRAPHS: LEN ZELL.

Goniastrea aspera

VERRILL, 1905

TYPE LOCALITY
Hong Kong.

IDENTIFYING CHARACTERS
Colonies are massive to
encrusting. Calices are 7-10 mm
in diameter and are angular.
Septa generally alternate,
paliform lobes are well developed
in coralla from turbid water to
absent in coralla from very
exposed habitats.

COLOUR
Usually pale brown; corallite
centres are often cream.

SIMILAR SPECIES
Like *G. retiformis*, only larger.

DISTRIBUTION
From the Mergui Archipelago
east to Indonesia, Palau and New
Caledonia.
Around Australia: the Great
Barrier Reef in the east, and
south to Geographe Bay on the
west coast.

ABUNDANCE
Common in intertidal habitats
where different colonies may
adjoin to form flat expanses
frequently over 5 m in diameter.
Also occurs in very protected
turbid environments.

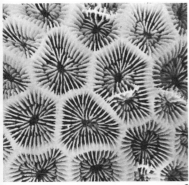

x2.5

1. A *Goniastrea aspera* colony projecting
high above the surrounding outer reef flat
of Scott Reef, Western Australia.
PHOTOGRAPH: AUTHOR.

2. A small colony of *Goniastrea aspera*.
PHOTOGRAPH: JOHN BARNETT.

3. All *Goniastrea* species are tolerant of
aerial exposure and are often the
dominant corals of intertidal flats around
the mainland or high islands. Here, masses
of *G. aspera* are exposed at low tide.
PHOTOGRAPH: LEN ZELL.

4. The polyps of *Goniastrea aspera*
showing elongate, cream-coloured
paliform lobes.
PHOTOGRAPH: LEN ZELL.

Goniastrea pectinata

(EHRENBERG, 1834)

TYPE LOCALITY
Red Sea.

IDENTIFYING CHARACTERS
Colonies are submassive or encrusting. Corallites are cerioid to submeandroid usually with less than four centres. Walls are thick, paliform lobes are well developed.

COLOUR
Pale brown or pink, dark brown in deep or turbid water.

SIMILAR SPECIES
G. edwardsi is similar but has markedly smaller corallites. *G. australensis* has valleys of similar width but is fully meandroid.

DISTRIBUTION
Red Sea east to Samoa. Around Australia: the Great Barrier Reef, Coral Sea and south to Lord Howe Island in the east, and south to Houtman Abrolhos Islands on the west coast.

ABUNDANCE
Very common in most shallow-water habitats.

 x2.5

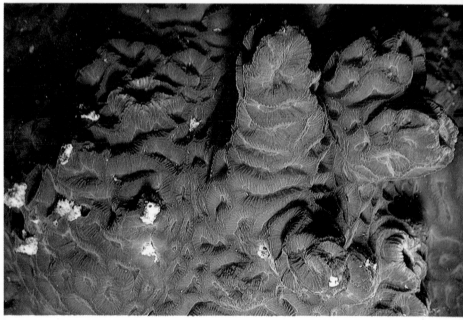

1. *Goniastrea pectinata* at the Swain Reefs, Great Barrier Reef.
PHOTOGRAPH: ED LOVELL.

2. The characteristic appearance of *Goniastrea pectinata* in shallow water. The pinkish skeleton has an almost translucent appearance.
PHOTOGRAPH: LEN ZELL.

3. *Goniastrea pectinata* often forms columnar colonies at the Houtman Abrolhos Islands, Western Australia.
PHOTOGRAPH: ED LOVELL.

Goniastrea australensis

(EDWARDS & HAIME, 1857)

TYPE LOCALITY
"Australia".

IDENTIFYING CHARACTERS
Colonies are submassive or encrusting, meandroid with sinuous valleys. Columella centres and paliform lobes are well developed.

COLOUR
Very variable but commonly a uniform dull green or brown or with walls and valley floors of different dull or bright colours.

SIMILAR SPECIES
G. australensis is the only fully meandroid *Goniastrea*. Under water it may be difficult to distinguish from *Platygyra*, but coralla are readily distinguished by their well-developed columellae and paliform lobes.

DISTRIBUTION
Australia and the western Pacific from Japan in the north to the Kermadec Islands in the south. Around Australia: the Great Barrier Reef and Coral Sea south to Lord Howe and Solitary Islands in the east, and south to Geographe Bay on the west coast.

ABUNDANCE
Common in shallow or clear water. May be a dominant of temperate reefs.

×2.5

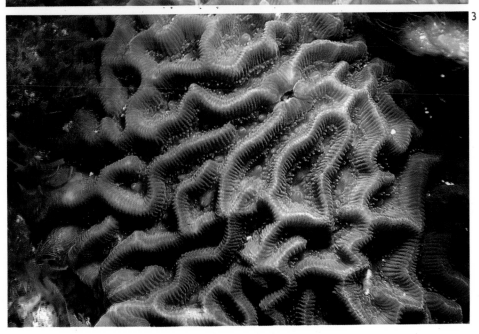

1,2. The most common appearance of *Goniastrea australensis* on tropical reefs. These may be impossible to distinguish from *Platygyra daedalea* under water.
PHOTOGRAPHS: ED LOVELL (1) AND RON AND VALERIE TAYLOR (2).

3. At Lord Howe Island, eastern Australia, *Goniastrea australensis* is a uniform brown and has large irregular valleys.
PHOTOGRAPH: JOHN BARNETT.

1. There are many colour variants of
Goniastrea australensis, but is most cases,
valleys and walls are differently coloured.
PHOTOGRAPH: RON AND VALERIE TAYLOR.

2. *Goniastrea australensis* at Dampier
Archipelago, Western Australia.
PHOTOGRAPH: ED LOVELL.

Goniastrea palauensis

(YABE, SUGIYAMA & EGUCHI, 1936)

TYPE LOCALITY

Palau.

IDENTIFYING CHARACTERS

Colonies are massive, usually flattened or hillocky, cerioid, with thick thecae. Columellae are small and are surrounded by a crown of tall paliform lobes. Septa are straight with a neat appearance.

COLOUR

Pale brown or dull green, becoming dark in deep water. Oral discs are usually cream but may be bright green in Western Australia.

SIMILAR SPECIES

Unlike other *Goniastrea* but can be confused with *Favites russelli*. The latter is usually subplocoid, has smaller corallites, relatively irregular septa and smaller paliform lobes.

DISTRIBUTION

Palau, New Caledonia and Australia.
Around Australia: the Great Barrier Reef and Elizabeth and Middleton Reefs in the east, and south to Fremantle on the west coast.

ABUNDANCE

Occupies a wide range of habitats but is seldom common.

x2.5

1. A small colony of *Goniastrea palauensis* at the Palm Islands, Great Barrier Reef.
PHOTOGRAPH: ED LOVELL.

2. The polyps of *Goniastrea palauensis*— these are usually deep and angular. A neat circle of paliform lobes around the mouth can usually be distinguished under water.
PHOTOGRAPH: ED LOVELL.

3. *Goniastrea palauensis* is occasionally very brightly coloured.
PHOTOGRAPH: AUTHOR.

GENUS
PLATYGYRA
(pronounced platy-dgai-ra)

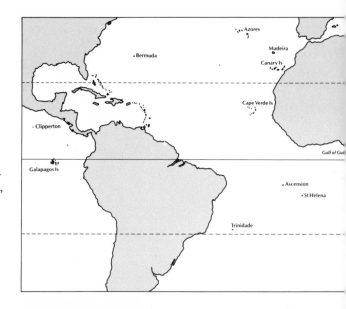

Ehrenberg, 1834

Some species of *Platygyra* may be difficult to separate unless they are found in the same habitat. Thus, deep-water *P. daedalea* can look much like shallow-water *P. lamellina*, and *P. sinensis* can be confused with *P. pini*.

Platygyra are commonly found on upper reef slopes, back reef margins and on reef flats, with *P. daedalea* being by far the most common species.

TYPE SPECIES
Platygyra labyrinthica Ehrenberg, 1834 from the Red Sea.

WELL-KNOWN SYNONYM
Coeloria Edwards & Haime, 1843.

FOSSIL RECORD
Eocene to Recent from Europe and the Indo-Pacific.

NUMBER OF SPECIES
Approximately 26 nominal species, five true species from Australia.

CHARACTERS
Colonies are massive, either flat or dome-shaped. Corallites are rarely cerioid, commonly meandroid. Paliform lobes are not developed, columellae seldom form centres and are a continuous tangle of spines. Polyps are usually extended only at night.

SIMILAR GENERA
Platygyra is similar to *Goniastrea* and also *Australogyra* and *Leptoria*.
Australogyra has *Platygyra*-like skeletal structures but has a branching growth form and no columellae.
Leptoria is more meandroid than *Platygyra*, has distinctive wall-like columellae and has very uniformly spaced septa of equal size.

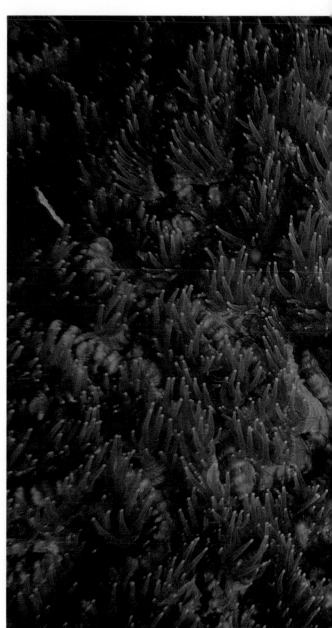

Platygyra **with polyps extended at night.**
PHOTOGRAPH: LEN ZELL.

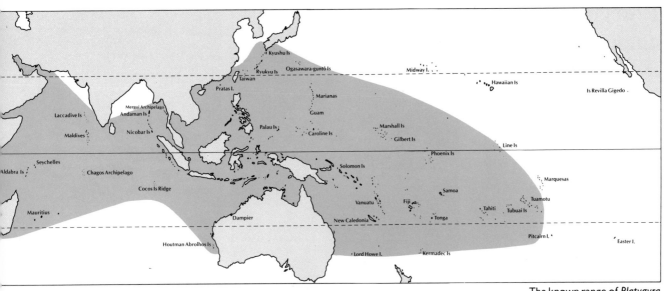

The known range of *Platygyra*.

Platygyra verweyi
WIJSMAN-BEST, 1976

TYPE LOCALITY
Indonesia.

IDENTIFYING CHARACTERS
Colonies are massive, subcerioid to submeandroid with thin acute walls. Septa are thin and uniformly spaced. Columellae are weakly developed or absent.

COLOUR
Not known.

SIMILAR SPECIES
P. sinensis is usually more meandroid and has shallower calices; *P. pini* has more widely spaced, more irregular septa. In general appearance *P. verweyi* has a *Goniastrea*-like neat skeletal structure.

DISTRIBUTION
Recorded only from Indonesia and Australia.
Around Australia: south to the Ningaloo Reef Tract on the west coast, not found in the east.

ABUNDANCE
Reported to be common on reef flats near Darwin.

×1

Platygyra daedalea

(ELLIS & SOLANDER, 1786)

TYPE LOCALITY
Fiji.

IDENTIFYING CHARACTERS
Colonies are massive to encrusting, meandroid or submeandroid, with thick walls. Septa are exsert and have a characteristically ragged appearance.

COLOUR
Usually brightly coloured, most commonly with brown walls and grey or green valleys.

SIMILAR SPECIES
P. lamellina is distinguished by its neat rounded septa. See also *Goniastrea australensis*.

DISTRIBUTION
From the Red Sea east to the Marshall Islands.
Around Australia: the Great Barrier Reef, Coral Sea and south to Lord Howe and Solitary Islands in the east, and south to Houtman Abrolhos Islands on the west coast.

ABUNDANCE
Common over a wide range of habitats, especially back reef margins.

×1

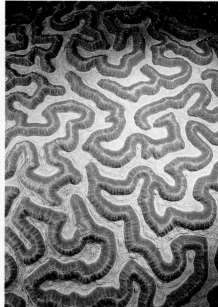

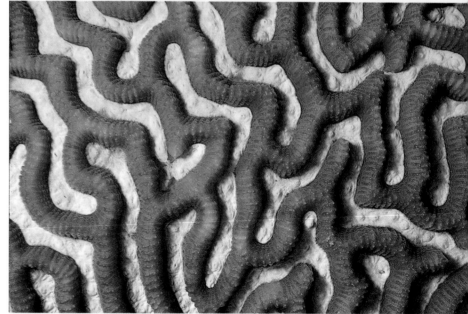

1. *Platygyra daedalea* at Broadhurst Reef, Great Barrier Reef, showing a common colony shape and general appearance.
PHOTOGRAPH: ED LOVELL.

2. The usual appearance of sinuous valleys of *Platygyra daedalea*. This species is difficult to distinguish from *Goniastrea australensis* under water.
PHOTOGRAPH: ED LOVELL.

3,4. Two common colour combinations of *Platygyra daedalea*.
PHOTOGRAPHS: ED LOVELL (3) AND RON AND VALERIE TAYLOR (4).

490

Platygyra lamellina

(EHRENBERG, 1834)

TYPE LOCALITY
Red Sea.

IDENTIFYING CHARACTERS
Colonies are massive, meandroid, with thick walls. Septa are uniformly exsert and are neat and rounded.

COLOUR
Usually brown or with brown walls and grey or green valleys.

SIMILAR SPECIES
P. daedalea.

DISTRIBUTION
From the Red Sea east to Polynesia.
Around Australia: the Great Barrier Reef, Elizabeth and Middleton Reefs and Solitary Islands in the east, and south to Houtman Abrolhos Islands on the west coast.

ABUNDANCE
Usually uncommon.

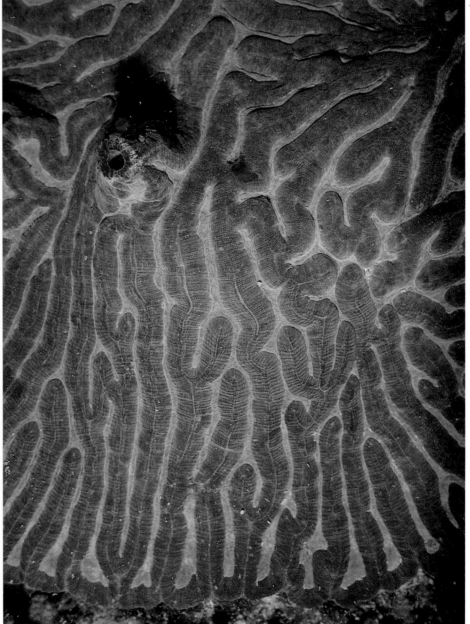

×1

1,2. *Platygyra lamellina* has thick walls between shallow valleys, and it has many colour combinations.
PHOTOGRAPHS: ED LOVELL.

Platygyra sinensis

(EDWARDS & HAIME, 1849)

TYPE LOCALITY
"China Sea".

IDENTIFYING CHARACTERS
Colonies are massive or flat, subcerioid to meandroid, with thin walls. Septa are thin, slightly exsert.

COLOUR
Variable dull or bright colours.

SIMILAR SPECIES
P. pini, also *Goniastrea favulus* under water.

DISTRIBUTION
Red Sea to Samoa. Around Australia: the Great Barrier Reef, Coral Sea and south to Elizabeth and Middleton Reefs in the east, and south to Port Gregory on the west coast.

ABUNDANCE
Usually uncommon.

×1

1. *Platygyra sinensis* at the Swain Reefs, Great Barrier Reef.
PHOTOGRAPH: ED LOVELL.

2. The usual appearance of *Platygyra sinensis* valleys: some elongate with several mouths, some with only one mouth.
PHOTOGRAPH: RON AND VALERIE TAYLOR.

492

Platygyra pini

CHEVALIER, 1975

TYPE LOCALITY
Chesterfield Reefs, eastern Coral Sea.

IDENTIFYING CHARACTERS
Colonies are massive to encrusting, subcerioid to submeandroid with thick walls. Septa are thin and widely spaced. There may be some development of columella centres and/or paliform lobes.

COLOUR
Grey- or yellow-brown with green or cream centres.

SIMILAR SPECIES
Submeandroid *P. sinensis* is distinguished by its thinner walls and more compact septa. Submeandroid *P. daedalea* is usually distinguished by exsert septa and the occasional presence of elongate valleys.

DISTRIBUTION
Australia and western Pacific, but the distribution is largely unknown.
Around Australia: the Great Barrier Reef and Coral Sea in the east, and North West Cape on the west coast.

ABUNDANCE
Usually uncommon.

x1

1,2. Two colour combinations of *Platygyra pini*.
PHOTOGRAPHS: ED LOVELL.

3,4. *Platygyra pini*. Valleys are short with thick walls.
PHOTOGRAPHS: ED LOVELL (3) AND AUTHOR (4).

GENUS
AUSTRALOGYRA
(pronounced ostral-oh-dgai-ra)

Veron & Pichon, 1982

TYPE SPECIES
Platygyra zelli (Veron, Pichon & Wijsman-Best, 1977).

FOSSIL RECORD
None.

NUMBER OF SPECIES
One.

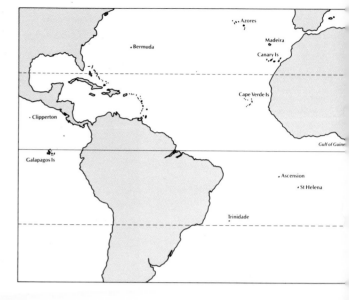

Australogyra zelli
(VERON, PICHON & WIJSMAN-BEST, 1977)

TYPE LOCALITY
Palm Islands, Great Barrier Reef.

IDENTIFYING CHARACTERS
Colonies have a branching growth form.
Corallites are meandroid, forming short valleys.
Columellae are absent.
Polyps are extended only at night.

COLOUR
Grey-green to brown.

SIMILAR SPECIES
Australogyra is similar to *Platygyra*. It also resembles superficially branching *Hydnophora*, but the latter have distinctive hydnophores.

DISTRIBUTION
Around Australia: the Great Barrier Reef and Elizabeth and Middleton Reefs in the east; not found on the west coast.

ABUNDANCE
Usually found in turbid waters around high islands, such as the Palm Islands, but rare elsewhere.

x1

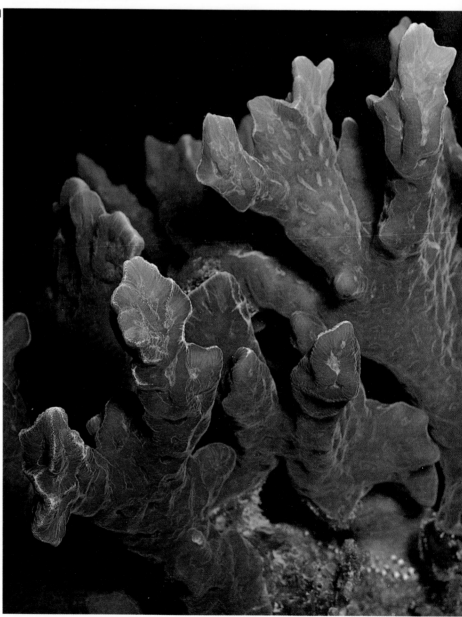

1,2. *Australogyra zelli*, named after Len Zell, who took many photographs in this book. This uncommon coral usually has a beautifully sculptured appearance.
PHOTOGRAPHS: ED LOVELL.

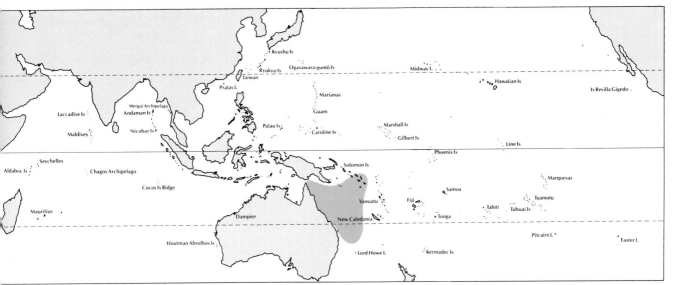

The known range of *Australogyra zelli*.

2

GENUS
LEPTORIA

(pronounced lep-tor-ee-a)

Edwards & Haime, 1848

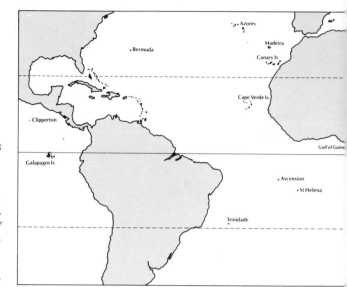

The genus having been known as Leptoria *for 80 years, Matthai's unravelling of Ehrenberg's mistakes is nothing but a misfortune . . . Matthai's discussion of Ehrenberg's confusion is a good example of the useless labour a rabbinical adherence to the rule of priority imposes upon men whose time is far too valuable for such rooting in old, and in this case, useless books.*

Cyril Crossland,
*Scientific Reports of the Great Barrier
Reef Expedition, 1928-29,* Volume 6, 1952.

Leptoria has been called *Platygyra* in several older scientific publications, but there can be no doubt that the present name is correct.

Like *Goniastrea,* the septa of *Leptoria* have a neat orderly arrangement. Valleys are also of very uniform width. They sometimes run parallel to each other, but more often form fascinatingly complex mazes.

TYPE SPECIES
Madrepora phrygia Ellis & Solander, 1786.

FOSSIL RECORD
Upper Cretaceous to Recent from Europe and the Indo-Pacific.

NUMBER OF SPECIES
Three nominal species, one true species.

1. *Leptoria phrygia* often forms lobed colonies which have a sculptured appearance.
PHOTOGRAPH: ED LOVELL.

2. The usual surface appearance of *Leptoria phrygia.* This species is not difficult to distinguish from *Platygyra* under water.
PHOTOGRAPH: ED LOVELL.

3,4. Surface detail of *Leptoria phrygia* colonies. This species is the most meandroid of all corals, forming mazes of neat, sinuous valleys.
PHOTOGRAPHS: RON AND VALERIE TAYLOR.

×2.5

Leptoria phrygia
(ELLIS & SOLANDER, 1786)

TYPE LOCALITY
"Pacific Ocean".

IDENTIFYING CHARACTERS
Colonies are massive with an even surface and dense skeleton. Corallite valleys are highly meandroid and very uniform. Septa are uniformly spaced and are of equal size. Columellae are wall-like with a lobed upper margin and do not form centres. Paliform lobes are absent. Polyps are extended only at night.

COLOUR
Cream, brown or green, with walls and valleys of different colours.

SIMILAR SPECIES
Leptoria is similar to *Platygyra* and also *Goniastrea.*
Goniastrea is less meandroid than *Leptoria,* has columellae forming distinct centres and well-developed paliform lobes.

DISTRIBUTION
Around Australia: the Great Barrier Reef, Coral Sea and south to Elizabeth Reef in the east, and south to Ningaloo Reef Tract on the west coast.

ABUNDANCE
Occurs in most reef environments except where the water is turbid. Often common on upper reef slopes.

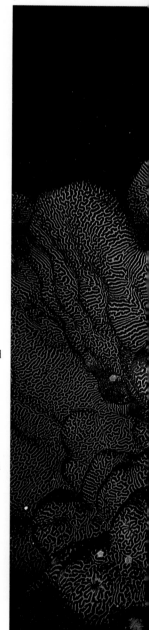

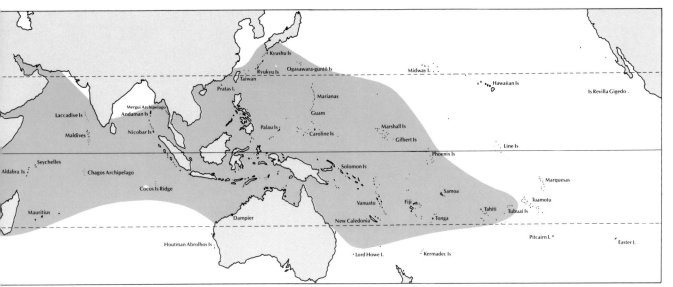

The known range of *Leptoria phrygia*.

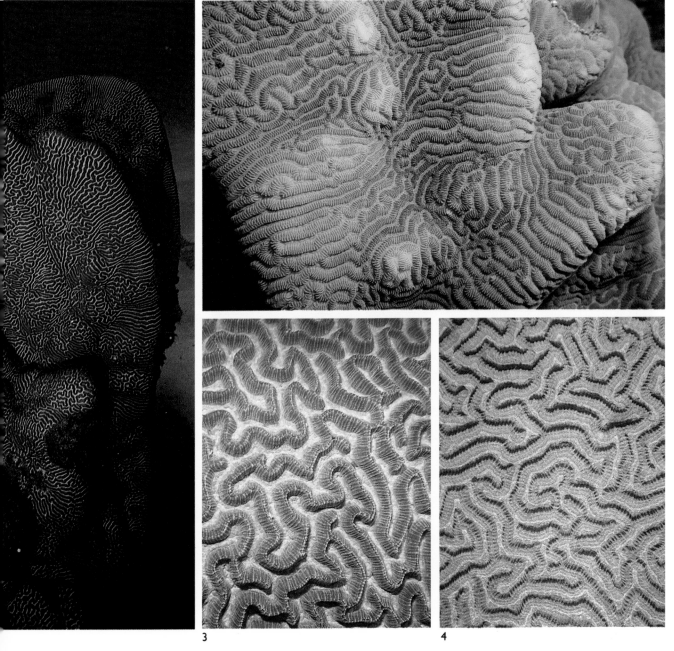

2

3

4

GENUS
OULOPHYLLIA

(pronounced oo-loh-fill-ee-a)

Edwards & Haime, 1848

TYPE SPECIES
Maeandrina crispa Lamarck, 1816.

FOSSIL RECORD
Oligocene to Recent from Europe and the Indo-Pacific.

NUMBER OF SPECIES
Approximately 11 nominal species, probably three true
species.

CHARACTERS
Colonies are massive, monocentric to meandroid,
composed of large valleys with widely spaced, ragged
septa and acute thin walls. Paliform lobes are usually
present.

SIMILAR GENERA
Platygyra and *Favites*.

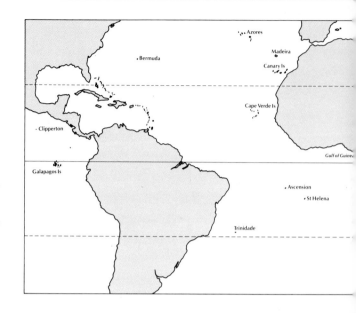

Oulophyllia
crispa

(LAMARCK, 1816)

TYPE LOCALITY
  "Indian Ocean".

IDENTIFYING CHARACTERS
  Colonies are usually massive and
  frequently exceed 1 m in
  diameter.
  Valleys are broad (up to 20 mm)
  and V-shaped. Septa are usually
  thin and slope uniformly to the
  columellae which usually form
  well-defined centres. Paliform
  lobes may be present. Valley
  walls have acute upper margins.
  Polyps are extended only at night
  and are large and fleshy with
  conspicuous white tips to the
  tentacles. When retracted, polyps
  have a coarse reptilian texture.
  Mouths are conspicuous.

COLOUR
  Brown walls with pale-cream or
  pink valley floors.

SIMILAR SPECIES
  O. bennettae.

DISTRIBUTION
  Probably the full range of the
  genus.
  Around Australia: the Great
  Barrier Reef, Coral Sea and
  Elizabeth and Middleton Reefs in

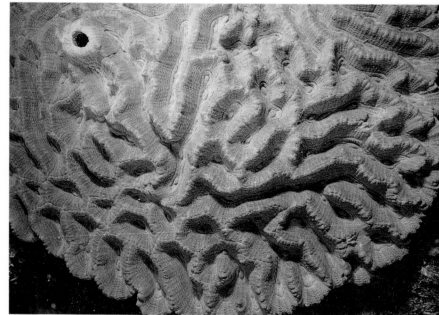

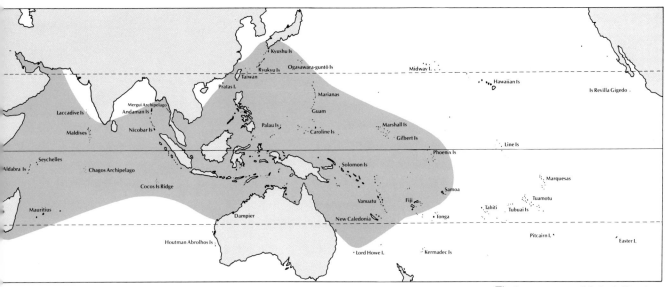

The known range of *Oulophyllia crispa*.

3

the east, and south to the Ningaloo Reef Tract on the west coast.

ABUNDANCE
Occurs in most reef environments, especially in reef lagoons, but is seldom a major component of any coral community.

x1

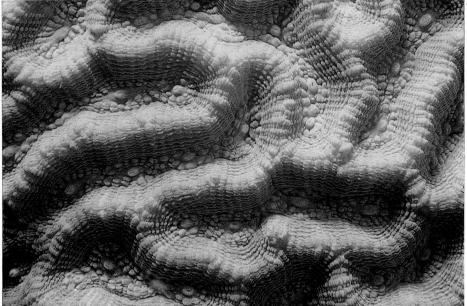

4

1. The valleys of *Oulophyllia crispa* are usually wide and V-shaped in section.
PHOTOGRAPH: ED LOVELL.

2,3. *Oulophyllia crispa* has larger valleys than other faviids.
PHOTOGRAPHS: AUTHOR (2) AND RUSS BABOCK (3).

4. *Oulophyllia crispa*. The mouths are always large and distinct.
PHOTOGRAPH: ED LOVELL.

Oulophyllia bennettae

(VERON, PICHON & WIJSMAN-BEST, 1977)

TYPE LOCALITY
Palm Islands, Great Barrier Reef.

IDENTIFYING CHARACTERS
Colonies are massive with large angular corallites which may have up to three columellae. Septa are widely spaced with large rounded teeth and some development of paliform lobes. Septa of adjacent corallites are aligned.

COLOUR
Greenish-grey with pinkish oral discs (east coast), or brown with green oral discs (west coast).

SIMILAR SPECIES
Resembles *O. crispa* more than any other coral but remains very distinct. Was formerly considered to belong to the genus *Favites* rather than *Oulophyllia*.

DISTRIBUTION
Known only from Australia: the Great Barrier Reef and Lord Howe Island in the east, and south to Passage Island on the west coast.

ABUNDANCE
Seldom common but very conspicuous.

x l

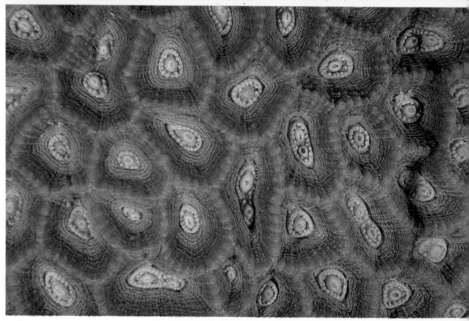

1. *Oulophyllia bennettae* on the west coast of Australia has a different colour to that on the east coast.
PHOTOGRAPH: ED LOVELL.

2,3. The polyps of *Oulophyllia bennettae*. This species was named after Isobel Bennett, author of *The Great Barrier Reef* and several other books about Australia's marine life.
PHOTOGRAPHS: ED LOVELL.

4. A large colony of *Oulophyllia bennettae* at the Palm Islands, Great Barrier Reef.
PHOTOGRAPH: ED LOVELL.

4

GENUS
MONTASTREA
(pronounced mont-ass-tree-a)

de Blainville, 1830

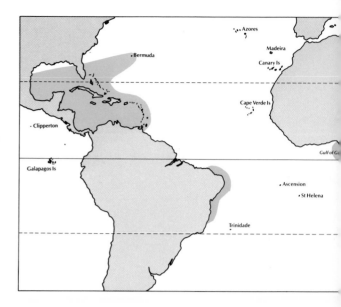

The distinction between *Montastrea* and *Favia* genera, in theory at least, is that *Montastrea* forms new corallites by extratentacular budding, while in *Favia*, budding is intratentacular. This distinction may be confused because some species of both genera exhibit both types of budding, even in the same colony. Also, the two types of budding can be distinguished only in the early stages and those may not be represented in colonies that are not actively growing. Fortunately, whether budding is taking place or not, these problems do not prevent species being recognisable.

Two species of *Montastrea*, *M. annuligera* and *M. valenciennesi*, have tiny grooves and/or tubercles between their corallites. They can occur in other genera, but in these species they are virtually always present. They are actually made of the coral's epitheca which is moulded in some way by the tiny polychaete worm *Toposyllis*. The tubercles help in the identification of these species, especially in distinguishing *M. annuligera* from the much more common *M. curta*.

TYPE SPECIES
Astraea guettardi Defrance, 1826 from an unknown locality.

FOSSIL RECORD
Jurassic or Cretaceous to Recent from the West Indies and Indo-Pacific.

NUMBER OF SPECIES
Ten nominal species, seven from the Indo-Pacific, five true species known from Australia.

CHARACTERS
Colonies are massive, either flat or dome-shaped. Corallites are monocentric and plocoid. Daughter corallites are predominantly formed by extratentacular budding, that is, budding from the wall of parent corallites. Some intratentacular budding may also occur.

SIMILAR GENERA
Montastrea is an ill-defined genus, but the species within it are usually recognised easily. It is separated readily from the other massive faviid genera with extratentacular budding (*Plesiastrea, Diploastrea, Leptastrea, Cyphastrea*) because each of these has well-defined characters.

Montastrea curta showing daughter polyps forming by extratentacular budding. Colonies of this colour are found in slightly shaded situations.
PHOTOGRAPH: RON AND VALERIE TAYLOR.

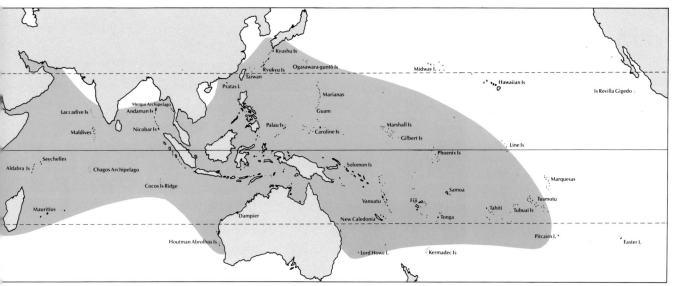

The known range of *Montastrea*.

Montastrea curta

(DANA, 1846)

TYPE LOCALITY
Fiji.

IDENTIFYING CHARACTERS
Colonies are spherical or flattened.
Corallites are circular or squeezed together, with calices 2.5-7.5 mm in diameter. Long and short septa alternate. Small paliform lobes are usually developed.

COLOUR
Cream or orange on reef flats, often with colours concentric to the mouths. Usually dark brown in shaded habitats.

SIMILAR SPECIES
M. annuligera.

DISTRIBUTION
From Madagascar east to the Tuamotu Archipelago.
Around Australia: the Great Barrier Reef, Coral Sea and South to Lord Howe Island in the east, and south to Perth on the west coast.

ABUNDANCE
Common, especially on reef flats.

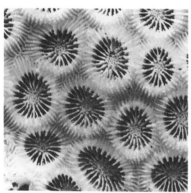

x2.5

1. A small colony of *Montastrea curta*, showing the conical polyps with concentric colours.
PHOTOGRAPH: LEN ZELL.

2. *Montastrea curta* at the Houtman Abrolhos Islands, Western Australia, with polyps partly extended.
PHOTOGRAPH: PAT BAKER.

3. The usual appearance of *Montastrea curta* polyps.
PHOTOGRAPH: RON AND VALERIE TAYLOR.

Montastrea annuligera

(EDWARDS & HAIME, 1849)

TYPE LOCALITY
"Australia".

IDENTIFYING CHARACTERS
Colonies are irregular or encrusting.
Corallites are circular with calices 3-4 mm in diameter. Septa taper from the wall to the columella and are in three cycles, those of the primary cycle being widely spaced with well-developed paliform lobes. Most colonies have at least some development of a groove and tubercle system.

COLOUR
Mottled or uniform green and brown, with darker calices.

SIMILAR SPECIES
M. curta. M. valenciennesi also has a groove and tubercle system.

DISTRIBUTION
From the Red Sea east to the Philippines and New Caledonia. Around Australia: the Great Barrier Reef and Flinders Reef (Moreton Bay) in the east; not found on the west coast.

ABUNDANCE
Uncommon.

 x2.5

1. *Montastrea annuligera.*
PHOTOGRAPH: LEN ZELL.

2. A mottled, cryptic colony of *Montastrea annuligera.*
PHOTOGRAPH: AUTHOR.

Montastrea magnistellata

CHEVALIER, 1971

TYPE LOCALITY
New Caledonia.

IDENTIFYING CHARACTERS
Colonies are massive with round corallites of varying sizes. Calices are shallow, approximately 6–13 mm in diameter, with tightly compacted septa. Columellae are large and small paliform lobes are usually developed.

COLOUR
Very variable but usually several colours, including grey, green, orange and pink, are arranged concentrically to the corallites.

SIMILAR SPECIES
None.

DISTRIBUTION
Indonesia, Australia and New Caledonia.
Around Australia: the Great Barrier Reef, Coral Sea and Flinders Reef (Moreton Bay) in the east, and south to Houtman Abrolhos Islands on the west coast.

ABUNDANCE
Usually uncommon, found on protected reef slopes.

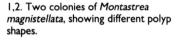

×1

1,2. Two colonies of *Montastrea magnistellata*, showing different polyp shapes.

PHOTOGRAPHS: ED LOVELL (1) AND RON AND VALERIE TAYLOR (2).

Montastrea valenciennesi

(EDWARDS & HAIME, 1848)

TYPE LOCALITY
Unrecorded.

IDENTIFYING CHARACTERS
Colonies are submassive to encrusting, with angular corallites. Calices are 8-15 mm in diameter. A groove and tubercle system is well developed.

COLOUR
Usually green or yellow with cream septa and sometimes with green oral discs.

SIMILAR SPECIES
None.

DISTRIBUTION
From Madagascar east to the Marshall Islands.
Around Australia: the Great Barrier Reef, Coral Sea and Flinders Reef (Moreton Bay) in the east, and south to Houtman Abrolhos Islands on the west coast.

ABUNDANCE
Usually uncommon but occurs in a wide variety of habitats.

x1

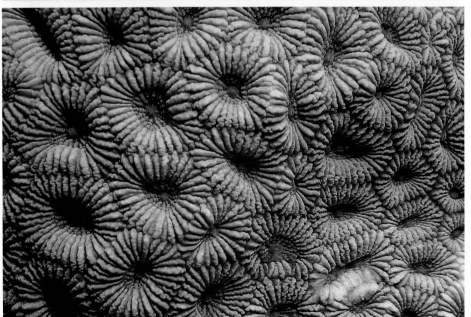

1. The usual appearance of a colony of *Montastrea valenciennesi.*
PHOTOGRAPH: ED LOVELL.

2,3. Variation in the shapes and colours of *Montastrea valenciennesi.*
PHOTOGRAPHS: RON AND VALERIE TAYLOR (2) AND ED LOVELL (3).

507

GENUS
OULASTREA

(pronounced oo-las-tree-a)

Edwards & Haime, 1848

TYPE SPECIES
Astrea crispata Lamarck, 1816.

FOSSIL RECORD
Pleistocene.

NUMBER OF SPECIES
Three nominal species, probably one true species.

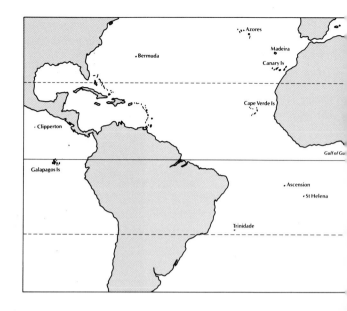

Oulastrea crispata

(LAMARCK, 1816)

TYPE LOCALITY
Unrecorded.

IDENTIFYING CHARACTERS
Colonies are encrusting and grow to only a few centimetres in diameter. Corallites are like a small *Montastrea*. The skeleton remains black with white septa when dried.

COLOURS
Living colonies are black and white, like the dried coralla.

SIMILAR SPECIES
None.

DISTRIBUTION
Around Australia: Admiralty Gulf on the west coast; not found in the east.

ABUNDANCE
Known in Australia from a single specimen. Elsewhere this species is found only in shallow water, attached to wave-washed rock.

×2.5

The polyps of *Oulastrea crispata*. This species shows very little variation.
PHOTOGRAPH: AUTHOR.

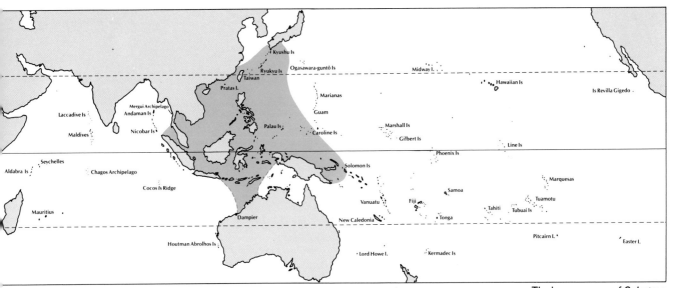

The known range of *Oulastrea*.

GENUS
PLESIASTREA

(pronounced plees-ee-ass-tree-a)

Edwards & Haime, 1848

TYPE SPECIES
Astraea versipora Lamarck, 1816.

FOSSIL RECORD
Eocene from the East Indies and Miocene from Europe and the Indo-Pacific.

NUMBER OF SPECIES
Nine nominal species, two true species, one from Australia.

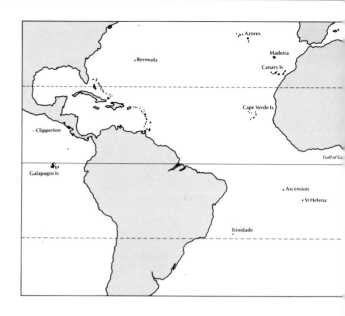

Plesiastrea versipora

(LAMARCK, 1816)

SYNONYM
Plesiastrea urvillei Edwards & Haime, 1849.

TYPE LOCALITY
Red Sea.

IDENTIFYING CHARACTERS
Colonies are flat and are frequently lobed.
Corallites are monocentric and plocoid. Daughter corallites are produced by extratentacular budding. Corallites have calices approximately 2.5 mm in diameter. Paliform lobes form a neat circle around small columellae. Polyps are usually extended only at night. Tentacles are short and are of two alternating sizes.

COLOUR
Yellow, cream, green or brown, usually pale-coloured in the tropics and brightly coloured (green or brown) in high latitude areas.

SIMILAR SPECIES
P. *versipora* is close to *Montastrea* but has smaller corallites with better-developed paliform lobes. It is more readily confused with other faviid species with corallites of similar size and shape, notably *Favia stelligera* and *Cyphastrea* species.
Favia stelligera has more conical corallites with thicker walls and intratentacular budding.
Cyphastrea has usually poorly developed paliform lobes and the coenosteum between corallites is characteristically covered with granules.

DISTRIBUTION
The full range of the genus. Around Australia: recorded from the entire mainland coastline including St Vincent's Gulf, South Australia and the south coast of Western Australia.

ABUNDANCE
In high latitudes it occurs in a wide range of non-reefal environments protected from strong wave action, and colonies may attain 3 m in diameter. Occurs in most reef environments but large colonies usually occur only in shaded places, such as under overhangs, and are seldom common.

×2.5

1. *Plesiastrea versipora* at Sydney, with tentacles extended.
PHOTOGRAPH: RUDI KUITER.

2. *Plesiastrea versipora* at Carnac Island, Western Australia.
PHOTOGRAPH: CLAY BRYCE.

3. Polyps of *Plesiastrea versipora*.
PHOTOGRAPH: NEVILLE COLEMAN. A.M.P.I.

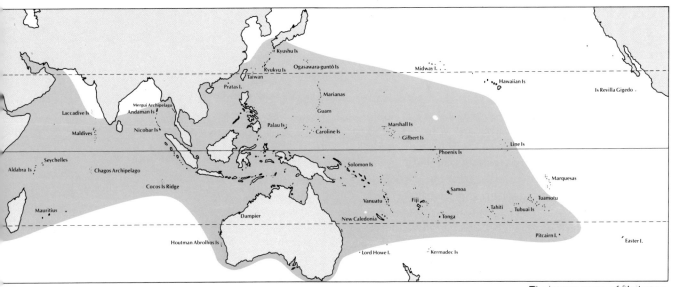

The known range of *Plesiastrea*.

2

3

GENUS
DIPLOASTREA

(pronounced diplo-ass-tree-a)

Matthai, 1914

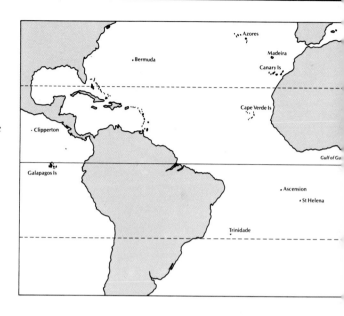

This is one of the few common corals that have only one name which is always correctly used. It is very distinct from all other corals alive today, and also has a long fossil history as a single recognisable species.

D. *heliopora* has a dense skeleton which is seldom penetrated by boring organisms and it is also seldom grazed by fish. Even the crown-of-thorns starfish is reluctant to attack it, which is probably why colonies may attain very large sizes, larger than any other faviid.

TYPE SPECIES
Astraea heliopora Lamarck, 1816.

FOSSIL RECORD
Cretaceous to Recent from Europe, North and South America and the Indo-Pacific.

NUMBER OF SPECIES
One.

Diploastrea heliopora
(LAMARCK, 1816)

TYPE LOCALITY
   "Indian Ocean".

IDENTIFYING CHARACTERS
   Colonies are dome-shaped with a very even surface and may be up to 2 m high and 7 m in diameter. The skeleton is very dense. Corallites are plocoid. Columellae are large. Septa are equal and are thick at the wall and thin where they join the columellae.
   Polyps are extended only at night.

COLOUR
   Usually uniform cream or grey, sometimes greenish.

SIMILAR SPECIES
   None. This is one of the most easily recognised of all corals.

DISTRIBUTION
   Around Australia: the Great Barrier Reef and Coral Sea in the east, and south to the Ningaloo Reef Tract on the west coast.

ABUNDANCE
   Occurs in both exposed and protected reef habitats but is usually uncommon except on some back reef margins.

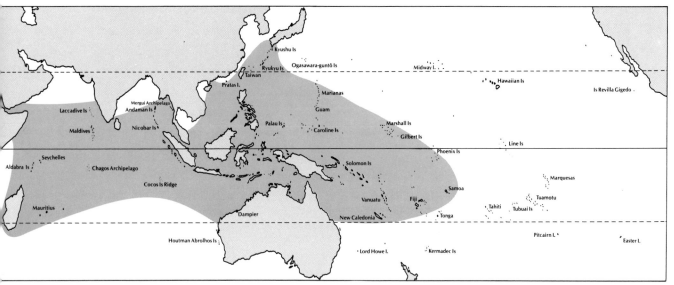

The known range of *Diploastrea heliopora*.

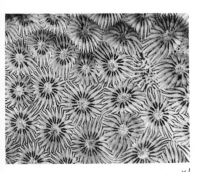

×1

3

4

1. The flat surface of a large *Diploastrea heliopora* colony. This species forms the largest colonies of all faviids.
PHOTOGRAPH: ED LOVELL.

2. The most common colour of *Diploastrea heliopora*.
PHOTOGRAPH: RON AND VALERIE TAYLOR.

3. *Diploastrea heliopora* occasionally has polyps with pale calices and tops of walls.
PHOTOGRAPH: RON AND VALERIE TAYLOR.

4. The polyps of *Diploastrea heliopora*. These are very distinct from those of other faviids and show little variability.
PHOTOGRAPH: ED LOVELL.

GENUS
LEPTASTREA

(pronounced lepta-stree-a)

Edwards & Haime, 1848

Of the five Australian species, two are readily
recognised: *L. bewickensis*, which is known only from a
few specimens, and *L. inaequalis* (often called *L. bottae*),
which is common on the Great Barrier Reef and
elsewhere. The three remaining species may be difficult
to identify from specimens. Under water, *L. pruinosa* is
easily identified because it has polyps extended during
the day (so also has *L. purpurea* at the Houtman
Abrolhos Islands).

   L. inaequalis has the same sort of groove and
tubercle formation described for *Montastrea*, except that
the epitheca is missing.

TYPE SPECIES
Leptastrea roissyana Edwards & Haime, 1848 from the
"Indian Ocean".

FOSSIL RECORD
Oligocene to Recent from the Indo-Pacific.

NUMBER OF SPECIES
Sixteen nominal species, six to eight true species, five
from Australia.

CHARACTERS
Colonies are massive, usually flat or dome-shaped.
Corallites are subcerioid to plocoid. Costae are poorly
developed or absent. Columellae consist of vertical
pinnules. Septa have inward-projecting teeth.
Polyps are usually extended only at night (except
L. pruinosa).

SIMILAR GENERA
Leptastrea is a well-defined genus. The only point of
close similarity with another genus is between
L. inaequalis and *Montastrea annuligera*. The former is
distinguished by its smaller corallites, well-defined first
cycle septa and columellae with vertical pinnules.

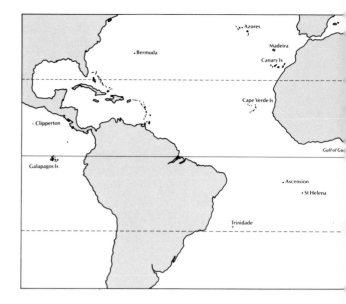

Leptastrea inaequalis
KLUNZINGER, 1879

TYPE LOCALITY
   Red Sea.

IDENTIFYING CHARACTERS
   Colonies are massive, plocoid,
   with conical corallites irregularly
   separated by deep grooves.

COLOUR
   Usually cream or yellow with
   black calices.

SIMILAR SPECIES
   None.

DISTRIBUTION
   From the Red Sea east to Hawaii.
   Around Australia: the Great
   Barrier Reef, Coral Sea and
   Elizabeth and Middleton Reefs in
   the east, and Rowley Shoals and
   Scott Reef on the west coast.

ABUNDANCE
   Sometimes common and occurs
   in a wide range of habitats.

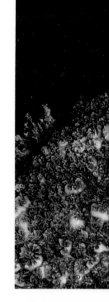

1. The usual colouration of *Leptastrea
inaequalis*.
PHOTOGRAPH: LEN ZELL.

2. *Leptastrea inaequalis* is usually a very
distinctive species.
PHOTOGRAPH: LEN ZELL.

3. Polyps of *Leptastrea inaequalis*.
PHOTOGRAPH: RON AND VALERIE TAYLOR.

x2.5

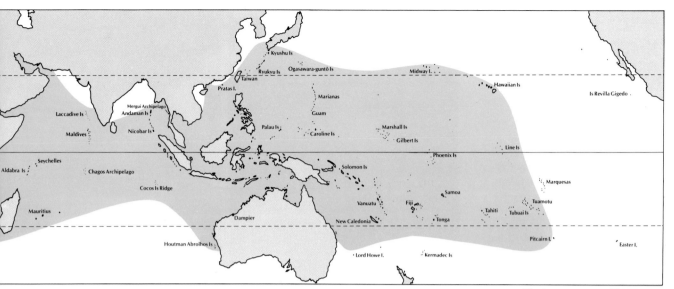

The known range of *Leptastrea*.

3

Leptastrea purpurea

(DANA, 1846)

TYPE LOCALITY
Fiji.

IDENTIFYING CHARACTERS
Colonies are flat with angular subcerioid corallites of very variable size. Septa are tightly compact. Columellae are small and compact.

COLOUR
Usually pale yellow or cream on the upper surface with dark sides (Great Barrier Reef), grey with pale oral discs (Houtman Abrolhos Islands).

SIMILAR SPECIES
L. transversa is very similar but has more uniformly sized corallites, and septa have steeply plunging inner margins.
L. pruinosa is also very similar.

DISTRIBUTION
From the Red Sea east to Hawaii. Around Australia: the Great Barrier Reef, Coral Sea and Elizabeth and Middleton Reefs in the east, and south to Houtman Abrolhos Islands on the west coast.

ABUNDANCE
Common and occurs in a wide range of habitats.

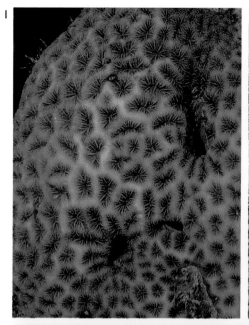

×2.5

1. *Leptastrea purpurea*, showing the most common colour form for the Great Barrier Reef.
PHOTOGRAPH: ED LOVELL.

2. Polyps of the same *Leptastrea purpurea* as 3, showing polyps extended during the day. This gives colonies a very different appearance compared with those of the Great Barrier Reef.
PHOTOGRAPH: ED LOVELL.

3. *Leptastrea purpurea* at the Houtman Abrolhos Islands, Western Australia, showing polyps encrusting the tubes of tube worms.
PHOTOGRAPH: ED LOVELL.

Leptastrea transversa
KLUNZINGER, 1879

TYPE LOCALITY
Red Sea.

IDENTIFYING CHARACTERS
Colonies are flat with angular, subcerioid corallites. Septa plunge steeply near the columella which consists usually of a few pinnules.

COLOUR
Usually grey or yellow with dark sides to the colony.

SIMILAR SPECIES
L. purpurea.

DISTRIBUTION
New Caledonia and Australia. Around Australia: the Great Barrier Reef, Coral Sea and south to Lord Howe Island in the east, and south to the Ningaloo Reef Tract on the west coast.

ABUNDANCE
Uncommon but occurs in a wide range of habitats.

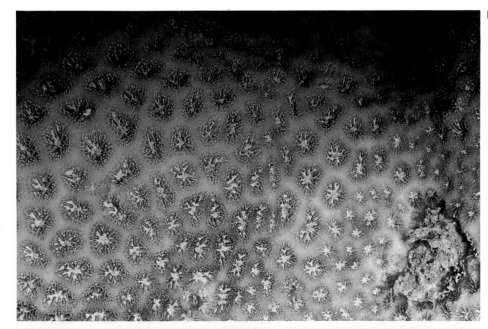

×2.5

1. One of a number of colour variations of *Leptastrea transversa*.
PHOTOGRAPH: LEN ZELL.

2. The usual appearance of *Leptastrea transversa*. This species closely resembles *L. purpurea* under water.
PHOTOGRAPH: ED LOVELL.

Leptastrea pruinosa

CROSSLAND, 1952

TYPE LOCALITY
Low Isles, Great Barrier Reef.

IDENTIFYING CHARACTERS
Colonies are flat with angular subcerioid corallites. Septa have granulated sides and margins. Polyps are extended usually during the day.

COLOUR
Usually chocolate-brown with green or cream oral discs.

SIMILAR SPECIES
L. pruinosa is readily identified under water but coralla are only differentiated from *L. purpurea* by the granulated septa, giving a frosted appearance.

DISTRIBUTION
New Caledonia and Australia. Around Australia: the Great Barrier Reef, Coral Sea and Elizabeth and Middleton Reefs in the east, and south to Houtman Abrolhos Islands on the west coast.

ABUNDANCE
Common in shallow clear water.

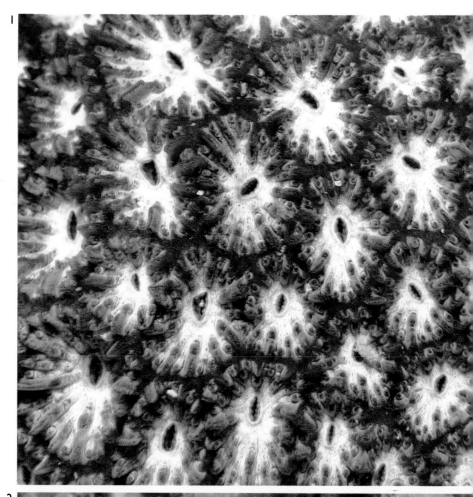

x2.5

1. *Leptastrea pruinosa* is one of the most colourful faviids. Polyps are usually extended during the day.
PHOTOGRAPH: ED LOVELL.

2. The polyps of *Leptastrea pruinosa*.
PHOTOGRAPH: ED LOVELL.

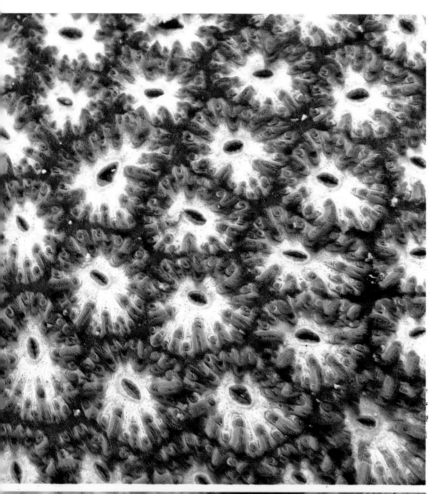

Leptastrea bewickensis

VERON, PICHON & WIJSMAN-BEST, 1977

TYPE LOCALITY
Bewick Island, Great Barrier Reef.

IDENTIFYING CHARACTERS
Colonies are flat or hillocky. Septa are in distinct cycles with six exsert primary septa plunging down to a very small columella, which is a simple fused ridge.

COLOUR
Grey.

SIMILAR SPECIES
None.

DISTRIBUTION
Known only from Australia: the Great Barrier Reef and south to Elizabeth Reef in the east; not found on the west coast.

ABUNDANCE
Rare.

x2.5

GENUS •
CYPHASTREA

(pronounced sigh-fass-tree-a)

Edwards & Haime, 1848

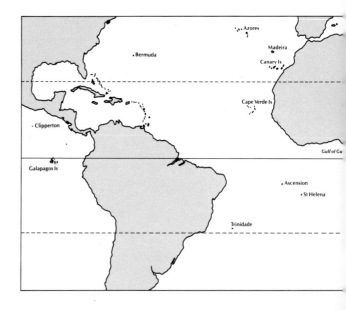

This genus is easily recognised and very common. The species are also more readily identified than those of most faviid genera if it is remembered that *C. serailia* is by far the most common and varied species, and that even colonies growing in the same place show much variation.

TYPE SPECIES
Astraea microphthalma Lamarck, 1816.

FOSSIL RECORD
Oligocene to Recent in Europe, the West Indies and Indo-Pacific.

NUMBER OF SPECIES
Approximately 26 nominal species, probably less than eight true species.

CHARACTERS
All species, except for *C. japonica* (which is arborescent with axial and radial corallites), are massive or encrusting.
Corallites are plocoid, with calices less than 3 mm in diameter. Costae are generally restricted to the corallite wall; the coenosteum is granulated.
Polyps are extended only at night.

SIMILAR GENERA
Cyphastrea is a well-defined genus. It resembles *Echinopora* and *Plesiastrea versipora*, which is distinguished by having larger corallites with better-developed paliform lobes and by having costae of adjacent corallites in contact, with no coenosteum granules.

1. A *Cyphastrea* just prior to spawning at night after the full moon in October. Pink egg masses can be seen in the mouths of the polyps.
PHOTOGRAPH: BETTE WILLIS.

2. *and I next page:* Variation in the appearance of polyps of two *Cyphastrea serailia* colonies.
PHOTOGRAPHS: ED LOVELL.

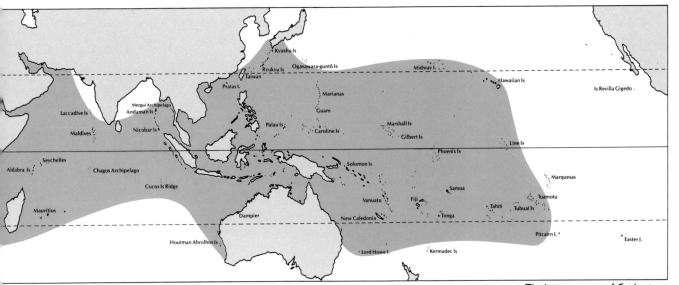

The known range of *Cyphastrea*.

2

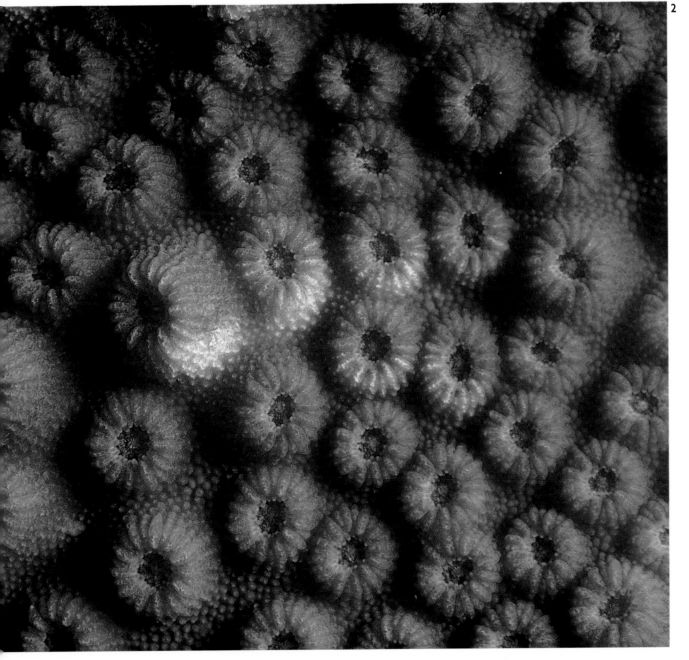

Cyphastrea serailia

(FORSKÅL, 1775)

TYPE LOCALITY
Red Sea.

IDENTIFYING CHARACTERS
Corallites have costae which do not alternate strongly. There are 12 primary septa.

COLOUR
Usually grey, brown or cream.

SIMILAR SPECIES
C. serailia corallites have a very wide range of variation so that colonies from different habitats may appear to be different species. Nevertheless, it is readily distinguished from *C. chalcidicum* by the costae and from *C. microphthalma* by the number of septa.

DISTRIBUTION
From the Red Sea east to the Marshall Islands.
Around Australia: the Great Barrier Reef, Coral Sea and south to Solitary Islands in the east, and south to Cockburn Sound on the west coast.

ABUNDANCE
Very common and occurs in all reef habitats.

 x5

1. See previous page.
2. *Cyphastrea serailia* is the most common and also the most variable of the *Cyphastrea* species.

PHOTOGRAPH: LEN ZELL.

522

Cyphastrea chalcidicum

(FORSKÅL, 1775)

TYPE LOCALITY
"?Red Sea".

IDENTIFYING CHARACTERS
Corallites have clearly alternating costae (easily visible under water). There are 12 primary septa.

COLOUR
Usually brown, green or cream.

SIMILAR SPECIES
C. serailia.

DISTRIBUTION
From the Red Sea east to the Marshall Islands.
Around Australia: the Great Barrier Reef and Coral Sea in the east, and south to the Ningaloo Reef Tract on the west coast.

ABUNDANCE
Common, but less so than C. serailia.

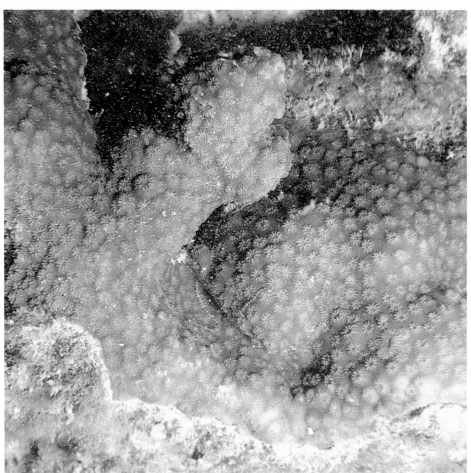

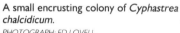
x5

A small encrusting colony of *Cyphastrea chalcidicum.*
PHOTOGRAPH: ED LOVELL.

Cyphastrea microphthalma

(LAMARCK, 1816)

TYPE LOCALITY
"Indian Ocean".

IDENTIFYING CHARACTERS
Most corallites have 10 primary septa.

COLOUR
Brown, cream or green.

SIMILAR SPECIES
C. microphthalma is readily identified by its 10 primary septa (which can be counted under water).

DISTRIBUTION
From the Red Sea east to Samoa and Tahiti.
Around Australia: the Great Barrier Reef, Elizabeth and Middleton Reefs and Lord Howe Island in the east, and south to Houtman Abrolhos Islands on the west coast.

ABUNDANCE
Common, but less so than *C. serailia*.

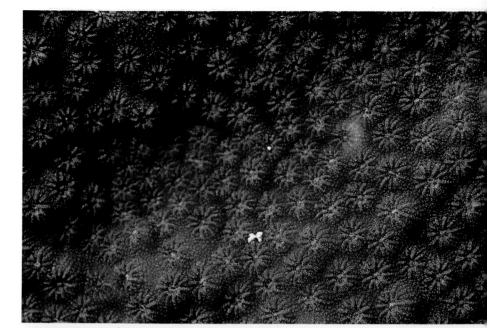

×5

1,3. The polyps of *Cyphastrea microphthalma* with 10 rather than the usual 12 primary septa.
PHOTOGRAPHS: AUTHOR.

2. *Cyphastrea microphthalma.*
PHOTOGRAPH: AUTHOR.

Cyphastrea japonica

YABE & SUGIYAMA, 1932

TYPE LOCALITY
Japan.

IDENTIFYING CHARACTERS
Colonies are branching, with axial and radial corallites.

COLOUR
Green, yellow or brown with pale-brown or white axial corallites.

SIMILAR SPECIES
None.

DISTRIBUTION
Japan, the Philippines and Australia.
Around Australia: the Great Barrier Reef in the east; not found on the west coast.

ABUNDANCE
Usually uncommon, but more conspicuous than other *Cyphastrea*.

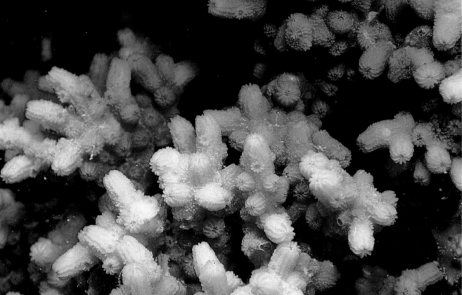

x5

1. *Cyphastrea japonica* at the Swain Reefs, Great Barrier Reef. The growth form is quite unlike any other *Cyphastrea*.
PHOTOGRAPH: ED LOVELL.

2. Polyps of *Cyphastrea japonica*.
PHOTOGRAPH: ED LOVELL.

3. A compact colony of *Cyphastrea japonica*.
PHOTOGRAPH: AUTHOR.

GENUS
ECHINOPORA
(pronounced ek-kine-oh-por-a)

Lamarck, 1816

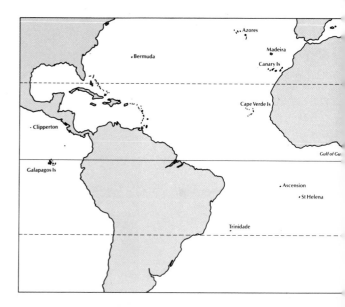

More than any other genus of corals (except perhaps *Merulina*), *Echinopora* colonies have widely varying growth forms. Encrusting plates may develop branches and these may, in turn, develop more plates higher up. Other colonies may be all plates, others all branches. Just what controls these forms is unclear as they occur in a wide range of environments. Nevertheless, common species of *Echinopora* are not difficult to identify, even if the result may seem to be an improbable combination of specimens.

TYPE SPECIES
Echinopora rosularia Lamarck, 1816 from the "Indian Ocean".

FOSSIL RECORD
Miocene to Recent in the Indo-Pacific.

NUMBER OF SPECIES
Approximately 30 nominal species, five to seven true species, five from Australia.

CHARACTERS
Colonies are massive, arborescent or foliaceous or mixtures of these forms.
Corallites are plocoid with calices up to 5 mm in diameter. Septa are exsert and irregular. Columellae are usually prominent. Costae are usually restricted to the corallite wall. The coenosteum is granulated (except *E. mammiformis*).
Polyps are extended only at night.

SIMILAR GENERA
Echinopora is a well-defined genus. It is closest to *Cyphastrea* which is distinguished by its massive or encrusting growth form (except *C. japonica*). The corallites of these genera are similar; those of *Echinopora* are usually larger, with thicker walls and more prominent columellae and septa.
Echinopora has a superficial resemblance to *Echinophyllia echinoporoides*.

SPECIES
Three species, *E. lamellosa, E. horrida* and
E. mammiformis, may all occur in large stands, especially in lagoons or elsewhere where the water is turbid. Two other species have also been recognised in the Great Barrier Reef, *E. hirsutissima* and *E. gemmacea*, both of which are common in the western Indian Ocean.

Echinopora lamellosa forming wide, flat sheets at the Swain Reefs, Great Barrier Reef.
PHOTOGRAPH: ED LOVELL.

526

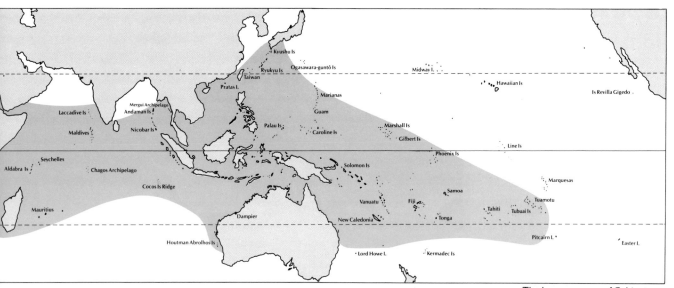

The known range of *Echinopora*

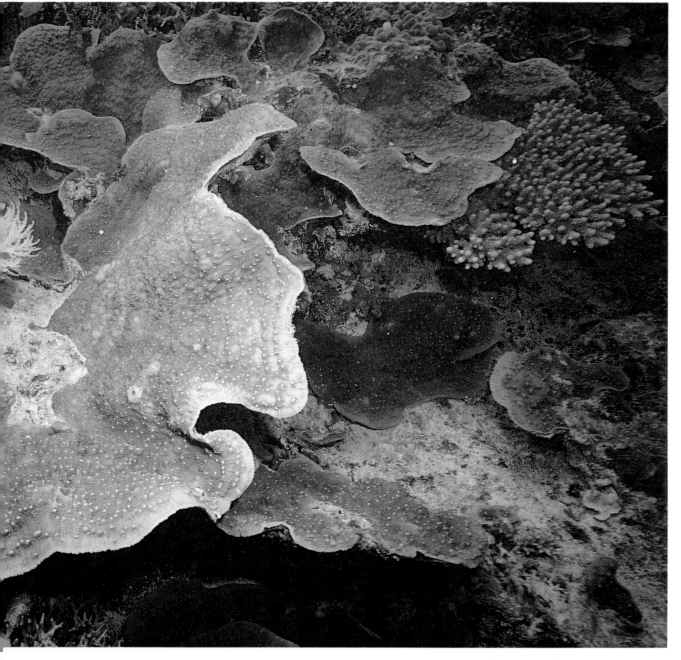

Echinopora lamellosa

(ESPER, 1795)

TYPE LOCALITY
Unrecorded.

IDENTIFYING CHARACTERS
Colonies consist of thin laminae arranged in whorls or tiers or, rarely, forming tubes. Corallites are relatively thin-walled and have calices 2.5-4.0 mm in diameter. Columellae are small and compact, and paliform lobes are well developed.

COLOUR
Amber, pale to dark brown or greenish, often with darker-brown or green calices.

SIMILAR SPECIES
E. gemmacea.

DISTRIBUTION
From the Red Sea east to the Marshall Islands and Samoa. Around Australia: the Great Barrier Reef, Coral Sea and Elizabeth and Middleton Reefs in the east, and south to Coral Bay on the west coast.

ABUNDANCE
Common and may be dominant in shallow-water habitats with flat substrates.

×5

1. Two colonies of *Echinopora lamellosa* competing for space at the Dampier Archipelago, Western Australia.
PHOTOGRAPH: ED LOVELL.

2. An uncommon tubular growth form of *Echinopora lamellosa* at the Rowley Shoals, Western Australia.
PHOTOGRAPH: AUTHOR.

3. Polyps of *Echinopora lamellosa.*
PHOTOGRAPH: ED LOVELL.

4. *Echinopora lamellosa* forming chimney-like tubes.
PHOTOGRAPH: RON AND VALERIE TAYLOR.

Echinopora gemmacea

LAMARCK, 1816

TYPE LOCALITY
"Indian Ocean".

IDENTIFYING CHARACTERS
Colonies are laminar, bifacial, sometimes forming contorted branches.
Corallites have calices 3.5–4.5 mm in diameter. Columellae are large, and paliform lobes are not well developed. Primary septa may be very thick and are always exsert.

COLOUR
Pale cream to dark brown or green.

SIMILAR SPECIES
E. lamellosa is similar but does not form branches. Corallites are smaller with smaller columellae and distinct paliform lobes.
E. horrida has very similar skeletal characters. It is usually branching whereas *E. gemmacea* is usually laminar.

DISTRIBUTION
From the Red Sea east to New Caledonia.
Around Australia: the Great Barrier Reef in the east; not found on the west coast.

ABUNDANCE
Usually uncommon.

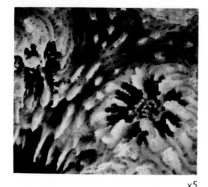

x5

1. An encrusting colony of *Echinopora gemmacea*, showing the most common colouration.
PHOTOGRAPH: LEN ZELL.

2. A frond of *Echinopora gemmacea*. Polyps are found on both faces of the frond.
PHOTOGRAPH: ED LOVELL.

530

2

Echinopora hirsutissima

EDWARDS & HAIME, 1849

TYPE LOCALITY
"Indian Ocean".

IDENTIFYING CHARACTERS
Colonies are encrusting laminae or columnar. Corallites are large and thick-walled. The coenosteum is densely covered with thick spinules which have fine elaborations.

COLOUR
Mustard.

SIMILAR SPECIES
E. hirsutissima has characters in common with other *Echinopora*, but is best recognised by its thickened skeletal structures.

DISTRIBUTION
From the Red Sea east to Australia.
Around Australia: the Great Barrier Reef in the east, and Dampier Archipelago and Scott Reef on the west coast.

ABUNDANCE
Very rare.

x5

Echinopora horrida

DANA, 1846

TYPE LOCALITY
  Fiji.

IDENTIFYING CHARACTERS
  Colonies are composed of
  contorted branches with flat
  laminar bases. Corallites are
  thick-walled and have six thick
  primary septa. The coenosteum is
  covered with tall spinules.

COLOUR
  Dark brown, cream or green.

SIMILAR SPECIES
  E. gemmacea and *E. mammiformis*.

DISTRIBUTION
  From Singapore east to the
  Philippines, New Caledonia and
  Fiji.
  Around Australia: the Great
  Barrier Reef in the east, and
  south to Exmouth Gulf on the
  west coast.

ABUNDANCE
  Seldom common, but may form
  large stands on protected
  horizontal substrates including
  lagoons.

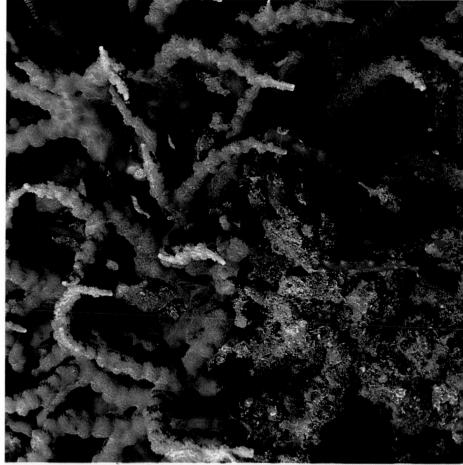

x5

1. The twisted, pointed branches of
Echinopora horrida.
PHOTOGRAPH: RON AND VALERIE TAYLOR.

2. Polyps at a branch tip of *Echinopora
horrida*.
PHOTOGRAPH: ED LOVELL.

Echinopora mammiformis

(NEMENZO, 1959)

TYPE LOCALITY
  The Philippines.

IDENTIFYING CHARACTERS
  Colonies are composed of contorted branches and flat plates and are rarely submassive. Despite this range of growth form, it is easily identified by the coenosteum which is smooth, and devoid of spinules.

COLOUR
  Cream with pink or purple corallites.

SIMILAR SPECIES
  E. horrida and *E. gemmacea* may both have the same growth forms. *E. mammiformis* is recognised readily by its smooth coenosteum.

DISTRIBUTION
  The Philippines, Australia and New Caledonia.
  Around Australia: the Great Barrier Reef in the east; Scott Reef on the west coast.

ABUNDANCE
  Very common, forms extensive stands in turbid water, especially lagoons and back reef margins.

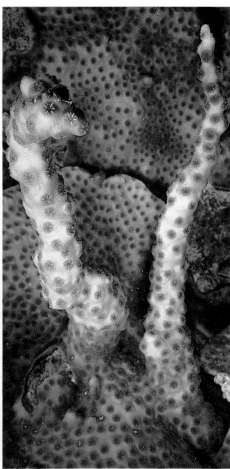

×5

1. *Echinopora mammiformis* at Lizard Island, Great Barrier Reef, showing the species's common general appearance.
PHOTOGRAPH: LEN ZELL.

2. The two growth forms of *Echinopora mammiformis*, plates and twisted branches, in the same colony.
PHOTOGRAPH: ED LOVELL.

3. The polyps of *Echinopora mammiformis*.
PHOTOGRAPH: ED LOVELL.

Genus
MOSELEYA

(pronounced moh-sa-lee-a)

Quelch, 1884

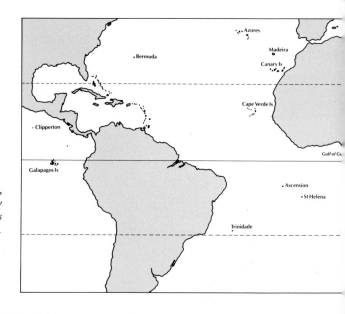

Considering the extremely interesting relationships of Moseleya it must be looked upon as one of the most remarkable types of structure brought to light by the Challenger.

John Quelch,
Report on the Reef Corals Collected by H.M.S. Challenger *During the Years 1873-76, 1886.*

The relationships of *Moseleya* remain somewhat obscure. It is a very distinctly and beautifully sculptured genus and symmetrical specimens are often sought by collectors.

TYPE SPECIES
Moseleya latistellata Quelch, 1884.

FOSSIL RECORD
None.

NUMBER OF SPECIES
One.

Moseleya latistellata

QUELCH, 1884

TYPE LOCALITY
Torres Strait.

IDENTIFYING CHARACTERS
Colonies are flat, submassive, usually disc-like, and sometimes free-living.
Corallites are cerioid with a large central corallite (up to 35 mm in diameter) surrounded concentrically with angular daughter corallites. Septa have fine teeth and usually prominent paliform lobes.
Polyps are extended only on dark nights.

COLOUR
Pale to deep green or brown.

SIMILAR SPECIES
None. *Moseleya* may resemble *Acanthastrea* (especially *A. hillae*) which can have the same colony and corallite shapes. *Acanthastrea* has more fleshy polyps, much larger septal teeth and never has paliform lobes.

DISTRIBUTION
Around Australia: the northern and central Great Barrier Reef in the east, and south to Houtman Abrolhos Islands on the west coast.

ABUNDANCE
Usually uncommon and restricted to turbid water with muddy substrates. Also occurs in muddy areas exposed at low tide.

×1

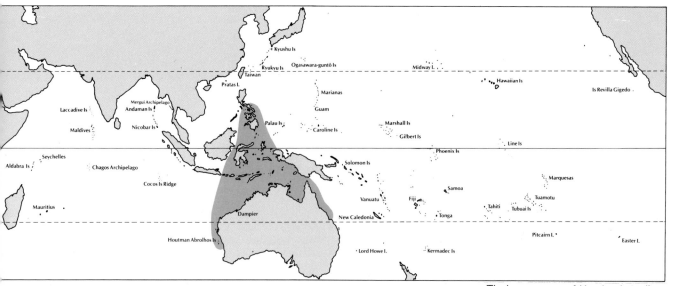

The known range of *Moseleya latistellata*.

1,3. The polyps of *Moseleya latistellata*. Polyps become progressively smaller away from the central polyp. New polyps are budded at the edge of the colony, giving the species a distinctive pattern.
PHOTOGRAPHS: AUTHOR (1) AND ED LOVELL (3).

2. *Moseleya latistellata* at the Houtman Abrolhos Islands, Western Australia.
PHOTOGRAPH: ED LOVELL.

Family
TRACHYPHYLLIIDAE

(pronounced trak-ee-fill-ee-id-ee)

VERRILL, 1901

CHARACTERS

Solitary to colonial, hermatypic.
The family is separated from the Faviidae by growth form and by the presence of large paliform lobes and fine teeth on the septa.

RELATED FAMILY

Trachyphylliidae is very close to the Faviidae, especially to the genus *Moseleya*, and so much so that its status is somewhat arbitrary.

THE GENERA

The family contains only two genera, *Trachyphyllia* and *Wellsophyllia*, both from Australia, although the latter is presently known in Australia only from museum specimens.

Opposite: *Trachyphyllia geoffroyi* with tentacles extended at night. Batteries of stinging cells can be seen.
PHOTOGRAPH: ED LOVELL.

GENUS
TRACHYPHYLLIA
(pronounced <u>trak</u>-ee-<u>fill</u>-ee-a)

Edwards & Haime, 1848

TYPE SPECIES
Turbinolia geoffroyi Audouin, 1826.

FOSSIL RECORD
Miocene to Recent from the Indo-Pacific.

NUMBER OF SPECIES
Probably six nominal species, two true species.

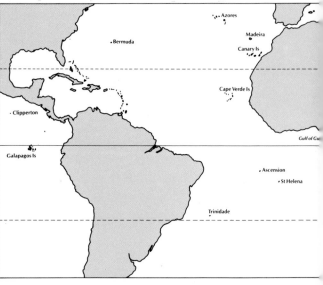

Trachyphyllia geoffroyi
AUDOUIN, 1826

TYPE LOCALITY
  Red Sea.

IDENTIFYING CHARACTERS
  Colonies are flabello-meandroid
  and free-living. They are usually
  bilaterally symmetrical, up to
  80 mm in length with one to
  three separate mouths. Large,
  fully flabello-meandroid colonies
  are uncommon.
  Valleys have large, regular septa
  and paliform lobes and a large
  columella tangle.
  Polyps are fleshy. When retracted
  during the day, a large mantle
  extends well beyond the
  perimeter of the skeleton, but this
  retracts if disturbed. At night,
  tentacles in several rows are
  extended from the expanded oral
  disc inside the mantle. The
  mouth is about 10 mm across.

COLOUR
  Polyps, especially the mantles,
  are brightly coloured and are
  commonly yellow, brown, blue
  or green.

SIMILAR SPECIES
  Wellsophyllia radiata.

DISTRIBUTION
  The full range of the genus.
  Around Australia: the Great
  Barrier Reef in the east, and
  south to Passage Island on the
  west coast.

ABUNDANCE
  Rare on reefs, common around
  continental islands and some
  inter-reef areas. Frequently found
  with other free-living corals
  (*Heteropsammia, Heterocyathus,
  Cycloseris* and *Diaseris*). Large
  colonies are found only in certain
  protected shallow island
  embayments.

×*1*

1,2. Two *Trachyphyllia* colonies composed
of contorted valleys at Dampier
Archipelago, Western Australia.
PHOTOGRAPHS: ED LOVELL.

3,4. *Trachyphyllia geoffroyi* has many
different colour variations. The species
usually grows no larger than these solitary
individuals but can form large flabello-
meandroid colonies.
PHOTOGRAPHS: ED LOVELL.

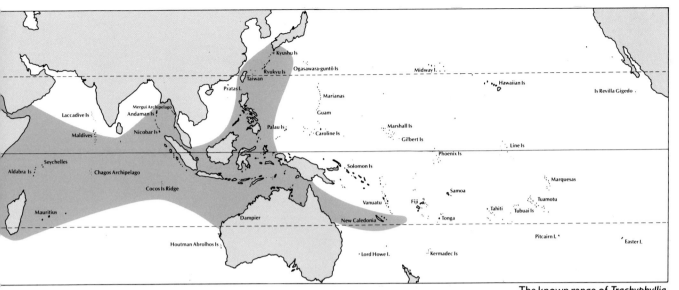

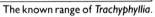

The known range of *Trachyphyllia*.

3

4

GENUS
WELLSOPHYLLIA
(pronounced wells-oh-fill-ee-a)

Pichon, 1980

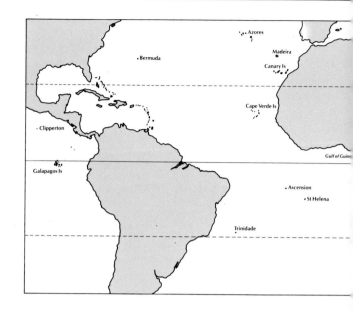

TYPE SPECIES
Callogyra formosa Bedot, 1907 from Indonesia.

FOSSIL RECORD
None.

NUMBER OF SPECIES
One. The validity of this genus is doubtful.

Wellsophyllia radiata
PICHON, 1980

TYPE LOCALITY
  Indonesia.

IDENTIFYING CHARACTERS
  Colonies are hemispherical, like
  Trachyphyllia, but adjacent
  valleys become fused.

COLOUR
  Unknown.

SIMILAR SPECIES
  Trachyphyllia geoffroyi is similar,
  but walls of adjacent valleys are
  not fused.

DISTRIBUTION
  Around Australia: the north-west
  coast; not found in the east.

ABUNDANCE
  The only Australian specimens
  known are two specimens in the
  British Museum (Natural
  History).

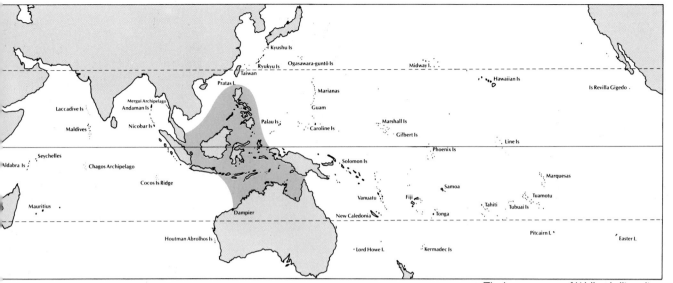

The known range of *Wellsophyllia radiata*.

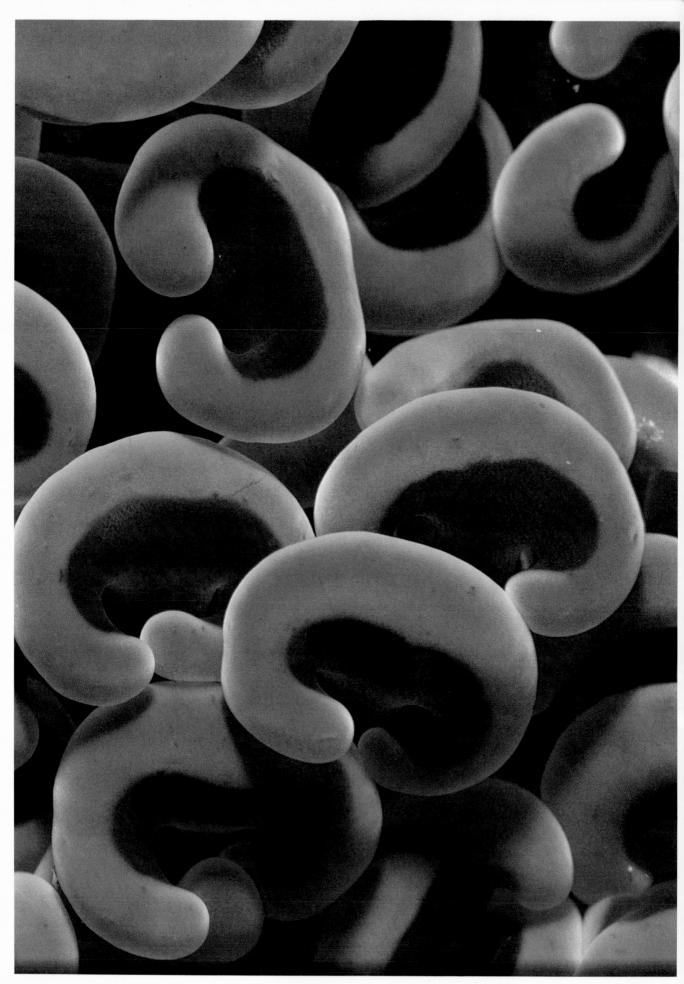

FAMILY
CARYOPHYLLIIDAE

(*pronounced karry-oh-fill-ee-id-ee*)

GRAY, 1847

CHARACTERS

This large family is usually divided into six subfamilies, only one of which is hermatypic. The latter have phaceloid, meandroid or flabello-meandroid colonies with large, unperforated and widely spaced septa with little or no ornamentation. Corallite walls are of similar structure. The ahermatypic subfamilies are solitary or form phaceloid or dendroid colonies, usually with large-lobed septa and paliform lobes. All Caryophylliidae have a membraneous epitheca.

RELATED FAMILY
Flabellidae.

EARLIEST FOSSILS
Jurassic.

THE GENERA

Hermatypes: of the eight extant genera, five are Australian and include *Euphyllia*, *Catalaphyllia*, *Plerogyra*, *Physogyra* and *Montigyra*. Of the remainder, *Nemenzophyllia* is from the Philippines, *Gyrosmilia* is restricted to the western Indian Ocean and the Red Sea, and *Eusmilia* occurs in the West Indies.

Ahermatypes: 23 genera have been recorded from eastern and southern Australia. Most occur in deep water where little or no light penetrates, but some occur in reefal areas, usually in caves or under rocks. Except for *Heterocyathus*, they are all poorly known and seldom encountered. *Heterocyathus* is partly hermatypic and is structurally equivalent to *Heteropsammia*.

Opposite: Fully developed kidney-shaped tentacle ends such as these are commonly seen on large east Australian *Euphyllia ancora* colonies.
PHOTOGRAPH: RON AND VALERIE TAYLOR.

GENUS EUPHYLLIA

(pronounced you-fill-ee-a)

Dana, 1846

For two centuries, corals have been identified entirely by their skeletons. In more recent times, the appearance of the living polyp has been used to help identification, but only in *Euphyllia* is it mandatory to use the appearance of the living polyp to separate two species. Fortunately, these polyps are large and very distinctive. Just why the tentacles of different species have such different shapes is unknown, but it probably bears some relation to specialised feeding habits. The tentacles never have stinging cells grouped into batteries, unlike those of most corals, and they may be adapted to capturing food particles in the water using mucus and cilia.

Euphyllia have separate sexes and most release gametes for external fertilisation. In equatorial localities, however, some may brood larvae.

TYPE SPECIES
Caryophyllia glabrescens Chamisso & Eysenhardt, 1821.

FOSSIL RECORD
Eocene to Recent from Eurasia and the Indo-Pacific.

NUMBER OF SPECIES
Fifteen nominal species, four true species from Australia.

CHARACTERS
Colonies are flabelloid, phaceloid or meandro-phaceloid, the latter usually dome-shaped.
Walls are thin and imperforate. Columellae are mostly absent. Septa are prominent, smooth-edged and imperforate.
Polyps are extended day and night, are large and fleshy and have tentacles which vary in shape for each species.
Two species, *E. divisa* and *E. ancora*, can be distinguished only by their tentacles.

SIMILAR GENERA
Catalaphyllia is very similar, but septa have straight margins forming V-shaped valleys, and polyps are very distinctive.
Euphyllia and *Plerogyra* coralla may be similar, but living polyps are completely different.

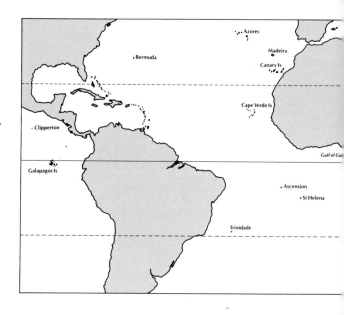

Euphyllia glabrescens

(CHAMISSO & EYSENHARDT, 1821)

TYPE LOCALITY
Radack Archipelago.

IDENTIFYING CHARACTERS
Colonies are phaceloid, and corallites are usually separated by 0.5-1 corallite diameters. Septa are not strongly exsert. Polyps have tubular tentacles.

COLOUR
Grey-blue to grey-green with cream, green or white tips to the tentacles.

SIMILAR SPECIES
E. cristata, which has much more compact corallites with more exsert primary septa.

DISTRIBUTION
From the Red Sea east to the Marshall Islands and Samoa. Around Australia: the Great Barrier Reef and Coral Sea in the east, and south to Houtman Abrolhos Islands on the west coast.

ABUNDANCE
Uncommon but conspicuous. Occupies a wide range of habitats.

xl

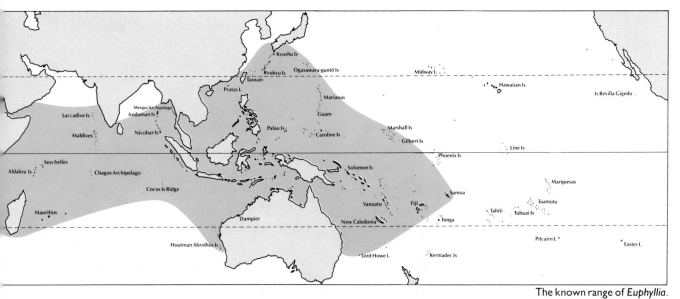

The known range of *Euphyllia*.

2

1. *Euphyllia glabrescens*. This species shows little variation except that it may be different colours in different geographic regions—for example, at the Marshall Islands it is mustard colour.
PHOTOGRAPH: RON AND VALERIE TAYLOR.

2. *Euphyllia glabrescens* with tentacles fully extended.
PHOTOGRAPH: AUTHOR.

Euphyllia cristata

CHEVALIER, 1971

TYPE LOCALITY
New Caledonia.

IDENTIFYING CHARACTERS
Colonies are phaceloid with closely compacted corallites. Primary septa are very exsert. Polyps have tubular tentacles.

COLOUR
Green, with pale-orange, yellow or cream tips to the tentacles.

SIMILAR SPECIES
E. glabrescens. Small *Plerogyra sinuosa* have similar coralla, but living colonies bear no resemblance.

DISTRIBUTION
New Caledonia and Australia. Around Australia: the Great Barrier Reef in the east, and south to Dampier Archipelago on the west coast.

ABUNDANCE
Uncommon but conspicuous.

1. A large colony of *Euphyllia cristata* at the Palm Islands, Great Barrier Reef.
PHOTOGRAPH: ED LOVELL.

2. *Euphyllia cristata*. The tentacles are similar to those of *E. glabrescens*, but the species has tall septa which can be seen between the tentacles.
PHOTOGRAPH: RON AND VALERIE TAYLOR.

546

Euphyllia ancora

VERON & PICHON, 1980

TYPE LOCALITY
   Jewell Reef, Great Barrier Reef.

IDENTIFYING CHARACTERS
   Colonies are phacelo-meandroid
   with exsert septa which plunge
   near the valley centre. Polyps
   have tubular tentacles without
   side branches but with an anchor-
   or T-shaped tip.

COLOUR
   Blue-grey to orange with a pale-
   cream or green outer border to
   the terminal structure of the
   tentacle.

SIMILAR SPECIES
   E. divisa has an identical skeleton
   but very distinctive polyps.

DISTRIBUTION
   As for *E. divisa*, also Japan.
   Around Australia: the Great
   Barrier Reef and south to
   Elizabeth Reef in the east, and
   south to North West Cape on the
   west coast.

ABUNDANCE
   Seldom common but may be a
   dominant species on deep
   horizontal substrates. Colonies
   are the same size and shape as
   E. divisa and are likewise
   conspicuous.

x1

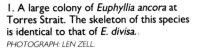

1. A large colony of *Euphyllia ancora* at
Torres Strait. The skeleton of this species
is identical to that of *E. divisa*.
PHOTOGRAPH: LEN ZELL.

2. Tentacle ends of a small *Euphyllia
ancora* colony.
PHOTOGRAPH: LEN ZELL.

547

Euphyllia divisa

VERON & PICHON, 1980

TYPE LOCALITY
 Whitsunday Islands, Great
 Barrier Reef.

IDENTIFYING CHARACTERS
 Colonies are phacelo-meandroid
 with exsert septa which plunge
 near the valley centre. Polyps
 have tubular tentacles which have
 smaller side branches.

COLOUR
 Pale, translucent cream or green
 with pale tentacle tips.

SIMILAR SPECIES
 E. ancora has an identical skeleton
 but very distinctive polyps.

DISTRIBUTION
 As coralla of this species cannot
 be distinguished from *E. ancora*
 and possibly other *Euphyllia*, its
 distribution cannot be determined
 from published records. Living
 colonies have been identified
 from the Philippines, Indonesia
 and Fiji, as well as Australia.
 Around Australia: the Great
 Barrier Reef in the east, and
 south to Houtman Abrolhos
 Islands on the west coast.

ABUNDANCE
 Seldom common except at the
 Houtman Abrolhos Islands.
 Colonies frequently exceed 1 m
 in diameter on flat muddy
 substrates and are conspicuous.

x1

1. *Euphyllia divisa* is a common species at
the Houtman Abrolhos Islands, Western
Australia.
PHOTOGRAPH: ED LOVELL.

2. A large colony of *Euphyllia divisa*. The
mass of tentacles completely obscures the
underlying skeleton.
PHOTOGRAPH: LEN ZELL.

548

3

4

3. *Euphyllia divisa* is one of the most beautiful of all corals. Polyps are extended day and night and frequently harbour small shrimps.
PHOTOGRAPH: ED LOVELL.

4. *Euphyllia divisa* with a curtain of long tentacles fully extended.
PHOTOGRAPH: LEN ZELL.

Genus
CATALAPHYLLIA
(pronounced ca-tar-la-fill-ee-a)

Wells, 1971

Named after Dr Rene Catala, author of *Carnaval sous la Mer*, this coral makes an excellent aquarium exhibit. Under natural light its colours are striking enough, but under ultraviolet light the oral disc is brilliant green and the tentacles are bright blue with red–violet tips.

Catalaphyllia has very obvious similarities with Euphyllia, so much so that the separation of these genera is more a result of historical custom than major morphological division.

TYPE SPECIES
Pectinia jardinei Saville-Kent, 1893.

FOSSIL RECORD
None.

NUMBER OF SPECIES
Probably one.

SIMILAR GENUS
Euphyllia.

Catalaphyllia jardinei
(SAVILLE-KENT, 1893)

TYPE LOCALITY
Great Barrier Reef.

IDENTIFYING CHARACTERS
Colonies are flabello-meandroid with straight-edged septa forming V-shaped valleys. Polyps have tubular tentacles extending from a large, fleshy oral disc.

COLOUR
Green with pink tentacle tips and a striped oral disc.

DISTRIBUTION
Around Australia: the Great Barrier Reef in the east, and south to Dampier Archipelago on the west coast.

ABUNDANCE
Occurs only in turbid water. Seldom common but very conspicuous.

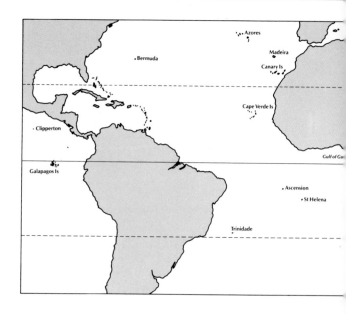

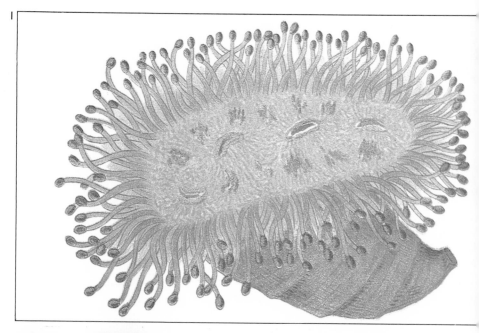

×1

1. *Catalaphyllia jardinei* as illustrated by W. Saville-Kent in his book *The Great Barrier Reef*, the first book about the Great Barrier Reef, and published in 1893.
2. A portrait of *Catalaphyllia jardinei*. Polyps remain extended day and night.
PHOTOGRAPH: ED LOVELL.

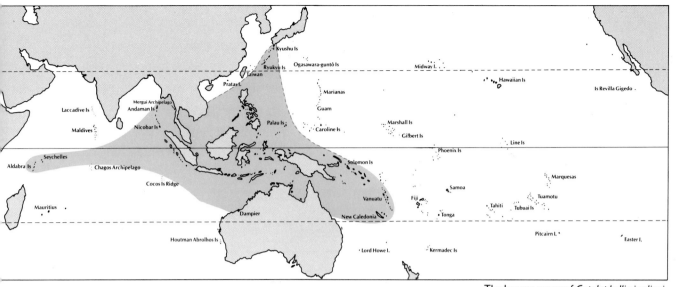

The known range of *Catalaphyllia jardinei*.

GENUS
PLEROGYRA

(pronounced plero-dgai-ra)

Edwards & Haime, 1848

These are the "grape corals", so called because colonies look like bunches of large grey grapes under water. These vesicles hide the underlying skeleton and possibly have a protective function. There are no batteries of nematocysts on the "grapes" as there are on the tentacles, but nevertheless, *Plerogyra* is one of the few corals sufficiently well armed to be able to sting a human on the back of the hand or on the arm.

TYPE SPECIES
Plerogyra laxa Edwards & Haime, 1848 from Singapore.

FOSSIL RECORD
None.

NUMBER OF SPECIES
Six nominal species, three true species, one of which is Australian.

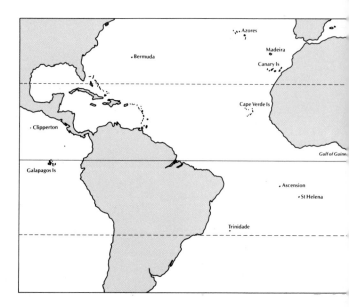

Plerogyra sinuosa

(DANA, 1846)

TYPE LOCALITY
    "East Indies".

IDENTIFYING CHARACTERS
    Colonies are phaceloid to flabello-meandroid with valleys more or less connected by a light blistery coenosteum.
    Septa are large, imperforate, smooth-edged, very exsert and widely spaced. Walls are imperforate. Columellae are absent.
    Polyps are extended only at night. During the day, polyps extend clusters of grey vesicles the size and shape of large grapes. These retract slowly, if at all, when disturbed.

COLOUR
    Bluish-grey.

SIMILAR SPECIES
    Living colonies of *Plerogyra* resemble those of *Physogyra*, except that the polyp vesicles of the latter are smaller and more retractable. Skeletons of *Physogyra* are meandroid, not meandro-phaceloid as with *Plerogyra*.
    Plerogyra skeletons may resemble *Euphyllia* as both have imperforate walls and septa and similar growth forms. *Euphyllia*

has less exsert, more numerous and more regular septa and there is little development of a blistery coenosteum. Living colonies are distinct, *Euphyllia* having tentacles, *Plerogyra* having vesicles during the day.

DISTRIBUTION
    From the Red Sea east to the Marshall Islands.
    Around Australia: the Great Barrier Reef in the east, and the Ningaloo Reef Tract on the west coast.

ABUNDANCE
    Restricted to protected caves or crevices where it grows on vertical faces or under overhangs. Large colonies are sometimes found on flat substrates in partly turbid water. Usually uncommon.

x0.5

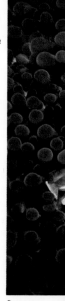

1. *Plerogyra sinuosa* during the day when tentacles are retracted. The large vesicles seen here can be retracted when disturbed, but only slowly. They may have a protective function as they contain stinging cells which can irritate human skin.
PHOTOGRAPH: ED LOVELL.

2. *Plerogyra sinuosa* on the Great Barrier Reef. This species looks like a bunch of grapes under water.
PHOTOGRAPH: ED LOVELL.

3. Adjacent colonies of *Physogyra lichtensteini* (left) and *Plerogyra sinuosa* (right). These species are usually found in the same habitat where light intensity is low and where there is little competition for space.
PHOTOGRAPH: RON AND VALERIE TAYLOR.

4. The vesicles of *Plerogyra sinuosa*. These are the size of large grapes and large colonies may have hundreds of them.
PHOTOGRAPH: RON AND VALERIE TAYLOR.

3

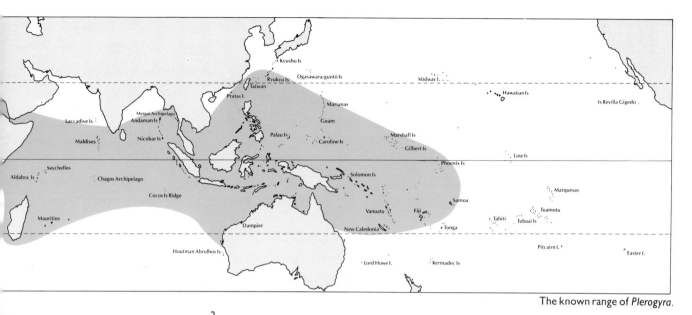

The known range of *Plerogyra*.

2

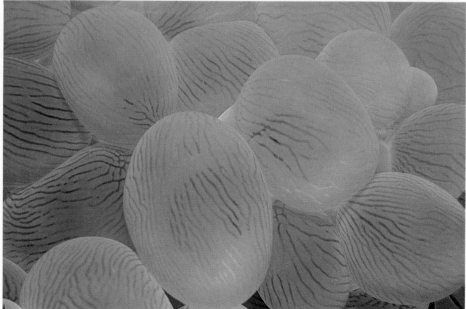

4

GENUS
PHYSOGYRA
(pronounced *fye-soh-dgai-ra*)

Quelch, 1884

Like *Plerogyra*, *Physogyra* is capable of stinging humans. They have similar vesicles which resemble masses of bubbles. These are smaller than those of *Plerogyra*, are extended during the day and can be retracted readily if disturbed. Often small shrimp, transparent except for small blue or pink skeletal plates, are found crawling over the colony surface.

The skeleton of *Physogyra* is mostly constructed of thin blistery plates. It can be cut with a knife and floats easily on water when dried.

Physogyra have separate sexes and release gametes for external fertilisation.

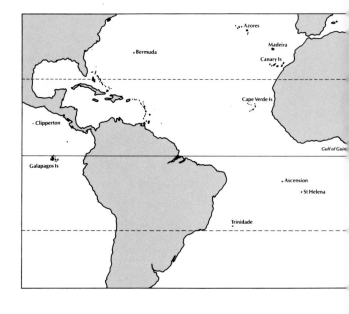

TYPE SPECIES
Physogyra aperta Quelch, 1884
from Indonesia.

FOSSIL RECORD
None.

NUMBER OF SPECIES
Five nominal species, three true species, one of which is Australian.

Physogyra lichtensteini
EDWARDS & HAIME, 1851

TYPE LOCALITY
"East Indies".

IDENTIFYING CHARACTERS
Colonies are meandroid with short, widely separated valleys interconnected with a light blistery coenosteum.
Septa are large, imperforate, smooth-edged, exsert and widely spaced. Walls are imperforate. Columellae are absent.
Polyps are extended only at night. During the day the whole colony surface is covered with a mass of vesicles the size and shape of small grapes. These retract when disturbed.

COLOUR
Pale grey, sometimes dull green.

SIMILAR SPECIES
Physogyra resembles only *Plerogyra*.

DISTRIBUTION
From Madagascar east to the Marshall Islands.
Around Australia: the Great Barrier Reef and Coral Sea in the east, and south to Ningaloo Reef Tract on the west coast.

ABUNDANCE
Common in protected habitats, such as crevices and overhangs, especially in turbid water with tidal currents.

×1

1. *Physogyra lichtensteini* with tentacles extended at night—this is always a beautiful sight.
PHOTOGRAPH: ED LOVELL.

2. A large colony of *Physogyra lichtensteini* at Torres Strait.
PHOTOGRAPH: LEN ZELL.

3,5. The surface of a *Physogyra lichtensteini* colony with vesicles extended (3), and retracted after being disturbed (5).
PHOTOGRAPH: RON AND VALERIE TAYLOR.

4. At night the tentacles of *Physogyra lichtensteini* are extended from the base of the vesicles. The latter do not contract, unlike the extended polyp wall of *Cynarina lacrymalis*.
PHOTOGRAPH: DAVE FISK.

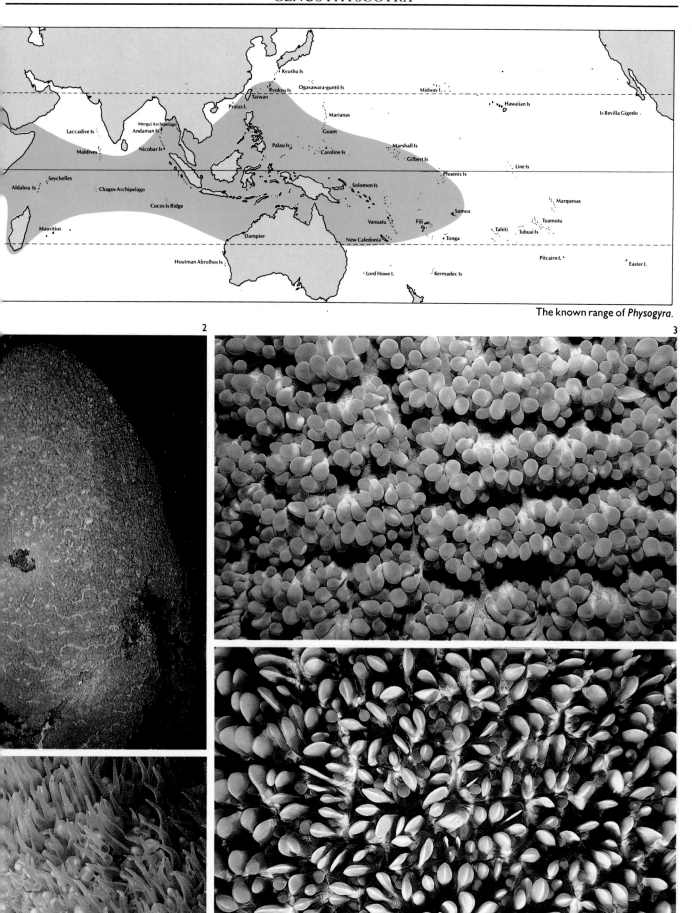

The known range of *Physogyra*.

Genus
MONTIGYRA
(pronounced monty-dgai-ra)

Matthai, 1928

TYPE SPECIES
Montigyra kenti Matthai, 1928.

FOSSIL RECORD
None.

NUMBER OF SPECIES
Probably one true species.

SIMILAR GENERA
Gyrosmilia.

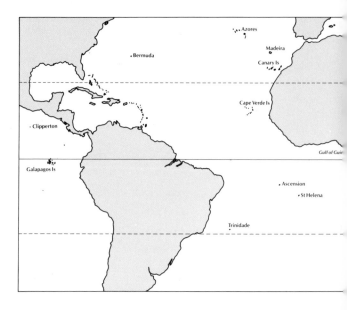

Montigyra kenti
MATTHAI, 1928

TYPE LOCALITY
Lacepede Islands, north-west Australia.

IDENTIFYING CHARACTERS
This species and genus is known from a single specimen. It is hemispherical and submeandroid with groups of septa fused into hydnophores. Septa are thin and compact.
Neither the genus nor the species have any clear affinities.

DISTRIBUTION
Known only from Australia: the Lacepede Islands on the north-west coast; not found in the east.

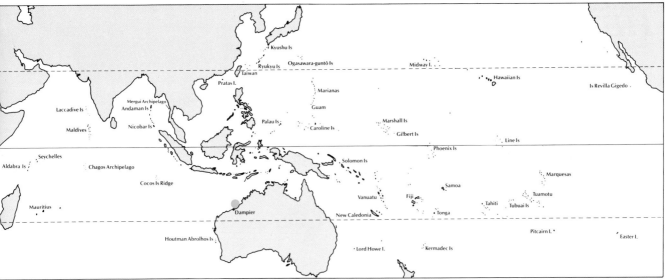

The known range of *Montigyra kenti*.

GENUS
HETEROCYATHUS
(pronounced het-a-roe-sigh-aith-us)

Edwards & Haime, 1848

TYPE SPECIES
Heterocyathus aequicostatus Edwards & Haime, 1848.

FOSSIL RECORD
Pliocene to Recent from the Indo-Pacific.

NUMBER OF SPECIES
Eleven nominal species, an unknown number of true species, one from Australia.

Heterocyathus aequicostatus
EDWARDS & HAIME, 1848

TYPE LOCALITY
Unrecorded.

IDENTIFYING CHARACTERS
Sometimes hermatypic. Corals are solitary, free-living, and have a flat base. They have a commensal relationship with a sipunculid worm (*Aspidosiphon corallicola*). The sipunculid moves the coral about on soft substrates and prevents it from becoming buried.
Polyps are extended only at night. Polyp larvae settle initially on dead micro-molluscs which become embedded in the corallum.

COLOUR
Pale brown, often with a greenish oral disc.

SIMILAR SPECIES
Heterocyathus and *Heteropsammia* are structural and ecological equivalents.

DISTRIBUTION
Unknown, but widely distributed in the Indo-Pacific. Around Australia: the Great Barrier Reef in the east, and between Dampier Archipelago and Shark Bay on the west coast.

ABUNDANCE
Always found on soft horizontal substrates at depths of 20 m or more, usually in association with *Heteropsammia cochlea* and *Cycloseris cyclolites*. May be very abundant (up to 40 individuals per square metre).

x5

Heterocyathus aequicostatus at Wistari Reef, Great Barrier Reef.
PHOTOGRAPH: DAVE FISK.

FAMILY
DENDROPHYLLIIDAE

(pronounced den-dro-fill-ee-id-ee)

GRAY, 1847

CHARACTERS

Solitary or colonial, mostly ahermatypic. Corallite walls are porous, usually composed of coenosteum. Septa are fused in a distinctive pattern (Pourtalès Plan), at least in immature corallites.

RELATED FAMILIES
None.

EARLIEST FOSSILS
Cretaceous.

THE GENERA

Hermatypes: the family contains only three hermatypic genera which are all Australian. Superficially they are completely different: *Turbinaria* forms large colonies with a primarily laminar growth form, and is very common and widespread with many species; *Duncanopsammia* forms dendroid colonies, and is rare with one species; *Heteropsammia* is small, free-living and usually solitary.

Ahermatypes: seven genera have been recorded from Australia. These are mostly from deep water but include the three most prominent ahermatypic genera from reef waters, *Dendrophyllia, Tubastrea* and *Balanophyllia.*

Opposite: The Family Dendrophylliidae contain hermatypic and ahermatypic genera of very different appearance.
In all cases however, the polyps are large with long tapering tentacles.
This species is the spectacular ahermatype *Tubastraea micrantha.*
PHOTOGRAPH: ALASTAIR BIRTLES.

GENUS
TURBINARIA

(pronounced ter-bin-air-ee-a)

Oken, 1815

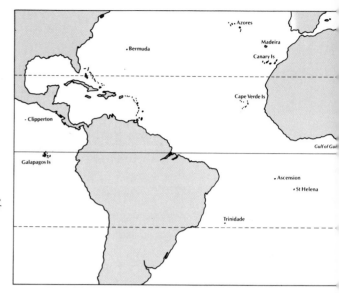

A knowledge of this variability will help us to understand the difficulty which, it is well known, all students of coral have in determining specimens of the genus Turbinaria. *By specimens here I mean, of course, those more or less scrappy pieces which have hitherto satisfied the collector.*

F. Bell,
On the Variation Observed in Large Masses of
Turbinaria, 1895.

Some species of *Turbinaria* are among the most variable of all corals, so much so that colonies growing in very shallow water have almost no specific characters in common with nearby colonies of the same species in deeper water. This variation is due to differences in available light, and recent studies have shown that if colonies are transplanted from shallow to deeper water, and *vice versa*, they will change their growth form to that which is normal for the changed depth.

Unlike most corals, *Turbinaria* breed in the autumn when the sea temperature falls. They have separate sexes and, as far as is known, they release gametes for external fertilisation. The unusual breeding time may be one reason why *Turbinaria* are particularly successful in higher latitudes, where they compete with kelp for space and light.

TYPE SPECIES
Madrepora crater Pallas, 1766 from the "East Indies".

FOSSIL RECORD
Oligocene to Recent from Europe and the Indo-Pacific.

NUMBER OF SPECIES
Eighty nominal species, 10 true species from Australia.

CHARACTERS
Colonies are massive, columnar, laminar or foliaceous with foliae frequently contorted.
Corallites are round, immersed to tubular and have porous walls with the same structure as the surrounding coenosteum. Septa are short and neat, columellae are broad and compact.
Polyps, except for those of *T. peltata*, are usually extended only at night.

SIMILAR GENERA
Turbinaria is a well-defined genus which does not resemble any other, except occasionally *Astreopora*.

I. The most common of the many growth forms of *Turbinaria peltata*.
PHOTOGRAPH: ED LOVELL.

2. The polyps of *Turbinaria peltata*, the largest of all the *Turbinaria* species.
PHOTOGRAPH: AUTHOR.

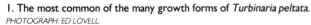

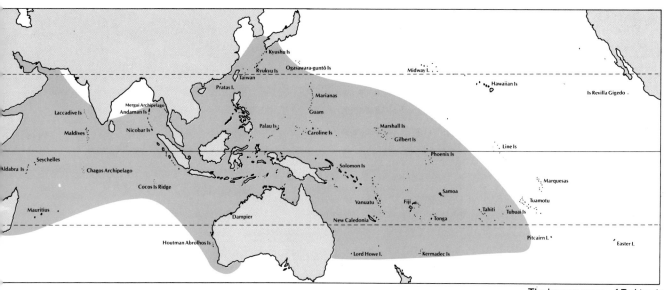

The known range of *Turbinaria*.

2

Turbinaria peltata
(ESPER, 1794)

TYPE LOCALITY
"China Sea".

IDENTIFYING CHARACTERS
Colonies are flat plates, often in overlapping tiers, and are sometimes columnar. Corallites are immersed to tubular, with calices 3–5 mm in diameter. Large polyps are frequently extended during the day.

COLOUR
Usually grey, sometimes brown.

SIMILAR SPECIES
T. patula.

DISTRIBUTION
From east Africa east to the Marshall Islands, with a wide latitudinal range.
Around Australia: the Great Barrier Reef, Coral Sea and south to Lord Howe Island and the Solitary Islands in the east, and south to Cape Naturaliste on the west coast.

ABUNDANCE
Common in a wide range of habitats and may form conspicuous colonies several metres in diameter.

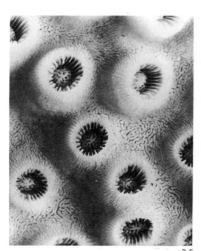

x2.5

1. The appearance of *Turbinaria peltata* after polyps have retracted.
PHOTOGRAPH: LEN ZELL.

2. The polyps of *Turbinaria peltata* are often extended during the day, giving the colony surface a carpet-like appearance.
PHOTOGRAPH: ED LOVELL.

Turbinaria patula

(DANA, 1846)

TYPE LOCALITY
Unrecorded.

IDENTIFYING CHARACTERS
Colonies are usually irregularly folded, unifacial, upright fronds with long, tubular, appressed corallites, strongly inclined towards the margins. Calices are elliptical, approximately 3.5 mm in diameter.

COLOUR
Pale brown, green or grey.

SIMILAR SPECIES
T. peltata, which has larger, less tubular corallites and *T. frondens*, which has smaller corallites.

DISTRIBUTION
Australia and Fiji.
Around Australia: the Great Barrier Reef and south to Lord Howe Island in the east, and south to Dampier Archipelago on the west coast.

ABUNDANCE
Uncommon except in temperate localities.

x2.5

Turbinaria patula is an uncommon species in the tropics. Tentacles are often extended during the day.
PHOTOGRAPH: LEN ZELL.

Turbinaria frondens

(DANA, 1846)

TYPE LOCALITY
Fiji.

IDENTIFYING CHARACTERS
Colonies are initially cup-shaped, developing broad, unifacial, upright to horizontal fronds, or becoming irregularly contorted. Corallites are immersed to long and tubular, the latter being strongly appressed on upright fronds. Calices are 1.5-2.5 mm in diameter.

COLOUR
Usually a uniform dark or greenish-brown, yellowish to grey.

SIMILAR SPECIES
T. patula.

DISTRIBUTION
From western Thailand north to Japan and east to Fiji and Samoa. Around Australia: the Great Barrier Reef, Coral Sea and south to Lord Howe Island in the east, and south to Duke of Orleans Bay on the west coast.

ABUNDANCE
Common in a wide range of reef habitats. In deep water, colonies are flat with mostly immersed corallites.

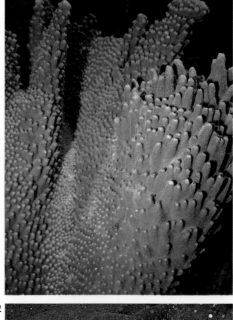

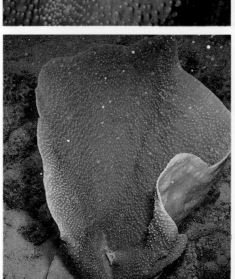

x2.5

1. *Turbinaria frondens* at Eagle Bay, Western Australia, showing the distinctive appearance of the species at southern localities. Only in the tropics does it become frond-like.
PHOTOGRAPH: BARRY WILSON.

2. *Turbinaria frondens* at the Palm Islands, Great Barrier Reef, showing the usual appearance of this species on lower reef slopes in tropical localities.
PHOTOGRAPH: LEN ZELL.

3. *Turbinaria frondens* from Torres Strait, showing a mixture of growth forms in the one colony.
PHOTOGRAPH: LEN ZELL.

4. The characteristic appearance of *Turbinaria frondens* polyps.
PHOTOGRAPH: LEN ZELL.

5. Polyps of *Turbinaria frondens* extended at night.
PHOTOGRAPH: ED LOVELL.

Turbinaria mesenterina

(LAMARCK, 1816)

TYPE LOCALITY
"Indian Ocean"

IDENTIFYING CHARACTERS
Colonies are composed of unifacial laminae which are highly contorted and anastomosed in subtidal habitats, are upright or tiered fronds on upper reef slopes and are horizontal fronds in deeper water, according to light availability. Corallites are crowded, slightly exsert, with calices 1.3-2 mm in diameter.

COLOUR
Usually grey-green or grey-brown.

SIMILAR SPECIES
T. frondens and, especially, *T. reniformis*, which can usually be recognised under water by its colour, its more horizontal than vertical fronds and its more immersed corallites, which give a smooth appearance.

DISTRIBUTION
From east Africa and the Red Sea east to Fiji and the Marshall Islands.
Around Australia: the Great Barrier Reef, Coral Sea and south to Elizabeth Reef in the east, and south to Recherche Archipelago on the west coast.

ABUNDANCE
Very common and may be dominant in shallow turbid-water habitats. Colonies are usually less than 1 m in diameter but may be much larger on fringing reefs.

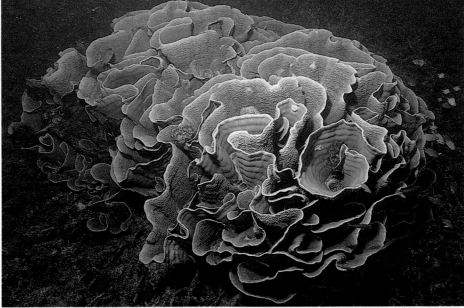

x2.5

1. Cabbage-like convolutions of a large *Turbinaria mesenterina* colony on the slope of a fringing reef.
PHOTOGRAPH: AUTHOR.

2. *Turbinaria mesenterina* from a lower reef slope showing the growth form of the species in deep or turbid water. As depth of water decreases, the laminae gradually become more upright and contorted.
PHOTOGRAPH: LEN ZELL.

3. Small *Turbinaria mesenterina* colonies at Pandora Reef, Great Barrier Reef, showing development of a convoluted growth form.
PHOTOGRAPH: ED LOVELL.

4. In very shallow water, *Turbinaria mesenterina* is highly convoluted.
PHOTOGRAPH: ED LOVELL.

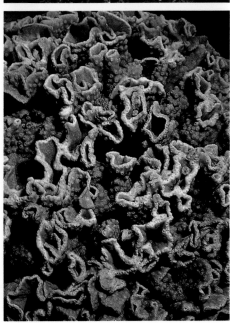

Turbinaria reniformis

BERNARD, 1896

TYPE LOCALITY
Palm Islands, Great Barrier Reef.

IDENTIFYING CHARACTERS
Colonies are composed of unifacial laminae, sometimes forming tiers, but mostly they are horizontal. Corallites are widely spaced, thick-walled, and immersed to conical in shape, with calices 1.5-2 mm in diameter.

COLOUR
Usually yellow-green with distinct margins.

SIMILAR SPECIES
T. mesenterina.

DISTRIBUTION
From the Nicobar Islands east to Tonga and the Cook Islands. Around Australia: the Great Barrier Reef in the east, and south to Recherche Archipelago on the west coast.

ABUNDANCE
Sometimes common and may form large stands on fringing reefs where the water is turbid.

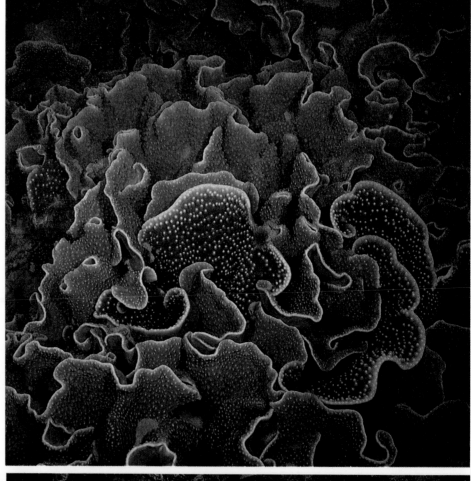

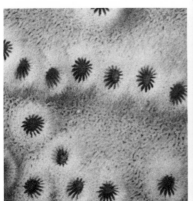

×2.5

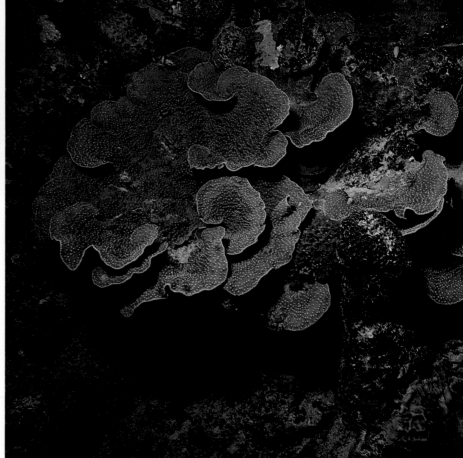

1. In shallow water, *Turbinaria reniformis* colonies (yellow) develop a growth form, similar to that of *T. mesenterina* (brown).
PHOTOGRAPH: LEN ZELL.

2. Characteristic colouration of *Turbinaria reniformis* at the Ryukyu Islands.
PHOTOGRAPH: AUTHOR.

568

Turbinaria stellulata

(LAMARCK, 1816)

TYPE LOCALITY
Unrecorded.

IDENTIFYING CHARACTERS
Colonies are submassive, usually with encrusting margins. Corallites are thick-walled, conical, with calices approximately 2 mm in diameter.

COLOUR
Usually brown or green but may be a wide range of other colours.

SIMILAR SPECIES
No other *Turbinaria* species is submassive, but small colonies are similar to *T. radicalis*.

DISTRIBUTION
From the South China Sea east to the Marshall Islands. Around Australia: the Great Barrier Reef and Flinders Reef (Moreton Bay) in the east, and south to King George Sound on the west coast.

ABUNDANCE
Usually uncommon but may form conspicuous dome-shaped colonies on upper reef slopes. Unlike other *Turbinaria*, this species is seldom found in turbid waters.

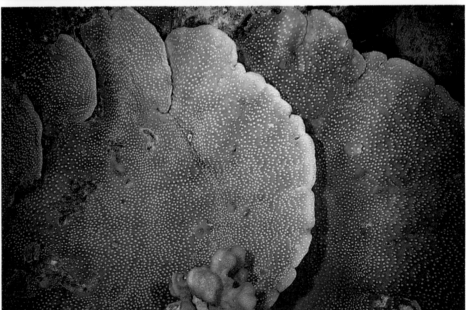

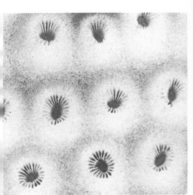

x2.5

1. A solid colony of *Turbinaria stellulata* at Broadhurst Reef, Great Barrier Reef.
PHOTOGRAPH: ED LOVELL.

2,4. *Turbinaria stellulata* most commonly occurs as encrusting colonies with irregular polyps.
PHOTOGRAPHS: LEN ZELL (2) AND AUTHOR (4).

3. *Turbinaria stellulata* forming flat plates.
PHOTOGRAPH: LEN ZELL.

Turbinaria bifrons

BRÜGGEMANN, 1877

TYPE LOCALITY
Unrecorded.

IDENTIFYING CHARACTERS
Colonies are initially flat laminae which develop elongate, upright, bifacial fronds. Corallites are conical, regularly spaced and have a uniform appearance.

COLOUR
Usually grey, green or brown with darker calices.

SIMILAR SPECIES
No other *Turbinaria* species except *T. conspicua* has bifacial fronds (except where unifacial fronds are fused back to back). Small colonies which have not developed bifacial fronds are difficult to distinguish from *T. frondens*.

DISTRIBUTION
Australia and Japan.
Around Australia: the Great Barrier Reef and Flinders Reef (Moreton Bay) in the east, and south to Houtman Abrolhos Islands on the west coast.

ABUNDANCE
Rare except in temperate localities (east coast); usually uncommon (west coast).

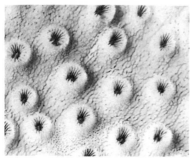

x2.5

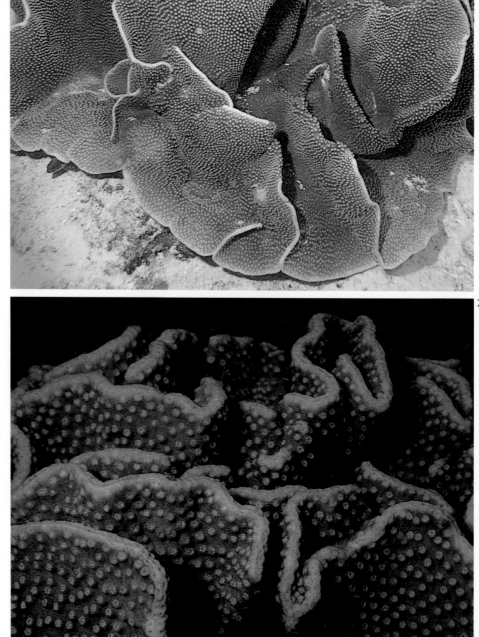

1. *Turbinaria bifrons* is easily recognised when upright fronds develop. Unlike other Australian species, except *T. conspicua*, polyps grow equally on both sides.
PHOTOGRAPH: LEN ZELL.

2. The fronds of *Turbinaria bifrons*.
PHOTOGRAPH: ED LOVELL.

570

Turbinaria conspicua

BERNARD, 1896

TYPE LOCALITY
  Shark Bay, Western Australia.

IDENTIFYING CHARACTERS
  Colonies are composed of thin, upright, bifacial fronds. Corallites are small, immersed and widely separated with very small calices.

COLOUR
  Pale brown or cream.

SIMILAR SPECIES
  T. bifrons has thicker fronds and larger corallites, which are conical with large calices.

DISTRIBUTION
  Known only from Australia: south to Port Denison Islands on the west coast; not found in the east.

ABUNDANCE
  Uncommon, except at Dampier Archipelago where it occurs with *T. bifrons* in equal abundance.

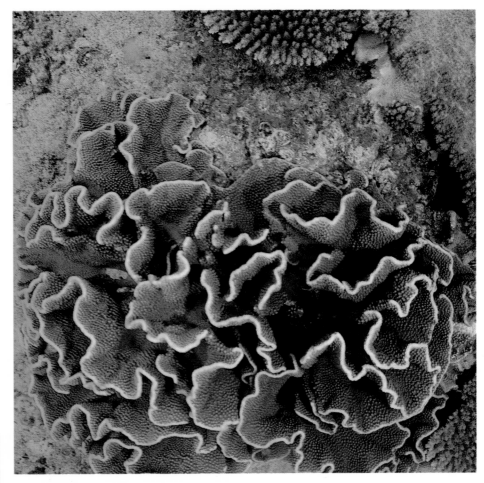

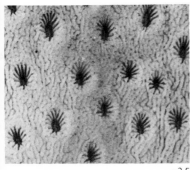

x2.5

Turbinaria conspicua at the Dampier Archipelago, Western Australia. This species is like *T. bifrons* but is finer, with smaller polyps.
PHOTOGRAPH: ED LOVELL.

Turbinaria radicalis

BERNARD, 1896

TYPE LOCALITY
  Great Barrier Reef.

IDENTIFYING CHARACTERS
  Colonies are encrusting laminae which have rootlets growing down into the substrate. Corallites may be aligned in irregular rows and are low cones or immersed.

COLOUR
  Pale to dark brown or green.

SIMILAR SPECIES
  No other *Turbinaria* species has rootlets. If these are not developed, *T. radicalis* may be difficult to distinguish from *T. mesenterina.*

DISTRIBUTION
  Known only from Australia: south to Lord Howe and Solitary Islands in the east; not found on the west coast.

ABUNDANCE
  Rare except in temperate localities.

x2.5

Turbinaria heronensis

WELLS, 1958

TYPE LOCALITY
  Heron Island, Great Barrier Reef.

IDENTIFYING CHARACTERS
  Colonies have highly divided, irregular laminae with very long tubular corallites.

COLOUR
  Dark browns and greens becoming pale on lower reef slopes.

SIMILAR SPECIES
  None.

DISTRIBUTION
  Known only from Australia: the Great Barrier Reef and Elizabeth and Middleton Reefs in the east; not found on the west coast.

ABUNDANCE
  Rare in the tropics, but common on the upper slopes and outer flats of temperate reefs.

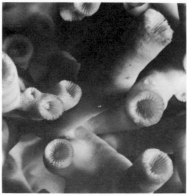

x2.5

1. *Turbinaria heronensis* often forms a thicket of tubular polyps.
PHOTOGRAPH: ED LOVELL.

2. *Turbinaria heronensis* at Heron Island, Great Barrier Reef. The growth form of this species is unlike that of any other coral.
PHOTOGRAPH: LEN ZELL.

3. Polyps of *Turbinaria heronensis*.
PHOTOGRAPH: RON AND VALERIE TAYLOR.

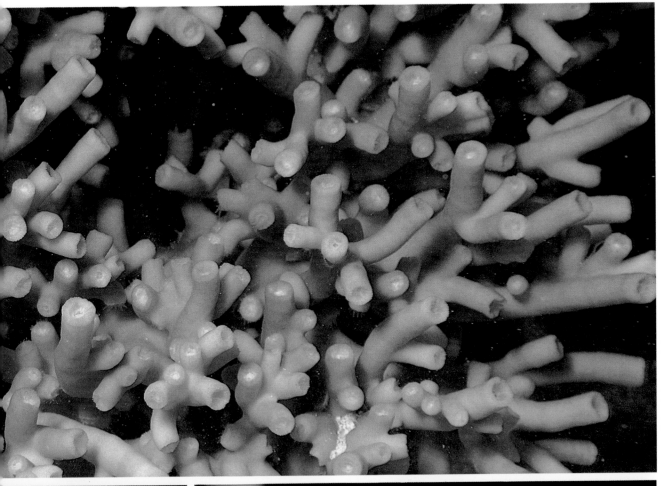

3

GENUS DUNCANOP-SAMMIA

(pronounced dun-kan-op-sam-ee-a)

Wells, 1936

TYPE SPECIES
Dendrophyllia axifuga Edwards & Haime, 1848.

FOSSIL RECORD
Miocene to Recent from the western Pacific.

NUMBER OF SPECIES
One.

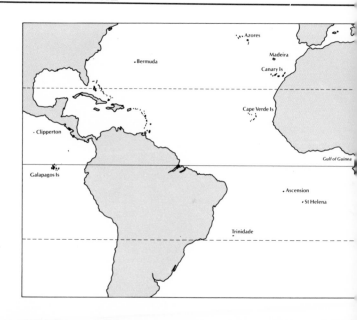

Duncanop-sammia axifuga

(EDWARDS & HAIME, 1848)

TYPE LOCALITY
Western Australia.

IDENTIFYING CHARACTERS
Colonies are dendroid, composed of long tubular corallites, which all face upward.
Corallites are round, 10-14 mm in diameter, have well-developed septa which follow Pourtalès Plan, broad deep-seated columelláe, and walls composed of porous coenosteum.
Polyps are extended day and night. Tentacles form a continuous mat concealing the shape of the underlying colony.

COLOUR
Green or blue-grey.

SIMILAR SPECIES
None.

DISTRIBUTION
Around Australia: the northern and central Great Barrier Reef in the east, and south to Houtman Abrolhos Islands on the west coast.

ABUNDANCE
Rare, usually occurs only in deep water (over 20 m) attached to a solid substrate, but in areas where soft horizontal substrates predominate.

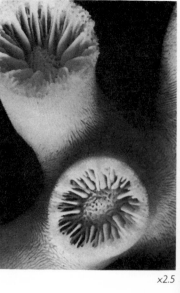

x2.5

1. *Duncanopsammia axifuga* with polyps extended during the day. The polyps to the right of the colony are in the process of contracting after being disturbed.
PHOTOGRAPH: CLAY BRYCE.

2. *Duncanopsammia axifuga* at the Houtman Abrolhos Islands, Western Australia. Contracted polyps reveal the presence of the underlying skeleton.
PHOTOGRAPH: CLAY BRYCE.

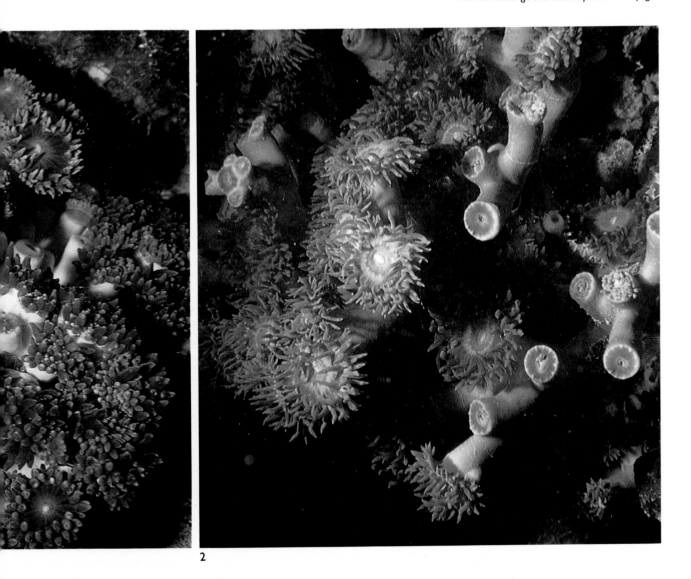

The known range of *Duncanopsammia axifuga*.

2

Genus *HETEROPSAMMIA*

(pronounced het-a-rop-sam-ee-a)

Edwards & Haime, 1848

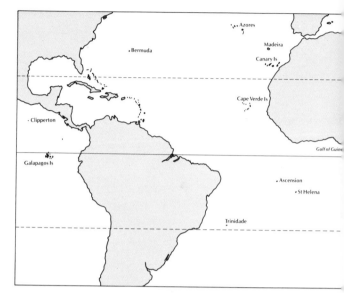

These fascinating little corals are found only on horizontal soft substrates between reefs and are thus seldom seen by divers. When they are found, however, thousands of individuals are often clustered together. All are free-living and highly mobile, and the mobility results from an extraordinary symbiotic relationship with a "peanut" (sipunculid) worm. This association involves a specialised life-cycle. Coral larvae settle initially on small gastropod shells of various species. During subsequent growth, the coral engulfs the shell, the shape of which can usually be seen in all but fully grown corals. Before the shell is fully engulfed, it must become occupied by the worm. The worm then builds and maintains a horizontal tube inside the coral leading from the shell to an opening in the side of the coral. As the coral grows, the tube is continually extended in an arc around the gastropod. Apart from the main opening, the tube is connected to the outside of the coral by a series of pores which may have a respiratory function. The worm is readily able to move the coral in short jerks by repeatedly extending and contracting its trunk-like proboscis.

Heteropsammia always has worms and thus appears to be dependent on them. These two organisms are often joined by a third, a parasitic mussel, which forms a second opening just above, and frequently connected to, that of the worm.

Heteropsammia is well adapted to life on soft substrates. It has special ciliary tracts capable of collecting organic food, and other tracts, working in the opposite direction, which keep the coral free of sediment.

It is extraordinary that the same symbiotic relationship, life-cycle and structure, are repeated in two other corals, *Heterocyathus* and *Psammoceris*—the former is a caryophylliid, the latter is another dendrophylliid. These two genera are included in this book as non-reefal corals because both are probably primarily ahermatypic, but it is likely that all three genera may be hermatypic to varying degrees.

Heteropsammia has separate sexes and, as far as is known, it releases gametes for external fertilisation.

TYPE SPECIES
Heteropsammia michelini Edwards & Haime, 1848 from the South China Sea.

FOSSIL RECORD
Pleistocene to Recent from the Indo-Pacific.

NUMBER OF SPECIES
Nine nominal species, but probably only one true species.

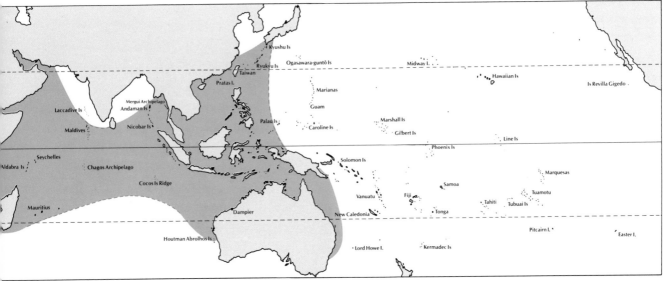

The known range of *Heteropsammia*.

1. The most common shape of *Heteropsammia cochlea*, with two partly separated polyps.
PHOTOGRAPH: DAVE FISK.

2. *Heteropsammia cochlea* with tentacles extended in an aquarium at night.
PHOTOGRAPH: DAVE FISK.

Heteropsammia cochlea

(SPENGLER, 1781)

TYPE LOCALITY
Bay of Bengal.

IDENTIFYING CHARACTERS
Corals are solitary or form small colonies, and are free-living with one or two calices on a base that is flat or keeled according to the nature of the substrate. They have an obligate commensal relationship with a sipunculid worm (*Aspidosiphon corallicola*) and usually have one parasitic mussel (*Lithophaga lessepsiana*) embedded above the sipunculid. The sipunculid moves the coral about on soft substrates and prevents it from becoming buried.

Corallites are round or laterally compressed, up to 25 mm in diameter, have well-developed septa which follow Pourtalès Plan, broad, compact, deep-seated columellae, and walls composed of porous coenosteum. Polyps are extended only at night. They are hermatypic in tropical localities, but are possibly ahermatypic in high latitude locations.

COLOUR
Grey or brown.

SIMILAR SPECIES
Heteropsammia and *Heterocyathus* are structural and ecological equivalents; *Psammoseris* is at least a structural equivalent.

DISTRIBUTION
From the east coast of Africa and the Persian Gulf east to the Coral Sea.

Around Australia: the Great Barrier Reef, Coral Sea and south to Sydney in the east; and south to Houtman Abrolhos Islands on the west coast.

ABUNDANCE
Always found on soft horizontal substrates at depths of 20 m or more. Where it does occur, it is usually very abundant (up to approximately 300 individuals per square metre having been recorded at Heron and Lizard Islands). Usually occurs in association with *Heterocyathus aequicostatus* and *Cycloseris cyclolites*.

x2.5

GENUS
DENDROPHYLLIA
(pronounced den-dro-fill-ee-a)

de Blainville, 1830

Three genera of ahermatypic corals, *Dendrophyllia,*
Tubastraea and *Balanophyllia*, are frequently found on
reefs and thus are included in this section rather than
with the non-reefal corals. However, they never have
algae in their tissues and their bright colours result only
from the coral's own pigments. Being ahermatypic, and
therefore not confined to reefs, they are more widely
distributed than hermatypic corals, and are even found
in the Mediterranean. Even single species (such as
Tubastraea faulkneri) may be cosmopolitan. Ecologically
they are also distinct from other reef corals. They are
not dependent on light and can thus colonise the roofs of
caves and other dark places where hermatypes cannot
grow. Only the large dendroid *Tubastraea micrantha* can
compete directly with the hermatypes and may do so
very successfully in communities not dominated by
Acropora.

All of these corals are voracious zooplankton
feeders. At night, when they usually extend their
tentacles, divers can easily attract fast-swimming
polychaete worms and other plankton to the corals by
shining a torch light on them. The corals catch the
plankton in their tentacles and promptly stuff them into
their mouths.

As far as is known, these genera all have separate
sexes. Fertilisation is internal and larvae are brooded.
These may be over 1 mm long and they crawl along the
substrate or swim for a short period after release.

TYPE SPECIES
Madrepora ramea Linnaeus, 1758 from an unrecorded
locality.

FOSSIL RECORD
Eocene to Recent, cosmopolitan.

CHARACTERS
Ahermatypic, colonies are dendroid becoming bushy by
extratentacular budding.
Corallites are tubular with septa fused according to
Pourtalès Plan.
Polyps are extended mostly at night and are large and
fleshy.

SIMILAR GENERA
Dendrophyllia resembles only *Tubastraea* and can be
distinguished by the latter's mature corallites not having
septa clearly arranged according to Pourtalès Plan.

DISTRIBUTION
Indo-Pacific and Atlantic Oceans and the Mediterranean.
Around Australia: occurs around the whole coastline, at
a depth of 2–85 m.

ABUNDANCE
Uncommon except in caves.

x5

AUSTRALIAN SPECIES
Six species have been recorded: *D. arbuscula* Horst, 1922;
D. gracilis Edwards & Haime, 1848; *D. atrata* Dennant,
1906; *D. fistula* Alcock, 1902; *D. praecipua* Gardiner &
Waugh, 1939; and *D. velata* Crossland, 1952.

1. *Dendrophyllia gracilis* at Heron Island, Great Barrier Reef.
PHOTOGRAPH: RON AND VALERIE TAYLOR.

2. A polyp of *Dendrophyllia.*
PHOTOGRAPH: RON AND VALERIE TAYLOR.

3. *Tubastraea* or *Dendrophyllia* with polyps retracted. These genera are not usually separable under water. They are sometimes called "turret corals" as the polyps look like projecting gun barrels.
PHOTOGRAPH: RON AND VALERIE TAYLOR.

4. *Dendrophyllia* species near Perth at night.
PHOTOGRAPH: CLAY BRYCE.

GENUS
TUBASTRAEA

(pronounced tube-ass-tree-a)

Lesson, 1829

TYPES SPECIES
Tubastraea coccinea Lesson, 1829 from Bora Bora.

FOSSIL RECORD
None.

CHARACTERS
Ahermatypic, colonies are dendroid, up to 1 m tall.
Corallites are tubular with septa of immature corallites
only following Pourtalès Plan.
Polyps are extended mostly at night and are large and
fleshy.

SIMILAR GENERA
Tubastraea resembles *Dendrophyllia*.

DISTRIBUTION
Indo-Pacific and Atlantic Oceans.
Around Australia: occurs along the tropical coastline and
south to Sydney in the east and south to Jurien Bay on
the west coast, at a depth of 1–40 m.

ABUNDANCE
Usually found only in caves (except *T. micrantha* which
may be abundant, even dominant, below 15 m in areas
exposed to currents).

AUSTRALIAN SPECIES
Four species have been recorded: *T. coccinea* Lesson,
1829; *T. diaphana* Dana, 1846; *T. faulkneri* Wells, 1982;
and *T. micrantha* Ehrenberg, 1834.

×5

A polyp of *Tubastraea coccinea*.
PHOTOGRAPH: ED LOVELL.

1. A polyp of *Tubastraea faulkneri*.
PHOTOGRAPH: RON AND VALERIE TAYLOR.

2. *Tubastraea diaphana* with polyps extended at night.
PHOTOGRAPH: CLAY BRYCE.

3. *Tubastraea micrantha* at Murray Island, Torres Strait, where it forms large stands with colonies over 1 m high.
PHOTOGRAPH: JOHN BARNETT.

4. Gaudy colours of a *Tubastraea* at night.
PHOTOGRAPH: RON AND VALERIE TAYLOR.

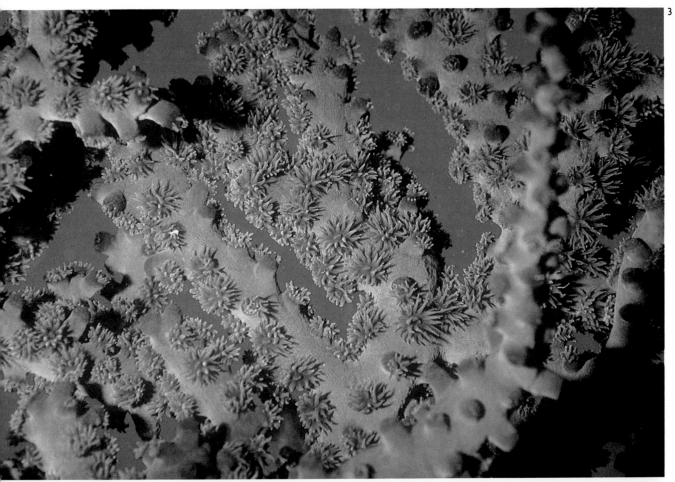

3

4

2

3

7

1. *Tubastraea aurea* near Perth, Western Australia, with polyps extended at night.
PHOTOGRAPH: CLAY BRYCE.

2. *Tubastraea faulkneri* at the Solitary Islands, eastern Australia. The same species is common around the world and is known to many a winner of photographic competitions.
PHOTOGRAPH: ED LOVELL.

3. *Tubastraea micrantha* with polyps extended. This species is one of the most distinctive of all corals and is a favourite subject of underwater photographers.
PHOTOGRAPH: RON AND VALERIE TAYLOR.

4. *Tubastraea coccinea* at the Swain Reefs, Great Barrier Reef.
PHOTOGRAPH: LEN ZELL.

Centre: *Tubastraea diaphana* as it is usually seen during the day with polyps retracted.
PHOTOGRAPH: RON AND VALERIE TAYLOR.

5. *Tubastraea* are voracious carnivores. This is the beginning of the end for a polychaete worm.
PHOTOGRAPH: RON AND VALERIE TAYLOR.

6. *Tubastraea faulkneri* as it usually appears during the day with polyps retracted.
PHOTOGRAPH: CLAY BRYCE.

7. *Tubastraea micrantha* as depicted by James Dana in his *Atlas of Zoophytes* in 1849. He called the species *Dendrophyllia nigrescens*, which is still the name most commonly used.

GENUS
BALANOPHYLLIA

(pronounced bal-an-oh-fill-ee-a)

Wood, 1844

TYPE SPECIES
Balanophyllia calyculus Wood, 1844 from Pliocene, Norfolk, England.

FOSSIL RECORD
Eocene to Recent, cosmopolitan.

CHARACTERS
Ahermatypic and solitary, or corallites in small attached clumps.

Corallites are elongate, tapering towards their base, elliptical in cross-section. Walls are thick, composed of coenosteum with costae. Septa are fused according to Pourtalès Plan.

Polyps are usually extended during the day.

SIMILAR GENERA
Dendrophyllia and *Tubastraea*. Both have thinner and less porous walls. Living colonies of these genera are usually difficult to distinguish as all may have similar black, bright-orange or yellow polyps.

DISTRIBUTION
Cosmopolitan.

Around Australia: occurs around the whole coastline, at a depth of 1-128 m.

ABUNDANCE
Common only on the roofs of caves. Found at any depth.

AUSTRALIAN SPECIES
Ten species are known, seven of which have been named: *B. bairdiana* Edwards & Haime, 1848; *B. buccina* Tenison-Woods, 1878; *B. dentata* Tenison-Woods, 1879; *B. dilatata* Dennant, 1904; *B. eguchii* Wells, 1982; *B. incisa* Crossland, 1952; and *B. yongei* Crossland, 1952.

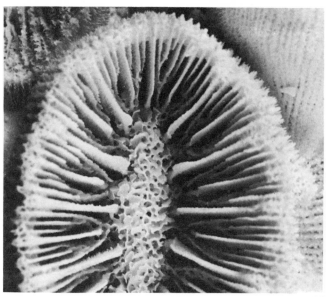

×8.5

4

5

4. The beautiful *Balanophyllia bairdiana*
om southern and south-east Australia.

*OTOGRAPHS: DAVID STAPLES (1 AND 4) AND
VILLE COLEMAN, A.M.P.I. (2 AND 3).*

A side view of *Balanophyllia bairdiana.*
OTOGRAPH: DAVID STAPLES.

REEF-BUILDING SCLERACTINIA
Non-Australian Genera

With only two exceptions, all non-Australian hermatypic genera are monospecific, and several of these are of doubtful validity.

Four distinct genera occur in the western Pacific but have not so far been found in Australia. *Zoopilus*, a large and very distinctive compound free-living fungiid is found from Japan to the Philippines, Indonesia and New Guinea and extends south-east to Fiji. *Physophyllia* (two or three species), a pectiniid, occurs from the Solomon Islands to Japan and west to Africa and the Red Sea, and is by far the most widespread non-Australian genus. *Boninastrea* from Japan and Taiwan and *Nemenzophyllia* from the Philippines are little-known but distinctive genera.

Three genera of siderastreids, *Siderastrea*, *Anomas-traea* and *Horastrea*, are all found in the Indian Ocean. *Siderastrea*, of which there are several Indo-Pacific species, also occurs in the Atlantic Ocean and one of these, *S. radians*, is probably the only hermatypic species common to both the Atlantic and Indo-Pacific Oceans.

At least four more valid genera, *Gyrosmilia*, *Erythrastrea*, *Astreosmilia* and *Ctenella*, have been described from the central and western Indian Ocean. Of these, *Ctenella* is of particular interest as it is found only at the Chagos Archipelago where it appears to be a relict of the otherwise Atlantic family, Meandrinidae.

There are several other monospecific genera known to the author which have not yet been described, and several more which have been described but which are of doubtful validity.

Opposite: *Zoopilus echinatus* next to *Euphyllia ancora* at the Ryukyu Islands.
PHOTOGRAPH: AUTHOR.

FAMILY *SIDERASTREIDAE* Vaughan & Wells, 1943

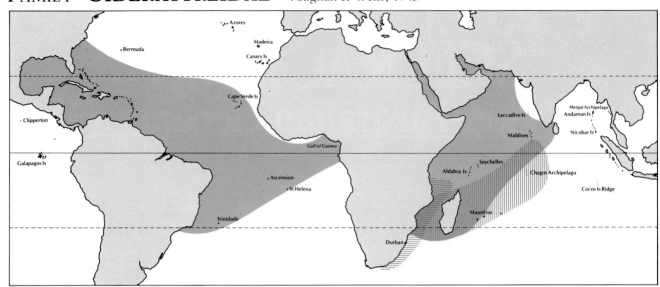

The known range of *Siderastrea* ▨ *Anomastraea irregularis* ▤ and *Horastrea indica* ▥

GENUS
Siderastrea
DE BLAINVILLE, 1830

CHARACTERS
Colonies are usually massive, sometimes branching or encrusting. Corallites are cerioid, formed by extratentacular budding, and are like those of *Pseudosiderastrea*, except that the walls are thicker, are composed of concentric rods, and septa do not fuse.

SIMILAR GENERA
Pseudosiderastrea and *Anomastraea*.

SPECIES
Approximately 11 nominal species, an unknown number of true species.

×5

GENUS
Anomastraea
VON MARENZELLER, 1908

CHARACTERS
Colonies are massive. Corallites are submeandroid to cerioid and are formed by intratentacular budding. Walls are thin and septa have irregularly fused inner margins.

SIMILAR GENERA
Closest to *Siderastrea* but distinct, especially as the latter has extratentacular budding.

SPECIES
One species: *A. irregularis* von Marenzeller, 1901.

×5

GENUS
Horastrea
PICHON, 1971

CHARACTERS
Colonies are massive. Corallites are plocoid, tending to become ploco-meandroid with several centres.

SIMILAR GENERA
None.

SPECIES
One species: *H. indica* Pichon, 1971.

×1

590

FAMILY *FUNGIIDAE* Dana, 1846

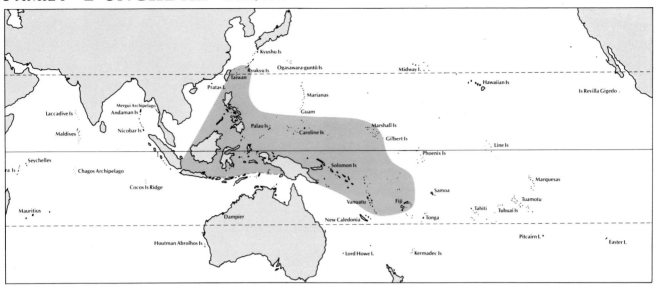

The known range of *Zoopilus echinatus*.

GENUS

Zoopilus

DANA, 1846

CHARACTERS
Free-living, colonial, similar to *Halomitra* but more delicate. Skeletal structures are similar to those of *Fungia (Ctenactis) echinata*.

SIMILAR GENERA
Closest to *Halomitra*.

SPECIES
One species: *Z. echinatus* Dana, 1846.

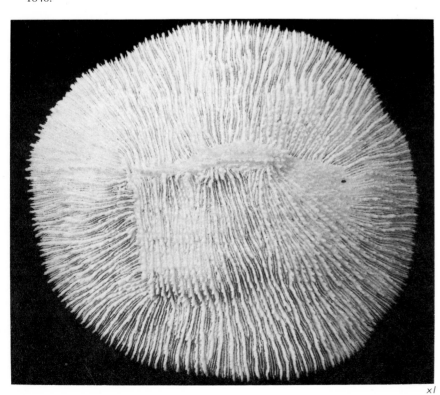

×1

FAMILY *PECTINIIDAE* Vaughan & Wells, 1943

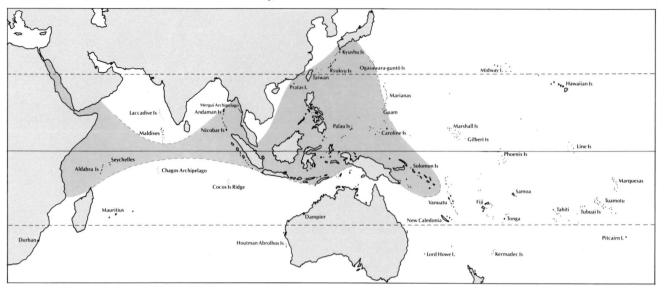

The known range of *Physophyllia*.

GENUS

Physophyllia

DUNCAN, 1884

CHARACTERS

Colonies are plate-like, combining many of the characters of *Pectinia* and *Echinophyllia*. Corallites are widely spaced, open and shallow. The coenosteum is thin and blistery and tends to develop *Pectinia*-like walls.

SIMILAR GENERA

Pectinia does not form flat plates. *Echinophyllia* has much better-defined corallites, with distinct walls.

SPECIES

Three species have been described: *P. ayleni* (Wells, 1934); *P. wellsi* Nemenzo, 1971; and *P. patula* Hodgson & Ross, 1981.

x0.5

FAMILY *MEANDRINIDAE* Gray, 1847

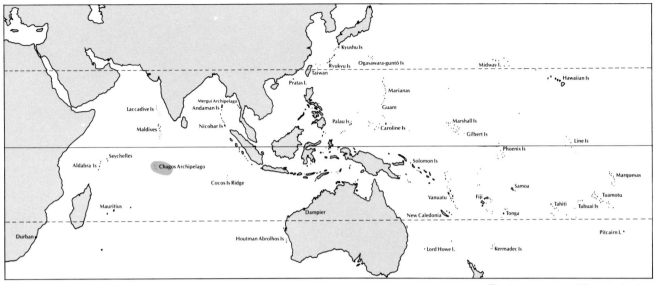

The known range of *Ctenella chagius*.

GENUS
Ctenella
MATTHAI, 1928

CHARACTERS
Colonies are massive and meandroid. Valleys and walls are of uniform width. Septa are fine and regular, columellae are septa-like, without centres.

SIMILAR GENUS
Superficially resembles *Leptoria* but is larger with smooth, caryophylliid-like septa.

SPECIES
One species: *C. chagius* Matthai, 1928.

×5

FAMILY *MERULINIDAE* Verrill, 1866

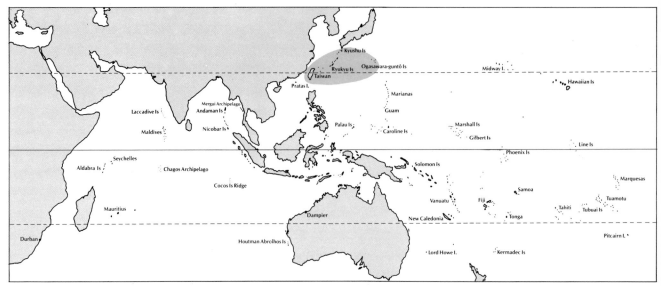

The known range of *Boninastrea boninensis*.

GENUS

Boninastrea

YABE & SUGIYAMA, 1935

CHARACTERS
Colonies are submassive with a contorted surface of cerioid corallites, each with one to three centres.

SIMILAR GENUS
Merulina. This genus was originally considered to be a mussid.

SPECIES
Only one species: *B. boninensis* Yabe & Sugiyama, 1935.

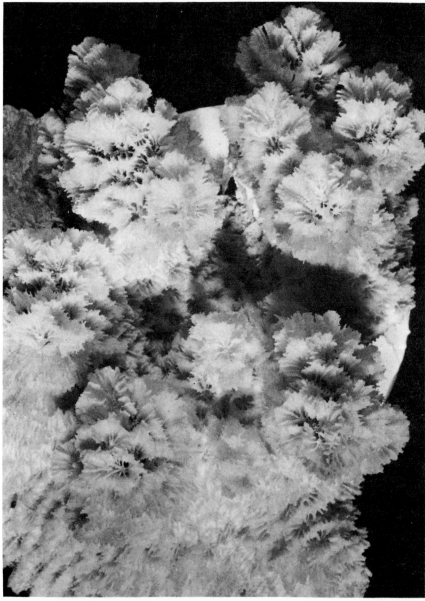

x1

FAMILY *FAVIIDAE* Gregory, 1900

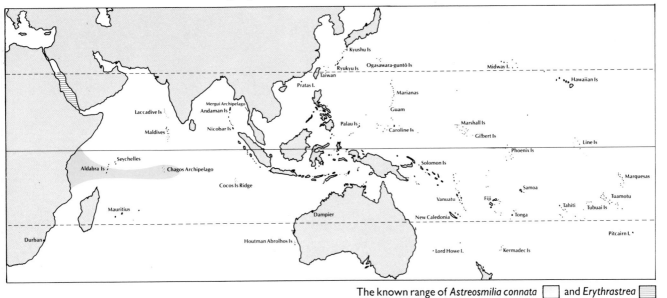

The known range of *Astreosmilia connata* ☐ and *Erythrastrea* ▨

GENUS
Astreosmilia
ORTMANN, 1892

CHARACTERS
Colonies are massive with corallites like *Caulastrea* but subplocoid.

SIMILAR GENUS
Caulastrea, which is phaceloid.

SPECIES
One species: *A. connata* Ortmann, 1892, only a few specimens of which have been recorded.

GENUS
Erythrastrea
PICHON, SCHEER & PILLAI, MS

CHARACTERS
Colonies are flabello-meandroid with thin walls and distinct columellae.

SIMILAR GENERA
Skeletal structures are like *Caulastrea*. *Erythrastrea* superficially resembles *Trachyphyllia* and *Nemenzophyllia*, all of which are flabello-meandroid.

SPECIES
Two nominal species: *E. wellsi* (Ma, 1959); and *E. flabellata* Pichon, Scheer & Pillai, ms.

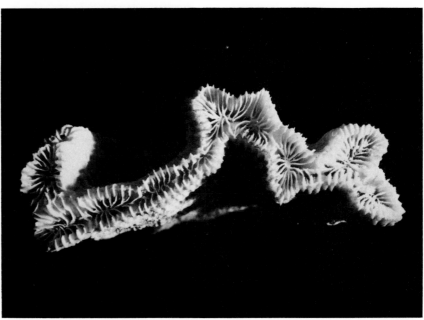

x2.5

FAMILY *CARYOPHYLLIIDAE* Gray, 1847

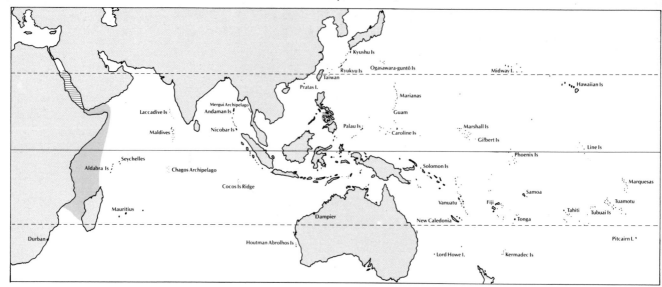

The known range of *Nemenzophyllia turbida* ▨ and *Gyrosmilia* *interrupta* ▨

GENUS
Nemenzophyllia
HODGSON & ROSS, 1981

CHARACTERS
Colonies are flabello-meandroid with thin fragile walls and septa. The columella extends down the centre of the valleys as a single elongate septum.

SIMILAR GENERA
This is a doubtful genus closest to *Plerogyra*. It also resembles *Erythrastrea*.

SPECIES
Only one species: *N. turbida* Hodgson & Ross, 1981.

GENUS
Gyrosmilia
EDWARDS & HAIME, 1851

CHARACTERS
Colonies are submassive to encrusting. Valleys are meandroid with compact *Euphyllia*-like septa and little or no development of columellae.

SIMILAR GENERA
Superficially resembles *Ctenella*; also resembles *Montigyra*.

SPECIES
One species is known: *G. interrupta* (Ehrenberg, 1834).

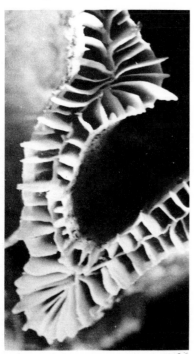

x2.5

x2.5

NON-REEFAL AUSTRALIAN SCLERACTINIA

The following is a summary of the corals that are not usually associated with coral reefs. They are all ahermatypic, that is, they have no symbiotic algae in their tissues. Some are found only in shallow water but the majority occur in the darkness of deep offshore waters. These have been collected only by dredging and very little is known of their distribution, depth range or habitat.

Most ahermatypes found in shallow water are attached to a solid substrate, while those from deep water are generally solitary and free-living. The latter may be known from a few specimens only, but others, notably *Flabellum* and *Caryophyllia*, are frequently dredged up in large numbers. In these cases, it appears that particular species have specific depth ranges or habitat preferences.

Three ahermatypic dendrophylliids, *Dendrophyllia*, *Tubastraea* and *Balanophyllia*, are commonly found in reefal habitats and are therefore included in this book with the reef corals, rather than with the other ahermatypes. Three other genera, *Heteropsammia* *Heterocyathus* and *Psammoseris*, which are superficially similar because they associate with symbiotic sipunculid worms to give them mobility on soft substrates, appear to be partial ahermatypes. The former two (which are commonly found in the vicinity of reefs) are included with the reef corals, while the latter (which is known only from a few specimens and which may be entirely ahermatypic) is described below.

Only the larger ahermatypes are illustrated by photographs. Identification of the remainder is usually a specialist's task requiring a microscope and more details of the skeletal characters than are given here.

Duncanopsammia axifuga has a skeletal structure and growth form intermediate between its hermatypic and its ahermatypic relatives, providing convincing proof of their common ancestry within the Dendrophylliidae. Both hermatypic and ahermatypic species occur on reefs, hence both are included with reef corals above.
PHOTOGRAPH: AUTHOR.

FAMILY *MICRABACIIDAE* Vaughan, 1905

CHARACTERS
Solitary, free-living, button-shaped. Walls are absent, costae alternate in position with septa.

RELATED FAMILIES
None closely related.

THE GENERA
The family contains only four genera, all from deep water, one being Australian.

GENUS
Letepsammia
YABE & EGUCHI, 1932

CHARACTERS
Solitary, free-living, button-shaped. There is no corallite wall and costae alternate in position with the septa, the latter having spine-like teeth.

DISTRIBUTION
Not known.
Around Australia: east coast at a depth of 165-457 m; not found on the west coast.

AUSTRALIAN SPECIES
Only one unnamed species known.

FAMILY *FUNGIIDAE* Dana, 1846

GENUS
Fungiacyathus
SARS, 1872

CHARACTERS
Solitary, free-living, disc- or button-shaped. Costae and septa are thin and spiny.

DISTRIBUTION
Cosmopolitan.
Around Australia: southern Queensland, Great Australian Bight and Western Australia from Port Hedland to Rowley Shoals and Scott Reef, at a depth of 190-600 m.

AUSTRALIAN SPECIES
Three Australian species are known: *F. marenzelleri* Vaughan, 1906; *F. palifera* (Alcock, 1902); and *F. symmetrica* (Pourtalès, 1871).

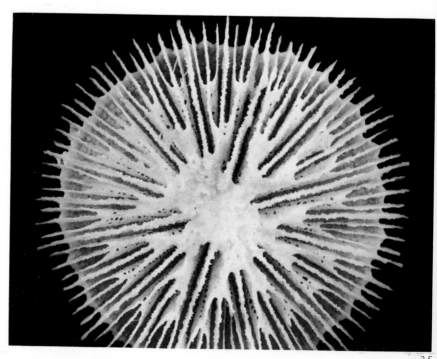

x2.5

FAMILY *OCULINIDAE* Gray, 1847

GENUS
Madrepora
LINNAEUS, 1758

CHARACTERS
Colonial, dendroid, with more or less alternate budding. Pali are absent, columellae are weakly developed.

SIMILAR GENUS
Archohelia.

DISTRIBUTION
Cosmopolitan.
Around Australia: recorded only from the Great Barrier Reef and south-western Australia, at a depth of 55-450 m.

AUSTRALIAN SPECIES
Three Australian species are known: *M. porcellana* (Moseley, 1881); *M. kauaiensis* Vaughan, 1907; and an unnamed species.

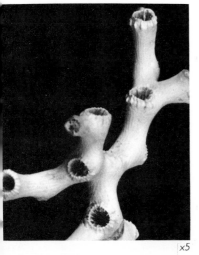

x5

GENUS
Archohelia
VAUGHAN, 1919

CHARACTERS
Colonial, attached and ramose. Has an axial corallite as in *Acropora*.

SIMILAR GENUS
Madrepora.

DISTRIBUTION
Except for Australia, known only as fossils from the West Indies and North and Central America. Around Australia: known only from a shallow-water locality (3.5 m depth) near Gladstone, Great Barrier Reef which is the only living record of the genus.

AUSTRALIAN SPECIES
Only one species is known: *A. rediviva* Well & Alderslade, 1979.

x5

GENUS
Cyathelia
EDWARDS & HAIME, 1849

CHARACTERS
Colonial, attached and branching. Has alternate budding of corallites with no axial corallites.

DISTRIBUTION
Indo-Pacific.
Around Australia: known only from Recherche Archipelago, Western Australia, at a depth of 40 m.

AUSTRALIAN SPECIES
Only one species is known: *C. axillaris* (Ellis & Solander, 1786).

x5

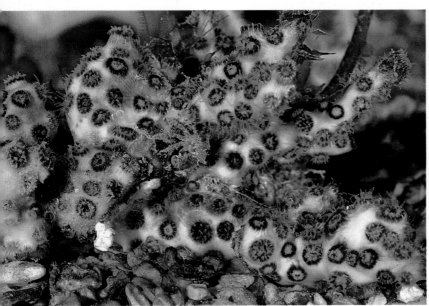

2

1. *Archohelia rediviva.*
PHOTOGRAPH: PHIL ALDERSLADE.

2. *Cyathelia axillaris* at the Recherche Archipelago, Western Australia.
PHOTOGRAPH: CLAY BRYCE.

FAMILY *RHIZANGIIDAE* d'Orbigny, 1851

CHARACTERS
Ahermatypic colonial corals
reproducing from stolons.
Corallites are small, with simple septa.

RELATED FAMILY
Oculinidae.

EARLIEST FOSSILS
Cretaceous.

THE GENERA
There are two Australian genera,
Culicia and *Astrangia*, both occurring
in shallow water on vertical or
overhung rock walls and caverns.
These genera differ primarily in their
reproductive stolons which are
temporary in *Culicia* and permanent
and conspicuous in *Astrangia*.

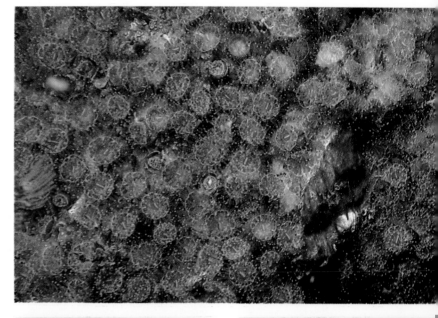

GENUS
Culicia
DANA, 1846

TYPE SPECIES
Culicia stellata Dana, 1846 from
Singapore.

FOSSIL RECORD
Miocene to Recent from the Indo-
Pacific.

NUMBER OF SPECIES
At least 12 nominal species, an
unknown number of true species.

CHARACTERS
Colonial, budding occurs from
rootlets but these are seen during
early stages only.
Corallites are tubular with thin
walls, thin, weakly toothed septa
and weakly developed columellae.
Polyps are extended day and
night. They are small with short,
straight radiating tentacles.

SIMILAR GENUS
Culicia is close to *Astrangia*.

DISTRIBUTION
Throughout the Indo-Pacific.
Around Australia: the entire
coastline including Tasmania
from intertidal rocky shores to a
depth of 128 m.

AUSTRALIAN SPECIES
Six species are known: *C. tenella*
Dana, 1846; *C. hoffmeisteri*
Squires, 1966; *C. rubeola* (Quoy &
Gaimard, 1833); *C. australiensis*
Hoffmeister, 1933; *C. smithi*
Edwards & Haime, 1850. and *C.
verreauxi* Edwards & Haime,
1850.

×10

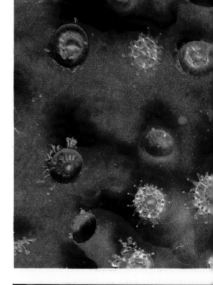

1. *Culicia tenella* at the Solitary Islands,
eastern Australia.
PHOTOGRAPH: ED LOVELL.

2. *Culicia tenella* imbedded in a sponge.
Polyps show differing degrees of
extension.
PHOTOGRAPH: NEVILLE COLEMAN, A.M.P.I.

3. Partly extended polyps of *Culicia
tenella*.
PHOTOGRAPH: ED LOVELL.

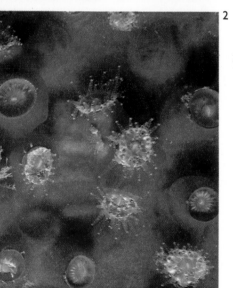

GENUS
Astrangia
EDWARDS & HAIME, 1848

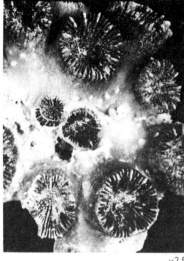

CHARACTERS
Solitary, attached and cylindrical. Corallites are in close clusters linked by rootlets, all septa are toothed. Cleaned skeletons of some species remain dark-coloured.

SIMILAR GENUS
Culicia.

DISTRIBUTION
Indo-Pacific and Atlantic. Around Australia: recorded from the entire southern half of the continent from southern Queensland in the east, and north to Derby in the west.

AUSTRALIAN SPECIES
Two species are known: *A. woodsi* Wells, 1955 and *A. ?rathbuni* Vaughan, 1906.

x2.5

Astrangia woodsi at Malabar, southern Australia. The dark colour of the corallum remains after bleaching.
PHOTOGRAPH: RUDI KUITER.

 2

3

FAMILY *FLABELLIDAE* Bourne, 1905

CHARACTERS
Ahermatypic, solitary, free-living corals with non-exsert septa, no paliform lobes and thin walls primarily composed of epitheca.

RELATED FAMILY
Caryophylliidae.

THE GENERA
Three genera have been recorded from Australia. *Flabellum* is the most common coral of deep inter-reef areas and occurs around Australia. *Placotrochus*, which is like *Flabellum* but has a flat columella, has been recorded only from inter-reef areas of the Great Barrier Reef. *Monomyces* has been recorded only from the southern Australian coastline.

EARLIEST FOSSILS
Cretaceous.

1. *Flabellum stokesi* with tentacles partly extended in an aquarium.
PHOTOGRAPH: LEN ZELL.

2. A *Flabellum* with tentacles partly extended.
PHOTOGRAPH: NEVILLE COLEMAN, A.M.P.I.

GENUS
Flabellum
LESSON, 1831

TYPE SPECIES
  Flabellum pavoninum Lesson, 1831.

FOSSIL RECORD
  Eocene to Recent, cosmopolitan.

NUMBER OF SPECIES
  Over 100 nominal species, an unknown number of true species.

CHARACTERS
  Solitary, free-living corals that are purse-shaped with or without rootlets.
  Septa are very fine and numerous. Columellae are absent or nearly so.
  Polyps are extended day and night and are large, like *Tubastraea*.

SIMILAR GENUS
  Flabellum is like *Placotrochus* but has no columella.

DISTRIBUTION
  Cosmopolitan.
  Around Australia: the entire coastline, at a depth of 10-824 m.

AUSTRALIAN SPECIES
  Fifteen nominal species have been recorded, some of which are of doubtful validity: *F. stokesi* Edwards & Haime, 1848 (a species complex); *?F. rubrum* (Quoy & Gaimard, 1833); *?F. spinosum* Edwards & Haime, 1848; *?F. mortensi* Studer, 1877; *F. irregulare* Tenison-Woods, 1878; *?F. australe* Moseley, 1881; *F. elongatum* Moseley, 1881; *F. pavoninum* Lesson, 1831 (a species complex); *F. japonicum* Moseley, 1881; *F. deludens* von Marenzeller, 1904; *F. distinctum* Edwards & Haime, 1848; *F. patens* Moseley, 1881; *F. transversale* Moseley, 1881; *F. tubuliferum* Tenison-Woods, 1880; and *F. tuthilli* Hoffmeister, 1933.

x1

GENUS
Placotrochus
EDWARDS & HAIME, 1848

CHARACTERS
  Solitary, free-living and purse-shaped. A thin, plate-like columella is present.

SIMILAR GENUS
  Flabellum.

DISTRIBUTION
  Indo-Pacific, from deep water.
  Around Australia: known only from the Great Barrier Reef, on soft substrates to a depth of 188 m.

AUSTRALIAN SPECIES
  Three nominal species, which may be only one true species, have been recorded: *P. candeanus* Edwards & Haime, 1848; *P. laevis* Edwards & Haime, 1848; and *P. pedicellatus* Tenison-Woods, 1879.

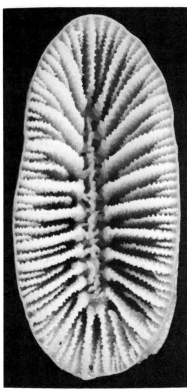

x5

GENUS
Monomyces
EHRENBERG, 1834

CHARACTERS
  Solitary, attached, shaped like an inverted cone or trumpet-shaped. Lateral rootlets are present, and columellae are absent.

DISTRIBUTION
  Indo-Pacific.
  Around Australia: recorded from South Australia and Cape Leeuwin, south-western Australia, at a depth of 3-40 m.

AUSTRALIAN SPECIES
  Two species have been recorded: *M. radiatus* (Dennant, 1904) and *M. levidensis* (Gardiner, 1899)

GENUS
Gardineria
VAUGHAN, 1907

CHARACTERS
  Solitary, attached, shaped like an inverted cone with rootlets. Has relatively few septa.

DISTRIBUTION
  Pacific and Atlantic Oceans.
  Around Australia: the Great Barrier Reef, at a depth of 55 m.

AUSTRALIAN SPECIES
  Only one, probably unnamed, species is known.

FAMILY *ANTHEMIPHYLLIIDAE* Vaughan, 1907

CHARACTERS
Solitary, free-living, button-like and ahermatypic; septa have well-developed teeth, other skeletal elements reduced or absent.

RELATED FAMILIES
None closely related.

THE GENERA
The family contains two genera, *Anthemiphyllia* and *Bathytrochus*.

GENUS
Anthemiphyllia
POURTALÈS, 1878

CHARACTERS
As for family. Columellae are present.

RELATED GENUS
Bathytrochus, which lacks a columella.

DISTRIBUTION
West Indies and Pacific Ocean. Around Australia: the eastern and southern coastline to a depth of 210 m.

SPECIES
Only one species is known: *A. dentata* (Alcock, 1902)

FAMILY *CARYOPHYLLIIDAE* Gray, 1847

GENUS
Caryophyllia
LAMARCK, 1801

CHARACTERS
Solitary, ahermatypic, attached or free-living, mostly cylindrical or horn-shaped. Septa are thin and straight with smooth margins. Pali and columellae are present.

SIMILAR GENERA
Cyathoceras, *Premocyathus*.

DISTRIBUTION
Cosmopolitan.
Around Australia: occurs around the whole coastline, at a depth of 119-1006 m.

AUSTRALIAN SPECIES
Six species have been recorded, four of which are named: *C. communis* (Seguenza, 1863); *C. cultrifera* Alcock, 1902; *C. planilamellata* Dennant, 1906; and *C. ?rugosa* Mosely, 1881.

×1.5

Most of what is known of deep-water corals comes from dredge samples such as this. This sample contained mostly *Caryophyllia* from a depth of about 150 m.
PHOTOGRAPH: ALASTAIR BIRTLES.

GENUS
Tethocyathus
KÜHN, 1913

CHARACTERS
Solitary, free-living, cylindrical, with epithecal walls.

DISTRIBUTION
Unknown.
Around Australia: the Great Barrier Reef in the east.

AUSTRALIAN SPECIES
Only one doubtful species has been recorded: *T. minor* Gardiner, 1899.

GENUS
Premocyathus
YABE & EGUCHI, 1942

CHARACTERS
Solitary, free-living or attached and compressed elliptical in cross-section with end costae extended into a keel on convex sides.

SIMILAR GENUS
Caryophyllia.

DISTRIBUTION
Cosmopolitan.
Around Australia: the Great Barrier Reef in the east, and Point Cloates, Western Australia, at a depth of 20-230 m.

AUSTRALIAN SPECIES
Only one doubtful species has been recorded: *P. ?compressus*, Yabe & Eguchi, 1942.

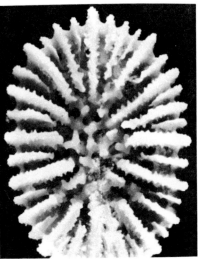

×15

GENUS
Cyathoceras
MOSELEY, 1881

CHARACTERS
Solitary, attached or free-living, cylindrical or horn-shaped. Septa are thin and straight with smooth margins. Columellae are present, pali are absent.

SIMILAR GENUS
Caryophyllia.

DISTRIBUTION
Indo-Pacific and Atlantic Oceans. Around Australia: occurs around the southern and eastern coastline, at a depth of 86-766 m.

AUSTRALIAN SPECIES
Four species have been recorded, three of which are named: C. woodsi Wells, 1964; C. cornu Moseley, 1881; and C. inornatus (Tenison-Woods, 1878).

×3

GENUS
Trochocyathus
EDWARDS & HAIME, 1848

CHARACTERS
Solitary, attached or free-living, and horn-shaped. Pali are in two circles, the epitheca is weak.

SIMILAR GENUS
Tethocyathus.

DISTRIBUTION
Cosmopolitan. Around Australia: recorded from southern Queensland and New South Wales, at a depth of 86-531 m.

AUSTRALIAN SPECIES
Four species have been recorded: T. virgatus Alcock, 1902; T. petterdi Dennant, 1906; T. victoriae Duncan, 1870; and T. meridionalis Duncan, 1870.

GENUS
Deltocyathus
EDWARDS & HAIME, 1848

CHARACTERS
Solitary, free-living and disc-shaped. Pali form "deltas"

SIMILAR GENERA
None.

DISTRIBUTION
Cosmopolitan. Around Australia: New South Wales, Victorian and South Australian coastlines, at a depth of 16-531 m.

AUSTRALIAN SPECIES
Three species have been recorded: D. vincentinus Dennant, 1904; D. andamanicus Alcock, 1902; and D. ?ornatus Gardiner, 1899.

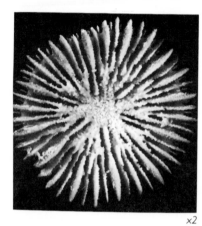

×2

GENUS
Bourneotrochus
WELLS, 1984

CHARACTERS
Solitary, free-living, disc-shaped, asexually reproducing by transverse (horizontal) division.

SIMILAR GENUS
Deltocyathus.

DISTRIBUTION
Vanuatu, Hawaii and Australia. Around Australia: the southern Great Barrier Reef, at a depth of 210-531 m.

AUSTRALIAN SPECIES
One species is known: B. stellulatus (Cairns 1984).

GENUS
Sphenotrochus
EDWARDS & HAIME, 1848

CHARACTERS
Solitary, free-living and compressed conical. Costae are usually absent except from the upper corallite wall, pali are absent.

SIMILAR GENERA
Dunocyathus, Platytrochus.

DISTRIBUTION
Cosmopolitan. Around Australia: New South Wales, from deep water.

AUSTRALIAN SPECIES
One species has been recorded: S. excavatus Tenison Woods, 1878.

GENUS
Polycyathus
DUNCAN, 1876

CHARACTERS
Solitary, attached, forming small colonies by budding from the sides of parent polyps.

SIMILAR GENUS
Paracyathus.

DISTRIBUTION
Cosmopolitan. Around Australia: recorded from the Great Barrier Reef and the south-west coast, over a depth of 40 m.

AUSTRALIAN SPECIES
Only one unnamed species is known.

×5

GENUS
Aulocyathus
VON MARENZELLER, 1904

CHARACTERS
Solitary, attached or free-living, horn-shaped. Columellae are compact, the corallum tends to split lengthwise.

DISTRIBUTION
Cosmopolitan.
Around Australia: South Australia, at a depth of 163-190 m.

AUSTRALIAN SPECIES
Only one species has been recorded: *A. recidivus* Dennant, 1906.

GENUS
Conotrochus
SEGUENZA, 1864

CHARACTERS
Solitary, attached or free-living, horn-shaped. The wall is composed of epitheca. Septa are only slightly exsert, and pali are absent.

SIMILAR GENUS
Ceratotrochus.

DISTRIBUTION
Indo-Pacific and Atlantic Oceans. Around Australia: from the Great Barrier Reef to Bass Strait, at a depth of 210-365 m.

AUSTRALIAN SPECIES
One species has been recorded: *C. brunneus* Moseley, 1881.

×5

GENUS
Stephanocyathus
SEGUENZA, 1864

CHARACTERS
Solitary, free-living, disc- or bowl-shaped with a pointed base. Costae are well developed, pali are weak or absent.

DISTRIBUTION
Cosmopolitan.
Around Australia: from the northern Great Barrier Reef and along the southern coast to Rottnest Island, at a depth of 366-1006 m.

AUSTRALIAN SPECIES
Four species have been recorded: *S. nobilis* (Moseley, 1881); *S. platypus* (Moseley, 1881); *S. spiniger* von Marenzeller, 1888; and *S. coronatus* (Pourtalès, 1867).

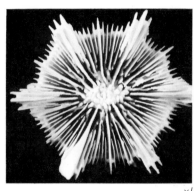

×1

GENUS
Oryzotrochus
WELLS, 1959

CHARACTERS
Solitary, free-living, shaped like a grain of rice, with prominent costae.

SIMILAR GENUS
Conocyathus.

DISTRIBUTION
Murray Islands, at a depth of 9-15 m.

AUSTRALIAN SPECIES
Only one species has been recorded: *O. stephensoni* Wells, 1959.

GENUS
Conocyathus
D'ORBIGNY, 1851

CHARACTERS
Solitary, free-living, cone-shaped. The wall is perforated between costae, pali are absent.

SIMILAR GENERA
Trematotrochus, Oryzotrochus.

DISTRIBUTION
Indo-Pacific.
Around Australia: occurs along the east Australian coastline, at a depth of 8-22 m.

AUSTRALIAN SPECIES
One species has been recorded, *C. zelandiae* Duncan, 1876.

GENUS
Trematotrochus
TENISON-WOODS, 1879

CHARACTERS
Solitary, free-living, cone-shaped. Walls are perforated, septa and costae are granulated and pali are reduced or absent.

SIMILAR GENERA
Conocyathus.

DISTRIBUTION
Australia, New Zealand and the Caribbean.
Around Australia: New South Wales and South Australia from a depth of 27 m to deep water.

AUSTRALIAN SPECIES
Two species have been recorded: *T. hedleyi* Dennant, 1906 and *T. verconis* Dennant, 1904.

GENUS
Dunocyathus
TENISON-WOODS, 1878

CHARACTERS
Solitary, free-living, and shaped like a disc or an inverted cone. Costae are weakly developed and alternate in position with septa. Pali are absent.

SIMILAR GENERA
Sphenotrochus, Platytrochus.

DISTRIBUTION
Known only from Australia: from southern Queensland to Tasmania, at a depth of 100-531 m.

AUSTRALIAN SPECIES
One species has been recorded: *D. parasiticus* Tenison-Woods, 1878.

607

GENUS
Paracyathus
EDWARDS & HAIME, 1848

CHARACTERS
Solitary, attached, and tapering to a pointed base. Pali merge with the columella.

SIMILAR GENUS
Polycyathus.

DISTRIBUTION
Cosmopolitan.
Around Australia: occurs along the eastern, southern and southwestern coastline, over 20 m depth.

AUSTRALIAN SPECIES
Four species have been recorded, three of which are named: *P. conceptus* Gardiner & Waugh, 1938; *P. vittatus* Dennant, 1906; and *P. porphyreus* Alcock, 1904.

×5

GENUS
Platytrochus
EDWARDS & HAIME, 1848

CHARACTERS
Solitary, free-living and compressed conical. Costae are thickened on the upper wall. Columellae are composed of twisted spines.

SIMILAR GENERA
Sphenotrochus, Dunocyathus.

DISTRIBUTION
Indo-Pacific.
Around Australia: recorded from the New South Wales, Victorian and South Australian coasts, at a depth of 28-183 m.

AUSTRALIAN SPECIES
Two species have been recorded: *P. compressus* (Tenison-Woods, 1878) and *P. hastatus* Dennant, 1902.

GENUS
Cylindrophyllia
YABE & EGUCHI, 1937

CHARACTERS
Solitary, free-living and barrel-shaped. Septa are in three cycles, and columellae are simple papillae.

DISTRIBUTION
Pacific Ocean.
Around Australia: New South Wales from deep water.

AUSTRALIAN SPECIES
Only one species has been recorded, probably undescribed.

GENUS
Peponocyathus
GRAVIER, 1905

CHARACTERS
Solitary, free-living, globular or bottle-shaped, pali are in two crowns.

SIMILAR GENUS
Cylindrophyllia.

DISTRIBUTION
Cosmopolitan.
Around Australia: the southern Great Barrier Reef, at a depth of 339-365 m.

AUSTRALIAN SPECIES
One species has been recorded: *P. orientalis* (Duncan, 1876).

GENUS
Holcotrochus
DENNANT, 1902

CHARACTERS
Solitary, free-living and compressed conical. Costae are broad and spiny. Septa are thick, equal and few in number.

DISTRIBUTION
Known only from Australia: recorded from the Great Barrier Reef and South Australia, at a depth of 11-183 m.

AUSTRALIAN SPECIES
Two species are known: *H. scriptus* Dennant, 1902 and *H. crenulatus* Dennant, 1904.

GENUS
Desmophyllum
EHRENBERG, 1834

CHARACTERS
Solitary, attached, horn-shaped. Costae are well developed only on the upper wall.

SIMILAR GENERA
None.

DISTRIBUTION
Cosmopolitan.
Around Australia: the Great Barrier Reef and New South Wales, at a depth of 6-860 m.

AUSTRALIAN SPECIES
Two species have been recorded: *D. cristagalli* Edwards & Haime, 1848 and *D. tenuescens* Gardiner, 1899.

×1.5

GENUS
Solenosmilia
DUNCAN, 1873

CHARACTERS
Colonial, attached, and dendroid to phaceloid. Corallites are cylindrical, septa are sparse and columellae are weak to absent.

SIMILAR GENERA
None.

DISTRIBUTION
Indo-Pacific and Atlantic Oceans.
Around Australia: New South Wales, at a depth of 860 m.

AUSTRALIAN SPECIES
One species has been recorded: *S. variabilis* Duncan, 1873.

FAMILY *GUYNIIDAE* Hickson, 1910

CHARACTERS
Solitary, free-living or attached, and tubular. Walls are composed of epitheca with pores between septa. Septa are few, not exsert, with smooth margins.

RELATED FAMILY
Flabellidae.

THE GENERA
The family contains three modern genera, two from the Atlantic, and *Stenocyathus*.

GENUS
Stenocyathus
POURTALÈS, 1871

CHARACTERS
Elongate, horn-shaped, and free-living or attached. The wall is composed of layers and pali are in a crown of six.

SIMILAR GENERA
None.

DISTRIBUTION
Atlantic, Mediterranean, Indian Ocean, New Zealand and Australia.
Around Australia: the southern Great Barrier Reef and New South Wales, at a depth of 455-531 m.

AUSTRALIAN SPECIES
One species has been recorded: *S. vermiformis* (Pourtalès, 1868).

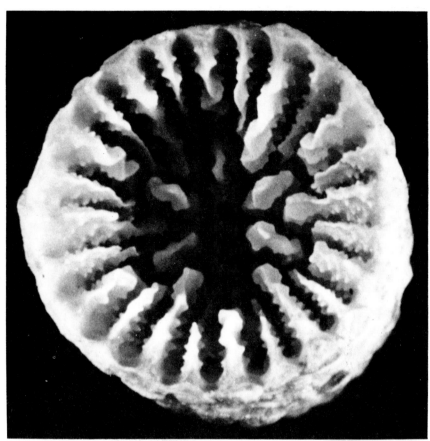

x25

FAMILY *DENDROPHYLLIIDAE* Gray, 1847

GENUS
Psammoseris
EDWARDS & HAIME, 1851

CHARACTERS
Solitary, probably ahermatypic, free-living, disc-shaped, with thick spongy costae and septa. With a commensal sipunculid worm.

SIMILAR GENUS
Resembles a flattened *Heteropsammia* and has similar worm-holes.

DISTRIBUTION
Indo-Pacific.
Around Australia: near Houtman Abrolhos Islands on the west coast.

AUSTRALIAN SPECIES
One species has been recorded: *P. hemispherica* (Gray, 1850).

×5

GENUS
Leptopsammia
EDWARDS & HAIME, 1848

CHARACTERS
Mostly solitary, attached, tubular, tapering towards the base and elliptical in cross-section. Septa are not fused according to Pourtalès Plan.

SIMILAR GENUS
Balanophyllia, which differs in having septa arranged according to Pourtalès Plan.

DISTRIBUTION
Indo-Pacific and Mediterranean.
Around Australia: recorded only from southern Queensland, at a depth of 8-86 m.

AUSTRALIAN SPECIES
One species has been recorded: *L. queenslandiae* Wells, 1964.

GENUS
Endopachys
LONSDALE, 1845

CHARACTERS
Solitary, free-living, and compressed conical. Costae have extensions near the longer axis. Septa are fused according to Pourtalès Plan.

SIMILAR GENERA
Structurally like *Balanophyllia*, but wedge-shaped.

DISTRIBUTION
Indo-Pacific.
Around Australia: New South Wales, and north of Shark Bay on the west coast, in deep water.

AUSTRALIAN SPECIES
Two species have been recorded: *E. australiae* Tenison-Woods, 1878 and *E. grayi* Edwards & Haime, 1848.

×3

GENUS
Notophyllia
DENNANT, 1899

CHARACTERS
Solitary, free-living, and purse- or wedge-shaped. Septa are confused.

SIMILAR GENUS
Endopachys.

DISTRIBUTION
Known only from south-eastern Australia, at a depth of 36-457 m.

SPECIES
Three species have been recorded: *N. etheridgei* Hoffmeister, 1933; *N. variolaris* (Tenison-Woods, 1877) and *N. recta* Dennant, 1906.

GENUS
Cladopsammia
LACAZE-DUTHIERS, 1897

CHARACTERS
Colonial, attached, forming small phaceloid colonies by extratentacular budding.

SIMILAR GENUS
Balanophyllia.

DISTRIBUTION
Cosmopolitan.
Around Australia: the Great Barrier Reef, at a depth of 6-10 m.

AUSTRALIAN SPECIES
Only one unnamed species is known.

GENUS
Endopsammia
EDWARDS & HAIME, 1848

CHARACTERS
Solitary, free-living or attached and cylindrical. Septa are thin, confused, and columellae are weakly developed.

SIMILAR GENUS
None.

DISTRIBUTION
Indo-Pacific, South Atlantic and Mediterranean.
Around Australia: recorded only from the Great Barrier Reef in the east.

AUSTRALIAN SPECIES
One species has been recorded, *E. philippinensis* Edwards & Haime, 1848.

GENUS
Thecopsammia
POURTALÈS, 1868

CHARACTERS
Solitary, attached, with costae reduced to granulations.

DISTRIBUTION
Cosmopolitan.
Around Australia: southern Queensland, at a depth of 270 m.

AUSTRALIAN SPECIES
One species has been recorded, *T. elongata* Moseley, 1881.

NON-SCLERACTINIAN CORALS

Although scleractinian corals overwhelmingly dominate most reef communities, there are many other groups of organisms that compete with the scleractinians for space and other resources. The vast majority of these do not build calcareous skeletons; some do, however, and these include a wide range of coelenterates which are sometimes called "false corals". The more common ones are included here. As with the Scleractinia, they include both hermatypes and ahermatypes, this division being reflected in their differing distribution patterns and habitats.

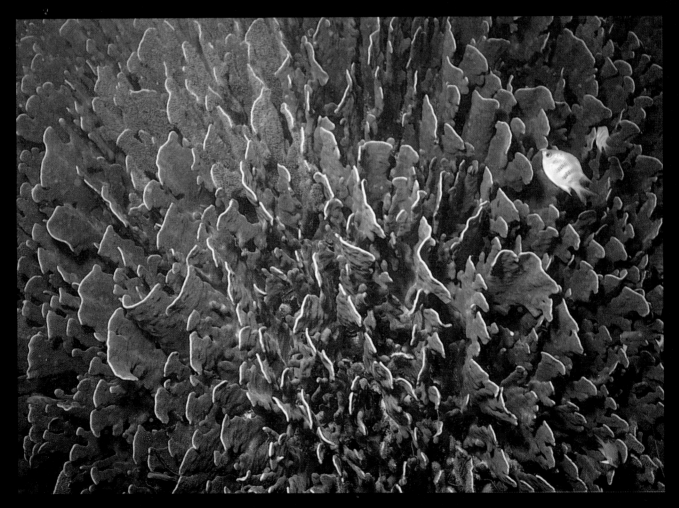

Shiraho Lagoon, Ishigaki Island, Japan, probably contains the world's largest colonies of *Heliopora coerulea*. This species is truely a "living fossil", with an ancestry that can be traced back to the Mesozoic Era.
PHOTOGRAPH: AUTHOR.

ORDER STOLONIFERA Hickson, 1833

FAMILY *TUBIPORIDAE* *(pronounced tube-ee-por-id-ee)* Ehrenberg, 1828

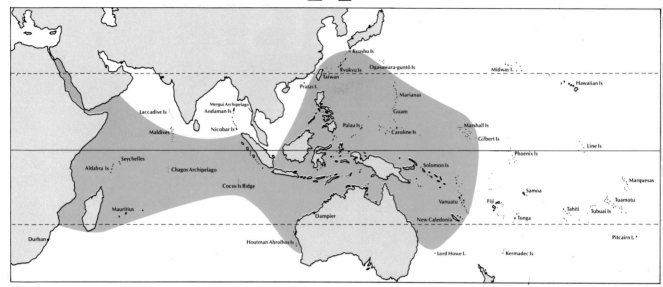

The known range of *Tubipora musica*.

CHARACTERS
Colonies are massive, formed by parallel tubes connected by horizontal platforms. The tubes contain the polyps, each of which has eight feather-like tentacles. The skeleton is a permanent dark-red colour.

RELATED FAMILIES
None.

EARLIEST FOSSILS
No fossil records.

THE GENERA
Only one, *Tubipora*.

GENUS
Tubipora
(pronounced tube-ee-por-a)
LINNAEUS, 1758

We had in the way of curiosity much better success, meeting with many curious fish and mollusca besides corals of many species, all alive among which was the Tubipora musica. I have often lamented that we had not time to make proper observations upon this curious tribe of animals but we were so entirely taken up with the more conspicuous links of the chain of creation as fish, plants, birds, etc. etc. that it was impossible.
The Endeavour *journal of Sir Joseph Banks, 1768-1771.*

This is the well-known "organ pipe" coral. Because the skeleton is permanently coloured it is often used for ornaments and jewellery. The living colony, however, is much less attractive, and usually remains unnoticed and unrecognised by divers.

TYPE SPECIES
Tubipora musica Linnaeus, 1758 from Micronesia.

NUMBER OF SPECIES
Four nominal species, probably one true species.

CHARACTERS
As for Family Tubiporidae.

COLOUR
Greenish-brown or grey when polyps are extended.

DISTRIBUTION
Around Australia: the Great Barrier Reef, Coral Sea and south to Elizabeth Reef in the east, and south to Houtman Abrolhos Islands on the west coast.

ABUNDANCE
Common on reef slopes, but inconspicuous as the skeleton is concealed below greenish-brown or grey polyps.

1. A colony of *Tubipora musica*. The "organ pipe" skeleton is seen only when polyps are fully retracted.
PHOTOGRAPH: ED LOVELL.

2. The polyps of the organ-pipe coral, *Tubipora musica*. Each polyp has eight feather-like tentacles which are folded at the slightest disturbance.
PHOTOGRAPH: ED LOVELL.

3. The skeleton of the organ-pipe coral, *Tubipora musica*. This drawing, made on Joseph Banks's expedition and published in 1792, is one of the oldest illustrations of an Australian coral and is completely accurate.

4. *Tubipora musica*.
PHOTOGRAPH: AUTHOR.

ORDER COENOTHECALIA Bourne, 1895

FAMILY *HELIOPORIDAE* (pronounced heel-ee-oh-pore-id-ee) Moseley, 1876

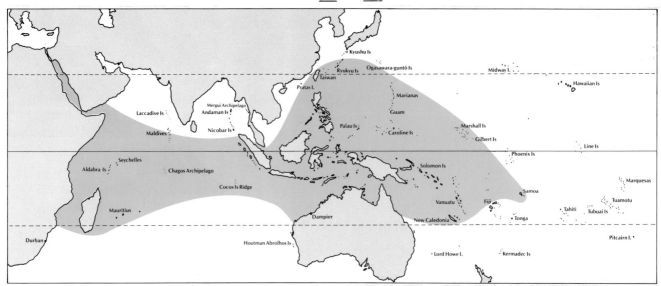

The known range of *Heliopora coerulea*.

CHARACTERS
Colonial and hermatypic. Colonies are arborescent, plate-like or columnar. The skeleton is composed of a matrix of fibrocrystalline aragonite penetrated by closely compacted circular tubes containing the polyps as well as finer tubes of a canal system. The skeleton is a permanent blue colour.

RELATED FAMILIES
None.

EARLIEST FOSSILS
No fossil record.

THE GENERA
Only one extant genus, *Heliopora*.

1. *Heliopora coerulea* at North West Cape, Western Australia. One of the columns has been broken off, revealing the permanently blue colour of the skeleton.
PHOTOGRAPH: CLAY BRYCE.

2. *Heliopora coerulea* at Broadhurst Reef, the southernmost record of the species on the Great Barrier Reef.
PHOTOGRAPH: ED LOVELL.

3,4. Two growth forms of *Heliopora coerulea* at Scott Reef, north-western Australia. In the lagoon (1), colonies may be 2 m high, while stunted colonies are very common on the reef flat (2).
PHOTOGRAPHS: AUTHOR.

GENUS
Heliopora
(pronounced heel-ee-oh-pore-a)
DE BLAINVILLE, 1830

The genus has one species only which is the well-known "blue coral". Like *Tubipora*, the living colony is not recognised easily under water as it looks very like the much more common *Millepora*. The colonies may vary enormously in size and shape but, unlike similar variation seen in *Millepora*, there is a clear correlation between colony shape and environmental conditions.

TYPE SPECIES
Millepora coerulea Pallas, 1766 from the "East Indies".

NUMBER OF SPECIES
One.

CHARACTERS
As for Family Helioporidae.

COLOUR
Greenish-grey with white polyps.

DISTRIBUTION
Around Australia: the northern and central Great Barrier Reef and Coral Sea in the east, and south to North West Cape on the west coast.

ABUNDANCE
Common, sometimes dominant, on northern tropical reef flats and upper reef slopes.

CLASS HYDROZOA Owen, 1843

ORDER MILLEPORINA Hickson, 1901

FAMILY *MILLEPORIDAE* (pronounced mill-ee-pore-id-ee) Fleming, 1828

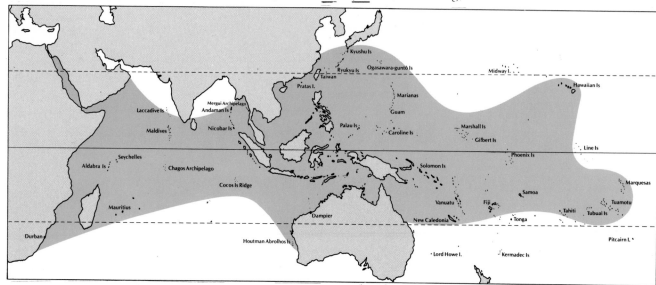

The known range of Indo-Pacific *Millepora*.

CHARACTERS
Colonial and hermatypic. Colonies are arborescent, plate-like, columnar or encrusting, with a smooth surface perforated by near-microscopic pores of two sizes: the larger are the gastropores, each of which is surrounded by five to seven smaller dactylopores. Fine straight hairs, visible under water, project from the colony surface. Minute free-swimming medusae larvae are produced in sexual generations.

RELATED FAMILIES
None.

EARLIEST FOSSILS
Cretaceous.

THE GENERA
Only one extant genus, *Millepora*.

GENUS
Millepora
(pronounced mill-ee-por-a)
LINNAEUS, 1758

It appears to me that these investigations present very strong reasons for believing that there is only one species of Millepora.

S. J. Hickson,
On the Species of the
Genus Millepora, 1898.

These are the common "stinging corals" or "fire corals" which cause a burning sensation if touched. The sting is usually mild and only soft skin is susceptible.

Millepora are often found on projecting parts of the reef where tidal currents are strong. They are also abundant on upper reef slopes and in lagoons and may be a dominant component of some coral communities.

The skeletons of most *Millepora* are brittle and can be broken easily. Others are thick and may form sturdy colonies capable of withstanding the strongest wave action. These different growth forms generally represent different species, but earlier this century it was widely believed that one species only was involved. The history of *Millepora* taxonomy has therefore been the opposite of scleractinian taxonomy, where each minor growth form was often described as a new species.

TYPE SPECIES
Millepora alcicornis Linnaeus, 1758 from an unrecorded locality.

NUMBER OF SPECIES
At least 48 nominal species, an unknown number of true species.

CHARACTERS
As for Family Milleporidae.

COLOUR
Green, cream or yellow.

DISTRIBUTION
Around Australia: the Great Barrier Reef and Coral Sea in the east, and south to Houtman Abrolhos Islands on the west coast.

ABUNDANCE
Common on most reef slopes and may be dominant on projecting parts of reefs exposed to strong currents.

1. The tip of a *Millepora* column at Myrmidon Reef, Great Barrier Reef.
PHOTOGRAPH: ED LOVELL.

2. *Millepora platyphylla* consists of fused vertical plates.
PHOTOGRAPH: AUTHOR.

3. Large colonies of *Millepora tenella*.
PHOTOGRAPH: AUTHOR.

4. A colony of *Millepora exaesa*, showing the characteristic mixture of encrusting and columnar growth forms.
PHOTOGRAPH: ED LOVELL.

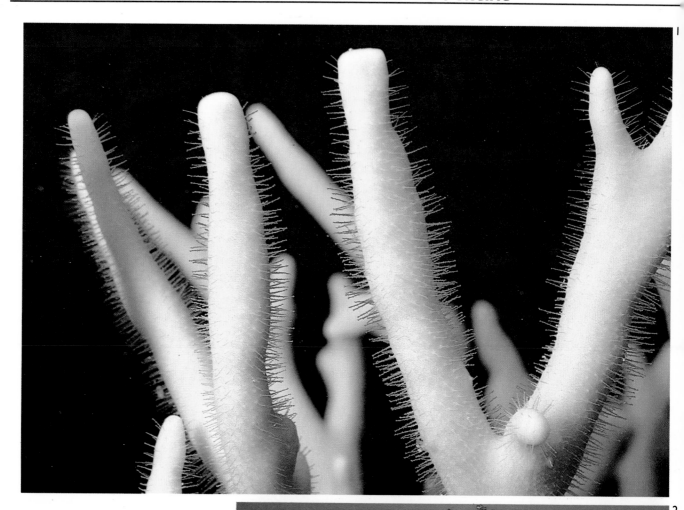

1. Tactile hairs projecting from *Millepora* branches.
PHOTOGRAPH: ED LOVELL.

2. A diver examining a forest of *Millepora tenella* on an outer reef slope of the Swain Reefs, Great Barrier Reef.
PHOTOGRAPH: ED LOVELL.

3. On Western Australian reefs this *Millepora* often forms large colonies of fused columns.
PHOTOGRAPH: ED LOVELL.

4. The branches of *Millepora* form different patterns according to species and environments.
PHOTOGRAPH: RON AND VALERIE TAYLOR.

3

4

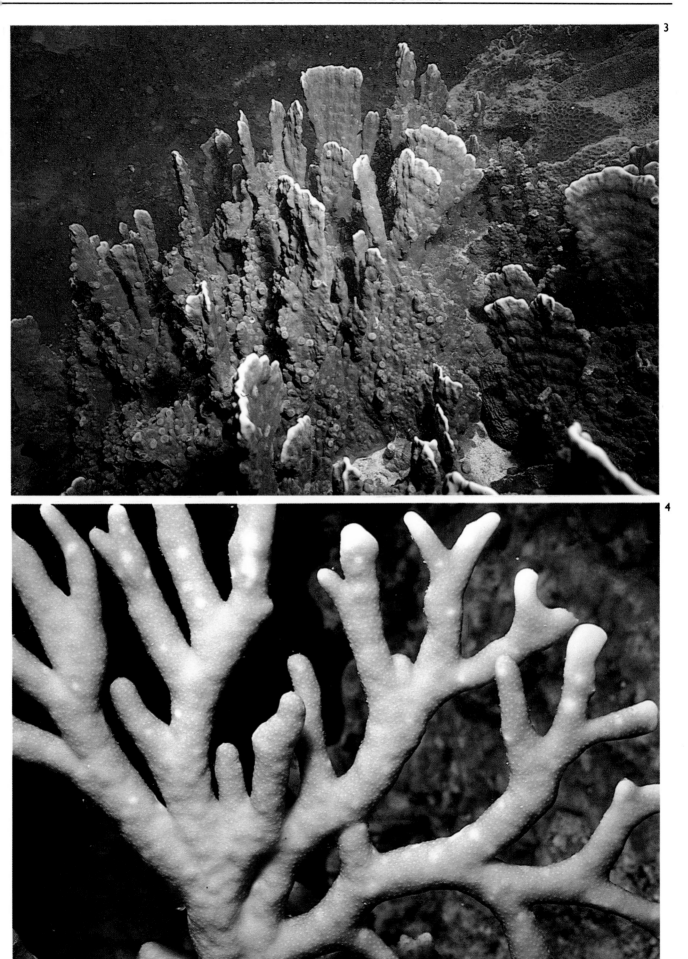

ORDER STYLASTERINA Hickson & England, 1905

FAMILY *STYLASTERIDAE* *(pronounced style-ass-terr-id-ee)* Gray, 1847

CHARACTERS
Colonial, ahermatypic, usually arborescent, with tubular gastropores surrounded by smaller dactylopores and usually forming cyclosystems. Sexual individuals, the gonophores, develop in ampullae between the gastropores and release planula larvae.

RELATED FAMILIES
None.

EARLIEST FOSSILS
Cretaceous.

THE GENERA
Approximately 15, all extant. These include two common Australian genera, *Stylaster* and *Distichopora*.

I. A large colony of *Stylaster*. These corals maintain their colour and delicate beauty when collected.
PHOTOGRAPH: RON AND VALERIE TAYLOR.

2, 3. Large colonies of *Distichopora* such as these are usually found in caves, where they live in semi-darkness.
PHOTOGRAPHS: RON AND VALERIE TAYLOR.

4. A common *Distichopora* of the Great Barrier Reef.
PHOTOGRAPH: RON AND VALERIE TAYLOR.

GENUS
Stylaster
(pronounced style-aster)
GRAY, 1831

TYPE SPECIES
Madrepora rosea Pallas, 1766 from the Caribbean.

FOSSIL RECORD
Eocene to Recent.

NUMBER OF SPECIES
At least 48 nominal species, an unknown number of true species.

CHARACTERS
Colonies are arborescent with fine branches, growing in one plane, which seldom anastomose. Cyclosystems alternate left and right sides of branches.

SIMILAR GENUS
Distichopora is readily distinguished by its thick branches without cyclosystems.

DISTRIBUTION
Worldwide, extending to the Arctic and Antarctic.

ABUNDANCE
Sometimes common under overhangs or on the roof of caves.

GENUS
Distichopora
(pronounced dis-tee-cop-or-a)
LAMARCK, 1816

TYPE SPECIES
Millepora violacea (Pallas, 1766) from an unrecorded locality.

FOSSIL RECORD
Eocene to Recent.

NUMBER OF SPECIES
At least 34 nominal species from the Indo-Pacific, an unknown number of true species.

CHARACTERS
Colonies are arborescent with flattened, blunt-ended, non-anastomosing branches of uniform width, growing in the one plane. There are no cyclosystems; gastropores are aligned along the lateral margins of branches with rows of dactylopores on either side.

SIMILAR GENUS
Stylaster.

DISTRIBUTION
Around Australia: found around the whole coastline.

ABUNDANCE
Sometimes common under overhangs or on the roof of caves.

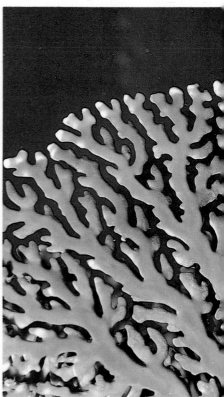

I

2

GEOLOGICAL HISTORY

. . . in honest moments we must admit that the history of complex life is more a story of multifarious variation about a set of basic designs than a saga of accumulating excellence.
Stephen Gould, The Ediacaran Experiment,
Natural History, 1984.

Era	Period	Epoch	Millions of years before present
Cainozoic	Quaternary	Holocene	
			0.01
		Pleistocene	
			1.8
	Tertiary	Pliocene	
			5
		Miocene	
			25
		Oligocene	
			37
		Eocene	
			54
		Palaeocene	
			65
Mesozoic	Cretaceous		
			140
	Jurassic		
			210
	Triassic		
			245
Palaeozoic	Permian		
			290
	Carboniferous		
			365
	Devonian		
			413
	Silurian		
			441
	Ordivician		
			504
	Cambrian		
			570
Precambrian			

Reefs, the greatest structures made by life on earth, seem ageless, immovable and indestructable. Yet they are none of these things. Rather, they are the end products of a combination of geological and climatic events which have acted to change the face of the earth, as well as the products of an evolutionary process which started well before the appearance on earth of any fauna that we now recognise.

The Earliest Reefs

The history of almost all forms of life is one of evolutionary expansion alternating with periods of mass extinctions. Palaeontologists have long recognised these periods and have used them to mark the major divisions in the geological time scale.

The greatest of all evolutionary expansions, that of the Cambrian Period, some 570 million years ago, heralded the first appearance in the fossil record of nearly all major groups of invertebrates with hard parts. Before then, nature made one "experiment" with soft-bodied animals in the form of a variety of marine invertebrates that resembled jellyfish, soft corals like "sea pens" and flat segmented worms. This, the relatively recently discovered Ediacaran fauna, was doomed to extinction and the record of its fossil remains ends just before the beginning of the Cambrian.

To find the earliest structures that we might be

***Opposite* 1.** A tabulate coral with individual corallites similar in size and shape to honeycomb. These extinct, almost invariably Palaeozoic corals are always colonial. The corallites consist of slender tubes which are crossed by transverse partitions called tabulae. Septa are poorly formed or absent. Specimen courtesy of Geology Department, James Cook University of North Queensland.
PHOTOGRAPH: AUTHOR.

2, 3. Rugose corals are an extinct Palaeozoic group which may be solitary (2) or colonial (3). In either case, corallites have a wide range of shapes and sizes. They contain tabulae (like tabulate corals) and septa (like scleractinian corals), the latter usually being much more prominent. Specimens courtesy of the Geology Department, James Cook University of North Queensland.
PHOTOGRAPHS: AUTHOR.

Diagram 22. The geological time scale.

vaguely tempted to call reefs, we can go back at least 2000 million years, to a time well before the evolution of animals, when life consisted only of simple plants—bacteria and algae. The first limestone accumulations, known in Precambrian rocks the world over, were formed from stromatolites. These ancient hemispherical mounds were probably composed of blue-green algae which entrapped fine sediment in much the same way that now-living stromatolites do. At this time there was no animal life to feed on planktonic algae. The algae probably turned the surface of the ocean into a veritable vegetable soup, blocking out light and saturating the water with oxygen. This abundance of food and oxygen probably set the stage for the evolution of animal life, and at the beginning of the Cambrian, over a period of only a few million years, the great evolutionary explosion took place. With algal growth held in check by animal life, light penetrated the shallower seas and the first limestone structures of animal origin appeared, the first of these being the sponge-like archaeocyathids, which formed calcareous thickets in very shallow water.

By the mid-Ordovician, complex algae and invertebrate reefal communities had become well established. The archaeocyathids had long become extinct and the stromatolites were replaced largely by a combination of red coralline algae, stony bryozoans, stromatoporoid "sponges" and tabulate and rugose corals. These are the oldest-known true "coral reef" communities and it is likely they captured the sun's energy by many of the methods used by modern reef communities. This may well be when algal symbiosis first evolved and it may have done so in both corals and sponges. For at least 150 million years, different combinations of these sponges and tabulate and rugose corals, as well as other organisms, built reefs around the world. It is interesting to speculate that the dominant organisms at any one time may have been the ones that had the best-developed algal symbiosis, for many of the reefs they built have an extraordinary resemblance in shape and structure to the reefs of today.

By the Late Devonian, reef development had occurred on a grand scale, rivalling that of any other period in the earth's history (including the present) but, for reasons still unexplained, the close of the Devonian saw the virtual end of major reef development until the end of the Palaeozoic Era.

As far as the fossil record shows, the evolution of marine life owes little to reef development. There was a proliferation of life in the Cambrian before major reef development occurred and another proliferation in the late Palaeozoic, so that during the Permian the diversity of marine benthic life may have been close to rivalling that of modern coral reefs. At the close of the Permian, however, another mass extinction overtook more than half the families and perhaps over 90 per cent of all the species of the world's marine invertebrates. Among the casualties were the remnants of the rugose and tabulate corals.

Scleractinian Reefs

The scleractinian (or modern) corals first appeared on the shores of the western Tethys Sea (see map, below), now southern Europe and the Mediterranean. They gradually moved into that important ecological niche that had long been unoccupied or sparsely occupied by coelenterates since the catastrophic decline of the tabulate corals and stromatoporoid sponges in the middle Palaeozoic.

The first scleractinians, progenitors of modern corals, now found in the remains of scattered European fossil reef patches, were composed of six distinct families, all of which appeared in the middle Triassic (230 million years ago). Throughout the Triassic these scleractinians were generally subordinate to other reef-builders, especially sphinctozoan sponges, but individual colonies sometimes exceeded one metre in diameter.

By the late Jurassic (150 million years ago), scleractinian corals had undergone a period of great diversification and global spreading. Most of the families we know today had evolved (see the "family tree", p. 61) and these corals were building reefs around the tropical shorelines of the Jurassic world.

Little or no reef development is known from the early Cretaceous—perhaps the climate was adverse worldwide. But by the end of the Cretaceous, both hermatypic and ahermatypic corals flourished much as they do today. They built reefs much like their modern

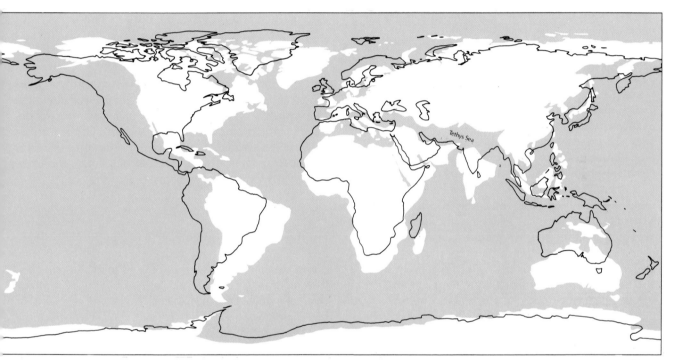

Tethys Sea

2

Continental drift — the gradual movement of the world's continental masses — has resulted in the opening and closing of the world's great oceans and the formation and break-up of the ocean currents that control the dispersal of marine life. The last 60 million years have seen the gradual break-up of the circumglobal Tethys seaway, the shores of which were home for corals throughout most of their evolution. The map shows the positions of the shorelines 40 million years ago.

1 (Opposite). A reef slope of a fossil reef near Charters Towers, eastern Queensland. Like the Canning Basin reefs, these are Devonian in age and contain beautifully preserved fossils.
PHOTOGRAPH: AUTHOR.

2. A river cutting through a huge fossil reef in the Canning Basin of north-western Australia. The reef, over 100 m high in places, was built by stromatoporoid sponges, algae and corals in the Devonian Period, long before modern corals evolved. Although built by different organisms, these reefs have the same basic structures as modern reefs.
PHOTOGRAPH: COLIN SCRUTTON.

counterparts and they probably differed from modern corals in general appearance no more than Caribbean corals now differ from those of the Indo-Pacific.

THE TERTIARY

The worldwide collapse and reordering of many animal groups at the close of the Cretaceous is the best known (although not the greatest) of all mass extinctions that have taken place during the earth's history. There have been many suggested causes, but the result was that nearly one-third of all animal families, including the dinosaurs, became extinct. Marine fauna and flora, including plankton and reef communities, were affected like all the others, and for 10 million years reefs did not recover. During all this time, not a single new genus of hermatypic coral appears in the fossil record.

Throughout the Tertiary, the gradual process of continental drift (see map, p. 625) continued. The shapes of all the continental coastlines during the early Tertiary differed substantially from the present. The most important of these differences, as far as reefs are concerned, lay in the separation of the two American continents. Thus with the presence of the Tethys Sea and the absence of the Isthmus of Panama, the tropical and subtropic northern hemisphere had a fully circumglobal seaway.

There were also major climatic differences. For much of the Mesozoic and the Tertiary until the Miocene, there were no polar icecaps. The world probably had a more equable marine climate than it does today and the northern continents were warmer. Because major oceans were less divided than they are today and had less latitudinal variation in temperature, surface-water movements (both equatorial and circumpolar) and their associated climatic influences, would have been less marked.

A minor radiation of hermatypic corals occurred in the Eocene and many of these genera now survive. A further radiation followed in the Miocene, and it is here that we find the readily recognisable immediate origins of many of today's corals.

By early Miocene times, about 25 million years ago, the continents had moved close to their present positions. The Tethys Sea had been reduced to a narrow passage connecting the Indian Ocean with the developing Mediterranean, approximately via the present Persian Gulf. The present Red Sea was periodically connected to the Mediterranean but was closed to the Indian Ocean. During the Miocene, mild climates gave away to cooler and more seasonal ones. The oceans developed marked temperature ranges and the Antarctic icecap was born. The tropical seas were also divided up (as they now are) and centres of coral diversity and reef growth became established in the western Atlantic (Caribbean region) and the Indo-west Pacific. These provinces were not separated by land as they are today, but by the vast emptiness of the eastern Pacific, which probably acted more as a selective filter to coral migration than as a complete barrier.

It was not until the Pliocene, five million years ago, that the Red Sea was opened to the Indian Ocean, but by then it was closed to the Mediterranean and did not connect the western Pacific to the Atlantic. Also in the Pliocene, the Isthmus of Panama was finally closed, completely separating the eastern Pacific from the Atlantic.

Many coral genera now restricted to the Indo-Pacific are known to have thrived in the Caribbean before the closure of the Isthmus of Panama and these included highly successful genera like *Pocillopora*. The reason for their extinction there is unclear, except that these reefs were much more affected by the Ice Age glaciation than were the Indo-Pacific reefs. After closure of the isthmus, what was left of Caribbean fauna in the eastern Pacific was also extinguished. Today there are only a few species of corals in the eastern Pacific and these all have their affinities with the species of the western Pacific.

During the late Pliocene, about two million years ago, reef development became well established along the Queensland coast. There had been extensive reef development since the Miocene in and around the borders of what is now the Papuan Basin, but in terms of major reef development in other parts of the world, the Great Barrier Reef is relatively young.

THE ICE AGES

By the close of the Pliocene, with the world's oceans divided up as they are today, geological events had ceased to be of general significance to marine organisms. Instead, this period has been one of enormous climatic changes which have had drastic effects on all forms of life, including corals. The Pleistocene is the epoch of the Ice Ages, and in it there have been several major periods of glaciation separated by warm periods, such as we have at present. During each glaciation, the polar icecaps build up and their volume becomes so great that the sea-level falls. During the last glaciation (20,000 years ago), the sea fell to over 100 metres below its present level. The shape of coastlines changed and land barriers emerged. All former coral reefs were high and dry. The number of extinctions that resulted is unknown, but it is probable that coral populations existed only in relatively isolated areas, which lacked the range of habitats usually associated with the reefs of today.

This happened in very recent times, even by human standards, so much so that it is not unreasonable to suppose that Australian Aborigines once lived and hunted on a flat grassy or forest plain with limestone hills that now, 20,000 years later, are under what we call the Great Barrier Reef. Indeed, our modern sea-level is no more than 6000 years old. This is probably time enough for most reefs to achieve some sort of stability, but more widespread genetic adjustments to corals, resulting from recombinations of populations that were isolated for thousands of years, are probably still in progress.

1 An intact thicket of fossil *Acropora* [on t]he Houtman Abrolhos Islands, [we]stern Australia. The thicket is [pro]bably Pleistocene in age and grew at a [tim]e when the sea-level was higher than it [n]ow.
[PHO]TOGRAPH: ED LOVELL.

2 An assemblage of fossil reef corals at [Eva]ns Head, eastern New South Wales. [Th]e assemblage contains at least 20 [spe]cies and grew approximately 120,000 [yea]rs ago, before the last major Ice Age [wh]en the sea-level was higher than it is [now] and tropical conditions were [pro]bably more widespread.
[PHO]TOGRAPH: JOHN PICKETT.

3 A stromatoporoid "sponge" standing [ove]r 2 m high near Charters Towers, [nor]thern Queensland. These huge [str]uctures were one of the main reef-[bui]lders of the Devonian Period and may [hav]e contained symbiotic algae to assist [the]ir growth.
[PHO]TOGRAPH: CLIVE WILKINSON.

BIOGEOGRAPHY

What are they? Where are they? Why are they where they are? These questions have been asked about corals ever since sea-going explorers first returned to their homelands with coral specimens for study and stories about the size and dangers of the reefs they saw.

Most of this book has been devoted to answering the "what" and "where" questions, as these are mostly matters of identification and distribution. The answer to the third question, why are they where they are, involves a complex and intriguing mixture of geological history, physical oceanography and coral biology, and one made all the more complicated because ever since Darwin and Wallace first proposed their theory of natural selection and survival of the fittest, the subject of the distribution of species and the subject of the origin of species have been bound together by a wealth of biogeographic and evolutionary theory, some of which is conflicting and much of which is highly controversial.

Modern Coral Distributions

The great difference between hermatypic and ahermatypic corals is nowhere more apparent than in their distribution patterns. Ahermatypic corals are not restricted by temperature or light. Each species appears to have a highly individual set of habitat requirements: some are restricted to specific places on continental slopes, while others are spaced throughout the dark, freezing ocean depths, irrespective of where these oceans may be. Hermatypic corals, on the other hand, are all limited by the demands of their symbiotic algae and, in the long term, are probably dependent on the reefs they build for their continuing survival.

SPATIAL SCALES

The patterns of distribution of hermatypic corals vary at different distances or scales (from tens of metres to

A coral community near the northern latitudinal limit of the Indo-west Pacific centre of high diversity (southern Ryukyu Islands). Of the 242 species (69 genera) present, all but 27 species (5 genera) are found on the Great Barrier Reef.
PHOTOGRAPH: AUTHOR.

thousands of kilometres).

Corals are distributed over the surface of a *single reef*, thereby creating patterns of community types and primarily reflecting conditions of the physical environment, especially depth and the amount of wave action, light and sediment.

Within a whole *region* (such as along the east or west coast of Australia), corals are distributed primarily according to ocean currents and temperatures, the availability of suitable substrates or "stepping stones" or sites for colonisation, the capacity of larvae to disperse over long distances and ecological conditions at the limit of their range.

Within the entire *Indo-Pacific*, and around the whole world, corals are distributed according to a mosaic of regional patterns, each with its own characteristics, superimposed upon a geological background of continental drift and of constantly changing sea-levels and climatic and ocean circulation patterns.

The distributions of almost all reef-building corals are controlled by various combinations of all these factors. Within these limitations, however, the different genera and species show markedly different patterns.

THE DISTRIBUTION OF GENERA

As the accompanying map (p. 631) shows, the highest number of genera are found in the reef complexes of the central Indo-Pacific south to the southern Great Barrier Reef and north to the northern Philippines. This belt occurs within the tropics, beyond which the diversity decreases abruptly. Eastwards across the Pacific, there is a progressive decrease in diversity. Westwards across the Indian Ocean, diversity remains relatively constant, the 50-genera contour extending from north-western Australia to the central Red Sea.

The Atlantic is much less rich in corals than the Indo-Pacific and most of the genera are concentrated in the Caribbean, with secondary centres occurring off Brazil in the south-western tropics and off the Gulf of Guinea in the east. There are no hermatypic corals in the Mediterranean.

THE DISTRIBUTION OF SPEICES

All published accounts of coral distributions (as with the one above) are based on genera, but many genera have only one species, while others have large numbers of them. The true distributions of corals, their causes and controls, will not be known until the distribution of species is known in detail, for it is the species, not the genera (which are artificially created), that are the fundamental units of biology.

To date, only the distribution of corals around Australia is known at species level, but this may be a useful indicator of more global patterns. These patterns may be inferred by comparing the numbers and identities of species from different Australian locations. As the adjacent map shows, northern tropical localities with a high diversity are generally similar while high latitude localities are distinct from each other. The vast majority of Australian species are also found on other central Indo-Pacific reefs and many range across the Indian Ocean to the Red Sea in the west, and across the Pacific to various south Pacific islands in the east. A few, in contrast, are restricted to particular localities, some to far-southern non-reefal areas, others to particular groups of reefs.

The abundance of individual species also changes over long distances, this being very marked south of the tropics. Some of the common species in southern localities are very rare in the tropics and *vice versa*. This pattern appears to be repeated in the northern hemisphere, where the same genera, and in some cases the same species, have similar distributions and abundances north from the Philippines. Thus, to some extent, the range and abundance of species of the two hemispheres are mirror images of each other.

Within the Great Barrier Reef, the distribution and abundance of species is more uniform. Some are more common in the muddy waters near the coastline, others are more common in the clear waters of outer reefs. Only the most southern (Capricorn and Bunker) groups

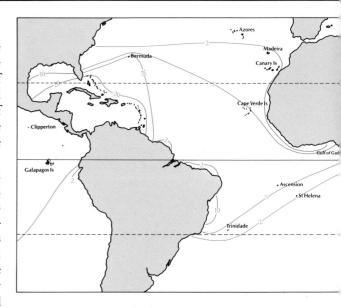

of reefs show a significant reduction in the number of species compared with the rest of the Great Barrier Reef. South of the Great Barrier Reef, the number of species decreases rapidly.

On the west coast of Australia, reefs are much fewer and are more widely spaced, with a general absence of intermediate reef types between them. As a result they show a high degree of individuality in species composition and abundance. However, the species that are most abundant in the far south of western Australia (for example, species of *Acanthastrea, Turbinaria* and *Pocillopora*) are usually also common along the southern coastal localities of the east coast.

The Origins of Coral Distributions

THE GEOLOGICAL BACKGROUND

For 90 per cent of their 240-million-year history, reef-building corals have occupied a tropical circumglobal seaway with the only barriers to dispersal being the

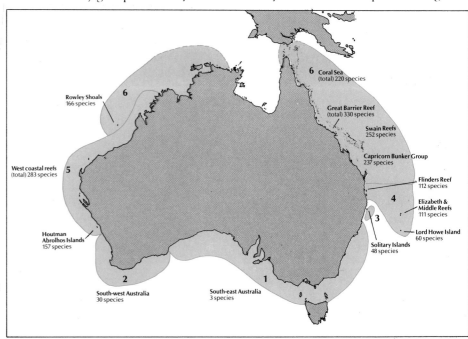

Numbers of species of hermatypic corals in the Australian waters. A computer measurement of similarity divides Australian corals into the six regions shown.

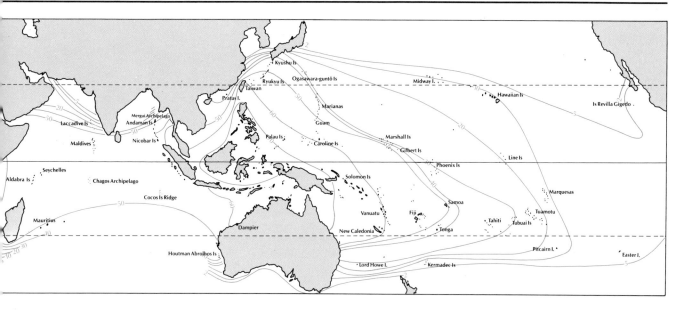

great open distances of the eastern Pacific and the gra-dually widening Atlantic. Throughout most of this time, the tropical world was a single, relatively uniform region, with coral distributions determined primarily by the availability of shallow-ocean areas suitable for reef development.

With the closure of the Tethys Sea and the isolation (and likely drying up) of the Mediterranean in the Miocene Epoch, two coral faunas began to develop: that of the Atlantic and far-eastern Pacific and that of the Indian Ocean and western Pacific. The subsequent clos-ure of the Isthmus of Panama reinforced this division, and after the extinction of the corals on both sides of the isthmus during the Ice Ages, the Atlantic and Indo-Pacific corals have remained very distinct. Only seven genera pre-dating the closure have survived the Ice Ages in the Atlantic and are now found in both the Atlantic and Indo-Pacific.

The Ice Ages also had major local effects on coral distribution which may well have given rise to new species. During glacial periods, falls in sea-levels forced reef-building corals away from the reefs to colonise the upper continental slopes. This caused their distributions to contract and perhaps divided their range into different isolated regions. If this isolation was maintained for long enough, the processes of genetic change might have caused what was once a single species to be divided into genetically distinct populations. When these populations recombined after the return of high sea-level, some may no longer have been able to interbreed, and so what was once a single species may have become two or more separate species. The Ice Ages may thus have been responsible for the formation of some of the more recently evolved species of corals, such as some species of *Acropora*.

THE PHYSICAL ENVIRONMENT

Of the main factors that determine the distribution of corals on a reef—depth on the reef slope, wave action, light and sediments—only the latter may be of regional importance, such as when sand or mud prevents further

Generic richness of hermatypic corals. This map was compiled by combining all the distribution maps of this book and similar maps of Atlantic genera. The contours show the maximum number of genera likely to be found at a given locality, not necessarily the number that does occur there. For large reef complexes, the real number is likely to be as shown; but for small isolated reefs, it is likely to be less.

reef development (for example, as it does at the southern end of the Great Barrier Reef).

There are, however, three aspects of the physical environment that clearly exert major global controls: ocean-circulation patterns, temperature and bathymetry.

Ocean-circulation patterns have an enormous influence on coral distributions. On a global scale, the impedi-ment to eastward migration of larvae can been seen on the map (see p. 632). In the Atlantic there are no tropical currents flowing from the Caribbean to other reef areas. In the Pacific there are two easterly tropical currents, but neither are good vehicles for larval transport. The main current flows north of the equator and misses complete-ly most reef areas. The second is the weaker "South Equatorial Counter Current", which in most years would probably be of little use in transporting coral larvae. However, every 10 to 15 years a major change occurs in the earth's atmosphere and ocean circulation patterns (the El Niño phenomenon) which greatly in-creases the strength of this current. This may well have provided the vehicle for most eastward coral migrations. The Indian Ocean currents offer much better transport opportunities, the only impediment to dispersal being the great distance between "stepping stones."

Currents also have profound effects on regional dis-tributions. Production of coral planula larvae is usually a seasonal event and larvae of individual species are trans-ported only by the currents that prevail at that particular time. Nevertheless, throughout the whole Great Barrier Reef and to a lesser extent along most of the west Australian coast, currents are sufficiently variable at the time of planula dispersal to provide adequate transport in any direction. This probably explains why the Hout-man Abrolhos Islands, so far south of other coral reefs, have so many genera and species, and it also explains why most east Australian species are distributed uniformly throughout most of the Great Barrier Reef. Southward from the Great Barrier Reef, the "East Australian Current" flows southward constantly and larvae can travel only south on non-return journeys. This is probably why some species that are common on southern reefs are absent from the Great Barrier Reef— they have become trapped in the south and will remain so as long as the "East Australian Current" prevails.

Temperature has long been considered the primary factor limiting corals to tropical and subtropical localities, and it is generally thought to do so by affecting the coral reproductive cycle, although this has yet to be demonstrated. Alternatively, the effects of temperature may be indirect. Below about 18°C, the rate of calcification is slowed and corals may require more light to grow. The effect of decreasing temperature may therefore be to decrease their depth limit and this may finally limit the capacity of corals to build reefs.

Although it might be expected that corals growing at the extreme limit of their distributional range would show some effects of an adverse environment, the opposite is the usual case. Such colonies are often bigger, more robust and more colourful than their tropical counterparts.

Bathymetry is an important factor limiting coral distribution because so much of the major oceans are deeper than the 50 metres or so depth limit for reef development. The most important of all bathymetric limitations to coral distribution is the "eastern Pacific barrier". This vast and geologically ancient expanse of deep ocean, without any shoreline within the reach of tropical organisms, is the main reason why so few corals have colonised the west coast of the Americas.

Bathymetry may limit coral growth along some coastlines but these effects are of regional importance only. Reefs are known to develop on very steeply sloping substrates, provided that there is some protection from extreme wave action. Shallow substrates are more limiting, especially where there is a lot of sediment build-up and also where there are major rivers.

BIOLOGICAL CONSTRAINTS

Most animals that live on land are mobile, and it is the adult phase of their life-cycle that is primarily responsible for the dispersal of the species. In the sea the reverse is the case. The ocean currents provide such a good vehicle for dispersal that a large proportion of marine species, including corals, have immobile adults, leaving the task of dispersal to the young. Consequently, the vast majority of marine species have planktonic young, usually larvae, which look nothing like the adult of the species.

The capacity of corals to disperse depends on the amount of time their larvae can remain afloat, their capacity to find a suitable substrate on which to settle and whether or not they can grow into an adult after settlement. Unfortunately, very little is known about any of these subjects.

Planula larvae of many species can be kept readily in an aquarium for several weeks (in one instance, three

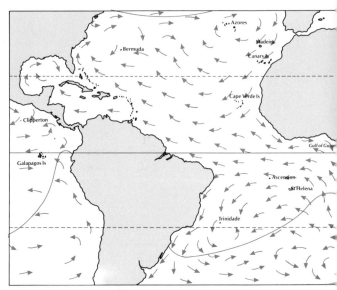

months), which is time enough for them to make ocean voyages of hundreds of kilometres. Species with such long-lived larvae would have great powers of dispersal, but the chances that these larvae would find a suitable substrate to colonise would be much less than species with larvae that settle promptly on the same or a nearby reef. So capacity for local population increase must be balanced against capacity for long-distance dispersal. Perhaps larvae change their role from the former to the latter as they mature without finding a suitable substrate on which to settle. Just how they detect the presence of a substrate, or if they can, is not known.

After settlement, the planula larva must develop into a reproducing adult before its task of dispersal is complete. Only a very small proportion of larvae that settle survives long enough to do this, as each must face all the environmental rigors and competitive interactions of the community in which it finds itself. These ecological limitations probably play a major role in restricting distribution in higher latitudes where kelp, *Sargassum* and other macro-algae exclude all but the toughest corals by simple competition for space and light.

The Origins of Coral Species

Echoes from the explosive impact Charles Darwin made on the religious and philosophical foundation of the civilised world by the publication of his book *On the Origin of Species* in 1859 are still being heard loudly today. That species have evolved has long ceased to be rationally questioned, but debate over the mechanisms involved goes ever on.

Perhaps Darwin's greatest achievement was that his theory—that species evolve by natural selection and survival of the fittest—was all-encompassing: it could be applied to all forms of life, present as well as past, and to the finest details of speciation as well as to the evolution of the broadest divisions in the plant and animal kingdoms.

Darwin proposed that as species evolved, the more advanced forms displaced the more primitive from their centre of origin. Thus the most advanced (youngest) species are found at the centre and the least advanced

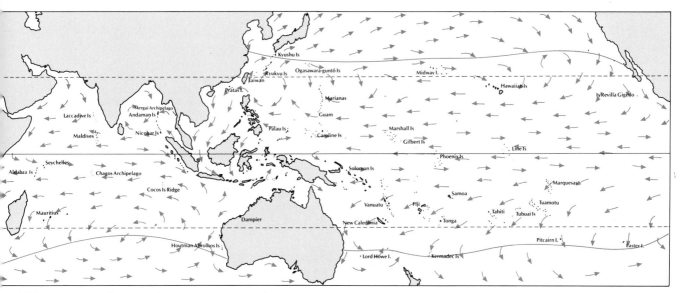

The major ocean surface circulation patterns (during winter). The lines are the 18°C boundary (isotherm) of average winter minimum sea temperature.

(oldest) are at the periphery. Ever since then, species origins and species distributions have been linked together, with observations on the distribution of species being used to support or denounce theories about their origin.

The strongest denunciation of this particular theory of Darwin's comes from a school of biogeographers who contend that speciation is the result of the formation and removal of "barriers", rather than the result of dispersal from a centre of origin. If species gradually change with time, the dividing of a species distribution by a "barrier" will cause the two halves to change independently. If the barrier is then removed, the two halves may no longer be able to interbreed and thus they will have become different species. The origin of species, this school believes, has absolutely nothing to do with Darwin's centres of origin.

Where do corals belong in such a debate? Perhaps, as previously mentioned, some of the more recent species owe their origins to barriers created by sea-level changes during the Ice Ages, but most coral species are far too old to have evolved at this time. The weight of evidence presented in this book suggests that these theories, and others like them, are not applied easily to marine organisms, such as corals, which have a great capacity for rapid long-distance dispersal. Most corals are not restricted to a particular region, but are widely distributed according to their individual characteristics and capacities, a distribution which probably has little or nothing to do with their place of origin. A high proportion of coral species probably occur in the Indo-west Pacific because this is the region that has the greatest concentration of reefs and the greatest range of habitats.

Because coral species are few in number, are widely dispersed and have long geological histories, the formation of a new species must be a rare event. To find the origins of most of them, we should probably look to an earlier age of long-term climatic stability, when species were dispersed to their limits, when tropical conditions prevailed over most of the earth's surface and ocean currents did not provide the communication between reefs that they now do and would have done during the Ice Ages.

GLOSSARY

Note: As technical terminology has been minimised in this book, some terms used,
and the explanations given for them, are not necessarily applicable to technical publications.

acanthocauli
juvenile *Fungia* attached to the substrate. See p. 330.

ahermatypic
without symbiotic algae. See pp. 1, 45.

algae
simple photosynthetic plants which may be single-celled or multicellular (macro-algae, filamentous algae, kelp). Usually initially classified according to their pigments, hence blue-green algae, brown algae, red algae (includes coralline algae) and green algae (includes *Halimeda*).

anastomose
to re-fuse (branches, columns etcetera).

appressed corallite
corallite presses against the coenosteum. See p. 128.

arborescent
a colony shape composed of elongate, tree-like branches. See p. 126.

atoll
a group of reefs and islands that surround a central lagoon.
See p. 12.

axial corallite
the corallite that runs down the centre (or axis) of a branch. See p. 126.

axial furrow
the groove along the top of fungiid corals.

bail-out
a form of asexual reproduction in corals. See p. 47.

bathymetry
sea-floor shape or topography, usually mapped by depth contours.

bifacial
corallites occur on both sides of a plate or frond.

bottlebrush
a growth form of *Acropora*. See p. 129.

budding
the process of polyp duplication in colony formation. See p. 58.

caespitose
a growth form of *Acropora*. See p. 126

calice
the opening of the corallite, bounded by the wall.

Cambrian
a geological Period. See p. 623.

cays
islands formed by the accumulation of sand on a coral reef. These are distinct from "high islands" which do not have a reefal origin.

centres
the positions of mouths or columellae.

cerioid
a type of colony formation where polyps share common walls. See p. 58.

cilia
microscopic hairs forming a brush-like surface to the ectodermis. See p. 57.

coelenterates
a phylum of aquatic animals including corals, jellyfish, soft corals, anemones and hydroids. See p. 55.

coenosteum
the skeletal matrix around corallites. See p. 56.

colony
a group of polyps formed from a common parent by budding. See p. 58.

columellae
skeletal structures at the centre of corallites. See p. 56.

columnar
a colony shape where columns are formed. See p. 60.

commensals
organisms that normally live together, usually with mutual benefit.

coral polyp
an anemone-like animal composed of fleshy tissues and a skeleton. See p. 55.

corallite
the skeleton of an individual polyp. See p. 55.

corallum
the skeleton of a coral.

corymbose
a growth form of *Acropora*. See p. 126.

costae
radial elements of corallites situated outside the corallite wall. See p. 56.

Cretaceous
a geological Period. See p. 623.

cryptic
well camouflaged, usually not noticed.

cyclosystems
groups of dactylozooids and gastrozooids in *Millepora* and Stylasteridae.

dactylopores
the smaller of the two pore sizes of *Millepora* and Stylasteridae. See p. 616.

dendroid
a type of colony formation where tubular corallites form a zigzag pattern, see *Tubastraea micrantha*, p. 583.

denticles
pali-like granules on the septa of *Porites*, see p. 218.

Devonian
a geological Period. See p. 623.

digitate
a colony shape composed of short finger-like branches. See p. 126.

dioecious
corals having separate male and female colonies. See p. 48.

directive septa
septa about which a corallite is bilaterally symmetrical. Especially important in *Porites*, see p. 217.

disc
the circular corallum of solitary, free-living fungiids.

dorsal directive septum
part of the septal configuration of *Porites* corallites. See p. 217.

ectodermis
the outer cell layer of the polyp body wall. See p. 57.

Ediacaran fauna
a group of soft-bodied Precambrian invertebrates. See p. 623.

encrusting
a colony shape where the colony forms a thin layer over the substrate. See pp. 60, 129.

Eocene
a geological Epoch. See p. 623.

epitheca
a fine skeletal layer which sometimes surrounds corallites. See p. 56.

exsert
projecting above the surrounding structure. Exsert septa project well above the corallite wall.

extant
now living (as opposed to extinct).

extratentacular budding
a type of polyp duplication where daughter polyps form on the side of a parent polyp. See p. 58.

635

family
a grouping of related genera with common characteristics. See p. 61.
flabellate
a type of colony (or individual polyp) formation where short valleys (or elongate calices) have separate walls.
flabello-meandroid
a type of colony formation where valleys are elongate and have separate walls. See p. 58.
foliaceous
a colony shape where the colony is composed of thin leaf-like sheets. See p. 60.
fossil
the remains of an organism that existed in former geological times.
free-living
not attached to a substrate.
frond
a thin, fern-like branch.
gastrodermis
the inner cell layer of the polyp body wall. See p. 57.
gastropods
snails and snail-like animals.
gastropores
the larger of the two pore sizes of *Millepora* and Stylasteridae.
genus
a grouping of related species with common characteristics. See p. 61.
gonads
reproductive organs; testes in males and ovaries in females. See pp. 57, 58.
gonophores
sexually reproducing individuals of *Millepora*, Stylasteridae and other coelenterates.
gonochoristic corals
corals having separate male and female colonies. See p. 48.
habitat
the locality in which a plant or animal lives.
hermaphrodite polyps
individuals containing both male and female gonads. See pp. 48, 58.
hermatypic
with symbiotic algae present in the polyp tissue. Almost all reef corals are hermatypic. See pp. 1, 45.
high islands
islands composed of non-reefal rock. These are distinct from cays which have a reefal origin.
hydnophores
conical structures developed between the corallite centres of some corals, especially *Hydnophora*. See p. 428.
immersed corallite
corallite that does not protrude from the coenosteum.
intratentacular budding
a type of polyp duplication where the polyp divides into two or more polyps. See p. 58.
Jurassic
a geological Period. See p. 623.
laminar
a colony shape where the colony forms flat horizontal plates. See p. 60.

lateral pairs
part of the septal configuration of *Porites* corallites. See p. 217.
mantle
a fleshy disc extended by some corals when tentacles are retracted.
massive
a colony shape where all dimensions are approximately the same. See pp. 60, 129.
meandroid
a type of colony formation where polyps form valleys. See p. 58.
mesenteric filaments
coiled tubular structures within the polyp body cavity. See p. 57.
mesoglea
a non-cellular layer of the body wall between the ectodermis and gastrodermis. See p. 57.
Mesozoic
a geological Era. See p. 623.
Miocene
a geological Epoch. See p. 623.
monocentric
with one columella centre per corallite.
monospecific stands
a conspicuous community of one species.
nariform corallite
Acropora corallite shaped like an upside-down Roman nose. See p. 128.
nematocysts
stinging cells. See p. 57.
nominal species
a species by name only. See p. 3.
orders (of septa or costae)
each order is composed of septa or costae of similar size (usually one or more cycles, see p. 56). First order (or primary) septa or costae are often derived from several cycles.
Ordivician
a geological Period See p. 623.
ovaries
female gonads.
Palaeozoic
a geological Era. See p. 623.
pali
a type of paliform lobe found in some corals, such as *Porites*, see p. 218.
paliform lobes
large, vertical teeth situated above the inner margins of septa. See p. 56.
papillae
reticulum structures of *Montipora* which are smaller than the corallites. See p. 94.
parasites
organisms that live on another organism (the host) from which they obtain food. shelter and other requirements.
petaloid
the raindrop-like shape of septo-costae formed when both ends are submerged in coenosteum. Best developed in *Polyphyllia* and *Psammocora*.
phaceloid
a type of colony formation where individual polyps are very prominent. See p. 58.
pharynx
a tube connecting the polyp body

cavity to the mouth. See p. 57.
phytoplankton
minute plants, mostly algae, which float near the water surface.
pits
holes or depressions in the coenosteum at the point of formation (or insertion) of costae. Of taxonomic use in fungiids and *Echinophyllia*, see pp. 333, 372.
plankton
minute plants and animals (phytoplankton and zooplankton) which occur in the water column.
planulae
free-swimming larvae of corals and other coelentrates. See p. 49.
Pleistocene
a geological Epoch. See p. 623.
Pliocene
a geological Epoch. See p. 623.
plocoid
a type of colony formation where polyps have separate walls. See p. 58.
polycentric
with more than one columella centre per corallite.
polymorphism
where individual species have more than one form or shape. See p. 60.
Pourtalès Plan
an arrangement of septa used in identification. See p. 56.
Precambrian
a geological Era. See p. 623.
primary septa
the largest septa of a corallite, composed of the first cycle only, or several cycles. See p. 56.
prostrate
a colony shape where branches sprawl over the substrate. See p. 129.
radial corallite
corallites that surround the axial corallite of *Acropora*. See pp. 128, 129.
radii
skeletal rods linking the columella to septa in *Porites*. See p. 218.
ramose
a colony shape where branches are present.
reticulum
the coenosteum and associated structures of *Montipora*. See p. 94.
rootlets
tongues of coenosteum which grow down into the substrate anchoring the colony.
rugose corals
a major group of corals which became extinct before the evolution of the Scleractinia. See p. 622.
Scleractinia
stony or hard corals excluding the extinct rugose and tabulate corals.
secondary septa
general term for the smaller septa of a corallite. See p. 56.
septa
radial elements of corallites situated inside the corallite wall. See pp. 56, 57.
septal deltas
groups of septa fused to form a segment of the columella.

septal teeth
lobes or spines along the margins of septa. See p. 54.

septo–costae
radial elements of corallites. See p. 56.

solitary
not colonial.

species
a group of organisms that, under normal circumstances, can interbreed. See pp. 2, 3, 60, 61.

spinules
minute spines in the coenosteum.

stromatolites
hemispherical mounds of blue-green filamentous algae of Precambrian origin. See p. 624.

stromatoporoids
reef-building sponges that were a major component of many Palaeozoic reefs. See p. 624.

sub-
a prefix much used in taxonomy which means "less than". Hence submassive, subplocoid etcetera.

sweeper tentacles
tentacles used in aggressive encounters between corals. See p. 50.

symbiosis
a close relationship between two differing types of organisms where both derive benefit.

synonym
an invalid name for a species. See p. 3.

tabulate corals
a major group of corals which became extinct before the evolution of the *Scleractinia*. See p. 622.

terete
of uniform thickness, without tapering.

Tertiary
a geological Period. See p. 623.

testes
male gonads.

Tethys Sea
an ancient tropical ocean that existed before the continents came to their present positions. See p. 625.

thecal
belonging to the corallite wall.

tiered colonies
where colonies are composed of several horizontal plates arranged one above the other. See p. 60.

Triassic
a geological Period. See p. 623.

triplet
part of the septal configuration of *Porites* corallites. See p. 217.

tuberculae
reticulum structures of *Montipora* which are larger than the corallites. See p. 94.

tubular corallite
corallite shaped like a tube. See p. 128.

type locality
the place where a species was originally recorded or collected. See p. 3.

type specimens
specimens on which species descriptions are based. See p. 3.

unifacial
corallites occur on one side of a plate or frond.

valleys
the equivalent of calices in meandroid and flabello-meandroid colonies.

ventral directive septum
part of the septal configuration of *Porites* corallites. See p. 217.

verrucae
wart-like nodules on *Pocillopora* colonies which contain polyps. See p. 71.

wall
part of a corallite. See p. 56.

whorls
a colony shape where the colony grows as a spiral sheet. See p. 60.

zooplankton
minute animals which swim in the water column.

zooxanthellae
symbiotic algae of coral and other organisms. See p. 45.

INDEX

Page numbers in bold type indicate the main reference.